BIAFRA

Selected Speeches
and Random Thoughts
of
C. ODUMEGWU OJUKWU

General of the People's Army

BIAFRA

Selected Speeches
and Random Thoughts
of
C. ODUMEGWU OJUKWU

General of the People's Army

With Diaries of Events

1817

Harper & Row, Publishers
New York, Evanston, and London

*To the many sons and daughters
whose fathers toiled and tramped with me,
and are gone.*

Contents

Foreword

. . . Colonial state generates a colonial posture. This posture automates a series of complexes which remain with the African long after the colonial stimulus has ceased to have direct contact. The continuation of these complexes is seen in a state of mind which permits colonialism as a reflex. During this period the remoteness of the stimulus is often misinterpreted as nonexistent, thus generating a false sense of security in the minds of Africans lately out of bondage. The stimulus exists, its virulence undiminished. In fact, what happens is that the imperial power at this time, finding itself undisturbed, conserves energy, spreads its contagion, prepares the ground, and concentrates all its efforts toward the achievement of its main objective—that of economic exploitation. . . .

These were my views as a student, discovered in a pile of my student-day essays. Today, after fifteen years, my views remain substantially unchanged. The future of Africa depends entirely on the ability of the African to overcome his own colonial mentality, which permits his erstwhile colonial masters to manage him by impulses generated from a remote control station, usually some European capital.

For the African, therefore, to measure up as a man in the full sense of the word, for him to be truly free, it becomes imperative that he must first understand himself, his psychological disability, then recognize his enemy—still his erstwhile colonial master—recognize the fact of neocolonialism, its destructive potential, and then take urgent and drastic steps to rid himself of this malignant blight which, if left unchecked, will surely destroy him. This is why I believe that the black will not emerge until he is able to build modern states based on a compelling African ideology. The need for an

African ideology arises from the fact that the withdrawal of the colonial masters and the effect of a long period under tutelage left most emergent African countries with an ideological vacuum. In order to fill this vacuum, the battle for men's minds continues in Africa today. The African leader is often left with very little to choose between one ideology or the other, each designed to serve needs other than his own. It is this that creates in Africa a state of instability, and this instability is bound to continue until Africa generates from within an ideology of equal dynamism that can fill the vacuum and act as a bulwark against foreign impositions. Our struggle, therefore, is African nationalism conscious of itself and fully aware of the powers with which it is contending.

For two years now the Gowon junta, with the direct and active support of the British government and Russia, has been waging a hideous and vicious war against the innocent people of what is now Biafra. The real intention is the destruction of a people and nation— genocide behind the façade of maintaining Nigerian unity, or keeping Nigeria one, as their slogan goes. Unity is, of course, a very important aim in a world so interdependent and yet so deficient. The term is so attractive and impressive that an evildoer needs only to invoke it for the less wary world to be mesmerized. In a political context, unity is not definitive but a definable term. When, therefore, Gowon and Harold Wilson talk of unity, one is apt to wonder what exactly they mean.

In spite of all efforts since the famous Amalgamation of Northern Nigeria and Southern Nigeria in 1914, an act which all Northern Nigerian leaders to this day consistently and publicly condemn as a mistake, Nigeria as a united country was nothing but a fiction. Certain basic features mark a country out as united. Some of these features are:

1. Common or similar culture, as well as social system.

2. Common citizenship, with equal rights and privileges for all men anywhere in the country.
3. Common laws and a common judicial system.
4. A common electoral system.
5. Equal rights of all citizens before the law.
6. Rights to acquire property and make a living anywhere in the country.
7. Equal rights to employment anywhere in the country.
8. Equal rights to protection of life and property.

All these features, and more, were completely lacking in Nigeria between the peoples of the North and those of the South. While the people of the South made strenuous efforts at Nigerian unity, the people of the North did everything to stultify, indeed kill, anything that would foster it.

The constitutional arrangements of Nigeria, as imposed upon the people by the erstwhile British rulers, were nothing but an implicit acceptance of the fact that there was no basis for Nigerian unity, a fact categorically echoed by Gowon in his first broadcast to Nigeria after his rebellion and his usurpation of power on August 1, 1966. The Federal Nigerian Constitution was designed primarily to hinder all attempts by Nigerians to progress. Its aim was to create a healthy atmosphere for further imperialist exploitation after the imperial master should have withdrawn. The problems that beset Nigeria after independence were, therefore, the problems of neocolonialism—problems that have beset every country in Africa since the attainment of independent status.

The crises which rocked Nigeria from the start of independence came as a result of efforts of progressive nationalists to rid themselves and posterity of the stranglehold of neocolonialism. For this, Biafrans in Nigeria were stigmatized and singled out for extermination. In imperialist thinking, only phony independence was acceptable for the Africans. Any attempt at true independence was a nuisance which had to be abated.

The sponsorship of Nigeria by the imperialists is, therefore, not surprising, nor has it been disinterested. These sponsors are concerned only with the preservation of that corrupt and rickety structure of a Nigeria in a perpetual state of powerlessness to check foreign economic exploitation.

People have sought in various ways to dismiss our struggle as a tribal conflict. People have attributed it to the greed of a fictitious power-seeking clique anxious to carve out an empire to rule, to dominate, and to exploit. This is not so. Our cause is transparently just, and no amount of propaganda can detract from it. Our struggle is of far greater significance. It is a total, vehement rejection of all those evils that blighted Nigeria—evils which were bound to lead to the disintegration of that ill-fated federation. Our struggle is a positive commitment to build a healthy, dynamic, and progressive state which will be a bulwark against neo-colonialism, and the pride of black men the world over. The failure of the Nigerian experiment was a tragic result of a refusal by both Nigeria and the world to recognize, accept, and accommodate the obvious and painful fact that Nigeria was not and could never be a nation. The nations comprising the Federation lacked all the necessary factors for cohesion, and her peoples the necessary will. The center, therefore, could not hold. Yet for a long time I believed it was just possible that parts of Nigeria might find mutual accommodation in a structure less tight than that envisaged by the federal constitution. I made proposals to this effect at Aburi. What Nigeria needed was time—time to get over her colonial past, time to recognize that political independence as it came to Africa was only a first step, at best an unsure step, toward true independence. In granting independence, the imperialist enemy had merely made a tactical withdrawal. Africa won a battle, perhaps, but the war was still raging. The enemy only moved to a better defensive position, from where he could more easily deal a death blow to the rather bumptious colonies girt in their new robes of liberty. Nigeria never understood the nature of neocolonialism, nor did she ever recognize the virulence of this new aspect of imperialism. Believing the war was over, she settled down to an orgy of loot; brother fought brother for the imaginary spoils of victory, and, tragically for us, those spoils turned out to be our patrimony. The orgy led to disorders and riots, ending with the massacre of 50,000 people of Eastern Nigeria origin, and unleashed a war the magnitude and totality of which Africa had never before witnessed.

It is during the course of this war, with all the many distractions attendant upon the leadership of a national struggle of this nature, that I have tried to put together in this volume my essential thoughts on the predicaments of my people. I have done this in acceptance of the many requests from citizens and friends from within and outside Biafra to publish selected speeches of mine since my appointment by Major General J. T. U. Aguiyi-Ironsi, Nigerian Head of State and Supreme Commander of the Armed Forces, and my mandate as the Biafran Head of State following my people's declaration of independence and assumption of sovereignty on May 30, 1967. I do this in the belief that: (a) the speeches will show my humble, sincere, but abortive efforts in trying to save what could be saved of Nigeria; (b) the speeches will show the world that for which Biafra stands, for what she has made such sacrifice, and the reason of our commitment to this struggle.

The speeches are published in sections arranged according to significance. To each section or group I have added a short introduction in the form of a diary, which I hope will be of some historical value. The random thoughts in the second volume arise from discussions and interviews I have held in the course of this struggle. I have added them in the hope that they will stimulate African thought and, in some way, assist and encourage the black man to understand his predicament in the struggle for his self-realization.

The circumstances of this publication are by no means ideal. It is therefore possible that some of the thoughts are yet incomplete. I make no apologies for this, as my intention is merely to present, as a kaleidoscope, thoughts as they occurred to me in the very heat of this struggle.

Finally, let me place on record my gratitude to Douglas Ngwube and Uche Chukwumerije for collecting and compiling both the speeches and the random thoughts, to the stenographers of the State House and the Ministry of Information, in particular Dan Anazonwu and Michael Nwokoye, for their tireless efforts in presenting the manuscript in readable fashion. My thanks also go to Ntienyong Akpan, Sylvanus Cookey, Francis Nwokedi, Godwin Onyegbula, and Emeka Mojekwu for their advice and comments throughout the preparation of this volume; to Ifeyinwa Okeke, my personal secretary, whose safekeeping of the various documents made this publication possible, and to a host of others too many to mention by name but without whom the preparation of both the document and the development of the thoughts could never have been presented.

C. ODUMEGWU OJUKWU

Biafra Lodge, Biafra
May 30, 1969

Introduction:
Their Bones Shall Rise

The history of the world is a chronicle of oppression. The true measure of man is the degree of his success in meeting the challenge posed by this oppression. Man, therefore, is born oppressed, his life is a struggle and his fulfillment freedom. Of all peoples the most oppressed is the black man, his true measure as man is mirrored only by the degree of his success in meeting the challenge posed by imperialism. The story of Biafra is an account of the heroic efforts of the Biafran people to meet the challenge of colonialism in all its forms.

Historical precedents, while constantly reaffirming the unchanging pattern of oppression, continually indicate that revolution is the only means left to a people for changing or breaking off the shackles of colonial oppression. Since oppression is maintained by force, it is only possible to remove that force by a counter force. Because force to maintain colonialism is always material —the products of a sophisticated network of industry and technology—because this force is often denied the oppressed, force becomes the major weapon in the revolutionary arsenal of an oppressed people. It is this force, which is moral, that enables a total mobilization of the oppressed people to combat the oppressor. This force—the revolution within—so changes the oppressed people that almost overnight the stigmatized, lazy, cowardly, primitive people, without initiative, without stamina, at once becomes hard-working, courageous, ingenious, persistent, modern. The metamorphosis is so complete, the result so unlike the original that the imperial giant finds itself fighting the unknown—an

enemy it made no plans to meet. It is the nature of
this change that forces the oppressor to make wrong
assessments, continually to miscalculate. He stumbles
from one objective to another, from one dateline to
another dateline, and from one final offensive to another. The war is prolonged, and he has no explanation.
His soldiers get disillusioned, his people bewildered.
For the enemy, war becomes an exercise in futility—
shadow-boxing of the worst type—until finally he col-
lapses through the sheer weight of frustration.

To us, war becomes a David-and-Goliath struggle—
a struggle which David inevitably must win. The oppressed people of Biafra believe in this moral force that
will inevitably humble the Nigerian giant and her bloodthirsty collaborators. In the course of this war, by a
system of constant analysis and deduction, we have set
out to remove the internal contradictions in our society
and to purify our body politic. This becomes the bed-
rock upon which our nation is founded.

• Hence, revolution for a colonized people is not a
series of acts of violence, which in themselves are often
revolutionary, but an indeterminate sequence of social
changes punctuated and supported by various acts of
violence..The complexities, the varied aspects, the full
ramifications of colonialism are such that they at once
make the struggle for freedom total and absolute. This
demands of the oppressed first an identification, then a
rejection of everything colonial, finally a determination,
lest it should ever recur, totally to eliminate all vestiges
of colonialism wherever it is found.

Colonial peoples today have variedly become aware
of the unnatural limitations imposed on progress by a
colonial status—as a people we have partially identified
and in identifying partially rejected its various aspects.
It is this that has made possible a new form of colonialism in which oppression is no longer by direct application but by distant impulses and self-imposed by reflex
action. Neocolonialism came to Africa by subterfuge,
by diverting the tide of nationalism before it had gath-

ered full momentum, by luring the unwary nationalist
away from his people's declared objectives with premature victories and by clothing the imperialist in the
false garb of defeat. Africa today has recognized this
subterfuge, Africa now understands the tactics of the
enemy—the tactical withdrawal which has lured her
into a hasty pursuit without the protection of her flanks
and rear. We have learned lately that the intention of
the imperialist is to cut the vanguard of our struggle
from the rear, to destroy that vanguard, and finally, to
retake the reins of power—a project made easy by the
demise of vanguard leadership—and impose a subjugation more total and a slavery more abject.

It is this discovery that has changed the pattern of
revolutionary struggle in Africa. Countries with nom-
inal independence have become aware that colonialism
does not die with the granting of independence.• They
have come to learn belatedly that independence—true
independence—is never granted but seized by the determined will of the people.• They know that true independence—freedom—comes only through revolution.
Countries not yet independent, with awareness of and
learning from the mistakes of the past, will no longer
take the easy way but will embark upon a revolution
as the sure road to freedom and fulfillment. For Africa
today, life takes on the aspect of a protracted war. We
learn that the enemy is not simply white, not simply the
colonial or ex-colonial master, but that the enemy is
neocolonialism; it is everything that threatens to destroy
African dignity both within the African state and without. We can be, and frequently are, our own enemies.
We have learned today what many on other continents
have learned before us: that it is only in the unequal
war which characterizes the struggle for national liberation that a people rid themselves of the myriads of
shackles backing each and every sinew that impede their
march to self-realization and fulfillment.

Arising from Africa's failure in the first pitched battle
against colonialism, arising from the ease with which

Africa's vanguard leaders were lured deep into the ambush which left the leaders prisoners of war with rights, as it were, under the Geneva Convention and her people subjected to moral occupation, the whole problem of leadership in a revolutionary struggle for a people's self-determination becomes a major preoccupation with the people in their determination to succeed. The structure of power and the control by the people of those who exercise power on their behalf becomes the ground floor of the revolutionary edifice.

To understand the anti-colonialist struggle one has to see the struggle in its true guise—a struggle for human dignity. This is the essence of the Biafran struggle; in this context only can one understand our attitude to our sufferings, deprivations, to brutality, to our friends, to our enemies, and to the future. We do not ask for pity, we make no apologies for the social phenomenon known as the Biafran revolution; rather, we proclaim with pride the inevitability of our struggle, the indestructibility of our people, and the assured finality of our success. We do not claim to be unique either in our suffering or in our achievement. What we proclaim is that we follow a laid-down pattern for man.
• The course is pre-set, as is the pattern of our revolutionary struggle. For South Sudan, for Vietnam, for Ireland, in Africa, in Asia, in Europe, for black, for yellow, for white, the pattern is the same whenever man at any stage in his history decides and sets out to assert his dignity and freedom.

Biafra is a child of circumstance. Like a premature baby born by Caesarean section, anemic and sustained by blood transfusion, destined, like the original Caesar for great works. His existence and survival are always a marvel, sometimes bordering on a miracle. His life is a tribute to man, his courage is his endurance, his ingenuity his humanity. There was never a laid-down plan—no long-haired intellectuals burning midnight oil in downtown cafes—no plotters, no systematic indoctrination, no cruelly induced conformity. The Biafran is a victim, a victim of a series of actions directed at his destruction. The only thing positive is his reflex to live, to prevent further death—a rejection of genocide. From the dawn of history he has been visited with many scourges—first, for his strength, he was made slave and in slavery his ability marked him out for resentment and persecution. In persecution his resilience led from murder to massacre, massacre to pogrom and to genocide. These self-same attributes—strength, ability, and resilience—ensure for him the fulfillment of his destiny.

Thoughts in this section of the book are random thoughts. They are, perhaps reflecting our circumstances, my reactions to the ever-changing circumstance of a vicious and unequal war. The thoughts are, of course, colored sometimes by the elation of a not-too-frequent military or diplomatic success, sometimes by the depression of a near calamitous setback. Through them emerges the essence of this phenomenon known as the Biafran Revolution, through them the logic of our struggle, through them the meaning of our sacrifice.

A great deal has been said about the Biafran struggle, a great deal has been written; yet a series of questions persist. While I do not provide the final answer, the careful reader will find indications of the attitude of mind that has governed my reactions and those of my people in this struggle. It is impossible in one work to set out in detail the full dimension of this African tragedy and the entire complex nature of this drama.

The war has continued, bringing with it increasing misery for the Biafran people. The apathy and direct collaboration of the great powers has continued to sidetrack the main issues, and all indications are that the world has and will continue to sentence Biafra to death.

Apologists of the illegal régime in Lagos under Gowon have accused Biafra of playing politics with her people's misery. Our answer is simple: "We do not play politics. We are not masochists; rather, we are a people who choose to hunger a little to remain alive instead of feeding fat to become respectable corpses."

We have been accused of flirtation on the one side with
socialism and communism, on the other side with imperialism and capitalism. To this we say we do neither:
we are simply a Biafran people, an African people, a
black people. What we seek is no slogan, our aim is
not an attachment to any one group in the present-day
world power conflict. Perhaps on reading through some
of my thoughts in this volume I would be accused of
being racist. This could not be further from the truth.
I do not believe in racism but I acknowledge fully the
existence of race. I believe that the future in Africa
today demands of Africans this formal acknowledg-
ment. We cannot go on pretending that there are no
immigrant populations on the African soil. My contention is that co-existence would be the ideal, since we
cannot either subscribe to a genocide or a mass deporta-
tion of populations, having ourselves been victims of
such an attempt. I believe that the ideal would be a
form of co-existence based on mutual respect and equality, a meaningful dialogue with those neighbors with
whom we have to co-exist. To generate mutual respect
and equality, it is necessary for the black man first to
purify himself and to make his own achievements.

Our struggle has been balked by the bogey of Balkanization. I reject this. Europe found peace through Balkanization, why not Africa through Biafranization? By
Balkanization, Europe gave proof to the truth that all
conflict has as its root cause the desire of one party to
dominate the other. We propose the same answer—
sovereignty for nations that assert their rights to self-
determination. Some critics have wondered why we
cannot accept a re-incorporation into Nigeria. The
answer is simple, we are not Nigerians, the Nigerians
have made us learn this to our bitter cost. Besides, what
can Nigeria hold for a re-incorporated Biafra? The
thousands massacred, the scores of unrelenting waves
of atrocities, the ruins of enterprise, the destitution
caused by total dispossession, the despoliation of life,
institution and livelihood—what reparations can Nigeria

offer? Without reparations, what life can Nigeria offer Biafrans? Nigeria has neither the means nor the will to re-incorporate Biafra into a meaningful existence in one political entity.

I have been unabashed in my commentary on the Organization of African Unity and the problems of African Unity. This is because of my absolute conviction that there is nothing exclusive in the term "Unity." I believe that unity for Africa holds out the best chance for progress when that unity is a unity of purpose rather than the present hollow approach to unity for the sake of unity. For unity to be meaningful it has to be creative, not the unity of Jonah in the whale but the unity of holy matrimony. The first can only lead to defecation, the second to procreation.

Perhaps the reader will ask, "Why continue?" My reply is simple, "Today I live because I have my rifle. I cannot, I must not give up my rifle. Having a rifle is the only chance I still have of giving meaning to my death."

My people live, you ask . . . How? Simply by living —we are human. We live. We fight, fight because the decision to be free is a decision taken freely and collectively, because to become involved in the violent struggle for freedom is the only honor left to an oppressed people threatened with genocide, because in the final analysis the only true bulwark against death is to live. Biafra rejects death . . . so Biafra lives.

C. ODUMEGWU OJUKWU

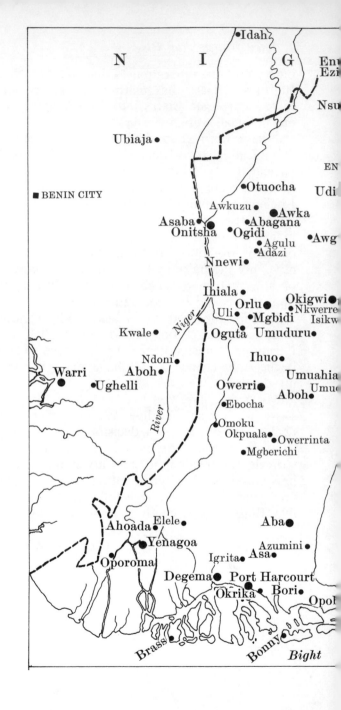

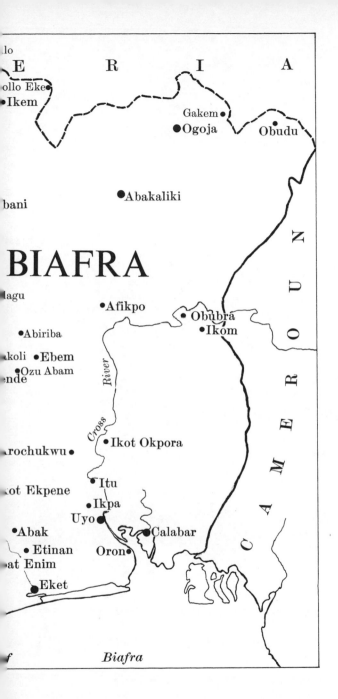

BIAFRA

1
Selected Speeches

I

The Blood of Martyrs

Nigeria never was and can never be a united country. The very nature of Nigeria inevitably gave rise to political power groups, goaded by sectional rather than national interests. These groups were clearly defined and perpetuated by the constitution itself. The veneer of unity generated and maintained by the veiled threat implicit in an imperial presence became exposed with the coming of independence, and left Nigeria a disjointed mass. Her only claim to form and sense was to be found in the nostalgic ruminations of the withered minds of ex-colonial office wallahs. Nigeria was not united—the Nigerians knew it.

From the moment of independence, all forms of corruption in public life found a good thriving ground in Nigeria, as also the different forms of injustices, oppression, discrimination, rivalry, suspicion, and hate. The country creaked and groaned; her institutions, structures, and organizations began to crack and cracked fast. Chaos was growing. Civil strife was evident. Lives and property were destroyed. All to satisfy political ambitions and fulfill sectional interests. The Nigerian colossus showed its feet of clay, and it became a question of time when the grandiose edifice would disintegrate and crumble to dust. The 1965 general elections in Western Nigeria brought all these acts and manifestations to their heights, and the inevitable consequence was a civil war.

To stem the disaster, a group of young army officers and men, drawn from all sections of the country, acted on January 15, 1966. The civilian governments of Ni-

1

geria had no alternative but to hand over power, in a formal way, to the army. Major General Aguiyi-Ironsi, the most senior officer and head of the Nigerian army, became Supreme Commander and Head of the State of Nigeria. He appointed military governors to the different regions (then to be known as groups of provinces to foreshadow the regime's determination to correct the past). I was appointed military governor for the eastern group of provinces. The Supreme Military Council and the Federal Executive Council were established for the Federation, while the governors were empowered to establish their own executive councils in the groups of provinces for which they were responsible.

The generality of the people welcomed the change with jubilation and relief. All political parties did the same. Even the feudalistic rulers of the North could not be outdone in their public expression of enthusiasm and a feeling of relief. Everyone promised support. Everyone saw the change as a needed chance for survival, an opportunity to avoid chaos, civil war, and the disintegration of the country. They saw the change as the key and gateway to justice, stability, and unity.

The military governments were determined to meet the people's wishes and aspirations. Their aim was to correct the past and lay foundations for a better future. All their pledges to the country were to this end. The people wanted unity; they wanted peace; they wanted progress; they wanted stability and fairness; they wanted to live, act, and be treated as real and true citizens of one country. Thirty-three decrees were passed within a period of four months—all in furtherance of the people's desires and yearnings. But these decrees turned out to be nothing but pious hopes, without getting at the roots of the problems.

On May 24, 1966, Decree No. 34 was promulgated. Its aim was principally to attune the country's administration to the existing unified command made necessary by the fact of military rule. Even in this, the government could not rise under the crushing weight of the white elephant of the North. What set out in concept to decree unity was watered down to mere centralization. The enlightened sections of the country welcomed and acclaimed the decree as a step, though belated, in the right direction. The North saw it as unifying the country, a development which they abhorred. They decided to act and took the law into their own hands, and the federal government appeared helpless.

Easterners resident in the North were massacred in the first pogrom of May 29, 1966. According to the usually conservative police estimate, 3,300 men, women, and children of Eastern Nigerian origin were massacred in the North as a result. It was not a spontaneous but a premeditated and deliberate act—diabolical in concept and maniacal in execution.

Our people began to run home from the North in fear and panic. A number of them came to me personally as the military governor of the Eastern group of provinces. While sympathizing with their pitiable condition, I gave them assurances that justice would be done and persuaded them to return to the North. They took my word and returned. My belief and interest in the oneness and unity of Nigeria remained overriding, as further evidenced by my appointment of the Emir of Kano as the chancellor of the University of Nigeria, Nsukka, in replacement of Dr. Nnamdi Azikiwe, that much beloved and revered son of Biafra.

The Supreme Military Council met, as did the Federal Executive Council. A decision was taken to set up a Commission of Inquiry under a British judge of the High Court. As soon as this decision was known, the emirs met and sent a short note of insult and defiance to the federal government that they would never tolerate such an inquiry. They eventually had their way.

Instead of acting firmly to call the Northern bluff and put an end to their defiance, the Federal Military Government resorted to the oft-tried and unrewarding practice of appeasement. Major General Aguiyi-Ironsi decided to go to the North personally to reassure the emirs. Indeed, if anything, Major General Aguiyi-Ironsi's approach to the North was so partial that it caused a number of people in the South some embarrassment. Federal funds for a crash educational program in the North were hurriedly increased as an earnest of the federal government's desire to bridge the educational gap existing between the North and the South.

Major General Ironsi's commitment to peace and unity in Nigeria was a personal obsession, but his appeasement policy satisfied neither the North nor the South. While he was in the North, the plan for his elimination was completed by Gowon, the main instrument of the feudal North.

On July 29, 1966, while Major General Aguiyi-Ironsi was on a visit to Ibadan, where he was to meet and explain his government's intentions to all the chiefs and traditional rulers of Nigeria, Northern soldiers under Gowon's illegal orders abducted and killed him, and with him his gallant host, Lieutenant Colonel Fajuyi. Simultaneous with the abduction and murder of Major General Aguiyi-Ironsi, officers and men of Eastern Nigerian origin then in the army were set upon and many were massacred. Those of us in the then Eastern Nigeria were saved by sheer providence following a mysterious but timely telephone call from Abeokuta. I rushed to the army barracks only to find the Northern soldiers already in battle uniform and about to break into the magazine for weapons to destroy me and my colleagues. I had to abandon my official residence and take refuge in the police headquarters.

I got in touch with Brigadier Ogundipe on telephone and tried to persuade him to step in and arrest the situation. His state of mind was one of utter helplessness, incoherent and inept. He abandoned his responsibility and fled his post. Later, I got in touch with Gowon, the architect of the mutiny. I impressed upon him the need to stop the bloodshed. On his insistence that he assume supreme command, I made it quite clear to him that I could not recognize him as the Head of the Federal Military Government and Supreme Commander. I urged a meeting of the Supreme Military Council to regularize the question of leadership in accordance with military practice, having regard to the established hierarchy. In spite of this warning, Gowon went on the air and announced himself as the Supreme Commander and Head of the Federal Military Government.

It is worthwhile mentioning here that following the abduction and massacre of the Supreme Commander, the intention of Gowon and his fellow Northerners was to secede.

Gowon, in fact, personally told me over the phone (and the conversation was duly recorded) that the North wanted to secede. Much as the idea shocked me at the time, I told him that if that would lead to peace, they could go ahead. Gowon had left the Lagos island to go to Ikeja barracks, where the Northern flag of the new Republic of the North was flown. A speech had been prepared for him, announcing the secession of the North from the rest of Nigeria. Meanwhile Northern Nigerian personnel and families were evacuated in commandeered aircrafts of the BOAC. It was the British and American diplomatic representatives in Lagos who intervened and stopped the North from seceding as had been their definite plan. There is evidence that the British High Commissioner in Lagos, after expounding to Gowon the opportunities now offered to him and the Northern people for the domination of Nigeria, also assured Gowon of the British government's pledge to give him every support to maintain that domination. As a result, the speech as finally delivered by Gowon bore traces of very hasty amendment and edition which did not conceal the real underlining reason for the mutiny—that the basis of unity in Nigeria did not exist.

At my own insistence, a meeting of the representatives of the military governors was held on August 9, 1966, where the following decisions were taken:

(1) Immediate steps should be taken by the Supreme Commander to post military personnel to barracks within their respective regions of origin.

(2) Having regard to its peculiar position the question of maintenance of peace and security in Lagos should be left to the Supreme Commander in consultation with the military governors.

(3) A meeting of this committee or an enlarged body should take place in a week's time to recommend in broad outlines the form of political association which the country should adopt in the future.

(4) Immediate steps should be taken to nullify or modify any provisions of any decree which assumes extreme centralization.

(5) The Supreme Commander should make conditions suitable for a meeting of the Supreme Military Council urgently as a further means of lowering tension.

None of the above decisions was implemented apart from that, because of my insistence and pressure, Northern soldiers were removed from Eastern Nigeria. Those of our officers and men who were sent back to the East from the North returned unarmed, even though, on agreement with Gowon, I allowed the Northern troops to take away their weapons, which were never returned.

As seen above, the meeting of the military governors' representatives had decided that a meeting of that committee or an enlarged one "should take place in a week's time to recommend in broad outlines the form of political association which the country should adopt in the future." That meeting did not take place until several weeks later when the Ad Hoc Constitutional Committee held its first meeting on September 12, 1966. It is significant that of all the memoranda submitted to that Ad Hoc Constitutional Conference the one submitted by the Eastern Nigeria delegation contained features for closer association among the peoples of Nigeria than those submitted by the North and the West. Indeed, in spite of the activities of the British High Commission behind the scenes, the meeting was able to take important decisions toward a confederal system of government. The subtleties of the behind-the-scene maneuvers was beyond the rude mind of the North, and it became necessary to halt the conference. The Northern delegation returned to the North and conferred with the British High Commission. A decision was taken to halt "the dangerous drift" into confederacy.

To effect this, while the meeting was still being held, the North unleashed another pogrom, which started on September 29, 1966, and eventually resulted in the massacre of more than 30,000 persons of Eastern Nigeria origin. (A special commission set up by the Eastern Nigeria government has since put the figure at 50,000.) Those massacred were not confined to any one ethnic group in Eastern Nigeria but involved everybody known to have hailed from the area. Apart from the massacres in the North, there were sporadic killings of Eastern Nigerians in Lagos and Western Nigeria. The people of Eastern Nigeria became disillusioned and realized rather belatedly that Nigeria, a country for the unity of which they had sacrificed and invested more than any other people to build, offered them security neither of person nor of property. They fled back to the East to their homes as a final place of refuge. More than 2,000,000 of them returned, with a good fraction of them maimed and practically all of them without their material possessions.

Before this influx of dispossessed and destitute Easterners, the Eastern Nigeria government was already catering for 12,400,000 people under a tight budget resulting from an unfair system of revenue allocation of the time—an arrangement which made Eastern Nigeria contribute more to the revenue of the federal government than any other region. All appeals to the federal government to assist toward the rehabilitation of our people who had returned failed. Later on, Gowon and his junta, instead of assisting, added to the sufferings by refusing to pay those federal Nigerian employees who had returned to the East.

Rising to its responsibility, the government of the then Eastern Nigeria established a Rehabilitation Commission with an initial grant of £1,000,000. Typical of the people of Eastern Nigeria, now Biafra, the people collectively and individually rose to the occasion by giving all they could and making sacrifices in order to absorb their kith and kin now back to them for refuge. The value of our extended family system stood the test, and foreigners who visited us were amazed that people were not found sleeping in the streets or begging for food. Here I must mention that the National Red Cross and some commercial firms, both foreign and indigenous, did a great deal to help.

Writing about the refugees streaming into Eastern Nigeria at the time, a correspondent commented, in the *London Observer* of October 16, 1966: "After a fortnight, the scene in the Eastern region continues to be reminiscent of the ingathering of exiles into Israel after the end of the last war. The parallel is not fanciful. . . ."

Diary of Events: January 1–25, 1966

January 1–15: Violent riots in Middle Belt of Northern Nigeria continue. Intensification of popular resistance (under code name of Operation E-Wet-ie)* in Western Nigeria.

* A Yoruba corruption of the English word "wet." The operation involved wetting people, opponents especially, with petrol or other inflammables and setting fire to them.

January 14: Secret meeting in Kaduna, capital city of Northern Nigeria, between Sir Ahmadu Bello, Northern Nigerian Premier, Chief S. L. Akintola, Western Nigerian Premier, and some senior army officers, to finalize their plan for a coup on January 17. . . . Delivery of arms and money to Isaac Boro (who later became major in Nigerian army, killed at Port Harcourt in 1968), to start preliminary violent disturbances in the Riverine area of Eastern Nigeria.

January 15: Military coup by some young army officers. The most prominent members of the Command Group are Major Ademuyiga (Western Nigeria), Major Nzeogwu (Midwestern Nigeria) and Major Ifeajuna (Eastern Nigeria).

January 16: Tense atmosphere in the country. Nobody seems to know what has happened. As the officer commanding the 5th Battalion in Kano, Northern Nigeria, I anxiously spend the day trying to get Lagos on the phone. After many efforts and blank replies, I finally get Major General Aguiyi-Ironsi. . . . Late-afternoon announcement by the federal government:

. . . For some time now there have been escalating political disturbances in parts of Nigeria with increasing loss of faith between political parties, and between political leaders themselves. This crisis of confidence reached a head during the elections in the Western Region in October last year. There were charges by the opposition parties of rigging of the elections and general abuse of power by the regional government in the conduct of the elections. Riots, arson, murder, and looting became widespread in Western Nigeria since last October. The situation deteriorated and certain army officers attempted to seize power. . . .

The Council of Ministers of the federal government met and appraised the problems confronting the government. They appreciated the immediate need to control the serious situation which threatened the Federation. On Sunday, January 16, the Council of Ministers unanimously decided to hand over voluntarily the administration of the country, with immediate effect to the Nigerian army . . . the Nigerian armed forces have been invited to form an interim military government for the purpose of maintaining law and order and of maintaining essential services.

The invitation has been accepted and I, General Johnson Thomas Umunnakwe Aguiyi-Ironsi, the general officer commanding the Nigerian army, have been formally vested with authority as Head of the Federal Military Government and Supreme Commander of the Nigerian armed forces.

Popular disturbances in Western Nigeria and the Middle Belt cease.

January 17: Appointment of military governors to the Regions by Major General Aguiyi-Ironsi: Lieutenant Colonel Adekunle Fajuyi for Western Region, Lieutenant Colonel David Ejoor for Midwestern Region, Lieutenant Colonel Hassan Katsina for Northern Region, I for Eastern Region. . . . Major Nzeogwu, representing the coup command group in Kaduna, announces the formation of the "Supreme Council of the Revolution" in a press conference in Kaduna, appoints an eighteen-man revolutionary council and a government of civil servants for Northern Nigeria. . . .

January 17–19: Editorial comments in all Nigerian papers welcoming the January 15 revolution. Pledges of support from all political parties. Congratulatory messages from labor unions, students, and other groups.

January 18: Surrender of the Supreme Council of the revolution on the conditions that "the people (all former politicians) whom we sought to remove will not be returned to office . . . *and amnesty is granted to all the leaders of the January 15 Revolution.*" I sought amnesty—not granted unconditionally.

January 19: Gowon mandated to conduct full investigation. . . . Before he leaves under escort for Lagos, Nzeogwu introduces, at a press conference, Usman Hassan Katsina as the new military governor of Northern Nigeria. Nzeogwu describes Katsina as a faithful ally who in the critical moment gave his support to the revolution. Usman Katsina replies: "I have been able to help Nzeogwu with some of his problems during the past few days. I am his good friend and I am sure that he will now help me. We will work together for the betterment of our country." . . . I arrive in Lagos from Kano for the first consultation of all the military governors. . . . The establishment of Supreme Military Council and Federal Executive Council of the Federal Military Government. . . . I leave for Enugu, capital of Eastern Nigeria, to assume duty as the military governor of Eastern Nigeria. Speaking to the press at Enugu airport, I emphasize: "The Federal Military Government is determined to prevent Nigeria from disintegration and to maintain law and order by correcting a number of wrongs committed in the name of politics."

January 23: First Nigeria police security report discloses that 34 officers and more than 500 other ranks from all parts and ethnic groups in the Federation took part in the January 15 coup. . . . The report speculates that the coup is masterminded by Chief Obafemi Awolowo (now Nigerian Commissioner of Finance). . . . Leaders and participants in the coup are being detained as they emerge from hiding.

January 25: My first broadcast to the people of the Eastern Region.

High Hopes for Nigeria

(Broadcast, January 25, 1966)

This is a crucial moment in the history of our country—the dramatic culmination of ten wasted years of planlessness, incompetence, inefficiency, gross abuse of office, corruption, avarice, and gross disregard of the interests of the common man.

The financial institutions and statutory corporations have been completely misused for the self-aggrandizement of a number of adventurers in positions of power and influence. Under the system, mediocrities were transplanted overnight from situations of obscurity into positions of affluence and corrupt power.

Key projects in the National Development Plan were not pursued with necessary vigor. Instead of these, palaces were constructed for the indulgence of ministers and other holders of public offices—men supposed to serve the interest of the common man. Expensive fleets of flamboyant and luxurious cars were purchased. Taxpayers' money was wasted on unnecessary foreign travel by ministers, each competing with the other only in their unbridled excesses.

This has disrupted the economy, depressed the standard of living of the toiling masses, spiraled prices, and made the rich richer and the poor poorer. Internal squabbles for parochial and clannish patronage took the place of purposeful coordinated service of the people. Land, the basic heritage of the people, was converted into the private estates of rapacious individuals who, thus trampling on the rights of the people, violated their sacred trust under this system. The public service was being increasingly demoralized. Nepotism became rife. Tribalism became the order of the day. In appointments and promotions mere lip service was paid to honesty and hard work.

Under the system, efficiency inevitably declined. All this led inevitably to the complete loss of moral and political authority by the former regime.

You are aware of the dramatic events of the past few days which led to the self-liquidation of the federal government and its abandonment of power to the armed forces. You are also aware of the immediate steps taken by the Supreme Commander to set up an effective administration and to repair the damage done to the country by gangster politicians, and to set the country on the path of true progress and greatness—the creation of the Supreme Military Council, the appointment of military governors to administer the former regions under the direction of the Supreme Commander and Head of the Executive Council.

In the Eastern provinces, all executive powers are now vested in the military governor. In the day-to-day business of government, I have appointed an executive committee which will assist me. The executive committee will be composed of: (1) the military governor, (2) the commanding officer of the army in the Eastern provinces, (3) the commissioner of police, (4) the chief law officer, (5) the chief secretary, (6) the permanent secretary, Ministry of Finance.

All other permanent secretaries will be coopted to participate in the discussions of the business of their respective ministries.

It is our intention to stamp out inefficiency, corruption, and dishonesty in all facets of public life, to create the consciousness of national unity, and to lead the citizens of Nigeria as one disciplined people in a purposeful march to maximum realization of the country's potential.

The citizens of Nigeria must therefore realize that we are determined to turn our back forever on the unproductive drift of yesteryears. To this end, the following will come into immediate effect:

• All the powers and functions formerly vested in or exercised by the former governor, premier, and ministers have been vested in and will be exercised by the military governor.

• The Regional Public Service Commission shall no longer be responsible for the appointment and promotions of senior staff in the public service of the Eastern provinces. In the future, the Public Service Commission will act in an advisory capacity to the military governor in relation to the appointment, promotion, and discipline of senior members of the public service of the Eastern provinces.

• All provincial assemblies in Eastern Nigeria are abolished.

• The former regional governor, premier, ministers, provincial commissioners and parliamentary secretaries shall, if they have not already done so, vacate their former official residences and surrender any government property, including cars, in their possession forthwith.

- The post of agent-general for Eastern Nigeria in the United Kingdom is abolished.
- All photographs of the former president, prime minister, regional governors, premiers, and ministers shall be immediately removed from all public buildings in the Eastern provinces.
- These photographs shall be replaced with the photograph of His Excellency, the Head of the Military Government and Supreme Commander of the Nigerian armed forces, Major General J. T. U. Aguiyi-Ironsi.
- No person in the Eastern provinces, except the military governor, shall fly any flag on cars and private residences.
- The salaries of all members of boards of statutory corporations and companies, solely owned by the government of Eastern Nigeria, are hereby suspended until further notice. They will, however, be entitled to their present sitting allowances.
- All debtors to government or government-sponsored financial institutions are warned in their own interests to liquidate such debts without delay in order to avoid the use of drastic measures in their recovery.
- The public is hereby warned against bribery, nepotism, and other forms of corruption in public life. This warning is directed particularly to the holders of public offices in the police force, civil service, judiciary (including customary court judges), local government bodies, statutory corporations, and trade unions.
- All doctors, pharmacists, nurses, and other workers in hospitals are reminded of their responsibility for the health of the members of the public.
- The military government will not tolerate acts of irresponsibility, dereliction of duty, and corruption in government hospitals, maternities, health centers, and dispensaries. The military government will deal firmly with any case that comes to its notice.
- The public is warned against careless talk, acts, and gestures contemptuous of all sections of the public, calculated to incite or cause disaffection among any section of the community. Such acts will be deemed to constitute an offense against public order and will be dealt with summarily with firm measures.
- The activities of the regional and provincial scholarship

boards are suspended until further notice. In the future, scholarships will be awarded purely on the basis of merit to enable us to solve our urgent high-level manpower needs.

• The law establishing the University of Nsukka will be reviewed to ensure that matters academic are left entirely in the hands of the academicians, subject to the overall direction of the country's manpower needs as recommended by the National Universities Commission.

• The appointment of chairmen and members of statutory corporations will be reviewed, and any future appointment or reappointment will be based entirely on qualifications and merit.

I hereby call on all citizens, whether working in government or private organizations, to give to the military government both loyalty and hard work.

The military government will regard disloyalty, inefficiency, bribery, corruption, nepotism, abuse of public office, and squandering of public funds as acts of sabotage against the regime and will not hesitate to invoke summary measures against any offenders in any position.

Finally, I thank you for your widespread expressions of good will and support. Fellow citizens, I shall count on you.

Diary of Events: January 28 – May 30, 1966

January 28: Major General Aguiyi-Ironsi broadcasts to the nation. He announces that the Federal Military Government will take measures *inter alia*: (a) to end regionalism, tribal loyalties and activities which promote tribal consciousness and sectional interests; (b) to preserve Nigeria as one strong nation with a firm, honest, and disciplined leadership; (c) to stamp out corruption and dishonesty in public life and restore integrity and self-respect in public affairs; (d) to introduce administrative reforms and pursue with vigor the implementation of the Six-Year Development Plan.

February 2:   The first meeting of the Supreme Military Council in Lagos.

February 9:   I cut down ministries in the Eastern Region from fifteen to twelve as an economic measure.

February 10:   Measures by Federal Military Government on some national problems—abolition of prerevolution political parties, ban on tribal unions, etc.

February 11:   Enactment of the Detention (of Peoples) Decree by the Federal Military Government. Under this decree, Dr. M. I. Okpara, former Eastern Region premier, and some other prominent politicians in Southern Nigeria are detained. The Northern Nigerian politicians are left free.

February 24:   I appoint a ten-man Economic Advisory Committee for Eastern Region.

February 25:   Establishment by Federal Military Government of study groups on various obstacles to national unity and peace: Constitutional Review Group, Working Party on Primary and Secondary Education in Nigeria, Working Party on Technical, Commercial, and Vocational Education in Nigeria.

March 1:   My government's edict dissolving all local government councils in Eastern Nigeria. . . . Appointment of Dr. N. B. Graham-Douglas as attorney general for Eastern Nigeria.

March 3–6:   Meeting of the Supreme Military Council to discuss *inter alia* the national budget for the next financial year.

March 8:   I appoint Alhaji Ado Bayero, Emir of Kano, Northern Nigeria, as new chancellor of the University of Nigeria, Nsukka, Eastern Nigeria.

March 9–10:   Beginning of insinuations in Hausa-language section of Northern Nigerian press against national unity and activities of Federal Military Government. Reports of suspicious movements of British nationals in Northern Nigeria.

March 31: National Budget Broadcast by Major General Aguiyi-Ironsi—"Unity Budget." He announces federal government's plan to: (a) alleviate the suffering of the lower-income group; (b) develop the North educationally in order to lessen the disparity between the feudal North and the progressive South; (c) expedite development programs for the whole nation.

April 3: My budget speech, presenting the regional budget for the new financial year. I declare: "As you no doubt have realized from the Supreme Commander's budget speech, unity is the keynote of this year's budget. Unity of the people of Nigeria. The military government is determined that the word "unity" shall no longer be a catchword or an empty slogan. Unity must be practiced and carried to its logical conclusion. Unity therefore means having uniform standards throughout the whole republic. . . ."

May 24: Decree No. 34 substituting the phrase "group of provinces" to "region" and formalizing as an interim administrative measure the unified nature of army command for the convenience of the Federal Military Government. . . . Mr. S. S. Richardson, the British expatriate deputy vice-chancellor and director of the Institute of Administration, Ahmadu Bello University, tells groups of Northern Nigerian students that if they protest against measures decreed by the Federal Military Government they will be considered as defending their right and fighting for a good cause. . . . In the night, the Northern Students Association, a student wing of the Northern People's Congress, holds a secret meeting in Ahmadu Bello University, Zaria.

May 25: The Northern students send a secret delegation to the Northern military governor and hold secret talks in Kaduna with top civil servants. . . . British lecturers in Zaria and politicians of Northern People's Congress intensify midnight campaign against national unity and the Federal Military Government.

May 27: After a meeting to finalize plans for a positive action against closer national unity, and against

Eastern Nigerians resident in the region, Northern Nigerian students dispatch coordinators to all the main centers of the region to liaise with emirs and their feudal
district heads on the execution of the planned action.

May 28:   Truckloads of armed students and thugs
begin to arrive in major towns of Northern Nigeria. . . .
A meeting of the Northern Students Association, which
lasts until early hours of Sunday, May 29. A Britisher,
Major Boyle (the estate manager of the university),
presides over the meeting.

May 29–30:   At 7 A.M. (Sunday), Northern students troop out of the university campus and fan out
in prearranged squads to Zaria, Kaduna, and other
towns in Northern Nigeria. They spearhead demonstrations in the North against Nigerian unity. The demonstrators carry placards demanding the secession of
Northern Region from the rest of Nigeria. Armed with
knives, clubs, and stones, they invade the churches, attack and massacre Eastern Nigerian worshipers. They
spread to all streets in Sabon-gari ("Strangers' " Quarters), massacring Eastern Nigerians and looting their
property. More than 3,000 Eastern Nigerians are massacred.

May 30:   Eastern Nigerian residents, no longer sure
of their safety in Northern region, begin to flock back
as refugees to their region of origin.

May 29 Pogrom

(Broadcast May 30, 1966)

In the past twenty-four hours there have been disturbances in certain parts of the Northern provinces.
These disturbances are a sequel to the promulgation on
national unity, which the Head of the National Military
Government and Supreme Commander made a few
days ago.

Many of you will no doubt have heard the statement of the Supreme Commander yesterday in which he stated that these disturbances are being caused by a few misguided Nigerians in collusion with foreign nationals whose objective is the sowing of discord among sections of the population. You will also no doubt have heard the broadcast of the military governor of the Northern provinces in which he stated that active steps were being taken to contain the situation.

Since its assumption of office five months ago, the National Military Government has been making strenuous efforts to create an atmosphere in which Nigerians can live and work together as brothers.

It is a matter for deep regret that some people by their ill-considered actions are trying to set the hands of the clock back. The military government is committed to the forging and maintenance of national unity and cannot be diverted from these objectives by these events.

I wish to assure all of you that the National Military Government is taking all necessary steps to bring the situation back to normal. The steps taken so far have had a salutary effect. Those Nigerians who are fomenting these disturbances will face the consequences of their actions, and their foreign backers will be dealt with in an appropriate manner.

I wish also to assure all of you, especially those of you who have relatives in the disturbed areas, that there is no cause for panic or alarm. All necessary action will be taken by the military government. No one must take the law into his own hands or use this as an opportunity of starting other troubles in these provinces. Everyone must go about his or her business peacefully and rest assured that the government has the situation well in hand.

Finally, I must repeat my earlier warning against careless talk and rumor-mongering. In times like this, these can only exacerbate the situation.

Diary of Events:
May 31–June 15, 1966

May 31: The slaughter of Easterners continues simultaneously in some Northern Nigeria towns. Some British expatriates provide vehicles to transport Northern looters and arms from the villages to planned targets of attacks (Easterners) in the towns. . . . I fly to Lagos to ask for an emergency meeting of the Supreme Military Council, which will initiate measures to stop the bloodshed.

June 1: Northern Nigerian emirs and the Northern military governor hold a secret meeting in Kaduna. In the meeting, they agree to oppose the implementation of Decree No. 34 and to pull Northern Nigeria out of the Federation if the Federal Military Government takes more measures to foster national unity. . . . The meeting of the Supreme Military Council on May 29 pogrom. The council decides to appoint a Commission of Inquiry under the chairmanship of a British High Court judge to investigate the pogrom. It also agrees on assurances of safety to Easterners and guarantees that there will be no more pogroms against Easterners.

June 5: More massacres of Easterners and the looting of their property occur in Gombe, Kaura Namoda, and Katsina, towns of Northern Nigeria.

June 6–8: Northern emirs meet and send this message to the Federal Military Government: *"We have received with dismay your intention to hold a Commission of Inquiry. We wish to inform you that this will be held over our dead bodies."* . . . Rumors of Northern Nigeria's plan to secede from the Federation sweep through Lagos.

June 8–15: Increase of appeasement gestures toward the North by Major General Aguiyi-Ironsi: accelerated promotions of Northern Nigerians in the federal service, profuse explanations by federal information services that Decree 34 is not intended to impose a unitary system of government on the country and that the future of the country will be decided by the people themselves. Speeding up of plan to divert federal funds to Northern Nigeria for a crash education program.

June 15: My appeals to Eastern Nigerians who fled the North to return to Northern Nigeria and my assurance that Northern Nigeria is now safe for all Nigerians. ... Easterners promptly heed my appeal and begin to return to their places of work in Northern Nigeria.

The Last Sacrifice

(Speech at state banquet in honor of the Emir of Kano, June 27, 1966)

I am sure that I shall be expressing the minds and feelings of all who are gathered here when I say that we are extremely happy to have in our midst, as the guest of honor tonight, His Highness Alhaji Ado Bayero, the Emir of Kano. His Highness and I are old friends. We met some five years ago under rather different circumstances—His Highness was then a chief of the Kano native administration police, and I was a young major in the brigade headquarters in Kaduna. We met again soon after my arrival in Kano in January, 1964, as commander of the 5th Battalion of the Nigerian army. It was during this period, through constant official and social contacts, that our acquaintance blossomed into what I am proud to call firm friendship. Unfortunately, when the time came for me to leave Kano the circumstances were such that it was impossible for me to take leave and to thank him for his great sympathy and charity. I was in command at Kano during the crisis of January 15, and I judge it a great tribute to our friendship that in close cooperation, Kano was kept insulated throughout from the turmoil and bloodshed of those days. I therefore feel honored and privileged to be able to say both welcome and thank you to an old and trusted friend.

Your Highness, may I start by offering you once again our heartiest congratulations and very best wishes on your appointment as the chancellor of the University of Nigeria, in which office you were installed with appropriate pomp and dignity yesterday. You must yourself have sensed the unfathomable depth of goodwill generated and transparently shown for you by the people on that occasion. . . .

The University of Nigeria is a young but great institution, full of hope and promise for this country; so also, if I may be permitted to say so, are you as a person. At your early age of thirty-six (or is it thirty-five?) you have distinguished yourself as an individual, independently of your birth and heritage. A prince though you were, you chose early in life to tread the path of the ordinary man, and this is now helping you, as one of the powerful potentates of this country, to have the right insight into, and understanding of, the needs and aspirations of the commonality of this country. This understanding and insight have made you one of the most highly respected figures in this country and beyond.

As a rich agricultural belt, center of trade and of growing industries, the increasing role that the emirate must play in the overall development of this country cannot be minimized. It is against this background that the cosmopolitan and heterogeneous character of the area can be understood. This is something which has augured well for this country—a country earnestly striving to weld its people together in love, mutual understanding, and respect.

The Kano dynasty, of which you are the worthy heir, is long established. Over it reigned an almost unbroken succession of forty-three kings through the centuries until 1807. Your illustrious father, His Highness Alhaji

Abdulahi Bayero, who reigned for twenty-seven long years from 1926 to 1953, earned a reputation in history as a reformist ruler, on account of the emphasis he placed on education, transport, communication, and other modern amenities for the advancement of this city-state. Indeed, the era of reform begun by your father and continued by you has had deep roots in the modern story of Kano.

Here, Your Highness, I must extend to you and the people of your emirate the sympathy of the people of this group of provinces on the sad and tragic events of recent weeks, events which erupted in parts of the Northern group of provinces, including your area of authority. I know that those events have greatly distressed you, as they have all well-meaning Nigerians and friends of Nigeria.

We must thank Providence that the situation has been brought under control. The military government has already reaffirmed its reliance on the good sense and mature leadership of the emirs and all traditional rulers of the country to ensure that that sort of episode is never allowed to occur again.

Meanwhile, we must accept the sad events as a challenge to all who have dedicated their energies to the tasks of unity for the country. No doubt, enemies and cynics have taken false comfort in those events. It is for the forces of construction and unity to go on marching to the promised land of brotherhood and oneness for the country.

Lives and property have been lost; many have been made homeless; others have been bereft of their loved ones; confidence has been shaken; fear has replaced faith in one toward the other. These are sad reflections which must remain a source of guilt and shame for all who, by deliberate acts and insinuations, were responsible, directly or indirectly, for them. We cannot restore the lives which have been lost nor the blood which has been shed. But we should not ignore the fact that they have been valuable lives and blood. It must, therefore, be our prayer that the innocent blood thus shed will be accepted as the supreme purchase price for the solid and everlasting unity of this country, and that the events which had led to the situation will, forever, be the worst that this country should experience.

We are passing through an exciting and delicate period in our national life. It would be naïve to think that that passage will be smooth at all times and places. We have as our goals progress and unity for this country. Our journey to these goals, fast and imaginative as it must be, is bound to take us through rough portions and periods. That must be so if we are truly to appreciate and value what we shall have achieved.

The aims of the military government have been repeatedly stated in clear and unmistakable terms. Those aims conform with the statement of a great American philosopher who said: "The purpose of military rule is to provide time for moral ideas to take root; the ideas of justice; the ideas of fairness; the ideas of merit; the ideas of unity and solidarity." The military government is in power in Nigeria today because the nation needed a corrective force which would foster and enthrone those ideals—ideals which were being desecrated, debased, and virtually destroyed.

It is the place of the armed forces to protect and defend the country, and not its place to govern or rule. But when it is necessary for them to assume political power, it is always for definite objectives which they must allow nothing to stand in their way of achieving. Those objectives for us are fairness and fair play, justice, merit, and unity and solidarity.

Ours is to "provide time for these ideas to take root" —or, at least, to provide the necessary conditions for these ideas to grow and thrive. As military men we do not claim to have cut-and-dried answers to all the problems now confronting the nation. It is therefore totally unfair and unjustified for anyone to fear that the army is out to impose permanent arrangements on the people. Any such fears must be dislodged and destroyed from any minds where they may be lurking.

As Nigerians, we naturally have ideas of the areas from which the national ills and ailments have in the past emanated. In order to find out and provide the right remedies, we have set up many expert committees and commissions to have a detached and objective look into these areas and suggest remedies which will make them cease to be sources of discomfort for the nation. When they have finished their work, their recommendations will be placed before the people for consideration before adoption. Let me repeat and emphasize that everyone will be involved and expected to participate in that final exercise. Meanwhile it is the duty of everyone to give the expert bodies and commissions, now engaged on the essential groundwork, every cooperation. I have said that fairness and national unity and solidarity are among our objectives. Let me try to say a few words about these two objectives.

First, *fairness*. We are aware of the uneven development of this country; we know that wealth and opportunities are not the same for all areas. We know the basic factors which influence all these. Those factors are *education, economic activities,* and *health*. In the past, under the old regime with its regional and rival setups, these vital factors were sectionally controlled and selfishly managed, with the result that the gaps of unevenness kept widening rather than narrowing, and the country's natural resources, human and material, were not closely coordinated for the general good. As an integral whole, this country must present equal opportunities for all everywhere; we must pool our resources for the benefit of *all* sections.

It was precisely in order to achieve these that the military government took the earliest possible steps to make education, agriculture, industries, commerce, and health national responsibilities and not sectional ones as they were before. Undertaken and coordinated at the national level, the even development of the country will be pursued to achievement. We shall be able to use our common national earnings to bring up the standards of education and living where they have been lagging behind; we shall ensure maximum productivity by moving trained and experienced personnel about; we shall modernize our agriculture in order to provide adequate food for our teeming population and also obtain the best marketing facilities and prices for their exports; we shall use the wealth gained from our unlimited natural resources such as oil and gas, iron and ore, lead and zinc, uranium, etc., for the overall economic and social development of the country.

I have talked of ensuring maximum productivity through the deployment of trained and experienced personnel according to need. That is the sole motive behind the national government's unification of the civil service. Far from this being done in order to place any person or group of persons at a disadvantage, it is to help ourselves by utilizing to the full what we have. What is the sense of allowing schools in some areas to starve of trained teachers while some areas are having enough and even to spare? What is the sense in going overseas to beg for help without first exhausting what we have? Why restrict the varying experience of the civil service to compartments when the best could be made of it in an open and common pool?

I now come to the objective of national unity and solidarity. For years this country has striven for unity. In this we have met and passed many hurdles. All the danger points of disintegration have been passed. The common generality of the people of this country have come to regard one another as brothers and sisters. The conscious and unconscious apostles of disunity are not the common men and women of this country. They are the few with vested interests, selfish and inordinate ambition for power and wealth, men who fear losing their positions and privileges, who care more for self than for the nation and the common good. These men have tried to exploit our differences to the detriment of the country, when they should be expected to work for the removal of those differences. They have tried to make unhealthy capital of our diversity, when a healthy perception of our diversity could be turned to our national advantage as a source of strength—diversity of culture, of background, of outlook, of experience, of education, of upbringings. Our diversity is not confined to our environments and other things I have named. It embraces our natural resources and facilities.

I have shown how the military government is already trying to pool and coordinate these for the common good. Why can't we accept that we can make similar use of other diversities? What makes Russia with its 230,000,000 people, China with its 500,000,000, great? It is their very diversities. According to the last census, Nigeria is only 55,000,000. In terms of size these other countries are several times that of Nigeria. Why is it that these countries have succeeded in unity? Why should Nigerians who have known of these facts continue to allow themselves to be ridden with fears, hesitations, and doubts? Why should we continue to allow ourselves to be deceived? Even historic experiences have demonstrated that diversity in religion, rather than militate against unity, has tended to have a stabilizing effect on societies.

That we should, after having gone this far, still be talking of lack of unity shows that there is something basically wrong with what has been our system thus far. We must find out what that is and correct it. It may be something requiring more than the mere administration of oral medicine or a panacea. It may require some surgical operation. I am personally convinced that it is a surgical operation that is required. Surgical operations are usually painful and uncomfortable when conducted, and may be for some time afterward. But once the patient survives the operation, and after pains, he is able to survive as a healthy and strong individual. And the success of a surgical operation depends on the promptness, decisiveness, and courage of the doctor—otherwise it may be too late.

Let us be true to ourselves. *Nigeria is now having its last chance to make permanent arrangements for last-*

ing unity. That chance may never occur again. Our very
survival is through unity; without it we shall perish.
Without it our people will remain weak and poor. We
shall lose our chance of influence in a shrinking world.
Let us not forget that we have been blessed with a number of things which have rightly been the envy of many,
who have been ready to cash in when they can.

We must be prepared to approach this issue of unity
and national solidarity realistically, selflessly, and fearlessly. We must be prepared for sacrifices in the spirit
of give and take. We must overcome old prejudices and
entrenched interests.

It is the aim of the military government to uphold,
protect, and strengthen our traditional institutions. We
respect the position and influence of traditional rulers
who must increasingly be recognized as the healthy
arms of government. Through a process of modernization and evolution, we want to preserve our special
identity as a race and people. Unfortunately, the politics
of the last regime did not allow anything to stand in its
way and rode roughshod over our traditional institutions, even halting the growth of national industries in
certain areas as a political reprisal. All this the military
government is committed to eradicate.

We in this country are a deeply religious people. The
two principal religions, Islam and Christianity, have a
lot in common for the general good. They both believe
in the brotherhood of man, they believe in truth and
justice, they believe in love and humility, they believe
in self-sacrifice. They are both outward-looking, with
a deep concern for others and their needs. They seek
the right human understanding as a means of service
to mankind.

All these are what have brought us so far. We must
not do anything which would be a betrayal of these
great ideals.

Your Highness, I have said a lot of what our feelings
are. As an old friend, I know that you share these feelings. We admire your progressive ideas and your great
efforts in trying to improve the lot of your people, par-

ticularly in the field of education. You are the very embodiment of the true aspiration of our Northern brothers: youthful yet dignified, detribalized and broad-minded yet traditional, cultured without bigotry, a unifying force for our peoples, and the very index of what Nigeria stands for. A reformist emir in the tradition of your father, we commend to you for protection and guidance not only your own traditional subjects of Kano but also several others who are now resident in your city, which they have made their home.

As the chancellor of the University of Nigeria we expect you to be coming here often. We also believe that you will, during one of such visits, manage to travel around and see things for yourself and afford the people of these provinces the opportunity of knowing you. This must now be your second home.

Finally, I thank all the distinguished guests who have come from all over the Republic to honor this occasion. I thank in particular His Highness Oba Akenzua II of Benin, one of the foremost traditional rulers of our country. We welcome you.

May I take this opportunity also to thank the outgoing vice-chancellor of this university, Dr. Glen Taggart, once again for his magnificent effort in holding our new university in the best tradition. I am sure that all of you here would wish to join me in saying good-bye and good luck to a sincere friend.

Finally, I crave your indulgence a little longer so as to make a presentation on behalf of the entire people of this group of provinces to Your Highness. These gifts, which are all of local manufacture, are symbolic of our industry and of our esteem of Your Highness. The spear represents authority, which you so ably wield; the elephant tusk is a symbol of honor, so visible in you; and the carved stool stands for majesty, so well represented in you.

I consider this visit perhaps the best and most significant act of faith in the unity of this country, the oneness of our people, and the singularity of our purpose.

Diary of Events:
July 5–August 26, 1966

July 5–25: Appeasement measures by Major General Ironsi continue. Efforts at personal friendship and alliance with Northern Emirs. Sultan of Sokoto visits Lagos. Persistent rumors of Northern Nigeria's plan to secede from the Federation. Meeting of the Supreme Military Council. The Council endorses the Supreme Commander's plan to undertake an educate-the-people tour of the country.

July 25: Major General Aguiyi-Ironsi begins national tour with a two-day visit to Northern Nigeria. . . . Series of dramatic and bloody events follow in cities and towns of Nigeria.

July 25–27, Ikeja (near Lagos): A Northern Nigerian basketball team from Abeokuta barracks arrives in battle order to rehearse and reconnoiter for undisclosed "impending operations." . . . Secret meetings of Northern Nigerian army officers with Lieutenant Colonel Gowon, Lieutenant Colonel Mohammed, and Major Alao in Ikeja garrison.

July 28, Ibadan (capital of Western Nigeria): The Supreme Commander, Major General Ironsi, addresses a meeting of traditional rulers. . . . In Lagos, Lieutenant Colonel Mohammed, Major Alao, and Major Martin Adamu alert and address the Northern soldiers in secret. This is followed by the disarming of Southern soldiers, seizure of the armory, and distribution of arms and ammunition to Northern troops. . . . *Abeokuta* (Western Nigeria): two sections of Northern Nigerian troops break into a meeting of officers in the officers' mess and kill Major Obienu, Lieutenant Orok, and Lieutenant Colonel Okonweze—all Eastern and Midwestern officers. . . . *Ibadan:* Southern troops in the Supreme Commander's bodyguard at Ibadan Government House are removed and disarmed by troops sent by Lieutenant Colonel Gowon. The Northerners among the bodyguard are reinforced by a special contingent of 24 Northern soldiers. . . . *Midnight, Ikeja:* The stage is set for a coup. The leader of the coup, Lieutenant Colonel Gowon, moves into his rebel headquarters at Ikeja barracks. The code word for the coup is ARABA DAY—SECESSION DAY.

July 29, Ibadan: The Northern troops kidnap and murder the Supreme Commander and the military governor of Western Region, Lieutenant Colonel F. A. Fajuyi, in Ibadan.

July 29–30, Ikeja: Eastern Nigerian officers and soldiers are lined out and shot, along with some Eastern Nigerian policemen and civilians. . . . *Abeokuta:* Northern troops disarm Southern soldiers among the guards, break into armory, arm all Northern troops, arrest and detain all Southern soldiers. The Eastern Nigerian soldiers among those arrested are sorted out and shot. . . . Captain Ogbonna (an Easterner) manages to escape from Abeokuta and telephone Enugu to alert me of the coup. This is my first knowledge of what is happening. . . . *Kaduna* (capital of Northern Nigeria): Eastern Nigerian commanding officer of 3d Battalion, Lieutenant Colonel Okoro, is shot by two Northern Nigerian officers, Lieutenant Dambo and Lieutenant Dinka. . . . Alarm is sounded early in the morning and all troops assemble at the hockey pitch, which is surrounded by Northern troops. All the Eastern Nigerian soldiers are shot dead. . . . *Ibadan:* Lieutenant Colonel J. R. I. Akahan, commanding officer of 4th Battalion, convenes a meeting of his officers. When the officers arrive, 74 of them who are Easterners are arrested and shot. . . . Looting of property and raping of wives of Eastern Nigerian soldiers by Northern troops begin. . . . Lieutenant Colonel Akahan later gives an assurance to Eastern Nigerian soldiers in hiding that there will be no more bloodshed. The soldiers come out of their hiding places and are massacred by Northern troops. . . . *Enugu* (capital of

Eastern Nigeria, now Biafra): Northern Nigerian troops attempt to seize the armory and arm themselves, to carry out their scheduled assignment in the coup. The attempt is foiled by the precautionary measure of Lieutenant Colonel Ogunewe, who is already alerted by the telephone call from Abeokuta.

July 30: Some Northern Nigerian political leaders and their Western allies of the Nigeria National Democratic Party hold a series of secret meetings with Northern army officers to finalize plans for the breakup of the country. . . . Lieutenant Colonel Gowon hoists and flies in front of the 2d Battalion headquarters at Ikeja (his temporary headquarters) a flag in red, yellow, black, green, and khaki colors—the new flag for the "Republic of the North." . . . Telephone conversation with the Chief of Staff, Supreme Headquarters, Brigadier Ogundipe. He says that Northern troops are determined to continue bloodshed until Northern Nigeria is allowed to secede from the Federation. I agree to the terms to stop further bloodshed. . . . Situation deteriorates. Increased massacre of Easterners by Northern troops. Brigadier Ogundipe flees.

July 31: Telephone conversations with Lieutenant Colonel Gowon. He confirms the mutineers' terms mentioned yesterday by Brigadier Ogundipe. I agree. I pledge my cooperation to help stop the bloodshed before we call on the people to decide the future of the country. I warn him that my government does not recognize the mutiny and that he should not announce himself as Supreme Commander.

August 1: Scheduled day for beginning of the Commission of Inquiry into May 29 pogrom. Thwarted by July 29 mutiny. . . . British High Commissioner, Cumming-Bruce, has top-secret talks with Lieutenant Colonel Gowon and sends envoys to Northern Nigerian emirs to dissuade Northern Nigeria from secession. . . . Lieutenant Colonel Gowon appoints himself Supreme Commander and Head of the Federal Military Government of Nigeria. In the broadcast, he declares that there is no basis for Nigerian Unity. . . . Major Ekanem, provost marshal, reporting for duty in response to Lieutenant Colonel Gowon's assurance of safety, is shot dead on Carter Bridge in Lagos by Lieutenant Numan, a Northern Nigerian officer.

August 2:   Release of Western Nigeria army officers who took part in the January 15, 1966, revolution. At the same time their Eastern Nigerian counterparts who were detained in the North are shot by Northern officers at a spot 19 miles from Kaduna.

August 8:   At the army workshop, Yaba, all Eastern Nigeria army personnel are ordered to leave on pain of execution.

August 9:   Meeting of representatives of the military governors is convened in Lagos to consider what immediate steps are to be taken to stop further bloodshed and reduce the extremely high tension existing in the country.

August 12:   Mass arrest of all NCO's of Eastern Nigeria origin in Apapa, Yaba, and Surulere.

August 16:   Army officers of Eastern Nigeria origin are abducted from Benin prisons and shot by Northern Nigerian troops. The rebel troops at the same time release the Northern Nigerian soldiers who are in detention with the Easterners for their participation in the January 15 revolution. Major Daramola orders the shooting of 15 Eastern soldiers.

August 18:   Atmosphere of insecurity heightens in the country. I assure a delegation of oil companies of the maximum protection of their business by my government.

August 20:   Following the decision to return troops to their regions of origin, I send for Eastern Nigerian soldiers. To forestall this, Lieutenant Nuhu gives orders for the execution of 22 Eastern Nigerian noncommissioned officers detained by the mutineers in Ikeja barracks.

August 25:   Influx of refugees from all parts of Nigeria back to the region increases by the hour. . . . I give directives to ministries and departments to absorb as many refugee civil servants as they can.

August 26: I set up the Rehabilitation Commission with an initial sum of £1,000,000.

July 29 Mutiny and Massacre

(Broadcast, August 1, 1966)

I have considered with my Executive Committee the very grave events in some parts of the country regarding the rebellion by some sections of the Nigerian army against the National Military Government, which resulted in the kidnapping of His Excellency the Head of the National Military Government and Supreme Commander of the Armed Forces, Major General J. T. U. Aguiyi-Ironsi, and the cold premeditated murder of officers of Eastern Nigerian origin.

In the course of this rebellion, I had discussions with the Chief of Staff, Supreme Headquarters, Brigadier Ogundipe, who, as the next most senior officer in the absence of the Supreme Commander, should have assumed command of the army; my colleagues, the other military governors; and the Chief of Staff, Army Headquarters, Lieutenant Colonel Gowon. During these discussions it was understood that the only conditions on which the rebels would agree to a cease-fire were:

(1) that the Republic of Nigeria be split into its component parts;
(2) that all Southerners resident in the North be repatriated to the South, and all Northerners resident in the South repatriated to the North.

In spite of the fact that the only representations made at these cease-fire negotiations were those of the rebels and their supporters in the North, and notwithstanding that the views of the people of the Eastern group of provinces had not been ascertained, it was agreed to accept these proposals and stop further bloodshed.

The public is aware of the wanton and deliberate massacre of several people of Eastern Nigerian origin in last May's disturbances in parts of the Northern group of provinces. In view of the very strong feelings aroused among the people of the East at that time as to whether their membership in the Nigerian nation was desirable, I appealed to chiefs and leaders of the people to use their influence to stop any retaliation or precipitate action, in the hope that this would be the final act of sacrifice Easterners would be called upon to make in the interest of Nigerian unity. However, the brutal and planned annihilation of officers of Eastern Nigerian origin in the last few days has again cast serious doubts as to whether the people of Nigeria, after these cruel and bloody atrocities, can ever sincerely live together as members of the same nation.

I have noted the action taken to stop bloodshed in the country, and I now consider that the next step is to open discussions at the appropriate level to allow other sections of the Nigerian people to express their views, as their Northern compatriots have recently done, as to what form of association they desire for themselves in accordance with the cease-fire terms.

As a result of the pressures and representations now being made to me by the chiefs, leaders, and organizations in the Eastern group of provinces, I am arranging for representatives of chiefs and organizations in these provinces to meet and advise me.

Meanwhile, I appeal to our people of these provinces not to give expression to their feelings in any violent form but to cooperate with the law enforcement authorities in the assurance that their rights of self-determination will be guaranteed.

I have further conveyed to the Chief of Staff at Supreme Headquarters, my fellow military governors, and the Chief of Staff at Army Headquarters my understanding that the only intention of the announcement made by the Chief of Staff at Army Headquarters today is the restoration of peace in the country, while immediate negotiations are begun, to allow the people of Nigeria to determine the form of their future association.

Preparation for Talks on the Future of Nigeria

(Speech at meeting of the Consultative Assembly. August 31, 1966)

I welcome you all to this first meeting of the consultative body which I have set up for the Eastern group of provinces. . . . I have indicated that this body will consist of representatives drawn on an equal basis from each of our administrative divisions, in addition to representatives of special interests. . . .

On January 15, 1966, a section of the Nigerian army was involved in a rebellion which brought to an end the last civilian regime in this country. This rebellion, which was led by a number of officers from various parts of the country, brought to an end the series of political crises which the country witnessed within the last four years. Faced with the bleak prospects of a total breakdown of law and order, the then federal government, or what remained of it, unanimously invited the armed forces to take over the government. The general officer commanding the Nigerian army, Major General J. T. U. Aguiyi-Ironsi, on behalf of the entire armed forces of the Federation, accepted the mantle which had been thrust on the army and set up a military administration for the whole of Nigeria.

You are all living witnesses to the steps taken by the Supreme Commander since January 15, to inculcate the spirit of oneness among all Nigerians. In furtherance of this objective, the Supreme Military Council unanimously decided in May this year to establish a centralized form of administration. After the approval of its text by the Council, His Excellency the Supreme Commander promulgated Decree No. 34. Five days later, disturbances started simultaneously in all the major towns of the Northern group of provinces, the sole object of which was a massacre of thousands of innocent civilians of Eastern origin resident in the North. This led to the exodus of Easterners back to the East. During these events, I broadcast an appeal to the people of these provinces to remain calm and to accept our losses in men and property only as our last sacrifice in the interest of Nigerian unity.

In the early hours of Friday, July 29, 1966, the Northern soldiers in the army put into execution a diabolic plan, the object of which was to eliminate all officers of Eastern Nigeria origin in the Nigerian army. His Excellency the Supreme Commander was kidnapped as well as the military governor of the Western group of provinces, Lieutenant Colonel Fajuyi, with whom he was staying at the Government House, Ibadan, while attending a conference of natural rulers. A great many officers of Eastern origin were slaughtered in army contingents in Abeokuta, Ibadan, Ikeja, Kaduna, and Kano.

In spite of all these provocations, the people of Eastern Nigeria remained calm and disciplined. In order to stop the bloodbath, I opened informal contacts with Lieutenant Colonel Gowon and the remaining senior officers of the army. The Northerners insisted that the only condition on which they would cease fire would be for the North to be allowed to secede: the Southerners living in the North to be repatriated to the South, and Northerners living in the South to be repatriated to the North. To avoid further bloodshed, I accepted these two conditions. I was later to learn that Gowon denied ever giving these conditions, though I still have in my possession the records of these conversations.

I made it quite clear to Gowon that, in view of what had happened, the Nigerian army could no longer be one. We both then agreed to a general disengagement of troops, that is, that troops should return to their region of origin.

We demonstrated our good faith by repatriating all the Northern soldiers who were in the East back to the North. Gowon did not keep his word but retained as hostages some 30 percent of officers and men of Eastern Nigeria origin. With this breach of agreement, I wonder how far one can go on negotiating with a party who is either unwilling or unable to implement agreements.

You no doubt have heard that molestations of Easterners in the North have continued. Also some of our army officers who, after escaping, returned to work following assurances of their safety by Gowon are known to have been shot. It has been confirmed that infiltrators have been dispatched into Eastern Nigeria to wreak further havoc in the East.

My fellow countrymen, I must be very frank with you. The situation in the country today is very tense and dangerous. Two days ago you all heard that the road linking Ijebu-Ode and Benin had been immobilized due to a vital bridge being blown up. This naturally makes it difficult for Easterners residing in the West and in Lagos to return home. There have been further reports that Northern troops are now massed at our border with Northern Nigeria. The East has remained calm and peaceful in spite of all these provocations. There has been no breakdown of law and order in these provinces. I have therefore informed Gowon that any movement of troops into any part of the East would be regarded as an act of aggression which would be resisted with all the forces at our command.

We have made so many sacrifices in the past, and I am sure that you all agree with me that we cannot continue making sacrifices indefinitely. We now have our back to the wall. One more push and we either have to fight back or else be crushed. There must come a time when we must call a halt to all these atrocities, humiliations, and insults directed against our people.

We are now engaged in a struggle for survival, and there is need above all else for solidarity among all the people of Eastern Nigeria. People may try to weaken our resolve and threaten our solidarity by emphasizing the differences between various groups in Eastern Nigeria. However, anthropologists inform us that while there are 18 ethnic groups in Eastern Nigeria, there are some 200 in Northern Nigeria. If Northern Nigeria can afford to face all of us with a common determination, what excuse can we have for being disunited in our hour of greatest danger? The ethnic differences between the various communities in the East are small when compared with the differences between the tribes which inhabit Northern Nigeria. I say this not to minimize the need for finding ways of bringing our various groups closer together but simply to emphasize that these things can be looked after in their own time. I have, in the last few weeks, been holding consultations with representatives of various groups in Eastern Nigeria, and hope to continue this exchange with a view to finding ways of promoting greater solidarity among our people. Right now we are faced with a common danger, a danger which does not discriminate between us. I can hardly emphasize that at no time has there been a greater need for us in the East to remain united as now. Very soon the second round of talks on the future association of the component parts of the Republic will open in Lagos. You will, therefore, have to consider at this meeting the form of association which we want the Eastern provinces to have with the rest of the country. We have tried a unitary system of government in Nigeria; and we have also tried a federal system. Your deliberations, therefore, will have the advantage of the experience of all these attempts.

One of the features of our last constitution was the

imbalance that existed between the component regions, contrary to all concepts of true federalism. The North was in a position of dominance over the other regions. It is now alleged that the North is willing to agree to be split into a number of states. However, in view of their joint responsibility for the sad events of July 29, the split, even if it materializes, will only be on paper, as the component states will tend to gang up in their common interest. There are also other points which you must not fail to consider. You have to suggest, for example, what should be the position of the armed forces in any new association, bearing in mind what I have said earlier, namely, that the basis for unified military command in Nigeria no longer exists.

You have to consider what economic ties will bind the component parts of Nigeria, to ensure our unrestricted economic development, and that our funds are not unnecessarily diverted to others.

You have to consider where the responsibility for foreign affairs will lie and to what extent the region will cooperate in the formulation of foreign policy, bearing in mind the necessity of exercising full control over our economic and defense agreements, and to establish friendly relations with countries of our choice.

You will have to consider the political arrangements for the supervision of the common services.

You will also consider what type of constitution will be best suited to Eastern Nigeria.

These few points only serve to indicate the wide field to be covered by your discussions. But I wish to remind you that you will be failing in your duty if your suggestions do not envisage the solution which would bring to an end the indignities, molestations, and atrocities directed against the people of Eastern Nigeria. You are men of the world and of experience, and I have no doubt that under the able chairmanship of Professor Eni Njoku you will give due consideration to all these matters. Your deliberations will be conducted in complete secrecy so as to ensure a frank exchange of views.

Diary of Events:
September 1–12, 1966

September 1: After their August 31 session, the Consultative Assembly and the Advisory Committee of Chiefs and Elders of Eastern Nigeria pass the following resolution:

1. We, the representatives of the various communities in Eastern Nigeria gathered in this Consultative Assembly, hereby declare our implicit confidence in the military governor for Eastern Nigeria, Lieutenant Colonel Odumegwu Ojukwu, in all the actions he has so far taken to deal with the situation which has arisen in Nigeria Since May 29, 1966.
2. In view of the grave threat to our survival as a unit in the Republic of Nigeria, we hereby urge and empower/ advise him to take all such actions that might be necessary to protect the integrity of Eastern Nigeria and the lives and property of its inhabitants.
3. We advise constant consultation by His Excellency with the Consultative Assembly.
4. In view of the gravity of the present situation, we affirm complete faith in and urge the need for solidarity of Eastern Nigeria as a unit.

September 12: The Ad Hoc Constitutional Conference begins sitting in Lagos.

Talks on the Future of Nigeria

(Broadcast, September 12, 1966)

Our team of thirteen people of this region, accompanied by two officials, leaves this morning for Lagos. There they are to join the teams of other regions of this

Federal Republic in deliberations about the future of this country. Their foremost task will be that of finding solutions to the unfortunate problems which now beset a country we have all come to love so much—problems which have in recent months, and more so in recent weeks, assumed disastrous and bloody proportions. You are aware of the sad and tragic circumstances of our predicament, and I will not this morning disturb your minds with their memories.

For the past five weeks, I have been in continuous consultations, day and night, with all sections and shades of opinion represented in this region. The sole purpose of these consultations has been to ascertain the stand of the people of this virile region about recent and current events, and their wishes for the future. I have on all these occasions without exception been encouraged by your frankness, objectivity, and sense of responsibility in examining and tackling the vexing problems now confronting the nation as a whole and our people in particular. For this I thank you all.

I have seen elders and chiefs in groups and as individuals; I have seen representatives of commerce, trade, and industries, representatives of labor unions, representatives of administrative divisions and provinces, of professions, of social and cultural organizations. I have also seen former politicians of different shades of opinion.

Apart from these direct personal consultations, I have during the past two weeks convened a consultative assembly of representatives of administrative divisions and of the different interests already mentioned, followed by an advisory body of chiefs, elders, statesmen, and other men and women of experience and maturity, to consider the problems and advise me. You have all done this in a most encouraging and unimpeachable spirit. In order to allow you full opportunity for honest and objective expressions, these meetings have all been held in secret, free from the glare of the press and of the public.

Your resolutions and recommendations, as well as

views expressed in private letters and private audiences, have been submitted to a constitutional committee of experts and harmonized for the use of our delegates to Lagos.

All of you have expressed grave doubts and fears about the safety of our delegates to Lagos. You have urged me to arrange with others concerned for the meeting to be held elsewhere than Lagos. I have all along appreciated your fears, which I confess I have had occasions to share myself. It is mainly for this reason that I have until now withheld the names of the delegates who are to represent us.

I have done all that is humanly possible to secure firm guarantees for the safety of our delegates. I have been in constant discussions with Lieutenant Colonel Gowon. On each occasion, he has given me his word of faith and honor that he has accepted personal responsibility for the safety and free conduct of our delegates. He has confirmed this telephone assurance in a lengthy coded message. Without doubting that the coded message came from him, I insisted and obtained his undertaking to send the guarantee in writing under his personal signature. Yesterday morning, I heard news of some disturbances in Lagos. I renewed my fears and plea for assurances, which he unstintedly and readily gave. As a soldier, Lieutenant Colonel Gowon must be trusted to keep his word of faith and honor.

I believe that our delegates will all be safe. I could have insisted on your strong representations that the conference be held outside Lagos, possibly outside Nigeria. But that would cause further delay, while we continue to live under explosive tension guised in treacherous calm. Let us all believe and hope that others in the country share our views and belief that we cannot afford to wait much longer before starting to talk, particularly when this conference was expected to be held a month ago.

At this conference our delegates will put forward plans to ensure equality and fair play for all citizens of this country; to minimize friction in appointments and in the distribution of national amenities; to eliminate the possibility of any region controlling the central authorities to the detriment of other regions and forever remove the possibility of any one region holding the others to ransom; to ensure maximum protection for the citizen outside his region of origin; to ensure the orderly development of each region at its own pace, and to generate mutual confidence and responsibility between the various regions of this country. I have every confidence that with our firm resolve to put a halt to the recent disastrous trend of events, Nigeria will emerge stronger and at peace with herself as a result of these deliberations.

Meanwhile, to advise me during the course of this conference on issues which may arise, I have summoned an advisory committee of trusted and experienced citizens. This committee will meet here in Enugu daily throughout the duration of the conference.

God bless Nigeria.

Diary of Events:
Sept. 13 – Nov. 17, 1966

September 13:   The various memoranda from the delegations generally agree on confederation. The Northern Nigerian memorandum advocates that "each of the existing four regions should be constituted into an autonomous state and that subjects or groups of subjects which are of common interest . . . should be delegated to a Common Services Commission. . . ."

September 15:   Fresh waves of massacres of Eastern Nigerians breaks out in Makurdi, Minna, Gboko, and Kaduna in Northern Nigeria.

September 17:   The Ad Hoc Constitutional Conference adjourns for three days. Chief Awolowo warns that "some people wanted a more prolonged approach to the work of this Conference. . . . If one section of the country feels that because they are in control and in occupation therefore the conference may go to hell that does not suit this delegation."

September 18: Northern delegates fly to Kaduna for consultations. Lieutenant Colonel Hassan Katsina flies to Lagos for consultations with Lieutenant Colonel Gowon. Gowon goes to British High Commission for secret talks. . . . Meeting between Lieutenant Colonel Gowon, Joseph Tarka, and Middle Belt leaders. Decision to use the first opportunity offered by Gowon's accession to power to get their long-desired state.

September 19: I appoint Consultative Committee on Constitution for Eastern Nigeria with Dr. Graham Douglas, Attorney General, as chairman.

September 20: The Ad Hoc Constitutional talks resume.

September 28: An Eastern Nigerian, Mr. S. O. Achilefu, personnel manager of Nigeria Airways, is kidnapped and murdered by Northern Nigerian soldiers off Agege motor road in Lagos.

September 29: More than 400 Eastern Nigerians waiting for evacuation at Kano international airport in Northern Nigeria are murdered by armed Northern soldiers and civilians.

September 30: Northern Nigerian soldiers from Abeokuta garrison swoop on a group of railway workers at Lafenwa, Western Nigeria, and kill the Easterners among them.

October 2: The BBC begins a campaign that "massacre" of Hausas has begun in Port Harcourt. My government promptly denies this as most untrue.

October 3: Airlifts back to the East of maimed and injured in most pathetic conditions. Many more coming by land and rail. Tension rising in Eastern Nigeria. . . . Rehabilitation Commission chairman, Mr. F. O. Ihenacho, appeals to all industrialists and employees of labor to assist them both individually and collectively. He says that although the government has set aside £1,000,000 for rehabilitation, this sum is very inadequate. He discloses that the number of refugees has now risen to 60,000. . . . Ever-mounting tension and police report of the danger of unpleasant incidents. I give orders that persons of non-Eastern origin resident in the region should return to their regions of origin as a purely temporary measure. My government takes measures to protect the houses and property of non-Easterners.

October 4: Second Session of the Consultative Assembly meets in Enugu.

October 5: The federal government orders the summary dismissal of all Eastern Nigerian civil servants who have fled from the pogroms if they do not return to Lagos by October 15, 1966.

October 8–9: 18 railway coaches conveying Eastern Nigerian refugees to the East are stopped at Makurdi and the inmates massacred by Northern Nigerians.

October 16: Colin Legum of the London *Observer* describes the September-October pogrom: *"For fear of promoting an even greater tragedy, the Nigerians have been sheltered from knowing the full magnitude of the disaster that has overtaken the Ibos in the Northern Region. The danger is that the truth will not be believed and so no proper lessons learnt, once the horror is over. . . . Men, women and children arrived with arms and legs broken, hands hacked off, mouths split open. Pregnant women were cut open and the unborn children killed."*

October 19: Lieutenant Colonel Gowon imposes a food blockade on Eastern Nigeria.

October 22: Easterners press for withdrawal of Northern soldiers from Lagos. . . . Leaders of Thought Conference of Western Region ask for withdrawal of Northern soldiers from Lagos and Western Region.

October 23: Third meeting of the Ad Hoc Constitutional Conference resumes in Lagos without the Eastern delegates participating.

October 31: In a letter to fellow military governors, I make compromise proposals to restore confidence in

the army and in the public, I declare: ". . . *I implore you all to consider the above proposals in the faith and spirit in which I have put them forward. We must take the decision quickly. The country is exploding, and we must stop the explosion. I do hope that we shall accept the above proposals of compromise, and not allow personal considerations or external forces to prevent us from doing the best possible to save the country. . . ."*
Delegation of Yorubas in Katsina, Northern Nigeria, meet the Emir of Katsina and thank him for protecting the Yorubas during the pogroms against Ibos.

November 1–5: Mounting criticism in the press, especially *Daily Sketch* (published in Western Nigeria), against the refusal of Lagos regime to repatriate Northern troops from Lagos and Western Region in accordance with the August 9, 1966, decision of the Ad Hoc Committee.

November 2: An Ibadan-based Eastern Nigerian photographer, Emmanuel Ogbonna, is kidnapped from his studio by Northern soldiers and shot dead.

November 3: I convene for November 4, 1966, the meeting of the members and advisers of the Eastern Nigeria delegation to the Ad Hoc Constitutional Conference.

November 7: Chief Awolowo, leader of the Yorubas, heads a high-powered deputation of Yorubas which urges the Lagos clique:

(1) All troops of Northern Nigeria and non-Yoruba origin should be withdrawn from the West and Lagos, with the proviso that the Supreme Commander's bodyguards should consist of such men and be of such strength as the Supreme Commander himself may from time to time decide.

(2) All troops of Western Nigeria and Lagos origin should be posted to these territories.

(3) Any shortfall in the existing strength of the troops in Western Nigeria and Lagos and the number of Yoruba soldiers in the army should be made up by the recruitment and training of an equivalent number of Yoruba troops.

November 8:   In a supplementary preface to his book *Thoughts on Nigerian Constitution,* Chief Awolowo adds in a press release: ". . . The most realistic approach to our constitutional problems is, therefore, clear. If we would save the Federation from complete disintegration, and the constituent units from mutual destruction, we must embark on a four- or five-year venture of confederalism. . . ."

November 9:   Western Nigeria Obas and chiefs arrive in Enugu to see the magnitude of the refugee problem and gauge the mood of the people.

November 13:   Fleeing Easterners from Northern Nigeria change route and begin to infiltrate home throught West and Midwest because of the constant waylaying of refugees in the trains by Northern Nigerians. Disruption of North–East rail line.

November 15:   Eastern Nigeria government warns that any refusal by the federal government-owned companies and corporations to continue to employ all refugee staff of Eastern Nigerian origin returning to the region will be "regarded as unfriendly and a further act of confrontation."

November 16:   An anonymous philanthropist from outside Eastern Nigeria donates £2,000 to the Rehabilitation Commission. . . . Plot to overthrow Western Nigeria government uncovered.

November 17:   Meeting of the Ad Hoc Constitutional Conference, due to resume tomorrow, is indefinitely adjourned by Lieutenant Colonel Gowon.

September 29 Pogrom

(Address to Second Meeting of Consultative Assembly, October 4, 1966)

The events of the past two months in this country are well known to every one of us. They have been events tragic in the extreme. The people of Eastern

Nigeria, be they Ibo, Efik, Ibibio, Ijaw, or anybody else, have been the direct and unmistaken targets of murderous onslaughts.

In May, thousands of our people, resident in Northern Nigeria, were slaughtered in cold blood like rats. This well-planned and efficiently executed massacre involved innocent civilians. This is not an occasion to stir up emotions, but it is impossible to forget that men, women, and children of our kith and kin were taken out of their beds and slaughtered, they were murdered in hospitals, including women in labor rooms—yes, women in pains trying to deliver children!—they were massacred in places of worship, in the streets, in marketplaces, and in vehicles trying to carry them to safety.

Emotions in this Region rose to the highest pitch as news of these atrocities flowed in, as we saw our relations coming back stripped naked and, having abandoned all they had, in flight for their dear lives; as we saw wives wailing for their husbands brutally massacred before their very eyes; as we witnessed the arrival of bewildered and nonunderstanding children deprived of their dear parents, of wealthy and comfortable businessmen now penniless and in rags and often covered with severe and deadly wounds. The perpetrators of these atrocities did not discriminate between the different communities in Eastern Nigeria in these wanton acts hardly surpassed in the world's dark history of man's inhumanity to man, not in the history of murderous treachery among a people of common citizenship and destiny.

I spared no efforts in calming our people, who naturally, understandably, and justifiably were itching for revenge. We all know that they had the will, the ability, and the means to revenge. Our people, who have all along worked for and believed in the unity and oneness of this country, heeded my appeal and abandoned all intentions to retaliate. I assured them, and publicly expressed my sincere belief, that the dear blood of our kith and kin thus wantonly shed by those we had come to regard and accept as our brothers and sisters would mark the last and supreme act of sacrifice for national unity. With the assurances of the Supreme Commander and the head of the then military government and of my fellow military governors, all of whom had agreed to an immediate meeting of the Supreme Council to find the means of a just and lasting settlement of the issues involved, I personally appealed to our people to return to Northern Nigeria and resume their normal occupations. They respected and answered my appeal. I have now found that I was mistaken and must ask you all to forgive my innocent miscalculations, which have since led to greater misfortunes and calamities for our people. I never intended, and could never have consciously done anything, to betray them.

Then came the event of July 29, 1966. On and from that date officers and men of the Nigerian army who happened to have their origin from Eastern Nigeria were unashamedly, systematically, and callously killed by soldiers from the North, where the news of what had happened was received and celebrated with open and proud jubilation. I and Eastern Nigerian officers even here in the East soon realized that our blood was also in demand. My duty to the people of Eastern Nigeria of all sections became clear. That duty was to preserve the integrity of this Region and to protect its inhabitants from any violence, be it external or internal.

Fellow countrymen, on September 29, 1966, another wave of violence was unleashed in the Northern Region against men, women, and children of Eastern Nigeria origin. The mass slaughter of our people, which started on that day, has been far greater in magnitude and callousness than what occurred and shocked the world in May. Two days ago, the soldiers in Kano, Northern Nigeria, were reported to have mutinied and joined the civilians in the crusade of annihilation directed against Easterners. These people, soldiers and civilians, went to Kano international airport and slaughtered Easterners —men, women and children—waiting to board a plane in flight for safety.

As a result of these new waves of atrocious killings directed against our kith and kin, it has been necessary to evacuate, from the North to the East, all Easterners still alive. The killings were not confined to Kano—indeed, Kano was the latest place to be affected. What has made the killings in Kano different is that, unlike in Zaria, Minna, Maiduguri, Kaduna, and other places in Northern Nigeria, where we have no evidence thus far that soldiers openly took part against unarmed Eastern civilians, soldiers openly did so in Kano.

For the past two months, I have overstrained all in my power to keep the people of this Region calm. In this I have received unreserved cooperation which has impressed our friends and caused our foes to marvel. The minor incident two Saturdays ago, which led to the killing by a Northerner in Enugu, Eastern Nigeria, of two innocent children of this Region playing in the street and the molestation of a few Northerners was quickly brought under control. It is significant that our detractors in this country and abroad, including a section of their press, thought it fair to exaggerate that incident out of all proportions, trying in a mean and disgraceful way even to compare it with the happenings in the North.

With the present waves of violence and massive losses of life which have led to the evacuation of all Easterners found alive to the East, I have lost confidence in the effectiveness of my ability to continue restraining the violently injured feelings of the people of this Region, particularly those returning from the jaws of cruel death, against non-Easterners resident in this Region. I still believe that two wrongs cannot make a right. I still feel a sense of duty to ensure the safety of all persons under my protection. In the face of the present situation, two days ago, I directed that all non-Easterns residing in this Region be repatriated to their home regions under protection. I would like to think that this is going to be no more than a temporary measure taken in the interests of the persons concerned. To this end, I have sent a telegram to Lieutenant Colonel Gowon and all the military governors about my decision, and I have directed the provincial secretaries to do everything to ensure the safe conduct of those who want to leave.

I still believe that Nigeria can be saved. Let us therefore continue in our efforts to find a satisfactory and lasting solution to our enormous and delicate problems. To succeed we must approach the issue with sincerity and realism. But, as I have said, no settlement will be acceptable to the Eastern Region which does not include reparation and compensation for lives and property lost by Easterners in these disturbances. I believe also that continued acts of vicious deprivations such as have now become a monthly norm in our society will have only one effect, and that is to make it increasingly more difficult to see and gather the threads of our togetherness. I have said before that the East will not secede unless she is forced out. . . . Fellow countrymen, the push has started.

During the negotiations which immediately followed the incident of July 29, 1966, I was prepared to do anything which could lead to the stoppage of further loss of lives. When I was told that the only condition on which the Northern soldiers could stop killing our people was that of secession, whereby the North would secede from the South and all Northern nationals resident in the South be repatriated to the North and vice versa, I advised that the condition be accepted if that would stop the killings. The idea was a painful one, considering the amount of contributions and sacrifices by the people of this Region to build a strong and united Nigeria. I, like everyone else in this Region, do not believe in secession, since secession means a direct negation of all that we have stood and fought for all these years.

Following wild and mischievous accusations and allegations about this Region's imaginary intention to secede, I recently called in the British and American diplomatic representatives and explained to them the position of Eastern Nigeria. I left them in no doubt that "we do not here in the East wish for, neither have we worked for, secession! If, however, circumstances place us outside what is now known as Nigeria, you may be certain then that we shall have been forced out."

By agreement with Lieutenant Colonel Gowon and all the other regional governors, a meeting of personal representatives of the military governors was held in Lagos on August 9, 1966. The aim of the meeting was to consider what immediate steps to take to reduce the extremely high tension of the time. In spite of the personal risks involved, considering that Eastern Nigerians were targets for the constant killings of those days, I dispatched a high-powered three-man delegation to attend the meeting. The meeting did useful work and reached the following decisions:

- Immediate steps should be taken by the Supreme Commander to post military personnel to barracks within their respective regions of origin.
- Having regard to its peculiar position, the question of maintenance of peace and security in Lagos should be left to the Supreme Commander in consultation with military governors.
- A meeting of this committee or an enlarged body should take place in a week's time to recommend in broad outlines the form of political association which the country should adopt in the future.
- Immediate steps should be taken to nullify or modify any provisions of any decree which assumes extreme centralization.
- The Supreme Commander should make conditions suitable for a meeting of the Supreme Military Council urgently as a further means of lowering tension.

(I have merely quoted the actual conclusions of that meeting.)

One would have thought that since the representatives to the said meeting were the personal and accredited representatives of the military governors, members of the Supreme Council who found it impossible to meet personally, its conclusions should be accepted as binding for implementation. But only the first recommendation has been implemented, and then partially. Not all army personnel of Eastern Nigeria origin have been repatriated to the East. Soldiers in the North are not confined to barracks and have been responsible for the frequent killings and molestations of the people of this Region still resident or working in the North. The third recommendation is only now being implemented, after more than a month from the recommended date! Apart from the repeal of the now "obnoxious" Decree 34, which has not gone far enough, the fourth recommendation has not been implemented.

However, in anticipation of the projected representative conference to consider the future constitutional arrangements for the country, I started consulting all and sundry shades of opinion represented in this Region. These consultations culminated in the first and smaller meeting of this Assembly from August 31 to September 2, 1966, followed by that of an advisory council of chiefs and elders, former legislators, and other leading personalities in the Region.

The advent of the military regime in January of this year was universally welcomed as a corrective force. As a soldier, I have no political ambitions. I have been trained, as a member of a disciplined force, to defend the country and its people against aggression. I cannot, therefore, claim to be an expert in political matters or in the art of government. In any case, I still uphold and stand by the original aims of the military government following the transfer of power in January. Ours is no more than a corrective interregnum, out to lay the foundation for a return to civilian rule in which there should be peace and harmony among the people, where the bases and sources of friction, injustice, threats to progress and stability, and other evils of the past will be eliminated.

I shall pursue my task of purging our public life of all sorts of corruption, injustice, and nepotism. The ban on politics and other partisan activities will be maintained. Inquiries and investigation aimed at exposing and punishing those in public life who have abused their positions of trust for private gains and self-enrichment will continue. Our people must for once realize that they cannot use their public positions to cheat those they are meant to serve.

It is against this background that I place the highest premium on close consultation with the people. In these consultations, I firmly believe that every man and woman of knowledge, experience, and influence should be involved. I am not interested in what might have been such a person's past political and other affiliations. It was in order to ensure this that I took upon myself to select those who came to the first meeting of this Consultative Assembly. In carrying out that exercise of selection, I acted upon the best possible advice. Only a handful of the people selected were known to me personally. In my meetings with the various provincial groups, I explained to them how they were selected and admitted that I could not claim perfection over those selections, and I reserved the right, in the light of future experience, to enlarge, contract, or even change the composition of the different representative groups. I can claim to have done more than any other government in this matter of consultation with the people.

Typical of democratic and vociferous Eastern Nigeria, I have been criticized for not allowing the people to choose their own representatives, even when such critics have been honest enough to admit that my choice was not bad! Well, in obedience to public opinion, I have now given the people the chance to choose their representatives, and I hope we shall now have peace and confidence.

The first meeting of this assembly considered the general situation in the country and made recommendations about the future. Of their own volition, those who attended divided themselves into four committees or study groups, which later submitted their conclusions to a plenary session of the assembly. One such committee was the one which considered the position, fears, and claims of the minority groups in this Region, to which I shall return later.

The recommendations of the Consultative Assembly were submitted subsequently to the Advisory Council of Chiefs and Elders for their views. The recommendations of the two bodies included suggestions about the type of association Nigeria should have in the future. These suggestions were submitted to a Constitutional Committee under the chairmanship of the late Attorney General of this Region, Dr. Graham-Douglas, for examination and advice. I emphasize that that Constitutional Committee concerned itself mainly with the type of constitutional arrangements best suited for Nigeria as a whole. It was not set up to consider a constitution for Eastern Nigeria as such, with a view to secession, which, I understand, is what some of our detractors would like to have people believe. If, as they naturally had to do, members of that committee found themselves having to examine the constitution for Eastern Nigeria, that was because there is, under the existing constitutional arrangements for Nigeria, a separate constitution for Eastern Nigeria.

The recommendations of this Constitutional Committee, along with those made by the Consultative Assembly, as endorsed by the Advisory Council of Chiefs, Elders, and others, formed the basis of the briefs with which our delegates to the current constitutional talks went to Lagos.

The main preoccupation of the people of this Region, whether as members invited to the Consultative Assembly or the Advisory Council of Chiefs and Elders or even as individuals consulted, was how to remove the highly charged tension in the country as a whole, with a view to ensuring the security of life and property, and removing causes of fear, friction, and panic.

The army, trained and disciplined to regard one another as comrades and dedicated to the defense of the country against an external enemy, had turned against itself, with members from one section, having the advantage of arms, turning against the members of a particular section and killing them as enemies. As a result, the army has become disintegrated and for the most part completely out of control. The Lagos Ad Hoc conference of August 9, 1966, faced this reality by recommending the separation of army personnel and their posting to barracks in their respective regions. We of this Region have implemented that recommendation faithfully and fully; but we have not been able to have back all our army personnel from other parts of the country.

In the Northern Region, the army is still largely out of control. Our people are still being molested and killed by both the army and civilians in that part of the country. The authorities in Lagos and in the North know this and have been making genuine but unsuccessful appeals to their people to behave in a civilized way.

Is it not a painful irony of fate that we, who had to be turned to by the United Nations to go and help restore law and order in the strife-torn Congo, and there discharged that duty creditably to the admiration and praise of the world, should today find ourselves unable to do the same in our own country? It is a shame for the whole country which all must share. We of this Region are prepared, as usual, to play our full part in the restoration of law and order in the disturbed areas of the North, if called upon to do so and if guaranteed the necessary cooperation in the discharge of that duty so absolutely necessary for the honor and prestige of our country.

In his very first broadcast to the nation on assumption of office on August 1 this year, Lieutenant Colonel Gowon categorically declared that the basis of unity did not exist for the people of this country. This statement was frequently echoed in the discussions which took place in this House between August 31 and September 2, and on September 7. In his second broadcast to the nation on August 8 (prior to the meeting of the military governors' representatives on the ninth), Lieutenant Colonel Gowon stated: "The basic point which has emerged from recent events is that we as a people are quite aware that this great country of ours has much to benefit in remaining a single entity in one form or another. Our difficulties in the past have been how to agree on the form which such association should take. . . . In the past we have been too presumptuous and have acted on such presumptions."

I consider those statements realistic. Most of our troubles and conflicts in the recent past have emanated from a desire to control the central government in Lagos. Fear, distrust, and suspicion, buttressed by ambitions for power, have led to political struggles and the commission of crimes and fraud. Our delegates went to Lagos determined to do all in their power to see that this state of affairs was not allowed to occur again. Based on the views and opinions expressed by our people, they went to Lagos with a mandate to work on the following broad principles:

- To acknowledge that the country is on the brink of anarchy, and everything must be done to ensure the security of life and property
- All deep-rooted differences in religion, culture, attitude, outlook, and rate of development existing in the country should be recognized and accepted.
- Each region must be allowed to develop in its own way and at its own pace.
- Since the control of the center has been the ever-living main source of friction and tension between the different regions, thereby threatening national solidarity, and integrity, the distribution of functions between the regions and the center should be reviewed and so arranged that only such subjects and functions as will engender the minimum of suspicion and friction among different groups are allowed in the hands of the federal government.

- The composition of the organs of the federal government should be arranged as to give no one region an advantage over the other.
- The subject of representation and the method of selecting such representatives should be carefully gone into. We would like to see the practice of federal general election abandoned.

Fellow countrymen, there is one vital point which I must here emphasize to you and make the world know. No attempts to settle our problems will succeed without the existence of confidence built on sound and transparent foundation. It is not enough to preach and shout about the need to establish confidence. It is a case of practice being much better and more convincing than precept.

As we engage in discussions and consultations, as we try to make gestures to reassure one another of our intentions, things keep on happening through the actions of our friends to make one wonder whether those with whom we are dealing are prepared to keep faith. A few instances will bring out what I mean.

- I have already mentioned the agreements reached by the representatives of military governors at a meeting held in Lagos on August 9, 1966. We saw there that not all the agreements reached have been implemented. Where attempts have been made to implement some of the agreements it has been a question of half-measures.
- The federal government has made recent important diplomatic and civil service appointments—to wit, ambassadors and permanent secretaries. People of Eastern Nigerian origin, with full claims and qualifications for consideration, have not been given fair treatment.
- Following recent happenings, many Eastern Nigerians fled their jobs for dear life. Appeals were issued by those in authority for their return with firm assurances about their personal safety. Trusting these assurances, our people have returned to their posts in the disturbed areas from which they fled, only to be murdered in cold blood.
- Early this year, the Supreme Council under the leader-

ship of Major General Aguiyi-Ironsi set up a Constitutional Study Group, under the chairmanship of Chief Rotimi Williams. All that the group had done was to receive memoranda and hold preliminary discussions, at which one of the things agreed was to tour the different parts of the country and collect additional evidence before settling down to business. When the tragic events of July 29 intervened and rendered irrelevant the existence and continued operation of that study groupy, Dr. T. O. Elias, an international lawyer of repute, who could not be mistaken regarding the implications of the events which followed July 29 insofar as the study group was concerned, formally submitted his resignation from membership of the group in August, 1966.

- We have now heard with some astonishment that the chairman of that group has taken upon himself to write his own report in the name of the group and has submitted such a report to Lieutenant Colonel Gowon, who has gratefully accepted it. With the abrogation of Decree Number 34, and the return to the federal form of government for the country, one would have thought that no head of one government could accept such a report without prior consultation with the other governments— that is, even if, which was not the case, the report had been the product of the full committee and its relevance still existed.

- Last Friday, members of the Constitutional Committee meeting in Lagos submitted an interim report to Lieutenant Colonel Gowon. Some members of the delegations from other parts of the country suggested that the terms of the report be published. Our delegation raised, in very strong terms, serious objections to the publication of the contents of the reports before the delegates, who were not plenipotentiaries, had had time to report to their principals. This important point of principle was ignored by Lieutenant Colonel Gowon, who promptly made public the contents of the interim report, a copy of which I have not before now officially received. It is difficult not to take the action as a direct spite for the East. Other delegations whose governments were close to Lagos might have had the advantage, which the Eastern delegation had not, of consulting their principals. Again, why should the federal government take upon itself to publish the text of such an important report without the prior consent of the regional governments?

- I have in my possession an intercepted instruction from Kaduna to the provincial secretaries in the North to recruit even citizens of the Chad resident in Maiduguri for guerrilla warfare! Well, you know what that means. The first law of nature is self-preservation. We must keep our vigilance.

- Recently, some Ibos of the Midwest expressed their honest views and desires following certain developments at the constitutional talks. I am now informed that the first reaction of the government of the Midwest has been to detain three of the chiefs associated with those views and expressions.

- Our refugees and repatriated soldiers arrived back in the East unclothed and unarmed. They are now without shelter. All appeals to supply these soldiers with basic necessities have not been answered. As these men, who joined the army in order to serve the nation, cannot indefinitely remain in this deplorable state, I am going ahead to provide them with clothing and shelter.

It is for the world to judge whether these are acts which can lay solid foundations for mutual confidence and trust, without which all our labors directed toward the solutions of our grave problems might be in vain.

The Issue of New States

I now come to the important issue of the creation of new states within the country. This is a question which I invited you to regard as the central theme of this meeting. As I have said, the Consultative Assembly, which met from August 31 to September 2, 1966, appointed a special committee to go into this matter. Representatives of all the administrative divisions sat on that committee, which was chairmaned by Dr. Okoi Arikpo (now Nigerian Commissioner of External Affairs), who, I understand, also served as its secretary. According to the report, which I later received, all the issues involved in the creation of states were thoroughly debated and analyzed. The representatives of the minority areas spoke frankly and forthrightly, pointing to what they considered acts and instances of neglect and injustice. Most of them made the point that the majority tribe inhabiting this Region was using its majority to oppress and cheat them. They had no sense of belonging, and so on.

The committee eventually agreed that the fears of the minorities could be assuaged and their rights safeguarded in some ways other than the creation of autonomous states leading to further fragmentation of the Region, which has already lost the Southern Cameroons. Having thus agreed, members sat down to finding ways and means of safeguarding the rights of minorities and allaying their fears. It was the consensus of the committee that a reorientation of the present system of provincial administration would provide the answer.

It was therefore recommended that a new constitution should contain provisions for the devolution of certain legislative and executive functions and powers upon provincial units which should be guaranteed a reasonable degree of autonomy. That committee also made recommendations about representation in the legislature and about other government organs. Those recommendations were accepted by the Consultative Assembly and later endorsed by the Advisory Council of Chiefs and Elders.

The Constitutional Committee, chairmaned by Dr. Graham-Douglas, then the Attorney General of this Region, also accepted those recommendations and went further to spell out those functions in respect of which they felt the provinces might be vested by the Constitution of Eastern Nigeria with legislative and executive powers, with the proviso that the regional government should have concurrent powers with the provincial administrations in respect of those functions. The functions suggested included local government and chieftaincy affairs; town and country planning; health; education at primary and secondary levels (excluding the maintenance of standards); customary marriages and succession; markets; roads; water supply; distribution of electricity; agriculture; fisheries; cooperatives; promotion of tourist traffic; quarantine; local development generally.

The Constitutional Committee also recommended that provisions should be inserted in the Constitution to enable provincial cooperation in the provision and the maintenance of joint services, as well as enable any two or more provinces to be merged, or more provinces to be created.

There is one point on which the Consultative Assembly was not clear. It was the only point upon which the Special Committee set up by that body was not unanimous. That point was the size and number of provincial units. On the number, there were suggestions of twelve on the basis of existing provinces, five on the basis of the old provinces, four on a basis to be determined, and twenty-nine on the basis of existing administrative divisions. It will be left to you, if the idea of establishing provincial units on the lines and for the purposes suggested by the different bodies mentioned above appeals to you as a means of allaying the fears of the minorities and guaranteeing their rights to manage their affairs, to reexamine the proposals and advise me.

A lasting and realistic solution could be found. I have mentioned that the list of subjects which the Constitutional Committee suggested could fall within the competence of the Provinces. . . . For the exercise to be fruitful and healthy and to the satisfaction of the people, the size of the units must be very carefully considered, bearing in mind that the executive and legislative functions which should devolve on such units would be directly influenced by their sizes. It is also pertinent to mention that this exercise may most probably necessitate the readjustment of existing administrative boundaries.

During the time of the meetings of the Consultative Assembly, I arranged for and met in long sessions, and

on separate occasions, representatives from the Old
Calabar Province, the Old Rivers Province, and representatives of the Old Ogoja Province. At these meetings
the people spoke out their minds boldly, frankly, and
fearlessly. They complained that they lacked a sense of
belonging, owing to the attitude of the majority group.
They pointed to alleged injustices which they had suffered in the distribution of amenities, the siting of industries, and appointments to public offices, boards,
and corporations. They therefore felt that a separate
state for them would cure all those ills.

It was not difficult to sense in their attitudes and
sentiments the ghosts, and perhaps even the living
spirits, of past prejudices, suspicion, and hate. I was,
however, encouraged by the fact that those before me
were sincere and responsible people who were prepared
to admit that the mere creation of states could not
be a panacea for the fears and rights of minorities. It is
impossible in a society such as ours to remove the
problem of minority, no matter how far you may go.
There would be that problem even if every village were
converted into a "state." I was finally left with the
impression, and this applied practically to all the
groups with whom I had discussed, that all they wanted
was to feel that they belong, on a perfect footing of
equality, to the Eastern Nigeria community, where all
vestiges and grounds of domination of one group by
another are removed, where social amenities and other
government benefits are fairly and justly distributed.

I expressed an honest sympathy with, and understanding of, their feelings and assured them that it was
precisely those types of things that the military government was here to put right.

Nobody in this Region is opposed to the creation of
states for healthy objectives. All right-thinking persons
who believe in a Nigeria governed and run on sound
democratic principles have advocated this. The creation
of states has in the past been advocated as a means of
founding a true federal country where no one or two
sections could use their size and numbers to dominate

and hold the rest of the country to ransom. The ills of the first Republic are directly relevant to the fact that this country did not have such an arrangement. We shall agree to any arrangement about the creation of states based on sound principles of democracy. *I am loathe to be party to any discussion about the creation of states on the poisoned principles of hate, fear, and spite, because that means laying foundation for a worse country than anything we have so far known. It would be an open betrayal of the trust and pledges of the military government.*

Our enemies and detractors, aided and abetted by people with an ax to grind or with selfish ambitions, have done their worst during the past few weeks to undermine the position of this Region over this issue. Our delegates to the Lagos talks have been denied the sympathy and understanding they need in the discharge of their delicate and difficult task. They have been maligned, misrepresented, and misinterpreted.

What are the facts?

Our people arrived at Lagos with the clear mandate I earlier quoted to you. In his opening address, Lieutenant Colonel Gowon laid down useful guidelines in the following terms:

It is very clear to me that it will be economically and politically suicidal to harbor any idea of a complete break-up of the Federation. Therefore, we seem to be left with the alternatives of:

- a federation with a strong central government;
- a federation with a weak central government;
- a confederation.

    On the other hand, it may be that through your deliberations which commence here today we may be able to devise a form of association with an entirely new name yet to be found in any political dictionary in the world but peculiar to Nigeria.

Depending on the choice that you eventually recommend you may later have to consider such matters as:

- the distribution of powers between the regional government and the central government;

- the territorial divisions of the country;
- the system for selecting representatives to the legislatures.

For three full days nothing concrete was done by the conference. Those who felt they had something to gain by it adopted delaying and frustrating tactics. Eventually, the different delegations submitted their proposals. It turned out that the North, the West, and the East wanted a loose association for the country, based on the existing regions. The Northern delegation, apart from advocating a loose association, also wanted a secession clause inserted in whatever new constitution might evolve for the country. Our own proposals never contained anything about a secession clause. Only the Midwest delegation took an entirely different view from that of the other delegations. They wanted new states created for the country. Eventually, on the insistence of the Midwest delegation, the conference was adjourned on Friday the sixteenth of last month, to resume on Tuesday the twentieth at 3 P.M., when the Midwest delegation would have had time to obtain a new mandate in the light of what they had seen of the attitude of the other delegations.

A whole week had thus been wasted, to the irritation of our delegates, who felt that the other delegations did not feel the same sense of urgency as our people.

When the conference reassembled on Wednesday, our delegation was startled by the Northern delegation, which suddenly declared that they wanted a strong and effective federal government in Lagos, no longer wanted any secession clause inserted in any new constitution, and were willing to consider the question of creating more states. The Western, Lagos, and, of course, Midwestern delegations promptly supported the Northern stand, the aim being perhaps to isolate the Eastern delegation.

This prompted the Eastern delegation to make the statement which has been so widely and in some cases mischievously misquoted and misinterpreted. The opening sentences of that statement read, and I quote the exact words:

The Eastern Nigerian delegation does not believe that the splitting up of the country into more states at this stage is what we need in order to normalize conditions of life in this country and provide a security for its inhabitants.

At the moment the country is in the grip of fear, suspicion, and mistrust. We believe that in order to save the existence of the country before it is too late, immediate constitutional arrangements for the country as a whole should be made on the basis of the existing regions.

The statements then went further to show how the question of creating more states now in the country could becloud the main issues confronting the nation, apart from causing delays.

The Eastern delegation wanted first things considered first. There was nothing in the statement to show that the Eastern delegation was opposed to the creation of states. If anything, nothing would gladden them more than to see the giant North broken up. As far as the East was concerned, they left here with the firm and honest impression that we of this Region had reached an internal agreement satisfactory to all.

It is now clear that all that the North is prepared to concede in this issue of states, and that because of great and understandable pressure, is the creation of a Middle Belt State, an exercise which has been long overdue. They do not want the Moslem North with its more than 20,000,000 souls touched!

Let us look at this matter from another angle. Chief Awolowo's philosophy is that of creating states based on tribal, linguistic, or ethnic groupings. Would states created on such basis ever make for stability and harmony in the country? Considering the fact that the North would not want its Moslem section touched, the fact that some tribal groupings would be extremely large as compared with very small tribes as exist—for instance, in this Region—and the fact that the army is likely to be based on regions or states of origin, would that make for a truly federal country where no one group or a combination of groups could use their size and numbers to dominate others?

I have done my best to keep this Region together as one people, which they are. But I am not out to impose my will on anyone. If, in spite of all these facts, you want this Region to disintegrate, I shall be disappointed and sad. But history will know whom to blame. No one who is honest and fair will at any time accuse me of dereliction of duty. No one with unbiased and objective mind will doubt my sincere and genuine efforts and intentions.

We have so far stood solidly and impregnably together. Whatever may be the future of this Region, which this assembly will help to determine, we have stood and suffered together with unalloyed pride and patriotism for the land and Region we share in common. My respect and gratitude to you all!

Please, God, forgive our enemies!

Failure of Talks

(Speech at Meeting of the Consultative
Assembly, November 23, 1966)

Circumstances have made it necessary for me to reconvene this assembly in order to bring you up to date on the developments which have taken place since your last meeting. At that last meeting you considered in detail the problems besetting the country, with particular reference to the constitutional talks which had taken place in Lagos and the issues raised there. You heard the report of your delegates to that conference and at the end agreed on certain lines of action. You specifically laid down the conditions under which our men should participate in further discussions.

I naturally pondered over your recommendations for

several days, during which I was in constant touch with Lieutenant Colonel Gowon with a view to seeing whether we could meet somewhere in our demands. Apart from telephone conversations, I wrote a letter to Lieutenant Colonel Gowon, with copies to the military governors, setting out clearly the position of this region and conveying to him the conditions and proposals which you had made about future meetings. Nothing favorable came out of those contacts.

On Saturday, October 22, 1966, I made a broadcast to the nation on the position of Eastern Nigeria with regard to participation at the conference which was scheduled to resume on October 24. The only reaction from Lagos was a statement that the meeting would still be held, and it was indeed held without our participation. By November 1, 1966, the other delegations after, as their release showed, consultations with Lieutenant Colonel Gowon, decided to adjourn the meeting until November 17, when it was hoped conditions would be created which would make it possible for all delegations to attend the discussions in an atmosphere of freedom conducive to personal safety. The communiqué issued by the delegations from the North, the West, Midwest, and Lagos blamed the noncontinuance of the talks on the inability of the East to accept suggested venues for the meeting. That communiqué was promptly replied by this government.

During the adjournment, a delegation of eminent and respected obas and chiefs from the West visited this region. They were able to meet and discuss with their counterparts and other leaders in this region. They also had a long session with me in the presence of some of the Eastern members of the Ad Hoc Committee. The discussions were free, frank, and detailed. That visit also afforded them a good opportunity of seeing a few things for themselves.

Besides those respected emissaries from the West, individuals from other parts of the country (except, of course, the North) as well as non-Nigerians, including diplomats, have also visited us in the East. One important fact which came out most clearly from those visits was that all of them, without a single exception, openly confessed that they had been grossly kept in the dark about the true position of things. There were occasions when the visitors lost their stomach for food after visiting the injured, the maimed, and the dismembered in the hospital. Sometimes they had not the tongue to speak, or spoke to me in tears following what they had seen. And yet anything they saw at that late time did not tell even a tenth of the story. They only saw those admitted in the Enugu General Hospital; and even here they had arrived too late to meet those whose lives could not be saved. They could not go to other hospitals which also had these unfortunate persons. There was not one of these visitors who did not openly agree that our fears and stand were justified, nor failed to praise us for our restraint. . . .

We had expected that the different visits made to this region by people who are friends of this country and anxious to safeguard its existence would lead to Lieutenant Colonel Gowon reviewing his stand and approaching the situation realistically. One way of doing this should have been to create the necessary conditions for further participation by the East at the conference. Nothing of the sort was done. However, we continued to wait hopefully.

In the course of my several telephone conversations with him, Lieutenant Colonel Gowon suggested Ghana or Fernando Po or any nearby country in Africa as a possible venue for the resumed conference. I readily agreed to his suggestion. He then returned to the question of Benin, which I had previously suggested. I agreed that the Ad Hoc Committee should meet in Benin subject to one qualification. I insisted that Northern Nigeria troops in the Western Region should be returned to the North. I was prepared to agree to the retention of a sufficient number of Northern Nigeria troops in Lagos for his own personal security, but bearing in mind that only last August, Northern Nigeria troops traveled from the West to Benin, broke into a prison, removed soldier-detainees of Eastern Nigeria origin, and shot five of them, I could not but insist on the removal of these unruly soldiers from Western Nigeria to the North before our delegation could attend the conference. Lieutenant Colonel Gowon informed me that the Northern delegation would not come to Benin. As regards the alternative venues proposed by Lieutenant Colonel Gowon himself, the public would no doubt wish to know which regions had refused to accept any one of them.

On Wednesday last week, less than twenty-four hours to the time when the Ad Hoc Committee was scheduled to resume its meeting, an announcement came out of Lagos dismissing the Ad Hoc Committee.

Since then many of you in the East and beyond have got in touch with me and asked a number of questions. Uppermost in everyone's mind is the question: Where do we go from here? . . .

Before commenting on Lieutenant Colonel Gowon's statement dismissing the Ad Hoc Committee, I should like to make it clear that I was at no time consulted before this action was taken nor am I aware that the other military governors had prior knowledge of Lieutenant Colonel Gowon's intention. The only conclusion to be drawn from the unilateral and dictatorial decision is that we are entering a new phase in the struggle for national existence.

You will observe from Lieutenant Colonel Gowon's statement of last week, and from what I have just told you about his suggestions with regard to venue for the meeting, that it is no longer a lack of acceptable venue which has necessitated the indefinite adjournment of the conference. This fact is clearly borne out by that portion of Lieutenant Colonel Gowon's statements which reads:

Even if an alternative venue was acceptable to all, the stand of some of the delegates, as evidenced from their last memoranda and the discussions which Lieutenant Colonel Gowon had with some of them, left one in no doubt that no useful purpose will be achieved by the continued sitting of the conference.

In its place, Lieutenant Colonel Gowon had himself drawn up "proposals for lessening tension and for constitutional reforms which would be discussed with the military governors."

This statement has worried everyone since its announcement. I am myself worried about it. We had accepted to go to Ghana, Fernando Po, and, of course, Benin, provided Northern troops were removed from the West. Who were the others who found these venues unacceptable, and why? There has, of course, been no evidence that Lieutenant Colonel Gowon had given any constructive thought to the conditions which this region wanted fulfilled to enable its delegates to participate at the conference. It now appears that such considerations were irrelevant to Lieutenant Colonel Gowon, so long as he became personally convinced that no useful purpose would be served by the continuation of the conference.

Lieutenant Colonel Gowon's statement could mean a lot of things. One is that he has abandoned faith in negotiations as a means of settlement. A statement was credited to a leading member of the Northern delegation to the effect that their aim was to settle the issues by *"negotiations or otherwise."* A request by this government for clarification of that statement has not yet been met. We wanted them to say what means they had in mind for settling our problems other than by negotiation.

Lieutenant Colonel Gowon has now decided to take upon himself to draw up proposals for lessening tension and for constitutional reforms. I must praise him for his courage in taking upon himself this extremely delicate and involved task, and for accepting, by implication, the enormous consequences of what will result from failure to produce something which can satisfy the aspirations of Nigeria. Constitution-making is not the task of a soldier, and all of us have publicly admitted that we were not trained to do that type of thing. That was precisely the reason why it was found necessary to set up the Ad Hoc Committee on the future constitution of Nigeria.

Despite solemn assurances by the National Military Government, headed by Major General J. T. U. Aguiyi-Ironsi, that military government would never impose a constitution on the people of this country and that it was entirely a matter which the people themselves must determine—an assurance which the military governors and Lieutenant Colonel Gowon have repeatedly supported in public declarations—Lieutenant Colonel Gowon, in complete disregard of this pledge and assurance, now proposes to draw up a constitution without consultation.

Lieutenant Colonel Gowon has stated that from the memoranda submitted by the different delegations, no one can be left in any doubt that no useful purpose would be achieved by the continued sitting of the conference. It would be interesting to know what was the purpose of convening the conference in the first instance. Was it not in order to iron out differences? Why should one discontinue the conference merely because the memoranda submitted by the different delegations contained different proposals? There would have been no need to meet at all if there were no differences of opinion, which it was the duty of the delegations to bring out in their different memoranda. This region did appreciate the fact that there must be such differences, hence its insistence that regional memoranda should be circulated in advance as previously agreed, in order that each delegation might be in a position to know the feelings of others and go to the conference prepared to discuss and make necessary concessions in the interest of all.

I have myself read all the memoranda submitted by the different delegations. As far as I can see, only the Northern memoranda differ in substantial points from the rest. With the type of people of high integrity and responsibility which every region had appointed as its delegates to the conference, one should have thought that these people should be allowed to go to the conference table and argue out the different points, with a view to reaching agreement by means of necessary adjustments and concessions. It is unfortunate that Lieutenant Colonel Gowon should have given the impression that because the rest of the delegations did not submit memoranda which conformed to the views of the North, there could be no meeting, and that it must now be left to him, in his wisdom, to draw up something which can be satisfactory to all. He is doing this without prior consultation with the military governors, who must wait to receive what he has decided to hand down to them.

Now that it is no longer possible for the people's representatives to participate in the constitution-making process, I owe it as a duty to you all to publish in full the proposals of the various regions which have resulted in the high-handed dismissal of the Ad Hoc Committee. The people must not be kept in the dark; they have a right to know the facts.

If, as I have evidence to support, the intention of Lieutenant Colonel Gowon and his advisers is to use the so-called Rotimi Williams Report as a basis for his proposals for a constitution which will reduce tension and create confidence, then one cannot help but tell him that he has not been properly advised. To start with, whatever report Chief Rotimi Williams must have submitted to him could not be regarded as something in which this region was associated. The representatives of this region, on the Rotimi Williams Commission set up by the former national government, have already declared their stand on the report, as was reported to you during your last meeting. The present federal Attorney-General, Dr. Elias, openly admitted the irrelevance of that committee, which was described as defunct and overtaken by the events of July 29, 1966.

Even if this were not the case, there is the fact that that commission was set up with objectives which no longer hold in our present situation. At that time, there was every hope and intention to work for more centralization than anything we have known before the same considerations which led to the promulgation of the fateful Decree No. 34. It would, therefore, be unrealistic to think that whatever Chief Rotimi Williams included in his report could be rightly and properly used as a basis for settling the present constitutional crisis in the country.

I can well understand Lieutenant Colonel Gowon's predicament in some of these matters. His particular interest in the creation of states is all too obvious. We wish him luck. We in this region have made our stand clear on this issue. What is needed in Nigeria today is a return to normalcy before anything else. The extreme sufferings and loss of life and property by Easterners dictate no other policy.

There is clear evidence, from information reaching me, that Lagos is still living in its world of unreality with regard to the present situation in the country. Perhaps in this, one may tend to sympathize with, rather than blame, Lieutenant Colonel Gowon. He has a group of senior civil servants in Lagos who, because of their vested interests, are blind to realities. I understand that this group of people in Lagos still believe that a strong central or federal government is feasible in this country in the near future. To this end they have advised on proposals which will lead to the creation of smaller and weaker states, with a view to ensuring a strong center. This again is evidence of the utter ignorance which appears to have engulfed Lagos in the treacherous clouds of idealism. The reality is that you cannot have a strong central or federal government without a unified, integrated, and intermingled army, living and working together in genuine comradeship and confidence. With the events of recent times, it is surprising that anybody could work on the assumption that soldiers from the

Eastern Region can in the foreseeable future share the same camp, sleep in the same barracks, and drink in the same mess in confidence and comradeship with soldiers from the Northern Region. Once a person can appreciate this fact and genuinely try to lay foundations for the future possibility of having a coherent country, he should address his mind to the inevitability of pulling the different sections further apart.

The basis of economic and political togetherness is that of population togetherness. Because of the recent pogroms in the North, no Eastern trader, carpenter, teacher, or civil servant can go and live among Northerners. The wholesale population movement of Easterners from the North to the South has pulled the people of the two areas apart, and this is a fact that no objective and right-thinking person should ignore when considering the question of political and economic association for the country. Unless the people of the North are able to live in the East and enjoy all the benefits offered in the East, there is no reason why the East should expect the North to contribute toward the services and amenities available in its area. The same thing must apply in reverse, and in any such circumstance.

I have often repeated that such a pulling apart could last for, say, five years. Whatever interim constitution is agreed upon could have that period entrenched in it, as should the imperativeness of automatic review of any such interim constitution at the end of that period. By this time, tempers would really have cooled down and the different sections would have had an opportunity of looking back and reassessing things. Such a reassessment could convince all concerned of the need for closer relationship, of interdependence, and, so, of respect for the rights and persons of others. Strong countries of the world started in this way. The United States, for instance, started as a confederation and has since been pulling closer and closer for a stronger and stronger federal government. Because this has been brought about by a genuine realization of the need for

closer association, the arrangement has been accepted
by all and has lasted.

I want to make it quite clear here that I cannot forget my position as a member of an interim administration which set itself the clear objective of performing
specific duties for a nation in the grip of disaster.

I have within the last few weeks addressed important
letters to Lieutenant Colonel Gowon and my other military colleagues at the helm of affairs in this distressed
country. In one of those letters, dated October 25, 1966,
I drew the attention of my colleagues to the heavy responsibilities which the army owed to the nation. Part
of that letter read as follows:

After long and serious reflections, I feel compelled to
address you this letter. I am doing this with a very heavy
heart and deep sense of responsibility and duty, and have
no doubt that you will share in full those feelings.

I write first as a Nigerian citizen who saw in the army
government a source of good, of dedication, and of courage
to do the best for the nation. The boundless feelings and
expressions of joy and hope which pervaded every inch of
this nation bear witness to this fact. Second, I write as a
soldier who, like you and others, answered the call of duty
and accepted positions of responsibility for bringing our
beloved country back from the path of madness and ruin
to that of sanity and progress.

The foremost duty of a soldier is to protect the integrity
of his country. In the discharge of this duty no price can
be too high for him to pay. He is not trained to govern
but to defend his country. If, however, circumstances compel him to interfere with the government of his country, he
does so as a corrective duty. As a nonpartisan member of
his country's community, his path of duty is expected to
be clear and objective, free from encumbrances and extraneous distraction.

Let me come directly to the point. No matter how or
what we may feel about the circumstances which brought
the army into power, we have committed ourselves to specific duties to the country. The country expects us to discharge certain responsibilities from which we cannot honorably escape. Our failure will be disastrous both to the

army and to the nation. It will be a betrayal of trust and a breach of faith.

I wonder how many of us have been able at times to take our minds from the pressing and tragic problems, which now make so many demands on us, to reflect, even for a few minutes, on the events of the past ten months in this country. It can be quite challenging to go back and read the feelings of the people as expressed through the different information media in the country following the event of January 15. To read the newspapers of those days will pointedly remind us of our responsibility to this country and its people; it will bring us to the full appreciation of the hope and faith which the total generality of the people of this country placed in us; it will bring back their expectations and make us search our minds and examine our actions and attitudes to see whether we are really living up to the trust and the expectations of the people and the world.

Are we discharging our duty, keeping our faith, keeping our honor, and facing our commitments? If we can be misguided enough to think that we can honestly and honorably answer those questions in the affirmative, then it is high time we knew that the public cannot be, and have not been, deceived.

Unfortunately and tragically, we seem already to be showing the people who had reposed such extreme confidence in us, the world who saw the army as a beacon of hope for a potentially great but politically betrayed country, that we are not equal to the task. We seem, consciously or unconsciously, to be reassuring the corrupt and the bad, who brought the country to the verge of destruction but for the transfer of power to the army, that they will soon return to their former positions of power unscathed. Quite a number of them are already making arrangements to return and with a vengeance.

The public is becoming apprehensive, frightened, and disappointed. It appears to them that the army, which they saw as their last source of hope and salvation, is not only shirking its responsibility but is in fact becoming apologetic for being given the honor of salvaging the nation. Our actions and public words seem to show that we shared and liked all the ills of the past which we are sorry to have been made to interrupt. The utterly discredited forces of the past seem now to be the powers influencing the army and its actions behind the scenes. The federal *Government Statements on the Current Nigerian Situation*, recently published, virtually admits this. Even more clearly, and disappointingly to the public, we have been giving indications that our duty is no longer the avowed one of correcting past ills but of running away from a difficult situation and handing power to the very people whose avarice, greed, and corruption compelled the army to abandon its natural duty of defending the nation for that of salvaging it. We are lending ourselves to the popular fear that we have allowed sectionalism, prejudice, lack of direction, and inadequacy to take us off the path of duty and honor.

The attemped coup of January 15, 1966, was a failure. But in spite of what might have been the motives and aims of the leaders of the attemped coup, the nation and the world welcomed without reservations the dethronement of the civilian governments, which at that moment of crisis suddenly realized their failings and handed over power to the army which had remained loyal to them. The leaders of those Governments were among the first to wish the army well in the needed and urgent task of national reconstruction. All sections of the country, collectively and individually, united in a single voice and pledged their loyalty and support for the army.

It was against this background that the military government announced its programs and intentions. Its early pronouncements were universally acclaimed, and the army was held as the saving Messiah for the country. It is true that some of our programs of reconstruction have been discredited and forcefully abandoned; for example, those set out in Decree 34 are now repealed. Maybe here the army was a little overzealous or misguided—as any human organization could be. But because a mistake has been made in one direction should not make us abdicate our responsibility and abandon the other programs which we set ourselves to execute.

Such programs included that of purging the country of corruption, of making sure that ill-gotten goods were disgorged, of making the public and those who abused their positions of trust to feel that such actions do not pay, and of setting the country on the path of fairness and justice. To achieve these aims, we set up a number of commissions of inquiry and investigations into public institutions and completed plans for inquiries into private wealth in order to sweep clean the public life of this country. All these were done at both federal and regional levels. A number of commissions of inquiry still exist; their reports will have to be examined and implemented. In some cases work has not even begun, but it is a work which the public does not expect us to abandon.

Apart from this there are other matters which constituted the baneful ills of the past to which the army ought—and the public expect it—to address itself. One has in mind the census issue. There are also the deep wounds and scars which have been caused to the Nigeria body politic as a result of events subsequent to January 15. These are legacies the army cannot morally leave to someone else. To heal the wounds and cover the scars cannot be a matter of months; and yet we do not seem to show by either our words or our actions that we are seriously considering these issues. Instead, we are giving the world and the public totally different impressions.

What do we mean by constantly repeating to the world and the Nigerian public that our main concern now is to return to barracks and hand over powers to the former politicians? By this, does it mean that we have completed our assignments? Does it mean that our duty is now different from what we claimed in January, to the relief and unbounded jubilation of men, women, and children of this country and to our friends both at home and abroad? Or are we abdicating our responsibilities? If so, let the army state that and admit its failure and betrayal of trust to the people, and return at once to the barracks with eternal dishonor, contempt and shame.

The rest of the letter, which was very long, dealt with the position of the army and ended with a suggestion for a meeting of the military governors with Lieutenant Colonel Gowon under guaranteed conditions. That letter was followed a week later by another one dated October 31, dealing with even more intimate problems about the position of the army and its duty. In this last letter, I made sincere and concrete proposals on how the armed forces could reorganize itself in a way which could put it in a position to discharge its responsibilities to the nation. To this day, I have received no replies from Lieutenant Colonel Gowon to the above letters.

Those letters were highly classified documents. But I have now been forced to a position where I shall soon make those letters public.

Fellow countrymen, there can be no doubt that the people in Lagos do not fully appreciate the sense of urgency for which the present situation in the country calls. It is difficult to explain such a destructive attitude in the face of the disintegration threatening the nation. I have been trying to conjecture but cannot really be sure. It is possible that they are living in a fool's paradise and thinking that things are settling down or solving themselves; it could be that they are deplorably ignorant of the true position of things. Perhaps we should give them allowance for ignorance, since it is difficult to understand why anybody who had the full appreciation of the dangers attendant upon procrastination and callous attitudes would have failed to face realities. If indeed they are ignorant of the possible consequences of their position, arising from their own complacency, they will have themselves to blame. However, I have reason to believe that the assumption of dictatorial powers by Lieutenant Colonel Gowon is the first of a series of arbitrary measures taken unilaterally which the country may expect in the coming months.

Last week, the country was shocked by the sad revelation by the Western Nigeria military government of a plot to overthrow that government. We must thank God that that bloody plot was uncovered in time, because its success could have had wider implications and consequences than perhaps the plotters contemplated or Lagos would be prepared to accept. We have been told by the military governor of Western Nigeria, Colonel R. Adebayo, that persons inside and outside the Western Region, including Lagos, were involved in this plot.

It is not for me to speculate on the mastermind behind the plot to overthrow the military government of Western Nigeria.

I must here warn the people of this region that that sort of thing will not be tolerated in this region. We must be alert to the fact that our enemies and detractors will spare no pains, and nothing will give them greater satisfaction than to disturb the stability and solidarity of this region.

As I rightly pointed out in my letter to Lieutenant Colonel Gowon, the truth is that the public is becoming impatient, disappointed, and frustrated, all because the military regime does not seem to be on the move. Under such circumstances it may be impossible to restrain the public from violence born of impatience and a sense of betrayal. The public want the army to solve its problems and carry out the tasks to which it publicly dedicated itself, and which it can shirk only with shame and dishonor.

The attitude of Lagos to this region remains one of callous indifference. They do nothing to show either sympathy or remorse for the atrocities which have been directed against us. . . .

Our people, for the sake of their dear lives, have found it necessary to flee their places of work and return to their home region. These people include civil servants and employees of public corporations. We are doing our best to absorb them at considerable expense and inconvenience.

This absorption has involved overestablishing practically all posts in the regional civil service, in addition to filling existing vacancies with these refugees. This, as you know, is bound to create more unemployment for people due to leave our schools and colleges at the end of this year. But we accept this as a problem which we have to solve.

While this is being done, the federal government has issued instructions to federal corporations operating in this region not to absorb or even pay the salaries of

Easterners who have fled Lagos, the reasons for the action of such employees notwithstanding. If they had taken the trouble to consider, even on grounds of humanity, the plight and positions of these people, they would have at least authorized the federal corporations existing in this region to pay the salaries of these fleeing employees, while early steps were being taken to normalize conditions in the country with a view to enabling the persons concerned to return to Lagos and the West. To do that, of course, would contradict the general attitude of Lieutenant Colonel Gowon and other Northerners toward the East, and this is something which they cannot do. . . .

This region owes a duty to these sons and daughters of ours who have managed to escape the clutches of death and return to us for safety. Their specialties and technical know-how must not be allowed to go to waste. With the specialized skills that these people have possessed, it is not possible to absorb them in ordinary government departments or regional corporations, because their skills will not be needed there. It follows then that if they are to be given employment it must be in the establishments or corporations for which they have acquired the specialized skills and knowledge.

It was against this background that I had to issue, last week, a stern warning to the corporations serving in this region to ensure that their employees from other parts of the country are fully absorbed. I sincerely hope that nobody, whether in the corporations or in the federal government, will take this warning lightly. If they fail to heed it, it will be the duty of this government to take appropriate steps to ensure that these people continue to exercise their skills in the areas and for the services requiring such skills.

I could give several examples of the hostile attitude of the federal government toward Eastern Nigeria. I could cite projects which have been stopped or which, having been completed by the federal government, are not allowed to operate. I could mention the fact that

Eastern officers in foreign missions are already being forced into positions where they have to return home and seek a transfer to the Eastern public service. All these are pointers to things to come.

Respected countrymen, we in this region are very disappointed that it has not been possible to continue with the constitutional talks which we were sure could produce useful and beneficial results to all if pursued in the right spirit. We still believe that all sections of this country will stand to gain by remaining together in some realistic form. We shall continue to pray and work for a peaceful solution of our problems and for the saving of this country. But it takes more than one to make a bargain. If our efforts are not matched by those of others, if we continue to be suspected even when we mean the best in our approaches and actions, then God alone knows where we shall all land.

I cannot omit making reference to our repeated demand for implementation of the unanimous agreements reached by the representatives of the military governors on August 9 for the repatriation of troops to their regions of origin and their confinement to barracks. The continued refusal of Lieutenant Colonel Gowon to implement this unanimous decision exposes him to a breach of faith. This is causing tension, particularly in the West, and strong representations made by the leaders of the West have not even convinced Lieutenant Colonel Gowon that an explosive situation is fast developing in that part of the country.

Ours in this region is to preserve the integrity of the region. This is a foremost responsibility, and we are determined to discharge it. We shall work on definite principles toward the solution of our problems. But this region will be neither bought nor sold. It will not be vanquished so long as we maintain and intensify our vigilance.

Let me now touch on more domestic matters. I am setting up a high-powered fact-finding commission to collect and collate evidence and stories about the atrocities which our people have suffered in the North. Along with this fact-finding commission a medical committee is being set up to examine, interpret, and record the medical cases which have come to our notice. We are doing this because it is important to keep a permanent record of these tragic events in our history as a people.

I have now signed a Customary Courts Edict, reorganizing and reorientating our customary courts system. What remains now is the appointment of the customary court judges, and this I am going to pursue with expedition.

An expert committee is now working on the details of our proposed new system of provincial administration, to which will be devolved legislative and executive powers. These powers will be entrenched in the constitution as recommended by this assembly. Soon after the publication of the necessary White Paper, I hope to appoint provincial administrators, and one of the duties of the provincial authorities will be to advise me on local government matters.

With the completion of these exercises I shall be in a position to appoint civilians to my executive committee on the basis of equal representation for the provinces.

One of the final duties of the military government will be to prepare a code of conduct which may, if necessary, be entrenched in our constitution for future holders of public office in this region. I consider this a matter of great importance, since the youth of this and future days will never again tolerate the type of things which have brought this country to its present grief.

Finally, I thank you for your confidence, cooperation, advice, and encouragement at all times. Without these from you, I would have found my position and task impossible at this critical and crucial time.

May God not destroy our souls with the wicked, nor our lives with men of blood.

II

The Seeds of Wrath

In spite of all that had happened to shatter the basis
for Nigeria's corporate existence, I still believed that a
lot could be salvaged from the debris. As a result of
persistent requests from me, Gowon finally agreed to a
meeting of Nigeria's military leaders outside Nigeria.
The famous Aburi meeting was the result. This was the
first meeting of the Supreme Military Council since the
July, 1966 massacre. The decisions reached were:

A. *Renunciation of the Use of Force:*

Council unanimously adopted a declaration proposed
by Lieutenant Colonel Ojukwu that all members:

(a) renounce the use of force as a means of settling
the Nigerian crisis;

(b) reaffirm their faith in discussions and negotiation
as the only peaceful way of resolving the Nigerian
crisis;

(c) agree to exchange information on the quantity of
arms and ammunition available in each unit of
the army in each region and in the unallocated
stores, and to share out such arms equitably to
the various commands;

(d) agree that there should be no more importation
of arms and ammunition until normalcy is restored.

B. *Reorganization and Control of the Army:*

(a) Army to be governed by the Supreme Military
Council under a chairman to be known as Commander-in-Chief of the Armed Forces and Head
of the Federal Military Government.

(b) Establishment of a military headquarters comprising equal representation from the regions and headed by a Chief of Staff.

(c) Creation of area commands corresponding to existing regions and under the charge of area commanders.

(d) Matters of policy, including appointments and promotion to top executive posts in the armed forces and the police, to be dealt with by the Supreme Military Council.

(e) During the period of the military government, military governors will have control over area commands for internal security.

(f) Creation of a Lagos garrison, including Ikeja barracks. . . .

After a lengthy discussion of the subject, the Council agreed to set up a military committee, on which each region will be represented, to prepare statistics which will show:

    i. present strength of Nigerian army;

    ii. deficiency in each sector of each unit;

    iii. the size appropriate for the country and each area command. The committee is to meet and report to Council within two weeks from the date of receipt of instructions.

C. *Appointments to Certain Posts:*

The following appointments must be approved by the Supreme Military Council:

    i. diplomatic and consular posts;

    ii. senior posts in the armed forces and the police;

    iii. superscale federal civil service and federal corporation posts.

D. *On Functioning of the Supreme Military Council:*

Any decision affecting the whole country must be determined by the Supreme Military Council. Where a meeting is not possible, such a matter must be referred to military governors for comment and concurrence.

E. *Repeal of Decrees:*

That all the law officers of the Federation should meet in Benin on *January 14, 1967,* and list out all the Decrees and provisions of Decrees concerned so that they may be repealed not later than *January 21, 1967.*

F. *On Military Government:*

That for at least the next six months, there should be purely a military government, having nothing to do whatever with politicians.

G. *On Rehabilitating of Displaced Persons:*

(a) That Finance Permanent Secretaries should resume their meeting within two weeks and submit recommendations and that each region should send three representatives to the meeting.

(b) On employment and recovery of property, that civil servants and corporation staff (including daily paid employees) who have not been absorbed should continue to be paid their full salaries until March 31, 1967, provided they have not got alternative employment, and that the military governors of the East, West, and Midwest should send representatives (police commissioners) to meet and discuss the problem of recovery of property left behind by displaced persons.

The urgency of the decisions, as an earnest for the restoration of mutual confidence in Nigeria, was indicated by the deadlines set for their implementation.

Thanks to the good offices of Lieutenant General Ankrah, then chairman of the National Liberation Council of Ghana, the Aburi proceedings and decisions were tape-recorded and copies made available to each delegation. There was therefore no reason for any good-intentioned and honest person to harbor any doubts as to the authenticity of what actually took place. I personally never even imagined that anyone of us who were parties to the decisions could hesitate to accept them as totally binding. The decisions were taken freely and deliberately by the highest authority of the land.

For the first three days after our return home, Gowon tried to act in the spirit of Aburi. On each of the three days, we were in constant telephone contact with each other, discussing matters in the most friendly terms. During one of those conversations Gowon told me about a pamphlet prepared by his government for publication. The document was so anti-Eastern Nigeria and so libelous against me personally that we agreed that it would be against the spirit of the Aburi Accord to go on with its publication. Gowon gave me his word that the publication of the booklet would be withheld if not cancelled. Gowon did not keep his word. On January 15, 1967, the anniversary of the 1966 incident, the pamphlet was launched with fanfare in all the Nigerian embassies abroad and carried over the world radio network. When contacted about the breach of faith, Gowon's only explanation was that it was a leak.

Soon information reached us that the officials of the British High Commission in Lagos had looked at the Aburi decisions and advised Gowon against accepting them. That apart, full minutes of a meeting held by a group of permanent secretaries in Lagos reached us. In essence, the document revealed that those top-ranking civil servants had decided to veto the decisions taken by the cabinet of the country—the Supreme Military Council—and that Gowon had accepted their stand. All these developments appeared to me quite incredible until I began to notice definite changes in Gowon's attitude. Our daily telephone contacts were no longer regular or cordial. Gowon's conversations became cold and peremptory. The different meetings for which deadlines had been set were not held. The salaries of Eastner Nigerian refugees were not paid. Nothing was done to relieve the sufferings of other refugees. After a lot of wrangling and pressure, Gowon came out with a decree purporting to implement the Aburi decisions but which in fact contradicted every aspect of those decisions. We, of course, refused to be party to such a fraud.

Meanwhile, our people were suffering. Our lawyers could not go to Lagos to practice their profession while Northern soldiers were still in that city. Employees of the federal government and those of federal corporations were starving along with their families for lack of pay. Educational institutions and examinations federally controlled were closed to our people in Eastern Nigeria. In the face of all these deprivations, the government of Eastern Nigeria saw no alternative but to discharge its responsibility to the people by introducing appropriate measures. The Survival Edicts were issued, namely,

The Revenue Collection Edict—designed with exactitude only to enable the Eastern government to fulfill federal government obligations to their employees as agreed at Aburi.

The Legal Education Edict—designed to safeguard the careers of Eastern Nigeria law students who had fled other parts of the Federation as a result of federal government inability to afford them basic protection of life and property.

The Court of Appeal Edict—designed to maintain the rule of law in Eastern Nigeria after all efforts to convince the federal government of the necessity for the Federal Supreme Court to hold session in Eastern Nigeria as was customary from time to time.

All these edicts were fully self-explanatory and designed precisely to meet specific responsibilities abandoned by the federal government.

Gowon's answer to these legitimate steps was to impose a blockade on Eastern Nigeria; first, by banning all flights by Nigeria Airways to Eastern Nigeria. In addition, foreign exchange credits of all concerns owned by the Eastern Nigerian government were frozen. Eastern Nigerian businessmen were denied import licenses. Lagos ordered all foreign ships to avoid Eastern Nigerian ports, and the British High Commission helped to ensure that the ban was enforced by British shipping lines. Ships carrying goods imported by Eastern Nigerian traders were diverted to Lagos, where the cargoes were impounded. Foreign savings and deposits, premium bonds and stamps sold in Eastern Nigeria, were declared null and void. Passports of Eastern Nigerians were nullified, and salaries of employees of federal-owned concerns operating in Eastern Nigeria were stopped. The people of Eastern Nigeria were denied postal and telecommunication facilities outside the region, and all post office savings held outside Eastern Nigeria by Easterners were frozen. Foreign savings of Eastern Nigerians were blocked and the assets of the Eastern Nigeria Marketing Board frozen. In addition, Gowon issued threats of force against Eastern Nigeria.

The economic blockade in the forms already mentioned was supplemented by another kind of blockade —the *"blockade of truth,"* by which Nigeria and the British government used all diplomatic channels to mislead the world and black out any truth about what was happening in Eastern Nigeria.

Eventually, in the face of great pressure from within and outside Nigeria, Gowon produced Decree No. 8 (the fifth in the series of such exercises to implement the Aburi Accord!) and convened a meeting of the Supreme Military Council with Benin as the venue. It later transpired that the real aim was to induce me to leave the Eastern Region to Benin, where there were still Northern Nigerian soldiers, who had been ordered to kidnap me during my visit to Benin.

Right through this whole period, I wrote several letters of strong appeal to Gowon and other military governors, pleading that the Aburi Agreements be implemented and also warning about the implications of failure to do so. I also made a journey to Ghana, where I pleaded with Lieutenant General Ankrah to use his influence on Gowon to see that the Aburi Agreements were implemented. I seized every opportunity of a meeting with every visitor of influence to Enugu to stress the need to get Gowon to implement the agreements before March 31. All these were of no avail. Throughout this period, the one man who could have saved the situation was none other than Lieutenant General Ankrah, under whose auspices the Aburi Accord was reached and into whose care copies of all the records were entrusted. For certain considerations per-

sonal to him, he said nothing—not even a word merely
to establish the terms of the accord. He only could have
averted this war—his silence made the war inevitable
and enhanced its pace once it started.

Significantly, whether acting on their own or inspired
by Lagos, important visitors to Enugu, among them
leading journalists and diplomats, almost invariably
wanted to know from me under what circumstances
Eastern Nigeria would secede from the rest of the Federation. We gave four conditions under which we would
finally be convinced that we were no longer wanted in
Nigeria. These conditions were: (a) nonimplementa-
tion of the Aburi Agreements; (b) imposition of economic blockade; (c) use of force or any threat thereof;
(d) interference with the territorial integrity of Eastern
Nigeria. Our position was that *any one* of the above
developments would compel Eastern Nigeria to secede.

As has been shown, Gowon systematically and pro-
vocatively proceeded to impose all those conditions
which we had publicly and repeatedly stated would
drive us out of the ill-fated Federation. He failed to
implement the Aburi Agreements; he imposed a total
economic blockade against Eastern Nigeria; he threatened the use of force and, finally, on May 27, 1967,
interfered with the territorial integrity of Eastern Nigeria by his arbitrary creation of states. This last act
was timed to coincide with the joint meeting of chiefs,
elders, and members of the Consultative Assembly
which began in Enugu on Friday, May 26, 1967.

The fact that we chose to wait until this last act, even
when we had repeatedly made it quite clear that the
imposition of any of the conditions mentioned would
compel us to leave Nigeria, is further evidence of our
patience and desire to save what could be saved of
Nigeria. Gowon's arbitrary and final act of creating
states in Eastern Nigeria, thereby interfering with the
territorial integrity of our region, became the last straw
and left us with no alternative but to take the historic
and proud step of declaring our independence and as-
suming our sovereignty.

In the joint session of the Council of Chiefs and Elders and of the Consultative Assembly held May 26–27, 1967, the people mandated me to take the final appropriate step for the redemption of our people. On May 30, 1967, I acted on the people's mandate and proclaimed what was known as Eastern Nigeria the sovereign and independent State of Biafra.

Diary of Events: November 26–30, 1966

November 26: Rehabilitation Day in the East. In my broadcast I appeal to individuals and some establishments in the region to contribute generously to funds for relieving the sufferings of the refugees. I also warn that my government might be forced to a position where drastic action will have to be taken to protect refugees against "those organizations and individuals who are exploiting our present difficulties for selfish gains, whether by raising rents or doubling prices. . . ." I implore those establishments, whether private or public, to show human consideration and not to increase the unemployment situation in the region for selfish ends.

November 28: Port Harcourt workers of Nigerian Ports Authority stage protest march against the decision of their chairman, Andrew Wilson, to transfer the sum of £150,000 of NPA's account from Port Harcourt to Lagos.

November 29: More than 2,000 refugee employees of the Nigerian Railway Corporation travel to Enugu from their villages to receive their arrears of salaries to the end of November. They are told by the railway authorities that Lagos has not sent any money. A violent protest demonstration to me by the railway staff is forestalled by the intervention and promises of the railway district superintendent, J. A. Anozie.

November 30: In a broadcast, Lieutenant Colonel

Gowon continues his bogey of "East's plan to secede"
and threatens to use force to maintain the "integrity of
the country." He indefinitely adjourns Ad Hoc Committee because its sitting "will serve no useful purpose."
. . . In a direct rejection of the increasing popular demand for a temporary confederation, Lieutenant
Colonel Gowon declares: "I should emphasize that the
idea of a temporary confederation is unworkable. . . ."

Provincial Administration

(Address to joint meeting of the Advisory Committee
of Chiefs and Elders and the Consultative Assembly,
November 10, 1966)

During the meeting of last week, I made two promises. The first was that I would be making available to
you and the public the different memoranda submitted
by the different delegations of the country to the Ad
Hoc Conference on the Nigerian Constitution, and the
second that I would soon be publishing a White Paper
about the new system of provincial administration.
These two documents are now ready.

We in this region sincerely want this country to remain one, with its component parts associating in a
realistic way. In order to achieve this, all those who
have the power and responsibility to make decisions
must be prepared to eschew personal pride, prejudices,
and vested interests, and look at the problems in a
practical and disinterested way. Unfortunately, the people in Lagos whose responsibility it is to create the
necessary conditions and atmosphere for a right solution of these pressing problems seem to be living in a
world of fantasy. They appear to ignore, or dismiss too
lightly, the glaring and inevitable facts.

It seems to be their attitude that things are solving
themselves, tempers are cooling, and the past is being

forgotten. The more I become conscious of this untenable attitude from Lagos, the more I am inclined to be sorry for them and for the country.

The pogroms carried out by the people of the North against our people of this region have set a pattern of population distribution which cannot be ignored or changed in the next few years. There has been virtually a wholesale population movement of Easterners from the North to the East, and this has pulled the people of the East and the North apart.

Let me make it clear in unmistakable terms that no one from any section of the East will in the immediate future find it possible to live side by side with people in the North or any section of the North, even if the North were divided into thirty states. The crime of genocide was committed jointly by all sections of the North against all sections of the East.

Politically and economically, therefore, the people of the East and the North cannot have the same type of associations which they have had in the past. That being the case, any talk of plans for a political arrangement which will pool the resources of the two groups is, to say the least, fatuous. Once the most important of these resources, namely the human, has been thus torn apart, it is nonsense to talk about pooling material resources. We in this region have always been aware and conscious of this fact. That is why we have said, as a proof of our sincerity about the need to keep Nigeria in existence, that what is needed now is to work toward a loose association of the existing component parts of the country, and that such arrangement could be limited to a specified period, at the end of which there could be an automatic review. I have even gone further to suggest that such a period could be five to ten years—in other words, the equivalent of one to two terms of the normal life of a parliament to which we have been accustomed in this country.

As usual, this suggestion does not seem to have registered with the authorities in Lagos. A group of people

there are afraid of losing their positions or even having
such positions diminished. They are using every means
—personal overtures and even a section of the press—
to pressure the military government in Lagos. Their
aim is to have a strong center—indeed a center even
stronger than what had been known before. To them
this is the most urgent need for saving the nation. As a
means of achieving their ends they are urging as a
priority the creation of states through breaking the
country into a number of small and weak units, resulting in a stronger federal government than before.

Unconsciously, they want to achieve some of the very
ends of the fateful Decree No. 34, which was used as a
pretext for the first wholesale massacre of Easterners
by Northerners in May this year.

Their attitude is an embarrassing contradiction of
the clear and categorical declaration of Lieutenant
Colonel Gowon on August 1 this year that the basis for
Nigerian unity did not exist. It is a departure from the
unanimous decision of the personal representatives of
the military governors at their meeting on August 9,
1966, that everything making for overcentralization
should be removed.

We in this region have rightly been conscious of these
facts, and all our proposals have been influenced by
them. During the first meeting of the Ad Hoc Committee of the Constitutional Conference, certain agreements
were reached. One of those agreements was that Nigeria
should remain as a unit, but nothing in that agreement
envisaged anything but a loose association, even if that
was called a "federation."

Turning to the different proposals submitted by the
different delegations, I need to make only one or two
comments. The first is that the joint Western and
Lagos position is very close to our own. Here it is
worth mentioning that for the meeting which lasted
from September 12 until the end of that month, the
West had not really made up its mind. The result was
that they submitted alternative proposals. Thanks, however, to the statesmanship of Chief Awolowo and other

leaders of the West, their latest memoranda contain definite and firm proposals for a loose federation. The Midwest also in its latest proposals supports a loose federation. None of them now advocates the creation of states. It is to us encouraging to know that there exist in this country people who are prepared to see and tackle the problems in the way that they ought to be seen and tackled. In spite of the sufferings and deprivations which we in the East have endured, we have tried to be quite objective in our approach. I am sure that if it is possible for the Ad Hoc Committee to continue its work, and delegates go there with open minds, even those who at present differ from us in their stand will be in a position, after hearing the arguments from all sides, to face realities and agree on arrangements which are congenial to the present circumstances.

The position of Northern Nigeria is rather interesting. They seem to be shifting grounds in the opposite direction from their original stand. We know for a fact that following the event of July 29, the main interest of the North was to secede, and they would have done so but for the intervention of friends of this country. When the Ad Hoc Committee met on September 12, their memoranda contained proposals which envisaged a customs union, something similar to the type of association they advocated in 1953. In support of their case, they added as an appendix to their memoranda a paper on the East African Common Services Organization. Their proposals even included a right of secession by any component part of the country. Nothing in their proposals supported the creation of states.

Before the end of that session, however, the North shifted its ground and declared for a federal government with an effective center, recanted their doctrine of secession, and said they would be prepared to consider the question of creating states! We have since known that the change of position was not unconnected with a calculated attempt to embarrass and confuse the delegation and people of this region.

Their latest memoranda have shown further inconsistencies and shifts of ground. They want a powerful center and have virtually abandoned their support for the creation of states, because the principle they suggest for doing this is hardly workable. It would be quite interesting and instructive to know the true motives of Northern Nigeria in these their chameleonic somersaults.

We have been consistent in the central principle that areas of conflict, which our sad experiences of the past have brought out, should be avoided. The struggle to control the center has been the main source of strife, leading to suspicion, distrust, and even hate among the different peoples of this country. If we want to stop this strife and conflict without destroying what we know today as Nigeria, we must, even if only for a period, render the central authority less powerful and so less attractive to ambitious and power-seeking individuals in this country. During the interim period everybody will have time to reflect on general issues, so that when we come to review whatever might be the interim constitution prepared for this country, we shall be able to evolve a practical constitution which would remove all fears and provide a basis for justice and mutual confidence. It is our position that if states are to be created, this would be the time to consider that, if it becomes necessary to have a strong central government in a more coherent country.

I shall now say a few words on the White Paper on the provincial administration. You are free to express your views on the proposals contained therein before I consider the final edict on the subject.

You will recall that the first meeting of this Consultative Assembly appointed a committee to consider and advise on what ways the fears of the minorities could be assuaged, and injustices and imbalances redressed. During that meeting I was able to speak to different groups and classes of people and became convinced that the fears and sense of injustice, shown and expressed by certain sections, were in a number of cases justified. I was accordingly determined to see that the sources of those fears, injustices, and grievances were removed. I was therefore particularly interested in what the committee set up by the first Consultative Assembly has to say.

That committee, which was chairmaned by Dr. Okoi Arikpo [now Nigerian Commissioner of External Affairs], submitted its report to the plenary session of this assembly, which acclaimed and accepted the broad recommendations. The only point in those recommendations, and in the decision of the assembly, which had not been finally settled was that of the number of provincial units. The committee has mentioned four, five, twelve, and twenty-seven units, but left the final decision to me.

Those recommendations were later submitted to the Constitutional Committee, headed by the late Attorney General, Dr. Graham Douglas, for a closer and more detailed study. The Constitutional Committee confirmed that the establishment of a provincial system, involving the devolution of executive and legislative powers on provinces, would satisfy the aspirations of certain areas in the region which had been complaining of neglect and exploitation.

Then came the return of our delegation from the Lagos conference on the constitutional future of this country. During their meeting in Lagos, other delegations had attempted to bring in the red herring of state creation. Our delegates made a public statement about the position of this region on that issue, and that statement was misrepresented and misinterpreted by our detractors. Our delegates on return reported everything in full to the Consultative Assembly, which had now been enlarged, and later to the Advisory Council of Chiefs and Elders. You, after hearing the report and considering all the issues, reaffirmed that a provincial system of administration in this region, given adequate powers and responsibilities, would be a satisfactory means of satisfying the aspiration of minorities and of removing all sources of injustice.

Following this recommendation I reconstituted the

Constitutional Committee and ensured that every province was represented on it. This new committee examined the proposals and finally recommended that fifteen provinces be created. I have, for the past few weeks, been studying this recommendation very carefully. After taking all the factors into consideration, my proposals are now contained in the White Paper. The capital city, Enugu, will be administered separately, with its own administrator. The principles governing this arrangement have been set out in the White Paper, and I want to draw your attention particularly to one of the objectives of this exercise, namely, that of ensuring even development and fair distribution of amenities.

We want to work toward a situation in this region in which no part will be looked upon as backward, in which every part of this region will be attractive enough for anyone to live and work in.

In this regard we can and shall turn what has appeared to us as misfortune into a blessing. With the return to this region of our sons and daughters who helped to build and develop other parts of the country, only eventually to be driven away from those places with great losses of life and property, we now have sufficient talent, manpower, and human resources which we can harness to our own good and to the shame of our enemy. It is for this reason that I attach very great importance to one of the functions which has been proposed for the new provinces, namely, that of local development, which includes town and country planning. This will present a challenge to the provincial government organs. The aim must be so to develop our areas that, within the next few years, the word "rural" or "backward" will have been banished from our social dictionary; and the drift to the important towns by school leavers will have stopped, everywhere being good enough for our young men and women to stay and make a living.

A regrouping of areas has been proposed. These regroupings have been influenced by two factors—affinity of the people and population. Since the finances of the provinces will come principally from the regional government, the population sizes had to play a good part in determining the regroupings in order to ensure fair distribution of funds.

I thank you all for being able to come to this meeting. Please, God, grant us peace.

Diary of Events:
Dec. 1, 1966—Jan. 5, 1967

December 1–4:   Demonstrations by refugee workers in Enugu against the denial of their salaries by Lagos. . . . Many organizations in Lagos and Western Nigeria press for withdrawal of Northern Nigeria and non-Yoruba troops from Lagos and the West. Northern troops in these areas are described as *"occupation troops in a protectorate"* by Yorubas. . . . Radio Kaduna, Northern Nigeria, jeers that Easterners "got what they deserved [the pogroms]" and appeals to Gowon not to aid the refugee problem of my government. The jeers are followed up by the launching of a book by the Current Issues Society, an organization hastily founded by Northern Nigerian students and supervised by British staff of the Ahmadu Bello University. The propaganda pamphlet contains fictitious atrocities committed against Northerners by Easterners. . . . Discovery of a plot by Gowon government to subvert Eastern Region and topple my government.

December 8:   I formally implement the report of the region's Constitutional Committee and establish the new Provincial Administrative System.

December 14:   I set up a tribunal "to inquire into the atrocities and other inhuman acts committed against persons of Eastern origin in Northern Nigeria and other parts of the Federal Republic of Nigeria during the month of May, 1966. The chairman of the tribunal is Mr. G. C. M. Onyiuke, now justice of the Biafra Court of Appeal.

December 31: In New Year's Eve broadcast, I urge that instead of launching campaign of calumny and raising bogies of the imaginary plan of the Eastern people to secede or revenge the pogroms, all that Northern Nigeria should do is to offer open repentance for the pogroms. This will lower the high tension in the East and reassure the people. . . . I contact Lieutenant Colonel Gowon on the phone and in a long conversation plead that the new year should bring peace to Nigeria. I renew my pleas for a meeting of the country's military governors outside Nigeria, since he is unwilling to carry out August 9 agreement on repatriation of troops to regions of origin.

January 2–4: Preparations for Aburi talks.

January 4–5: Meeting of all military leaders of Nigeria at Aburi, Ghana. This is the first meeting of the Supreme Military Council since the July 29, 1966, massacre-mutiny.

Aburi Meeting

(Press Conference, January 6, 1967)

You are already aware that we have just ended the meeting of the Supreme Military Council in Ghana.

It has come to my notice that the public is anxious to have more details of decisions taken.

The meeting opened with a joint declaration by all of us, the military leaders, renouncing the use of force as a means of settling the present crisis in Nigeria and holding ourselves in honor bound by that declaration. That declaration also reaffirmed our faith in discussions and negotiations as the only peaceful means of resolving the Nigerian crisis.

Having regard to the great fear and suspicion on all

parts about the use of force, we thought that this declaration should precede any other business; and I am sure that all Nigerians will welcome it as a source of great relief.

The next important matter discussed, and upon which a lot of other things hinged, was the organization of the Nigerian army. Let me say here that our discussions right through went on in a calm atmosphere, understanding, and realism. We in the East have always felt that realism and understanding were lacking in the past in the approach to our problems, and it was very encouraging that our meetings on the two days showed the sincere determination by all to find realistic solutions to our problems.

It was agreed that the army will henceforth be governed by the Supreme Military Council, the chairman of which will be known as Commander-in-Chief and Head of the Federal Military Government. There is to be a military headquarters on which the regions will be equally represented and which will be headed by a Chief of Staff. There shall be an area command in each region under the charge of an area commander—the regions corresponding to the existing ones. There will be a Lagos garrison, which will include Ikeja. For the duration of the military government, military governors will have control over their area commands in matters of internal security. All matters of policy, including appointments and promotions of persons in the executive posts in the armed forces and the police, shall be dealt with by the Supreme Military Council. Any decision affecting the whole country must be determined by the Supreme Military Council, and when a meeting is not possible, such a matter must be referred to the military governors for comments and concurrence.

Subject to the above arrangements, we felt that the existing governmental institutions, namely, the Supreme Military Council and the Federal Executive Council, as well as regional executive councils, are workable and should be retained.

It was agreed that the Supreme Military Council

must collectively approve appointments to the following offices: (a) diplomatic and consular posts; (b) senior posts in the armed forces and the police; (c) superscale federal civil service and federal corporation posts.

This particular decision was made as a means of removing friction, it being our unfortunate experience that friction and misunderstanding had in the past bedeviled these appointments. What it means is that no one person will have the right and power to make these appointments alone in the future.

Politically, it was unanimously agreed that it was in the interest of the safety of this nation that the regions should move slightly further apart than before. As a prelude to this, it was decided that all decrees and parts of decrees promulgated since the military regime, and which detracted from the previous powers of the regional governments, should be repealed by the twenty-first of this month. Once this is done and the agreements are implemented, the aim of allowing the regions to operate more independently and of ensuring fairness to all will be achieved.

The question of displaced persons was exhaustively discussed. As regards civil servants and employees of government corporations who had to flee their places of work as a result of the current situation, it was decided that such people will be paid their full salaries up to the end of March this year, unless they have found alternative employment.

On the question of other displaced persons, it was decided to set up a committee to look into the problems of rehabilitation and recovery of property. I took that opportunity to repeat my assurance that those non-Easterners who had to be ordered to leave the region in the interest of their own safety would be welcomed back as soon as conditions become more normal.

I have hurried to make this statement to you because of the misgivings which I understand are prevalent in the region as a result of this meeting. I recall that just before my departure, when the public did not even know that our meeting was so close, students and other groups of individuals issued resolutions advising me against attending any meeting with my counterparts. You will now be convinced that this meeting was more than necessary and worthwhile. Our duty is to reduce or remove tension, in order to leave ourselves free to tackle the most urgent and constructive tasks of economic and social development, which cannot be possible in a state of tension and fear. I have no doubt that all of us who participated in the last discussions are determined to implement the agreements reached. Once this is done, we shall have gone a long way to relieving tension and banishing fear among us. It is our plan to meet again soon, this time in Nigeria, to consider other matters arising from our last discussions and those which were not touched.

I want here to place on record my personal indebtedness to the government and people of Ghana for making a plane available to convey me to and from the meetings on the two days, and for making other arrangements to make this meeting possible. Provided our aims are achieved, we in this country will have cause to remain eternally grateful to Ghana for their constructive initiative.

For our part in this country, we must keep calm and avoid actions or words which might create difficulties for our progress in the solution of our problems.

God will certainly rescue this nation from collapse and perdition.

Diary of Events: Jan. 10—Feb. 18, 1967

January 10: Top secret meeting of federal permanent secretaries in Lagos with members of the Federal Executive Council (without Eastern members). The permanent secretaries criticize Aburi decisions and advise against implementation.

January 14: Meeting of law officers of the Federation in Benin to discuss the legal implications of the Aburi decisions and to list out all decrees which are to be repealed by February 21, 1966.

January 16: Articles in the Eastern Nigerian press praising Aburi decisions and expressing hope for the future. Lessening of tension.

January 17–18: Law officials of the five governments of the Nigerian Federation resume Benin meeting on a draft decree on decentralization.

January 19: My first telegram to Gowon expressing joy that the repealing decree is being drafted.

January 20: Body of late Major General J. T. U. Aguiyi-Ironsi is flown to Enugu, from where it is conveyed by train to Umuahia for interment. . . . Chief secretary to the federal government circulates Permanent Secretaries' *Comments on the Accra Decisions* to members of the Supreme Military Council and Federal Executive Council (Eastern members excluded). The comments urge rejection of Aburi decisions. . . . Draft of the decree on decentralization is completed by Lagos regime. The draft, which is a complete departure from Aburi, is rejected by both Eastern and Western Nigeria.

January 21: Aburi's deadline on decentralization decree expires.

January 26: Gowon's press conference on the Aburi Accord, in which he repudiates the Aburi decisions, in accordance with Permanent Secretaries' *Comments on the Accra Decisions.*

January 28: Aburi's date for the meeting of the Supreme Military Council. No meeting because implementation of Aburi decisions, which was to be a prelude to the council's meeting, has not been carried out.

January 30: I address another letter to Gowon, in which I appeal to him to implement the Aburi Accord in order "to avoid disintegration of Nigeria." . . . Another decree is prepared by Lagos, and a clause in it arrogates to Gowon the power to declare a state of emergency in any region. The East promptly raises objection.

February 1: The Atrocities Commission ends its 49-day public sitting with recorded sworn evidence from 253 witnesses and a total of 498 exhibits.

February 15–24: Eastern Nigeria tries without success to present her case of genocide against Nigeria before the Commission of Human Rights of the United Nations. The delegation forward our case in "MEMORANDUM ON THE DELIBERATE AND CONTINUOUS CONTRAVENTIONS BY NIGERIA OF THE UNITED NATIONS CHARTER ON HUMAN RIGHTS AND HER PRACTICE OF GENOCIDE."

February 17–18: Secretaries to the military governments and other officials meet in Benin on a second draft decree on decentralization.

Breach of Aburi Accord

(Broadcast, February 25, 1967)

A little over a month ago, the whole country rejoiced at the prospect of a fast return to normal conditions. This was after the historic meeting at Aburi in Ghana, where Nigerian military leaders held their first meeting since the tragic events of July 29, 1966. We reached unanimous agreement on a wide range of matters.

Today all the high hopes and confidence borne out of Aburi seem to be waning. There is evidence that those in authority in Lagos are determined to repudiate or evade the agreements reached unanimously. Unnecessary confusion has been infused into the whole issue both from within and from without, and the country is once again drifting dangerously.

Eastern Nigeria has gone through terrible tragedies in recent months. Apart from the wounds of the recent pogrom, we have on our hands 1,800,000 refugees who must be catered for. The people of this region have a right to decent life, peace, and harmony. Conscious of the gravity of the situation, I have spared no effort to inspire a sense of realism and sanity in the approach to the crisis so that we might preserve the integrity of this country and enable our people to embark upon the enormous task of reconstruction without fear of molestation. I tried hard for several months to persuade my colleagues to hold a meeting outside Nigeria, where the security of all the participants would be assured. For long, this suggestion was treated with levity by Lieutenant Colonel Gowon, but eventually it was unanimously agreed that the meeting should be held in Ghana.

Why did I go to Aburi? First, because after the events of July 29, 1966, there was no single authority in Nigeria which could command the allegiance and obedience of the entire peoples of Nigeria or give protection to their lives and property. It became imperative, therefore, to re-create the Supreme Military Council in such a manner as to reestablish its authority and ensure its impartiality in matters affecting Nigeria as a whole, thus removing the possibility of the central authority being solely controlled by a Northerner, an Easterner, a Westerner, or a Midwesterner. Second, in order to preserve the integrity of the country, a solution had to be found to the question of national leadership and chain of command within the armed forces. The Aburi meeting was intended to provide and did provide a working basis for solving the problem. Third, it was necessary to arrest the drift in the country and to control the situation so as to enable constitutional arrangements to be made in an atmosphere devoid of fear, tension and suspicion. I did not go to Aburi as an Easterner; I went there as a Nigerian seeking a satisfactory solution to a Nigerian problem. I did not go to Aburi to seek powers for myself, nor did I go there for a picnic. I went there to work in order to save this country from disintegration. The solutions proposed were accepted without equivocation at Aburi. They were accepted because we all saw in them the *only* formula that can keep Nigeria together. I am, therefore, irrevocably committed to seeing that the Aburi decisions are fully implemented.

My position regarding the implementation of the Aburi Agreements has been repeatedly made clear. Apart from my public statements on the subject, I have written a number of letters to my colleagues, all urging that the Aburi Agreements be implemented without unnecessary delay.

Having regard, however, to the volume of letters and other forms of inquiries, and the great uneasiness, which appear to be pervading the region as a result of actions on the part of the government in Lagos such as the nonpayment of salaries to both its direct employees and those of its statutory corporations, I have no alternative but to make this statement for two reasons. First, to assure the people of this region that I am bound in honor to the Aburi Agreements, and second, to call for continued calm and intensified vigilance.

Soon after our return from Aburi, Lieutenant Colonel Gowon got in touch with me and informed me that the government in Lagos had prepared a publication called *Nigeria '66*. He wanted my views as to whether the publication of that booklet would be contrary to the decision reached not to publish anything which would detract from the spirit of Aburi. I personally saw in this approach an encouraging sign for future cooperation and confidence. We discussed and agreed that since the publication had not been put out to the public it would be wise to withhold it. On January 15, 1967, that publication was released, its sole objective being to denigrate Eastern Nigerians, living and dead. I got in touch with Lieutenant Colonel Gowon, and he assured me that it was not a deliberate act but a leakage. This information turned out to be untrue because evidence soon came through that the publication was, in fact, formally launched in Washington, London, Cotonou and other foreign capitals. What is more, its introduction shows that the draft was completed after the Aburi meeting, most likely even after our discussion. It was the first act from Lagos after Aburi which shook my confidence in what we tried to do at Aburi.

Then came Lieutenant Colonel Gowon's press conference to the world on the Aburi meeting, which virtually amounted to a denunciation of the agreements
reached at that meeting.

Contrary to the decisions at Aburi, recruitment into
the army has continued in different parts of the country
except the East; contrary to those agreements, important diplomatic and other public appointments have
been made without reference to the Supreme Military
Council as clearly agreed at Aburi; contrary to the
agreements, purchase and importation of arms have
continued. The meeting of military officers to discuss
the reorganization of the army as agreed at Aburi has
been unilaterally postponed by Lagos. The meeting of
finance officials, with particular reference to the problem of rehabilitation, has not even been held because
officials in Lagos do not think it will serve any useful
purpose.

At a meeting of representatives of the military governors held in Lagos on August 9, 1966, it was agreed
that all decrees or provisions of decrees which detracted
from the previous powers and position of the regional
governments should be repealed. The government in
Lagos failed to implement that decision. At the Aburi
meeting, all the military governors insisted that that decision of August 9, 1966, be fully implemented, and it
was agreed that solicitors-general should meet on January 14, 1967, to identify those decrees or provisions
of decrees so that they could be repealed by January
21, 1967. The solicitors-general met and identified those
decrees or provisions of decrees affected. Naturally they
also discussed other aspects of the Aburi decisions and
sought guidance on some of them.

Since they had pinpointed the decrees or sections of
decrees to be repealed, there should be no difficulty in
repealing those decrees, while leaving the other questions asked by the solicitors-general to the Supreme
Military Council. After strong pressures from me and
the military governor of the West, the government in

Lagos produced a draft decree which for all intents and purposes aimed at strengthening the powers of the government at the expense of the regions: the very opposite of what the Aburi decisions envisaged. The draft was, of course, not acceptable, and so that decree has not yet been published.

At the Aburi meeting, the question came up of employees of government and public corporations who found it necessary to flee their places of work because of the disturbances. On the suggestion and personal initiative of Lieutenant Colonel Gowon himself, we decided that such employees should be paid their salaries until March 31, 1967, unless they had in the meantime found alternative employment. This decision has not been implemented. Indeed, instructions have been received from Lagos that people of Eastern Nigerian origin should not be paid their salaries.

In support of their defaults, the Lagos government has looked for one reason or another. There have been suggestions that the Aburi Agreements should be reviewed if not abandoned because some members did not understand their implications. Others have said that they went there unprepared. As it was our first meeting since July 29, 1966, we certainly could not have gone to Aburi unprepared. The agenda was prepared beforehand in consultation with all the governments concerned. If anybody went to that meeting unprepared, then one can only infer that he was not seriously concerned with the problems which had beset the country, let alone with how to solve them.

In support of the Lagos government's refusal to honor the Aburi Agreements as they affected the payment of fleeing employees up to the end of March, the fact that a number of railway wagons are now in the East has been proffered as an excuse. When the decision was taken at Aburi, everybody knew that those wagons were here. One should have thought that the implementation of the Aburi Agreements would be a precondition for the release of these wagons and not the other way around. The government in Lagos further complicated matters by denying the coal corporation the right to collect their just debts from the Nigerian Railway Corporation, and have refused to send the necessary funds for the payment of salaries for railway workers. These acts are nothing but a deliberate attempt to cause trouble and disaffection among the people of Eastern Nigeria, because they know the large number of persons involved and the seriousness of their dissatisfaction following nonpayment of their salaries at the beginning of a new year, when they have to meet commitments for their children's school fees and other personal matters.

The authorities in Lagos have not stopped there. They are using all their power to impede the smooth operation of private industries in this region. Not only are they doing everything to obstruct investors and industrialists coming to do business here, they are doing everything they can to kill even those industries which are operating in this region. I am aware also that plans to carry out a blockade of the East are being hatched.

On the political front, I have evidence that the governments in Lagos and Kaduna are encouraging acts of subversion and sabotage within this region. These Northern-controlled governments are prepared to sink their tribal and political differences in order to achieve an objective nearest to their hearts, namely, to dominate and rule the Southern regions. It is this same policy that is now driving this country to the verge of disintegration. I, therefore, take this opportunity to call on the peoples of Southern Nigeria to open their eyes and see the handwriting on the wall.

It has now become imperative that an end be put to all this. As a people who once claimed the honor of being looked upon as the most mature in Africa, the leaders of this country must show that maturity by honoring agreements. The survival of this country, its normalcy and peace, hinges on the implementation of the Aburi Agreements.

The secretaries to the military governments and other officials have recently held a meeting in Benin to advise on the implementation of the Aburi Agreements. I sincerely hope they will bring home to all concerned the pressing need to give immediate effect to the Aburi decisions. Friends of Nigeria in Africa and the rest of the world, and particularly in Ghana, are watching our actions with deep concern. Once the agreements are implemented, Nigerians will be assured of a faster and more peaceful march to the goal of normalcy.

I feel I must say something about the position of non-Easterners whom circumstances compelled me to ask to leave this region some months ago. While at Aburi, I gave assurance that this order will "be kept under constant review with a view to its being lifted as soon as practicable." It is not true, as has frequently been suggested in different quarters, that I undertook to ask them to return as soon as we got back from Accra. I reserved my position in this respect because I felt that the implementation of the Aburi decisions would create the atmosphere conducive to their early return. I am anxious for this occasion to come and sincerely hope that conditions will soon materialize for this to be done.

Finally, I must warn all Easterners once again to remain vigilant. The East will never be intimidated, nor will she acquiesce to any form of dictation. It is not the intention of the East to play the aggressor. Nonetheless, it is not our intention to be slaughtered in our beds. We are ready to defend our homeland. We are prepared to crush any aggressors.

Fellow countrymen and women, on Aburi We Stand. There will be no compromise! God grant peace in our time.

Diary of Events:
February 26—March 12, 1967

February 26–28: Tension high again. Mass demonstrations and rallies in major towns of Eastern Nigeria, calling for the implementation of Aburi decisions. . . . I give a public notice that faced with unending delays by Lagos and indefinite prolongation of the stalemate in the crisis, my government will take certain measures within the context of Aburi Accord if by March 31 the Lagos regime has not yet implemented the agreements.

March 1: Lieutenant Colonel Gowon addresses a secret meeting of Heads of African Diplomatic Missions in Nigeria on the Aburi decisions. Pressmen are not invited to the conference. He distorts the Aburi decisions, raises the usual hoax of secession and threatens use of force against Eastern Region.

March 10: Lieutenant Colonel Gowon's Supreme Military Council, meeting at Benin without my participation, approves another draft of decentralization decree prepared by Lagos.

March 10–12: Mass demonstrations in Calabar, Enugu, Port Harcourt, Uyo, and Degema in protest against Lagos strong-arm measures and in support of the adoption of a confederal system of government for Nigeria.

Distortion of Aburi Accord

(Statement, March 2, 1967)

Yesterday, March 1, Lieutenant Colonel Yakubu Gowon summoned the Heads of the Diplomatic Missions in Nigeria to what was no less than a secret meeting. From the opening address delivered by him to them, it is clear that his intention was to use his position and access to the Heads of Diplomatic Missions in Lagos for blackmail.

He made no secret of this intention, because he excluded the press and enjoined the Heads of Diplomatic Missions to regard everything he said as a matter of confidence and to send dispatches to their governments based on the distorted information he gave out to them.

He started his address by talking of "various interpretations that have been given to the conclusion reached at Aburi." The Aburi decisions as contained in the statements and communiqués issued at that meeting, as well as in the official minutes issued from the Cabinet office in Lagos, were put in language and phrases which for their simplicity allowed no ambiguity.

Lieutenant Colonel Yakubu Gowon made it "abundantly clear"—and these are his very words—that he had abandoned faith in the joint declaration to eschew the use of force in the settlement of our problems. For this statement he owes Nigeria and the whole world personal responsibility for whatever may be the consequences of any attempt to employ force in the settlement of our current problems.

As far as the East is concerned, it has been made repeatedly clear that we cannot be intimidated and that we are prepared to match any force with force. He would be a fool who thought that the East would be sleeping and therefore not apprehensive of intentions on the part of Lagos and the North to destroy or enslave it by force.

Anybody who was present at the Aburi meeting or has read the minutes, communiqués, statements, and verbatim reports would be surprised that a person who calls himself a Head of State could so deliberately mislead accredited representatives of foreign governments by saying that the implementation of each item of the conclusions required prior detailed examination by the administrative and professional experts in the various fields. The conclusions in Aburi were no proposals but decisions taken by the highest authority in the land.

What happened in fact was that specific matters, namely, the decrees and sections of decrees to be repealed, the mechanics of army reorganization, and the question of rehabilitation of refugees, were referred to experts. The meeting of the financial experts to consider the question of rehabilitation of displaced persons has not been held because the federal permanent secretary of the Ministry of Finance does not think that such a meeting would serve any useful purpose. The army experts met and started discussions, but the federal representatives suddenly caused the meeting to be discontinued. The legal experts met and reached agreements, but these were rejected.

To talk of any of the decisions reached requiring further clarification and further decisions by the Supreme Military Council before the relevant Aburi "understandings" can be given effect in concrete legislation is dishonest and cannot therefore do any credit to Nigeria in the eyes of an inquisitive and understanding world.

Lieutenant Colonel Yakubu Gowon told the Heads of Missions that the agreement about returning the regions to the positions before January 17 also meant in effect that the federal government in Lagos would continue to carry on its functions as before. He failed to inform the world that by the decisions taken at Aburi, the federal government meant no more than the Supreme Military Council. No one of course who knows the sort of advice Lieutenant Colonel Gowon is receiving in Lagos would be surprised by this suppression and distortion of the truth.

The actual Aburi decisions read as follows:

● Members agreed that the legislative and executive authority of the Federal Military Government should remain in the Supreme Military Council, to which any decision affecting the whole country shall be referred for determination provided that where it is not possible for a meeting to be held the matter requiring determination must be referred to military governors for their comment and concurrence.

● Specifically, the council agreed that appointments to senior ranks in the police, diplomatic, and consular services as well as appointments to superscale posts in the federal civil service and the equivalent posts in statutory corporations must be approved by the Supreme Military Council.

● The regional members felt that all the decrees or provisions of decrees passed since January 15, 1966, and which detracted from the previous powers and positions of regional governments, should be repealed if mutual confidence is to be restored.

It is difficult to understand the introduction of the word "veto" into the matter. The Aburi Agreement was that any decision which affected the whole country must receive the concurrence of all the military governors because of their special responsibilities in their different areas of authority and so to the country as a corporate whole.

On the reorganization of the army, it is for Lieutenant Colonel Gowon to explain to the world what he means by the "army continuing to be under one command," when in the very next sentence of his statement he also speaks of an agreement to establish area commands corresponding with the existing regional boundaries. This contradiction in itself tells the truth, and one does not need to belabor the point.

The actual decision of the Supreme Military Council as recorded in the official minutes reads as follows:

The Council decided that:

(i) on the reorganization of the army:
  (a) Army to be governed by the Supreme Military Council under a chairman to be known as Commander-in-Chief of the Armed Forces and Head of the Federal Military Government.
  (b) Establishment of a military headquarters comprising equal representation from the regions and headed by a Chief of Staff.
  (c) Creation of area commands corresponding to existing regions and under the charge of area commanders.

(d) Matters of policy, including appointments and promotion to top executive posts in the armed forces and the police, to be dealt with by the Supreme Military Council.

(e) During the period of the military government, military governors will have control over area commands for internal security.

(f) Creation of a Lagos garrison, including Ikeja barracks.

It is clear from the Aburi decisions that what was envisaged was a loosely knit army administered by a representative military headquarters under the charge of a Chief of Staff and commanded by the Supreme Military Council, not by Lieutenant Colonel Gowon as he claimed in his present statement to the diplomats.

Significantly, Lieutenant Colonel Yakubu Gowon merely made a passing reference to the pervading question of rehabilitation of displaced persons and says that things are moving in the right direction. Judging from what is happening, one would agree that things are moving in the right direction as Gowon would like it in that the hated East is bearing the heaviest brunt in this misfortune. So long as this is so and the East is suffering under the heavy burden, Gowon and his accomplices can remain satisfied that things are moving in the right direction.

One does not need to mention his statement that the Aburi decisions discussed the restoration of essential services, such as the disruption of railway services. In my recent broadcast, I touched on this point and told the country that the restoration of these services was to follow the general course of a return to normalcy following the implementation of the Aburi Agreements.

Lieutenant Colonel Yakubu Gowon informed the accredited assembly of world representatives that the decision of the Aburi meeting relating to appointments to diplomatic and consular posts as well as to senior posts in the federal civil service and public corporations was confined to the posts of permanent secretaries and principal representatives abroad.

Nowhere in the decisions were the words "permanent secretaries" or "principal representatives abroad" mentioned. Such limitations never occurred in anybody's mind. The words used were "appointments to diplomatic and consular posts" as well as to "senior posts in the federal civil service and public corporations."

According to the Aburi Agreements "the following appointments must be approved by the Supreme Military Council: (a) diplomatic and consular posts; (b) senior posts in the armed forces and the police; (c) superscale federal civil service and federal corporation posts."

Everyone with even the most superficial acquaintance with the Nigerian civil service knows what those expressions mean and connote.

To confuse issues, Lieutenant Colonel Gowon gave the impression that the main difference between him and me on this particular decision was that I insisted on cancelling the appointments of existing civil servants. I can think of nothing more slanderous. At my press conference on January 6, explaining to the public what had happened at Aburi, I had this to say on this subject:

On the question of public appointments, it was agreed that the Supreme Military Council must collectively approve appointments to the following offices: diplomatic and consular posts, senior posts in the armed forces and police, superscale federal civil service and federal corporation posts.

This particular decision was made as a means of removing friction; it has been our unfortunate experience that friction and misunderstanding had in fact bedeviled these appointments. What it means is that no one person will have the right and powers to make these appointments alone in the future.

Nothing in that statement can be interpreted by any honest person to mean that my intention was that existing appointments should be cancelled. The sum total of all this is to further confuse the situation in a deliberate attempt to hoodwink the diplomats. For this I apologize to them on behalf of all honest Nigerians.

Since it is now clear that Lieutenant Colonel Yakubu Gowon and his aides in and outside Lagos now want to resort to blackmail and deceit, I am dispatching to all embassies in Nigeria all relevant and authentic documents available to me in connection with Aburi.

It is hoped that the federal government will not interfere with the movement of these documents and that those concerned will be able to base their dispatches on the truth. As accredited representatives of their countries, they must not lend themselves to blackmail, deceit, or intimidation.

It is clear from Gowon's statement in question that he is prepared to distort the verbatim reports of the Aburi meeting. To keep the public informed, the Eastern Nigerian Broadcasting Service will be playing the tape records of the proceedings live at scheduled times as from today. Arrangements have been completed to transform those tape recordings to long-playing gramophone records for those who may wish to have them to play at leisure. We are also going ahead to print and publish the documents and records of the Aburi meeting.

Finally Gowon, closing his statement, wanted reassurance from the respective governments through the embassies that they will cooperate with him and do nothing whatsoever to give any form of recognition or support to dissident elements opposed to his government. The question that one would like to ask Gowon is: "Who are the dissident elements and which is his government?" At the Aburi meeting I made it perfectly clear that the East did not recognize Gowon as the Head of the Federal Military Government because he usurped that position. To talk, therefore, of his government is presumptuous.

We in the East are anxious to see that our difficulties are resolved by peaceful means and that Nigeria is preserved as a unit, but it is doubtful, and the world must judge whether Lieutenant Colonel Gowon's attitudes and other exhibitions of his insincerity are something which can lead to a return of normalcy and confidence in the country.

Diary of Events: March 14—April 24, 1967

March 14: Popular tension running higher. More mass demonstrations in support of Aburi Accord in Umuahia and Owerri.

March 17: Lieutenant Colonel Gowon breaks the Aburi Agreements on consensus and issues the distorted decree on decentralization, despite the open opposition of my government and the mute opposition of Midwestern and Western regions.

March 26: I pay a visit to Ghana to personally request General Ankrah to persuade the Lagos regime to honor the Aburi Agreements and pay federal debts to Eastern Region (£11.8 million) before March 31, 1967.

March 27: I hold a meeting with a peace-seeking delegation (comprising Commodore Wey, Police Deputy Inspector-General Omo-Bare, and Colonel Adebayo of Western Region) at Onitsha, Eastern Nigeria. Delegation undertake to: (a) Make sure that the debt owed to Eastern Nigeria by the federal government is paid by March 31, 1967; (b) Ensure that either Decree No. 8 is suspended or those sections which are unacceptable to the East are repealed; (c) Ensure that the North expresses public apology to the East for the pogroms.

March 29: Financial representatives of the government of Nigeria meet in Ghana, and the federal officials make it clear that the Lagos regime has no intention of paying the federal debts to Eastern Nigeria.

March 31: Issue of the first of the Survival Edicts by my government. The Revenue Collection Edict—to ensure that the federal government is no longer in a position to owe the East its statutory revenues.

April 4:   Nigeria Airways is ordered by the Nigerian federal government to stop all flights to Eastern Nigeria. . . . Stoppage of payment of salaries to staff of all federal-owned concerns in Eastern Region. . . . Stoppage of all postal order transactions with Eastern Nigeria. . . . Blockade of foreign exchange against Eastern Nigeria government, corporations, and other institutions. . . . Eastern Nigerian importers are denied licenses. . . . Nigeria Produce Marketing Company, Lagos, issued directives to firms to deal directly with it to the exclusion of Eastern Nigerian Marketing Board. . . . Seizure by Lagos of all foreign exchange standing in the credit of Eastern Nigeria government, etc., and private establishments in which the government of Eastern Nigeria had financial interest.

April 13:   Irate Eastern Nigerians hijack a Nigerian Airways F-27 aircraft in the Midwest.

April 17:   Legal Education Edict establishing Eastern Nigeria Law School. . . . Establishment of Eastern Nigerian Medical School and Teaching Hospital.

April 18:   The court of Appeal Edict intended to clear the backlog in appeal cases concerning Easterners.

April 19:   Marketing Board Edict designed to enable Eastern Nigeria to market its produce.

April 23:   In a letter of resignation from the Ad Hoc Constitutional Committee, Chief Awolowo (leader of Western Nigeria and now the Nigerian Commissioner of Finance) declares:

. . . there are powerful reasons in support of this demand [withdrawal of Northern troops from Western Region and West]:

1. It was in pursuance of the decision of a meeting of representatives of regional military governors which had been implemented with immediate effect in respect of not only the East, but also of the Midwest.

2. It was also in pursuance of one of the decisions taken at Aburi on 5th January 1967.

3. The consensus of opinion among the vast majority of people in Western Nigeria and Lagos is that Northern troops in the two territories constitute an army of occupation and that their nonremoval has virtually reduced the said territories to the status of a "protectorate." These views have been repeatedly expressed in the press.

4. There is a growing disaffection and bitter resentment toward Northerners because of the presence of Northern soldiers in the West and Lagos. . . .

5. . . . One of the conditions—the most important and about the only one which remains unfulfilled—which Lieutenant Colonel Ojukwu stipulated for attending a meeting of the Supreme Military Council convened for a venue in Midwest, West, or Lagos is the withdrawal of Northern troops from the West and Lagos. . . . It is also my considered view that both the projected military and the prevailing economic warfares could be avoided if it is possible for Lieutenant Colonel Ojukwu to attend meetings of the Supreme Military Council in Nigeria. And it is believed that this will be possible if the Agreement reached in Lagos on 9th August 1966 and reaffirmed in Aburi on 5th January 1967, in respect of the posting of army personnel, is implemented.

On the other hand, if after the implementation of these agreements the military governor of the East continues to be absent from the meetings of the Supreme Military Council, then he would be having the rest of the country, without exception, ranged against himself for deliberately setting out to destroy the Federation. . . .

. . . it appears to me that what some people of influence in government circles now want is to help the Eastern Region out of Nigeria, and to try and form a new Federation, on terms which are already cut and dried by them, from among the remaining units.

April 24: Lieutenant Colonel Gowon's Supreme Military Council announces "stern measures" against Eastern Nigeria for alleged "defiance of federal authority." The Council also ratifies the British High Commission's political and administrative program of action for preserving the Federation of Nigeria, which is presented through Lieutenant Colonel Hassan and Gowon. . . .

In an address to the Anglican Synod meeting in Onitsha, I repeat my warning that any attempt by the Lagos government to implement any of the measures that will lead to the diplomatic, economic, and military strangulation of Eastern Nigeria will have the effect of taking the East out of the Federation of Nigeria.

Economic Blockade

(Address to diplomatic representatives in Eastern Nigeria, April 24, 1967)

I have called you in on this occasion to bring directly to your notice once more another proof of bad faith and duplicity on the part of Lagos and the North. As the accredited representatives of your governments in this region, you are in a position to know and assess the real feelings of the people of this region, and how much I have been trying to contain those feelings.

I shall presently be handing to you a copy of a memorandum submitted by Lieutenant Colonel Gowon to the present meeting of some members of the Supreme Military Council in Lagos. The sole purpose of that memorandum is the immediate destruction of the East, economically, politically, militarily, and diplomatically. The text of that memorandum has been broadcast in full to the public by the Eastern Nigeria radio network since last night.

You will study that memorandum and judge for yourselves how anyone in this region can ever trust Lagos and the North, or even take them seriously, when they speak of peace. Some people, your principals in Lagos not excepted, have often misunderstood our position and have branded us as being difficult. But, as God would have it, facts keep revealing themselves, almost daily, to vindicate our positions and attitudes.

You will notice that Lieutenant Colonel Gowon

approved the memorandum on Wednesday, the nineteenth of this month. I draw attention to this fact because of what it proves—duplicity. It was on that very day that Lieutenant Colonel Gowon spoke to me for the first time in several weeks. We were on the telephone for nearly an hour. From him it was all protestations for peace, and how to settle our present problems peacefully.

The points agreed during that telephone discussion included: an urgent meeting outside Nigeria; establishment of close contacts by means of a hot telephone line; visit to me by Mr. Omo-Bare, deputy inspector-general of police, for discussions and report, after the current Lagos meeting; above all, agreement on the non-use of force in the current dispute.

I have, of course, known Lagos well enough not to be taken in too readily by such protestations. All the same, I was prepared to concede to be once again disillusioned—this time, yet more conclusively, and when serious plans were being made for us, the military leaders, to meet and discuss at an acceptable venue.

As far as international and diplomatic interests are concerned, I would like to draw attention to one or two points contained in Lieutenant Colonel Gowon's memorandum.

There is the assertion that foreign shipping companies have made it clear to the Gowon government that they will not send their ships to Eastern ports if the Lagos government so directs. If that assertion is true, then foreign powers who own those ships have pledged their support to Gowon in his efforts to destroy the East. It would be an interference in the internal affairs of Nigeria and a breach of diplomatic impartiality.

It has been proposed that our border with the Cameroun should be closed and with it the Cameroun consulate here. We do not believe that the Cameroun government can succumb to such blackmail, which will be regarded as nothing but an unfriendly act. Already the Cameroun government appears to have given in to

Gowon's pressure not to allow Cameroun aircraft to come into this region.

Then there is the question of withdrawal of passports, both diplomatic and ordinary, from the people of this region. Every national has a right to his country's passport. If Lagos carries out its proposal, it will mean that they no longer accept the East as part of Nigeria. The path open to us in that event is clear, and I shall have no alternative but to take it.

Let it not be forgotten that they are already carrying out an economic blockade of this region. They have interfered with banking and blocked our rights to foreign exchange. The poor traders of this region who have placed orders for goods and issued bills of exchange are not in a position to meet their contractual obligations because of their inability to obtain foreign exchange with which to pay for the goods ordered. I do not need to mention the closure of Calabar as a customs airport, the refusal to pay employees of federal establishments in the East, and other measures well known to you.

I want to leave you and everybody else in no doubt that if that vicious memorandum of aggression against the East is accepted by those now meeting in Lagos and even a single step is taken to carry its terms out, that will be the certain end.

If you have been listening to our local news, you will have heard reports that Lieutenant Colonel Hassan was to submit to the meeting plans to resolve the problems and that a statement would be issued at the end of the current meeting in Lagos. Again you will be interested to know that the projected statement had already been prepared in advance and numbered SMC 67/43.

That statement is a so-called program before the return to civil government. The program includes the creation of states, the drawing up of a new constitution, economic reconstruction, including restoration of economic links, a new development plan, purging of corrupt elements and restoration of ill-gotten gains, and the supervision of election for a civilian regime.

The program then sets out in detail various dates, beginning from April 30 this year and extending to March 20, 1969, by which date the various stages must be completed. All these are to happen after, or in the course of, economic, political, military, and diplomatic elimination of this region! It is our knowledge that for some days now troops in all other parts of the country have been placed on the alert!

An interesting thing about their program is that it is proposed to create states, or decide on their creation, even before the meeting of the proposed Constituent Assembly and the drafting of the country's constitution. I once said that the vested interest of certain quarters in the creation of states has obsessed their minds and blackened their vision. Naturally there were protests and denials by those quarters at the time. But truth can never be destroyed, or hidden indefinitely.

Gentlemen, these, in ominous brief, are the Lagos and North ideas and methods of settling the current Nigerian problems peacefully and realistically!

My purpose of calling you is to inform you in no uncertain terms so that you can intimate your governments of what is about to happen. I repeat again that anything done to carry out any of the proposals in Lieutenant Colonel Gowon's memorandum will mark the certain end for us as part of Nigeria. The consequences will be grave and even bloody. But we are neither intimidated nor afraid.

God bless Nigeria.

Survival Budget

(Address to Consultative Assembly,
April 24, 1967)

When last year I spoke to you on an occasion like this, I spoke with great excitement and expectations. The glorious vision of a country truly united pulsated

everyone's blood. The army takeover and its corrective
mission had raised the hopes of our people in their
desire to see an end to the hideous evils of tribalism,
corruption, and nepotism. The army professed to turn
Nigeria into a land where no one should feel a stranger
in his own country, where he would be free to live and
work anywhere without fear or molestation, discrimination, or oppression.

Sad to relate, the events of May, July, and September, 1966, and thereafter, have shattered those pious
hopes and plunged Nigeria into uncertainty, drift, and
confusion. Wanton and premeditated acts of destruction against this Region and its people have compelled
them to reappraise their attitudes. Confidence and faith
have been destroyed. The people have been disillusioned. We have reached a stage where I am unalter-
ably convinced that to save the very semblance of
Nigeria as one country, we must drift a little apart.
Call it "confederation," "federation," "loose association," or whatever you will. It is the only way for
survival, not only for ourselves but also for the country.
Nigeria can never be the same again. Of that we are
sure. If it is to remain one entity, everyone must wake
up from stupor and work hard and fast to reach a
realistic solution. Otherwise we cannot avoid disintegration.

The disturbances have imposed on this region unfore-
seen burdens and responsibilities, the most pressing of
which is resettling refugees. There is hardly any family
in the East which has not suffered directly or indirectly
by the well-planned pogrom inflicted on the people of
this region.

By tradition our fiscal year begins April 1 of each
year. Before then it is normally the practice to publish
the budget for the public, showing what expenditures
are envisaged and the sources of revenue to meet those
expenditures. Unfortunately, circumstances did not allow such publication this year, and I know that the
public has been anxious.

The budget for this year has been delayed thus far because we wanted to prepare a realistic budget reflecting our determination to survive as a people. We wanted it to be forward-looking, for "where there is no vision the people perish." Our budget this year can, therefore, be appropriately described as a "survival budget."

The problem of resettling our refugees is an exercise in economic development and social readjustment. We have got to develop and expand the agricultural and industrial setup of our economy, provide our greatly increased population with the means of acquiring enough food, clothing, shelter, and other basic necessities of life; expand our health and other social services for the care and welfare of our people, and thereby minimize suffering and unhappiness among our people.

I want to commend the sense of determination and sacrifice which has pervaded the length and breadth of this Region. The generous contributions voluntarily made by the people for the resettling of our refugees have been staggering. Every day the people show new determination and devise new means of sacrifice for the welfare of all. The latest example is the voluntary decision by civil servants and some other sectors of the wage-earning class in this Region to forgo a percentage of their incomes in favor of the emergency. Our budget for this year has taken good advantage of this general mood on the part of the people, and I have no doubt that the various sacrifices entailed in the budget will be willingly and gladly accepted by all.

I have today signed an Appropriation Edict which envisages a revenue estimate of £39.5 million, as against last year's revenue of £30.6 million—an increase of nearly £9 million. Against this estimated revenue is the estimated expenditure of £39.1 million as against last year's expenditure of £29.6 million, an increase of £9.5 million. There is a very small budget surplus of slightly more than £400,000. Slim though this budget is, taken together with our reserves and in spite of the heavy expenditure which we have borne in the past year, there will be at the end of March, 1968, a consolidated revenue fund of £2.79 million.

Of our revenue estimates, nearly £20 million is expected to come from our statutory share of federal revenues based on the existing formula, a drop of £2.5 million from last year's estimated revenue from the same source.

This leads me to the Revenue Collection Edict, which was promulgated at the end of last month. This edict is designed to serve three simple purposes:

(1) To make sure that what is statutorily due to us from the federal government comes to us promptly;

(2) to recover federal indebtedness to us;

(3) to prevent the authorities in Lagos from further accumulating their debts to us.

It can thus be seen that contrary to sinister attempts to read ulterior motive into the edict, there is nothing in the edict to show that I have unilaterally altered the existing formula for revenue allocation. But of course, the Lagos authorities are always prone to misunderstand. It is therefore no surprise that they should become so jittery and start taking the erratic steps so far announced. I understand they are contemplating more. God bless them!

The simple truth is that because of our refugee problem we require the use of every penny that is due to us. Lagos has been most unfeeling and unsympathetic in their approach to this problem. For a paltry grant of £350,000 they gave toward the refugees, trumpets have been sounded all over the world. But this problem is more than dishing out of funds, even if the federal government had the several hundred million pounds for resettling and re-establishing the refugees. The irreversible shift in population which has resulted in a population increase of 16 percent in this Region has rendered the present basis of revenue distribution illogical and untenable. It made some sense—even though still un-

fair to this Region—when every citizen had a right to
live, work, and earn his living in any part of the country, and so be able to share in the benefits from funds
spent from a common pool in such parts. Easterners
have now been excluded, permanently at least in the
foreseeable future, from two-thirds of the country. They
have been hounded from their usual places of residence
and work; they have been hunted in every other corner
of Nigeria; they have been driven from the federal and
Northern public services; they are now fleeing from the
police force; and they are now being withdrawn surreptitiously from the diplomatic and consular missions
of their country. As things are, no Easterner can hope
in the foreseeable future to be welcomed in many parts
of Nigeria or expect rights and justice there. Certainly
not in the North. It is therefore obvious that there must
be a new basis for arranging our economic and financial
affairs.

The real cost of resettling our refugees is extremely
high and is neither the £350,000 which the federal
government has given nor even the £4 million which
it has promised the whole country for the resettlement
of displaced persons. It will involve, in terms of investment, sums amounting to several hundred million
pounds. An important fact to appreciate is that there
is a world of difference between resettlement and relief.
One way of assessing the magnitude of our refugee
problem is by realizing that if houses were to be built
for housing all of them it would involve the total housing space of the whole of Lagos and Ibadan combined
for our refugees.

I have said that of the estimated revenue of £39.5
million, £20 million is expected from the federal statutory sources. The balance of £19.5 million will come
from purely regional sources. Compared to last year's
figures, revenues from regional sources show an increase
of £11.3 million or 137 percent. The often-vaunted
claims that two-thirds of this Region's revenues are
derived from federal sources are no longer valid.

Faced with the prospects of rising expenditure and

falling revenue from external sources, including statutory share from the federal government, we have had to explore various avenues of increasing revenues from local sources. This has entailed calling for greater sacrifices from the better-placed members of our community. I want us to work systematically toward the establishment of a good progressive and democratic society, in which all vestiges of privilege and social injustice will be abolished and the rich contribute more for the welfare of the poor.

It is on the basis of these principles that we expect to raise so much local revenue in this Region this financial year. Last year I announced the introduction of a flat rate tax of 10/- for the ordinary peasants and employees in the lowest income groups (which means those earning less than £100 per annum) as opposed to between £1:12s:6d and £8:16s:0d a year, which the majority of them were paying previously. At that time, too, I announced that we were going to adopt the federal system of income tax for others—my aim at that time being to ensure that there was a uniform system of taxation for the whole country which I then mistakenly believed would be a truly united country. The flat rate tax of 10/- will continue for the peasants and lower-income groups. All others who earn £100 per annum and above will pay the regional income tax to which they were accustomed before my announcement of last year. In addition, a graduated development tax ranging from as little as £1 for those earning £200 per annum, and rising to £10 per annum for those earning £2,000 and over, has been introduced.

Civil servants will now pay for their drugs and treatment in government hospitals, and to this end, the existing scale of fees for government hospitals has been revised. It does violence to my conscience and belief in social justice that the poor peasants in rural areas, attending voluntary agency and joint hospitals, and even government hospitals, should pay for their treatment, often very heavily, while the regular and well-paid civil servants and employees of government corporations pay little or nothing for medical attention. The new Hospital Fees Regulations, soon to be promulgated, will abolish this privilege for the financially better-placed members of our society.

Rents on government houses occupied by civil servants were increased last year and will remain in vogue. Regular basic allowances for motor vehicles owned by civil servants have been abolished. A new system of mileage allowance for those who use their cars regularly for government service has been introduced. The scales of mileage allowance introduced will adequately cover the cost of petrol and wear and tear on cars of touring officers who, in fact, may not lose by the abolition of basic allowances. The civil servants who will lose, and rightly, are heads of departments and others who do not use their cars on regular touring.

It has for some time now been the policy of the government that indigenous officers (except where it is in the public interest that those in certain posts should occupy government quarters) are not entitled to government quarters by right. It is the policy of this government to encourage officers to own their own houses. To this end, plans for low-cost housing are being made, and public servants will be able to buy such houses on convenient terms. Our public services are growing fast and manifold, making it practically impossible for the government to house all its servants, and there will be the injustice of housing some and leaving the others. Besides, the cost of maintaining government buildings has been very great and hardly covered by the amounts of rents paid by civil servants occupying those houses.

I proposed, in the course of this year, to set up an expert body to examine the structures and salary scales in our public services, the aim being to ensure that salaries attached to the different posts are realistic and equitable, having regard to the responsibilities attached to those posts and the level of our economic and social development. To this end, I want to see our negotiating machineries, such as the Whitley Councils, revived and revitalized. There must be regular consultations between employers and employees, on a basis of realism, mutual confidence, and respect. The importance of trade unions in the different facets of our economic and social development cannot be minimized—it must be recognized and constructively used.

Let me return again to the question of revenue and indicate to you how we expect to derive the revenues shown in the estimates. From the former Ministry of Agriculture we expect £2.5 million, including receipts from forest products, produce purchase tax, and sales of livestock foodstuff. From earnings arising out of interest and dividends from government investments of its surplus funds and industrial projects we expect more than £720,000. From direct and indirect taxes we expect £6.5 million, out of which we hope to get £4.4 million from personal income taxes, £1.3 million from motor vehicles taxes, £5 million as a result of the revision of the Hospital Fees Regulations, £500,000 from the operations of the Ministry of Lands and Survey, and £1.1 million from the activities of the Ministry of Works. Finally, we hope to get £5.8 million from Special Revenue.

You will recall that in recent weeks a number of edicts have been published for the operation and license of casinos, government pools, slot and amusement machines, government lotteries, etc. Although it is not possible at this stage to estimate accurately how much revenue will come from these sources, it is my belief that they will contribute considerably to our revenue.

I want to repeat my warning of last year that I shall regard any attempt to evade payment of tax as an act of sabotage. If this was my position last year, the present situation in the country makes it even more pertinent. I trust the loyalty and patriotism of all to pay their tax promptly and save me the painful duty of taking drastic steps against tax evaders. This appeal is addressed particularly to the self-employed, private businessmen, and small private industries, which have been known in the past not to declare their true incomes for the purpose of taxation. There must be better assessment and collection of tax.

On the expenditure side, I have already mentioned that this will be of the order of £39.1 million, an increase of £9.5 million or 32 percent over last year's figure of £29.6 million. This phenomenal increase is due to our having to provide a total sum of £3 million for the salaries of established refugee civil servants and a further £1 million to cover ancillary and other charges attributable to their absorption into the Eastern Nigeria public service.

We have provided slightly less than £2.27 million for servicing our public debts, which remain at the same level as for the 1965/66 financial year and represent only 5.8 percent of our total recurrent expenditure. This is well below the generally accepted margin of 10 percent and indeed compares very favorably with the provision of 23 percent of its revenue by the federal government for debts servicing. International lending agencies, especially the International Monetary Fund and the World Bank, have persistently warned against the utilization to any large extent of many offers of contractor finance, deferred payment, and other short-term finances frequently offered by machine dealers. We have religiously heeded the admonition of these international organizations, and that is why we have been able to keep expenditure on this score so low. Despite the need for rapid expansion and modernization of agriculture and the setting up of industries, I do not intend that we fall into the temptation of going all out for contractor-finance agreements and other short-term financial arrangements.

Another feature is the increased shortfall grants to our corporations. This, to a large extent, is due to the absorption by the corporations of a large number of refugees. These large shortfall grants reflect the government's firm policy that statutory corporations should forge ahead quickly toward the stage where they can be self-sufficient and no longer depend on the government for subventions. The shortfall grants total £1.24 million as against £450,000, or more than twice what they received last financial year.

Now that the government has been compelled to assume responsibility for federal corporations in this Region, it is planned to expand the scope and services of these corporations, notably the Electricity Corporation, in order to absorb the refugees who have returned or may be forced to return to this Region.

It is true that in discussing these estimates and the problem of refugees, mention has been made only to those refugees in regular salaried employments. I want to emphasize that the government is equally concerned about those who served in the private sectors of business or were self-employed. These categories of refugees are being handled by the Rehabilitation Commission.

It has become necessary to expand and strengthen considerably our Ministry of Information in order to get across to the general public both in and outside Nigeria the Eastern Nigerian version of the current political and constitutional struggle in the country. Because of this, expenditure in respect of the Ministry of Information has increased from slightly less than £728,000 in the last financial year to £1.43 million this financial year.

Let me here place on record my complete satisfaction with the way our finances have been managed in this Region. Had it not been for the prudence and general circumspection exercised by our financial experts, the increased burdens of last year, resulting in many unbudgeted expenditures, would have spelled doom for this Region, to the satisfaction and joy of our enemies.

I would like here to make special mention of education. Over the past year I have given very careful thought to the question of the falling standards in our primary schools. I had at one stage thought that a remedy would lie in reintroducing the eight-year elementary system, but after series of meetings and discussions at different levels I am now convinced that an eight-year elementary school would be a retrograde step, especially since we have increased the number of well-trained teachers and are introducing modern methods of teaching.

The heavy dropouts in our primary schools during the last three years have been a source of real worry and waste, which must be stopped. Under our present system the total fees payable by a pupil throughout his elementary school course is £21, the first three years being free. £5 is paid in Standard IV, and £8 each in Standards V and VI. It is the general belief that the sudden heavy expenditure of £5 in the fourth year of a child in school, by parents who had taken for granted the cost of education for their children during the previous three years, may have been the cause for the heavy dropouts. It is now proposed that from the next school year the same amount of total fees for primary education will still be paid but in smaller fees graduatedly distributed throughout all the classes. The new scale of fees which will come into operation from January 1, 1968, are:

Elementary	I	£1	Elementary IV	£4
Elementary	II	£2	Elementary V	£5
Elementary	III	£3	Elementary VI	£6

This means a reduction of £1 in the fees paid in Standard IV, £3 in Standard V, and £2 in Standard VI, making a total of £6, which is now redistributed between Elementaries I to III. In other words, there is no overall increase in the fees for a child's primary school education. In fact, you can say: "Tell me the fee of a primary school pupil and I will tell you his class."

Our projected recurrent expenditure on educational services accounts for £12.4 million, about 32 percent of our total recurrent expenditure. If to this are added recurrent grants to the university, the medical school, and the teaching hospital, the expenditure will total more than £ 14.5 million, or 37 percent of our total recurrent expenditure.

In the course of the last financial year a number of measures were introduced which affected the government and administration of this Region. The new estimate reflects those measures. I refer, for instance, to the new Customary Courts Edict, introducing district courts and customary courts of appeal, and the new provincial administration system. In these areas, the government's intention is to secure effective local participation in public affairs. To the extent that public-spirited and honest people come forward to the service of their fellow beings, to that extent will the new system serve the purposes for which it was produced.

In order to satisfy the needs of the new situation arising from the sudden movement of population and other problems associated with the disastrous events of 1966, the Six-Year Development Program, which was designed to last from 1962 to 1968, came to an abrupt end in the East at the end of the last financial year. In its stead, and in order to have more time to gather the necessary data and fashion a new plan to take into consideration all these new phenomena, a three-year interim development plan for the Region has now reached the final stages of preparation. Greater emphasis has been laid on agriculture, industrial expansion, and labor intensive programs. Both the interim plan and the capital estimates will reflect these.

One more thing which is a new feature in the estimates is the establishment of a new Ministry of Forestry and Animal Health. This new ministry has been excised from the former Ministry of Agriculture, which had become rather amorphous and unwieldy. Effective planning and supervision is impossible in a ministry which is too large, and I have no doubt that this new arrangement will facilitate matters.

I cannot overemphasize the necessity for all those

connected with public spending, from the highest departmental heads to the lowest officers, to practice very strict economy. This Region can no longer tolerate squandermania. To this end, an edict will shortly be enacted appointing a Public Accounts Committee, which will scrutinize government and corporation accounts, spotlight irregularities, and report to me. I have also directed that all financial lapses be very severely dealt with and all those responsible for such lapses be seriously disciplined. Little drops of water, they say, make a mighty ocean. Little pennies saved here and there will indeed go a long way to ensuring our safety and security.

Last week two edicts were published: the Statutory Bodies Edict, 1967, and the Legal Education Edict, 1967. More edicts will be published in the near future. As in the case of the Revenue Collection Edict, the sole aim is to safeguard the interest of this Region and all its people. It had been my sincere hope that our problems would have been solved by now to avoid unilateral actions like these, but there has been nothing to show any sense of urgency on the part of Lagos and the North to resolve the situation and save the country. The signs are clearly that this country is fast disintegrating because of the indifference and vindictive attitude of the Lagos government and the North.

Following the promulgation of the Revenue Collection Edict, the Lagos government saw fit to counteract with measures aimed at isolating this Region to strangulation. Employees of statutory bodies have been denied salaries and equipment for their jobs. As you heard over the weekend, even more vicious acts and measures have been proposed by the Lagos government and the North against the East. This government will be failing in its duty if it does not take appropriate steps to meet any contingencies and eventualities which may result from the aims and actions of Lagos and the North.

Lagos is doing everything to isolate Eastern Nigeria, strangle its trade and industry, and eliminate its people militarily, economically, politically, and diplomatically. I have, of course, made the position of the East clear and unmistakable in the face of Lagos' plans. If they want to save the country and avoid bloody civil war, they must think again and retrace their steps.

Before the leakage last week of the plans by Lieutenant Colonel Gowon, as contained in his memorandum to the recent meeting in Lagos, efforts had been afoot for the meeting of military leaders outside Nigeria. Whether that meeting will still be held after the last revelations of duplicity and hostile plans against the East is a matter yet to be determined. If and when, however, a meeting is held, it must be a meeting which will lead to definite decisions for the ending of the present stalemate and the return of peace and tranquility within the country. That being so, one should think that the agenda for that meeting would be discussed and settled in advance. This is vital because we do not want to meet merely to exchange pleasantries and shake hands. Still better, those participating should prepare and exchange memoranda before the meeting.

I have repeatedly called for such a meeting and given my conditions for attending. One of those conditions, and I regard it of the greatest importance, is that the meeting must be held in the presence of neutral bodies and outside the country. Unfortunately, whether out of ignorance or misplaced pride, lack of the right appreciation of the situation or sheer confused thinking, many people have tried to show why a meeting on those conditions should not be held.

The conditions which I have mentioned have not been presented for the fun of it. Confidence has been completely shattered, and a meeting held without neutral witnesses will end only in a stalemate and lead to a situation much worse than we are now experiencing. We must not forget the different interpretations, arguments, and misrepresentations which followed the Aburi meeting. The developments could have been much worse if the meeting had been held by ourselves without a predetermined agenda, proper records, and neutral witnesses. Having learned from this experience, the answer really is that we should go out of the country, meet before witnesses, and come back with agreements or decisions duly signed and witnessed by neutral persons. That would not wound our pride. It would merely show that we are prepared to go any length to find peaceful solutions to our problems.

Another point which commends meeting outside the country is the need to free our minds and actions from public pressures in order to reach decisions which will be realistic and in the overall interests of all.

As I see it, Lagos believes that the East will lose most by delays and procrastinations—or even by military, economic, and political sanctions. That may well be true as long as Lagos retains a number of powers now in their hands—powers they are now exercising in mean and vicious ways. If Lagos and the North expect that the East will sit back and fold its arms to violent and even slow death and destruction, then the time has come when they should start to disabuse their minds.

Fellow countrymen and women, the future is nebulous and bleak. It is in the interest of all to solve our problems peacefully and quickly. If this is not done, we must be prepared for a struggle to the bitter end to ensure our survival and integrity.

Diary of Events: April 25—May 26, 1967

April 25: Gowon, in an address to diplomats, threatens "to create the Calabar-Ogoja-River [C.O.R.] State by decree."

April 26: Nigeria's former Minister for the Navy, M. T. Mbu, in a press conference, describes Gowon's program on the creation of Calabar-Ogoja-River State as "detached from reality." He asks: "Is it being suggested that states be now created without reference to the people or without ascertaining the wishes of the people through a plebiscite?"

April 29:   Lagos declares that savings bank deposits made in Eastern Nigeria after March 31 as well as savings stamp certificates and premium bonds sold in Eastern Nigeria will not be recognized by the federal government.

April 30:   The Eastern Nigerian Ministry of Finance announces that it has spent by the end of April £600,000 as payment of salaries and wages to refugee civil servants, the employees of the federal corporations operating in the region and abandoned by the Lagos regime.

April 25–May 11:   The Lagos government issues directives to the national shipping line not to allow ships to call to Eastern ports. . . . The *Ahmadu Bello,* sailing from Liverpool and scheduled to arrive in Port Harcourt on May 17, is instructed not to accept cargo for Port Harcourt. . . . The *Nnamdi Azikiwe,* sailing for Port Harcourt, is instructed to discharge the cargo at Apapa. . . . The *M.V. El Kanemi,* due to arrive in Port Harcourt on May 24, is instructed not to accept cargo for Eastern ports. . . . Imported goods of traders of Eastern Nigeria origin are confiscated by the Lagos government. . . . Lieutenant Colonel Gowon warns foreign governments to recognize the crisis as an internal affair of Nigeria. . . . Eastern Nigeria's border with the Cameroun Republic is sealed off by Lagos government. . . . All passports issued to officers of Eastern Nigeria origin who transfer from the federal public service are canceled. . . . British shipping lines—Elder Dempster, John Holt, and the British-controlled West African Conference lines—stop carrying freight to Eastern ports. Lloyds of London declines to reinsure vessels bound for Port Harcourt. . . . British High Commission orders the evacuation of British citizens from Eastern Nigeria. The BBC begins to build hostile propaganda around the evacuation.

May 3: Mass demonstrations in Enugu. In their resolution, the demonstrators declare: "We hereby declare
that our government [my government] does not seem
to be willing to accept the logic of Gowon's push-out
measures. Further delay may be too late. How long
will Ojukwu trust untrustworthy Gowon?"

May 5: A private National Conciliation Committee
headed by Chief Awolowo visits Eastern Nigeria and
holds talks with me.

May 10: Thirty former councillors of the dissolved
Lagos City Council disassociate themselves from a
statement credited to Oba Adeyinka Oyekan of Lagos
and his white-cap chiefs [traditional rulers] demanding
a federal constitution for Nigeria with a strong center
and a Lagos state. They also demand that Northern
troops now stationed in Lagos must quit.

May 13: Demonstrations by students of the University of Nigeria, Nsukka. In a two-point resolution, the
students state:

i. Gowon's acts of perfidy, now combined with total
economic and diplomatic blockade of the East, amply show
that Eastern Region is no longer wanted in the Federation.

ii. To save the people of the region from strangulation,
the Eastern Nigerian government should make the only
logical break of the blockade by asserting our right to self-
determination. Our new state should be called Biafra.

May 14: Demonstrations of women in Enugu urging
me to "save us from Gowon's tightening noose."

May 15: Chief Awolowo warns that the Federal Military Government is not the right authority to try to
rebuild Nigeria politically. . . . Lieutenant Colonel
Adebayo of Western Nigeria, speaking in an official
ceremony in Chief Awolowo's house, spurs Yorubas
"to assert their rights." He calls on his people to meet
the challenge facing them as a component part of
Nigeria "whichever way the present crisis may turn"—
"It is only by this way can Yorubas help to lift the
ominous clouds hanging over Nigeria quickly. . . . The
moment calls for deep thought for a correct action to

assert our right without infringing those of others."
. . . Dr. Akanu Ibiam blames our intellectuals and
charges them to be active. Speaking at a luncheon after
the installation of Chief Awolowo as chancellor of Ife
University, Sir Ibiam says, "It seems to me that the
learned men in Nigeria are not giving the best of their
service to our country. . . ."

May 16: The military governor of the Midwest,
Lieutenant Colonel Ejoor, declares that his region is
not prepared to support any of the regions of the Federation against another "merely to keep the Federation
going on their own terms." He is speaking during a
farewell call on him by Mr. John Volkmar, director of
the International Dialogues of the American Quaker
Friendship Service Committee.

May 19: Adebayo opposes Gowon's plan to bring in
British troops to police the Midwest for a meeting of
the Supreme Military Council and calls for good will.
He declares: "We will not subscribe to the idea of
inviting British troops to Nigeria for the purpose of
holding a meeting of the country's military rulers. . . .
All military leaders should demonstrate good faith and
preparedness for peace and meet themselves instead of
meeting under the protection of foreign soldiers." His
speech follows Lieutenant Colonel Gowon's admission
that he will not object to Nigeria's military rulers meeting in a British warship or in a neutralized military
zone, policed by British troops anywhere in the country.
. . . Catholic bishops of Nigeria send messages of appeal to the military governors in Nigeria, calling for a
peaceful settlement of the Nigeria crisis through negotiation.

May 21: Radio announcement by Gowon that his
sanctions against the East will be lifted with effect from
May 23, 1967, and a suggestion that the East should
reciprocate by repealing the Survival Edicts and releas-
ing railway rolling stocks in the region. . . . News of a
plan to repatriate students of Eastern Nigeria origin in
the United States by the Lagos government. A cable

from Washington says Eastern Nigeria students studying in overseas countries are faced with the unpleasant
prospect of being repatriated and their scholarships
withdrawn by the Lagos government.

May 22–23: Demonstrations by women in Aba urging me to dismiss Gowon's announcement of May 21
as another trick. . . . Rallies by railway workers in
Enugu, asking Gowon to pay their "arrears of salaries
before the rolling stocks are released." Their placards
read: GOWON IS PUTTING THE CART BEFORE THE HORSE,
IF YOUR PURPORTED LIFT OF YOUR BLOCKADE IS NOT
PROPAGANDA STUNT, GOWON, PAY US OUR SALARIES.
. . . Demonstrations by University of Nigeria students.
In an open letter to me, they urge me to "go ahead and
not look back ". . . The Nigeria Workers Council describes the announcement as a tactical maneuver and
belated move because "it is a calculated attempt to
deceive the outside world into believing that Gowon is
making gestures for a settlement of the crisis."

May 24: More demand for separation. The demonstrations spread to all provinces. . . . Lagos government
stops financial assistance to Niger Delta Development
Board for capital projects "until the position improves."
Eastern Nigeria government, however, promises to help
the board to tide over its difficulties.

May 25: Demonstrations in Degema and Bonny
against Lagos' withdrawal of financial assistance from
Niger Delta Development Board and "Gowon's continuation of Northern tactics of using Rivers people
for politics.". . . Rallies by workers of the Nigeria Ports
Authority in Port Harcourt. In a resolution, they point
to the withdrawal of capital from the Niger Delta Development Board as "another evidence of the Lagos
junta's abandonment of its responsibilities and reckless
use of power." The resolution continues: "Our government [my government] is not in tune with the mood of
the people if it continues to display reluctance in acced-
ing to the people's unanimous wish for the emergence
of Eastern Region as a separate sovereign republic." . . .

Workers and farmers in Abakaliki demonstrate and
pass a resolution which *inter alia* reads: "Are we human
beings or trees? Only a tree stands when the forester
hacks it with an ax. Gowon is hacking us with axes."
. . . Workers in Obudu (Ogoja) hold a rally. In their
resolution, they declare: "We welcome our new provincial system and reject Gowon's C.O.R. State as mere
propaganda . . . whereas it is now clear that we are no
longer wanted in Nigeria . . . be it here resolved that
we ask our government to declare Eastern Region an
independent state."

May 26:   In view of the mood of the people and intensification of economic provocations by Lagos, I
summon a joint session of the Council of Elders and
Chiefs and the Consultative Assembly to advise my
government on the next line of action. . . . Demonstrations by all the people of Enugu outside the Assembly
Hall. The demonstrators carry placards calling on the
assembly to pull the Eastern Region out of the Nigerian Federation.

The People's Hour of Decision

(Address to joint meeting of Chiefs and Elders and
the Consultative Assembly, May 26, 1967)

Once again it is my privilege to welcome you to this
assembly. I do this with all humility and a sense of
duty. Your meeting today is very crucial. Eastern Nigeria is at the crossroads. Since our last meeting, everything possible has been done by enemies of the East to
escalate the crisis in an attempt to bring about the collapse of this Region. They have failed and will continue
to fail. Nevertheless, I find it necessary to put all the
facts before you, indicating the issues, the difficulties,
and the dangers, so that you can examine them fully
and advise me on the path we are to follow from now

on. As usual, I call upon you to be free, frank, and objective.

For a better understanding and a proper appreciation of the problems facing the country today, and in particular of the attitude of Eastern Nigeria to them, we need to go back to the historic statements on Nigerian unity made by leaders of Northern Nigeria.

We all know that before the amalgamation in 1914 of Southern and Northern Nigeria, the North was administered as an entity quite distinct from Southern Nigeria. The amalgamation was, however, not intended to, and did not in fact, result in a fusion either of the peoples of both areas or of their institutions. When, for example, a Legislative Council was established in 1922, it could not, and did not, legislate for the North; rather the governor-general in Lagos legislated for the North by means of proclamations. This was so because the amalgamation was forced on Northerners who made no secret of their dislike for it.

The late Sir Ahmadu Bello, in his book *My Life,* said:

The Colonial master who ruled Nigeria introduced a system of unitary government not for the present or future unity or well-being of all the indigenes of the country but for his own administrative convenience. Lord Lugard and his amalgamation were far from popular amongst us at that time (p. 135).

In 1953, the late Sir Abubakar Tafawa Balewa in a speech in the Legislative Council, said:

Since the amalgamation of the Southern and Northern Provinces in 1914, Nigeria has existed as one country only on paper. It is still far from being united. The country is inhabited by peoples and tribes who speak different languages, who have different religions, different customs, and traditions and entirely different historical backgrounds in their way of life, and who have also attained different stages of development. . . . We do not want our southern neighbors to interfere in our development. . . . But I should like to make it clear to you that if the British quitted Nigeria now at this stage the Northern people would continue their interrupted conquest to the sea.

"Interrupted conquest"! That has always been the Northern intention. Thank God that the East has now awakened to its responsibilities, and with that awakening, that ambitious dream will never be fulfilled in this country.

The self-government motion in the Central Legislature in March, 1953, evoked the following reply from the late Sir Ahmadu Bello:

It is true that we politicians delight in talking loosely about unity of Nigeria. . . . What is now called Nigeria consisted of large and small communities all of which were different in their outlooks and beliefs. The advent of the British and of Western education has not materially altered the situation and these many and varied communities have not knit themselves into composite unit. . . . In 1914, the North and South were amalgamated though the administration of the two sections are distinctly different. Since then, no serious attempt has been made by the British or by the people themselves to come together and each section has looked upon the other with suspicion and misgiving.

In supporting him, Isa Kaita said: "The mistake of 1914 has come to light and I should like to go no further."

During this period, secession was the talk of every Northern Nigeria leader, and Sir Ahmadu again said during one of the Legislative Council debates:

. . . There were agitations in favour of secession; we should set up on our own; we should cease to have anything more to do with the Southern people; we should take our own way.

I must say it looked very tempting. We were certainly "viable," to use the current phrase; we could run our own show; the Center would have to hand over to us our share of Nigeria's accumulated sterling assets. We had the men and production and minerals and the will to act.

The Northern House of Assembly debated the issue of self-government for Nigeria later that year, and in the course of this, her leaders adopted the now famous eight-point proposal, the purport of which is that the political arrangement best suited to Nigeria was complete regional autonomy with common services maintained by a central agency which would have neither legislative nor executive powers.

This attitude of the North delayed Nigerian independence for two years. History will record that leaders from Southern Nigeria, and from Eastern Nigeria in particular, preached and worked for twenty years to achieve the unity of this country. History will also bear witness to the fact that the North had for long resisted the idea of unity, and had, on four occasions in the recent past, expressed this resentment through brutal killings.

In 1964, when the most farcical election in Nigeria took place, a Northerner, Mallam Baba Garuba, published the following statement in the December 30 issue of the *West African Pilot:*

The conquest to the sea is now in sight. When our god-sent Ahmadu Bello said some years ago that our conquest will reach the seashores of Nigeria, some idiots in the South were doubting its possibilities.

Today have we not reached the sea? Lagos is reached. It remains Port Harcourt. It must be conquered and taken after December 30, 1964.

I remember when the N.C.N.C. and the A.G. were boasting about their daydreams of snatching power from us. Today, their great brains are in our bag. Imagine such personalities as Akintola, Benson, Davies, Akinjide, Olowofoyeku. . . .

I still hope that it will not be long when Okpara, Adegbenro and Aminu Kano will come to beg. Osadebay and other Midwest leaders are half way to us. As for Awo [Awolowo], he will spend the last day of his term of imprisonment there for his inordinate ambition. Some Southern fools must understand that to suggest secession after their defeat is suicide for them. Let them think about all these things and understand the implications in secession.

(a) Where is the Nigerian Military Academy? (b) Where is the Nigerian Air Force base built? All these are up here in our region.

After the election, we will call upon our leaders to make a Northerner the leader of the Nigerian Army. Those who propose Ironsi are daydreaming.

After the next five years those Southern so-called educated fools must realize where they are. Once we will be able to connect the Bornu Railway with those of our brothers in the neighbouring country and from there to Egypt, we can allow secession to take place.

Our exports could be sent out through that way. Thanks to Allah that the Kainji Dam will soon be completed. It is up to Tarka to come back now or face what will follow when we achieve our aim.

We must do anything possible to win the coming Jihad. But we must keep our weather eyes open on those from the West, as they could do anything at any time. Immediately we win, we can lose some members from the West at any time. We must not take things for granted.

With our 167 seats in the North we can go it alone. There is no need sharing the post of Prime Ministership and Presidentship with anyone. I have a genuine fear that we keep the posts and then concede some important ministries to some Yoruba members.

The time has come. We are going to show these intellectual fools that we are only in the morning of our leadership of this country.

We try N.N.D.P. in the next five years and see whether they will be too forward and ambitious as the ungrateful N.C.N.C. and A.G. If some still doubt that we haven't conquered our way to the sea, let them go through these facts.

(a) Who is the Prime Minister of the country?

(b) Who is the Minister of Lagos Affairs? Is Lagos not our capital?

Our only obstacle are the Ibos. They have played their card. They will sink.

This statement summarizes the stand of Northern Nigeria in relation to the rest of the country. In August, 1966, just after the murder of Major General Aguiyi-Ironsi, Gowon stated publicly that there was no basis for Nigerian unity.

I have quoted these and other statements in order to remind us of the consistency of the North in their feeling of separateness except where they are in relation to other peoples of Nigeria as master is to servant.

In May, 1966, the ill-fated Decree No. 34 was promulgated after it had been discussed and approved by General Aguiyi-Ironsi's Supreme Military Council, which was composed as follows:

North (two members):	Lt. Col. Hassan
	Lt. Col. Gowon
East (two members):	Lt. Col. Odumegwu Ojukwu
	Lt. Col. G. T. Kurubo
West and Lagos (three members):	Lt. Col. F. A. Fajuyi
	Commodore J. Wey
	Brigadier B. O. Ogundipe
Midwest (one member):	Lt. Col. D. Ejoor

At the same time, his Federal Executive Council consisted of:

North (three members):	Lt. Col. Hassan
	Lt. Col. Gowon
	Alhaji Kam Selem—Deputy Inspector-General of Police
East (three members):	Lt. Col. C. Odumegwu Ojukwu
	Mr. L. E. Edet, Inspector-General of Police
	Lt. Col. G. T. Kurubo
West and Lagos (three members):	Lt. Col. F. A. Fajuyi
	Commodore J. Wey
	Major M. Johnson
Midwest (one member):	Lt. Col. D. Ejoor

The heads of the federal civil service were distributed as follows:

Northern Nigeria:	8
Eastern Nigeria:	3
Western Nigeria and Lagos:	7
Midwestern Nigeria:	7

The heads of federal corporations and institutions then were distributed thus:

North:	6
East:	3
West:	12
Midwest:	1

I have given you these facts because after the promulgation of Decree No. 34, evil-minded persons in the North and elsewhere propagated the mischievous lie that Easterners were dominating the affairs of the country. At no time since independence did Easterners dominate the politics of the Federation.

The reaction of the North to Decree No. 34 was to massacre Easterners in the North and to loot their property in May, 1966.

Thereafter, the Supreme Military Council decided that a tribunal should be set up to inquire into the causes of that disturbance. Northern emirs rejected it and demanded the secession of the North from the Federation. Nonetheless, the tribunal was scheduled to begin its sittings on August 2, 1966. On July 29, and for several days thereafter, Northern soldiers in conspiracy with Northern civilians unleashed against defenseless Easterners the bloodiest acts of brutality. Major General Aguiyi-Ironsi was murdered. His host, Lieutenant Colonel Fajuyi, was also murdered. Dead they are, but their memories will live from age to age as shining examples of heroism, courage, and loyalty.

In the heat of these outrageous acts, Gowon, a fairly junior colonel in the army, and himself one of the rebels, hoisted himself onto the seat of the Supreme Commander; his first act was to demand secession for the North as a condition for stopping the massacre. I was left with no other alternative than to agree. However, on the advice of certain foreign nationals, he abandoned the idea, telling his people of the North that Allah had once more put the government of Nigeria into the hands of "another Northerner." . . .

The proposed Constitutional Conference began its sitting on September 12, 1966. Gowon charged it to discover a form of association suitable for Nigeria, no matter the name by which it may be called.

Memoranda were exchanged by the delegates, and vital features of some of them are as follows:

NORTHERN NIGERIA

A great deal of passion has been generated within the last six years between the peoples of this country. We have moved from one crisis to another and have on each occasion congratulated ourselves for that Nigerian spirit of compromise about which we have been flattered by the rest of the world. We have failed to accept that each crack, whether patched up or not, represented a progressive weakening of the base of our association.

All Nigerians realize the advantages of a united country which is economically strong, politically and socially stable, and respected all over Africa and the entire globe. This is the ideal which anyone will desire for his country if only because it is more comforting to feel that one belongs to a strong group.

In a young country as large as Nigeria, where the ethnic groups are not homogeneous, where the cultures differ and where values are not necessarily the same from one part of the country to another, the textbook rules for political association between the various groups will not necessarily be applicable.

The leaders of such a country must be ever prepared to grope for new ways of association which, while preserving the aspirations of the individual groups, will at the same time preserve some forms of association which will make possible cooperation in fields which are of mutual interest to all the groups without bringing the component groups into direct physical or economic conflict.

Recent events have shown that for Nigerian leaders to try to build a future for the country on rigid political ideology will be unrealistic and disastrous. We have pretended for too long that there are no differences between the peoples of this country. The hard fact which we must honestly accept as of paramount importance in the Nigerian experiment especially for the future is that we are different peoples brought together by recent accidents of history. To pretend otherwise will be folly.

We all have our fears of one another. Some fear that opportunities in their own areas are limited and they would therefore wish to expand and venture unhampered in other parts. Some fear the sheer weight of skills and the aggressive drive of other groups which they feel has to be regulated if they are not to be left as the economic, social, and possibly political underdogs in their own areas of origin in the very near future.

These fears may be real or imagined; they may be reasonable or petty. Whether they are genuine or not, they have to be taken account of because they influence to a considerable degree the actions of the groups toward one another and, more important perhaps, the daily actions of the individual in each group toward individuals from other groups.

The colonial master who ruled Nigeria introduced a system of unitary government not for the present or future unity or well-being of all the indigenes of the country but for his own administrative convenience. But even he had to devolve powers to his governors or commissioners in the provinces partly because of the difficulties of communication and partly because he realized that administrative needs and practices vary from one part of the country to the other because of the differences between the peoples.

The unitary system was changed to a federal system towards the end of colonial rule as the Nigerian was politically coming to his own and becoming increasingly vocal about his own affairs. The colonial masters accepted the federal system of government as being most suitable for the differing interests in Nigeria. This system was reviewed and modified, and it carried us into independence. We have since worked this system with varying degrees of success, but the fears which have earlier been listed constituted great snags in the working of the system.

In all, we have had two attempts at a unitary system of government. The first attempt proved unsatisfactory, and the second proved a disaster. We have also had two attempts at the federal system. The two attempts ended in chaos, and we are again presented with an opportunity to look dispassionately at our future association.

In putting forward its suggestions, the Northern delegation has taken into account the mood of the people and the mood of the army, which must be a matter for serious consideration if we are not to deceive ourselves. The delegation has also taken into account the very wise recommendations made recently by a meeting of the representatives of the regional governors that army personnel should be posted to barracks in their regions of origin. It has also taken into account the areas of lasting mutual trust, in whatever pockets they may exist, which have so far not been completely destroyed by recent events. It has also taken into account the need to preserve the economy of the component parts of the country and avoid as far as possible its disruption.

The Northern delegation advocates a system of government which differs from anything that has been attempted in Nigeria in the past. As each region has managed to preserve some measure of order and sense of unity within its confines, each region should be constituted into an autonomous state. Subjects or groups of subjects which are of common interest to the component states should be delegated to a Common Services Commission to operate.

The North then proposed:

(1) The new Nigeria shall comprise a number of autonomous states.

(2) The autonomous states of Nigeria, that is to say, Northern Nigeria, Eastern Nigeria, Western Nigeria, Midwestern Nigeria, or by whatever name they may choose to be called later, and such other states as may be formed subsequently, should agree to enter into a union which shall have a Central Executive Council, representation to which shall be on equal representation from all the states comprising the association. The powers of the Central Executive Council shall be delegated by the component states except that powers connected with external or foreign affairs, immigration, can be unilaterally withdrawn by the state government while all other functions or powers delegated to the Central Executive Council can only be withdrawn by the state governments after a unanimous decision by their representatives in the Central Executive Council.

The chairmanship of the Council shall rotate. Each chairman shall hold office for one year.

(3) Any member state of the union should reserve the right to secede completely and unilaterally from the union and to make arrangements for cooperation with the other members of the union in such a manner as they may severally or individually deem fit.

(4) Each state must have its own army, air force, police, civil service, and judiciary. There shall be a navy composed of personnel in proportion to the population of each state.

The Northern memorandum then went on to propose a detailed form of Common Services Organization within the existing regions as sovereign states. The terms of this memorandum are in consonance with the eight-point proposal adopted by the North on May 23, 1953.

WESTERN NIGERIA AND LAGOS:

The alternative proposal of the Delegates of Western Nigeria and Lagos is as follows:

In the event of the other regions feeling unable to accept the foregoing proposals for the establishment of true federalism in Nigeria, then it is proposed that what is now the Federation of Nigeria should become the Commonwealth of Nigeria, comprising the existing regions and such other regions as may be subsequently created, with Lagos forming part of the present Western Nigeria.

The government of each state within the Commonwealth shall be completely sovereign in all matters excepting those with respect to which responsibility is delegated to the Council of States.

You can see that the position of the West then was very similar to the Northern proposal which suggested the loosest type of association for Nigeria. In the words of the late Sir Ahmadu Bello, this association would be:

A looser structure for Nigeria while preserving its general pattern—a structure which would give the regions the greatest possible freedom of movement and action: a structure which would reduce the powers of the center to the absolute minimum.

The Gowon junta now preaches unity not because it believes in unity but because the dominating position of the North is threatened.

The Ad Hoc Constitutional Conference sat for about three weeks, and when it looked as if it was going to achieve a form of association unsuitable to Northerners, the pogrom of September and October was unleashed. The story of this pogrom is now being recorded by the Atrocities Commission in the interest of posterity.

The events of that period have made fundamental changes in the structure and pattern of Nigeria society and government. Some 2,000,000 Eastern Nigerians have returned to the East. All the Northerners in the East have gone home. Relationships between peoples of the two Regions have come to an end and, if ever revived, will be on an entirely different basis.

I refused to recognize Gowon for reasons which I gave at Aburi. To recognize him would mean to accept the authority of a rebel in the army, and that would be bad for discipline. The stalemate which followed culminated in the Aburi meeting.

It is to be noted that the meeting of January 4–5 at Aburi was held largely on my own initiative. Although I had strong forebodings about the outcome of the meeting, I went to it with a genuine desire to make it succeed. I decided that as soon as I set foot on Ghana soil, I should be nothing but a Nigerian. It was my aim that the military leaders must come to an arrangement whereby the right climate could be created for all of us to carry out the duties and responsibilities to which we had dedicated ourselves. I wanted an atmosphere created for a return of normalcy, peace, and confidence in the country, an atmosphere in which all sources of fear and suspicion would be removed.

My genuine desire for all these was borne out by the fact that, before the start of the meeting, I pressed for a resolution eschewing the use of force in the settlement of our problems. I did so because of the widespread fear and suspicion in other parts of the country that the East was planning an attack. Nobody with knowledge or discernment could doubt our ability, even at that time, to take effective actions of revenge against the North, or even Lagos, if we had wanted. But our aim was and has remained that we should avoid further bloodshed, even though it has been the innocent blood of Easterners that has been most wantonly shed. Subsequent events seem to indicate that our opponents mistook my action in pressing for that resolution on the use of force as a sign of weakness.

On the question of political and administrative control of the country as a whole, executive and legislative powers were vested in the Supreme Military Council. In other words, all of what used to be the legislative powers of the Nigerian Parliament, and what used to be the executive and policy-making powers of the Council of Ministers, under the civilian regime, were vested in the Supreme Military Council as a collective organ. To make sure that the regions had an effective voice in all decisions affecting the whole country, all such decisions had to receive the concurrence of all military governors; and where any military governor was unable to attend a meeting of the Supreme Military Council, any decision reached in his absence had to be referred to him for comments and concurrence.

This principle of concurrence by military governors was prompted by an appreciation of the special responsibilities which each military governor had over his area of authority. Having regard to the general welfare of the people under his charge, he should be in a position to delay any decision affecting the country as a whole until a consensus was reached.

As far as the regions were concerned, it was decided that all the powers vested by the Nigerian Constitution in the regions and which they exercised prior to January 15, 1966, should be restored to the regions. To this end, the Supreme Military Council decided that all decrees passed since the military takeover, and which tended to detract from the previous powers of the regions, should be replaced by January 21, after the law officers had met on January 14 to list all such decrees.

None of these agreements has been carried out. The meeting of military officers was abandoned because Gowon withdrew the federal representatives. The law officers met on January 14 as agreed and listed the relevant decrees which had detracted from the previous powers and positions of the regions, to enable the Supreme Military Council to promulgate the necessary decree by January 21 as decided at Aburi. The officers of the Ministry of Finance never met within the time stipulated at Aburi because the permanent secretary of the Federal Ministry of Finance did not consider that such a meeting would serve any useful purpose.

I have said that what the decisions at Aburi amounted to in terms of political and military control of the country was that the country should be governed as a confederation. As soon as we came back from Aburi, I considered it my duty to explain to the Eastern Nigeria public, through the press, the decisions taken at Aburi, and as far as my sense of responsibility allowed me, the implications. In Lagos, the permanent secretaries studied the recommendations and, to their credit, brought out clearly and unmistakenly their meanings and implications. Having seen these, however, they unfortunately went beyond their rights and duty as civil servants to advise against the implementation of the Aburi Agreement. From here our difficulties started and have taken us to our present stalemate.

This leads me to the publication by Lagos of the controversial Decree No. 8. That is the decree by which Gowon and his group claim to have implemented the Aburi Agreement. I have mentioned that aspect of the Aburi decisions which stipulated that a decree restoring the regions to their position before the military takeover should be passed by January 21, 1967. The law

officers met, as required, on January 14, but no signs
of action appeared forthcoming from Lagos after that
meeting. On or about January 19, I dispatched a telegram calling for the necessary draft decree to be circulated for concurrence.

Gowon's reply was the negative one of giving untenable reasons for his failure to carry out that aspect of
the Aburi decisions. He, however, assured me that the
decree was being drafted and asked for an urgent meeting of the Supreme Military Council. I promptly replied
to his telegram as follows:

Glad learn decree being drafted to repeal all decrees or
aspects of decrees which detracted from position and
powers of regional governments as they existed before January 15, 1966. Imperative that repealing decree be published immediately in order to confirm confidence and clear
way of meeting Supreme Military Council. I agree that
matters affecting constitution for which there were questions or reservations should be referred to Supreme Military
Council which should follow soon after publication of
decree repealing overcentralizing decrees or aspects of decrees. Surprised that my press statement embarrassed anyone. I know people with vested interests have tried through
representations to you and others to capitalize viciously on
that press conference. Honest acquaintance with and appreciation of feelings in East would show that it was in the
interest of all that the conference was given. Silence would
be misinterpreted here and difficulties created for smooth
return to normalcy and of confidence. Every word spoken
at press conference completely in accord with transcript of
Aburi meeting.

You will see in that telegram my willingness to attend the meeting of the Supreme Military Council provided the repealing decree acceptable to all was published without delay. Such an action on the part of
Gowon would have proved his sincerity to keep faith
and honor agreements in the interest of public confidence. I should add here that the West military gov-

ernor took the same stand with us on the need for an immediate publication of the repealing decree.

Eventually a draft decree came forward from Lagos; but it was a document which was a complete departure from, indeed the very opposite of, what was intended at Aburi. It was even at variance with the agreements reached by the solicitors-general at their Benin meeting of January 14, 1967. Both the West and ourselves rejected the draft outright. Then followed a period of public controversy, confusion, and uncertainty, until it was agreed that officials of the different governments, led by their respective secretaries to the military governments, should meet at Benin to advise on how best the Aburi Agreement should be implemented.

The officials of the five governments of the Federation held meetings on February 17–18, 1967, and at the end made recommendations which have since been published and which I believe you all have seen. Another draft decree was prepared by Lagos. Although it must be admitted that this draft (which incidentally was, I am told, the fifth attempt!) was an improvement on the first one, yet it contained extraneous features which, at best, went contrary to the agreements of the officials and, at worst, were directed against the East. We promptly raised our objections to these features, but without any further comments from the federal government a meeting of the Supreme Military Council was arranged to be held in Benin on March 10.

They expected me to attend that meeting even though they knew perfectly well that I could not do so for three obvious reasons. First, Northern troops were still present in the West and Lagos. Second, all the confidence and marks of good faith generated at Aburi had been systematically undermined by Lagos. Third, the passing of the right decree had been my precondition for attending such a meeting. However, they met on March 10 and, that very day, approved their Decree No. 8.

As if to underline their action of perfidy and double-dealing, a message was sent through, even after they had taken a final decision on the decree, for law officers of the regions to meet in Lagos to finalize a draft decree. As a mark of my genuine desire for a peaceful settlement and return to normalcy, I sent my law officers to the meeting in Benin, where they were simply told that since the decree had been passed by the Supreme Military Council, there was really nothing for them to do! All the same, our men reduced into writing and handed to their colleagues this region's objections. A few days later, on March 19, the decree was formally published.

The decree gave Gowon a veto power over the concurrence of all the military governors in matters affecting the exercise of legislative and executive powers of the Federation; it gave the Supreme Military Council power to declare a state of emergency in a region against the wishes of the governor. It is important that you should know that two days after the promulgation of the decree, Gowon requested the other members of the Supreme Military Council to approve his proposal for a declaration of a state of emergency in Eastern Nigeria. But for the wisdom of some members of the council who refused to be so used, the story of the past two months would have been different.

For the foregoing reasons, I found Decree No. 8 unacceptable and rejected it. It was a Northern instrument for political power over the South. An important fact to bear in mind is that at Aburi it was agreed that all the members of the Supreme Military Council should meet to appoint the Commander-in-Chief and Head of the Federal Military Government. Up until now that decision has not been implemented.

I think I should here tell you my personal efforts since July to ensure a quick, realistic, and peaceful settlement of our problems. Soon after the July 29 rebellion and the usurpation of office by Gowon, I told him that even though I was not prepared to accept him either as the Supreme Commander or the Head of the

Federal Government, I would be prepared to cooperate with him in the task of keeping the country together, stopping further bloodshed, and ensuring a quick return to normalcy.

It was for that reason that I sent representatives of this region to Lagos on August 8 although I knew perfectly well the type of risks to which they were at that time exposed. It was for that reason that I did everything to make it possible for the meeting of the Ad Hoc Constitutional Conference to be held in Lagos with our representatives attending. All along, Gowon and I were keeping in daily contact with each other on the telephone. Even after the pogrom which started on September 29 and which has, more than anything else, changed our previous conception of Nigeria as one country, I continued the daily dialogue with Gowon.

There was a meeting of secretaries to the military governments immediately followed by that of advisers to the military governors. The outcome of these efforts was the famous Aburi meeting of January 4–5.

Although the attitude of Lagos to the Aburi Agreement was nothing but a catalog of bad faith, I still felt that chances of peaceful settlement, which would lead to the maintenance of this country as a unit, had not all been lost. Meanwhile the federal government owed us heavy amounts of money as our right under the Constitution. I pressed that this debt should be paid promptly in view of our urgent needs for funds to meet our refugee problems. Nothing was done; the drift continued; the stalemate persisted, and the clouds thickened.

On February 16, I sent a lengthy letter to Gowon with copies to Commodore Wey and other military leaders. In it I brought out as forcefully as possible the dangers inherent in the continued stalemate. I pointed out to Gowon that, in spite of all his public protestations to that effect, he was not serious about saving the country. I repeated this region's absolute stand on the Aburi decisions. I then gave him a catalog of his acts of bad faith and perfidy following the Aburi meeting.

Finally I gave the warning that if by March 31 the Aburi Agreements were not implemented, I would have no alternative but to feel free to take whatever measure was possible to implement the decisions unilaterally. I ended my letter with these words:

I say this with the deepest sense of regret and fully conscious of the consequences of such unilateral action. But, I shall be able to tell the world when the time comes what part I have played at different stages and in different circumstances since the emergency which started in May last year, to avoid the situation. The responsibility will not be mine.

I still hope that good sense will prevail and that God will save us from such a bleak future. Let us at once implement the Aburi Agreements, and preserve the country as one.

There was no reaction from Gowon to that letter. We continued to drift. On March 10, a meeting of the Supreme Military Council was held in Benin, and on March 19, the so-called Decree No. 8 was promulgated. The financial year was coming to an end, as was fast approaching my deadline of March 31.

My aim was still to avoid a point of no return. Thus, on Easter Sunday, March 26, I paid a visit to Ghana for discussions with General Ankrah and his colleagues on the National Liberation Council. I explained to them the position of this region and the dangerous consequences of Gowon's continued indifference. I undertook not to take unilateral action provided Lagos paid its debt to us before March 31. General Ankrah and his colleagues for their part undertook to bring together in Ghana all the officials of the Nigerian governments to discuss the settlement of federal debts to this region.

On Monday, March 27, 1967, I held a meeting at Onitsha with Colonel Adebayo, Military Governor of Western Nigeria, accompanied by Commodore Wey, Head of the Navy, and Mr. Omo-Bare, Deputy Inspector-General of Police. We held a lengthy, detailed, and frank talk, in which I made the position of the East absolutely clear. The meeting ended on a high note of optimism. The delegation undertook to get Gowon to do two things: first to make sure that the debt owed to the East was paid by March 31; second, either to suspend Decree No. 8 or to repeal those sections which were obnoxious to the East. They also suggested that the North should express public apology to the East for their atrocities.

I should also have mentioned that I had previously paid a visit to my colleague and friend Lieutenant Colonel David Ejoor, with whom I held intimate discussions. I had made quite clear to him the course open to the East unless there was a change of attitude in Lagos.

True to their word, the Ghanaian authorities were able to bring together in Ghana representatives of the governments of the Federation, comprising economists, financial experts, and legal experts, for a meeting which was held on Wednesday, March 29, 1967. The painful result of that meeting was the knowledge that the federal government had no intention of paying to this region debts owed to it.

I must place on record my unqualified gratitude and tribute to General Ankrah and his colleagues for their untiring efforts in trying to help this country solve its problems. The sincerity in all their approaches has always been transparent. Apart from telephone contacts and letter correspondence, the Ghanaian government has sent representatives to Nigeria on several occasions to hold personal discussions, all aimed at helping us resolve our difficulties. Even if it turns out that Nigeria cannot remain as one, the efforts of Ghana in trying to avoid that situation will never be forgotten. If in the end some other solution is achieved, Nigeria will have yet greater reason to be grateful to the government and people of that sister country of Africa.

Eventually, the deadline of March 31 arrived, and I considered it my duty to take appropriate actions effect-

cd through edicts. Not surprisingly, the federal government and its associates immediately read everything
vicious into my action. I think I should here explain
again the reasons behind the various edicts passed since
March 31:

Revenue Collection Edict

The purpose of this edict was to make sure that the
federal government was no longer in a position to owe
this region its statutory revenues. It is legitimate that
we take what belongs to us; the edict did not attempt to
change the formula for revenue allocation as provided
in the Nigerian Constitution, nor take away what rightly
belonged to the federal government. The truth of this
statement is borne out in our estimates for this year,
where the revenues expected from federal sources have
been shown strictly on the existing formula.

Legal Education Edict

Following the disturbances of 1966, our students in
the Lagos Law School were compelled to return to this
region. As a result of the stalemate, it became clear that
they would never return to Lagos for their studies. We
asked Lagos to open a law school at our expense, but
they refused, even though under the act it was possible.
These students had a right to continue with their legal
studies and also to practice their chosen profession.
This government would have failed in its duty to them
if it did not take appropriate action to safeguard their
interests. Our action was guided by the same principle
that led us to establish a medical school and a teaching
hospital.

Statutory Bodies Council Edict

As part of its acts of retaliation and repression, the
federal government stopped the payment of salaries and
wages to the employees of the various federal statutory
bodies operating in this region, stopped the supply of

necessary equipment, material, and spare parts for them, and suspended the services of some of them, while making every effort to stifle others. The aim of the edict was to enable this region to take over the control and administration of these bodies to ensure coordination and efficient management. I do not need to mention that the federal government had failed to honor the Aburi Agreement to pay employees of governments and statutory corporations up to March 31. The result is that this government had to take over responsibility for the payment not only of the salaries and wages of refugees, but even of other employees of those corporations operating in this region. As at the end of April, this government had spent £600,000 on this account.

Court of Appeal Edict

This edict was enacted to ensure that our people have opportunities of prompt justice and redress. The Federal Supreme Court last held sessions in the East in February, 1965. As a result of the events which started in July, 1966, our people, as lawyers or clients, could not pursue their appeals in Lagos. As the Federal Chief Justice was unwilling to arrange sittings of the court in the East, the representative of Eastern Nigeria on the Supreme Court has since returned to the East, and the Bar Association of Eastern Nigeria has taken a resolute stand against its members going to Lagos for cases, we saw no alternative than to enact an edict establishing our own final Court of Appeal.

Registration of Companies Edict

This edict requires companies to be registered in Eastern Nigeria; it does not deal with incorporation. It will enable us to collect and collate statistics of businesses operating in this region for the purposes of planning.

No sooner had the Revenue Edict been passed than Lagos stopped all flights of Nigeria Airways, of which

this region is a joint owner, to the East. Business and
official travel has been disrupted, and movement of
mails has been disturbed.

In addition to this, Lagos ordered that federal employees serving in this region, whether in government
or corporations, should not be paid their salaries and
abandoned all financial responsibility for federal projects established in this region.

As if all these were not enough, Gowon convened a
meeting of his military colleagues and presented to
them a memorandum seeking authority for diplomatic,
military, and further economic sanctions against the
East.

You have heard about the withdrawal of diplomatic
passports from citizens of this region, the stoppage of
postal order transactions between this region and the
rest of the country. There is, of course, the blockage of
foreign exchange, not only against this government as
such but also against statutory corporations and institutions and even private industrial concerns in which
this government has a financial interest.

Importers from this region have been denied import
licenses, and our industries the right to import essential
raw materials for their operations. Further, Lagos has
sent emissaries abroad to interfere with this region's
sale of its produce. Lagos has done everything within
its power to strangle this region economically.

I think that here I must mention the radio announcement by Gowon that his sanctions against the East have
been lifted with effect from Tuesday the twenty-third
of this month. The unfortunate thing is that Gowon
should tag onto his announcement the suggestion that
the East should reciprocate by repealing the different
edicts which I have already mentioned and even the
release of railway rolling stock. If Gowon's action is to
be taken as a sign of a change of heart, belated though
it may be, let him go further and support it by paying
to the East all moneys owed by Lagos, pay all federal
corporation staff, reconstitute the Federal Supreme

Court in a manner acceptable to all. No, we have had and known enough of Lagos not to be so foolish as to take Gowon's words on their face value. There must be concrete proof of genuine intentions and good faith.

Let me give you the background to Gowon's announcement about the lifting of his sanctions against this region. I had repeatedly stated categorically that neither I nor my representatives would attend any further meeting to discuss the problems of Nigeria while the economic strangulation continued. I said it to the last delegation from Ghana; I said so to Mr. Justice Arthur Prest, who came here as a representative of a body called Nigerian Peace Committee; I said so to Chief Awolowo and others who came as the representatives of the so-called National Conciliation Committee.

Indeed I should say a little more on the visit of Chief Awolowo and his group. They had come, in the name of the so-called National Conciliation Committee, to plead with us to send delegates to attend a meeting of that committee. We could not understand the basis on which the committee was constituted; it contained two self-exiled Eastern Nigerians resident in Lagos, in whom we have no confidence. The committee has, however, invited two prominent men in this region to serve as members, Sir Francis Ibiam, my adviser, and Sir Louis Mbanefo, my respected Chief Justice. I informed the delegation that, as my adviser, Sir Francis could not be expected to serve on a committee to mediate between me and other military leaders; I told them that in this region we regard the judiciary as sacrosanct and would not want it involved in political matters of this nature.

However, we offered concrete proposals which were reduced into writing as follows:

1. The East is willing, and indeed prepared, to participate in discussions designed to resolve the present Nigerian crisis.
2. With regard to the request made by the delegates of the Conciliation Committee that the Eastern govern-

ment should appoint representatives to the committee,
it would appear anomalous that while the other members of the committee have been personally invited by
the sponsors/conveners, the Eastern delegates should
be appointed by their own government.

3. Other members of the committee, therefore, ought
   also to be appointed by their respective governments.
   A committee constituted in this way would be in a
   better position to achieve effective results.

4. Such a committee should be set up in such a way that
   it is made up of people who have the authority and
   mandate of their governments, with the regions having equal representation and equality of status.

5. Necessary preparations should be made to ensure that
   there are:
   (a) agreed agenda, with emphasis on the terms of
       association between the regions;
   (b) an acceptable venue, with due regard to condi-
       tions of safety and free discussion; and
   (c) a time limit set for the completion of the work
       of the committee so that the discussions do not
       become unduly protracted.

6. If the delegates are to participate in the discussion in
   an atmosphere of freedom and equality, then:
   (a) the economic strangulation of the East should be
       discontinued;
   (b) the occupation of West and Lagos by Northern
       troops should end.

We have heard that the committee subsequently met
and submitted recommendations to Gowon, who has
accepted them. Gowon is, of course, always prepared to
accept recommendations from any body or any organization provided the Eastern viewpoint is not represented.

Last week, Gowon sent me a telegram informing me
that he had arranged with the British government to
supply two companies of British troops to neutralize
Benin or nearby so that the military leaders might meet,
and that as an alternative to the supply of troops the
British government had agreed to make available an
aircraft carrier or frigate on which we could hold a

meeting. I, of course, promptly rejected the proposals in a telegram which read:

Reference British invasion Midwest. Proposal not acceptable for following reasons—
(1) Meeting of military leaders without proper preparation and agreed agenda cannot achieve good results;
(2) Request for British troops without prior consultation with East makes whole business suspicious in the extreme;
(3) British agreement not in consonance with their policy of non-intervention nor your declared policy of non-internationalization of crisis;
(4) Presence of British troops in Benin will be regarded as inimical to East.
In view of British attitude in present crisis other alternative not acceptable. East will resist British or Northern incursion into Midwest with force.
If, however, you are now prepared to approach matter with realism and sincerity, meeting of military leaders should be preceded by meeting of government representatives on an agenda mutually agreed. Representatives would be fully briefed by respective military leaders so that they can reach agreement for ratification by military leaders or place proposals for them to decide upon. In any case, the East will not, repeat *not*, attend any meeting while subject to economic strangulation.

Two days before, I had addressed what I regarded as a final letter to him, part of which read as follows:

The purpose of this letter is to tell you that in the face of all these unfriendly and destructive acts, deliberate and well calculated against this region, we have no alternative but to make plans for a separate existence in the interest of self-preservation. Contrary to what you have chosen to believe, and have taken great pains to get the world to believe, it has always been my genuine desire to keep this country in existence. But for this desire, I could have taken all the measures now taken, or proposed to be taken, six months ago, and there would have been no power to stop us. I believe that this country should exist as one in a real-

istic form of association. Since this wish cannot be fulfilled
the responsibility is yours and history will know where to
lay the blame.

Before I go on, I should like here to stress that while
Gowon is only too anxious to ask Britain for troops, his
attitude toward the efforts of African Heads of State
and the OAU to mediate has been one of stout and
consistent rebuff bordering on contempt.

Having said that, there are certain facts which we
must bear in mind. In the context of Nigeria, the history
of this region has been one of retarded progress because
we are too prone to compromise and sacrifice in the
interest of national unity.

The year 1966 has been for us a year of great lessons,
opening our eyes to realities and dispelling our illusions.
We came to this position months ago, but unfortunately
we were alone. We had seen the need that if this
country was to be saved, its component parts were to
move apart. For this we were misunderstood and even
abused. But because we believed our stand to be right
we stuck to it.

One thing that has come out of the evils of 1966 is
that they have clearly identified for us areas of conflict
and friction as well as what powers can be used or
abused by one authority to the detriment of others.

I am happy that at last our brothers in the South
have come to realize the wisdom and sanity of what we
have been advocating these last months. A great deal
has, however, happened, that our people are now demanding sovereignty.

Another good sign of the recent weeks is the ac-
knowledgment by the people of the South that the stand
of the East against the North has not been a mere
struggle for itself, but a struggle against all forms of
injustice and for the natural rights of every citizen to
have and enjoy life and property in an atmosphere and
under environments free from fear and molestation. It
has been a struggle of progress against reaction. If then,

by hitherto standing alone, we have been able to convince others that we have been championing their cause as well as ours, we have every reason to feel proud of our stand, without regret for whatever sacrifices we have so far sustained.

Those of you who have been following the utterances in the North and Lagos during the past months have heard threats of force against this region. May I take this opportunity to assure you all that there is no power in this country, or in black Africa, to subdue us by force. I make this statement not to intimidate anyone but to reassure you all, as well as to warn those who might be misguided.

As I pointed out in my letter of May 16, 1967, to Gowon, he seems to believe that time is on his side and against us. We know that the federal government has been importing arms and preparing troops for purposes best known to them. We shall not launch an attack on anybody. But should anybody want to use force against this region, he will find us neither unprepared nor inadequate. I think a word to the wise should be sufficient.

No Easterner would want to pass through the events of the past ten months again. Only a loose association, call it confederation or what you may, can ensure this. But Gowon and the North have categorically rejected confederation. The position of the East, and indeed the West and Midwest, on the one hand, and that of the North on the other, are at once irreconcilable.

It is for you as the representatives of the 14,000,000 people of Eastern Nigeria to choose from (a) accepting the terms of the North and Gowon and thereby submit to domination by the North, or (b) continuing the present stalemate and drift, or (c) ensuring the survival of our people by asserting our autonomy.

If we have no alternative to the third choice, we shall leave the door open for association with any of the other regions of the country that accept the principle of association of autonomous units.

In such a situation the present units of the country

would emerge as sovereign units, each capable of maintaining its integrity at home and abroad but at the same time cooperating in the operation of common services in such fields as transport and communications, particularly shipping, harbors and ports, railways and airways. This form of association would envisage the movement of goods and services across the borders without customs restrictions. Appropriate machinery could be devised for coordination in currency management and monetary policy.

While I cannot here go into the details of this arrangement, the association could provide for dual citizenship so that nationals of the associating units need not carry passports from one territory to another.

It is my belief that such arrangements are the only practicable and realistic ones in the present circumstances and hold greater promise for the future than complete disintegration. Given good faith on all sides, we cannot rule out the possibility of closer ties in the near future.

I consider it my duty to warn that if we are compelled to take that decision, we must be prepared for a period of real sacrifice, hardship, and inconvenience. To start with, we may be without friends for a period. We may have to face the hostilities of the North acting in desperation. For a time there will be financial and economic difficulties. There will be the problem of external communications, of immigration, including passports.

All these would prove uncomfortable but only for a while. But we are bound to pull through it all. We have already made contingency plans to mitigate as much of those difficulties as possible. I shall not pursue the point, except to warn that time is running out. The people of this region are totally tired of the present stalemate and state of uncertainty. We do not have much longer to wait. If Lagos and the North are now prepared to settle the matter peacefully, they must act quickly.

We have a way of life and proud heritage to defend and preserve. We want to preserve our democratic and free institutions as a progressive society, unhampered in its progress and development by the feudalistic and reactionary forces with which it has been our misfortune to contend all these years.

As I said, I shall need your advice and guidance on the path we are to follow from now on. If, as is now customary, the Lagos and Kaduna authorities continue to spurn our genuine proposals for a form of association of sovereign units, merely because they wish to dominate the entire country through a strong central government, I would expect the people of this region to resist to the last man their aggressive designs on this region. I am encouraged by the massive demonstrations throughout the region supporting the government's stand in this crisis. There have also been persistent requests and appeals to me for a formal break with some parts of the country. I now look to this august assembly for clear guidance on what to do should all our peaceful and constructive overtures fail.

I should like to refer to a few matters which are of particular interest to everyone in this region at this moment. It has come to my notice that a number of expatriates have been worried about their future and personal safety. I want to assure them that Eastern Nigeria is safe for all friends; we need their services and their assistance and friendship. We guarantee them the safety and security not only of their persons but also of their property and business. I regret that in the past week or so circumstances have arisen where the people of this region have had to react unfavorably toward a long-established expatriate business in this region. I personally regret the incident and do sincerely hope that the type of circumstances borne out of the present crisis will not occur again.

Quite a number of you here might be wondering what this government has been doing to give effect to the new provincial administration system. I want to assure you that everything is being done in this direction. There have been many administrative and technical details to be completed before the system can come into full operation. What could be done has been done, such as the posting of administrative officers to the new divisions and provinces. What remains to be done will be done as expeditiously as possible.

I also appreciate the inconvenience which the absence of customary courts has caused to every man and woman of this region as well as to the local government authorities, which have been handicapped in the collection of rates and in the maintenance of law and order. Here again things have been moving as fast as practicable, and I hope, within a short time, to announce the constitution and members of the different courts.

Finally, I do not need to extol the value of your understanding and cooperation, which you have all along extended to me in the present crisis. The struggle has been the people's struggle, not the struggle of one individual. With God on our side we shall emerge from the dark clouds, now overshadowing us, into a glorious and happy future.

Diary of Events: May 27–30, 1967

May 27: Lieutenant Colonel Gowon announces the splitting up of Nigeria into twelve states. Eastern Nigeria is "split" into three states. . . . Lieutenant Colonel Gowon declares a state of emergency and assumes dictatorial powers. . . . Leaders of Western Nigeria hold discussions with their military governor, Colonel Adeyinka Adebayo, and express opposition to the creation of more states by decree. . . . Demonstrations are staged in all major towns in Eastern Region. The people welcome the decision of the Consultative Assembly, mandating me to proclaim the Eastern Region an independent Republic of Biafra.

May 28: An announcement that Nigeria's ammunition factory in Kaduna has begun to manufacture submachine guns. The general manager of the Nigerian Defense Industries Corporation presents one set of the weapons to the Permanent Secretary of the Ministry of Defense. . . . I appoint the provincial administrators to the new provinces under the Eastern Nigeria Provincial Administration Edict. . . . Statements by the Council of Labor, Civil Service Union, Students Union, Traders Association, and railway workers describing Gowon's creation of states as the last straw. Demonstrations by workers in Enugu. In their resolution, they declare: "Gowon's creation of states by decree is the red signal. If we wait a minute longer, we will all be dead. . . ."

May 29: A release by my government declares Gowon's unilateral paper creation of twelve states as dictatorial, unrealistic, and inapplicable to Eastern Region.

May 30: Proclamation of the Republic of Biafra.

The People's Choice

(Proclamation of the Republic of Biafra, May 30, 1967)

It is right and just that we of this generation of Eastern Nigeria should record for the benefit of posterity some of the reasons for the momentous decision we have taken at this crucial time in the history of our people.

The military government of Eastern Nigeria has, in a series of publications, traced the evils and injustices of the Nigerian political association through the dec-

ades, stating also the case and standpoint of Eastern
Nigeria in the recent crisis.

Throughout the period of Nigeria's precarious existence as a single political entity, Eastern Nigerians have
always believed in fundamental human rights and principles as they are accepted and enjoyed in civilized
communities. Impelled by their belief in these rights
and principles and in their common citizenship with
other Nigerians after Amalgamation, Eastern Nigerians
employed their ideas and skills, their resourcefulness
and dynamism, in the development of areas of Nigeria
outside the East. Eastern Nigerians opened up avenues
of trade and industry throughout the country; overlooked the neglect of their homeland in the disposition
of national institutions, projects, and utilities; made
available their own natural resources to the rest of the
country; and confidently invested in the general economic and social development of Nigeria. Politically,
Eastern Nigerians advocated a strong, united Nigeria:
for ONE COUNTRY, ONE CONSTITUTION, ONE DESTINY.
Eastern Nigerians were in the vanguard of the struggle
for national independence and made sacrifices and concessions for the cause of national unity. They conceded
the inauguration of a federal instead of a unitary system of government in Nigeria.

Leaders of Northern Nigeria have told us several
times that what our former colonial masters made into
"Nigeria" consisted of an agglomeration of people,
distinct in every way except in the color of their skins,
and organized as a unit for their own commercial interests and administrative convenience. The name "Nigeria" was regarded by many as a mere "geographical
expression."

In course of time, the peoples of the other parts of
Southern Nigeria found that they possessed many things
in common with those of Eastern Nigeria, and while the
colonial master made adjustments to accommodate
these common ties between the Southern inhabitants,
the peoples of the North insisted on maintaining their
separateness.

On October 1, 1960, independence was granted to the people of Nigeria in a form of "federation," based on artificially made units. The Nigerian Constitution installed the North in perpetual dominance over Nigeria. The Federation was predicated on the perpetual rule by one unit over the others. The Constitution itself contained provisions which negated the fundamental human freedoms which it purported to guarantee for the citizens. Thus were sown, by design or by default, the seeds of factionalism and hate, of struggle for power at the center, and of the worst types of political chicanery and abuse of power. One of two situations was bound to result from that arrangement: either perpetual domination of the rest of the country by the North, not by consent but by force and fraud, or a dissolution of the federation bond. National independence was followed by successive crises, each leading to near-disintegration of the country. Some of the major events which are directly attributable to the defective and inadequate Constitution may here be mentioned.

In 1962, an emergency was imposed on Western Nigeria. Jurists agree that the imposition was unconstitutional; it was a ruse to remove certain elements in Western Nigeria known to have taken a firm stand against the misuse of political power. A puppet of the North was maneuvered into power in Western Nigeria.

Also in 1962, and again in 1963, Nigerians tried for the first time to count themselves. What should ordinarily be a statistical and dull exercise was, because of the nature of the Constitution, turned into a fierce political struggle. The official figures established by these censuses have been discredited.

Federal elections followed in December, 1964—elections which have been described as the most farcical in our history. Candidates were kidnapped, killed, or forced to withdraw from the elections. Results announced were in direct opposition to the actual facts. The Southern parties had boycotted the election, and the deadlock which followed brought the country near to dissolution. The situation was patched up; the conflagration was brought under control, but its embers lay smoldering.

On October 11, 1965, elections were held to the Western House of Assembly. The puppet government of that region existed not by the will of the people of Western Nigeria but because of the combined power of the federal government and the Northern Nigeria government which installed it. The electorate of Western Nigeria was not permitted to declare its will in the elections. Fraud, foul play, and murder were committed with impunity. The smoldering embers of the recent past erupted with unquenchable virulence. The irate electorate showed its resentment in its own way. Complete disorder followed. Yet the federal government dominated by the North fiddled with the issue and even refused to recognize what the whole world had known, namely, that Nigeria was on the brink of disaster.

Only the armed forces remained politically uncommitted and nonpartisan. Some of their officers and men revolted against the injustices which were perpetrated before their very eyes and attempted to overthrow the federal government and regional governments. In desperation, the ministers of the federal government handed over power to the armed forces under the supreme command of Major General J. T. U. Aguiyi-Ironsi.

The military administration under Major General Aguiyi-Ironsi made the first real attempt to unite the country and its peoples. The Northerners saw in his efforts the possibility of losing their control of the affairs of the country. So while its leaders paid lip service to unity, they laid plans for making sure that it could never be achieved. Major General Aguiyi-Ironsi was, of course, an Easterner, but the majority of the individuals at the head of affairs were not. At no time under the civilian rule did Eastern Nigerians hold a dominating position in the government of the Federation.

On May 24, 1966, the military government issued a decree designed to provide a more unified administration in keeping with the military command. The people of Northern Nigeria protested against the decree, and on May 29, 1966, thousands of Easterners residing in the North were massacred by Northern civilians. They looted their property. The Supreme Military Council set up a tribunal to look into the causes of those unprovoked acts of murder and pillage and determine what compensations might be paid to the victims. The Northern emirs declared their intention to pull Northern Nigeria out of the Federation rather than face the tribunal. But the Supreme Military Council justly decided that the tribunal must do its duty.

Then, on July 29, 1966, two months after the May murders and despoliation, and four days before the tribunal was due to commence its sitting, the real pogrom against Eastern Nigerians residing in the Federation began. Major General Aguiyi-Ironsi and his host, Lieutenant Colonel Francis Fajuyi, were kidnapped at Ibadan and murdered. This time Northern soldiers acted in concert with Northern civilians. Defenseless men, women, and children were shot down or hacked to death; some were burned, and some buried alive. Women and young girls were ravished with unprecedented bestiality; unborn children were torn out of the womb of their mothers.

Again, on September 29, 1966, the pogrom was resumed. Thirty thousand Eastern Nigerians are known to have been killed by Northerners. They were killed in the North, in Western Nigeria, in Lagos; some Eastern soldiers in detention at Benin were forcibly removed from prison by Northern soldiers and murdered.

At the time of the incident, millions of Eastern Nigerians resided outside the East, and persons from other parts of the country lived in this region. While Eastern Nigerians who assembled at Northern airports, railway stations, and motor parks were set upon by Northern soldiers and civilians armed with machine

guns, rifles, daggers, and poisoned arrows, the army
and police in the East were specifically instructed to
shoot at sight any Eastern Nigerian found molesting
non-Easterners living in the region. By early October
the sight of mutilated refugees, orphaned children,
widowed mothers, and decapitated corpses of Eastern
Nigerians arriving at our airports and railway stations
inflamed passions to such an extent that it was found
necessary to ask all non-Easterners to leave the region
in their own interest. Since the events of July, 1966,
there has been a mass movement of population in this
country. Nigerian society has undergone a fundamental
change; it is no longer possible for Eastern Nigerians
to live outside their region without fear of loss of life
or of property.

Two facts emerge from the events described above.
The widespread nature of the massacre and its peri-
odicity—May 29, July 29, and September 29—show
first, that they were premeditated and planned, and
second, that Eastern Nigerians are no longer wanted
as equal partners in the Federation of Nigeria. It must
be recalled that this was the fourth in a series of massacres of Eastern Nigerians in the last two decades.

At the early stages of the crisis, the world was told
that it was a conflict between the North and the East.
That pretense collapsed when it became clear that
Northern soldiers moved into Western Nigeria and
Lagos as another step in Northern Nigeria's bid to
continue her so-called conquest to the sea. Belatedly,
it was generally accepted that the fundamental issue
was not a struggle between the East and the North, but
one involving the very existence of Nigeria as one political entity.

Throughout the Nigerian crises, some of the indigenous judges have been found quite unequal to their
calling by reason of their involvement in partisan politics. People soon lost faith in them and would not go
to their courts for redress. In some measure, they were
responsible for the collapse of the rule of law in certain

parts of Nigeria. Providence has spared us in the East from this terrible calamity.

It is now necessary to summarize the attempt of the government and people of Eastern Nigeria to solve the crisis, and the bad faith with which these attempts have been received.

On August 9, 1966, representatives of the military governors meeting in Lagos made decisions for restoring peace and for clearing the way for constitutional talks, notably the decision that troops be all repatriated to their region of origin. These decisions were not fully implemented.

On September 12, the Ad Hoc Constitutional Conference, consisting of delegates representing all the governments of the Federation, met in Lagos and for three weeks sought to discover a form of association best suited to Nigeria, having regard to the prevailing circumstances and their causes, and future possibilities. This conference was unilaterally dismissed by Lieutenant Colonel Gowon, the head of the Lagos government.

It had become then impossible for the Supreme Military Council, the highest governing body in the Federation, to meet on Nigerian soil. As long as Northern troops were in Lagos and the West, no venue could be found acceptable to all the military governors for a meeting of the Supreme Military Council in Nigeria. It met at Aburi in Ghana, January 4–5, 1967, on the basis of an agenda previously determined by the officials of the governments of the country and adopted by the Supreme Military Council. Decisions reached at the meeting were ignored by Lieutenant Colonel Gowon and the North. In the interest of this region and of the whole country, the East stood firmly by those decisions and warned that they would be applied to Eastern Nigeria if steps were not taken by the Lagos government to apply them generally. The East rejected all measures which did not reflect the decisions at Aburi.

The Aburi Accord was not implemented by the

Lagos government. All the meetings of military leaders held since Aburi were held without the East. All the decisions taken by Lagos were taken without comment and concurrence from the East.

It became evident that each time Nigerians came close to a realistic solution to the current crisis by moving toward a loose form of association or confederation, Lieutenant Colonel Gowon unilaterally frustrated their efforts. When the representatives of the military governors decided on August 9, 1966, that troops be repatriated to their regions of origin, and it appeared to him that this would lead to confederation, he unilaterally refused to fully implement that decision. When in September, 1967, the Ad Hoc Constitutional Conference appeared near to agreement on a loose federation, he unilaterally dismissed them indefinitely. When in January, 1967, the military leaders agreed at Aburi on what the federal permanent secretaries correctly interpreted as confederation, he unilaterally rejected the agreement to which he had voluntarily subscribed. When in May, 1967, all the Southern military governors and the Leaders of Thought of their regions spoke out in favor of confederation, he dismissed the Supreme Military Council and proclaimed himself the dictator of Nigeria—an act which, to say the least, is treasonable.

Following the pogrom of 1966, some 2,000,000 Eastern Nigerians have returned from other regions, refugees in their own country. Money was needed to care for them—not to give them mere relief but to rehabilitate them and, in time, restore their outraged feelings. The Lagos government was urged to give the Eastern Nigeria government its share of the statutory revenues. Lieutenant Colonel Gowon refused to do so in the hope that the weight of the burden would lead to the economic collapse of Eastern Nigeria.

Ultimately, and beginning from April 1, 1967, steps were taken to recover what was due to Eastern Nigeria and to enable this region and her people to survive.

These are the Survival Edicts: the Revenue Collection Edict, the Legal Education (Eastern Nigeria) Edict, the Statutory Bodies Edict, and the Court of Appeal Edict.

At each stage during the crisis, in accordance with the democratic and republican spirit of Eastern Nigerians, the people were fully consulted for their advice and guidance.

On August 31, 1966, the first Consultative Assembly and the Advisory Committee of Chiefs and Elders, consisting of four representatives from each administrative division, and other interests were summoned and the facts relating to the crisis put before them. Their advice was as follows:

Be it resolved as follows:

1. We, the representatives of the various communities in Eastern Nigeria gathered in this Consultative Assembly, hereby declare our implicit confidence in the military governor for Eastern Nigeria, Lieutenant Colonel Odumegwu Ojukwu, in all the actions he has so far taken to deal with the situation which has arisen in Nigeria since May 29, 1966.

2. In view of the grave threat to our survival as a unit in the Republic of Nigeria, we hereby urge and empower/advise him to take all such actions that might be necessary to protect the integrity of Eastern Nigeria and the lives and property of its inhabitants.

3. We advise constant consultation by His Excellency with the Consultative Assembly.

4. In view of the gravity of the present situation we affirm complete faith in and urge the need for solidarity of Eastern Nigeria as a unit.

5. In view of the present situation of things no delegates be sent to Lagos for any constitutional talks unless the safety of the delegates is guaranteed.

After the adjournment of the Ad Hoc Constitutional Conference, those bodies, now enlarged to consist of ten representatives from each administrative division in Eastern Nigeria, and other sectors of the community were summoned. The delegates to the Ad Hoc Constitutional Conference placed a full report before them, and by a resolution dated October 7, 1966, the Consultative Assembly and the Advisory Committee of Chiefs and Elders advised as follows:

1. PLACES on record its deep gratitude to the Eastern Nigeria delegation to the Constitutional Conference in Lagos for the diligent and faithful way in which, under conditions of severe strain, tension, and fear, they carried out the mandate given to them by the Consultative Assembly and the Chiefs and Elders of Eastern Nigeria.

2. ENDORSES the stand of the Eastern delegation at the Lagos Constitutional Conference.

3. URGES that as an interim measure, a beginning be made to implement those aspects of the recommendations as relate to the armed forces at least to the extent of returning them to their regions of origin and vesting the operational control of the regional contingents in the respective military governors.

4. REAFFIRMS its acceptance of the report of the Committee on the Pattern of Constitution for Eastern Nigeria within the Federation of Nigeria and the additional suggestions proposed by the Graham-Douglas Constitutional Committee regarding the legislative and executive functions to be devolved upon the provincial units, and urges that the Constitutional Committee should forthwith study the details of the scheme, with particular reference to the number and size of provinces, the distribution of functions between the provinces and the regional government, financial arrangements, and the method and timing of implementation.

5. ENDORSES both the principle of the creation of more states in Nigeria and the statement of the Eastern delegation to the Lagos Constitutional Conference to the effect that the splitting up of the country at this stage is not what is needed to normalize conditions of life in the country and provide a sense of security for its inhabitants, and that immediate constitutional arrangements for the country as a whole should be made on the basis of the existing regions in order to save the country from impending disintegration.

6. SINCE the issue of the creation of more states is a vital

and inevitable item on the agenda of the Lagos Constitutional Conference, RECOMMENDS the following as the conditions upon which the creation of states should proceed:

(a) The basis for the creation of states must be mutually agreed upon beforehand and must be uniformly and consistently applied throughout the country.

(b) The creation of states must take place simultaneously throughout the country.

(c) The creation of any new state must be based upon the consent of the people of the area which is to be included in the proposed state, and where two or more distinct tribal groupings are comprised within such area the wishes of each such grouping must be separately ascertained and respected.

(d) The population, area, and economic resources of any new state which it is proposed to create must be reasonably commensurate to the enormous functions which the states will be expected to perform under the new constitutional arrangements envisaged for Nigeria.

7. IN VIEW OF the fact that the desire on the part of the minority groups for self-determination is the active force behind the demand for the creation of more states, and since in the context of present-day Nigeria minorities are defined by reference to tribe, AFFIRMS its belief that the best hope for a satisfactory solution to the problems of Nigeria lies in the recognition and preservation of the separate identity of the various tribal or linguistic groupings and their right to develop each along its own line and at its own pace; accordingly RECOMMENDS that the creation of states throughout Nigeria should be on the basis of tribal or linguistic groupings or mutual consent between the linguistic groupings.

8. ADVISES that, until the agreements reached by the personal representatives of the military governors on August 8 and 9 are fully implemented, and until immediate compensation is paid by the Federal Military Government for the lives and property of Easterners lost in the disturbed areas of Nigeria, the Eastern Nigeria delegation should no longer participate in future Constitutional Conferences.

9. SATISFIED that the interim report of the Constitutional
Conference has been completely overtaken by the most
recent events in the country, ADVISES that the only possible and logical solution to the problem of political
association for Nigeria lies in the organization and running of common services.

A. IKOKU
Chairman

DATED 7th October, 1966.

On November 23, 1966, they met again to consider
the progress of the crisis. They resolved as follows:

RECALLING the atrocious murders of persons of Eastern
Nigeria origin and other acts of barbarism and inhumanity
committed against us in other parts of Nigeria by fellow
countrymen among whom they lawfully resided;

AWARE of the planned and determined effort to exclude
Eastern Nigeria and the people from the public affairs and
public offices of the Federal Republic of Nigeria;

CONSCIOUS of the attempt made and being made, by the
government and people of Eastern Nigeria, in spite of the
wrongs done to Eastern Nigerians, to promote peace and
salvage what is left of Nigeria and her honor;

DETERMINED to protect and defend the integrity of Eastern Nigeria and the dignity of her people;

CONFIRMING the mandate given by us to our delegates
to the Ad Hoc Constitutional Conference, and our confidence in them, and having noted with regret the indefinite
adjournment of the meeting of the Ad Hoc Constitutional
Conference by Lieutenant Colonel Yakubu Gowon for
alleged inability to agree upon the venue of the meeting as
well as according to him, because of other difficulties which
he has not named;

OBSERVING that, even though the decision to appoint the
Ad Hoc Constitutional Conference was a unanimous agreement of the governments of the Federation, yet the adjournment was made without consultation with or consent by
the Eastern Nigeria government;

HAVING also noted the many acts of bad faith on the part
of the Gowon government and its inability to fulfill promises or implement agreements unanimously reached;

FINDING now that there is a plot hatched up by certain

civil servants and other officials with the active involvement
of Lieutenant Colonel Yakubu Gowon to impose a constitution and certain other measures on Nigeria;

REAFFIRMING the implicit confidence of the people of
Eastern Nigeria in His Excellency, Lieutenant Colonel
Odumegwu Ojukwu, and assuring him of the solidarity of
Eastern Nigeria and their support and admiration for the
way he has handled the present crisis facing Nigeria;

ALSO ASSURING HIS EXCELLENCY of the admiration of the
people of Eastern Nigeria in the military government of
Eastern Nigeria and their desire for its continued administration until it has achieved its objective of creating a new
society in Eastern Nigeria;

WE DO HEREBY RESOLVE that our military governor be
advised as follows:

(1) To take any measures he considers appropriate for
the defense and protection of the integrity of Eastern Nigeria, the lives and property of its inhabitants.

(2) To maintain utmost vigilance against subversion of
the government of Eastern Nigeria not only from
outside the region, but also from within and to deal
ruthlessly with anybody, high or low, engaged in
subversion.

(3) To resist the imposition on the people of Eastern
Nigeria of any constitutional, administrative, or legislative measures taken without prior consultation
and agreement.

(4) To reject any solution which will undermine the
economic and industrial progress and prosperity of
Eastern Nigeria or which will tend to sow the seeds
of future friction among the regions of this country.

(5) To continue with the good progress made so far in
the rehabilitation of refugees.

(6) To speed up the implementation of provincial administration with legislative and executive powers,
and the reestablishment of customary courts.

(7) To spare no efforts at the right time to purge former
holders of public offices of corrupt practices so as
to set a shining example for the youths of this region, and inculcate into the people the spirit of
honesty, integrity, fair play, mutual trust, and a
feeling of oneness which will provide the basis for
our future progress.

(8) To continue Your Excellency's efforts to bring about
     a meeting of military leaders and the reconvening
     of the Ad Hoc Constitutional Conference under
     conditions of adequate security satisfactory to Your
     Excellency.

(9) To ensure that only men and women of integrity
     and merit are appointed to public offices in the re-
     gion and that a code of conduct for public officers
     be drawn up for Eastern Nigeria.

LASTLY, we assure Your Excellency that no Eastern Nigerian, whether living inside or outside this region, has the
mandate or support of the people of this region to speak
for or represent them UNLESS appointed with the recommendation and approval of Your Excellency acting on behalf of Eastern Nigeria.

A. IKOKU
Chairman

Eastern Nigeria Consultative Assembly Meeting
Dated 23 November, 1966.

Since that date, matters became worse; sanctions
were imposed on Eastern Nigeria; warlike preparations
were made against her; her isolation was complete.
Men and women in the region, incensed by the treatment meted out to them by an unrepentant Lagos and
the North, called for the declaration of Eastern Nigeria
as a sovereign independent state.

In these circumstances, the joint meeting of the
Consultative Assembly and the Advisory Committee of
Chiefs and Elders was reconvened for a clear statement on the future course of action. After an appraisal
of the developments in the Nigerian crises past and
present had been presented to the joint session, a telegram just received from the Lagos government was
read. The full text is as follows:

FURTHER MY TELEX OF TWENTIETH MAY X I HAVE JUST
RECEIVED YOUR LETTER PG/0897/11 OF MAY 16, 1967 X AS
YOU ARE AWARE ECONOMIC MEASURES COMPLAINED OF
WERE LIFTED IN RESPONSE TO RECOMMENDATIONS OF
NATIONAL CONCILIATION COMMITTEE WITH EFFECT FROM
MAY 23 X THEREFORE DEEPLY DISAPPOINTED THAT YOU

HAVE NOT RESPONDED POSITIVELY X IT IS NOT TOO LATE
TO COMMENCE MEASURES TO RESOLVE CRISIS WITHOUT
BLOODSHED AND KEEP THE COUNTRY TOGETHER X

IT IS DESIRABLE YOU DECLARE YOUR AGREEMENT WITH
POLITICAL AND ADMINISTRATIVE PROGRAM RECENTLY PRO-
CLAIMED BY THE SUPREME MILITARY COUNCIL X THIS YOU
WILL RECALL REQUIRES THE URGENT CREATION OF STATES
SIMULTANEOUSLY ALL OVER THE COUNTRY TO REMOVE
THREAT OF DOMINATION, PREPARATION OF NEW CONSTITU-
TION ON THEIR BASIS X NEW CONSTITUTION CAN PROVIDE
ALL SAFEGUARDS CONSIDERED NECESSARY FOR STATES
GOVERNMENTS X ALSO PROGRAM ENVISAGES IMMEDIATE
APPOINTMENT OF A REVENUE ALLOCATION COMMISSION TO
FIND NEW FORMULA ON BASIS OF PRINCIPLE OF DERIVA-
TION AND NEED TO PROVIDE ADEQUATE FUNDS FOR ESSEN-
TIAL CENTRAL GOVERNMENT FUNCTIONS X PROGRAM WILL
ENSURE FAIR PLAY AND JUSTICE FOR ALL SECTIONS OF THE
COUNTRY X

THEREFORE I EARNESTLY APPEAL TO YOU TO COOPERATE
TO ARREST FURTHER DRIFT INTO DISINTEGRATION X ON
THE BASIS OF THE FOREGOING REPRESENTATIVES OF ALL
GOVERNMENTS CAN MEET WITHOUT FURTHER DELAY TO
PLAN FOR SMOOTH IMPLEMENTATION OF THE POLITICAL
AND ADMINISTRATIVE PROGRAM ADOPTED BY ALL YOUR
COLLEAGUES OF THE SUPREME MILITARY COUNCIL X

MOST IMMEDIATE

On the evening of Saturday, May 27, 1967, the joint
session of the enlarged Consultative Assembly and the
Advisory Committee of Chiefs and Elders, after full
deliberation, passed a resolution the text of which is
as follows:

WE, THE Chiefs, Elders, and Representatives of Eastern
Nigeria, gathered at this Joint Meeting of the Advisory
Committee of Chiefs and Elders and the Consultative As-
sembly, do solemnly declare as follows:

WHEREAS we have been in the vanguard of the national
movement for the building of a strong, united, and prosperous Nigeria where no man will be oppressed and have
devoted our efforts, talents, and resources to this end;

WHEREAS we cherish certain inalienable human rights
and state obligations such as the right to life, liberty, and

pursuit of happiness; the right to acquire, possess, and defend property; the provision of security; and the establishment of good and just government based on the consent of the governed;

WHEREAS in practical demonstration of these beliefs, our people settled in other parts of Nigeria, served their country in many capacities, and contributed immensely to the growth and development of Nigeria;

WHEREAS WE ARE LIVING WITNESSES OF INJUSTICES AND ATROCITIES COMMITTED against Eastern Nigeria, among which are the premeditated murder of over 30,000 of our innocent men, women, and children by Northern Nigerians, the calculated destruction of the property of our sons and daughters, the shameless conversion of 2,000,000 Eastern Nigerians into refugees in their own country, all this without remorse;

WHEREAS in consequence of these and other acts of discrimination and injustice, we have painfully realized that the Federation of Nigeria has failed, and has given us no protection;

WHEREAS in spite of these facts, the government and people of Eastern Nigeria have persisted in their efforts to find a practical and just solution that would preserve the continued existence of Nigeria as one corporate unit and restore peace and confidence as demonstrated by the initiative of our military governor in getting all the military leaders together at Aburi, Ghana;

WHEREAS the hopes which the Aburi Agreement engendered have proved to be misplaced and have been destroyed by a series of acts of bad faith and distortions and finally by a refusal on the part of the "Lagos Government" to implement these and other agreements notwithstanding the fact that they were freely and voluntarily entered into;

WHEREAS the Federation of Nigeria has forfeited any claim to our allegiance by these acts and by the economic, political, and diplomatic sanctions imposed against us by the so-called Federal Government;

AND WHEREAS the object of government is the good of the governed and the will of the people its ultimate sanction;

NOW, THEREFORE, in consideration of these and other facts and injustices, we, the Chiefs, Elders, and Representatives of all the twenty provinces of Eastern Nigeria, assembled in this Joint Meeting of the Advisory Committee of Chiefs and Elders and the Consultative Assembly, at Enugu this 27th day of May, 1967, hereby solemnly:

(a) MANDATE His Excellency Lieutenant Colonel Chukwuemeka Odumegwu Ojukwu, Military Governor of Eastern Nigeria, to declare at the earliest practicable date Eastern Nigeria a free, sovereign, and independent state by the name and title of the REPUBLIC OF BIAFRA.

(b) RESOLVE that the new REPUBLIC OF BIAFRA shall have the full and absolute powers of a sovereign state, and shall establish commerce, levy war, conclude peace, enter into diplomatic relations, and carry out, as of right, other sovereign responsibilities.

(c) DIRECT that the REPUBLIC OF BIAFRA may enter into arrangement with any sovereign unit or units in what remains of Nigeria or in any part of Africa desirous of association with us for the purpose of running a common services organization and for the establishment of economic ties.

(d) RECOMMEND that the REPUBLIC OF BIAFRA should become a member of the Commonwealth of Nations, the Organization of African Unity, and the United Nations Organization.

(e) RECOMMEND the adoption of a federal constitution based on the new provincial units.

(f) REAFFIRM His Excellency's assurance of protection for the persons, properties, and businesses of foreign nationals in our territory.

(g) DECLARE our unqualified confidence in the Military Governor of Eastern Nigeria, Lieutenant Colonel Chukwuemeka Odumegwu Ojukwu, and assure him of our unreserved support for the way and manner he has handled the crisis in the country.

So help us God.

THE DECLARATION

Fellow countrymen and women, YOU, the people of Eastern Nigeria:

CONSCIOUS of the supreme authority of Almighty God over all mankind, of your duty to yourselves and posterity;

AWARE that you can no longer be protected in your lives and in your property by any government based outside Eastern Nigeria;

BELIEVING that you are born free and have certain inalienable rights which can best be preserved by yourselves;

UNWILLING to be unfree partners in any association of a political or economic nature;

REJECTING the authority of any person or persons other than the Military Government of Eastern Nigeria to make any imposition of whatever kind or nature upon you;

DETERMINED to dissolve all political and other ties between you and the former Federal Republic of Nigeria;

PREPARED to enter into such association, treaty or alliance with any sovereign state within the former Federal Republic of Nigeria and elsewhere on such terms and conditions as best to subserve your common good;

AFFIRMING your trust and confidence in ME;

HAVING mandated ME to proclaim on your behalf, and in your name, that Eastern Nigeria be a sovereign independent Republic, NOW THEREFORE I, LIEUTENANT COLONEL CHUKWUEMEKA ODUMEGWU OJUKWU, MILITARY GOVERNOR OF EASTERN NIGERIA, BY VIRTUE OF THE AUTHORITY, AND PURSUANT TO THE PRINCIPLES, RECITED ABOVE, DO HEREBY SOLEMNLY PROCLAIM THAT THE TERRITORY AND REGION KNOWN AS AND CALLED EASTERN NIGERIA TOGETHER WITH HER CONTINENTAL SHELF AND TERRITORIAL WATERS SHALL HENCEFORTH BE AN INDEPENDENT SOVEREIGN STATE OF THE NAME AND TITLE OF "THE REPUBLIC OF BIAFRA." AND I DO DECLARE THAT:

> (i) all political ties between us and the Federal Republic of Nigeria are hereby totally dissolved;

(ii) all subsisting contractual obligations entered into by the Government of the Federal Republic of Nigeria or by any person, authority, organization, or government acting on its behalf, with any person, authority, or organization, or relating to any matter or thing, within the Republic of Biafra, shall henceforth be deemed to be entered into with the Military Governor of the Republic of Biafra for and on behalf of the Government and people of the Republic of Biafra, and the covenants thereof shall, subject to this Declaration, be performed by the parties according to their tenor;

(iii) all subsisting international treaties and obligations made on behalf of Eastern Nigeria by the Government of the Federal Republic of Nigeria shall be honored and respected;

(iv) Eastern Nigeria's due share of all subsisting international debts and obligations entered into by the Government of the Federal Republic of Nigeria on behalf of the Federation of Nigeria shall be honored and respected;

(v) steps will be taken to open discussions on the question of Eastern Nigeria's due share of the assets of the Federation of Nigeria and personal properties of the citizens of Biafra throughout the Federation of Nigeria;

(vi) the rights, privileges, pensions, etc., of all personnel of the Public Services, the Armed Forces, and the Police now serving in any capacity within the Republic of Biafra are hereby guaranteed;

(vii) we shall keep the door open for association with, and would welcome, any sovereign unit or units in the former Federation of Nigeria or in any other parts of Africa desirous of association with us for the purposes of running a common services organization and for the establishment of economic ties;

(viii) we shall protect the lives and property of all foreigners residing in Biafra; we shall extend the hand of friendship to those nations who respect our sovereignty, and shall repel any interference in our internal affairs;

(ix) we shall faithfully adhere to the Charter of the Organization of African Unity and of the United Nations Organization;

(x) it is our intention to remain a member of the British Commonwealth of Nations in our right as a sovereign independent nation.

LONG LIVE THE REPUBLIC OF BIAFRA!

AND MAY GOD PROTECT ALL WHO LIVE IN HER.

III
Harvest of Arms

In the early hours of July 6, 1969, Nigerian hordes crossed Biafran boundaries and invaded Biafra in three different points from the North. The Nigerian war slogan, blared in Hausa over the Nigerian radio network, was:

> Mu je Mu Kerkeshe Su,
> Tu Tatara Kayan Su,
> Mu Ber Su Suna Kukan Banza.

English translation:

> We go, we slaughter them,
> We ravish their precious wares,
> We abandon them crying useless tears.

Those who take seriously Gowon's glib protestations about Nigerian unity, or fighting "to keep Nigeria one," need to look at that slogan again in order to discover the true intentions of Gowon. Gowon and his Northern masters are not fighting to keep Nigeria one. Nigerian unity remains an abomination for them. The current fighting is simply an attempt to complete the Gowon coup d'etat by the continuation of the pogroms of 1966. It is a fulfillment of the long-cherished Fulani ambition to carry their conquest to the sea. The war began as a confrontation of the North with Biafra. All the soldiers who invaded our territory were soldiers of Northern Nigerian origin. The Yorubas openly declared that they would have nothing to do with the war. For that reason, no Yoruba soldier took part until later in the

war when, with defeat staring Gowon in the face, the
Yorubas were cajoled into entering the conflict.

Relying on the fact that Biafra was without arms
while he could count on the whole Nigerian arsenal
built up over the years, Gowon and his British planners
calculated that Biafra would be crushed within forty-
eight hours. The rest of the story and the "accuracy" of
that calculation are well known to the world.

They left a vital and an indestructible factor out of
their calculations—the will and the determination of the
Biafran people to survive. Every man, woman, and
child shared in that determination and will to survive;
and it is on these twin rocks that Nigerian military ambitions are bound to founder.

Within a few weeks of the war, our troops were in
control of the Midwest. Our motive was not territorial
ambition or the desire of conquest. We went into the
Midwest (later declared the Republic of Benin) purely
in an effort to seize the serpent by the head; every
other activity in that Republic was subordinated to
that single aim. We were going to Lagos to seize the
villain Gowon, and we took necessary military precau-
tions. To Gowon and his junta this was a clear sign of
defeat, as indeed it was. Panic gripped Lagos. Valuable
assets were evacuated from Lagos to the North. These
included bullions in the central bank. Gowon concluded
arrangements to flee and actually moved his personal
effects to the Ikeja airport.

Once again the British government and the Johnson
administration of America decided to intervene. Britain
and America advised Gowon against leaving Lagos. The
British government backed the advice with promises of
military supplies. Russia, sensing trouble, reacted in her
traditional manner and staked her claim to the debris.
The Johnson administration confined itself to diplomatic support. Military personnel from the Chad Republic and Egyptian pilots for the Russian jet planes,
British jet provosts from Sudan, arrived on the scene.
The war that had virtually come to an end acquired a

new lease of life. These points are important in order to know those who are really responsible for the prolongation of the conflict to this day, with all the human losses and sufferings entailed.

From that time on, the war became one of total commitment for the British government on the Nigerian side. Behind the position of the British government is Harold Wilson's contempt for African lives and the gigantic financial interests of Shell BP and big British commercial firms.

It is said that in international diplomacy, hypocrisy is the tribute which vice pays to virtue. British diplomacy in particular has traditionally prided itself on its dubious tools of duplicity, cunning, and perfidy. In this matter of Biafra, the British government under Harold Wilson shamelessly displayed at every turn its expertise in this ignoble art.

By the beginning of April, 1968, the truth about Biafra and the genocide being perpetrated by Nigerians was filtering in increasing volume to the outside world. The world was shocked. On the humanitarian side, various governments and relief organizations resolved that if they could not stop genocide, they could at least try to delay its completion by supplying relief materials to Biafrans. These organizations bravely scaled Anglo-Nigerian-created hurdles, ran the gauntlet of antiaircraft fire, and began the hazardous nightly airlifts of food into Biafra. First in France, then all over Western Europe and in the United States, Save Biafran People relief campaigns gathered momentum. When Britain's insistence that all relief materials should be channeled through Lagos failed, and Lagos' attempts to intercept relief planes were foiled, the Lagos mutinous regime resorted to obstructions on the ground. In Awgu, Nigerian troops commandeered Red Cross vehicles for military use. In Port Harcourt, the Nigerian commander not only banned all relief operations but also commandeered aircraft of the International Red Cross for military purposes. These cruel developments did not deter the relief workers. The moral conscience of humanity had been aroused.

Farsighted political statesmen realized that humanitarian relief was nothing but a palliative. It could not cure the carnage and devastation of war. The cure lay in cessation of hostilities. If both sides could lay down arms and go to the negotiating table, peace could be negotiated. Nigeria was not interested in peaceful negotiations. The British government and Nigeria adopted the policy of "quick kill."

More courageous statesmen took a more positive step. They realized that the only action which could impress an aggressor so lavishly armed and bent on military conquest was political recognition of Biafra. Within a period of six weeks, four African countries—Tanzania, Gabon, Ivory Coast, and Zambia—recognized the Republic of Biafra. They have since been joined by Haiti.

The recognitions achieved instant results. Britain and Nigeria suddenly agreed to peace talks. The mood of Africa and the world was such that Britain feared that more countries would immediately follow the realistic examples of the four African countries. Still more disconcerting to Britain was the increasing sympathy even beyond Africa for the rights of our people to self-determination. In the Scandinavian countries, workers and students staged protest demonstrations against the massacre of Biafrans. In Switzerland, the Action Pro-Biafra Committee was launched. In the United States, the Friends of Biafra Association emerged. In Britain, the press became more critical of Harold Wilson's militarism, and Parliamentary opposition against the government's policy grew louder. The highlight of increasing world sympathy was the declaration by the French government that it endorsed the principle of Biafra's right to self-determination.

"Peace" conferences have been held in Kampala, Niamey, Addis Ababa, and Monrovia. The Anglo-Nigerian attitude and tactics at these conferences have been the same. Three can be mentioned: (a) dilatory tactics —to delay the beginning of talks or, when the talks began, to prolong them as long as possible with irrelevancies; (b) carefully planned offers of terms which sought to reduce the peace talks to a surrender parley between a conqueror and the conquered; (c) diplomatic, economic, and military threats to certain member states of the OAU who show sympathy and understanding to the Biafran cause.

All the talks failed and will ever fail as long as both Gowon and Harold Wilson remain convinced that a military solution is both possible and desirable.

Diary of Events: May 31–June 30, 1967

May 31: Exodus of Biafrans from Nigeria back to their homeland. . . . Mammoth crowds gather on premises of Biafra Military Headquarters, volunteering to fight with the armed forces if Nigeria declares a war on Biafra. . . . Government of the Republic of Biafra designates Port Harcourt, Calabar, Degema, and Bonny as customs ports and calls on all ships bound for these ports to continue to use them. . . . Steep rise in people's donations to the Civil Defense Fund. By end of day, donations total £1.02 million. . . . Military governor of the North, Lieutenant Colonel Usman Hassan Katsina, orders immediate, total mobilization of all able-bodied youths in the North, adding that compulsory military service cannot be ruled out for Northerners. He boasts that Biafra will be overrun in "a matter of hours." . . . Gowon further tightens his ban on all foreign exchange transactions involving the government, corporate bodies, and individuals of the Republic of Biafra. He suspends public telecommunication services and postal services with Biafra. . . . British-owned Conference Lines requests its associates and other shipping companies to avoid Biafran ports.

June 2:   Abdul Attah, Permanent Secretary in the Federal Ministry of Finance, writes to Mallam Ahmed Tallib, Permanent Secretary, Northern Nigeria Ministry of Finance, explaining to him that for the economic interests of Northern Nigeria, "the East should not be allowed to secede." . . . Biafra cargoes in Apapa Wharf are confiscated by Lagos regime.

June 3:   Biafran government proclaims the Republic as a disturbed area under the Law and Order (Maintenance) Decree, 1967, and orders the total mobilization of the resources and people of Biafra. . . . Lagos regime begins to use its British-loaned "navy" to intercept oil tankers proceeding to the oil terminal of Bonny in Biafra.

June 6:   Two governing councils, the Armed Forces Council and the Executive Council, are set up in Biafra.

June 7:   The secretary of the Biafran Students Union writes to Chief of Staff, stating that all the students have resolutely declared their intention to join the National Freedom Defense Front.

June 8:   Biafran government announces to expatriates in Biafra that their visas can be extended.

June 18:   Lieutenant Colonel David Ejoor, military governor of the Midwest, addressing the people at Asaba, Midwest Nigeria, says that he will not live to see Midwestern Region turned into a battlefield.

June 26:   Dusk-to-dawn curfew is imposed on Ibadan following what is described as the discovery of explosives at the outskirts of the town. The government, unwilling to admit rising popular indignation against Northern occupation troops, blames the tension on resident Biafrans. Mass arrests.

June 29:   Biafran government informs oil companies that Revenue Collection Decree No. 2 applies to all companies of whatever description.

June 30: Massing of Nigerian troops (eight battalions) on Northern borders of Biafra.

The Zero Hour

(Broadcast, June 30, 1967)

It is a month today since we took the irrevocable decision to assert our autonomy and sovereignty by becoming the Republic of Biafra.

Gowon's immediate reaction to our decision was to vow to crush us. Since then, he has consistently described his decision as irrevocable. I have conclusive evidence that he and his Northern bandits have now finalized their plans to attack us in our home. They have taken all this time to prepare and accumulate arms.

For about four weeks, ships on the high seas bound for Biafran ports have been scared away by the Nigerian government led by Gowon.

As a young nation we have respected international law and conventions which guarantee the freedom of ships of all nations on the high seas in time of peace. Gowon has flouted those international conventions. While we should continue to uphold them, we must in the interest of survival do everything to keep our ports open.

We shall hold ourselves ready to exercise our right to self-preservation and of hot pursuit.

Yesterday, Gowon published and distributed a code of conduct for war: yesterday, he and his gangster Cabinet decided that the time had come to launch the long-awaited attack on Biafra; yesterday Gowon began troop movements to complete his concentration menacing our borders.

Furthermore, he has openly incited certain sections

of this Republic to insurrection and has tried to subvert the loyalty of the police of this Republic.

It is reliably learned that he has continued to negotiate for the passage of his troops through a neighboring country.

I wish to take this opportunity to make it crystal clear that any territory through which Gowon's troops pass shall be considered enemy territory.

Fellow countrymen and women, we have arrived at the zero hour. Gowon is determined to come into our homes and destroy us in order to carry away what belongs to us.

His psychological warfare of lying propaganda, calculated to create alarm, frighten our people, and cause dissension among us, has failed completely.

Gowon feels that he must play the man and carry out his suicidal threats to launch a physical attack on us.

I want you all to remain calm and determined, as you have always been.

Our soldiers are ready. While they will be fighting, our civil defense organizations, men, women, and children, must guard our homes.

If Gowon should make the mistake of crossing into our territory, even by a few yards, we shall immediately go into an open, outright, and total war against Nigeria.

Our conduct of the war will not be confined to our territorial boundaries. We shall take the opportunity to ensure that they do not repeat their adventure ever again.

This will be an opportunity for us to do honor to the memory of the thousands of our kith and kin savagely murdered last year by avenging their death.

If this is what the world wants in order to be convinced that we are determined to keep our sovereignty we now eagerly await the opportunity of giving that proof.

We shall not be blamed for the consequences of what is now imminent. Fellow countrymen, proud and courageous Biafrans, this is your moment.

When we go to war, it will be a war against Nigeria, for it is Nigeria that has vowed that we shall not exist.

With God on our side, we shall vanquish.

Long live the Republic of Biafra.

Diary of Events: July 1—October 15, 1967

July 1: Lieutenant Colonel Gowon prohibits people in Nigeria from tuning to Radio Biafra. Already 500 people have been detained by the Lagos regime.

July 2: In Western Nigeria the military governor, Colonel Adebayo, warns against demonstrations in favor of Central Yoruba State and other public issues. . . . Two bomb blasts in the Lagos areas of Obalande, Yaba, and Ebute-Metta by Yoruba dissidents. Six casualties.

July 3: In Umuahia, Aba, Abakaliki, Owerri, Enugu, and other major towns, the people of Biafra rename with Biafran names streets and lanes that bore Nigerian names.

July 5: A new decree changing the name of the Biafran state-owned university at Nsukka from University of Nigeria to University of Biafra.

July 6: Nigerians invade Biafra from three points in Biafra's northern border.

July 7: Lagos allows a British Royal Air Force Argosy aircraft to land in Kano.

July 8: Alhaji Kam Selem, Nigeria's Inspector-General of Police, issues a top secret memorandum entitled "Yoruba nationalism, the final solution," a blueprint which calls for mass arrest of Yoruba leaders

suspected of aiding Yoruba freedom fighters and recommends the immediate recruitment of more Northern
Nigerians into the police force.

July 11:   A spokesman of the United States State
Department announces in Washington that his government has indicated to Lieutenant Colonel Gowon, who
has requested American aid to deal "with the challenge
of his authority represented by Biafra," that America
considers the Nigeria-Biafra conflict an internal problem. The spokesman adds that the United States has not
provided Nigeria with military aid since 1964 and has
no intention of doing so.

July 18:   Tension still high in Lagos and Western
Region against Northern occupation troops. Bomb
blasts in Yaba.

July 19:   I hold a press conference and introduce to
foreign press five Biafran Army officers, claimed by
Gowon to have been killed on July 17, 1967. . . . Second
bomb explosion in Lagos, killing about ten and injuring
many.

July 20:   Nigerian troops enter Ogoja.

July 21:   First picture of the corpse of a white mercenary serving in the Nigerian army appears on the
front page of Biafra newspapers.

July 25:   Nigeria's invasion of Bonny with Shell BP
and U.A.C. [British company] vessels. . . . Biafra Air
Force destroys four enemy vessels which attack Bonny
oil installations. . . . Efik community in Aba declares
that minority problem is dead in Biafra. The declaration continues: "We are Biafrans and will always, both
by word and by deed, identify ourselves with the Republic of Biafra. We are equally committed to the survival of our country.

July 29:   Nigerian government sends emissaries to
Russia to sign already concluded deals for military aid
in the guise of "cultural agreement."

August 1:   Shell BP is ordered by Biafran government to stop operations following the company's failure

to pay Biafra the oil royalties due her on July 1, 1967.

August 2:   Biafra security unearths a plot for industrial unrest hatched by some British firms operating in Biafra.

August 5:   Nigerian troops start amassing troops and stockpiling large quantities of arms in the Midwest in preparation for an attack on Biafra.

August 6:   I publicly warn the Midwest government about the consequences of making Midwest a battleground and remind the military governor of his pledges to the people to keep the region neutral. . . . Biafran government sets up the Petroleum Management Committee to manage the assets of Shell BP.

August 8:   Nigerian government forges a document which it presents to the foreign press as a photostat of a document purported to show that Biafra has sold her oil concessions to France. . . . Biafra military intelligence confirms that Nigerian invasion of Biafra through Midwest will take place any time from now.

August 9:   In a quick countermove, Biafran forces take Nigeria's Midwest region.

August 10:   British High Commissioner in Benin, Mr. Bell, pays a secret visit to Brigadier Banjo, commander of the Biafran forces in the Midwest. . . . Biafra Ministry of External Affairs lodges formal protest with the Head of the British Mission in Enugu, Mr. J. R. W. Parker, against British Government's intervention in the conflict. . . . Banjo begins to make contacts and plan a coup against my government with British High Commissioner in Lagos, Sir David Hunt, through the British Deputy High Commissioner in Benin, Mr. Bell.

August 12:   Nigerian air raids on civilians begin with bombing of Enugu.

August 13:   Biafran forces capture three key towns in Northern Nigeria—Okene, Atanai, and Iloshi—located beyond the north border of Midwest Nigeria.

August 14:   Biafran homemade rocket is launched.

August 16:   Three international airlines based in

London—Caledonia Airways, British United Airways, and Transglobe—give notice of their intention not to carry further arms to Nigeria.

August 18:   Closure of Kano airport to civil flights and conversion of the airport to Russian military base. . . . Fleet of Russian Ilyushin air freighters arrive in Kano, containing a shipment of MIG-17 and MIG-15 jet fighters, with pilots, technicians, maintenance engineers, and military "advisers."

August 20:   Biafran forces in Midwest capture Ore —a town inside Western Region of Nigeria. . . . Biafran government offers peaceful settlement and publishes proposals for a basis of future relations between Nigeria and Biafra—"The Case for Biafra."

August 21:   The State Department in Washington warns on ideological dangers of Soviet military aid to Nigeria. . . . Biafrans capture five more towns beyond Midwest—Okitipupa, Atotogbo, Irele, Ute, and Sobe.

August 27:   I cable OAU and declare Biafra is ready to present its case before the next month's conference of the organization in Kinshasa.

August 28:   I announce to international press that although the war initiative is now in our hands, Biafra is prepared to cease hostilities immediately and negotiate with Nigeria.

August 30:   Biafran forces make further advances toward Lagos. Gowon plans to transfer his headquarters to Zaria as "a temporary measure." This is disclosed by Gowon to his Cabinet meeting. . . . More than 5,000 Aba women demonstrate against the role of Britain and Russia in the war.

September 2:   Biafran forces destroy two Nigerian war planes—one an L-29 jet fighter serial No. NAF.401 and the other a Piaggio—in Nsukka and Port Harcourt respectively.

September 5:   Dr. Akanu Ibiam, my adviser, renounces his British knighthood.

September 6:   Two enemy planes which are preparing to raid Biafra are destroyed on the ground at Makurdi airport by Biafran air force.

September 7: Thirty-seven eminent Biafrans renounce their British colonial honors.

September 10: Chief Awolowo, leader of the Nigerian delegation to OAU meeting in Kinshasa, leaves Lagos for Congo. He tells the press that before the end of the meeting Biafra will be crushed and the Biafran government will be overthrown.

September 11: OAU Summit opens in Kinshasa. Biafra's case is presented by delegation led by Dr. M. I. Okpara, the last Premier of former Eastern Nigeria and my political adviser.

September 13: Normal postal, telephone and telegraphic services between Biafra and Midwest are resumed. . . . OAU summit appoints a Consultative Committee under the chairmanship of Emperor Haile Selassie of Ethiopia to mediate between Nigeria and Biafra. . . . The summit also passes a resolution ordering that mercenaries be cleared from the continent. The summit ends.

September 15: Encirclement of Nigerian troops in Nsukka by Biafran forces.

September 17: Radio Togo warns Togolese against offering accommodation to more than 20,000 Nigerian refugees who arrived in Togo.

September 20: Declaration of the Republic of Benin by Major A. Okonkwo. . . . Liberation army under the order of Brigadier Banjo withdraws to Agbor from Benin, a distance of forty miles. . . . Fall of Benin to the Nigerian army.

September 21: "Kinshasa Special"—a coup to overthrow the Biafran Government—is uncovered. . . . Lieutenant Colonel E. M. Ifeajuna, one of the leaders of the coup, is apprehended while he is coming out of the premises of the British High Commission. . . . Security discovers in the flat of Brigadier Banjo, leader of the coup, thousands of Nigerian pounds given to him by the

British High Commission. . . . Security discovers that British-paid saboteurs have been indoctrinating our troops in their trenches against the cause of Biafra. Agents have also been infiltrated into Enugu for sabotage.

September 22:   I make a broadcast to the nation informing them of the fall of Benin through the deliberate withdrawal of our troops by the coup plotters.

September 23:   Court-martial of the four ringleaders of the coup.

September 26:   Mortaring of Enugu by British-financed agents begins. Fall of Nsukka and Opi.

September 27:   Biafran Security discovers that BBC and NBC (Nigerian Broadcasting Corporation) use certain names of towns as code words for British agents in Biafra.

October 1–3:   Fall of the Midwest. Massacre of more than 1,000 Ibos in Asaba by Nigerian troops. Enemy advance to 9-mile corner near Enugu.

October 6:   First invasion of Onitsha across River Niger by Nigeria with John Holt and U.A.C. vessels.

October 10:   Enemy enters Enugu. Fierce resistance by Biafran troops and people. . . . Onitsha invasion is repulsed. More than 2,000 Nigerian soldiers killed. Enemy burns down Onitsha £1,000,000 market before retreat.

October 11:   Seventh Session of the joint meeting of the Council of Elders and Chiefs and the Consultative Assembly at Umuahia.

October 15:   I address under-officers of the Biafra army at their passing-out parade and invite critical questions on wide range of subjects including international affairs and politics.*

* Every three Sundays, since October 15, 1967, I have always conducted the exercise.

A Coup by Britain-Nigeria

(Address to joint session of the Advisory Council of Chiefs and Elders and the Consultative Assembly, October 11, 1967)

Our very existence is being threatened by both external and internal foes. Of the two the latter is the more dangerous because they are within and around us.

At your last meeting, I gave you an up-to-date account of our struggle with Nigeria. After two days of deliberations, during which you considered all the facts before you, together with the implications and consequences of different alternatives open to us, you passed a number of resolutions and gave me a mandate.

The resolutions and mandate, clear and unequivocal, were arrived at without a dissident voice. The mandate was a clear one by the people to guide me in my dealings, on behalf of our people, with the rest of Nigeria of which we were then a part.

In my position as your servant and leader, I intended to use your resolutions and the mandate as a basis for bargaining with our opponents. I still believed, even at that time, that there was room for negotiations which could lead to a peaceful and amicable settlement of the problems then besetting Nigeria.

I held that belief, in spite of that iniquitous telegram of threat and blackmail which came through from Lagos while I was still addressing you at that meeting of May 26, 1967. The text of that telegram was read to you in full.

A number of you will recall my discussions with you and my intention to make further efforts toward a settlement by negotiation. But alas, while these consultations were still going on, and before I had actually received and studied your resolutions and mandate, Gowon promulgated his arbitrary, dictatorial, and tendentious decree on the creation of states, dismissed the Supreme Military Council, and declared a state of emergency all over the country.

The declaration of a state of emergency had two aims: to give Gowon cover to attack us by force and to stifle the aspirations of other parts of Southern Nigeria who were fast coming to our position and point of view.

It became clear that Gowon's unflinching aim was to push us out of the then Nigerian Federation. The arbitrary creation of states had been the last trump card toward this end; and was a direct infringement of even his much-vaunted Decree No. 8, which purported to guarantee the territorial integrity of the then existing regions of the Nigerian Federation.

We had repeatedly stated that our aim was to save the then Nigerian Federation in a realistic form and that we would be forced to leave that ill-fated Federation if Gowon and his clique did certain things, to wit: attack us economically and militarily or threaten our territorial integrity. By the time this august assembly met on May 26, Gowon had already imposed an economic blockade against the government of the then Eastern Nigeria and was openly making warlike preparations to attack us by force. By his high-handed and arbitrary action of May 27, I had no alternative but to carry out your mandate and declare our sovereignty on May 30, to universal relief, approbation, and jubilation right through the length and breadth of this young Republic.

In our declaration of sovereignty, we made it quite clear that we wished to remain friends with what remained of Nigeria. We kept the door open for mutual cooperation and even went further to guarantee whatever might be our own share of debts incurred by Nigeria while we were still a part of it. What more could we have done to show our good faith and continued affection for our former partners of the defunct Nigerian Federation?

Gowon and his Northern clique would not leave us to manage our own affairs in an atmosphere of peace, freedom, and equality. Nothing short of our complete subjugation to the North, or extermination by it, would satisfy Gowon, who openly vowed to use the military might of Nigeria, a might built over many years with our common resources, to destroy us. To buttress his iniquitous intentions, he set up a puppet government of ex-politicians well known for their antagonism against us. Included in his puppet government were a number of renegades from among us.

The members of that puppet government not only endorsed Gowon's evil plans against us but also gave him open support. All of them severally traveled overseas to purchase arms and hire mercenaries for the sole purpose of destroying us. For our part, we left no one in doubt of our intention to fight, and die if necessary, for our freedom and fatherland rather than allow ourselves to be enslaved or made second-class citizens by the Hausa-Fulani hegemony.

Meanwhile our people still resident in Lagos were subjected to increasing and humiliating molestations. They were asked to register as aliens and to go about with passes like slaves. Here we see another form of Gowon's tact. He singled out the Ibos of Biafra for these treatments not because he liked other citizens of Biafra but as a subtle means of furthering his determined plan to cause dissension among our people by pretending that there were people in this Republic who could be treated differently. In this, Gowon typically underrated the intelligence of our people, who could not so soon forget that the Northerners never differentiated between members of ethnic groups in this Republic in their pogrom of 1966.

On July 6, Gowon's hordes invaded the Republic of Biafra at three different points, two in the Ogoja front and one in the Nsukka sector. Because of the long and careful preparation by Lagos, and the superiority of the enemy in arms and numbers, Gowon and his clique planned to overrun this Republic within forty-eight hours.

He called his aggression a "police action," in order that the world might regard it as an internal affair of Nigeria and so fail to recognize and condemn the aggression. Our troops, ill-prepared, inadequate, and poorly equipped as they were, displayed such outstanding heroism that within the first two days of Nigerian aggression they not only withstood the aggressors but actually drove the enemy into his territory.

Weeks passed, and Gowon could not penetrate beyond the border areas. Contrary to all expectations, Gowon was defeated in his plan to overrun this Republic. The whole world wondered at and admired our heroism. Everywhere, Gowon's troops were humiliated, disgraced, and frustrated. The invasion of Bonny after nearly six weeks of war was made possible through the antics and collusion of certain foreign interests. I do not need to go into details of this event because they are well known.

Considering the initial achievements of our troops, their subsequent experience and the supply in sufficient quantities of weapons which our troops initially lacked, we had expected to finish the war in the defeat of the aggressors by the end of August—this in spite of the massive support of Nigeria by Britain and Russia. This expectation was properly founded by our successful liberation of the Midwest and advance into Western Nigeria.

But hardly could we know that a number of officers within our army did not share the aspirations of their people and had allowed themselves to be suborned and perverted by the enemy. Those in position of trust in the army shamelessly betrayed that trust against their people. Because of their positions, nobody could suspect them while they continued with their subtle and nefarious acts of demoralizing our troops and causing the destruction of those who could not succumb to their antics.

To the astonishment of all, the enthusiasm that our troops had shown from the start began to wane. Instead of making advances, they kept on leaving the door open for enemy advance. It was in this way that we lost Nsukka; it was in this way that we lost parts of Ogoja; it was in this way that the door was let open to the enemy through Opi to the suburbs of Enugu; it was in this way that the Midwest, which later proclaimed itself the Republic of Benin, was abandoned to the enemy.

You need to hear the stories of our soldiers to be able to appreciate the degree of sabotage and treachery which a number of our trusted army officers were engineering.

These young men, anxious to fight for the honor and survival of their country, will tell you how their officers were giving them wrong orders or ordering them not to fight in the face of the enemy.

They will tell you how their colleagues were shot and killed from behind, not by the enemy but by their fellow Biafran soldiers. Not suspecting that this sort of thing could be possible among us, I, as the Commander-in-Chief, never suspected such acts of sabotage and treachery. If anything, I put it all down for incompetence which could be forgiven.

These saboteurs and traitors did not stop at that. They entered into a bargain with Gowon and his clique for the overthrow of this government by a coup. This coup was to take place between September 18 and 19, after which those concerned would have compromised our position with the enemy. But as Providence would have it, this plot was discovered and foiled in time. It was not until after the discovery of the plot that we began to be circumspective and to discover what was happening within our camps.

I repeat that whatever success has been made by the enemy has been a success not of military valor or gallantry but of treachery by our own men. For days our own men, using our own weapons, were shelling Enugu to cause panic, and acting in collusion with the enemy, they have done the same thing in Onitsha.

Here let me record the debt of this Republic to our general public, whose vigilance has made it possible to foil many efforts by these saboteurs and traitors. We must intensify the vigilance.

Investigations and the vigilance of the general public have shown that there are people outside the army who either have encouraged these acts of treachery or at least have condoned them. To such people, I can only say woe betide them that they should sell their fatherland. Because of the acts of these people, Gowon and his clique have been confident of defeating us without merit. They know that they cannot defeat Biafra except through the use and help of Biafrans. Having succeeded in getting such support and help by treachery, they appear confident.

It is for you today to decide whether we are to go on with this fight of survival and ensure for our children and posterity freedom, security, fair play, and justice in their own homes and in their own way, or to capitulate to the enemy and forever remain a conquered, disgraced, and enslaved people.

The consequences of the latter are clear. Let the few who, whether for money, spite, unpatriotism, or sheer wickedness, have helped the enemy find no comfort. The consequences of our capitulation for them, their children, kith and kin, and posterity are clear. Capitulation or surrender would mean acceptance of defeat and slavery; it would mean the surrender of our sovereignty and survival as a people; it would mean perpetual exploitation and expropriation of our wealth by the conquerors; it would mean our ever remaining second-class citizens paying war reparations to the enemy for as long as they wish; it would mean lack of progress and development; it would mean poverty, disease, indeed everything that will make for anything but happiness and self-respect.

We do not need to be told that the North does not

want us in any association based on equality and respect. It is true that their concept of unity is unity of slave and master. Let us not forget how Major General Aguiyi-Ironsi, whose grave is next door to this building, died. Let us not forget why our officers and men in the Nigerian army were killed last year. Let us not forget the pogrom which cost us more than 50,000 people last year. Let us not forget the millions of pounds of investment which our people have lost in other parts of the former Federation of Nigeria by being forced to return home. Let us not forget that there is no place like home, and that having been killed in other lands and driven away from those lands, history will forever condemn us for betraying our soil and heritage to the enemy and allowing ourselves to be slaughtered even in our own homes. Most important of all, let us not forget our repeated vow that our sovereignty is not negotiable!

As for me, I see no hope for our people without victory in this war. As I have told this assembly, I have no personal ambition and have all along carried out what I consider my duty for the people of this Republic.

We have in recent weeks heard Lagos call upon you to choose a new leader, a suggestion which I should have thought every man and woman with soul in this Republic would regard as insulting. But if, considering what is happening, our enemy is echoing what they know to be the feelings in this Republic about leadership, it is for you to take a decision, uninfluenced by any external enemy.

God knows that I have done my best and I am prepared to continue to serve. But if in this war I am considered the Jonah in the ship of state, I am prepared to step down for another person who will be able to inspire sufficient confidence for the achievement of victory.

As a soldier, I know that no man is indispensable, and as a soldier, I also know that I owe my first duty to my country and my people. We are fighting a war of survival which we cannot afford to lose.

If we have personal grievances, if we have personal

animosities, should this be a reason for betraying our fatherland and condemning our children and generations unborn to eternal disgrace and servitude? Our sense of patriotism demands of us to fight and win this war in order to maintain our honor and identity as a people. After we have done this, we can do whatever we like to settle our grievances or redress wrongs.

Finally, in spite of all that has happened, I feel proud of the people of Biafra as a whole. We have worked together. We have sacrificed together. Our young men are dying for our survival. From the resolutions I have received and other expressions of support and determination, the present crisis has brought our people closer together.

The differences which once existed between the different ethnic groups are now a matter of the past. If we decide, as we must, to continue in this struggle, the enemy will be vanquished sooner than either we or the enemy expect. I commend your deliberations today to God's guidance and await your further instructions.

Diary of Events: Oct. 17—Dec. 11, 1967

October 17: Nigerian troops, under the command of a British naval officer, Commander J. Rawe, invade Calabar. The invasion is repulsed. . . . Chief Awolowo announces that Nigeria has so far spent £50,000,000 for the prosecution of the war.

October 27: Oil shortage hits Nigeria and ration system is adopted.

October 31: Biafra scientists start experimenting on the production of salt from the country's local resources —the Uburu salt deposit.

November 1: A member of the OAU Committee on Nigeria-Biafra war calls for United Nations intervention in the crisis. . . . Nigeria threatens Zambia for raising the Nigeria-Biafra issue at the United Nations.

November 18: Soviet Premier Alexi Kosygin, in a solidarity statement to Gowon, offers words of encouragement to Gowon "for his attempt to hold the Nigerian Federation together." . . . Nationalist activities are intensified in Lagos; telephone lines between the Nigerian capital and other towns—Ibadan, Oshogbo, Abeokuta, Ikorodu, and Agege—in Western Nigeria are cut by Yoruba dissidents.

November 7: Commenting on an article by William Norris in the London *Times* of October 12, 1967, in which reference is made to him, Dr. Nnamdi Azikiwe, former President of Nigeria, states that the only straightforward way to resolve the present Nigeria-Biafra war is to recognize the national and inalienable right of Biafrans to self-determination and the autonomous existence of the Republic of Biafra as a free, sovereign, and independent nation.

November 11: Lagos asks for three battalions of British troops. One of them is to be a marine battalion, and all three would be deployed against Biafra for the dual purpose of assisting in the fight and protecting Shell and other British investments.

November 12: Lagos government again appeals to the Soviet Union for financial aid to "repair roads and bridges" damaged in the current Nigerian war of aggression against Biafra.

November 14: Revolt against Gowon's plans to conscript civilians into his army erupts in Tiv division of Northern Nigeria, and troops are dispatched to quell the riots.

November 22: After almost nine weeks of its appointment in Kinshasa, the six-nation OAU Peace Committee arrives in Lagos.

November 24: In a communiqué, the OAU Peace Committee calls on Biafra to revoke her independence and return to Nigeria.

November 30: Swiss government expresses deep con-

cern at the violence of the war between Nigeria and
Biafra. . . . Nationals of four African states—Ghana,
Togo, Dahomey, and Upper Volta—resident in Biafra
say that the decision of the OAU delegation on the
Nigeria-Biafra war has exposed the OAU to ridicule in
the eyes of the world.

December 2: A Russian jet fighter is shot down at
Itam near Itu by Biafran forces.

December 6: Christian bodies in Britain express
concern over Britain's arms deal with underdeveloped
countries, particularly Nigeria, where the arms are being
misused.

December 9: I inaugurate Biafra's Court of Appeal.
The president of the new Court, Chief Justice Louis
Mbanefo, and two others, Justice Gabriel Onyiuke and
Moses Balonwu, are sworn in.

December 11: Lagos plans bacteriological warfare
—"Christmas Special." Beginning of smuggling of poisoned food into Biafra.

The Vision of Biafra

(Christmas broadcast, December 24, 1967)

It is with the confident assurance of our triumph in
this war that I send you this message of cheer and hope
for this year's Yuletide.

As I speak, my thoughts are one with our brave and
gallant fighting forces—the standard-bearers of our new
Republic—in their various theaters of war. I salute
them—heroes of Biafran revolution and independence
—in the battlefields, in the skies, on the high seas,
where they are demonstrating an iron resolve to crush
and conquer the enemies of our motherland. They are
fighting to uphold the territorial integrity and sovereignty of Biafra. They are at war to safeguard our
country, our beloved ones, our institutions and noble

heritage, against a plunder that is most brutal; against a genocide that is total; against a tyranny that is monstrous; against the military imperialism of the Soviet Union which enslaves, and, above all, against the economic imperialism of a bankrupt Britain. I salute the 14,000,000 virile and dynamic people of this Republic, who have given the government very solid moral and material support in the prosecution of the war to crush Nigerian aggression against Biafra. I also salute all countries, institutions, and individuals who have shown sympathy for, and understanding of, our cause.

As bells of Christian churches all over the world proclaim the birth of Christ, the bells bring again to a world distressed a message of peace and good will—a message of hope and comfort to the afflicted—a message of faith in the goodness of God.

Our young Republic of Biafra joins the rest of Christendom to celebrate Christmas, the birth of Christ, the Hope and Assurance of Peace, Freedom, and Survival. It is the first Christmas that we in Biafra are celebrating as a sovereign nation, the birth of which, seven months ago, was an occasion of hope, jubilation, and joy for all of us. Like the Jews of old, we saw in the birth of our young Republic the gateway to freedom and survival for our people. We saw in it the birth of a society of justice, brotherhood, and peace among our people. But like Herod, Nigeria under its hateful, greedy, and bloodthirsty rulers was totally unhappy about the prospects of our freedom and sovereignty. Like Herod, Nigeria embarked upon an adventure of indiscriminate slaughter and destruction in order to kill the new nation and frustrate all the hope and promises ushered in by its birth. And like Herod, Nigeria has failed. Yet I shudder to think that the leaders of the Christian world should watch in silence Nigeria's unprovoked war against Biafra in a devilish bid to complete the genocide which she began last year. I also shudder to think that the leaders of the Christian church, particularly in Europe and America, should stand dumb and silent while the war machines of Britain and of a godless Soviet Union are allowed to destroy our civilian institutions, and with their war planes slaughter innocent men, women, and children in their homes, in hospitals, and even in places of worship.

Seven months ago, a new nation state was born in Africa. For six months, she has been engaged in a war forced upon her by Nigerian vandals. Grim as the struggle has been, our victory over the enemy is assured though not yet complete. Biafra is bound to survive with all the promises and hope she brought to us at her birth on May 30 this year.

In spite of initial handicaps, our brave and gallant forces, on land, air, and sea, have not only held their own but are giving the enemy exactly what they deserve. The initiative has now passed permanently into our hands. The daily toll on enemy lives has been heavy and sometimes staggering. That the enemy has not called off their aggression in the face of their heavy losses in human lives is another evidence of their utter disregard for those lives. Our sympathy goes to those unfortunate wives, the innocent and common people of Western Nigeria and Lagos, whose children are daily lured to destruction in a war which they neither understand nor have faith in. We have destroyed the enemy in Bonny and liberated that ancient and historic island. The remnants of the enemy in the Enugu sector are being systematically destroyed. The same is true of the Nkalagu sector. In the Ogoja sector, our advances and successes have been steady and consistent. In the Calabar sector, the enemy is being starved to death.

To the discomfiture of our enemy, the world is beginning to see the justness of our cause. Many who were skeptical of our resolve or even our will and ability to defend our sovereignty at all costs have now begun to think again. The resourcefulness of our men, particularly of our scientists who are daily turning out effective defensive weapons, has been a baffle, and the complete willingness of our people to suffer and sacrifice a marvel, to all. The gallantry, valor, and achievements of our military commanders and men have astounded our foes and heartened our friends.

What are the secrets? What is the driving force behind our successes and resolve?

First and foremost, it is the absolute faith of our people in our young Republic and what it represents. There is the realization by all that our survival lies in the defeat of the enemy and the maintenance of our sovereignty; there is the universal feeling of wrong by our people; there is the insult of the enemy's naked aggression in an effort to destroy us in our own homes as they had done elsewhere; there is man's first instinct of self-preservation. All these have made our people absolutely one and determined in this struggle. It is this which has created the solidarity among us, and frustrated and foiled the efforts of the enemy, who, coming face to face with inevitable military defeat, resorted to subtle attempts to subvert our government and cause dissensions among our determined people.

We are a peaceful people. We love and cherish peace and would like to see an end to this conflict, with all its loss and destruction. But the initiative for ending this war must come from those who unleashed it. Let those who started the war stop it.

Born out of the gruesome murders and vandalism of yesterday, Biafra has come to stay as a historical reality. We believe that the future we face and our battle for survival cannot be won by bullets alone, but by brainpower, modern skills, and the determination to live and succeed.

Proud and courageous Biafrans, I see the birth of a new Biafran society out of the carnage and wreckage of the war.

I see a new breed of men and women, with new moral and spiritual values, building a new society—a renascent and strong Biafra.

I see the realization of all our cherished dreams and aspirations in a revolution which will not only guarantee our basic freedoms but usher in an era of equal opportunity and prosperity for all.

I see the evolution of a new democracy in Biafra as we advance as partners in our country's onward march to her destiny.

When I look into the future, I see Biafra transformed into a fully industrialized nation, wastelands and slums giving way to throbbing industrial centers and cities.

I see towns replanned and relocated in harmony with their surroundings.

I see agriculture mechanized by science and technology, which have already made their mark in the present war.

I see a Republic knit with arteries of roads and highways; a nation of free men and women dedicated to the noble attributes of justice and liberty for which our youth have shed their blood; a people with an art and literature rich and unrivaled.

I am sure all Biafrans, on this Christmas Day, share these hopes for our country's future and destiny.

In spite of the trials of the war, we must remember that Christmas is in essence a children's festival. We must therefore ensure that this is for them a happy and truly Christian Christmas.

A happy and cheerful Christmas to you all. Fellow citizens, we shall vanquish.

Diary of Events: Dec. 25, 1967–Jan. 27, 1968

December 25: Pope Paul VI sends two representatives to Lagos on a peace mission.

January 1: Gowon gives March 31, 1968, as the deadline for crushing Biafra . . . Lagos government announces change of currency as an economic measure against Biafra.

January 5: Gowon boasts about his "biggest military machine in Africa," which is to crush Biafra by March 31, 1968.

January 6: Colin C. MacDonald, headmaster, Hope Waddell Training Institute, Calabar, in a letter to the London *Times,* accuses the Lagos government of not providing the "fundamental requirements" of security of life and property for law-abiding citizens. This letter arouses protest from the International Red Cross against the conduct of the war by Gowon's troops.

January 16: Poisoned foodstuffs being smuggled to Biafra by Lagos government are seized by Nigerian troops at Ena Ora (Midwest) and mistakenly distributed to areas in Benin, Western Nigeria, and Okene in the North. Cases of death.

January 22: Nigerian currency notes cease to be legal tender.

January 27: Biafra new currency introduced at meeting of the 7th session of the Consultative Assembly and the Council of Chiefs and Elders.

Genocide

(Address to joint meeting of the Consultative Assembly and the Council of Chiefs and Elders, January 27, 1968)

It once again gives me great pleasure to welcome you all to this meeting. As you know, it has been my practice to consult you from time to time and to keep you informed about the latest developments in the conflict between our young Republic and Nigeria.

When I addressed this assembly in October, we were just recovering from the shock of the attempt by some of our misguided sons and non-Biafrans, to whom we had entrusted the command of our forces, to overthrow the government of this Republic. The disaster of our withdrawal from the capital city of Enugu was the direct consequence of that subversion organized by Gowon and his collaborators. Our situation at that time was grave. The enemy were in parts of our capital and we needed to drive them completely out of it; the enemy were pressing on us from Calabar where they had landed during the second week of October, 1967. We had to push them back to the beaches. In the Ogoja area, the enemy were seeking means of linking up with the forces in Calabar. We had to counter all these. At that time, I reviewed for you in detail the measures we were taking to restore confidence within the army and to give leadership to the lower ranks. I pledged my word before you that, subject only to your assent, the armed forces would continue to prosecute the war against our aggressors till victory is won. You, in this august assembly, signified your unanimous determination to prosecute the war to the bitterest end. For my part and that of the armed forces, we took up the challenge.

Today, three months since that date, we have not only succeeded in avoiding what had loomed as grave disaster, we have also been able to hold the enemy down in most of these sectors. . . .

In November, 1967, the enemy made another and more disastrous attempt to invade Onitsha. Five ships were sunk and more than two enemy battalions destroyed in the operations.

In the last several days, the enemy have opened a new front in the Nsukka West sector, with the aim of cutting our lines of communication between Udi and Onitsha and thereby imperiling our defense of the two positions. I am proud to say that our troops have been equal to the new assault and have dealt a drastic blow on the aggressors in that sector.

You have heard of the alleged plan of the British government to send 1,000 regular marines to aid the Nigerian offensives. The British government has denied it; and since that denial was made by British Ministers in and out of Parliament we are prepared to accept it, in spite of our previous unhappy experiences with British official denials. We in Biafra have a duty to ourselves, and I can assure this assembly that we have taken necessary steps to maximize our preparedness to deal with any renewed offensives from the enemy.

Gowon has been threatening to capture Port Harcourt in the very near future and has even set himself a date. As a man who cannot learn from bitter experience, he is certain to renew his suicidal offensive in the Port Harcourt-Bonny area. We know the strategic importance of Port Harcourt and shall do everything in our power to defend it. War is determination and victory the triumph of that determination.

The story of enemy presence in the Calabar area has been the same as in other areas where they were able to set foot. Mass killings, wanton molestation and harassment, wholesale looting, and assault have been the order of the day. Reports keep coming in of barbaric crimes and unspeakable cruelties. The enemy have not hidden the fact that it is their desire in their war to annihilate the people of this Republic and expropriate or destroy all their property.

The last few days have witnessed massive and desperate offensives by the enemy against our troops in all sectors. Two days ago the enemy virtually razed Slessor Memorial Hospital to the ground, killing the doctor and patients. But, in spite of these, our troops have remained undaunted and determined to resist until the enemy is vanquished.

In spite of the war, we have been doing other things than fighting Gowon and his men. On December 8, 1967, I inaugurated the Biafra Court of Appeal. Our peace-loving people are deeply committed to the rule of law and the proper administration of justice. It is therefore essential and proper that even at this perilous period of our history, the administration of justice should be upheld in all its independence and impartiality. It was a mark not only of our absolute belief in justice and the rights of the common people but also of our determination to maintain our sovereignty.

As Nigeria wages her war of genocide against the peaceful people of Biafra, Radio Nigeria continues to make the claim that Gowon and his Nigerian and foreign accomplices and collaborators are engaged in the nonsensical task of "keeping Nigeria one." It is revealing, however, that immediately after the enunciation of the slogan the Lagos propaganda medium proceeds to spell out in a war song the meaning of "keeping Nigeria one," namely, to pillage our property, ravish our womenfolk, murder our menfolk, and complete the pogrom of 1966. Significantly, and characteristically of Nigeria, this war song is yelled out in Hausa and is not reproduced in any other language of the country which they are claiming "to keep one." Not that this bothers us in Biafra; but its significance should be clear to those non-Hausas still remaining part of ill-fated Nigeria.

What concerns us is that the reaction of the world to the genocidal war being waged by Nigeria against Biafra has, for the most part, been one of silence and indifference and occasionally of veiled hostility to Biafra. It is, however, gratifying that signs of change are becoming evident. Expatriate doctors, clergymen, teachers, technicians, and businessmen who have been in Biafra and seen the truth have gone home to narrate to their people their personal observations and experiences. A number of independent observers and press correspondents have also come to Biafra to see things for themselves and have consequently been impelled to disturb the studied silence of their fellow countrymen. As a result, the case for Biafra has gradually begun to be heard and understood. I shall just reproduce a few random excerpts from foreign reports and comments on Gowon's conduct of the war:

The Lagos government . . . has failed to provide even that fundamental requirement which is taken for granted in the most totalitarian regimes, namely, security of life and property for law-abiding citizens. We have never heard that any attempt was made to bring to justice those responsible for atrocities of 1966, nor has court-martial action been taken against soldiers who murdered [Biafran] civilians in defiance of their "code of conduct," giving rise to protests from the International Red Cross. (C. MacDonald, headmaster, Hope Waddell Training Institute, Calabar, in a letter to the London *Times,* January 6, 1968.)

They [Nigerian army and navy officers] were interested in my experience but seemed not to share my views about the shooting of prisoners. I referred to the Geneva Convention, and one laughed and said, "They gave us a copy before we left, but I ripped up mine—never read it." Another had burned his. (The Reverend David T. Craig in the British *Presbyterian Record*, December, 1967.)

A Lagos police officer was quoted last month as saying that [Biafrans] "must be reduced considerably in number." (Dr. Conor Cruise O'Brien in the *New York Review*, December 21, 1967.)

The slaying of civilians appears to be mounting in areas overrun by Federal Nigerian troops. . . ." (Lloyd Garrison in the New York *Times*, July 21, 1967.)

A Nigerian pro-Federal writer in California, irritated by being reminded of such events [massacre of Biafran civilians], admirably summed up the Federalist position in the following words: "We have just to close our eyes to such things and to everything else and put unity first and reconciliation later." (Dr. O'Brien, *op. cit.*)

A question which must be posed is whether there is an uncontrollable genocidal movement in the [Nigerian] army. Evidence of indiscriminate killing of noncombat [Biafrans] is now incontrovertible, having been reported in recent weeks from Benin, Asaba and Calabar. Anxiety has been expressed in the corridors of the United Nations and in various leading newspapers, and some expatriates have reported their experiences. If politically neutral people see these events as a continuation of the pogrom, there can be no doubt of the feelings of Biafrans. (Dr. W. C. Shepherd, a medical missionary of the Presbyterian Church, Biafra, in the *British Weekly*, November 16, 1967.)

[Biafrans] saw a more concrete choice before them: survival or extermination. To talk to people whose families suffered in the Northern pogroms about the advantages of Federation is essentially equivalent to addressing Armenians of an earlier period about the advantages of that great supranational entity, the Ottoman Empire. In both cases, there is a gulf of experience between the man who advocated the abstraction and the man who has experienced the reality. (Dr. O'Brien, *op. cit.*)

Biafran civilians are aware that upwards of ten thousand noncombatants have recently been slaughtered by Federal troops in the combat areas. They experience little confusion, therefore, when they compare Federal broadcasts from Lagos promising safety to the somewhat more realistic broadcasts from Radio Kaduna in the Northern capital, discussing the final solution to the [Biafra] problem and dolefully listing names of [Biafra] leaders marked for execution. If the truculent Biafrans show no signs of giving up, it is bcause they at least know they are literally fighting for their lives.

Therein lies the major hypocrisy of the Nigerian disaster: The public posture of nearly everyone else reflects a pious concern for Nigerian unity, as if this were still possible. Diplomats, businessmen and other foreigners familiar with the situation knew very well that the [Ibos] and perhaps other tribes in Biafra face extermination in large numbers; that in the event of a Federal victory in the civil war the Eastern survivors will be pariahs. Gowon and his government maintain that Nigerian unity is the sole issue in the civil war; they claim such matters as the clash between Moslem and Christian ethics and suppression of the uppity Ibos do not exist. . . .

Religious conversions from animism in West Africa are being won by the Moslems, seven to three. To deny that there is religious involvement in the Nigerian impasse is fatuous nonsense, especially when it is realized that two directly opposite ways of looking at life are in clash between the North and the East: Moslem fatalism and Christion self-determination. A sort of jihad is in progress. (George T. Orick, [U.S.] *New Leader*.)

These excerpts speak for themselves. They expose the insincerity and hollowness of the Lagos professions. Gowon was reported to have boasted in the New Year that he would step up the tempo of the war because he was touched by "the suffering of innocent people"!

What Gowon really meant was that he would step up the tempo of his destruction of life and property in Biafra.

Although Gowon claims that his war against Biafra is an "internal" affair, its implications already transcend the boundaries of Biafra and Nigeria. For by the very commission of genocide by the soldiers and civilians whom he organized and led during the pogrom of 1966 and by the army over which he has claimed to be Commander-in-Chief since 1967, Gowon now stands condemned before the world.

At the end of the Second World War, although no international convention of genocide was in existence, the Nuremberg Tribunal, to the acclaim of the world, still condemned Hitler's Nazi officials who had organized the systematic extermination of Jews, Russians, Ukrainians, Byelorussians, and others. The members of the tribunal insisted that genocide was a crime against humanity. Shocked by revelations at the tribunal, the United Nations thereafter, on December 9, 1948, adopted the Convention for the Prevention and Punishment of the Crime of Genocide. By this convention, genocide stood formally condemned by the civilized world as a crime under international law and as contrary to the spirit and aims of the United Nations. International cooperation was therefore required "to liberate mankind from such an odious scourge."

The first four Articles of the Convention shed a great deal of light on the extreme gravity of the crime being committed by Gowon and his collaborators:

ARTICLE 1—The Contracting Parties confirm that genocide, whether committed in time of peace or in time of war, is a crime under international law which they undertake to prevent and punish. [Nigerians have committed genocide against Biafrans in time of war, but Gowon's government has taken no steps to prevent or punish the crime.]

ARTICLE 2—In the present Convention genocide means

any of the following acts committed with intent to destroy, in whole or in part, a national, ethnical, racial, or religious group, as such:

(a) Killing of members of the group [Nigerians killed, and are still killing, Biafrans];

(b) Causing serious bodily or mental harm to members of the group [Northern Nigerians maimed, burned, and tortured Biafrans];

(c) Deliberately inflicting on the group conditions of life calculated to bring about its physical destruction in whole or in part [In July–August, 1966, Biafrans at Ikeja barracks were fed on a mixture of rice and carbolic acid. In 1967 large quantities of salt poisoned with cyanide and arsenic acid were secretly introduced into the Biafran market by the Nigerian government];

(d) Imposing measures intended to prevent births within the group;

(e) Forcibly transferring children of the group to another group [Recently Gowon's men forcibly transferred Biafran children from Biafra to Nigeria under the pretext they were "refugees from liberated areas"].

ARTICLE 3—The following acts shall be punishable:

(a) Genocide;

(b) Conspiracy to commit genocide;

(c) Direct and public incitement to commit genocide;

(d) Attempt to commit genocide;

(e) Complicity in genocide.

ARTICLE 4—Persons committing genocide or any of the other acts enumerated in ARTICLE 3 shall be punished, whether they are constitutionally responsible rulers, public officials or private individuals [Although Gowon's tenure of office as Head of State and Commander-in-Chief of Nigeria is illegal and unconstitutional, himself, his War Council, his public officials, his army, navy and air Force personnel, and his other civilian collaborators are all involved in the crime of genocide committed against Biafra].

Genocide is, I repeat, proscribed by the United Nations Charter. It is a crime under the United Nations Convention on Human Rights. It is totally condemned by all the Christian churches. Yet Gowon claims to be "a Christian and the son of a Methodist minister"—a claim calculated to impress foreign churchmen and press correspondents who do not know that he is in reality the leader of a Muslim jihad directed toward the annihilation of Biafrans and the Islamization of Biafra.

Gowon and his supporters have gone to absurd lengths to hide the truth from the world and to ensure that our voice is not heard. They have mounted an intensive propaganda offensive based on falsehood and hypocrisy. In this Nigeria is aided by some foreign information media. You are already familiar with the false claims of Nigeria and her collaborators about the military situation: severe fighting where there has been none; combined land, sea, and air operations at a place like Onitsha which is not on the seacoast, the capture or occupation of places when Nigerian troops are nowhere in the neighborhood. All this has propaganda value for Gowon. It gives the outside world the impression of vigorous military activity on the part of Nigerian troops, of the great military pressure by Nigeria on Biafra, of the futility of assisting a Biafra on the brink of collapse.

Nigeria's hypocritical propaganda operates in directions other than the military. Gowon, for example, insults the intelligence of Biafrans by professing love for them. For the edification and benefit of his foreign supporters, he "assures" Biafrans of "security"—the kind of security he provided for them all through the pogrom of 1966 or when his troops entered Nsukka, Ogoja, Bonny, and Calabar. To make it appear as if the war

was over and things were returning to "normal," Gowon
and his collaborators speak of "a heavy political program" for 1968; of "a massive reconstruction program";
of plans for "a new deal," including "a new constitution
and rehabilitation of persons affected by the disruption
of the last two years." Gowon's policy, adopted on the
advice of his mentors, seems to be: "Do what you like
in actual practice but express it in benevolent language."

Even more serious for our cause than the current
propaganda is the previous conditioning of the Western
world in respect of the former Nigerian Federation.
Britain, the former colonial power, has painted for the
European and American public the picture of the now
dismantled Nigerian structure as the most stable and
promising in Africa, a country whose leaders were the
most mature, statesmanlike, and progressive on the
continent. Those who were opposed to these leaders
were sectionalist and regressive. But we who have lived
in this part of the world over the decades know that
this picture is not true. Nigeria was never really one
country and was never stable; it never even had a common colonial experience, for Britain, which ruled the
territory for years, pursued two radically different policies in the country.

Foreign commentators hardly realize this fact and
are therefore in no position to appreciate "the huge
human price which probably will have to be paid to
hold together physically a territory which spiritually and
psychologically was never one." The outside world was
also taken in by empty concepts such as "federation,"
"unity," "reconciliation," and the aura of sanctity sur-
rounding them. In the event, little or no attention was
paid to the substance of the slogans or the sincerity of
those who mouthed them. Terms like "rebel," "secessionist," and "tribalist" were used freely to condemn
without examination.

One further reason for the indifference of the Western world to our cause is that Biafra's struggle for
independence is simply the self-expression of an African
people struggling for survival. As it was not inspired by

any foreign interests and did not involve any global ideological issues, the Western world could not care less about what happens to African lives. And yet that very Western world would immediately show deep concern for the lives of white people destroyed in a hurricane or earthquake and even for the death of a white criminal serving a prison sentence in an African country.

A large number of people in Europe and America are still ill informed about the Biafra-Nigeria conflict because they have not been well served by their foreign missions and overseas correspondents. There appears to be no systematic effort on the part of some of these overseas missions and correspondents to examine and report objectively on the basic issues of the conflict. So when, occasionally, foreign correspondents do visit Biafra they are astonished to find that far from being dead and finished, Biafra is hale and hearty.

The involvement of certain foreign powers, notably Britain and Russia, in the present Biafra-Nigeria conflict deserves some mention. It is regrettable that these two powers should have openly identified themselves with the regime of force in Lagos and supplied weapons of destruction to Nigeria for continuing the aggression and genocide. Britain has been supplying Nigeria with military, naval, and air equipment and personnel before and since the war began. British naval experts planned and executed the operations against not only Bonny but also Calabar, the leading naval officer in the latter case being a Briton, Commander Rawe. More recently Britain, in spite of her financial difficulties, has granted a loan of £10,000,000 to Nigeria, as was announced at Kaduna, the real seat of power in Nigeria, by Sir David Hunt, the British High Commissioner.

Britain's Elder Dempster Lines, and the West African Conference Lines in which the Elder Dempster Lines is the leading firm, started the economic blockade of Biafra even before the measure was officially announced by Gowon. Shell BP Petroleum Company, a firm in which the British government has a preponderant financial interest, collaborated with Nigeria in the attack on

Bonny in July, 1967. A couple of months ago, Shell BP paid to Nigeria the oil royalties that properly belonged to Biafra. This is nothing but an act of war.

From the beginning of the crisis in 1966 to the present, British information media have not been fair to Biafra in their reports and comments. A home listener recently warned one of these media that it "must accept the grave responsibility of disseminating false ideas to millions" about the Biafra-Nigeria situation.

One should expect that Britain, as an ex-colonial power, should have done everything she could to prevent a shooting war and should have played a neutral role in view of her large investments and prospects in the two areas. She should have tried at all stages to mediate between the contending parties. Since the outbreak of the war, my government has taken steps to protect their property from damage except what has been caused by aircraft supplied to the enemy by Britain and Russia. It is unfortunate that British provocation reached the point where an angry mob set fire to two offices belonging to British companies in Port Harcourt. I must here condemn all acts of vandalism and lawlessness, whether in peace or in war. It is strange that Sir David Hunt, the British High Commissioner in Nigeria, should have stated that Britain reserved the right to ask for compensation for the property of the British companies destroyed during the demonstration while being silent about British property in Biafra destroyed by British planes.

In spite of so much water that has passed under the bridge, there is no antagonism between Biafrans and ordinary British citizens. This short extract from a letter written on January 6, 1968, to the *Times* of London by Mr. Colin G. MacDonald, headmaster, Hope Waddell Training Institute, Calabar—now at home in Scotland —is a tribute to us in Biafra:

There can be no doubt that Colonel Ojukwu has the support of most Biafrans, even in the minority area where I work. His government has upheld the principles of freedom even in time of war, and has shown a truly remarkable degree of maturity in its continued friendly attitude to British people in Biafra in spite of the hostility of the British government.

As for Russia, she has not had a long enough acquaintance with Africa to understand its peoples. She has had setbacks in the Congo (Kinshasa), Ghana, and Guinea and is naturally anxious to regain a foothold in West Africa, and so to further her political strategy in Africa, north and south of the Sahara. Russia and Czechoslovakia stepped in to sell jets to the Nigerian air force after the temporary refusal of Britain to do so. Russia has also delivered to Nigeria a number of coastal crafts. She and various other east European countries have offered Nigeria a loan totaling £33,000,000. Hitherto we have had no quarrel with Russia, and one would have thought she would understand the self-expression of our progressive people and our determination to be free from the fetters of neocolonialism which have immensely contributed to the present conflict.

With regard to African states and the Organization of African Unity, Nigeria has tried intimidation at one time and blackmail at another. For instance, she attacked two African nations through her radio and the press for raising the Biafra-Nigeria issue in the United Nations. She has threatened to foment communal strife in some African countries if they dared to raise their voice in support of Biafra. Nigeria has even gone so far as to rebuke certain Heads of State by name and threaten the withdrawal of technical aid from some African countries for showing pro-Biafran sympathies.

More serious still, Nigeria has blackmailed African states with what is variously referred to as the theory of "disintegrating dominoes" or "Balkanization." This is simply the idea that if Nigeria's disintegration is accepted, other African countries may also disintegrate. It goes without saying that this is a mere ruse. In the history of nations, no country has ever broken up simply because another did. Each case of dissolution of a political union has always been due to unique local factors. The breakup of the United Arab Republic of Egypt and Syria had nothing to do with the dissolution of the Mali Federation of Senegal and Mali, nor can the disintegration of the Federation of Nigeria be properly referred to the dismemberment of the Federation of Rhodesia and Nyasaland.

African leaders have also often been warned by Nigeria of their obligation, under the OAU Charter, to respect the territorial integrity of member states. Our understanding of that part of the charter is that it can legitimately be invoked if one member state attempts to enlarge its territory at the expense of another member state, but certainly not in respect of the emergence of new states arising from the disintegration of a member state.

Africans throughout the continent should waken to the grim prospect that if the current Nigerian position—"smite to unite"—is allowed to prevail, it may be good-bye to the promotion of peaceful and conciliatory solutions to any serious problems that may confront differing communities of any African state in the future. As a well-informed and independent writer has recently observed: "African and other opinion may yet come to regard the effort to hold the Federation [of Nigeria] together, and the means used for this purpose, as far more ominous for Africa than dissolution into the major units could have been." And whatever the predictions of the pessimists, we Biafrans are satisfied that Biafra may yet prove to be a beacon for the furtherance of unity in other states of Africa—and of the world, for that matter—rather than a precedent for their disintegration. Our unwavering stand against injustice, persecution, and genocide will always remain a shining example, particularly for heterogeneous communities in Africa. Never again on this continent of Africa will one section of a political community seek with impunity the total annihilation of another section—for any reason whatsoever—without contemplating the possible consequences of such an act in the light of the Nigeria-Biafra experience.

Thus, our African friends will see that by our separate existence we are not lost to Africa. Indeed, whatever attractive attributes we possessed in Nigeria we still possess in Biafra, in Africa. If anything, these attributes will now be in such a form of concentration and rationalization as will enable Biafrans to make their rightful contribution toward the enhancement of the dignity of man on this continent and the maintenance of universally accepted norms of civilized life.

Our foreign policy continues to be the establishment and maintenance of friendly relations with all nations which respect our sovereignty. We shall also continue to protect the life and property of all foreigners residing in Biafra and shall welcome foreign investments and technical cooperation from any quarter. This includes even those countries whose governments are currently aiding our enemy but whose policies are not shared by a number of their businessmen and people. Here I want to make it categorically clear that we have no animosity for the British people and businessmen. Our quarrel is with the policy of the British government in aiding and abetting genocide.

I must now say a word about Nigeria's recent change of currency. This exercise must be taken with the economic blockade, which was one of the instruments with which we were finally pushed out of Nigeria. The abrupt change was intended to be a financial coup de grace, aimed at accomplishing in one fell swoop the complete economic ruin and demoralization of Biafrans. It was really economic genocide. It was intended to render all the money in Biafra useless overnight and reduce all our 14,000,000 people to abject poverty. Once again, contrary to his professions, Gowon did not discriminate between one part of Biafra and another. Genocide for him has always been total. Gowon has now severed the last economic link Nigeria had with Biafra. The break is complete.

I have been greatly impressed by the calm and level-headed manner in which Biafrans have reacted to the change. We have demonstrated beyond any shadow of doubt that to us survival towers above everything else.

Fellow countrymen, I am happy to announce to you that I have today signed a decree introducing Biafran currency notes which will be the legal tender throughout the Republic of Biafra. By that same decree, Nigeria currency notes will cease to be legal tender in Biafra. Our new currency notes, along with our new postage stamps, will be issued to the public on January 29, 1968.

Gowon has been bewildered by the unity and solidarity of our people. Lagos has been frustrated by the utter failure of its propaganda media to cause dissension and disaffection among our people. The truth is that by intermarriage, cultural intercourse, and economic interdependence, Biafrans have developed common traditions and identity of outlook over the centuries. And for three-quarters of a century now, Biafra has been ruled as a single political unit; so that the vast majority of the population have grown accustomed to the fact of the uniqueness of the political entity which we now know as Biafra. Not even the divisive forces of the turbulent history of Nigeria have broken the cultural and economic homogeneity which has evolved within Biafran territory. Rather, their bitter experience of recent times has further strengthened the solidarity of all Biafrans. We all suffered together in Nigeria and are determined to survive together in Biafra.

All Biafrans are today united by a common experience, a common purpose, and a common destiny. This has been demonstrated more convincingly now than ever before. Biafrans now have an opportunity of building a nation that will reflect the fine qualities of their dynamic but peace-loving people.

We have stated over and over again that we are always ready for a cease-fire and a negotiated settlement. We in Biafra did not start the war; we fight in self-defense. What we wanted before the declaration of Gowon's genocidal war and what we want now is peace, so that we can proceed with the more urgent and more fruitful task of economic, social, and cultural development of our country.

But do we have this peace? No, because of Gowon's blatant rape of the United Nations Convention on Genocide.

Gowon conspired with his fellow Northern Nigerians to massacre more than 3,000 Eastern Nigerians in May, 1966. This is genocide.

Gowon murdered his supreme commander, stole his mantle of office, and proceeded to direct the extermination of army officers and men of Eastern Nigeria origin. This is genocide.

Gowon plotted and executed the wholesale massacre throughout Nigeria of persons of Eastern Nigeria origin in September, 1966, killing more than 30,000 defenseless men, women, and children. This is genocide.

Gowon, in 1966, organized the pillage and destruction of properties belonging to Eastern Nigerians in Northern Nigeria. This is genocide.

Gowon's genocidal acts precipitated the mass exodus of millions of Eastern Nigerians resident in different parts of Nigeria, abandoning all their properties, businesses, and means of livelihood. This is genocide.

Gowon refused to compensate Eastern Nigerians who had lost all their properties as a result of his activities. This is genocide.

Gowon permitted the wanton destruction of properties, looting, and rape throughout those areas of Biafra overrun by his troops. This is genocide.

Gowon ordered the forcible transfer of Biafran children from their homes in Biafra to Nigeria. This is genocide.

For all these acts, Gowon stands condemned for genocide—a crime condemned by the civilized world under international law, a crime against humanity, a crime against God.

The total commitment of all Biafrans to the current

war is no longer in doubt. Gowon and his collaborators have tried desperately to talk the world into thinking that this has been the struggle of what they call "Ojukwu and his rebel gang." The world, however, is beginning to understand that as far as Biafrans are concerned, it is a people's war of survival. The Biafra government has no war budget; rather, it depends on voluntary donations of the people. We are fighting the war entirely with an army, navy, and air force of volunteers. There is no conscription into the Biafran armed forces; instead, we are overwhelmed by the large crowds of able-bodied young men who come forward every day to enlist. Civilians in the towns and villages volunteer and train for service in the Red Cross, the civil defense, and the militia. Biafrans freely donate food and blood for the soldiers. Our men and women make the soldiers' clothes, and our women cook their food. The Biafran war of survival is not "Ojukwu's rebellion."

It has been reported that Gowon has nominated nineteen Biafrans with whom he is prepared to negotiate a peace settlement. I would hope that he will be gracious enough to send a plane, preferably a Fokker Friendship, to collect them! But on a more serious note, chiefs and elders, ladies and gentlemen, we are prepared to negotiate peace with Nigeria under the auspices of the Commonwealth, the United Nations, the OAU or any nonpolitical international organization.

After their experience of the last half-century, Biafrans can never again entrust their safety and security to people outside their homeland.

We appeal to the supporters of Nigeria in and outside Africa to pause and contemplate the human catastrophe they are precipitating in these parts, and to realize that they will be answerable at the bar of history for their contribution to the conscienceless attempt to eliminate a people from the face of the earth.

"Africa's newest venture in nation-building appears to have withstood the first tests of infancy." So ran the dispatch of Lloyd Garrison, correspondent of the New York *Times* news service, writing from Biafra at the end of July, 1967. Not only has Biafra withstood the first tests of infancy, but she has developed into a virile adult.

In more senses than one we are blazing a new trail in this part of the world. Alone we have taken a stand against the most heinous crime against humanity—genocide. Alone, and for the first time in postcolonial Africa, we are fighting a people's war and responding to its challenges in the true Biafran spirit: every Biafran is his brother's keeper. Alone, and in the course of prosecuting this war, we are calling forth the hitherto latent powers of scientific and technological invention of our people. Maybe there is something in the suggestion that our case, our success so far, is too good to be true. Be that as it may, we are used to pioneering in spite of odds. We pioneered the experiment in nation-building in the old Nigeria. But because others would not allow the experiment to succeed, because we were physically, economically, and diplomatically expelled from that country, we returned home to establish this Republic. Whatever we have done well in other lands we will do better in our own.

Since we have responded so well to the occasion and achieved so much so far, we are confident that final success will crown our efforts.

The end of our war of survival will mark the beginning of the war of reconstruction and development. That war will be carried to our educational institutions, to the factories, to commerce, to our farms and countryside, to our public institutions, and to our homes. It will be waged against disease, ignorance, and poverty. A cardinal objective will be the improvement and development of our villages, the reconstruction and modernization of our cities and towns, and the provision of employment opportunities and social amenities for all.

The current war has set the pattern. The performance of our armed forces, our chiefs and elders, our scientists, technologists, educationists, technicians, public servants, students, civil defense workers, and ordinary men, women, and children of Biafra during this struggle has brought out even more clearly our innate qualities and capacity to take advantage of the benefits of modern science and technology. The knowledge and experience and the abilities now demonstrated will no doubt be put to maximum advantage in the building of a new nation—a nation which provides opportunity for each individual citizen to participate in his own way in the national reconstruction and development, as is the case in our current struggle.

I should like once again to pay my warmest tribute to our armed forces for their resolute stand against the enemy. Their performance will go down in the history of our struggle. I have today signed a decree instituting Biafra national honors as a means of giving recognition to outstanding members of our armed forces, the police, and the civilian population. I have also today promoted Brigadier Philip Effiong, Chief of Staff, Defense, and Brigadier Alexander Madiebo, Commander of the Biafra Army, to the rank of Major General.

I have continuously been overwhelmed by the expressions of confidence and support, in speech and action, which I have enjoyed from all sections of our community since the crisis began and developed into a war.

Our cause is just. In this struggle for survival we continue to reaffirm our abiding faith in God, in His infinite wisdom and justice. Please, God, have mercy on Gowon.

Diary of Events: February 3—March 31, 1968

February 3:   Alhaji Adul Maliki, in a press conference in Paris, admits that Egyptian pilots are among those flying Nigerian war planes.

February 9:   His Holiness the Pope sends two special envoys to Biafra to bring the Pope's personal greetings; they express admiration for the courageous people of Biafra.

February 10: Nigerian soldiers enter West Niger Ibo area of Okpanam in Aniocha District, kill two school children, Oseloka Api and Awokome Awagali, and wound many others.

February 11: University Town of Nsukka and the two main towns between Enugu and Nsukka—Opi and Ukehe—are recaptured by Biafran forces.

February 15: In a broadcast, I express appreciation to the Vatican and World Council of Churches for coming to see things for themselves, reiterate my wish for a peaceful settlement, and ask for any peace formula which would guarantee the security of Biafrans in and outside Biafra's borders.

February 16: Tax riot in Tiv Division. Nigerian troops are sent to quell riots.

February 22: Red Cross representative in Geneva protests to the Nigerian government about bombing of civilian areas in Biafra.

February 26: Women demonstrate against Russian involvement in the conflict.

February 27: Roman Catholic charity organizations and pharmaceutical firms in the U.S. donate £84,000 worth of drugs, milk, etc., to Biafra.

February 29: Shell BP concludes a plan to drill Biafra's oil offshore after assurance of protection by British government.

March 5: Head of Biafra Air Force, Colonel Chude Sokei, dies in an accident. I mourn the death of a dear friend.

March 7: 40 Labour MP's call on Wilson administration to stop sending arms to Lagos.

March 9: Details of the resolution adopted at last month's meeting of the Executive Council of World Council of Churches have been released; the council calls on Britain and Russia to stop supplying arms to Lagos.

March 10: Official delegation from the combined churches of the United Kingdom, headed by the Bishop

of Birmingham, Dr. Leonard Wilson, as personal representative of the Archbishop of Canterbury, visits all
parts of Biafra and states that independence for Biafra
should be the wish of everyone. Dr. Wilson says it
would be "crass stupidity" to wish for anything else.

March 12:   In a press conference I reaffirm Biafra's
willingness to negotiate a peaceful solution to the war
without any preconditions.

March 20:   In Geneva and Rome the World Council
of Churches and the Roman Catholic Church call for
a cease-fire in the conflict.

March 22:   Soviet Union steps up supply of military
aircraft to Nigeria with the delivery of more Ilyushin-28
fighter-bombers. Foreign missionaries offer to join Biafran Civil Defense.

March 25:   20,000-strong Nigerian force repulsed at
Onitsha with heavy casualties after ten weeks' bloody
fighting; Nigeria's 102-vehicle convoy bound from
Enugu to Onitsha is completely destroyed in Abagana.

March 31:   Sinking of eight Nigerian boats which try
to invade Onitsha from Asaba. . . . Expiration of Lieutenant Colonel Gowon's March 31 deadline.

Gowon's March 31 Deadline

(Broadcast, March 31, 1968)

For nearly ten months now, we have been fighting a
hard and bitter war in defense of our lives and property
and the future of our children against Nigeria's calculated war of destruction and genocide. The immediate
tragic circumstances which culminated in this war are
well known to all of us. . . .

For nearly ten months now, we have successfully
resisted the "total war" declared on us by Nigeria and
her British and Russian supporters. We have fought
them with credit and with success in every sector of the

war in spite of the elaborate weapons of war and the huge arsenal bought or borrowed by the military junta in Lagos from Britain and Russia. We have proved to the Nigerian aggressors that our will to resist and our ability to succeed could never be destroyed.

Our policy was to fight the enemy until success was achieved or until Nigeria's leaders and their collaborators called off their genocidal war. This is still our policy today.

Before war actually broke out last year, we in this Republic made every possible effort to prevent it. Since armed hostilities broke out, reputable international organizations and personalities, including a number of leading African statesmen, have spoken out about the futility and the disaster of this war and have appealed most urgently and fervently for the cessation of hostilities and the settlement of the dispute through negotiation. Most of these African statesmen have openly rejected the principle of enforcing unity by conquest. Principal among the international organizations are the Vatican and the World Council of Churches, which sent reverend emissaries to us and to Lagos on this matter. Upon joint appeal of the Vatican and the World Council of Churches, we in Biafra have reaffirmed our readiness to stop fighting as soon as Nigeria abandons the use of force. Since we are fighting in self-defense, we shall have no reason to continue the war if Nigeria agrees to stop its war of aggression and genocide, and leaves us alone.

For his part, Gowon rejected both appeals with contempt and even dared to question the sincerity and impartiality of these two august bodies which had appealed for peace "in the name of God." Gowon and his collaborators chose instead to continue with the war.

In the knowledge that Britain and Russia would continue deliveries of deadly armaments to them, Gowon announced in January of this year that he was even stepping up the tempo of the war. Thenceforth Nigerian leaders in Lagos, in Kaduna, and on the warfronts

insisted on "a military solution" to the conflict and
boasted of total victory for them by March 31, 1968.

Today, March 31, 1968, Gowon's last deadline for
achieving this military solution has lapsed. Yet Gowon
is continuing his bloody war, to the shame of all Africa
and the dismay of humanity everywhere. A purposeless,
a senseless, an absurd war continues, and good men
everywhere watch, disgusted that Nigerians have not yet
learned the lesson of the futility of war in the settlement
of human problems.

In the past ten days, Gowon has been making totally
unfounded claims of victory on the battlefront. These
claims are undoubtedly intended to mislead the world
and to soothe his own disappointed people into a false
sense of their achievement.

A new financial year awaits Gowon tomorrow, and
he will then be seeking more credit abroad from governments and international agencies to buy more arms
and ammunition. He knows that his ten months of war
have won him nothing and cost him everything, including whatever honor is left for his tottering regime. In
these circumstances, Gowon is desperately making false
claims which are being faithfully echoed by interested
foreign stations, principally the British Broadcasting
Corporation.

We in Biafra know that these claims are false. Fortunately, several journalists and television cameramen
from Europe and America are here with us today and
are independent witnesses to the rank untruth of those
claims from Lagos. Only last Friday they went to see
for themselves the situation in the Onitsha sector, where
the "crack" 2d Division of the Nigerian army was totally
destroyed. Their reports and photographs are now on
their way to newspapers and radio and television stations of Europe and America. They will tell our part of
the story simply but eloquently and expose the deliberate falsehood being put out by Lagos and the BBC.

In the past week also, Lagos has been making wild
claims of victories in the Oron-Itu sector of the war,

where the Nigerian army has been so humiliated that their remnants have discarded their uniforms and now operate in hit-and-run terrorist gangs. In places like Uyo and Etinan where these terrorists have visited, they have caused panic among the civilian population. In situations such as this, Lagos claims to capture these places, some of them, interestingly enough, the second or third time over. All I can say now is that the pockets of these terrorist gangs have been located and within the last forty-eight hours are being systematically destroyed. We shall as always welcome any interested representatives of the world press to come to Biafra and see things for themselves.

Gowon has failed in his attempts to achieve a military solution but has succeeded in bringing tragedy and misery to thousands of Nigerian families and immense destruction of life and property to this Republic. He has authorized atrocities of every kind in this war. His soldiers have massacred thousands of defenseless civilians wherever they have entered in the Republic of Biafra, as they did in Sapele, Aboh, and Asaba in the Republic of Benin. His officers have organized the mass abduction of women and children from their homes to concentration camps outside this Republic. The Nigeria army has carried out wholesale burning of towns and villages in its path of advance or retreat.

Nigerian war planes have for months bombed schools, hospitals, Cheshire homes, refugee camps, churches, and other civilian centers; in the last six weeks they have bombed and strafed markets and hamlets in every province of this country. Napalm and other incendiary bombs have been used on civilians in Opobo, Nomeh, Onitsha, and Abakaliki; asphyxiating bombs have been used on Biafran troops at Ugwuoba and other sectors. There has been every manner of torture and degradation in the towns and villages overrun by Gowon's soldiers. These atrocities have shocked the conscience of all good men, and they have raised their voices in protest.

We take this opportunity to express our thanks to the individuals, governments, and other world organizations that have made strenuous and risky efforts to bring to an end these atrocities and pave the way for a peaceful settlement. We want especially to thank His Holiness, the Pope, and the Vatican, the World Council of Churches and its officers, the British Council of Churches and its bishops, the International Red Cross Society and the relief organizations working in cooperation with it. We thank them for their expressions of sympathy and consolation and for their material assistance of various kinds for the relief of our people. We have been the victims of this war, the object of the genocidal lust of Nigerians. To us, therefore, should belong anger and the urge for revenge. We nevertheless respect and accept the appeal of these august bodies made in the name of God and of all humanity for the cessation of hostilities.

We in Biafra, though justified in killing in self-defense, nevertheless hate to see blood let in a war which cannot, in any event, solve the fundamental conflict between Biafra and Nigeria. Political association, like all human relationships, cannot be secured by force of arms. War can never achieve political and social peace. As the World Council of Churches and the Vatican put it in their joint appeal, "War is inhuman and is a futile means to resolve differences and controversies. War only makes destruction greater and more lives are lost. If war is to be prolonged, neither side will be able to live in peace and prosperity."

It is now abundantly clear that Gowon will not willingly agree to the cessation of hostilities and the negotiation of a peaceful settlement. It is clear that he feels no concern for the misery and destruction which the continuation of this war is causing. It is also clear that Gowon will now want to buy more time, fix a new deadline, and again step up the scale of his atrocities in Biafra—and achieve practically nothing at the end of it.

We have survived to this day because we are united,

because we fully appreciate the gravity of our danger, and especially because of our attachment to this Republic of Biafra, which we founded on May 30 last year as our last place of refuge.

Our struggle to defend this Republic is not yet over. However, Gowon has not yet called off his war or altered his original plan to exterminate our people. Until he does, we have no choice but to fight on until the last remnants of his doomed and ill-fated army are destroyed in our land. We have already broken the backbone of the Nigerian army. We must therefore sustain and even increase our vigilance; we must intensify our involvement in this struggle in defense of our fatherland, particularly now that there are more reasons than ever before for us to believe that success in our struggle is in sight. Biafra has amply demonstrated that she can survive as a nation these months of independence and war. I am confident that the nations of the world will not fail to take note of this reality. God, in His goodness, has been kind to this young Republic and to her people. God bless our Republic.

Diary of Events:
April 1 – May 29, 1968

April 1: A report of a review of the progress of the war after nine months discloses that: (a) Russia has so far supplied nearly 50 MIG fighters and 15 Ilyushin bombers to Nigeria. The planes are flown by Russian, Egyptian, and British pilots. (b) The emirs of Northern Nigeria have used their considerable influence with their fellow Hausa-speaking people of the adjoining countries, especially Chad Republic, to engage the services of approximately 10,000 warriors, called Gwodogwodos. . . . Biafra government issues three defense bonds totaling £25,000,000.

April 2: Biafran-made gunboats counter Nigeria's

seaborne invasion attempt on Port Harcourt. In four-day encounter, the enemy lost eight out of nine attacking ships and more than 1,000 troops. Three of these vessels were captured intact as well as considerable quantities of heavy equipment (105-mm. artillery pieces, Oerlikon antiaircraft guns, rifles, ammunition, two electric generators, and a Land Rover).

April 12: I go on Retreat and Major-General Phillip Effiong, Chief of General Staff, takes over as Acting Head of State. . . . Biafra government asks foreign companies operating in Biafra to declare their intentions regarding their assets, since they have abandoned their businesses and their responsibility to their staff.

April 13: Republic of Tanzania recognizes Republic of Biafra.

April 19: Brigade of the Biafran 11th Division cross the Niger and capture Asaba, Ibusa, Ogwashiuku, and Oko. . . . I return from Retreat after seven days of meditation and take over from the Chief of General Staff.

April 23: Caritas Internationalis launches relief operation for Biafra with £200,000 worth of relief.

April 25: Czechoslovak government bans all shipments of arms to Nigeria.

April 26: Peace talks between Nigeria and Biafra begin in Niamey, Niger.

April 27: Nigerian air raid takes 148 civilian lives in Aba.

May 3: Russian war planes of Nigerian air force bomb and strafe Okigwi township and Orodo village in Owerri Division. 36 dead and 75 wounded.

May 6: Nigerian planes bomb Assa in Ngwa Division. 94 refugees in a church missionary school killed and 65 wounded.

May 7: Nigerian jet fighters raid Eleme near Port Harcourt. 19 dead.

May 8: Republic of Gabon recognizes Republic of Biafra.

May 9: Nigerian fighter and bomber planes attack

Umumasi and Umukoroshe near Port Harcourt. 87 dead (mostly women and children). . . . Mbawsi and Okpuala bombed. 60 killed and 140 injured.

May 11: Nigeria talks peace in London. . . . Obehie market near Aba bombed. 27 killed. . . . Ibiono near Umuahia bombed. 4 dead.

May 12: Nigerian planes bomb Port Harcourt Shell BP residential area and Elelenwa near Port Harcourt two times. 120 dead and 250 wounded.

May 14: Republic of Ivory Coast recognizes Republic of Biafra. . . . Air attack on Port Harcourt three times. 12 dead and 25 injured. . . . Owerrinta attacked by Nigerian fighter planes. 16 dead.

May 20: Republic of Zambia recognizes Republic of Biafra. . . . London *Times* reports that British-dominated Shell BP Company has expressed "guarded optimism about restarting the flow of oil from Biafra . . . following confirmation that Nigeria federal forces had gained control of the company's oil installations at Bonny and Ogoni in the break-away State of Biafra." . . . Nigerian offensives on Port Harcourt intensified. . . . Five British officers killed in Port Harcourt sector while fighting with Nigerian troops: Captains P. Boylen, R. Leigh, Aubrey, L. Darrel and D. Symonds.

May 23: Peace talks between Nigeria and Biafra open at Kampala, Uganda.

May 23–24: Nigerian soldiers enter Port Harcourt.

May 27: Biafran commandos, operating behind enemy lines, attack Enugu airport, destroy two Nigerian aircraft, and capture a Nigerian reconnaissance party.

May 28: With escalation of the war and aggravation of refugee problem in Biafra, humanitarian bodies take increasing interest in relief to Biafra.

May 29: Eve of Biafra's 1st Independence Anniversary.

State of the Nation

(Broadcast, May 30, 1968)

Twelve months ago today, our young Republic of Biafra was born. On May 30, 1967, we took the momentous decision and proclaimed the sovereign independence of our homeland, our last place of refuge, our fatherland. Today, May 30, 1968, I join all Biafrans everywhere in celebrating this first anniversary of our sovereignty and in rededicating ourselves anew to the defense and prosperity of our nation.

A year is a short period in the history of a nation. For us in Biafra, however, the experience of this first year of sovereignty has been like that of a century. In one short year we have had to tackle the very grave questions of life and death, war and peace, survival and extermination. We have been blockaded and isolated, shot and shelled, bombed and strafed; we have been insulted and taunted by our Nigerian enemies and their spokesmen, agents, and foreign collaborators. Through this period of great trial, we have stood up like men and held our heads high. We have fought back against the Nigerian aggressor, scorning his vainglorious threats and defying his borrowed might. Within the year we have made the world aware of our existence as a nation. We have stirred the conscience of the world to a just appreciation of our cause; we have earned the diplomatic recognition of our sovereignty and right to separate existence as a sure guarantee for survival, security, and prosperity.

We have a great deal to celebrate this day, a great deal to be thankful for. But because we are still at war, we cannot celebrate this occasion with all the spirit and fanfare it deserves.

I am confident that we all—men, women, and children, soldiers at the front and civilians supporting them, diplomats, students, and others abroad—will be able to give expression, each in his own way, to our common joy, our continuing struggle, and our expanding hope.

Let me, this auspicious morning, say how proud I have been of you, the people of this Republic—your faith, your courage, your endurance, and your loyalty— in the crucial months during which I have had the opportunity to lead this nation. I have drawn my own sustenance and faith from the intrepidity of you all. I feel today like fourteen million men because I know there are such lion-hearts behind me.

An anniversary such as this is an appropriate time for reflection and projection by the nation. Before our Proclamation of Independence our people were saddled with a host of social, economic, and political problems, created for us by Nigerians.

Following the atrocities committed against our people from May to October, 1966, we had in our midst refugees who had to be housed, fed, clothed, and employed. We had to do this without help and without sympathy from the government that held the common purse of the then Federation of Nigeria. The resource-fulness and the resilience of our social system were strained to the fullest as we tried to cope with the immense human problems which resettlement and re-habilitation involved. At the same time an economic blockade was mounted against us, thereby denying import of food, clothing, medicine, and other essential supplies to our people and making the export of our own products impossible. Our enemies expected the blockade to ruin our economy and destroy our people. They mounted a diplomatic offensive aimed at isolating us from the outside world as a prelude to their plan of invasion and annihilation. This attitude did not improve the political situation in Nigeria. The Lagos government tried to coerce our people into subjection by the imposition of arbitrary and unconstitutional decrees. They sought to foment strife and discord among our people, encouraging tendencies which they believed would lead to the political collapse of the administration. It was in pursuit of this aim that Gowon dictatorially created his three paper states out of our territory.

We refused to be intimidated; we refused to despair. We undertook immediately to rehabilitate and consolidate. New priorities were marked out. Food production was stepped up. Most refugees were catered for by the "extended family" system. Individually and collectively, we all became our brothers' keepers. Some who had the resources built new homes for themselves; others were provided for by the state. New settlements sprang up all over the country, and with them new markets. The old towns expanded incredibly to absorb increased populations. We began to lay plans for economic and industrial development which could absorb the repatriated skills and manpower. Although the current war has not allowed the full realization of our economic and industrial plans, all available skills have been harnessed for the prosecution of the war.

We were on the threshold of bringing security, peace, and material comfort to our people when Nigeria declared war on us on July 6 last year. At that date our army was just being assembled for the defense of the new nation, barely a month old. Arms were scanty, ammunition in short supply. Nigeria had the armory of the old Nigeria army at her disposal and had, besides, massive new supplies from Britain, and later from Russia as well.

We knew all this. But we also knew that we had to defend our lives.

Our will to survive was to us far more important than the arms or ammunition. And we have been proved right. The enemy that had boasted its determination to crush us in forty-eight hours was held down to within twenty miles of our northern borders in July, August, and September. By the middle of August, the eight battalions sent into that area, with all the support they got from British-manned Ferrets and Saladins, were virtually destroyed by the much smaller force of Biafran stalwarts. We have convinced the aggressors that force of arms alone cannot subdue a people, that Biafrans have chosen independence as the only guarantee of their survival and are prepared to die defending it.

On August 9, 1967, our forces entered and occupied the Midwest in a lightning campaign, conceived in the highest ideals of a Biafran revolution. The objective of the move was twofold. First, it was strategic in order to secure the western defense of Biafra. Second, it was to protect our kith and kin to the west of the Niger, who had suffered, like us, from the Nigerian atrocities of 1966. Contrary to what our enemies and detractors would like the world to believe, the move had nothing to do with territorial ambition. With the collapse of that operation through treachery, and the entry of the enemy into Enugu, the war which we had virtually won has taken a more arduous turn.

The massive military assistance which Nigeria received from Britain, Russia, and other countries encouraged Nigerians to build up an oversized army for her "total war" against us. Britain and Russia supplied the artillery bombs and mortar shells which have caused so much destruction in Biafran towns; they provided the planes and aerial bombs with which hundreds of defenseless civilians in our towns and villages, in refugee camps and settlements, have been killed. Those planes and aerial bombs have also destroyed our schools and colleges, markets, hospitals, and homes for the handicapped.

To a foe so callously minded and so generously supplied, we opposed with all our resources of mind and limb. With whatever we had, we fought. Our scientists and engineers designed new weapons or adapted old ones; our officers contributed new techniques to deal with the exigency. Our soldiers fought gallantly against a foe patently inferior to them in pure infantry combat. In that way, we made victory elude the Nigerians, who shifted from one deadline to another, from one vain hope to yet another. On New Year's Day, 1968, Gowon fixed March 31 for the defeat of our people. By March 31, to his discomfiture, we had destroyed the "crack" 2d Division of the Nigerian army en route to Onitsha, and a substantial part of the 3d Commando Division operating in the Bonny area.

As you already know, our position in the current struggle has been enhanced in the diplomatic field with the recognition accorded to our Republic by a number of African countries. We are no longer without friends. It is possible that Nigeria will no longer enjoy her superiority in the air, in the sea, and in infantry support. As I said recently, we are entering our second phase of the struggle. Henceforth, everyone owes a clear duty to this Republic to ensure that the enemy has neither peace nor respite until he leaves every inch of our territory where he has set foot. Young men will have to leave their refugee camps for training in order to operate against the enemy in their own areas. The pace of return to our native provinces, towns, and villages must be quickened into a flood which will sweep away the enemy. The enemy's lines of communication must be attacked and destroyed. He must be allowed no rest, comfort, or safety. Enemy agents and collaborators must not be allowed to thrive on our soil. They must be made to live in constant fear and peril.

The war has been hard on us. Many of our towns and villages have been shelled, bombed, and vandalized out of existence by the Nigerians. Thousands of our civilians have been slaughtered by hatred-ridden Nigerian vandals. Atrocities of many kinds have been perpetrated against our people—all in pursuance of the genocidal war which Nigeria is waging against us.

In spite of the military pressure on us in our first twelve months of existence, we have made good our accession to sovereign independence in social, economic, and political spheres.

Recognizing the diversity of local interests and the

need to promote harmony among the various communities in the country, the government of Biafra initiated discussions at all levels, and this led to the idea of a provincial system of government for the Republic. With the express mandate of the country's Council of Chiefs and Elders and the Consultative Assembly, the government inaugurated, and has successfully been operating, the provincial system of administration comprising the twenty federated units.

In keeping with the native instincts of her peace-loving people—a people deeply committed to the rule of law—Biafra has upheld the proper administration of justice, in all its independence and impartiality. As a mark of its belief in justice, in the principles of freedom, and in the rights of the common people, the Biafran government inaugurated in time of war (December, 1967) the Biafra Court of Appeal—a tribunal which has been in active operation ever since.

In addition to rehabilitating the 2,000,000 refugees expelled from various parts of Nigeria—an outstanding feat which has been independently assessed by foreign observers as one of the greatest achievements in modern history—Biafra is currently providing for nearly 4,000,000 people who have been forced to leave their homes for other places within Biafra since Nigeria started her war of annihilation.

The Biafran government has successfully organized other aspects of the economic life of its people. Besides the economic blockade of Biafra and other repressive measures, the Lagos government, after prosecuting its destructive war on Biafra for six months, announced on January 3, 1968, a change of currency—an operation intended to accomplish the economic ruin and total demoralization of our people. Yet there has been no upheaval in Biafra. Biafra has issued her own currency and postage stamps which have been popularly accepted by her citizens.

A number of alien companies operating in Biafra deliberately assisted our enemies by applying measures which damaged our economy and increased the hardship suffered by our people. They abandoned their businesses and neglected to arrange for the continued payment of their Biafran employees. We have, as you know, issued a notice to those firms and business establishments, requiring them to indicate whether they have abandoned these establishments and, if not, how they intend to resume their operations. Our policy toward foreign enterprise in this country has been made clear on several occasions, and no responsible opinion can claim that we have not been fair and even generous to these establishments which have been completely neglected by their owners for more than a year now. My government has considered the present position very carefully and has promulgated a decree which will enable us to act in respect of the companies which have not satisfied the requirements of our notice and to appoint boards to manage them. In this way, the government hopes to reestablish the economy of the country by salvaging what it can out of the wreckage into which it was deliberately plunged by these alien companies. We have a supreme responsibility to protect the interests of our country and people, especially in the midst of all their other sufferings as a result of the present war.

Nigeria's genocidal war has affected our communities in various other ways. The human suffering and hardship brought on by the economic blockade have been accentuated. The indiscriminate bombing of civilian populations has further caused disquiet, unsettlement, and grief throughout the country. Schools have been closed, the youths have been deprived of education, and new responsibilities have been imposed on parents and guardians. But the response of our people to this emergency has been marvelous. In spite of personal hardships and anxieties, our cooperation has helped the mobilization of all our resources to meet these challenges. It is to the eternal credit of our people, and a source of pride to me personally, that we have been able to maintain absolute law and order throughout this period of emergency.

Above all, Biafra has achieved the original purpose of her accession to a separate political existence. She has provided safety and security for her citizens in their homeland and has, with much success, stemmed a war of aggression and genocide directed against them by Nigerians.

Few communities could have faced our difficulties as bravely as we have. Our people are fighting for a cause and a faith. That cause is their right to security of life and property. That faith is in the possibility of creating and maintaining a nation in the service of man.

We owe this first anniversary primarily to the indomitable spirit of the people of this nation, to their understanding of the issues at stake, and to their confidence that Biafra will not let them down.

Biafra will not let them down. For the Biafra that will emerge from the present crisis and war will have to be faithful to the principles and values which inspired our people to found this Republic. Biafra will have to live up to the expectation of a world that has already come to see her as a new and salutary experience in the community of nations.

On this occasion of our first anniversary, let me restate these principles and values. First, Biafra believes in the sanctity of human life and in the sacredness of the human person. In our traditional society, the destruction of human life is not only a crime but a sacrilege. Having ourselves been subjected to humiliation, torture, and death at the hands of our enemies, we should now and always uphold and strengthen this traditional faith in the sacredness of human life. It is the duty of all Biafrans—now and in the future—to ensure that this principle is never assailed in their community. The government of Biafra will ensure that at all times the person of every individual Biafran is rendered worthy of respect; that all forms of disabilities and inequalities which derogate from the dignity of the individ

ual or destroy his sense of person are eliminated from
Biafran society.

Second, we as a people believe in hard work and
economic initiative. We believe that property legitimately acquired by the individual through his exertions
should not be taken away from him without just cause.
This concern for security of personal property derives
part of its logic from the view widespread among Biafrans that a certain degree of wantlessness and the
possession of personal property is essential to ensure
the dignity and respect of the individual, and that, con-
versely, utter destitution and lack of basic personal
property erode that dignity and respect. The government of Biafra will therefore ensure that the individual
is free, within legitimate bounds and subject to the
overriding considerations of collective well-being, to
work, to acquire and own property, and that property
so acquired is adequately protected by law. Our society, however, believes that every man belongs to his
community. Our people have developed a realistic world
view which accepts cooperation as the sanest and most
logical answer to the question of man's proper place in
society. This world view also recognizes a delicate but
workable balance between the claims of the individual
and those of society. As a result, our society has developed a most realistic and effective reciprocal relationship between man and society. Biafra must seek to
preserve this relationship.

Third, the ideal of the rule of law was one of the
driving forces behind the founding of the Republic of
Biafra. The future Biafra will be guided by this knowledge.

Law courts will have a crucial role to play in upholding and fostering this rule of law. In this country,
the process of law and justice will be speedy, efficient,
and honest. Justice will be accessible to all, irrespective
of their personal means, and ways will be devised to
protect the citizen from exploitation in his search for
justice.

Fourth, we believe in the right of every citizen to participate in the government of his country as a means of forestalling misrule and securing his rights and liberties. We believe that society should be organized to ensure social harmony and maximum scope for the individual to realize himself and attain personal happiness. Biafra believes in the communal democracy which gave stability and morality to the politics of our traditional society. We have always held that a sound structure of political power and the right relationship between that power and social responsibility hold the key to the well-being of society and the individual. Communal democracy, or government by consensus, is our own formula for good democratic government. Under this system, which has been with us for centuries, all political authority is derived from the community, and political decisions are based not solely on the view of the majority (as in conventional democracy) but on consensus. The result, in our traditional society, was that the structure of political power and governmental action was aimed at ensuring the good and well-being of all the people, as well as providing stability, peace, and justice within society. In the future Biafra, the government will ensure that the people have their opportunity to participate fully in the management of public affairs and that there are valid and dependable procedures available to them for doing this. Consensus will be the basis of government in Biafra.

Fifth, our society is a progressive and dynamic one. The people of Biafra have always striven to achieve a workable balance between the claims of tradition and the demand for change and betterment. We are an adaptable people because we are convinced that, as our people say, "no condition is really permanent," that human effort and will are necessary to bring about those changes and improvements in the condition of the individual and of society which they regard as desirable. Where others would accept an inferior position in life or communal backwardness with apathy or even as tho divine will of the Almighty, the Biafran sees it as a challenge to his God-given talent and initiative. He thus strives relentlessly to improve his lot and raise the general level of his community. The government of Biafra will make sure that our society remains progressive and dynamic through the discovery and development of local talent as well as the acceptance of progressive foreign ideas which do not detract from the identity of our culture.

Finally, our revolution and this war have brought home to us the fundamental need for social justice in our community. Our people have always rejected all forms of social injustice and disability; they have been unrelenting in their desire to overthrow all class and sectional privileges and all vestiges of official abuse and corruption. The government of Biafra is committed to the achievement of a just society in which every citizen will have the fullest opportunity for self-development and self-fulfillment; where a man can reach his just place in the community unimpeded by social, economic, or political inequalities or by the evil forces of corruption and nepotism. The government will strive to ensure for *all* Biafrans freedom from hunger, ignorance, want, and disease. These freedoms are the basic fruits of the Biafran revolution, and Biafrans are entitled to them not as privileges but as rights which they have dearly bought with their own sweat and blood.

Education will be the primary means of attaining this goal. The government of Biafra is therefore committed to a program of educational reform and expansion which will ensure that every Biafran child will receive the primary education which is considered the starting point in any meaningful program of equal opportunities. The nation is committed to a judicious and liberal scholarship policy, whereby no son of ours with the talent and the ability to profit from further education will be deprived of the opportunity through lack of means.

In the same spirit, the government will aim at equipping every citizen through education and training for full and useful service to the community. No citizen thus equipped will be prevented unjustly from seeking and obtaining the employment for which he is qualified or from receiving adequate reward for his work.

We assume it as the necessary fulfillment of our revolution that we can enthrone the human idea of the responsibility of society for the welfare of all its citizens, particularly those who are in need of special care—the sick, the disabled, the mentally ill, and the very old.

We are fortunate as a people to have developed a profound appreciation of the importance and dignity of labor. We believe that as long as a man does honest and useful work he is entitled to a fair appreciation and reward. Thus, the village farmer, the fisherman, the truck pusher, the artisan, the civil servant, the professional, the big business executive, the trader, and indeed every class of worker has an important part to play in the life of the community and should be proud of that part. We as a people have always believed that from humble beginnings a man can, through his own initiative, honesty, and hard work, rise to great heights from which he is able to make commensurate contribution to the well-being of society. The government of Biafra will do everything in its power to give to every worker in any field the respect and dignity due to him as an honest and hard-working citizen of Biafra. An honest and hard-working Biafran, whether he pushes a pen, a scalpel, or a truck, is a proud son of his country.

These objectives will require the direction of responsible political leadership and the exertions of a responsive and competent public service. And the people themselves will be the judge of this responsibility and this competence. In this connection, Biafra will reaffirm and enforce the principle of public accountability which was so central to our traditional society. Public office is public trust, and the community expects, and is entitled to, an account of services rendered in terms of both efficiency and integrity.

The Minister of State, as well as the Permanent Sec-

retary and the Corporation Manager, will bc required
to account to the community for the use he has made of
his opportunity to serve. Where inefficiency or impro-
priety is established, the head of that service, if found
guilty of dereliction of duty, must be made to accept
personal responsibility for such a situation. When the
situation is sufficiently grave, he should be made to bear
the full consequences of his neglect. The service of the
community must under no circumstances be hampered
or paralyzed by indolence, inefficiency, or corruption of
any public servant, however highly placed. In return
for his good work, the people will guarantee to the public servant his rights and liberties as a citizen, and the
honor and courtesy due to him as a leader or a servant
of his people.

This is the kind of society we are now fighting to create here in Biafra. For these values and principles we
are willing to endure our present hardships. Let us individually resolve to shape our own lives to accord with
these objectives of our nation. The individual Biafran
must today resolve to live like the ideal Biafran—a man
who believes in the existence of a supreme God, head
over all men; a man who accepts the obligation to
work hard; a man who believes in the dignity of work
and is diligent in all his exertions; a man who values
thrift and uses the resources of his head and hand to
find legitimate economic security for himself and his
family; a man who is original in his thinking and always
eager to experiment; above all, a man who is responsible, disciplined, efficient, but simple.

Our experience during over twelve months of economic blockade and eleven months of war has emphasized the propriety of the domestic and foreign economic policies of this government. During the current
hostilities, various latent qualities and resources in Biafra have been discovered. In particular, the government has been impressed by the quality and quantity of
the high-level manpower which has become available not
only for business management but for social, scientific,
and technological development. We have been able

through the resourcefulness of our people to maintain a high level of industrial production in spite of the blockade which denied us the essential materials and spare parts. This government will encourage the full exploitation of this manpower and resourcefulness. Biafra has also been able to sustain the strain of the war in her domestic economy through the energy and enterprise of her indigenous businessmen. The government will encourage such businessmen and, where necessary, promote the fullest partnership between them and foreign investors. In the rehabilitation of abandoned industries and commercial enterprises we shall make full use of our talents and qualities. We shall encourage our industries to continue to make the maximum use of our local raw materials. Attention will be given after the war to providing the necessary infrastructure for the development of industry and trade and to providing employment opportunities for all.

Our policy with regard to foreign investment and trade will be consistent with our policy of nonalignment as declared a year ago in our proclamation. Biafra will welcome all genuine friends who wish to join us in the development of our resources. In this connection we will subscribe to international agreements for trade and development. We will contribute toward the promotion of intra-African trade and will participate fully in the growth of regional economic groupings which make for the unity of the African continent. The fiscal policy of the government will be geared toward ensuring a safe and healthy environment for investors. Tax exemptions, import duty relief for productive enterprises, and customs drawback for all exports resulting from manufactured goods in Biafra are some of the incentives which will be available to genuine partners in the reconstruction and economic development of Biafra. To this end, the government will pursue stable monetary and fiscal policies which will maintain confidence in the economy and ensure its ability to sustain a steady growth. I appeal to all true lovers of humanity and believers in the progress of the African to join with us in Biafra in the fullest exploitation of our natural resources. I wish to assure all comers that there can be no discrimination against anybody on grounds of race or creed or political ideology.

In the meantime, we have the ravages of war to deal with—the dislocation of life, the displacement of populations, the anxieties of a nation under siege. The task of rebuilding our cities, our industries, our farms, indeed our total economy, will take time. So also will the more urgent task of healing the wounds of war, especially the psychological strains imposed on young and old alike by the trying events of the past two years. We will need time to seek out old friends and heal shattered relationships and even loves. We will need time to make Biafra a home again after the breaches and the desecration of hearth and home by Nigerians. We will need time to restore Biafran life to its original and appropriate fullness.

I must make a passing reference to the different offers of gifts by humanitarian and philanthropic international organizations to relieve suffering arising from the current Nigeria-Biafra war. We in Biafra heartily welcome and deeply appreciate such assistance. But it is worth warning those concerned against the possibility of some interested parties playing politics with the gifts. It would, for instance, be unrealistic to send gifts to Lagos, as some quarters have been reported to be contemplating, and expect such gifts to benefit displaced persons in Biafra. Such an action would be nothing but a partisan step in aid of Lagos against Biafra. Gifts intended for displaced persons in Biafra should be sent direct to Biafra. It has been reported that the International Red Cross has made gifts available for the relief of displaced persons or refugees. Their problem is that of transport. I hereby appeal to governments and organizations of the world who can help in the transportation of those gifts to Biafra to come to our assistance by contacting our representatives in London, Lisbon, Paris, New York, and friendly African countries.

While we seek to rebuild, Gowon continues a futile war which he believes he will win. Today it should be clear to him and to his supporters that he cannot. Peace talks are now going on in Kampala between us and Nigeria. Our delegates have gone there with a clear and unequivocal mandate to seek a cease-fire in the present conflict and thereafter to discuss with the Nigerians the basis of our future cooperation with them. Without a cease-fire, there can be no talks aimed at reaching a permanent settlement.

We have been watching with keen interest what is going on in Kampala. Already, there are signs of Nigeria's usual bad faith. They have been forced against their will, by a combination of circumstances, to the conference table. They believe in nothing but a military solution and would prefer that to peaceful negotiations. Their insincerity about the current talks has been borne out by Nigeria's delaying maneuvers, first during the preliminary talks and now during the full-scale negotiations. Nigeria and Britain will bear full responsibility for the failure of the talks.

As an example of our sincerity for successful negotiations, we have, right from the start of the Kampala conference, made generous offers of friendship and cooperation to Nigeria. We have offered to meet our share of Nigeria's obligations (including public debt) incurred before the crisis which brought us to the present state. We have offered sincere cooperation in economic, educational, cultural, and industrial fields. We have said that, if necessary, a plebiscite should be conducted in disputed areas to determine the wishes of the people. We have emphasized that no peaceful talks can have meaning while we are killing ourselves. No such gestures have come from Nigeria. Instead, only yesterday, Nigeria announced her so-called terms for the cessation of hostilities. Our only comment on that inane document is that it is as much an insult to Biafra as to humanity as a whole.

Only negotiations can settle the differences between

us and Nigeria. The world can assist in bringing about a just settlement by making it clear to Gowon that war cannot win anything. The world can help by getting Britain and Russia to discontinue their military assistance to Lagos. In the present circumstances, it will be cynical and immoral for the world to begin amassing grants-in-aid for reconstruction, whereas by exercising their moral and diplomatic influence on Nigeria they could bring this genocide and destruction to a speedy end.

As we celebrate this anniversary, let us remember that there are still a small number of Biafrans in Nigeria who were unable to return home before Nigeria declared war on us last July. Among these are businessmen, professionals, domestics, and others. Some, mainly technical people, were forced to remain in Nigeria to maintain that country's essential services. Others were enticed away from Biafra by offers of prominent and lucrative positions in the Nigeria government and by false assurance of swift Nigerian military victory over Biafra. Some of these people have regrettably been collaborating with, or otherwise aiding, the Nigerian aggressors. Biafra deplores the treacherous and patricidal activities of these persons. These deluded children of Biafra have for some time now been listening to the beneficent voices of sanity and humanity from various parts of the world, particularly from the continent of Africa and even from Nigeria itself, crying out against Nigeria's genocidal atrocities. Those voices proclaim that notwithstanding the shifting excuses advanced by Nigeria—whether it be the ostensible crushing of a rebellion or the professed maintenance of territorial integrity or the sacrosanctity of national unity—THERE CAN BE NO JUSTIFICATION WHATSOEVER for the heinous crimes being committed by Nigerians against Biafra.

This changing world attitude must be generating contrition and repentance in these erring children of Biafra. Their sense of filial pity must be compelling them to feel for their flesh and blood at home. Biafra appreciates that they have been led astray and calls upon her dutiful children at home to forgive these brothers abroad. Biafra will sincerely welcome the homecoming of her repentant children and will grant them forgiveness and safe conduct.

On this first anniversary, then, we call on these Biafrans to return to their fatherland. We have fought the gallant fight to defend the nation; we now ask them to return home to join in the rebuilding of their homesteads and their villages. We urge them not to miss this opportunity of playing some part in the foundation of this young Republic. We offer them the hospitality we Biafrans are enjoying today in our own homeland. Biafra needs all her sons and daughters, especially now.

Fellow countrymen and women, this Republic was born from tragic and unhappy circumstances. But it was born in faith and great expectations. For the past twelve months it has stood that test with increasing and unabashed faith. We have struggled together with unparalleled and indestructive resolve; we have been suffering and dying so that the young Republic may survive and play an honorable role in the comity of nations. May the blood of our youth, the tears of the bereaved, and the sweat of the suffering together water and foster, forever, the luxuriant growth of all the principles, ideals, and aspirations for which this Republic stands. With our faith fastened on God, we shall not fail.

HAIL the Republic of Biafra.

Diary of Events: May 30—June 28, 1968

May 30: Kampala peace talks break down as a result of Nigeria's insistence on "renunciation of secession" and unconditional surrender of Biafra before she will agree to cease-fire. . . . The *Spectator* (British) in a front-page article asserts that British government has become an accomplice in the slaughter of hundreds of thousands of men, women, and children. In fact, the paper emphasizes, the British government has become an accomplice in *genocide,* while "the British people averted their eyes." . . . Another British paper, the *Manchester Guardian,* comments: "The oil companies first decided to treat secession as a *force majeure* and pay royalties to Biafrans. But there were rapid second thoughts—apparently brought about by the official British calculation based on reports from Lagos, that the Federal side was sure to win a quick and easy victory."

June 3:   Shell BP begins to smuggle Biafran oil by offshore drilling under British protection.

June 7:   Government of Holland proclaims immediate and total ban on all arms shipments to Nigeria.

June 9:   British Deputy Commissioner in Benin restates Britain's determination to continue the supply of arms to Nigeria.

June 12:   France's Foreign Minister, Michel Debré, announces embargo on arms deliveries to Nigeria.

June 18:   British House of Commons holds emergency debate on British arms deliveries to Nigeria: Prime Minister Wilson does not allow the debate to come to a final vote, and arms supplies are to be continued.

June 26:   Red Cross food packets meant for refugees are discovered in Nigerian soldiers' trenches after they were pushed out of Ikot Ekpene.

June 28:   In acceptance and implementation of the suggestion of the International Committee of the Red Cross for a separate airport for relief flights, Biafran government opens a new airport, Uturu, and hands it over to relief agencies exclusively for relief flights.

Failure of the Kampala Talks

(Speech to a joint meeting of the Consultative
Assembly and the Council of Chiefs and Elders,
June 30, 1968)

I addressed this joint meeting five weeks ago, on the
eve of the departure of our delegation to the peace talks
with Nigeria at Kampala, Uganda. I outlined the devi-
ous tactics employed by London and Lagos to ward off
further support and recognition of our Republic by giving the world the false impression that they genuinely
wanted a peaceful settlement. I also indicated the stand
which our delegation would take at the talks: insistence
on a cease-fire before meaningful discussions on the settlement of the conflict. As you know, the Kampala talks
broke down. Our delegation, led by Justice Mbanefo,
O.M., has returned home.

Nigeria chose her delegation to Kampala very carefully to reflect the levity with which she regarded the
proposed proceedings at Kampala. Nigeria chose Chief
Anthony Enahoro—a fugitive offender, a felon—to lead
the delegation. He was assisted by Mallam Aminu Kano
and three renegades from Biafra—Dr. B. J. Ikpeme,
Brigadier George Kurubo, and Mr. Anthony Asika. No
delegation could be more unrepresentative of Nigeria,
none could have been more representative of the ad hoc
and illogical power combination which now calls itself
the government of Nigeria. It is certainly hard to believe
that the junta in Lagos was sincere about fruitful negotiations leading to a permanent settlement if they would
send a peace delegation from which the real Hausa-Fu-
lanis of Northern Nigeria and the Yorubas of Western
Nigeria were completely excluded. It is clear that what
went to Kampala to represent Nigeria was a gathering

of conscienceless fortune seekers, comrades in crime, representing no one but themselves.

We know that the deserved diplomatic recognition of our Republic by Tanzania, Gabon, Ivory Coast, and Zambia helped to force a reluctant Nigeria to Kampala. It was not difficult to see, right from the beginning, that Nigeria did not seriously want a peaceful settlement as long as Britain and America continued to assure her of arms supplies and diplomatic assistance, openly support her policies, and even help implement them.

In spite of all the bitterness of the past year and the grave sufferings we have undergone at the hands of the Nigerians, our delegation went to Kampala in faith and there made genuine and realistic proposals for the settlement of this conflict. We drew attention to the horrors of the present war, to the futility of military adventurism, and proposed the cessation of hostilities as a necessary preliminary to any serious talks of a permanent settlement. We therefore proposed: (1) immediate cessation of fighting on land, sea and air; (2) immediate removal of the economic blockade mounted by Nigeria against Biafra; and (3) the withdrawal of troops behind the prewar boundaries.

With regard to (1)—cessation of fighting—we shall be willing to agree to: (a) the policing of the cease-fire line by an international force, the composition of which must be agreed to by both sides; (b) a supervisory body, the composition and power of which are to be agreed, which will be stationed in the areas from which troops are withdrawn to ensure that the local population are not in any way victimized.

With regard to (2)—removal of the blockade—we shall be ready, if it is agreed, to accept the supervision at points of entry into Nigeria and Biafra to ensure that there is no arms buildup by either side while talks on Item 4 of the agenda—arrangements for a permanent settlement—continue. The aim should be to restore civilian life and administration back to normal in the war-ravaged areas as soon as possible.

Our delegation also proposed that once the cessation

of hostilities is achieved, the conference will, with confidence, examine whatever arrangements may be suggested for a permanent settlement. As has already been stated, we believe that sovereignty is the only possible way of ensuring that Biafrans have exclusive control of the protection of their own lives, liberty, and prosperity. Granted that, the Biafran delegation will propose for discussion under Item 4 of the agenda the following: (1) maximum economic cooperation and common services with Nigeria; (2) problems relating to the sharing of the assets and liabilities (including the external public debt) of the former Federation of Nigeria; (3) problems relating to the payment of compensation for the life and property of Biafrans which were lost during the pogrom and as a result of the war; and (4) the holding of a plebiscite in disputed areas in and outside Biafra.

From the personal conduct of Nigeria's delegates as individuals, from their official statements and delaying tactics at Kampala, and from the policy guidelines reportedly set out by Gowon in Lagos, it became clear that Nigeria's course was still that of war, conquest, and extermination. It is to this policy that we in Biafra must now seriously address ourselves. It is to the implications of this course, also, that we have been asking the world to address itself.

Nigeria, on the other hand, went to Kampala not to seek a peaceful end to the war but to achieve an accelerated imposition of its genocidal aims. It went to Kampala as a conqueror. Hence, the twelve-point proposal which the Nigerian delegation presented at the conference:

1. A date shall be agreed as cease-fire day.
2. A time on cease-fire day shall be agreed as cease-fire hour.
3. Twelve hours before cease-fire hour,
    (a) the rebels will renounce secession, order their troops to lay down their arms as from cease-fire hour, and announce the renunciation and the order publicly and simultaneously;
    (b) the Federal Government will order the army,

navy, and air force to cease military operations as from cease-fire hour and announce the order publicly;

(c) the Commonwealth Secretariat will make the same announcement as at (a) and (b).

4. At cease-fire hour, all troops will be frozen in their positions. An observer force drawn from a source agreed at this meeting shall take position at the cease-fire line.

5. Twenty-four hours after cease-fire hour, a mixed force shall enter rebel-held areas for the purpose of supervising the disarming of rebel forces. The mixed force shall consist of:

(a) elements of the federal army and police;

(b) elements of the observer force and

(c) Ibo policemen from police units established in liberated areas.

The mixed force shall cooperate with elements of the rebel forces.

6. Not later than seven days after cease-fire day, the administration of rebel-held areas will be handed over to the Federal Government.

7. Pending arrangements to bring the administration of the East Central State into line with the rest of the country, the Federal Government will appoint a commission to administer rebel-held areas. The commission shall consist of a chairman who is Ibo appointed by the Federal Government and a number of other members who are Ibos appointed by the Federal Government, half of whom shall be appointed in consultation with rebel leaders.

8. Law and order in the rebel areas will be the normal responsibility of the police.

9. The Federal Government will recruit persons of Ibo origin and integrate them with the Nigerian army.

10. As soon as possible, a person of East Central State origin will be appointed to the Federal Executive Council.

11. The Federal Government will, in respect of the organizers of the rebellion, grant amnesty in appropriate cases, and will, in respect of other persons connected with the rebellion, grant general amnesty.

12. Prisoners of war held by both sides and hostages taken by the rebels will be released.

These conditions would have to be accepted by our delegation before a cease-fire could be considered. The conditions were obviously unacceptable, and Nigeria must have anticipated this. But so crazed were they with their military power and the strength of the resources of Britain and other powers which stood behind them that they failed to remember that we are not a conquered nation, that we are a people determined, now as at any other time, to fight to death in defense of our nation, our survival and that of our posterity.

I wish here to express my personal thanks to the leader and the members of our delegation to Kampala for the very able way in which they represented us, for the commendable restraint they maintained in spite of grave provocations from the Nigerian side, and for the proud impression which they left behind them at Kampala of the dignity and sincerity of the people of Biafra.

It is to the justness of our position in this war and to the credit of our delegation to Kampala that the world has now placed the failures of the Kampala talks squarely at the feet of the Nigerian leadership. Almost every radio station or newspaper commentator in the world has condemned Nigeria and those who encouraged her to put forward the proposals she presented at Kampala. Distinguished leaders in Africa and in Europe have spoken out firmly in favor of our Republic.

In Britain, in particular, the public has been incensed at the callousness of the government's policy of continued armed assistance to Nigeria. The British press and public are now crying out against Nigeria's genocide and against the active participation of the British government in it; they are calling for the organization of assistance to the millions made destitute by the bombs, shells, and mortars being supplied by Britain to Nigeria; they are asking the British government to admit the justness of our cause, which has now been acknowledged in Africa and elsewhere.

Whether the British government will heed this wave of public opinion in Britain and the rest of the world is not certain; whether the British government will face up to the errors of its past policies and admit that the one-time Federation of Nigeria no longer exists and cannot be resuscitated even with the help of British mortar bombs and grenades is even more uncertain.

Three things have emerged from the events of the period since my last address to you. The first is the obvious determination of the leaders of the Lagos junta to continue in their bid for a military conquest of Biafra. To this end, they have been intensifying their military operations in a number of sectors, particularly in the Awgu and the Riverine areas of Port Harcourt, Degema, and Yenogoa provinces. The enemy, continuing to rely on massive military supplies from Britain, Russia, and other powers, has devastated most of these areas with bombs and artillery, and has rendered many more thousands of our people homeless.

The Nigerian atrocities in Biafra have continued undiminished. In Degema Province, for instance, hundreds of defenseless civilians have been tortured and killed because they refused to collaborate with the Nigerian aggressors. In some of the outlying areas, civilians caught behind enemy lines have been taken prisoners and transported to concentration camps outside their homes. In Annang, Uyo, and Eket, where our forces drove out the enemy, they found hundreds of starving and abused civilians huddled together in nasty heaps in detention centers. Some 8,000 detainees were released from several of these detention centers, and more than 3,000 from the local prisons. Among them were children, nursing mothers, and teen-age girls clearly ravished and now in dire need of medical care. The death rate in these camps was estimated by a minister gentleman who lived with and ministered to them at between twenty-five and thirty per day.

Even the food and medical supplies donated by international charitable organizations for the relief of needy Biafrans caught behind Nigerian lines have been denied them. The supplies have instead been diverted for the use of Nigerian troops. Senior representatives of some of these organizations have been able to visit these places to see things for themselves. It is idle, therefore, for the BBC and the British government now to try to hide these truths by talking of a change of policy in Lagos or by reporting the purported execution of Nigerian army officers convicted of killing innocent civilians in the Republic of Benin. These propaganda moves deceive no one, and the world knows that the genocidal policies of the Nigerian leadership are being as ruthlessly implemented now as they were this time last year.

Only last week, further firm evidence reached us of the extent of the atrocities being committed by Nigerian leaders and their agents in Annang and Uyo provinces —their so-called liberated areas of Biafra. There, the representatives of Esuene and Gowon's army officers, led by that notorious jailbird, Mr. E. O. Eyo, undertook the detention, torture, and systematic extermination of distinguished Biafran men and women who had championed the cause of the people throughout this period of crisis and war. Among the men now reported executed are such proud and illustrious sons of Biafra as:

Mr. A. A. Obot, principal of Lutheran High School and former member of Eastern House of Assembly. He was tied to a Land Rover and dragged to a gruesome death.

Prince Umo Ndak, member of the former Federal House of Representatives.

Mr. H. U. Akpabio, Minister in the former Eastern Nigeria government.

Mr. J. B. Umana, information attaché to the former Eastern Nigeria Deputy High Commissioner in London. His body was left for days to feed the vultures.

Chief O. U. Affiah, Minister in the former Eastern Nigeria government.

Mr. H. O. Akpan-Udo, member of the former Federal House of Representatives.

Chief R. A. Umo, member of the former Federal Nigerian Senate.

Mr. U. U. Okure, former member of the Public Service
Commission and later chairman of the Calabar Cement
Company.

Yet, in the face of all this, Lagos and the British government continue to talk of a change in Nigeria's genocidal policy. If such ghastly atrocities are perpetrated in
the non-Ibo areas of Biafra, the rest of the story is quite
obvious.

The second emergence since I last addressed you is
the apparent reassertion of the British government's attitude to the current Nigeria-Biafra conflict as revealed
by Lord Shepherd's recent activities and utterances.
History is replete with accurate parallels of the British
government's hypocrisy, duplicity, and blackmail in
their pursuit of economic or imperialist aims. As far as
those aims are concerned, considerations of morality
and humanity do not matter. Their behavior today
against Biafra coincides with their behavior in 1921–22
against another people struggling as we are doing today
for self-determination and security. The pattern is the
same. The scene, the background, and the actors are
different, but the characters, the characteristics, and the
London stage remain the same.

It was during that time that a noble British Lord proclaimed in the House of Lords: "I, as an Englishman,
rejoice to see them [the Irish people] making this effort.
If there are to be struggles and fisticuffs, and if blood
is to be shed, then in the first place it ought to be Irish
blood. . . . If the task is effectively carried out by them,
the fact that it should be done by them and not by us
will have resulted in an economy of English lives."

Those words could accurately and honestly be spoken
by Lord Shepherd today. As far as the British government is concerned, if it does not involve the loss of
British lives, there is nothing wrong in our current war,
where Africans kill fellow Africans, and Britain will
continue to supply one side with the means as she did in
the case of the Irish.

We have consistently said that the British government is our real enemy. It is the British government which goaded Nigeria into the current war of genocide, and it is the British government which has sustained Nigeria with arms and ammunition to carry out the massacre of Biafrans. In this, the British government has defied British and world public opinion.

The British government's maneuvers through Lord Shepherd were for purposes other than peace. The real aims were:

1. to assuage and stultify the mounting tide of British and world public opinion against the British government's role in this conflict;
2. to retrieve the diplomatic losses Nigeria suffered following the breakdown of the Kampala talks;
3. to lead the world to believe that the Kampala talks had in fact not broken down, thus holding back further diplomatic recognition by sympathetic and understanding countries of the world;
4. to allow Nigeria time to achieve the Anglo-Nigerian aim of a military solution.

Fortunately for us and the world, Lord Shepherd's much-vaunted visit to Lagos and the outcome of that visit have been revealing. During one of his meetings in London with our representative, Mr. Justice Mbanefo, Lord Shepherd put forward certain proposals which included the idea of a peace-keeping force following a cease-fire. He described the proposals as exploratory. Our delegate merely expressed his views on them. There was no real discussion, let alone an agreement which could only be reached after the necessary details had been worked out.

Lord Shepherd then went to Lagos, and after his two-day discussion with Gowon and his men, the BBC blared to the anxious world that the talks had been very satisfactory. So satisfied and happy were Lord Shepherd and his Nigerian friends that he had to postpone his departure by a day in order to celebrate and toast their achievement at the Lagos Island Club and to visit Calabar to witness a stage-managed demonstration of the people of Calabar in support of Britain and Nigeria.

On his return, Lord Shepherd elatedly spoke to reporters of "the joy of people of smaller tribes who live in that district."

The impressions of Lord Shepherd about his visit to Calabar are reminiscent of the impressions of another British peer who visited a European country under occupation and found the people "boundlessly happy to be overrun." Let me, in passing, assure Lord Shepherd that if he came to Biafra he would find Nigerian prisoners of war, including the Hausas, joyously telling him that they could find no greater heaven anywhere than in Biafra!

From the utterances of Lord Shepherd in and outside Parliament, and of Mr. Thompson in Parliament since Lord Shepherd's return, it is clear that, far from changing, the policy and attitude of the British government have actually hardened. The aim remains a military solution and the annihilation of the people of Biafra.

Asked about the question of a cease-fire, having regard to the positions of both sides, Lord Shepherd replied, "Well, as far as the federal government is concerned, they stand for a united Nigeria, and I think this makes sense."

He then plunged into antics of blackmail when he said, "Sir Louis Mbanefo said to me that the one reason why they wish to have sovereignty was for their own protection, i.e., the protection of the Ibos. Now, as you see in the communiqué, the federal government have agreed and so has Sir Louis Mbanefo agreed that there should be an external force, presumably from the Commonwealth, who would be going to give protection and security to the Ibos in that area, and I would have therefore thought that the main question of secession as now required by the Biafran authorities has been met."

Earlier, Lord Shepherd had told the world that Mr.

Justice Mbanefo had given him the mandate of deciding
for Biafra when there was satisfaction that there could
be meaningful talks with Nigeria, to enable our delegates to return. Our trusted and respected delegate
never did or said such things. It is nothing but gross
misrepresentations bordering on blackmail.

I must, at this juncture, inform the House that only
last night I received from our representative in London
the following extracts from a letter by Lord Shepherd:

> At the meeting on the 15 June, I obtained from Sir Louis
> an agreement that if I were able to give Sir Louis an as-
> surance that, in the view of Her Majesty's Government,
> the Federal Government of Nigeria were ready for genuine
> and meaningful talks, he would be prepared to restart in-
> formal discussions.
>
> At a subsequent meeting on 19 June I reported I was
> going to Lagos for the purpose of satisfying myself that
> Lagos was prepared to engage in meaningful informal talks
> in London. Sir Louis assured me that if I were satisfied,
> there was no doubt that a fully authorized Biafran repre-
> sentative would be available in London.
>
> I was in Lagos from 20 to 24 June and had full discus-
> sions against this background with the Lagos authorities.
> As a result I am satisfied that the Federal Government are
> prepared to engage in informal talks with Biafran repre-
> sentatives in London and that such talks can be meaningful.
> I am convinced that the Federal Government are genuine
> and hope that the Biafrans for their part may take this
> renewed opportunity to have discussions which can bring
> about a cease-fire and an end to the fighting.

There is nothing in the foregoing to show the grounds
of Lord Shepherd's satisfaction that the talks would be
meaningful. It is, therefore, quite clear that, as far as
Biafra is concerned, this particular Lord cannot be our
Shepherd.

Meanwhile, the British government stands by its policy of military solution, for which it must continue to
supply Nigeria with arms. Nigeria has been continuing
its offensives unabated—after all, the area left to be

conquered, according to Lord Shepherd, is very small. The British government will stop supplying arms only when there is a catastrophe, and what could that mean other than the complete extermination of Biafrans?

Yes, it is the British government against which we are fighting. That British troops have not been massively committed along with British arms against us arises mainly from two considerations—the fear of world opinion and the fear of losing British lives if they can avoid that.

Does the world want further proof of British interest and direct involvement in this war? Then let me tell them that only a few weeks ago the First Secretary of the British High Commission in Lagos was fatally wounded while touring the Port Harcourt front of the war in the company of Nigerian troops. What should have been the motive in a British diplomat visiting a war front if the government he represented was not actively involved in the war?

The third thing standing out of the events of the past month is the universal recognition of the human misery and suffering which the Nigerian war of genocide and aggression has brought to our people. There are in Biafra today more than 4,500,000 displaced persons, the great majority of whom come from the so-called minority tribes who inhabit the peripheries of Biafra. In recognition of the mortal danger they stand at the hands of the Nigerian aggressors, our people troop out of the disturbed areas to crowd our refugee camps, penniless and dejected, having abandoned all their property, to live under most appalling conditions. In the past few weeks, several world organizations and even governments have shown great interest in the plight of our people and are taking urgent steps to arrange for food and other relief to be assembled for Biafra.

It is a source of considerable comfort that, in the midst of the current conflict, every effort is being made by international organizations to bring in relief supplies to our suffering people. Some of these organizations

have in the past sent in aid direct to us in spite of
pressures put on them by the Lagos regime. Today, as
more organizations plan for more relief to us, Nigeria
is bringing pressure on them to play politics with the
gifts.

Some interested foreign governments will as usual
bring the weight of their influence to suggest that aid
to us be channeled through Nigeria. It should not be
necessary to comment on the absurdity of this suggestion. How unnatural and wicked it would be to have
relief meant for us to be channeled through the very
enemies with whom we have been at war for almost a
year, through those who refuse to have a cease-fire in
the very hostilities which brought about the present
hardships.

Would Britain have accepted such aid from Germany
in 1943? Some foreign governments otherwise in a position to be of great assistance to our suffering countrymen can choose to be cynical in the present circumstances and continue to send their million dollars' worth
of relief through Lagos. We cannot dictate to them.
But they hurt us immensely and unnecessarily by telling
the world that such aid is meant to bring relief to our
people.

On the purely technical level, it is obvious that if
supplies meant for Biafra are shipped to an airport or
seaport in Nigeria or areas of Biafra now controlled
by Nigeria, further arrangements will need to be made
for their trans-shipment in smaller consignments and for
their subsequent redistribution overland through several
fighting zones which will need very delicate and careful
policing, even if the bridges along the road have not
been blown. All this will entail many delays and immense difficulties. This is why we have offered an airport in Biafra which the relief organizations can use for
easy and quick shuttles from Sao Tome.

Our enemies cannot be our benefactors. And posterity will not forgive us if we compromise our ultimate
survival as a people (for which we are fighting against

the Nigerian aggressors) in order to accept relief channeled through Nigeria.

The British government still has an invaluable opportunity to think again. It is hypocritical in the extreme
for the British government now to appear to be interested in bringing relief by way of milk and butter to
Biafra when it is still adamant in its policy of sending
more arms and ammunition to Nigeria for the destruction of Biafrans. Britain cannot inspire world confidence
about her genuineness for peace until she publicly renounces her support for Nigeria's genocidal aggression
on Biafra.

The British government has for long continued to
argue that they require the continuation of arms supplies to Nigeria to be able to influence the Lagos junta.
From the statements and communiqué issued since Lord
Shepherd's visit to Nigeria, it is clear that this influence
is certainly for ill, encouraging Nigeria to impose a
military solution to a human problem.

All the arguments put forward by the British government for the continued supply of arms to Nigeria have
now been exploded, and the world, including the British
press, the British public, and British Members of Parliament, are no longer deceived. Britain is not the "traditional supplier" of arms to Nigeria. As I have said
on another occasion, Nigeria stopped the purchase of
rifles and machine guns from Britain in 1964. Nigeria
bought her 106 recoilless rifles and shells from America,
rifles from Italy, machine guns from Germany, artillery
guns from Italy, and mortars from Israel. As of 1964,
Britain supplied Nigeria with just twelve Ferret cars
and two Saladins.

A new but meaningless argument now advanced by
the British government is that her supply of arms represents only 15 percent of Nigeria's total requirements.
The mortar bombs, artillery shells, and Saladins which
have made Nigeria's large-scale devastation of our cities
and their penetration of our territory possible have been
British-supplied. Until Britain actually stops arms sup-

plies to Nigeria while proposing milk and butter for Biafra, Biafrans will be justified in believing that, to the British government, Biafrans are turkeys being fattened for some Christmas.

Since the last meeting of this Assembly, several countries, including France, Holland, and Czechoslovakia, have backed out of contracts for supplying arms to Nigeria. The actual position is that Britain is now one on a rapidly contracting list of arms suppliers. The rest are Russia, Belgium, and Spain.

Let us emphasize here and now that the Kampala talks have ended. Our chief delegate made the position quite clear that he would return to London only in the event of the prospects for a meaningful discussion emerging from the visit of Lord Shepherd to Lagos. In this we were to be the judge. As far as we can now see, such a situation has not emerged.

Many interested governments and organizations have sent observers to Biafra since the present war to acquaint themselves with the actual conditions in our Republic. Our door remains open for any interested government or organization to send a mission to Biafra to meet the people of this Republic and obtain a first-hand impression of the nature of the conflict and the feelings of the people.

The policy of the United States government in this matter is now a source of embarrassment to many friends of America in Biafra and to those who believed that America's public stance of neutrality in the present conflict was genuine. Obviously under the influence of its onetime ambassador to Lagos (Joseph Palmer), the United States government has now confirmed itself in a policy of open hostility to Biafra.

Surely the United States government cannot be ignorant of the destruction of life and property, the displacement of large populations, the general misery, which this senseless war they are supporting has brought about. Surely the United States government is aware of the wave of world opinion condemning the continuation

of the present war. Surely the United States government realizes that this destruction they now appear to
condone cannot possibly help bring about peace and
stability to this part of Africa. It is not too much to ask
of a major signatory to the Charter of the United
Nations Organization that she should cease to be an
accomplice in genocide.

The United States, as Britain's chief ally, can exert
a great deal of influence for good in the present crisis
by impressing on the British government the good sense
of our contention that peaceful settlement is possible
and that an immediate cease-fire is necessary to create
the atmosphere for such settlement.

If she could do this, a state of near-normalcy can be
reached for Nigeria and Biafra to work out the details
of their future association and of the possible areas of
cooperation between them. It should be possible for the
principals of both sides to meet after cease-fire to bring
up any point which may be a step in the direction of a
peaceful settlement.

I think we have made it abundantly clear to the
world that the only settlement we can accept is one
which satisfies the needs and the wishes of the people
for whom we speak and on whose undisputed mandate
we act. In the early months of this war, our struggle
was maliciously called "Ojukwu's rebellion" by our
enemies; later they began to call it the "Ibo resistance."
Sooner or later they are bound to accept realities and
admit that this struggle has been nothing short of a
struggle for survival and self-determination involving all
Biafrans.

Happily, the world is now beginning to hear something and acknowledge our people's expressions of their
right to self-determination. The issues involved in this
conflict affect the very lives of each and every one of
the 14,000,000 people of Biafra. No settlement is therefore valid which does not take very serious cognizance
of this fact. It cannot be an agreement among leaders
of the two countries, merely on paper; it cannot be

simply a face-saving arrangement intended to soothe the conscience of foreign ministers. It must be a settlement which fully satisfies the deepest urges of our men and women who have taken up arms against mighty odds to defend their lives and property and ensure that there is a homeland for the security of those that come after them.

It was from this conviction that we challenged the present leaders of Nigeria to accept a plebiscite in the disputed areas of Nigeria and Biafra to determine the true wishes of the people in those areas. Those who now lead Nigeria know too well the reality of the popular support in all the provinces of this Republic for our stand in this conflict to agree to such a plebiscite.

It has become abundantly clear to discerning observers inside and outside Nigeria that the leaders of the regime in Lagos are refusing to accept a cease-fire because only as long as the war continues can they hope to remain in power. Because they now control the military machine which Britain and other countries have lavishly made available, these so-called leaders are adamant in their ambition to impose their will on the Biafran people. In sharp contrast to the democratic practices of our government here in Biafra, the Lagos junta has on no occasion, or over any issue, gone to the people or to representatives chosen by them to ascertain their wishes. There is no form of representation by which they can hold effective consultations with their people. Contact between the junta and the general population is simply on the point of the rifle.

No wonder their leaders are adamant in their pursuit of a discredited and ruinous policy. And should there be any doubt about this contention, we dare the Nigerian leadership to hold general elections under international supervision in Nigeria within three months of a cease-fire to choose civilian leaders to represent the wishes of the people. We would ourselves be willing to do likewise in Biafra.

All of us had hoped that our efforts and sincerity for

an early return to peace would be rewarded. But Nigeria and the British government have continued in their intransigence. Their war of genocide continues, and so long as the enemy continues in his bid to exterminate us, so long shall we continue to resist. There is no question of going back, let alone failing to fulfill our duty to our people.

A few weeks ago I announced to the world that we had entered the second phase in this struggle. Our strategy is yielding devastating results against the enemy, and it is gathering momentum.

A problem no less momentous than the war itself is the problem of refugees. The government is doing its utmost to tackle it. In this, everyone in Biafra is, as usual, involved. And as I have said, we welcome any assistance from any part of the world coming from genuine and unadulterated motives. We are grateful to those who have risen to our needs.

The struggle continues, and no one can predict when it will end. But we know how it will end—in triumph for our right to survive as a people, in spite of all odds. We must remain resolute in our faith in God and in the cause for which we are struggling.

Diary of Events: July 3—August 5, 1968

July 3: It becomes known that two West Niger Ibos were in fact murdered in place of two "field commanders" who were said to have been executed in Benin. The two men were Nwabuofu Umunna of Ibusa and Theophilus Ofili of Asaba. They were accused of actively working in support of Biafra.

July 4: Belgium becomes fifth European country to ban arms exports to Nigeria.

July 8: Lagos announces that its air force commanders have been ordered to seek out and destroy all "unauthorized" aircraft, including Red Cross mercy flights.

July 11: World Jewish Congress calls on the United Nations to halt the Nigeria-Biafra war.

July 14: Swiss students collect more than £15,000 for war victims in Biafra.

July 15: Nationwide aid-Biafra campaign launched in Switzerland to alleviate suffering of Biafra war victims.

July 16: OAU consultative meeting invites Lt. Col. Gowon and me to attend the committee's meeting in Niamey.

July 17: French Foreign Minister, Michel Debré, announces relief supplies will be sent to suffering people of Biafra.

July 19: I address the OAU peace committee in Niamey. I propose two possible routes for land-sea corridors for relief supplies which would obviate dangers and doubts of contact with Nigerian forces. . . . Nigerian rebel junta announces that a final military solution in Biafra will be achieved within four to six weeks.

July 23: French newspaper *Le Monde* in an editorial emphasizes that without British and Soviet support, Gowon will not continue the war.

July 30: Five more army officers from Chad Republic join Nigeria army. The team is led by Captain C. Ahmed.

August 1: Plan by Nigeria army to carry out massive offensive air and land attack on three Biafran towns on August 3 is uncovered; 20 British officers and three squadrons of British parachutists to be involved in the operation.

August 2: West Germany makes further contribution of £500,000 to the victims of the war.

August 3: Twenty-four vehicles which Britain

claimed were sent to Nigeria for transporting relief supplies to Biafra are commissioned to military service by Nigerian soldiers in Enugu-Awgu sector.

August 5: Beginning of Addis Ababa peace talks.

Address at Addis Ababa

(August 5, 1968)

Your Imperial Majesty, Your Excellencies,

With all humility and the deepest respect, I salute you. I extend to you all the gratitude of the people of Biafra for your concern about the sufferings of our people, following the calculated and systematic acts of genocide and total extermination being carried out against them. We are extremely grateful that you have made it possible for us to state before you and the world our case and position with regard to this unfortunate conflict. Speaking for myself and the entirety of the afflicted people of Biafra, and having regard to our love of peace, progress, and justice in Africa, we feel totally ashamed that we should be associated with an unnecessary and futile war which has brought considerable discredit and shame to Africa.

There is no precedent for a people being victim of such injustice and being at present threatened by abandonment to its aggressor. Also there has never before been an example of any government proceeding to the systematic extermination of a nation by a barbarous means in violation of the most solemn promises made to all the nations of the earth.

It is in order to denounce to the civilized world the tortures inflicted upon my people that I resolved to come to Geneva.

I was defending the cause of all small people who are threatened by aggression. . . . It is us today. It will be you tomorrow.

"Today" was June 30, 1936. The speaker and circumstances are well known to all who have pride in Africa. The appeal was made to a world which seemed to have misplaced its conscience.

The appeal went unheeded to a world already deafened by the cacophony of clanging armor and rattling sabers of a war which was to bring misery to the world on an unprecedented scale. The League of Nations collapsed.

Today I stand before this august assembly because the lessons of this vivid past have not been learned. I stand before you because the prophetic tomorrow has all too soon become the lot of my people today.

For more than twelve months, a cruel and bloody war has been waged by Nigeria against the people of Biafra. During this period more lives have been lost and more property destroyed than at any other time in the known history of the African continent. An area of our continent noted for its promise and plenty, a region dedicated to justice, peace, and progress is being brutalized and turned into a spectacle of fear and famine, disease and death.

The people of Biafra have always maintained that war can solve none of the fundamental ills which have plagued our part of the continent for decades. If anything, it can only profit the enemies of Africa who dread the progress of the African and his determination to escape from their tutelage and dependence. That is why these enemies of African peace and progress are actively and shamelessly fanning the embers of a senseless and fratricidal war by supplying the weapons of destruction to one side and are doing everything to obstruct the way and efforts toward a just and honorable peace.

May I with all humility and respect venture to say that Your Excellencies have a special responsibility to both present and future generations of Africans to ensure that this war is brought to an immediate end.

Africa must demonstrate her capacity to settle her

own problems free from dictation by foreign vested interests. She must pledge herself to the preservation of those norms and practices that distinguish her from all other peoples.

The world has rightly focused her attention on this conference taking place in this great African city. The world challenges Africa to grapple, with sincerity and justice, the problem which she has set out to resolve. We cannot, we dare not, fail without compromising the self-respect, the maturity, and the dignity of the African race.

We, the people of Biafra, have come to this conference determined to ensure success for peace. Right from the beginning of the current conflict, and even before, we have always believed that this is an African problem which can be solved only by Africa. We as a people seek nothing but peace and security—peace to save us from extermination and security to enable us to develop our talents for the upliftment of Africa. We have no doubt that after hearing our case the problem which hitherto had seemed intractable will be easily amenable to your mediation.

Repeatedly, we have made appeals for the intervention of African states into the dispute. A number of African Heads of State have also offered their good offices in quest for a peaceful solution. It was Gowon who consistently and contemptuously spurned all such proposals on the fatuous pretext that the matter was an internal affair of Nigeria. For example, following the controversy resulting from Nigeria's failure to implement the Aburi Agreement we pressed that we should move out of Nigeria into a neighboring African state to iron out the differences. Gowon would not countenance such a move. Instead, he arranged a meeting of the Supreme Military Council in Benin and wanted to bring in British troops to ensure the security of those attending. It was with difficulty that Gowon was persuaded to agree to the holding of the last abortive peace talks in Africa. His choice had been London. For chairmanship of the talks, Nigeria wanted a non-African in the person of Mr. Arnold Smith of Canada. When we insisted on an African chairman, Nigeria preferred to have no chairman at all.

The whole background to this conflict is well known to all of you. Yet, this being a historic occasion, I implore you to bear with me while I recall in some detail the developments which not only form the background to the current conflict but will best clarify our position and aspirations.

Background to the Nigerian Crisis of 1966

Although the conglomeration of territories formerly known as Nigeria was now and then held up to the world, by those who created it, as "democracy's best hope in Africa," it was never a democracy. Furthermore, the former Federation of Nigeria encompassed peoples of such vast political, economic, religious, and cultural differences as could hardly ever have coexisted peacefully as one independent political entity.

In what was Eastern Nigeria—now Biafra—we found in Christianity much that corresponded to our own traditional outlook on life. We readily accepted the egalitarian and democratic ideas—and other things in their wake—introduced by Christian Europe and America.

On the other hand, as a result of the separatist attitude of feudal Northern Nigeria, a vast section of the Northern Nigeria public was left out of the mainstream of educational, technological, and industrial development which has taken place in the rest of Nigeria in the last hundred years. The government, the missionary houses, and the business firms wanted men and women to man their new establishments, and naturally they employed those Nigerians who had the requisite education and training. A considerable number of the employable men came from the then Eastern Nigeria, whose people had made progress in learning and adopting the new ideas and skills introduced by Europeans and Americans.

Our Role in the Development of Nigeria

Christian education and Western training stimulated and enriched our native resourcefulness, industry, and dynamism and so contributed in no small measure to the leading role we played in the development of Nigeria during the half century before 1966. In all spheres of life in the former Federation of Nigeria—economic, social, cultural, political, and constitutional—we were in the forefront of the struggle for unity and equality, justice and progress.

Economically, down to the late 1950's, our territory was relegated to the backwaters as a destitute area. National institutions, projects, and utilities were deliberately sited outside our territory. Nevertheless, we invested confidently in the development of the whole of Nigeria. We unhesitatingly built houses, hotels, shops, market stalls, etc., in various parts of the country, sometimes on the strength of mere certificates of occupancy which could be, and indeed often were, revoked at will in Northern Nigeria. We provided intermediate and high-level manpower for the development of Nigeria, only to be later frustrated and expelled from positions we had earned on merit.

After the fashion of the Christian missionaries, we built schools and colleges and supplied teachers and lecturers for general education throughout the country. In the same manner, we established hospitals and nursing homes and provided doctors and nurses for healing and tending the sick. We strove in every way to identify ourselves with the peoples of the areas in which we settled. We spoke their language; we intermarried with them; and Northern Nigerians even declared that, because we wore their dresses, they had conquered us culturally. Yet, in spite of all this, in Northern Nigeria we were physically and socially segregated from the indigenous people. In contrast, the people of Western Nigeria, who shared the same education and cultural experience, took pride in being "traditionally reluctant" to settle in and contribute to the development of places outside their region.

In the field of political and constitutional development, while we advocated a strong, united Nigeria and had for our watchword ONE COUNTRY, ONE CONSTITUTION, ONE DESTINY, Northern Nigerians consistently and openly maintained that the Amalgamation of Northern and Southern Nigeria in 1914 was "a mistake." Not surprisingly, in January, 1950, at the General Conference summoned at Ibadan to discuss proposals for the review of the Nigerian Constitution, the Northern Nigeria delegates announced that "unless the Northern Region was allowed 50 percent of the seats in the Central Legislature it would ask for separation from the rest of Nigeria on the arrangements existing before 1914." In other words, Northern Nigeria would secede. Eventually, to avoid breaking up the country, we conceded this demand.

At the Ibadan Conference of 1950, also, Northern Nigerians insisted that "only Northern Nigerian male adults of twenty-five years or more, resident in the Region for three years, should be qualified for election to the Northern House of Assembly." In reply, our delegates were obliged to enter a minority report in which they raised an issue of fundamental principle. They asserted:

It is in our view invidious that any Nigerian could under a Nigerian Constitution be deprived of the right of election to the House of Assembly in any region in which he for the time being—or permanently—has his abode, merely by reason of the accident of birth or ancestry.

Three years later, in May, 1953, during one of the recurrent constitutional crises of those years, Northern Nigeria again agitated for secession. They published an eight-point proposal for the establishment of a "Central Agency" to maintain what was in effect a Common Services Organization. To secure the implementation of this proposal by force, Northern Nigerian leaders organized and carried out violent demonstrations, during which they slaughtered and wounded hundreds of our people then resident in Kano, Northern Nigeria, acts of genocide which they had perpetrated at Jos in Northern Nigeria earlier in 1945. In the end, we had to abandon the idea of a strong and united country which we had been advocating and, with difficulty, persuaded Northern Nigerians to accept a stronger federal system of government than that which was envisaged by them.

The following year, as a result of its failure to absorb Lagos, Western Nigeria also threatened to secede and was only prevented from proceeding to make good the threat by a stern and timely warning from the British Secretary of State for the colonies, Mr. Oliver Lyttleton (afterward Lord Chandos).

Nigeria After Independence

It was in these precarious circumstances that Nigeria acceded to independence on October 1, 1960. Not unexpectedly, the five years immediately after that date were marked by successive crises; notably the Tiv Riots of 1960–66, the Western Nigeria Emergency of 1962, the National Census Controversy of 1962–63, the Federal Election Crisis of 1964–65, and the Western Election Crisis of 1965–66.

By January, 1966, it had become clear that unless the situation was arrested the successive crises experienced by the country before and since independence would certainly lead to unutterable disaster.

The existing Independence Constitution gave Northern Nigeria a built-in 50 percent representation in the federal Parliament, an arrangement which assured the region permanent control of the federal government. The *New Statesman* of London aptly described the Northern Nigerian Head of the federal government as *"Prime Minister in apparent perpetuity."*

Each crisis had been impossible to resolve satisfactorily, partly because of the men who handled it. A great number of the politicians and others in public life were known to be corrupt, ostentatious, and selfish. Bribery and nepotism were rife. There was widespread inordinate ambition for power, an evil mirrored in the prevalence of thuggery, hooliganism, and lawlessness. To win power or to keep themselves in power, public men had sown unhealthy rivalry, suspicion, and mistrust among the various communities of the country. Thus the unabashed rigging of the Western election of October, 1965, came to be the last straw. The widespread violence which it precipitated took thousands of lives. Law and order broke down in the Western Region. Since each of the other regions had an interest in the election, it was obvious that the country was on the brink of civil war. And yet the Northern Nigeria-controlled federal government, the last hope of the people, would not discharge its responsibility. Indeed many an objective observer interpreted its inaction in the face of the impending national collapse as virtual abdication.

January 15 Revolution

These were the circumstances in which some young army officers and men decided to act. They originated from all parts of Nigeria—North, West, Midwest, and East. It was a revolt against injustice and oppression. From available information, their aims were threefold: to put an end to the sufferings of Nigerian citizens in Tiv land and Western Nigeria, to dethrone corrupt and dishonest politicians, and to restore public faith at home and retrieve Nigeria's reputation abroad. They attempted to overthrow the federal and regional governments. In desperation the federal government handed over power to the armed forces under the general officer commanding the Nigerian army, Major General J. T. U. Aguiyi-Ironsi, who happened to originate from the then Eastern Nigeria and who had in no way been connected with the revolution. The revolution was spontaneously acclaimed inside and outside Nigeria. Nigerians basked in the general relief that a corrupt, unpopular, and unstable regime had been deposed.

The Ironsi Regime

The military administration of General Ironsi made the first real attempt to unite the country and its peoples. The general approached his enormous task with transparent honesty, unflinching confidence, and unalloyed patriotism. The main organs of the central government which he established—the Supreme Military Council and the Federal Executive Council—were representative of all the regions of the country. Whether it was the appointment of tribunals of inquiry into political activities, financial deals, and personal accounts of suspects or appointments to top posts in the federal public service and statutory corporations or the disposition of command in the army, General Ironsi promoted the interest of the country as a whole. He endeavored to accelerate the economic development of Northern Nigeria in order to bring the region in line with other parts of the country.

Genocide of 1966

On May 24, 1966, Major General Aguiyi-Ironsi promulgated Decree No. 34. That decree was the implementation of a decision of the Federal Supreme Military Council, in which all the regional military governors were represented. The decree was intended to establish a National Executive Council for the whole country with the regional military governors as members and to unify the top cadres of the civil service to ensure the efficient administration of the country for the duration of the military regime.

Ironically enough, it was this decree (popularly known as the Unification Decree) that sparked off widespread rioting and violence directed against the lives and property of Eastern Nigerians in Northern Nigeria. It did not seem to matter to the leaders who planned the riots that Eastern Nigerians were in a terrible minority (3 out of 9 members) in the Supreme Military Council that took the collective decision. The death toll of our people in the massacres of that month stood at 3,000. A high-powered commission was appointed by the Supreme Military Council to investigate the causes and the conduct of the May riots in Northern Nigeria. An English judge of the Supreme Court was appointed chairman. Northern Nigerian leaders never allowed that commission to meet.

In the meantime, firm assurances of personal safety for our people in Northern Nigeria had been given by the Supreme Military Council itself, and by the Sultan of Sokoto and the emirs of the North. On the strength of these assurances, we appealed to our people who had fled their stations to return to Northern Nigeria. They did.

At this point Major General Aguiyi-Ironsi undertook an extensive tour of Northern and Midwestern Nigeria and arranged to round off his tour at Ibadan in Western Nigeria with a meeting of traditional rulers and chiefs from all over Nigeria to seek their advice on matters affecting the future of the country. The meeting was scheduled for July 29, 1966. But in the morning of that day, a well-organized group of Northern soldiers kidnapped the Supreme Commander and his host, Lieutenant Colonel Adekunle Fajuyi, the military governor of Western Nigeria, and subsequently murdered them in very gruesome circumstances. The cruel massacre of more than 200 Eastern Nigerian army officers and men also took place.

The pace of violence seemed at the time to be quickening. Its character seemed also to be worsening. Brigadier Ogundipe, then the most senior officer in the army, was compelled to abandon his responsibility; he escaped from Nigeria and was later posted to London as Nigeria's High Commissioner to Britain. In the confusion and violence which followed all over Nigeria, we made efforts to get Lieutenant Colonel Yakubu Gowon, the coordinator and spokesman for the Northern Nigeria rebels, to stop the bloodshed. The rebels stipulated two conditions for doing so: (1) That the Republic of Nigeria be split into its component units. (2) That all Southern Nigerians resident in Northern Nigeria be repatriated to the South, and all Northerners resident in the South be repatriated to the North.

In pursuance of these demands, all available aircraft at Ikeja airport had been commandeered and used in repatriating the families and belongings of Northern Nigerian top civil servants and other officials the moment the rebellion of the Northern Nigerian army officers and men began in the Lagos area.

We had no alternative in the circumstances but to accept the Northern Nigerian terms for a cease-fire in order at least to bring a halt to the mass killings and the general breakdown of law and order in the country. It would also give the army itself the opportunity to decide on its leadership, a necessary condition for the restoration of normal conditions in the country.

It was well known before May, 1966, that there were very powerful moves in Northern Nigeria for secession from the federation. With the support of British government officials these interests—traditional rulers, politicians, civil servants, and intellectuals—were known to have planned and led the riots of May and the rebellion of July. Their July putsch was given the code name of ARABA, or secession. The purpose of the British government in supporting the riots was to restore Northern domination of the country. But Northern Nigerians understood this as support for the secession which they had been demanding over the years. In the event, Lieutenant Colonel Gowon was persuaded by the British High Commissioner in Nigeria, Sir Francis Cumming-Bruce, not to make his scheduled broadcast proclaiming the secession of Northern Nigeria. Nevertheless, in his first broadcast on August 1, 1966, Lieutenant Colonel Gowon declared: "Suffice it to say that putting all considerations to test, political, economic as well as social, the base for unity is not there."

The August Preliminary Meeting

On August 9, 1966, representatives of the military governors held a meeting with those of Lieutenant Colonel Gowon to propose some urgent steps to halt the pace of violence and destruction and reduce tension in the country. It was decided that an Ad Hoc Constitutional Conference made up of regional delegations be convened to recommend in broad outline the future form of association for the different regions of Nigeria. It was agreed that immediate steps be taken to return military personnel to barracks within their respective regions of origin. The maintenance of peace and security in the Lagos area was left to Lieutenant Colonel Gowon, acting in consultation with the military governors.

Had these basic decisions been implemented, promptly and completely, much of the history of the next several months might have been different. But Lieutenant Colonel Gowon did or wanted no such thing. With respect to Western Nigeria, for example, he refused to repatriate Northern Nigerian soldiers to their region of origin, in opposition to the demands of the chiefs, leaders, and people of Western Nigeria. We implemented the decisions fully. In keeping with an earlier agreement, Northern Nigerian soldiers then in our territory left for their home region with their arms and some quantity of ammunition for self-defense. On the other hand, our soldiers returning from Northern Nigeria were denied both arms and ammunition. Exposed and defenseless, these soldiers became easy victims of ridicule, molestation, and torture by Northern Nigerians.

In Lagos it was completely impossible to guarantee the personal safety of our military personnel. Major Ekanem, the provost marshal of Ikeja garrison, was shot dead on Carter Bridge, Lagos, in broad daylight; at Ikeja airport another of our officers, Captain Okoye, was captured and subsequently tortured to death. In

Yaba two officers, Lieutenant Colonel Eze and Captain Ilo, obeyed appeals from Gowon to return to duty. Captain Ilo was shot dead; Colonel Eze managed to escape with injuries.

About the same time, armed Northern Nigerian soldiers drove to the Benin prisons in Midwestern Nigeria and abducted army officers and men in detention there following the January 15 revolution. Their fellow Northern Nigerians among them were set free; the others, mainly our people, were murdered under very brutal circumstances.

Throughout this period our territory remained the only part of the former Federation of Nigeria which could boast of peace and order. Though there was bitterness at the treatment meted out to our people in parts of Nigeria, there was no attempt on the part of the people to avenge on Nigerians resident among us. Instead, our people remained calm and restrained in the face of overwhelming provocation. They were, of course, fully aware of the pattern of events throughout Lagos, Western Nigeria, and Northern Nigeria. They saw evidence of genocide in the killings. Somehow, they hoped that it would be possible to check the drift of events and that Nigeria could still be saved.

It is pertinent here to state categorically that we never recognized Gowon as the Head of the Nigerian Federal Military Government. Gowon is a rebel. I made this point convincingly clear during the Aburi meeting of January, 1967, and it was in acceptance of this fact that it was agreed at that meeting that one of the first things to do on our return from Aburi was to formally elect a Commander-in-Chief, whose duty would be to preside over the meetings of the Supreme Military Council.

As the days passed by in August, the wave of massacres in Northern Nigeria began to gather momentum. From even the remotest villages of the region, our people were fleeing for dear life to the bigger towns, from whence to return home. At Kaduna on August 30, and in the early days of September, our people fleeing Northern Nigeria were again attacked in the railway stations and several hundreds were killed. Those who escaped abandoned all their possessions. In Minna and many other Northern Nigerian towns, the African Continental Bank and other businesses owned by our government and people were attacked and looted. Their agents and owners fled back to their homeland, determined never to return.

The September Ad Hoc Constitutional Conference

These developments notwithstanding, and even though they were taking very serious personal risks, our delegates attended the Ad Hoc Constitutional Conference which began in Lagos on September 12, 1966. In his opening address to the conference, Lieutenant Colonel Gowon suggested the following alternative forms of association for Nigeria: "(a) a federal system with a strong central government; (b) a federal system with a weak central government; (c) a confederation; or (d) an entirely new arrangement which may be peculiar to Nigeria."

Faced with the realities of the Nigerian situation, the conference was veering toward recommending a loose form of association. The delegation from Northern Nigeria, in its original memorandum to the conference, proposed that the country be broken up into "a number of autonomous states . . . that is to say, Northern Nigeria, Eastern Nigeria, Western Nigeria, Midwestern Nigeria, or by whatever name they may choose to be called." The central government, according to the Northern Nigerian memorandum, was to be a mere "central authority," and its powers were to be "delegated by the component states except that powers connected with external or foreign affairs [and] immigration can be unilaterally withdrawn by the state government." "Nigerian" citizenship should be abolished and replaced by an "associate citizenship"; and in any case, "Any member state of the Union should reserve the right to

secede completely and unilaterally from the Union and
to make arrangement for cooperation with the other
members of the Union in such a manner as they may
severally or individually deem fit."

The joint memorandum from Lagos and Western
Nigeria proposed a "Commonwealth of Nigeria," if
federalism was unacceptable to other regions. This
Commonwealth would comprise "the existing regions
and such other regions as may be subsequently created.
The government of each state within the Commonwealth shall be completely sovereign in all matters
excepting those with respect to which responsibility is
delegated to the Council of State."

When the conference adjourned on October 3 for
three weeks, it had made some progress in spite of
pressures and intimidations. By September 18, within a
week of the opening of the conference, riots had broken
out in Makurdi, Minna, Gboko, and Kaduna in Northern Nigeria. Our people—men, women, and children—
became the targets of well-organized and systematic
mass murders. Our property fell to Northern Nigerian
looters and plunderers. By the third week of September,
the reign of terror had spread to Lagos and Western
Nigeria. Distinguished Biafrans in Ibadan and Oshogbo
were abducted by Nigerian soldiers and killed. In Lagos,
too, kidnapping of defenseless Biafran civilians by
armed soldiers became the order of the day. The climax
came with the massacres of September 29 and after,
when the Ad Hoc Constitutional Conference was still
sitting. On October 1, at Kano airport alone, more
than 400 Biafrans awaiting airlifts home were surrounded by armed Northern Nigerian soldiers and
civilians and massacred.

In the five months of massacres and atrocities, May
to October, 1966, over 50,000 of our people were shot,
hacked to death, burned, or buried alive; hundreds of
women and children were ravished; unborn children
were torn out of their mothers' wombs. Two million of
our people, deprived and dejected, were forced to seek
refuge in their homeland.

The September massacres marked a decisive turning point in the history of the crisis. Before that, we had hoped that the Ad Hoc Constitutional Conference would lead to some satisfactory solution. After the September massacres we were convinced beyond doubt that our security was entirely in our own hands as individuals and that our only hope lay in returning to our homeland, where we could be sure of protection from molestation and murder. Hence the mass return home — a mass movement on a scale for which there is no precedent in modern African history. The *London Observer* (October 16, 1966) described the scene in the Eastern Region within a fortnight of this mass return as "reminiscent of the ingathering of exiles into Israel after the end of the last war. The parallel is not fanciful." As Dr. Conor Cruise O'Brien remarked in an article in the *New York Review of Books* (December 21, 1967), "If this movement had taken place across international frontiers, it would have attracted worldwide attention. Because it was within the geographical unit called Nigeria, it drew no public comment and won no world sympathy." The experiences of those who came back were bitter, their hardship heartbreaking. Those at home who received them and cared for them were also shocked and embittered, especially when they saw the courtesy and kindness with which they continued to treat Nigerians among them.

The mass movement of population in October, 1966, complicated the problems of the country. It meant that thousands of our people could no longer participate in the functions of the federal government through employment with federal officers, statutory corporations, and organizations based elsewhere in the then Nigeria. It also meant that thousands of our people who were self-employed now had to make a livelihood out of the resources in our homeland and no more.

In short, then, while the Ad Hoc Conference was seeking a short-term solution to the country's constitutional problems, the organized massacres of September and October precipitated a further problem of mass population movements and all the attendant complications. The massacres meant that even long-term solutions were going to be very difficult to reach.

At no better time than during October could Lieutenant Colonel Gowon and his junta in Lagos have shown an appreciation of the peculiar hardships of the citizens of the former Eastern Nigeria. No more opportune moment could have been wished for by the junta to begin to rethink about the madness of their activities since the previous May. Sad to say, however, it was precisely at this time that Lieutenant Colonel Gowon and his advisers decided to deal what they hoped would be a deathblow to our people. On October 19, Lieutenant Colonel Gowon imposed a food blockade on us by prohibiting any diversion to us of what he called "food meant for consumption in Lagos." The police and the army were summoned to enforce the blockade at checkpoints throughout Lagos and Western and Midwestern Nigeria. Thanks to the determination of our people and their capacity for hard work, we had no food shortage. But our people did not miss the lesson of the blockade.

Meanwhile we had looked forward to the adoption of a new form of association in Nigeria, necessitated by the new situation created by Northern Nigerian brutality. We were willing to accept the loose association which the Northern Nigerians had been persistently demanding over the years.

Then, suddenly, the situation changed radically. Lieutenant Colonel Gowon and his fellow Northern Nigerians had been advised by the British that the association they were seeking would not be in the interest of their region, that their interest lay in a "strong federal" Nigeria which the Northern Nigerians were to dominate. On the basis of this advice, the Northern Nigerian delegation withdrew its original memorandum. Subsequently, on November 30, 1966, Lieutenant Colonel Gowon, without consultation with the military governors, unilaterally dismissed the Ad Hoc Constitutional Conference. In its place he appointed what he called a "drafting committee" to draw up a constitution on lines determined and approved by his British mentors. Thus, on top of the constitutional stalemate, complicated by the social and economic effects of the September massacres, Lieutenant Colonel Gowon was not going to allow the accredited representatives of the regions— representatives bearing the mandate of their regions —to suggest in what form they wanted to be associated. By his dismissal of the Ad Hoc Conference, Gowon destroyed the one hope we had of being represented in the determination of our place within the former Nigerian Federation. The dismissal of the Ad Hoc Constitutional Conference created the tragic and uneasy impasse that was not broken until the meeting of the Supreme Military Council at Aburi, Ghana, in January, 1967.

The Aburi Summit

The Aburi meeting was held at the instance and on the insistence of our people. We had pleaded with our counterparts in other regions that we should meet outside Nigeria (for obvious security reasons) to review realistically the very urgent problems facing the country—the army, the central government, finance, population, and rehabilitation.

It should be pointed out here that the Aburi meeting was held under the worst auguries possible. First, the pattern of bad faith had become all too evident to us: our people did not believe that Gowon and his fellow rebels had had the kind of change of heart that could give reasonable hope of success at the conference. Second, Gowon had begun to talk of the might of the federal military machine, suggesting that he would use force to achieve his ends. In spite of these doubts and uncertainties, however, the meeting was duly held, and several important and realistic decisions were taken:

(a) The use of force as a means of settling the problems confronting the country was renounced.
(b) It was agreed that the army, which was to be

governed by the Supreme Military Council under
the chairmanship of a Commander-in-Chief of the
armed forces, should be reorganized.

(c) The military leaders created area commands in the
various regions under the control of the regional
military governors; a Lagos garrison, including
Ikeja barracks, was also created; a military headquarters comprising equal representation from the
regions and headed by a Chief of Staff was proposed.

(d) The military leaders restated that Northern Nigerian soldiers should be repatriated from Western
Nigeria; a crash program of recruitment and training for Western Nigeria was approved.

(e) It was agreed that the legislative and executive
authority of the federal military government should
be vested in the Supreme Military Council, to
which any decision on matters affecting the whole
country should be referred for determination; where
it was not possible for a meeting to be held, the
matter requiring determination should be referred
to the regional military governors for their comments and concurrence.

(f) It was agreed that all matters of policy, including
appointments and promotions to commission or
senior posts in the armed forces and the police and
appointment to diplomatic and consular service as
well as to superscale posts in the federal public
service and equivalent functions in statutory corporations must be approved by the Supreme Military Council.

(g) It was agreed that all decrees or provisions of
decrees passed since January 15, 1966, which detracted from the previous powers and positions of
regional governments should be repealed; all the
law officers of the Federation should meet in Benin
on January 14, 1967, to list all the relevant decrees
for repeal not later than January 21, 1967, if
possible.

(h) It was decided that the Permanent Secretaries of
Ministries of Finance should meet within two weeks
to consider ways and means of solving the serious
problems posed by displaced persons; in the mean-

time displaced civil servants and corporation staff (including daily paid employees) should continue to be paid their full salaries until March 31, 1967.

(i) Finally, it was decided that the Ad Hoc Constitutional Conference should resume sitting as soon as possible.

Commenting on the Aburi episode, the present British Secretary of State for Commonwealth Affairs, George Thompson, recently said in the House of Commons: "It has been one of the tragedies of this story that the undertakings entered into at that meeting were given different interpretations by both sides and did not come into effect." There was no cause for any confusion or misinterpretation, since the meeting was tape-recorded and held before a third party. The truth, of course, is that there were no differences of interpretation. It is on record that Gowon's federal Permanent Secretaries and officials mostly of Northern origin advised him not to implement the decision largely because they were not in consonance with the avowed Northern Nigerian policy of dominating Nigeria under the supervision of the British government. Gowon consequently drafted decrees which at best circumvented the Aburi decisions, at worst contradicted them. Most dishonorable of all, Gowon included in one of these decrees a clause, not agreed on at Aburi, arrogating to himself the power to declare a state of emergency in any region—a dictatorial measure which completely nullified the whole Aburi Accord.

At this stage in the crisis, I appealed to some African Heads of State to use their good offices to effect a peaceful settlement of the dispute. But Gowon rejected the well-intentioned offers of mediation from those Heads of State. Gowon even went further. He took positive measures designed to expel us from Nigeria. In the face of the colossal problem of rehabilitating our refugees, his Lagos government, which was in possession of the central resources of Nigeria, would render no assistance. Instead the Lagos government complicated matters for our people by denying us the statutory periodic remittances to which we were entitled. In spite of the agreement at Aburi, our people in the employ of the federal government and its agencies were denied salaries and wages due to them between July, 1966, and March, 1967. The Lagos government also stopped the supply of the necessary equipment, material, and spare parts for federal statutory bodies operating in our territory.

On February 16, I was constrained to address the following letter to Gowon:

After the Aburi meeting, everybody rejoiced that it had been a success. From our mood in Ghana, I was convinced that this was the feeling of us all. Personally I returned to Enugu satisfied that we had faced our problems in earnest and realism. I therefore lost no time in reassuring the people of the East, who had good reasons to doubt the usefulness of our meeting, that they had been wrong in their doubts and misgivings. It is a shame that subsequent developments tend, in fact, to prove them right and me wrong.

At Aburi, certain decisions were taken by the Supreme Military Council—the highest authority of the land under the present regime. For my part, I became dedicated to those decisions, only to discover soon that you and your civil service advisers, along with selfish and disgruntled politicians in Lagos and perhaps elsewhere as well, did not feel the same. As a result you have seen to it that the decisions taken at Aburi are systematically vitiated or stalled.

Soon after our return from the Aburi meeting you, on your own volition, got in touch with me to discuss the federal publication *Nigeria '66*. You wondered if it would be advisable in the light of the spirit of Aburi to go ahead with publishing the document. We discussed and agreed that since the publication had not already been put out to the public it might be wise to withhold it at least for some time. On January 15 the publication came out. I got in touch with you and you assured me that it was not a deliberate act but a leakage. This information turned out to be a deceit because evidence soon came through that the publication was, in fact, formally launched in Washington, London, Cotonou, and other foreign capitals. What is more, its introduction shows that the draft was completed after the Aburi meeting, most likely even after our discussion.

Your press conference to the world on the Aburi meeting virtually amounted to a denunciation of the agreements reached at Aburi. At that press conference you even brought in issues which were never discussed at Aburi, no doubt in order to embarrass me and cause dissatisfaction in the East. My reaction to that press conference was clearly shown in my letter EMG/S.62/ of January 30, 1967, addressed to military governors and copied to you.

Contrary to the decisions at Aburi, recruitment into the army has continued with publicity in different parts of the country except the East; contrary to these agreements, you have proceeded to appoint ambassadors without reference to the Supreme Military Council; contrary to the agreements, purchase and importation of arms have continued. The meeting of military officers to discuss the reorganization of the army as agreed at Aburi has been unilaterally postponed by you. The meeting of finance officials, with particular reference to the problem of rehabilitation, has not even been held because your Finance Permanent Secretary in Lagos does not think it will serve any useful purpose.

You failed to publish the decree on January 21, repealing all decrees or aspects of decrees which detracted from the previous powers and positions of the regional governments. After strong pressure from me and the military governor of the West, you have got a comprehensive decree drafted which, for all intents and purposes, aims at strengthening the powers of the federal government at the expense of the regions. You have denounced the decision (which, incidentally, was taken on your own personal initiative and proposal at Aburi) to pay employees who had been compelled to flee their places of work in other parts of the country until March 31.

In support of these defaults on your part, you and your federal advisers have looked for one reason or another. You have described the press statement I gave soon after my return as causing "serious embarrassment to all," when, in fact, my honest motive was to assure the people of the East of the sincerity and determination of the military regime to face realities and save the country from ruin.

You have on another occasion accused me of distorting the decisions of Aburi, when in fact I was very careful in my choice of words to conform with the actual ones we used. Another reason to support your efforts to abandon the Aburi Agreement is the ridiculous one that I went to the meeting prepared while others were not. This is an information which has repeatedly filtered through to me, and it surprises me that mature people should expose themselves to such ridicule. It was our first meeting since July 29, and it certainly could not have been a picnic but business. The agenda was prepared beforehand in consultation with all concerned. If anybody went to that meeting unprepared, one can only infer that he was not seriously concerned with the sad problems which had beset the country, let alone with how to solve those problems.

Following your denunciation of the agreement to pay fleeing employees up to the end of March, your officials have given the fact that railway wagons are now in the East as an excuse. When the decision was taken at Aburi, everybody knew that those wagons were here. One should have thought that the implementation of the Aburi Agreement would be a precondition for the release of those wagons and not the other way around. Your government has further complicated matters by denying the Coal Corporation the right to collect their just debts from the Nigerian Railway Corporation and have refused to send the necessary funds for the payment of salaries for railway workers. These acts are nothing but a deliberate attempt to cause trouble and disaffection among the people of Eastern Nigeria, because you and your federal officials know the large number of persons involved and the seriousness of their dissatisfaction following nonpayment of their salaries at the beginning of a new year when they have to meet commitments for their children's school fees and other personal matters.

The authorities in Lagos have not stopped there. They are using all their power to impede the smooth operation of private industries in this region. Not only are they doing everything to obstruct investors and industrialists coming to do business here, they are doing everything they can to kill even those industries which are operating in this region.

On the political front, I have evidence that the federal

government is encouraging acts of subversion and sabotage within this region, all of which are unfriendly and unbecoming of a people who regard themselves as belonging to one corporate country.

I have in this letter tried to catalog some of the actions of the federal authorities which are nothing but breaches of faith and exhibition of hostility toward this region. I do not want to go over what I have often repeated, and of which you are well aware, of similar acts prior to the Aburi meeting and beginning from July 29.

Since your assumption of office you have constantly told me one thing and done another. You have never honored any of our mutual agreements, let alone those reached by accredited representatives of our governments at conferences. I had thought that the Aburi meeting would put an end to all these acts of hostility and deception.

As far as I am concerned, I have now on my hands 1,800,000 refugees who must be catered for. In addition to these people, thousands have left secondary schools and other training institutions and have entered the labor market looking for employment in the East. I accept with disfavor the attempts on the part of the federal authorities to increase this problem by refusing to pay the railway employees until March 31 as agreed, following your own personal suggestion at Aburi, and of doing everything to see that the Coal Corporation folds up. I have separately addressed you on the subject of the federal government's refusal to pay to this region its statutory share of revenue.

Now that I have been driven right to the wall, I have no alternative but to consider certain actions of which I have always hated to think. But I have a responsibility, and as a soldier of honor, I will not run away from it. The people of this region have a right to decent life, peace, and harmony. As a people who once claimed the honor of being looked upon as the most matured in Africa, the leaders of this country must show that maturity by honoring agreements. Organized society, confidence, good faith, and progress cannot exist if people who call themselves civilized cannot honor agreements voluntarily and maturely reached. The survival of this country, its normalcy, and its peace hinge on the implementation of the Aburi Agreement. I would be the last to say that those agreements were perfect. I have already said that I took them as no

more than interim arrangements for the smooth running
of the military regime. Having admitted that they could
not be perfect, I believed that they might have been modified in the light of experience in their operation.

We are coming to the end of our financial year, when
estimates must be finalized and plans made for the coming
year. These are not possible under the present stalemate
and unsettlement. If, therefore, the Aburi Agreement is
not implemented by March 31, I shall have no alternative
but to feel free to take whatever measure is unilaterally
possible to carry out the spirit of the Aburi Agreement.
I say this with the deepest sense of regret and fully conscious of the consequences of such unilateral action. But
I shall be able to tell the world when the time comes what
part I have played at different stages and in different circumstances, since the emergency which started in May of
last year, to avoid the situation. The responsibility will not
be mine. . . .

It cannot here be too strongly emphasized that if the
above letter had been heeded, and the Aburi Agreement fully implemented, the present conflict would
have been averted. No reply to this letter was received.

The Survival Edicts and the Blockade

In the face of the blatant refusal to implement the
Aburi Agreement, and the many acts of atrocities
against our people, we were forced to pass the Survival
Edicts. One of these, the Revenue Collection Edict, was
to prevent the Lagos government from owing us the
statutory revenues that legitimately belonged to us. The
Lagos government was then indebted to our government
to the tune of £11,800,000. Another, the Statutory
Bodies Edict, was to ensure the procurement of funds
for the maintenance of essential services. It must be
stated that these edicts did not alter the formula for
revenue allocation as provided in the Nigerian Constitution. In the annual estimates for 1967–68, the revenues
expected from federal sources were shown strictly in
accordance with the existing formula.

Gowon's reaction to these edicts was to impose further punitive measures on us. He informed major world and African powers that his actions against us were an internal affair and that their intervention would be regarded as a hostile act against Nigeria. He sealed off our border with the Republic of Cameroun and closed the Republic's consulate in Enugu. Gowon canceled the passports of all our people who transferred from the federal public service to our public service.

Gowon imposed a total economic blockade on us; suspended Nigeria Airways flights to our territory; closed all our airports to traffic; froze all our assets in Nigeria; froze all the assets we jointly owned with Nigerians abroad, and withdrew all foreign exchange facilities from us. He closed all our seaports to shipping and banned all export of produce other than through the Nigerian Produce Marketing Company in Lagos.

The people who were being so shabbily and callously treated were the selfsame people who had virtually created the prosperity and the dignity which Nigeria boasted of abroad. Our traders, businessmen, technicians, university teachers, civil servants, and others—men and women who had labored honestly and diligently for the development and progress of Nigeria—were now the object of Nigeria's gross violence, abject ridicule, and ruthless exploitation.

On May 26, 1967, a joint meeting of our Consultative Assembly and Council of Chiefs and Elders was convened to deliberate on these latest developments in the crisis and advise our governor what to do. But on May 27, while the meeting was still in session, Gowon illegally issued a decree arbitrarily amending the Constitution of Nigeria and unilaterally dividing Nigeria into twelve states, three of these being in our territory. Not only was this decree illegal and unconstitutional—it was a calculated slight on our people; it was an act of extreme provocation.

We were now thoroughly convinced that only our separate political existence could guarantee our basic needs of survival and security of life and property. On

May 30, 1967, we proclaimed the sovereign and independent Republic of Biafra.

The Nigeria-Biafra War

On July 6, 1967, Nigeria opened armed hostilities
against Biafra. They massed three brigades on our
Northern frontiers and opened four fronts—Okutu and
Obollo Afor in Nsukka, Gakem, and Obudu in Ogoja.
With massive artillery and infantry support, Nigerians
were able to overrun these border towns in the first
week of fighting. By the second week the provincial
capitals of Nsukka and Ogoja fell. Nigerian atrocities
began early enough in these towns. Arson, looting, rape,
and all kinds of torture became the order of the day.
Whole villages were remorselessly burned to ashes,
farms and barns were completely looted, churches and
shrines were outrageously desecrated. Defenseless civilians—men, women, and children fleeing their homes
—gave accounts of their experiences of horror and
anguish. Mothers told of the wholesale massacre and
torture of their sons and the rape and abduction of
their young daughters. Children trekked miles of bush
paths in tears, wailing the death at enemy hands of
mother and father, sister and brother, aunt and uncle.

Since those terrible days of July, 1967, the story has
not changed. If anything it has been further strengthened
by more violent, more gruesome murders, made all the
more unhuman because they are organized at the highest level and executed with the minutest deliberation.
In Benin and Warri, Agbor and Asaba, in August last
year, Nigerian soldiers under clear orders from their
superior officers machine-gunned hundreds of Biafrans
and Midwestern Ibos. Foreign reporters spoke of the
streets of Warri being strewn with dead bodies blocking
the flow of traffic. In Calabar, two months later, several
hundred noncombatants, many of them schoolchildren,
were similarly murdered under direct orders from
Nigerian officers. Children have been carried away
en-masse from their homes in Biafra to unknown desti-
nations.

Since January of this year, Nigerians have intensified their genocidal war with the indiscriminate bombing of civilians in their hearths and homes, in schools and hospitals, in churches and marketplaces. In February, the International Red Cross was so appalled after the bombing of the Awgu and Nomeh markets that their representative, Mr. Jean Pierroz, had to lodge a formal protest with the Nigerian government. The Red Cross observer in Biafra had earlier reported rocket and cannon onslaught on civilians in Aba, Port Harcourt, and other towns. These raids, he said, were "deliberate attacks on civilian population." Lagos, as usual, denied these charges, but in the week following the recognition of Biafra by Tanzania, Nigerian war planes killed 657 civilians in Aba, Owerri, Umuahia, and Port Harcourt. Reporting the bombing of civilians at Aba in the *Sunday Times* of London on April 28, William Norris declared:

I have seen things in Biafra this week which no man should have to see. Sights to scorch the mind and sicken the conscience. I have seen children roasted alive, young girls torn in two by shrapnel, pregnant woman eviscerated, and old men blown to fragments. I have seen these things and I have seen their cause: high-flying Russian Ilyushin jets operated by Federal Nigeria, dropping their bombs on civilian centres throughout Biafra.

All the main towns of Biafra have been raided by Nigerian war planes: Aba, Abakaliki, Afikpo, Arochuku, Awgu, Bonny, Brass, Degema, Ikot Ekpene, Itu, Okigwe, Onitsha, Opobo, Oron, Owerri, Port Harcourt, Umuahia, and Uyo. By the end of April, some of the tolls were: Aba: 279 killed; Port Harcourt: 272; Umuahia: 214; Owerri: 146. More than fifty villages have been bombed, the most murderous in one single raid being at Awgu (165 deaths) and Nomeh (105). Gowon's justification for all this: "TO KEEP NIGERIA ONE."

Nigeria's conduct of the war has left no doubt in the minds of our people that destruction and death are the mission of the Nigerian aggressors. In thirteen months

of war Nigerians have spared no pains to demonstrate
that no life in Biafra will be saved, no valuable asset
spared, in the process of realizing their vain hope of
victory. The University of Biafra, Nsukka, has been
almost entirely destroyed. The Onitsha market was
completely burned down by Nigerian soldiers. The industries at Nkalagu, Calabar, Enugu, Port Harcourt,
Aba, and other Biafran centers have been systematically
demolished.

This has been not only a most brutal and ruinous
but a most senseless and fruitless war. In all, some
100,000 Biafran civilians have been estimated killed in
the past thirteen months of war. In addition to the
original 2,000,000 refugees from Nigeria, the Republic
has to cater for another 4,500,000 fleeing the towns and
villages invaded by Nigerian soldiers. Of these, some
have found homes with relations of one kind or the
other, while the rest are in refugee centers in the country or hiding in the bush. According to the Biafran Red
Cross, about one-third to half of the refugees in camps
are children who require special foods and medicines.

The Pretext for Genocide

It has often been suggested that the Nigerian crisis
of 1966–67, followed by the Nigeria-Biafra war, had its
origins in the revolution of January, 1966. Nigerians
have tried to deceive the world into believing that the
inhuman atrocities they have been perpetrating against
Biafrans since 1966 were a spontaneous reaction to
"crimes" allegedly committed by Biafrans in January,
1966.

Nothing can be further from the truth. The immediate cause of the revolution of 1966 was the Western
election crisis of 1965–66. To many Nigerians it was
the final test before despairing of constitutional, political, and economic reform. The abuses went far beyond
the worst predictions of the pessimists. Law and order
completely broke down in Western Nigeria. On January 15, 1966, the very day of the revolution, the West

African correspondent of the *Economist* of London summarized in these words the state of affairs in Nigeria:

Three months after the disputed election, Western Nigeria shows no sign of settling down to life under its disputed government, and the situation now seriously threatens the prosperity of the region, the popularity of parliamentary institutions, and even the survival of the federation.

In the revolution the Prime Minister, the Federal Minister of Finance, the Premiers of Western and Northern Nigeria, and eight army officers of Northern, Western, Eastern, and Midwestern Nigerian origin—twelve persons in all—were killed.

Was it this revolution that motivated the inhuman atrocities of May to October, 1966, resulting in the death of more than 50,000 people? Was it this revolution that motivated the following utterances of hate by representatives of various parts of Northern Nigeria in the Northern House of Assembly as far back as February–March, 1964?

MALLAM MUHAMMADU MUSTAPHA MAUDE GYARI:

On the allocation of plots to Ibos, or allocation of stalls I would like to advise the minister that these people know how to make money and we do not know the way and manner of getting about this business. . . . We do not want Ibos to be allocated with plots, I do not want them to be given plots. . . .

MALLAM BASHARI UMARU:

I would like [you], as the Minister of Land and Survey, to revoke forthwith all certificates of occupancy from the hands of the Ibos resident in the Region [Applause]. . . .

MR. A. A. AGOGEDE:

I am very glad that we are in Moslem country, and the government of Northern Nigeria allowed some few Christians in the region to enjoy themselves according to the belief of their religion, but building of hotels should be taken away from the Ibos and even if we find some Christians who are interested in building hotels and have no money to do so, the government should aid them, instead of allowing Ibos to continue with the hotels.

DR. IYA ABUBAKAR *(Special Member: Lecturer, Ahmadu Bello University, Zaria)*:

I am one of the strong believers in Nigerian unity, and I have hoped for our having a united Nigeria, but certainly if the present trend of affairs continues, then I hope the government will investigate first the desirability and secondly the possibility of extending Northernization policy to the petty traders [Applause].

MALLAM MUKHTAR BELLO:

I would like to say something very important that the Minister should take my appeal to the federal government about the Ibos in the post office. I wish the numbers of these Ibos be reduced. . . . There are too many of them in the North. They were just like sardines and I think they were just too dangerous to the Region.

MALLAM IBRAHIM MUSE:

Mr. Chairman, sir, well, first and foremost, what I have to say before this hon. House is that we should send a delegate to meet our hon. Premier to move a Motion in this very Budget Session that all the Ibos working in the Civil Service of Northern Nigeria, including the native authorities, whether they are contractors, or not, should be repatriated at once. . . .

MALLAM BASHARI UMARU:

. . . there should be no contracts either from the government, native authorities, or private enterprises given to Ibo contractors. [*Government bench:* Good talk and shouts of "Fire the Southerners."] Again, Mr. Chairman, the foreign firms too should be given time limit to replace all Ibos in their firms by some other people.

THE PREMIER (ALHAJI THE HON. SIR AHMADU BELLO, K.B.E., SARDUANA OF SOKOTO):

It is my most earnest desire that every post in the region, however small it is, be filled by a Northerner [Applause].

ALHAJI USUMAN LIMAN:

What brought the Ibos into this region? They were here since the colonial days. Had it not been for the colonial rule there would hardly have been any Ibo in this region.

Now that there is no colonial rule the Ibos should go back to their region. There should be no hesitation about this matter. Mr. Chairman, North is for Northerners, East for Easterners, West for Westerners, and the Federation is for us all [Applause].

THE MINISTER OF LAND AND SURVEY (ALHAJI THE HON. IBRAHIM MUSA CASHASH, O.B.E.):

Mr. Chairman, sir, I do not like to take up much of the time of this House in making explanations, but I would like to assure members that having heard their demands about Ibos holding land in Northern Nigeria, my ministry will do all it can to see that the demands of members are met. How to do this, when to do it, all this should not be disclosed. In due course, you will all see what will happen [Applause].

The world has seen what has been happening since 1966.

The world has now come to understand that the present war has been nothing short of a continuation of the genocide of 1966 and earlier years. Thanks to the coverage now being given to the war by the world press in response to several protests from us and from many international organizations, the world has been able to read of the brutal nature of the war Nigeria is waging within our borders. The world has had the opportunity to read eyewitness accounts of the barbarity and savagery of this war and has seen photographic evidence of Nigeria's genocidal intentions.

Toward a Realistic Solution

What is quite appalling, in the context of Africa and Africa's aspirations, is that this palpable genocide is being openly financed and directed by major non-African powers whose interest is the economic and political advantage of their own countries. Russia has involved herself fully in the present war on Nigeria's side in return for assurances of military bases and a political and economic foothold in West Africa. In order to further their economic interests and their political influence in Africa, the British government, that most callous of

imperialistic governments, has proclaimed its determination "to found a single Federal Nigeria." To this end,
they have equipped the Nigerian government in every
conceivable way to wage the present war on such a
brutal scale. Every advance of Nigerian troops into Biafran territory has been made possible by the hundreds
of British Saladins and Ferrets. With thousands of British artillery shells and mortar bombs, the Nigerians
have destroyed many towns and villages in Biafra and
rendered their inhabitants destitute refugees. Africa
and the world are now in no doubt that Nigeria's war
against us is also Britain's war—a war for empire, natural resources, and markets.

Accordingly, the British government have made it
impossible for Africa to take the initiative in settling
this unique African problem. They have used and still
use all their political and diplomatic influence to sabotage every honest effort at genuine negotiations. They
have refused to stop arms supplies to Nigeria, but have
instead continued their policy of imposing their idea of
a solution on Biafra and the rest of Africa. In pursuance of their declared policy of support for Nigeria, the
British government have created obstacles in the way of
the international and private agencies willing to bring
aid direct to us. Adequate relief has not reached our
suffering refugees, thanks to the duplicity of the British
government and their schemes for diverting world opinion into a debate on the question of relief.

This question of relief, and the larger one of peace
between Nigeria and Biafra, belongs to Africa and cannot be resolved until Africa accepts it as her own responsibility. To be able to do this, African states must
completely insulate themselves from the influence of
these non-African powers who have, in any case, never
wished Africa well.

"Unity" and Nigeria

Like many people of good will throughout Africa,
Biafrans were disappointed to see the former Federation of Nigeria break up. Over many decades, in every

sphere of life, we struggled to make that Federation work. Our disappointment must be taken together with the circumstances and events which made unity in that country impossible. The world is now fully aware of the basic differences of culture, religion, education, and social and political organization within that country. We have already given a brief review of the immediate events which since independence in 1960 made Nigeria's survival as one nation impossible. In fact only the will to federate which was so strong among us saved Nigeria from disintegrating before and since independence. Year after year, we made concessions and compromises to ward off the secessionist threats of Northern Nigerians and save the unity of the Federation. The pogrom of 1966 ended all that, because it killed the will to maintain this precarious and inhuman association called Nigeria. Disappointment, therefore, at the disintegration of Nigeria is not a virtue in itself. It must be placed in a context. The lesson of today is that the incongruous and murderous association called Nigeria cannot and ought not now be restored in unity by either bombs or pious resolutions.

UNITY is a sacred word in Africa, and for good reasons. Yet unity is not a miracle but the consequence of a specific human condition. As President Houphouet-Boigny of the Ivory Coast declared on May 9 of this year, "Unity is the fruit of the common will to live together; it should not be imposed by force by one group upon another. If we all are in agreement in the OAU in recognizing the imperious necessity of unity, unity as the ideal framework for the full development of the African man, we admit, as for ourselves, that it should not become his grave. We say yes to unity in peace, unity in love and through brotherhood. Unity is for the living and not for the dead."

The Balkanization Theory

Will other African countries which are made up of several ethnic groups also break up simply because Biafra has survived? The answer is clearly "NO."

First, very few countries in Africa have a history of constitutional conflict and tribal power play such as Nigeria has had. In fact, many of these countries which are multitribal in composition have had a common colonial experience or a workable constitutional structure which now unites them in their pursuit of a common independent future. In any case, they have usually had the leadership to realize the need for the fullest cooperation, respect, and good will among their peoples, and also to realize that political power was never intended to be used to oppress and even exterminate a section of the community. Finally, these African countries can maintain their unity in a progressive environment because they have not come to think, as the Nigerians now do, that "national unity" should be based on common hatred of one section of the population by all the others. Contrary to the opinion of Africa's detractors, there are many countries in Africa today where unity can flourish because these ideals have been accepted and applied.

Within the past two decades, a number of African countries carved out by colonial powers have had to break up or had their patterns of association adjusted without bloodshed. In all these cases, it was generally accepted that all political associations have to be based on the will of the associates. From this point of view, every modern African country (including Biafra) is a new willing association of ethnic nationalities. In such countries, the first safeguard against disintegration is the protection of all communities and all individuals under the law. It would be tragic if Africa should consider the territorial structure of existing countries more sacrosanct than the safeguarding of the lives of persecuted communities in those countries. Fortunately, many African statesmen are beginning to realize this and to see that if the conflict between Biafra and Nigeria is solved by "the application of firepower," the result will be quite ominous for all Africa. As the Tanzanian government declared in their statement of April 13, 1968:

While people have a duty to defend the integrity of their state, and even to die in its defense, this duty stems from the fact that it is theirs, and that it is important to their well-being and to the future of their children. When the state ceases to stand for the honor, the protection, and the well-being of all its citizens, then it is no longer the instrument of those it has rejected.

This is the lesson of Biafra's bold stand against tyranny and genocide. The loss of this lesson on Africa could well lead to a dire harvest of intertribal vengeance within our continent.

The Minority Problem

There are 14,000,000 people involved in this Biafran resistance. They include the people of all the major tribal groups of Biafra who suffered from the pogrom of 1966 and whose accredited representatives took part in the consultations that led to the Proclamation of Independence. The Nigerians claim that they are waging a war to "liberate" the so-called minorities. Hence the arbitrary creation of twelve paper states imposed on the people by Gowon without any form of consultation. The world press has rightly seen this action as "extremely irresponsible" and a "disastrous political blunder." As *Africa and the World* of February, 1968, put it: "The circumstances which led to the secession were created by Gowon, and the secession itself was provoked by his unilateral declaration of twelve states."

The peoples of Biafra coexisted harmoniously for thousands of years before the creation of the political unit called Nigeria. The common traditions, outlook, and identity of Biafrans resulted from their centuries of intermarriage and their cultural and economic interdependence. The cultural and economic homogeneity which evolved within the Biafran territory remained unshaken even by the divisive forces of the turbulent politics of Nigeria.

The Ibos are, of course, the majority tribe in Biafra. It is true, nevertheless, that Biafra is the only part of the former Federation of Nigeria where there is no record of civil strife against minority groups. The Willink Minorities Commission, appointed by the British government in 1958, examined the place of the minorities in the whole of the former Federation of Nigeria. The commission concluded that the destiny of the "minorities" in our territory was traditionally and intimately interwoven with that of the rest. In the Rivers area, for instance, of the population of 747,000 (in 1958), 305,-000 were Ibo, 240,000 Ijaw, and 156,000 Ogoni. The commission did not recommend the creation of any states in our territory, although it strongly recommended the carving out of the Midwest from Western Nigeria and the Middle Belt State from Northern Nigeria. The Midwest State was subsequently created, following extensive consultations, approval by all the governments of the Federation, and a plebiscite among the people concerned. Northern Nigeria and the federal governments controlled by the Hausa-Fulani oligarchy opposed discussion and a plebiscite in connection with the Middle Belt State. The refusal to create this state led to the Tiv riots which lasted from before Nigeria's independence in October, 1960, to the military revolution of January, 1966.

Biafra has worked out and introduced a provincial administration system to meet the needs of local communities. This system was introduced after full consultations and discussions among the people; it has killed any residual fears. The result is that all Biafrans are cooperating fully and vigorously in the prosecution of the present war. It is worth pointing out that the present provincial administration system was closely studied and formulated by a committee headed by Mr. Okoi Arikpo, a member of the Consultative Assembly of Eastern Nigeria, who himself originates from one of the "minority" tribes in Biafra. Mr. Arikpo was later brought over by Gowon, who made him his Commissioner of External Affairs.

The uniqueness of the case for Biafra is that from

the start of the struggle with Nigeria, the people of the Republic have completely backed the mandate which they freely and unanimously gave to the government. One only has to consider the various stages of the war to appreciate the fact that no amount of regimentation could achieve the kind of solidarity in Biafra which is immediately visible to those who have visited our country. Fifteen months ago, Nigeria imposed a total economic blockade on our people, and since then our businesses and industries—our means of livelihood—were completely cut. Yet, our people have remained unflinching in their loyalty. This is the measure of confidence our government enjoys. In January of this year, the Lagos regime announced a change of currency. Overnight, the people of Biafra were dispossessed of all their worldly savings. When the Biafran government called on the people to surrender all the old Nigerian currency in return for mere official receipts, the exercise was completed smoothly and in record time. Again, that is clear evidence of the people's confidence in their government. Today, as I have said, Biafra has a refugee population of 4,500,000. Let us take even 1,000,000 or half that number—500,000. I wonder how many countries in the world would harbor that number of destitutes without any ripples in the quietude of the nation. Yet, as all observers have noted, Biafrans have borne their suffering without demonstrations or any breakdown of law and order. Again, that is indicative of the confidence which the Biafran government enjoys.

Some weeks ago, after the enemy had penetrated into the city of Port Harcourt, I summoned all the chiefs of Yenagoa Province, one of the so-called minority areas, and said to them that as a Christian I deplored the shedding of blood. I told them I was anxious to minimize the suffering of our people. I called on them to return home and consult their people again on whether they still wished to remain Biafrans. If they changed their mind I would readily withdraw Biafran troops from the province because the presence of those troops would

make the Nigerians even more bloodthirsty and more
blood would be spilled. However, if they remained
steadfast in their loyalty, I made it quite clear that I
could not promise them safety but all I could promise
was that the government would try its best. The chiefs
and leaders wished to give an immediate reply, but I
rejected this. I insisted that they must return home and
consult their people. Well, they did consult, and a decision was taken. They reaffirmed their loyalty and their
determination to continue the struggle. This mirrors
the feelings among all Biafrans for Biafra, irrespective
of ethnic origin.

The so-called states created by Gowon in our territory were not designed to serve the genuine interests
of the peoples but to spite them, cripple them, and eventually exterminate them. Early this year, a Swiss correspondent, Dr. Edmond C. Schwarzenbach, secured
an interview with a Nigerian commissioner whom he
described as "one of the most impressive in the present
military regime in Lagos." It was an interview which
he said, in the *Swiss Review of Africa* of February,
1968, provided him with a "significant insight into the
political aims of the federal government." Dr. Schwarzenbach continued:

The [Nigeria] war aim and "solution" . . . of the entire
problem was to "discriminate against the Ibos in the future
in their own interest." Such discrimination would include
above all the detachment of those oil-rich territories in the
Eastern Region which were not inhabited by them at the
beginning of the colonial period, on the lines of the projected twelve-state plan.

In addition, the Ibos' movement would be restricted, to
prevent their renewed penetration into the other parts of
the country. Leaving them any access to the sea, the commissioner declared, was quite out of the question.

Plebiscite

At the present moment, the Nigerian army has occupied some non-Ibo areas of Biafra. But this cannot be
regarded as a settlement of the "minority question."

This is why we have suggested a plebiscite. Under adequate international supervision, the people of these areas should be given a chance to choose whether they want to belong to Nigeria or to Biafra. Plebiscites have been used in the Southern Camerouns, in Togo, and in Midwestern Nigeria (and by the British recently in Gibraltar), to determine what grouping is most acceptable to the people of disputed areas. If Nigeria believes that she is really defending the true wishes of the minorities, she should accept our proposal for a plebiscite in the disputed areas of Nigeria and Biafra.

The Katanga Analogy

The comparison which the Nigerians make between the Biafran revolution and the Katanga crisis is ill-founded. In its history, motivation, leadership, and organization, the Katanga crisis has no parallels with our revolution. Moise Tshombe's Katanga was created to frustrate the national independence of the Congo under Patrice Lumumba and was planned and financed by the huge foreign mining combines in that province.

Katanga itself had a long tradition of separation, of which its secession in 1960 was simply the culmination. But in the former Federation of Nigeria, it was the Northern Region that had a history of repeated demands for and threats of secession. On the other hand, we made concessions and sacrifices for the maintenance of Nigerian unity, up until the eve of Biafran independence. Katanga Province voluntarily seceded from the Congo, whereas the massacres and other events of 1966 and 1967 forced Biafra out of the Nigerian association.

Biafra's revolution is, then, an indigenous expression of African self-determination. Dr. Conor Cruise O'Brien, who supervised the United Nations Force against Katanga, has spoken out against any comparison of Biafra with Katanga:

The difference is that the secession of Katanga, unlike that of Biafra, had been carried out at the instigation of Western interests and under the protection of an invading

force of the former colonial power. . . . The secession was
not an indigenous but an international phenomenon.

Because our independence is an indigenous expression of the people's will, it cannot be "crushed," as the
Katanga rebellion was, through the present military
campaign. When Nigeria opened armed hostilities
against us in July, 1967, we knew she had all the stores
and equipment and the bulk of the infantrymen of the
former Nigerian army. She had the naval base in Lagos
and the air force and munitions factory in Kaduna. On
our side, we had practically nothing. Our ports were
blockaded, our assets held jointly with Nigeria were
frozen, and contact with foreign governments was almost impossible. Hence, where the Nigerians invaded
our territory with a battalion and supporting weapons,
we opposed them with a company and a few rifles. It
was no surprise that Nigeria and her foreign advisers
concluded that we would be crushed within a fortnight.
That prediction has been proved wrong. The will of
the people, not firepower, is the force behind the Biafran resistance.

Ineffectiveness of Guarantees

We Biafrans assumed our political sovereignty because we were convinced that this was our only guarantee of safety and protection for our people in and
outside Biafra. That conviction grew out of our experience of Nigeria.

Some well-meaning people, anxious to maintain some
semblance of a united Nigeria, have suggested the provision of guarantees for the people of Biafra within a
Nigerian political framework. They admit that it would
be tragic for us to give up our sovereign independence
without adequate guarantees for our security of life and
property.

Two kinds of guarantees have been mentioned. It has
been suggested that the federal Nigerian government
should give direct definite guarantees that the lives and

property of Biafrans will be safe everywhere in Nigeria, as if the present Nigerian government has the ability, sincerity, and good faith to keep their word and that all succeeding governments in Nigeria will be equally able, sincere, and willing to honor their pledge.

In colonial Nigeria, not even the British government was in a position to guarantee these fundamental rights to us. The British administrator who investigated the 1953 massacre of our people in Kano emphasized that the tragic incidents would be repeated in the future.

Independent Nigeria had guarantees for the rights to life and property and the freedom of movement, religion, and belief, supposedly entrenched in her Constitution. Independent Nigeria also subscribed to the United Nations Charter and the United Nations Convention on Genocide. Yet these guarantees were unavailing during the pogrom of 1966.

During the crisis of 1966–67, the present leaders of Nigeria gave several assurances and guarantees to our people about the safety of their lives and property, and about the restoration of political and personal freedom within the Constitution. None of these assurances was honored. On the contrary, the Nigerian government went out of its way to demonstrate its repudiation of those assurances. There is, therefore, no precedent to recall and no reason to hope that a Nigerian government can give adequate guarantees for the security of Biafrans if they are part of Nigeria.

Direct international guarantees have been suggested. According to one suggestion, "the major world powers and the African states should be willing to add their guarantees to those given by the Nigerian federal government to ensure the safety of the Ibo people." The snag is that it is still the Nigerian government that would have the sovereign responsibility for providing this security. And, in the long run, an international involvement cannot last forever.

An international force which is used to keep Nigerians and Biafrans apart does not offer any greater security than could be obtained from a cease-fire which Nigeria honors. Even then, such an international force invited into a "reunited" Nigeria would operate under the sovereign authority of the Nigerian federal government, which could always mandate it out of Nigeria. Moreover, an international force would not only have to keep the two armies apart; it would also have to keep the two peoples apart, since no international force can provide security to Biafrans in the day-to-day process of living under Nigerian authority. An international force cannot prevent discrimination and ultimate extermination through pernicious national policies and impositions.

This is why we Biafrans have insisted that only a protective political sovereignty controlled by our own leaders will guarantee us safety at home and protection abroad. In the absence of that sovereignty, we will continue to be regarded as the internal problem of our enemies and die in the thousands as we have done in past years without help or support from the international community.

The Road to Peace

Today, Nigerians have us to talk to because we have been able to survive the massacres, for which they offered no apologies; the total blockade, which they have refused to lift; the "total war," which they are fiercely waging on us. Had it not been for our confidence in God, our belief in our sole responsibility for our survival, and our understanding of our predicament, we Biafrans would long ago have succumbed to the power of the Nigerian junta and to the extermination of our people.

Today, in response to the disturbed conscience of the world, Nigerians are here to negotiate peace with us, the Republic of Biafra. We join in the negotiations in all sincerity, believing, as we always have done, that there can be no other way for resolving the conflict between us.

While these peace discussions go on, let us not forget that four leading African countries—Tanzania, Gabon, Ivory Coast, and Zambia—have carefully considered the issues involved and have accorded us diplomatic recognition. These countries have also set out their reasons for considering our case just and our independence deserved. Briefly:

- They condemn the massacres and the continuing genocides.
- They are convinced that we sought every conceivable constitutional means to protect our lives and property and to get the leaders of Nigeria to accept and implement decisions intended to save the former Federation of Nigeria from collapse.
- They believe that self-determination is sacrosanct, and the willing consent of the people a supreme condition for all government.
- They are convinced that the sovereign independence of Biafra will promote humane and democratic rule throughout Africa.

In the words of Tanzania's statement of recognition, "Africa fought for freedom on the grounds of individual liberty and equality, and on the grounds that every people must have the right to determine for themselves the conditions under which they would be governed." The statement concludes that only by recognizing Biafra as an independent sovereign entity could Tanzania remain true to her "conviction that the purpose of society, and of all political organization, is the service of man."

Conclusion

The failure of the Nigerian experiment in political association is not the first of its kind in history. Among the territories of the former British empire, for instance, several political unions have broken up. These include the Federation of the West Indies, the Federation of Malaysia and Singapore, the Federation of Rhodesia and Nyasaland, and the Federation of South Arabia. But it is highly significant that against the disintegration of none of these political associations was a devastating war, wholly supported by Britain, ever fought, as is now the case with the collapse of the Nigerian federation.

It was certainly because he had the support of the British government, who believed that war could solve the human problems involved in the present conflict, that Lieutenant Colonel Yakubu Gowon could glibly say on March 31 of this year that since his New Year's message to his field commanders "to quicken the pace of the military operations, the rate of progress in all the war fronts has been most satisfactory," that progress, he concluded, would be continued "no matter the cost and how long it takes." That progress has indeed continued, and Gowon must now be quite happy with its enormous cost in lives and property.

It is always wise to dissolve an unhappy political union rather than to condemn its unfortunate partners to perpetual suffering and misery accompanied by unrelieved bitterness and rancor. Dissolution becomes imperative when one section of a political community is singled out by others for extermination.

The bitter experience of more than fifty years of association between Biafrans and Nigerians—experience which reached its climax in the events of 1966 and 1967 —has absolutely convinced Biafrans that only their separate political existence can guarantee their basic needs of survival and security of life and property as well as of progress. This conviction has been further strengthened by Nigeria's conduct of her current war of aggression and genocide.

There never was very much of a bond of union between us and Nigerians. According to the late Premier of Northern Nigeria, Sir Ahmadu Bello,

Politicians always delight in talking loosely about the unity of Nigeria. Sixty years ago there was no country called Nigeria. What is now Nigeria consisted of a number of large and small communities all of which were different in their outlooks and beliefs. The advent of the British and Western education has not materially altered the situation and these many varied communities have not knit themselves into a complete unit.

In the memorandum submitted to the Ad Hoc Conference on the Nigerian Constitution in September, 1966, the Northern Nigeria delegation declared:

We have pretended for too long that there are no differences between the peoples of [Nigeria]. The hard fact which we must honestly accept as of paramount importance in the Nigerian experiment especially for the future is that we are different peoples brought together by recent accidents of history. To pretend otherwise will be folly.

For a long time, we Biafrans continued to act and live as if these differences were not bitterly felt by our fellow Nigerians. We traveled extensively within that country, settled in large numbers in many parts of it, married from among all its people, set up business, provided educational and health facilities in every corner of it. Our investment in men ran to more than 3,000,-000; in buildings and other assets to several million pounds sterling. "If Great Britain had conjured up the entity designated Nigeria from a network of trading routes," wrote Professor Stanley Diamond of New York's New School last January, "it was the Biafrans who had dedicated themselves to the proposition of an internally coherent and unified state."

The massacres of our people in Jos in 1945 and in Kano in 1953 had indeed warned us of the little faith Northern Nigeria had in the idea of "Nigerian unity." The massacres brought home to many of us the immensity of the gulf of differences between our peoples.

Yet such was our faith and, in retrospect, our folly that our people ignored these early warnings and continued to preach and fight for a united Nigeria. In our folly we ignored the fundamental differences in religion, the differences in our social organization, the differences in political outlook. We continued to believe that our gestures of brotherhood and compromise, our efforts at understanding and unity, were serving a useful purpose. We continued to invest in Nigeria and placed all our security—of life as well as of property—in the hands of the Nigerian government and the Nigerian Constitution.

In 1966 our folly became real tragedy when massacre followed massacre in May, June, July, August, September, and October. We lost more than 50,000 of our kith and kin. We had to resettle more than 2,000,000 refugees, our people who had fled from all parts of Nigeria.

Throughout that period of crisis in 1966, no other people in Nigeria rose to condemn the genocide being perpetrated against our people; none pleaded for our protection. The Nigerian federal government, who were expected to honor the Constitution and defend the people, were themselves privy to the planning and the execution of the atrocities.

We came to our senses. We realized that the differences between us and other Nigerians were not only real: they were the perfect circumstances for genocide. We ruminated and resolved to build a security for ourselves, independent of those other peoples of Nigeria who were, and still are, seeking to exterminate us. We were forced to found the Republic of Biafra.

For more than twelve months Nigeria has sought unsuccessfully to destroy that Republic and its people. She has employed every known means for mass extermination which two world powers—Britain and Russia—have placed generously at her disposal. Biafrans have been bombed out of their homes, schools, churches, and hospitals. Their cities have been shelled, pillaged, and devastated. Their borders have been sealed off from the outside to ensure that they are totally starved to death. Food treated with arsenic has been passed from Nigeria to them for consumption. The war has claimed more than 100,000 Biafran civilian lives; between 200 and 300 Biafran men, women, and children are dying daily from starvation and disease; more than 4,500,000 have become refugees in the areas still under our control. Can it be doubted that the war has increased the bitterness between us and Nigeria? Is it possible to imagine that our people would now be ready to accept Nigerian rule?

What kind of confidence can Biafrans repose in the present Nigerian leadership after all that has happened?

- We accuse Gowon of murder, for plotting the death of his benefactor, Major General J. T. U. Aguiyi-Ironsi, late Supreme Commander and Head of the Nigerian Military Government.
- We accuse Gowon of duplicity and bad faith for consistently failing to honor agreements mutually arrived at.
- We accuse Gowon of genocide for seeking to exterminate 14,000,000 Biafrans in a most gruesome manner.
- We accuse Gowon of aspiring to be the Hitler of Africa.

This is the case of Biafra. It is the case of 14,000,000 people. We are a people who have suffered more ravage and endured more wrong from our fellow Africans than from our former European colonial oppressors. We seek nothing other than what every people in Africa have struggled to achieve for themselves—peace, self-determination, security, and progress. We have come to this ancient African country convinced that the rest of Africa cannot justly deny us what they themselves enjoy. We are confident that, if left alone, Africa can resolve this problem. Let therefore the people of Africa be the sole judges; let them resist the promptings and dictates of foreign vested interests; let them exercise the impartiality which alone can enhance the moral authority of the OAU.

Against all the background of suspicion, hate, conflict, and war, our survival cannot be separated from the sovereign independence of our state. No one who has studied the past contribution of our people to the cause of African freedom and unity can doubt our awareness of the need for the whole of Africa to unite. Nevertheless, we have learned by bitter experience that unity must come in stages through cooperation and mutual understanding. This was the purpose for which the OAU was established. In fulfillment of that purpose we offer to discuss with Nigeria the closest form of association which does not detract from our right to ensure our security at home and abroad.

All along, we in Biafra have made several proposals for a peaceful settlement of the crisis, even before the start of the shooting war. All those suggestions have been spurned by Gowon. I can see no better opportunity than now to ask Gowon to bring forward his own proposals for peace.

Finally, Your Imperial Majesty, Your Excellencies, as we sit here, thousands of God's sacred creation are perishing in Biafra. They are dying not so much from bullets supplied by Britain and Russia as from starvation imposed upon them by this inhuman war. God and humanity are owed a debt, a duty, that an immediate end be put to the suffering. The situation is of immediate urgency. The adversaries of Biafra are doing their best to exploit the sufferings of these helpless people for their political and military ends. I therefore call upon you, in the name of God, of humanity, and of Africa to expedite your deliberations and action at this conference.

Diary of Events:
August 5—September 21, 1968

August 5: Nigeria violates truce—attacks on Biafran troop positions in all fronts.

August 6: Addis Ababa peace talks between Nigeria and Biafra continue.

August 8: One of Nigeria's mercenary pilots, David Vaughan-Games, confesses to a London newspaper, *News of the World,* that Nigeria has been carrying out horrifying and indiscriminate bombing raids against Biafra. In a front-page article entitled "Paid in Girls to Bomb Biafra," the paper quotes Mr. Vaughan-Games as saying that mercenaries were promised £1,000 a month plus all the girls they wanted between the raids. The Nigerian Defense Ministry, the pilot confirms, authorized him to sign a chit for absolutely anything.

August 9: Spokesman of the Norwegian Embassy in Lagos is quoted by Radio (ORTF) Paris as disclosing that 400 tons of stockfish and medical supplies sent by Norway for victims of the Nigeria-Biafra war were grabbed by Nigerian troops on arrival in Calabar. . . . In Stockholm, Sweden, an open-air service marks the first step in an appeal by the World Council of Churches for the equivalent of *15 million Swedish kronor* to purchase and transport food to Biafra. . . . Massive peaceful demonstration by the American Committee to Keep Biafra Alive is staged outside United Nations Headquarters in New York to draw attention to the plight of Biafran refugees. . . . 21 major Jewish organizations announce the formation of an American-Jewish effort to bring relief to Biafra.

August 12: 97 Nigerian soldiers who surrendered to Biafran troops are handed over to the International Red Cross at a press briefing given by me.

August 13: The Hank Wharton Plot, hatched by British government and American CIA to sabotage Biafra and help Nigeria to carry through her "final thrust" into Biafran heartland. Cargoes of arms and ammunition bought by Biafra are dumped into the sea during airflight. Tons of new Biafran currency are dumped into the sea, to create artificial scarcity in the Republic.

August 14: More than 35,000 villagers around Umuagbai and Akwete, in Ukwa, Aba Province, are forced out of their homes as a result of intensified indiscriminate mortar and artillery bombardment of the areas by Nigerian troops. Nigerian bombardment of civilian concentrations around the Imo River basin is stepped up, resulting in the destruction of hundreds of houses and death of several people. . . . Announcement by a spokesman of the West German Parliamentary Committee on Overseas Aid and Development says West German people will not accept continued friendly relations with Nigeria, which has shamefully violated the most elementary laws of decency by firing at Red Cross planes on mercy flights.

August 16: Sweden earmarked £80,000 more in aid to victims of Nigeria-Biafra war. . . . Swiss government decides to contribute 2 million Swiss francs toward Biafra Relief Fund.

August 17: Nigerian soldiers who crossed the Imo River massacre 2,000 people at Owaza and more than 300 in Ozuaka and the Imo Gate areas of the Imo River Basin. . . . In Awka, Nigerian soldiers open fire on refugees, killing 375 inmates of the camps.

August 19: Nigerian officer, Lieutenant Araenia, captured by Biafran forces in Oke-Ehi village near Port Harcourt, discloses that Russian officers are leading the attack of the Nigerian infantry in course of the final thrust into the heart of Iboland. He says that twenty Russian officers are assigned to every brigade of the Nigeria army. . . . West German government protests to Lagos regime about statements credited to Nigerian army officer, Colonel Adekunle, in West German magazine *Stern*. *Stern* quotes Colonel Adekunle as saying that he does not want to see the Red Cross or any other relief body in his sector. He is also quoted as saying that as his troops march into Biafra territory every moving thing is shot.

August 24: Master Emmanuel Effiong, an eight-year-old orphan from Ikot-Ekpene, discloses that when Nigerian troops occupied the town, his parents were taken away to an unknown place. He, with many other orphans, ran down the Ikot-Ekpene/Abak road, where they lived in the bush until they were rescued by Biafran troops after the town had been liberated. . . . Seventy-year-old Madam Okure, rescued from Ikot-Ekpene, discloses that when Nigerian soldiers entered the town they killed all that could breathe, except the aged and the maimed—left to die of hunger and starvation. All her children living with her were slaughtered. She watched one of them as the Nigerian soldiers tied him up and shot him. . . . An Irish priest, Professor Heely, tells the French News Agency that during their advance the Nigerians killed everyone—men, women, and children.

August 26: Red Cross societies in Denmark, Sweden, Norway, and Finland make available four more aircraft to the International Red Cross for the airlift of relief supplies from Fernando Po to Biafra.

August 27: British television men witness killing of Biafran civilians at Ogwe (near Aba) by a Nigerian army officer, Lieutenant Macaulay Lamurde.

August 28: A Briton serving a jail term in London donates £1 for relief of Biafran victims of the war. . . . Editorials of most British newspapers condemn Britain's supply of arms to Nigeria. . . . Belgian television man, Roger Machieles, says he witnessed and filmed the killing of young Biafrans by Nigerian soldiers at Obokwe (15 miles south of Aba). Mr. Machieles confirms that women and children who could not escape were shot, and some women and children were rounded up and taken away to an unknown place. He reports a case in which 20 Nigerian soldiers surrounded a Biafran civilian, matcheted him twice in the forehead, and later shot him twice in the belly.

September 1: Increased Nigerian military pressure on Aba. Biafran troops run out of ammunition. Acute shortage of currency due to Hank Wharton's Plot. . . . In article titled "Bibles and Bullets Ship," Defense Correspondent of the *Sun* (London), Frank Dewer, reports shipment of 170 tons of British shells, cartridges, and other lethal weapons to Nigeria by Britain in Elder Dempster cargo ship *Ebani* also carrying Bibles and clothing gifts of Christian aid meant for Biafra!

September 3:   Five European countries—Denmark, Finland, Iceland, Norway, Sweden—call on United Nations Secretary U Thant to take new steps to relieve sufferings of Biafrans.

September 4:   Aba temporarily falls to the Nigerian troops. . . . Foreign Ministers of member states of the OAU open their conference in Algiers to prepare ground for the summit of OAU Heads of States scheduled for September 13.

September 5:   Report from Dublin that people of Ireland have raised £250,000 for relief of refugees in Biafra. . . . Jewish pilot and businessman, Abe Nathan, donates more than 118 tons of food of high protein content and medicine to the government of Biafra in aid of refugees. The food and medicine was raised in Israel in response to the Campaign for Biafra which he organized with Biafra students in Israel. . . . Caritas Internationalis representative in Biafra discloses to newsmen that his association had set aside £200,000 for the establishment of feeding centers in Biafra. . . . Addis Ababa talks between Nigeria and Biafra adjourned.

September 9:   U.S. Presidential candidate, Richard Nixon, commenting on the Nigeria-Biafra war, says: ". . . genocide is what is taking place right now, and starvation is the grim reaper. This is not the time to stand on ceremony. . . . I urge President Johnson to give to this crisis all the time and attention and energy he can muster. . . ."

September 10:   At the Afoagu market, Nigerian soldiers line up and shoot 47 men from Afiamanya in Udi Division for their refusal to organize and lead a solidarity demonstration in support of "one Nigeria."

September 12:   Nigerian troops enter Oguta in a bold attempt to seize the Uli airport nearby in broad daylight. I lead Biafran troops and, in four hours, defeat this attempt of the enemy to capture our most vital line of supply. From the bottom of Oguta Lake, the Biafra Navy later recovers Nigerian landing crafts and boats loaded with armored vehicles, arms, and ammunition (including heavy artillery guns) of the disastrous river-borne invasion.

September 14: Nigerian threats on Owerri mount; evacuation of the town starts.

September 16: Several hundred people of all races demonstrate in support of Biafra outside the United Nations, New York, calling for the "boycott" of Britain, who supplies arms to kill Biafran children. . . . Owerri temporarily falls to Nigerian troops.

September 17: Nigeria carries out its most reckless air raid—510 civilians killed and more than 1,000 injured when two Nigerian planes attack Otuocha market in Onitsha Province.

September 19: Swiss people's hostility to British alliance with Nigeria in the war against Biafra halts "British Week" commercial exhibition in Basle. . . . The Congolese paper *Lasumin Cathohe* describes the results of the OAU Algiers summit as "useless because of the prudent silence of the delegates which was not only disappointing but a clear admission of impotence." The attitude of the African leaders, the paper continues, "was not dictated by the massacres of an unarmed people but by the military superiority of Nigeria."

September 21: Dr. Emil Zinsou, President of Dahomey, suggests in Paris a confederal setup with the greatest possible independence for Biafra as solution to the Nigeria-Biafra war.

Failure of Addis Ababa Talks

(Address to a joint meeting of the Consultative Assembly and the Council of Chiefs and Elders, September 25, 1968)

Since our last meeting, a number of events of great moment have taken place. There were the preliminary talks at Niamey, to which I was invited, as had been

Gowon, with a view to preparing the ground for full-
scale and final negotiations at Addis Ababa. The invitation for me to attend that meeting reached me at midnight, Thursday, July 18, 1968. Prompted by my desire
for a peaceful settlement which would lead to the stoppage of bloodshed and suffering of our people, and in
spite of the extremely short notice, I traveled to Niamey the following day in the company of top personalities in Biafra. I met the members of the OAU
Consultative Committee and put before them as dispassionately and realistically as I could our case, our
efforts and belief in peace, and our position.

Two weeks after the Niamey meeting, a full-scale
meeting of the two sides was convened in Addis Ababa
for Monday, August 5. Invitations were extended to
both Gowon and myself by His Imperial Majesty, Haile
Selassie, of Ethiopia, chairman of the Consultative
Committee. As in the case of Niamey, I promptly accepted the invitation and proceeded to Addis Ababa
only to learn that Gowon had contemptuously turned
down the invitation of His Imperial Majesty, Haile Selassie, the Emperor of Ethiopia. Before I left Addis
Ababa on August 7, I learned on good authority that
the Emperor had sent at least three other urgent invitations to Gowon to attend in person and that these
invitations had successively been spurned.

All the same, I was personally able from the floor of
Africa Hall to put to Africa the full case of Biafra. All
indications of world reaction, as could be seen from
international press reports, show that we had a good
and convincing case.

The Nigerian delegation arrived there not to negotiate but to exact abject surrender from us. This was
consistently shown right through their stay at Addis
Ababa, in and outside the conference, in their statements
and general demeanor. My speech of course could not
please the Nigerian delegation because there was nothing in it to show that we were wavering in our resolve
to ensure security and survival for our people. The per-

formances and general attitude of the Nigerian delegation right from the beginning of the conference and to the end left no one in any doubt that without our open announcement of abject surrender by renouncing our sovereignty on Nigerian terms the Nigerian delegation saw no point in continuing with the negotiations. The clearest evidence of this was the abrupt departure from Addis Ababa of the leader of the Nigerian delegation, who went first to Nigeria and from there to England, where he finalized plans with the British government for the final extermination of our people. In this he did no more than carry out his threat that unless we agreed to settle the matter on their own terms at the conference table, Nigeria would do so by other means, namely, the military. The British government replenished further the Nigerian arsenal for what they considered the final military push.

Meanwhile, while the negotiations were going on in Addis Ababa, the British Parliament in an emergency session discussed the Nigeria-Biafra conflict. One relieving feature in the debate was the clear fact that the majority of the members of the House of Commons, as distinct from the Wilson government, fully saw the need for ending the Nigerian war of genocide and for Britain to stop the supply of lethal weapons to Nigeria with which to carry out her war of extermination against our people.

Three things can be said to have come clearly out of the debate in the British Parliament. The first is that the British government had actually and fully accepted responsibility for this war, which they were prepared to carry to its inhuman and grim conclusion at all cost. Second, like Nigeria, they could not tolerate a situation in which we had not abjectly surrendered and placed the fate and future of our people at the mercy of our enemies. Third, the conscience of the British public had been so violently incensed against the British complicity and open participation in the war of genocide against our people that they were not behind their own govern-

ment. The debate in the House of Commons ended in
an uproar followed by angry crowds smashing and destroying windows at No. 10 Downing Street, the official
residence of the British Prime Minister. But in spite of
all these open demonstrations of disapproval and condemnation of the British government, that government
announced its determination to ensure a massive "quick
kill" of our innocent people as the best means of ending the war and safeguarding their economic interests.

With the final plan for the extermination of the people of Biafra meticulously designed and concluded by
the British government for Nigeria, Gowon was able to
announce in a radio and television interview for overseas audiences on August 23, 1968 that the final offensive against our people had begun and that he hoped to
overrun every town, every village, and every nook and
corner of Biafra within four weeks of that date. The
televised interview was shown in many countries of Europe. On August 31, 1968 he broadcast to Nigeria and
the world the final orders for Biafra's destruction. As a
matter of fact, Gowon had actually given orders for
what he called the final push against the people of Biafra even before the start of the deceptive Addis Ababa
conference.

You will recall that as an earnest of my desire for
peace and in order at least to halt the destruction of innocent lives, I announced on the morning of my departure to Addis Ababa a unilateral truce by ordering our
troops not to fire on the enemy except in self-defense.
This was one of the points discussed exhaustively in
Niamey, and it appeared to have commended itself to
all the Heads of State forming the membership of the
OAU Consultative Committee. No sooner, however, had
Nigeria heard of my announcement of a unilateral truce
than they ordered a massive and most vicious thrust
further into our heartland. Indeed, Nigerian troops were
ordered to capture our airport to ensure that I and my
delegation never got back there. As God would have it,
they never succeeded.

Meanwhile, the talks in Addis Ababa had reached a stalemate. With the departure of the leader of the Nigerian delegation, nothing about a peaceful settlement of the dispute was discussed. Instead the delegates were made to while away their time in fatuous and meaningless discussions on how to bring relief to our people. In these discussions, Nigeria's insincerity could not be disguised. It soon became clear that the main reason for the Nigerian delegation to stay in Addis Ababa was to await the news of the final collapse and destruction of our people.

For our part, we faced the discussions with earnestness and sincerity. It was our people who were suffering most, and we owed them a relief. To that end, we made several realistic proposals to Nigeria—only to meet with rebuff and contempt from them. As far as they were concerned, they wanted a condition which would prove clearly to the world that we did not exist as a people and indeed depended on Nigeria even for relief coming to us from international humanitarian organizations. This of course we could not accept, and no progress, let alone an agreement, was made.

The so-called negotiations were formally called off by His Imperial Majesty a few days before the beginning of the meeting of the African Heads of State at Algiers. For a long time before the start of that meeting, the world had been told that one of the most important matters to be discussed at that meeting was the Nigeria-Biafra conflict. The world therefore pitched its hope on that meeting; and so did we. We had always made it quite clear that we considered the conflict between us and Nigeria essentially an African problem to be best dealt with by Africans. We therefore made every effort to attend the meeting and put forward our case to the African leaders. All these efforts were frustrated principally by the host country, Algeria, whose alignment with Nigeria had never been in doubt. On Nigeria's insistence, the OAU succumbed to the suggestion that our case should not even be discussed in public. In conse-

quence, the world has not been told what the OAU
Consultative Committee reported to the OAU at its full
meeting in Algiers. The world has not been told what
the exact recommendations were nor what arguments
were adduced by the participants before a resolution
was taken. Up until now nothing has been communi-
cated to us officially either by the OAU secretariat or
by the consultative committee which had actually heard
both sides to the dispute. All we have heard about the
happenings at the OAU, insofar as our war with Nigeria
is concerned, has come to us through world radio media
reporting what is alleged to have been the resolution
taken by the OAU. The BBC's headline was that the
OAU had called for an immediate cease-fire and had
appealed to us to cooperate with Nigeria for the purpose
of ensuring peace and unity.

Not having received an official communication about
the resolution, it is not possible for me to talk to you in
great detail. But there is one very significant thing about
the resolution, and that is that the BBC in particular,
and some other world radio media in general, have com-
peted with each other in emphasizing that the resolution
adopted by the OAU was exactly in accordance with
the wishes of Nigeria. They have even gone further to
report that the resolution had to be personally approved and perhaps drafted by Chief Awolowo, the
leader of the Nigerian delegation to the OAU Algiers
meeting. Well, if it is true, and we have no reason to
feel otherwise, that the resolution completely satisfied
Nigeria's aspirations, then the whole issue lends itself
to no further comments. There is nobody in Biafra who
does not know what Nigeria's intentions for us are.

One may ask: What have all those OAU peace conferences achieved? The preliminary talks in Niamey
lasted from July 20 to July 26th. For seven days, the
delegates only succeeded in agreeing on an agenda for
a substantive meeting. On the matter of relief, to which
the delegates devoted most of their attention, no agree-

ment was reached. The following conclusion is an example of the utter futility of this meeting:

Conclusion—The subcommittee could not reach any agreed conclusions on the proposals for the transportation by land, sea or air of relief supplies to the civilian victims of the war.

The Addis Ababa talks lasted from August 5 to September 1, 1968. It ended, as I have explained, with no agreement on any subject, and so was formally adjourned. On relief again, where the world expected that at least the Nigerians would make a gesture of humanity to the suffering victims, they proved intractable. They rejected our proposals for both air and land corridors. The Emperor made two compromise proposals, neither of which was acceptable to them. They insisted that, with regard to the air proposal, only a particular airport in Biafra would be acceptable to them, and not the one already handed over to the International Red Cross for this purpose by us. The second set of compromise proposals were still under discussion when Gowon made his broadcast in Nigeria on August 31, stating that Nigeria was intent on a military solution and that the final assault had in fact been launched to achieve it. Gowon's pronouncements had the effect of closing the door to further negotiations at Addis Ababa on any of the items on the agenda.

At Algiers, the OAU failed to call on Nigeria to stop her war of aggression but instead is said to have naïvely appealed to both parties to cease hostilities. This, my fellow countrymen and women, has always been our position. Even before this, many world organizations, including the Vatican and the World Council of Churches, had genuinely called for a cessation of hostilities. The OAU is also reported to have urged the "secessionists," presumably the freedom fighters of Biafra, to cooperate in restoring peace and unity. The whole world knows, and cannot forget, that the people of Biafra, as Eastern Nigerians, had, more than any other people in the then Nigerian Federation, worked for unity. But the OAU did not make it clear what type of unity it wanted: Unity for life or unity for death? Unity for survival or unity for destruction? The OAU resolution avoided, in fact, the main cause of the conflict with Nigeria, which is the lack of security for lives and property of Biafrans in the Nigerian community which previous guarantees and constitutional safeguards failed to provide. In our discussions with Nigeria, both in Kampala and at Addis Ababa, we challenged them to present their proposals for effective and lasting security for our people. Nigeria could not even consider such a proposal, but insisted that we must renounce our sovereignty and opt for unity which had cost our people several thousand lives and properties in the genocide of 1966 and thereafter.

The OAU Consultative Committee peace initiatives at Niamey and Addis Ababa represent an attempt to correct a basic defect in their handling of this crisis. You will recall that at Lagos in 1967 the committee reached its decision on the case as presented by one side to the conflict. Perhaps more important than this admission, these latter exercises reflect increasing African disquiet at the growing international concern in the human suffering involved in this futile war. Both exercises and the OAU Summit failed to resolve the conflict, and to redeem the image of an inept African organization, largely because those African governments represented at the OAU are not free agents but mere tools of British, American, and Russian imperialism. It is clear to all Biafrans by now that our salvation does not lie in an organization ostensibly African, but which in fact is manipulated by foreign powers.

When we last met, Anglo-Nigerian propaganda was full of professions that Lagos did not intend to advance into the Biafran heartland. This was, of course, nothing but a ruse to cover their preparation for the final military onslaught. The fact is that Gowon and his British masters have been doing their utmost to achieve a quick military solution of the conflict.

In this massive onslaught, backed by enormous military support by Britain and Russia, we have inevitably lost some ground. On the Onitsha-Awka axis our gallant troops have been able to check enemy incursion. In the Agwu-Afikpo sector, the enemy has been able to make some gains, thereby threatening our airstrip at Uturu. We have been able to halt their movement, but the position is far from comfortable. To the east our fortunes have fluctuated, but we have succeeded in keeping them on the other side of the Cross River on the Arochukwu-Ikot Okpora axis. We have again entered Ikot Ekpene and are advancing toward Uyo. On the Southern front, we have suffered our greatest reverses by the loss of Aba and Owerri. This further enemy incursion into our territory has had the effect of increasing the already acute refugee problem. In spite of it all, I am happy to inform you that we have been able to recoup most of our losses and will continue to do so.

We went into this war because we had no choice except to defend ourselves from extermination. Right from the start it has been an unequal war. Against the 150 rifles with which we started, Lagos had the whole armament belonging to the Nigerian Federation, accumulated over seventy years. With no allies on our side and deprived by the economic blockade of the opportunity of earning foreign exchange, we have had to fight against a deadly foe supported by the imperialist powers of Britain, Russia, and the United States.

Our aim all along has been to delay the enemy until the world conscience can effectively be aroused against genocide. We sought no conquests and cherished no territorial ambitions. Our real victory lies in our ability to prevent the extermination of our people by a heartless enemy. Insofar as these aims are concerned, we have not failed.

In spite of the enemy's borrowed might and attempt to sweep the main issues under the carpet, we have fought them back and have been able to hold off the enemy sufficiently to arouse world understanding and support. In this, you yourselves have seen mounting world concern, expressed through the public statements and actions of some governments and international organizations. Far from being discouraged by the reverses in the Southern sector, the increased international acceptance of our rights to self-determination and our improved supply position gives me more confidence in our ability to frustrate the enemy. We are stronger today than we were two weeks ago, and indications are that we shall continue to grow from strength to strength.

And for the enemy it has not been an easy or comfortable affair. They are paying a heavy price for their rash adventure. Foreign agencies, quoting Lagos sources, have estimated the cost to Nigeria, in men alone, during the two weeks of fighting for Aba as fifteen thousand. And this was merely to prove to the OAU Council of Ministers at their recent meeting in Algiers that they were winning the war. On August 23, 1968, Gowon felt confident to announce that within four weeks he would be able to overrun not only Aba, Owerri, and Umuahia but the entire Republic. No sooner was this four weeks about to elapse than he gave himself a further two months. It is a tribute to the fortitude, gallantry, and dedication of our troops that they have been able to frustrate the enemy in spite of its massive superiority in number and armaments. I am confident that they will continue to do so.

During that period the enemy also, in a combined land, sea, and air operation, invaded Oguta—that beautiful lake city of Biafra. Their aim had been to push through that area to capture our airport and cut across our country. Our troops not only checked the advance on Oguta but practically destroyed every Nigerian soldier that set foot in that city as well as whatever equipment they brought there. Barely two days afterward, everything had become completely normalized for the whole population, which had fled the place to return to their homes, where they are now living as normally as before and helping the armed forces in salvaging what they had lost. Only before coming here, I received a report that a Saladin has been salvaged.

The role of the British government in the whole tragic episode has been a most despicable one. Whatever the British government may think or feel, history will never forgive her for her role in this conflict—her refusal to respect her often professed love of humanity and justice; her moral enslavement to economic interests at the expense of human lives; her arrogant posture for prestige and her utter defiance and contempt for public opinion, both in Britain and the world over. All these have not only undermined her prestige and honor in the world—they may eventually destroy anything she has ever stood for over her long period of imperial history. She may succeed in destroying a people struggling for survival and freedom in which the British have for centuries claimed to be the foremost vindicators, but the consequences for her are yet to be assessed. That the British government has been so morally bankrupt and contradictory has been seen in her condemnation of Russia's action in recent weeks, when in fact Russia has done no more in Europe than Britain has been doing in Biafra. Indeed, Russian action may even be regarded as more respectable and more honorable, because she has acted openly and honestly and not with subtlety buttressed by lame excuses of legality and other such nonsense. The aspiration of Biafra which the British government has determined to crush are in no way different from the aspirations of peoples of the world who respect freedom and justice.

As far as the United States of America is concerned, one should not be surprised by the role played by the government of that country, because it conforms with its callous and inhuman attitude toward the black minorities of America.

Our improved military situation, recent setbacks notwithstanding, rule out such a consideration. We have fought this war from the beginning conscious of our disabilities. All our sacrifices in men and material would have been in vain if we were to give up at this stage. The fight for freedom has always been uneasy, but victory has always belonged to those who persevered.

I call on all of you to rededicate yourselves again to the struggle. The future belongs to us, and we can regain lost grounds by renewed effort. The enemy is fighting in our territory, and the initiative belongs to us. Our armed forces will continue with their conventional tactics, but I am glad to report that they are now supported effectively by guerrillas. I am convinced that combined conventional and guerrilla warfare will defeat the enemy.

Our wishful enemies and detractors have been telling the world that the war has come to an end. The foremost propagators to this bogy have been the BBC and the Voice of America. Such speculations and hopes are utter nonsense. In many respects, the war is far from ending. In fact it is just beginning. Our troops are poised for a harder fight. Our guerrillas are being trained and equipped in larger numbers. It is fantastic for foreign agents to talk in terms of a Biafran government in exile. With the will and the determination of our people to fight, Nigeria can never crush us. History bears eloquent evidence of the fact that no people have ever lost a war or struggle for freedom and survival.

This is a fitting opportunity to thank those governments and relief organizations who have so generously provided relief for our suffering people. The time has come, however, for them to reexamine the whole basis of this relief operation in light of the Nigerian determination to frustrate their efforts and to press on to a military solution. It is clear that no relief will be effective without a cessation of hostilities. Nigeria has refused to heed any appeal to this end. Biafrans are therefore compelled in self-defense to continue fighting for their lives and their rights as human beings. Those governments motivated by humanitarian considerations have a responsibility now to ensure that Biafrans are enabled to defend themselves by providing them the wherewithal so to do. While on this, it is gratifying to note the recent statement of the Canadian government to take the Biafra-Nigeria conflict before United Nations on *humanitarian grounds*. In her war of aggression against our people, Nigeria has conducted a war of genocide on our people. All countries which believe in human dignity and freedom have a duty to ensure that the Geneva Convention on Genocide is respected. We welcome the initiative also taken by the Nordic countries with the United Nations Secretary General. We salute the governments of such countries as France and the People's Republic of China, who have made statements affirming our rights to self-determination. We urge them to join our friends in Africa and all over the world to ensure the survival of the progressive people of Biafra. Let them all support the Canadian initiative.

I owe you and the country a duty to place on record the debt we owe to our fighting forces. We must salute them with the deepest respect, gratitude, and honor for their gallantry and all the qualities becoming to patriotic soldiers fighting in open and often fatal defiance of overwhelming odds before them—fighting for the honor of their country and the survival of their people. We owe the same praise and must accord the same place of honor to all who have been responsible for the different supporting services—our scientists, our engineers, our propaganda agents, the food producers, and all.

Respected chiefs and elders, ladies and gentlemen, our faith in God must continue and never falter.

IV
Leave Us Alone

The whole episode of the Biafran struggle for self-determination and survival has become, as one foreigner recently put it, a phenomenon—unique in its nature and far-reaching in its repercussions. Our survival to this day has become a marvel and a wonder which have frustrated all expert calculations and anticipations. Biafra is fighting not in order to conquer, subjugate, or exploit other people. It is not interested in territorial acquisitions; not even in revenge. In a sense it is fighting for the cause of black man everywhere. The implications of Biafra's struggle for Africa should therefore not be overlooked.

Biafra is fighting against *imperialism* and all the forces of *neocolonialism*. It is fighting for the true independence of Africa. It is fighting to show the world that the African can have a will of his own which cannot be destroyed by even the awful might of imperialism and neocolonialism, which to this day are bent to enslave and subjugate Africa. The failure then of Biafra in this struggle could mean the failure of Africa.

It is the first real revolution in Africa, a continent which imperialist economic interests and world political ideologies would like to keep in perpetual vassalage. There could be no other reason than this for the extraordinary and unholy alliance of Russia and Britain in their common determination to destroy Biafra. They see in Biafra talent, ingenuity, skill, and resourcefulness, which can bring out the true character and dignity of Africa and which could blaze the trail for Africa's true independence and initiatives.

They are afraid of such a development and are determined to crush it, using men like Gowon and some spineless African statesmen as their instruments.

For two years now we have struggled and have survived terrible onslaughts and baffled all military calculations. For a long time we were totally isolated and alone. Our voice was never heard in the world, nor our sufferings felt by those abroad who could arouse world conscience against the hideous crime of genocide. Thus blockaded, starved of food and sympathy, and under a siege capable of suffocating us to death as a nation, a large proportion of the world wrote us off as a lost cause. But soon the truth and the facts began to filter out. Men of conscience started to ask questions; journalists, members of humanitarian organizations, and representatives of the church began to visit Biafra at great personal risks. They witnessed on the spot the horrifying events daily happening and returned to their own countries to tell the story. Humanity was aroused, and relief in the form of food and medication started pouring into Biafra. Newspapers and other mass media published the horrors of the war for the outside world to see. The Biafra-Nigeria conflict could no longer be regarded as "the unknown or forgotten war," to use the words of one humanitarian. We are grateful to all those who have helped to bring this about.

Today, though still blockaded and under siege, we are no longer totally isolated. The world is now alive to our cause, and our struggle has become the topic of common discussion and concern in practically all countries of the world. World leaders have spoken out; a number of countries have given us diplomatic recognition.

In spite of the indescribable sufferings of our people, our will remains undaunted and our determination unshaken. A number of our people are now being enslaved by the enemy. Most of our lands are now beyond our reach; our cities are in ruins; our industries have been destroyed and our trade disrupted. But these have not affected our resolve to go on to the glorious end. We want nothing but to be left alone and, in the words of a Biafran popular song, to rebuild our land, heal our wounds, care for the wounded, the orphaned, and the widowed. We want to be left alone to develop in our own way and pace in order to be able to contribute to the development of our country, Africa, and the world. We ask the world nothing other than this. Leave us alone to heal our wounds. Leave us alone to feed our hungry, to clothe our naked and destitute. Leave us alone; we seek no vengeance but life to reconstruct our being, to chart our course, to map that course, to follow our chosen path. Leave us alone to weep our tears, to laugh our laughter, to make our mistakes, have our frustrations, do our right, and have our achievements. Leave us alone to live . . . our black lives.

Diary of Events: Sept. 30, 1968 – Jan. 30, 1969

September 30: Two delegates of the International Committee of the Red Cross and two relief workers of the World Council of Churches are cold-bloodedly shot dead outside their Red Cross-marked hospital by Nigerian troops in Okigwi, Biafra. . . . More than 200 Biafran civilians are murdered by Nigerian troops in Okigwi.

October 1: Red Cross DC-4 carrying 55 Nigerian soldiers to Port Harcourt crashes . . . Maxwell Cohen, American attorney, confirms that Nigeria is waging a war of genocide against Biafra. He describes the statement credited to Lord Shepherd that he has not seen any evidence of genocide in the Nigerian war against Biafra as a contemptuous, vicious, and shameless lie calculated to deceive the world.

October 3: I write to United Nation member states, drawing their attention to genocide and calling on them to use their position to enforce an immediate cease-fire and stop the genocide now being committed by Nigeria against Biafra. . . . Chinese government speaks in condemnation of Nigeria and her allies in crime of genocide against the people of Biafra. . . . French Foreign Minister Michel Debré, speaking in the National Assembly in Paris, says that genocide now going on in Biafra and the creation of phantom states by Gowon "cannot solve or ease the problem which brought the conflict."

October 4: German churches make available £10,-000 through the World Council of Churches for the maintenance of refugees in Biafra.

October 6: Gabonese chief delegate to the United Nations, speaking in the United Nations General Assembly, says UN cannot be indifferent to destruction of human lives in Nigeria's war of genocide. He says that the United Nations must intervene to end the massacres. . . . Speaking at the seventh anniversary of Uganda's independence, the President, Dr. Milton Obote, describes Nigeria as shame of Africa. He rules out Nigeria's vaunted military victory in her genocidal war against Biafra.

October 8: Stephen Lewis, leader of Canadian New Democratic Party and the third Canadian parliamentarian to visit Biafra, reports: "Genocide is an ugly impossible word. . . . There is genocide in Biafra—I saw it.". . . French Foreign Minister Debré tells 23d General Assembly of UN that every passing day shows more clearly than ever that self-determination represents only suitable solution for Biafra.

October 13: Action Association of Independent Germans, with headquarters in West Berlin, says that Britain and Russia are guilty of genocide for their support of extermination of Biafrans through the Lagos government.

October 21: Canadian missionary, Dr. E. H. John

son, addressing the Canadian Parliamentary Committee on Foreign Relations, says that Nigeria-Biafra war might have been averted "if Britain had not given overwhelming arms support to the Lagos government." Dr. Johnson observes: "The British people have a very bad conscience about arms shipment to Nigeria."

October 24: Observer team disagrees. Disagreement comes to light following report submitted by Canada's representative, General William Milroy, that Nigerian troops looted belongings of Biafran civilians wherever they set their feet in Biafra.

November 2: Dr. Tunji Otegbeye, a Nigerian, signs £10 million arms deal with Communist Bulgaria on behalf of Nigerian government.

November 10: Seventeen-year-old boy, Eugene Ofichi, tells how civilians in Awka are forced by Nigeria occupation troops to drink urine. Men and boys are brought out and flogged every morning by the occupation troops, and their women are sent to the soldiers at night.

November 11: President of Gabon, Albert Bongo, announces that his country will be at war with Nigeria if Nigeria carries out her plot to infiltrate agitators into Gabon. . . . Discovery of poisoned food supposed to have been introduced from Nigeria. Poisoned packets are identified as bearing the following Nos. AC.836; AC.832B; AC.833B; AC.836B; AC.837B; AC.838B; AC.839B.

November 12: Students in Zurich call on Swiss motorists to boycott English-made cars and English-refined gasoline and oil. Boycott is organized by Friends of Biafra Association.

November 14: Compilation by research and evaluation division of Biafra Information Services reveals that Nigerian air raids have killed more than 2,000 Biafran civilians and injured more than 5,000 in May to October, 1968.

November 24: Commenting on Biafra's charges of genocide against Nigeria, IRC chief delegate in Biafra,

Karl-Heinz Jaggi, compares Nigeria's conduct with what the Nazi Germans did to the Jews and declares: "I am not an international lawyer, but there are certain overtones of genocide."

November 25–27: Nigerian troops make massive thrusts into Adazi and Agulu, near Nnewi, and are decimated. . . . Mounting wave of unrest in Western Nigeria against the war and its cost.

November 27: Rioting in Western Nigeria. Several persons killed and many others injured when Nigerian soldiers open fire on a crowd of demonstrators in Ibadan, capital of Western Nigeria.

November 29: In Lokpa village of Okigwe, 60 people are lined up and shot by Nigerian soldiers.

December 1: President Albert Bongo of Gabon in an address to the representatives of the press in Paris, announces that the Republic of Gabon will continue to defend the interest of Biafra because she is convinced that Biafra's struggle is for human rights.

December 5: British member of Parliament, Dr. John Dunwoody, says after visit to Biafra that there can be no military solution to Nigeria-Biafra war.

December 6: Pope Paul VI expresses grave concern over the fate of human lives, particularly children, now exposed to danger as a result of the Nigerian war of genocide against the people of Biafra.

December 7: International Committee to Keep Biafra Alive organizes seminar in New York. Peter Enahoro, a Nigerian and brother of Gowon's Information-Labor Commissioner, describes Biafran people as "the pride of Africa and the black peoples of the world."

December 8: Violent riots in Ibadan, Shagamu, and Abeokuta in Western Nigeria against "heavy taxes." Massive repressive measures employed by Lagos to quell the riots.

December 9: A high-ranking Nigerian officer and a British purchasing agent reported combing Europe for 500 napalm flame-throwers for Nigerian army.

December 12: Swiss multiple chain store, Migros,

offers 1 Swiss franc for every franc collected by their customers in campaign to raise cash to pay transportation costs of relief supplies into Biafra and raises 1 million francs in less than two weeks.

December 25: Nigerian air force takes another delivery of two British jet planes, two Russian jet fighters, and one Russian jet bomber.

December 26: Violent demonstrations continue in the West.

January 1–5: University Students Association of East Africa passes resolution recognizing Biafra and condemning what it describes as genocide being perpetrated against Biafra.

January 8: I address the Biafra People's Seminar in the State House.[1]

January 14: Ivory Coast paper, *Fraternité Matin,* expresses regret over attitude of Commonwealth leaders in London by relegating to the background the Nigeria-Biafra war. The paper feels that Nigeria-Biafra war is "the only topic that merited every attention at the conference" and describes the war as "the tragedy of Biafra."

January 16: Riots in Nigeria's Abeokuta and Shagamu in Western Nigeria. Angry demonstrators in Abeokuta ambush Nigerian troops, killing 100 soldiers including four Nigerian captains. Military governor of Western Nigeria, Colonel R. Adebayo, flees to Benin in the Midwest for security. . . . Lord Fenner Brockway calls on United Nations to intervene in the Nigeria-Biafra war because if the war is left to linger on, "it will escalate into a conflict between the major powers."

January 17: I launch the Biafra Land Army campaign.

January 19: Radio Prague refutes Nigeria's claim

[1] Every Wednesday night from January 8, 1969, I address People's Seminar (or what could be described as People's Parliament) in the State House. The discussions, which cover a wide range of subjects including current matters and problems, are open to everybody: the taxi driver, housewife, farmer, professional, intellectual, policeman, soldier, priest, etc.

that "her war of genocide against Biafra is an internal affair." In comment on the Nigeria-Biafra situation, the Czech radio station observes that "right from the start, the war was internationalized by the arrival in Nigeria of the most modern armaments from abroad."

January 22: In my greeting to new American President Richard Nixon on the day of inauguration, I express hope that the new administration of the U.S.A. will call for a cease-fire and a halt to the Nigeria-Biafra war. ... Leading French citizens including diplomats, parliamentarians, and writers call for recognition of Biafra's independence and for an immediate cease-fire in Nigeria-Biafra war.

January 23: Riots continue in Abeokuta, Western Nigeria. Three army officers and 43 civilians killed. ... Tanzanian envoy criticizes Chief Obafemi Awolowo over his statement after the Commonwealth Conference. The envoy, Mr. Mure, describes as "fallacious and ridiculous" Chief Awolowo's report that both Dr. Julius Nyerere of Tanzania and Dr. Kenneth Kaunda of Zambia, both Presidents of their respective countries, regretted their recognition of Biafra.

January 30: French good-will mission led by Monsieur Raymond Offroy addresses a mass rally at Umuahia.

The People's Resistance Continues

(Address to joint meeting of the Council of Chiefs and Elders and the Consultative Assembly, February 10, 1969)

We met last in this assembly five months ago. We dispersed from that meeting with many not quite sure that we would meet again. It was probably the darkest hour in the history of our struggle. The atmosphere was tense. The prospect was gloomy. The enemy had entered Aba. Owerri fell. The OAU, by its resolution, had adopted a supine posture to this conflict with a majority of its members confirming themselves as stooges of neocolonialism. At home there was widespread anxiety. Abroad, a world, so willing to seal our fate, published once again our obituary and sent wreaths for our supposed funeral. In Britain the Harold Wilson government made elaborate preparations to induce crocodile tears while gloating beside the funeral pyre.

Lord Shepherd flew to Lagos to represent Harold Wilson at a planned victory parade. The BBC and other world media of information announced a blitzkrieg ending with the fictitious capture of Umuahia in forty-eight hours. Yet our faith remained, and our resolve was unshaken. Contrary to the belief and expectation of our enemies and their supporters, the nation met to discuss the situation and give directives for the moment and the future.

I can well recall the anxious faces of the gathering as I stood before you. But transcending your anxiety were the determined mind and undaunted spirit of Biafra. I could see, cutting through the dark atmosphere, streaks of hope and confidence, and I was encouraged.

I spoke to you first in a formal, and later in an informal, meeting. The waiting and keen world had pricked its ears for news of what they considered the inevitable outcome of the meeting—namely, an offer of surrender in a last-minute desperate effort to save what could be saved. All these were based on one basic miscalculation. They had failed to understand that Biafra is not towns but a people with heartbeats as regular and a pride as erect as the best on earth.

Biafra was determined to fight on and never to surrender. I told the world so in no uncertain terms. This assembly later reinforced, with a unanimous voice, our resolve to fight on. The world was astonished. Our people were happy and reassured. Our friends showed admiration, sympathy and understanding. Nigeria was nonplussed; Lord Shepherd expressed open disappointment. Harold Wilson publicly condemned our natural desire to survive. The United States was puzzled. France understood.

The war continued with our enemies more than ever determined not only to wipe us off the face of our God-given earth but to do so with such brutality and in so short a time as to be a lesson to us for daring.

Today, I am happy and proud to report that their miscalculations have persisted. Rather than destroy our gallant people, we have in the intervening period inflicted such casualties on the enemy that presently all hospitals in their doomed federation are overflowing with their wounded—that both their 1st and 2d divisions have had to be reconstituted and that rag-tag force known as their 3d Marine Commando has throughout only been retracing its steps and its commander swallowing back his words.

We have stabilized the fronts; we have built up our forces and seized certain initiatives, and the future prospect is one that can only generate confidence.

The position at present is: In the Onitsha area the position has remained relatively unchanged. Our troops are still in the precincts of the township and in some points inside it. BBC reports of the enemy thrust southward toward Nnewi are false, although troops labeled "Nnewi Task Force" are at this moment congregating in Asaba. We await them.

One of the areas in which enemy activity has been most felt is the Abagana-Awka axis. Here the enemy has been indiscriminately shelling neighboring villages and has made some advances. It is now in control from Ifite-Ukpo junction to Awkuzu market, but our troops have regained some of the ground lost in recent counter-attacks.

In the Agulu area the enemy has been beaten back and is located in Ipene village and the Ipene-Unwana road facing our troops in that area.

In the Ikot-Ekpene axis, while both sides have maintained their defensive positions, the past few days have witnessed heavy fighting, with the enemy trying to break through and suffering heavy losses. Enemy attack at Nyara Enyin was beaten back.

The enemy is still located in Aba township, but our troops have constantly conducted effective raids into every part of the town. Our attacks on the enemy in the Eberi-Obokwe-Ogwe axis have yielded good results. Fighting has continued along the Owerrinta-Okpuala axis after our troops successfully repulsed enemy offensives. The enemy is still located at the Okpuala junction.

Our troops on February 3 launched an attack against the enemy in all areas of Okigwe and seized the provincial office, police barracks, and the Ihube-Uturu-Okigwe junction. The past few days have witnessed fierce enemy counterattacks, and our own troops are maintaining their positions.

By far the fiercest scene of action has been Owerri, where for the past few weeks our troops have been trying to clear the town of enemy presence. Fighting is going on in many areas right inside the town. While the fighting for Owerri township continues, our troops are pushing toward Port Harcourt on the main Port Harcourt-Owerri road. It was as a result of this move that members of the so-called observer team were reported to have been cut off in Owerri.

In the Oguta sector, our troops in a lightning move cleared the enemy from Egbema beyond Ebocha, where the oil field is firmly in our hands. We are now fighting the enemy at Omoku.

The enemy, faced with so much frustration at every turn, has resorted to indiscriminate air raids against the civilian population, churches, schools, refugee camps, and everything not military. In the past weeks their raids have taken heaviest tolls in Orlu Province and at Okpuala market, where in one single raid they caused nearly 500 casualties, predominantly market women.

Today we are many times stronger than we were on the last occasion we met. Our regular forces have been increased, improved, and better armed. Our guerrilla forces operating behind enemy lines have struck terror in the minds of the aggressor and paralyzed its administration. The initiative has passed into our own hands. The enemy no longer dictates the pace and has been subjected to sustained harassments and destruction. Parts of our territories into which they had set their venomous foot have been wrested from them. A number of our displaced persons have been able to return home.

Last week we heard the enemy moaning about a series of air raids sometimes attributed to the relief agencies but oftimes attributed to the Biafran air force. Whichever way—praise be the Lord.

In the diplomatic field we have once more captured the initiative. The diplomatic activities of Harold Wilson's government and Joseph Palmer of the United States administration frustrated the Addis Ababa peace talks and cajoled the OAU into adopting an evasive and subjective resolution at Algiers. Using that meaningless resolution of the OAU, the British government and their agents stopped at nothing in their campaigns of calumny and blackmail against the leadership and people of Biafra.

For a while the world appeared to have lost interest in what was going on here. It did not take long before the dishonesty of the hired and so-called international observer team was exposed to ridicule. Misdirected by the Lagos propaganda that lies to friend and foe alike, they were cut off together with the remains of the Nigerian army in Owerri. If they are still there, I assure them that the Saracen armored car on standby will not guarantee them any safety. I therefore invite them not to miss this godsent opportunity for obtaining balanced information! Our troops have been ordered to treat them with the utmost courtesy.

The many faces of Harold Wilson, now unmasked, cannot bear the light of the day. Harold Wilson has

earned a place for himself in history as a ruler who has
defied the wishes of his people, his party, and a Parliament which he is supposed to serve and obey. Having
tried long and repeatedly to deceive the world about
the British government's efforts for peace and its influence in Lagos resulting from the supply of arms to
Nigeria, Harold Wilson recently had to confess before
the British House of Commons his utter failure and
total inability to influence Lagos and bring about a
cease-fire.

We have on our own side repeatedly pointed out that
it is their supply of arms that blur from Lagos the
vision of reason. We have repeatedly called for a total
embargo on the supply of arms to both sides; we have
called for unconditional cease-fire and negotiations without preconditions. Leaders throughout the world, heads
of states or governments, have made the same call for a
cease-fire followed by peaceful negotiation. The conscience of humanity has rallied to put a halt to this
wanton slaughter and sheer waste of human lives. All
over the world, ordinary people—men, women, children, both professionals and laborers, farmers, businessmen—have cried out for justice and the rights of our
persecuted people. In places, workers have refused to
load ships, students have gone on hunger strikes, organized labor has broken strikes to load a mercy ship—
the streets of the world are daily being tramped by
people of all races, all creeds, all sexes, and all ages
together to bring relief for a wronged people.

The support has been universal and has begun to have
effects on the governments of many countries. Our case
has been formally debated in the United States Congress, in the Swedish Parliament, many, many times
over in the British Parliament, discussed in the French
Assembly, and more recently in the Italian Parliament,
not to mention in Africa, where major discussions
finally crystallize around the issue of this conflict. It is
our founded belief that this support by the masses all
over the world will, in the year 1969, be translated into

support and positive action by their various governments. The signs are healthy.

Our struggle for freedom and self-determination has not been easy. We have been able to achieve our present successes because the dogged determination and indomitable will of our people have defied all difficulties, sufferings, and death. We have lived for two years with the hard and harsh conditions of an unjust war. Our experiences have no parallel in history. While those difficulties no longer frighten and intimidate us, while we do not for a moment like those unfortunate conditions, we cannot run away from them. Our people have continued to meet the challenge with growing efficiency, increased ingenuity, and greater cohesion and enterprise. There has been a growing mutual understanding among our people. Every difficulty, every hazard, has brought out the best in our people. Every new challenge has enhanced the resourcefulness of our people so much so that the past few months have witnessed a return to an almost prewar standard of normalcy.

We have been able to reopen our schools to enable our children to prepare themselves for the future task of reconstruction and the defense of our hard-won freedom. These schools are necessarily of a makeshift nature, reflecting naturally the limitations imposed by a cruel war. But they also reflect our absolute faith in the survival of our nation.

I must stress that it is on the minds of our younger generation that this unholy war and its vicious nature will make its most lasting imprint. Parents and guardians, teachers and elders, all have a greater responsibility for the physical and moral well-being of our youth. The many shifts of the battlefronts have uprooted our youth from the rigors of our tradition and society; already moral values have been assailed, and time has flown with such unsuspecting swiftness that those who were children before the war are no longer children. I would like to remind the older ones of us of our responsibility to this nation in building up our future generation. To exploit this disruption would be tantamount to aiding and abetting national suicide.

A few weeks ago I had the honor of launching the Land Army program, which calls for the cultivation of every available piece of land in Biafra so as to meet the challenge of hunger. The war against scarcity of food ranks equally with our war against the enemy on the battlefield. The Land Army must conquer starvation, it must conquer want, it must conquer waste, and above all, shoulder to shoulder with men of our fighting forces, it must conquer and secure our land. I want to make very clear to all true Biafrans that in the context of our struggle, no organization can be regarded as truly Biafran without that organization operating a farm. Every effort is being made to obtain farm implements to enable the tilling of our soil to go apace.

It is my sincere hope that every householder in this Republic will farm the precincts of his own domain. Every quarter, every village, every town, indeed, every clan and every tribe, will be judged Biafran to the degree of cultivation and the degree of total involvement in this Nigeria war against our nation. Let there be no wasteland, let there be no idle hands. I call upon you, fellow countrymen and women—men and women who have already conquered the myths of African servility and permanent dependence—to demonstrate once again that pride and resourcefulness, that independence, and that self-reliance which have enabled us to confound our enemies and have marked us for a unique role in the sociopolitical revolution of the black man on earth.

We are in a hurry. We must be in a hurry, for the period of want is upon us. The time for action is now, if you have not already started. The land is there yearning to be turned; hands are itching to be set on the plow. The organization is local and gives scope for the widest exploitation of local conditions and local talents. The government is yours to advise and to assist. If any group or any area suffers want after this program has gathered momentum, that person—yea, that group—will have nobody to blame but itself. Once again, I call upon you to join hands with me and save our generation. I call upon you to bend with me, to turn the sod with me, to bury Gowon with me.

Already I can see our farmers and all those who have helped to win this war against hunger and starvation with their hoes on their shoulders and matchetes in their hands, marching side by side with the members of our fighting forces and singing in unison with them our songs of freedom in honor of our nation on victory day. On that day, they will march forward together as partners.

I have also launched the national emergency medical service. This program is designed to bring medical care to every doorstep in our country. This program calls for the establishment of emergency health centers in all population areas. It is geared to bringing relief and comfort to the sick and afflicted. It is designed to seek out disease and effect its cure before it turns into epidemics. I appeal to all relief organizations to assist us in this program by bringing more drugs and to make available to us modern skills and equipment.

Many in our society have shown remarkable resilience to the vicissitudes of this war: our scientists are now producing more weapons of war than ever before; our farmers are producing more food, our traders and businessmen are showing remarkable enterprise and have started to bring in a variety of consumer goods. As conditions allow and as circumstances improve, it is the intention of this government to expand all activities in these directions.

Old habits die hard. If we are to build the new Biafra we are fighting for, we must shed Nigerianism, which symbolizes indolence, cheating, greed, and avarice. It is unfortunate that people should be found among us who are trying to exploit the current emergency and suffering of our people for their private ends—people who profiteer and those who cause scarcity of money through hoarding. Some people are even trading with the enemy behind the lines. All this must stop. We must make up our minds to change our attitudes. If by the end of the war we have not eschewed all the ill which contributed to the destruction of what used to be Nigeria, then we shall have lost half the cause for which we have fought.

I sincerely hope that these are temporary difficulties arising from the uniqueness of our revolution. Ours has been, as it were, a revolution in reverse. The conventional course of national revolutions is that they should be preceded by intensive preparation and education of the people, culminating in the revolutionary action, the seizure of power, the war of national liberation.

In our own case, the revolutionary act seized us before we were fully prepared for it. The result is that we have been placed in a situation where we are fighting a war of revolution, a war of national survival and independence, and at the same time educating our people about its implications. It is this lack of prior education which has led, on a number of occasions in the past, to acts and excesses of misdirected enthusiasm which could generate misunderstanding and aggravate hardships among our people. We owe it to our cause, and to those it is our privilege to lead, to preach and act the true philosophy of our revolution.

Let us always bear in mind, and let it be known to all, why we are fighting. Let us never lose sight of the goals of our struggle—the goal of justice, the goal of brotherhood, the goal of equal opportunity, and the goal of service to our country and humanity.

To those in public life—those who have the privilege of leading and serving the people—I remind them of the inalienable sovereignty of the people. The government and its agents are nothing but servants, the people their masters. The test of all our actions must be the good of the people whom it is our privilege to serve. We must act as though we are every hour, every minute, every second, accountable to the people, bearing in mind at all times that should we fail to give satisfaction the people reserve the right to remove us from office. To this end, I suggest that we at all times subject each and every action of ours to the triple test of the Biafran revolution. Whatever we do, we must ask: Is it good for the individual? Is it good for the group? Is it good for the nation? If the answer is yes to the three questions, let us go ahead without hesitation. If we answer yes to two, we should think again before proceeding. If yes applies only to one, we must abandon our intention. If we can answer yes to none, we are lunatic and must be hurried to a doctor.

The government has long been aware of the hardships of our people and our terrible fears of this war. I thank all of you who, faced with the enemy air menace, have contributed generously for the provision of air cover or at least some form of an answer to the enemy menace. I am happy to inform you that the government has been doing its best to meet your wishes, and while it would not be politic for me to give the details of our achievement in this direction, I will say this and only this: I will keep my promise.

The government has long been aware of the terrible experiences of our people over the issue of currency. The present difficulties started when early last year Nigeria, on the advice of Whitehall, suddenly decided on its wicked and diabolical plan to dispossess our people of their wealth by means of the notorious currency switch. We had to do something quickly to save the near-disastrous situation. New currency was introduced. With the short time at our disposal, we could only produce notes in denominations of £1 and 5/–; we could not produce coins. We had to arrange and conclude the exercise in a hurry. The production of our currency notes could not be of the highest quality. I am happy to announce to you that we have now been able to produce real Biafran currency of the highest quality. The new currency notes are of the wide range of £10, £5, £1, 10/– and 5/–.

This government has always been aware of the gen-

eral inconvenience and difficulties arising from shortage of coins. These difficulties have also been aggravat-
ed by the avarice of some unscrupulous traders who
have tried to debase our currency by using available
coins in their trade with the enemy. I am happy to inform you that our own coins have now been minted.

In view of the severe hardships already endured by
persons in the lower income group in our society, I have
directed that immediate steps be taken to pay salaries
to persons within this category and that until this is
done nobody in the senior service sector will be paid.
This exercise will begin with immediate effect.

Recently a great deal of time and energy have been
wasted on the question of relief. We, of course, have
always welcomed relief from genuine quarters, where
the method of giving such relief does not place the
security of our people in jeopardy. We want our people
to live. To this end we have made offers which have not
been taken up. We have offered land for the construction of an airstrip for those who find the present night
facilities inadequate and want to operate by daylight.
We have proposed a sea route which could bring in
more relief for those who would like to supplement air
transport with sea and land transport. None of these
offers has been taken up.

The other side, of course, is not interested in relief.
Nigeria has never made any secret of this. The British
government has further underlined the stand of Nigeria
by stating categorically that what Lagos is doing is a
siege warfare. But relief in the forms now being given
or proposed cannot serve as anything but a palliative.
The only way of providing true relief to our people is
to put a stop to hostilities to enable our people, now
refugees, to return to their homes and live normal lives.
For the purpose of bringing an end to hostilities, I
proposed in my New Year message:

On the vital question of cease-fire and negotiations, we
submit that a cease-fire more than any other plan or pro-

posal is the surest and most effective means of bringing relief to the people.

Hitherto, we have insisted that there must be a cease-fire before any negotiations; but considering the difficulties and delays associated with a cease-fire before it can be made effective, we propose a truce for a limited and specified period, during which arrangements for a cease-fire can be made. During that period, too, the much-needed relief supplies for the suffering on both sides of the conflict can be brought in without impediments.

We proposed that both the cease-fire and negotiations should be without preconditions.

As I have mentioned in my discussion with recent foreign visitors, there is a wide area of cooperation of great mutual advantage open to Nigeria and Biafra. Negotiations can cover a wide range of subjects, including economic relations and even the possibility of a commonwealth arrangement. The overriding requirement is good faith, free of prejudice and mistrust between the parties concerned.

Those proposals have been welcomed by unprejudiced sections of the world as reasonable, but our enemies appear not to react at all to them. Those proposals remain open, and we are prepared to meet anybody to clarify any of them if necessary.

About this time last year all of us, men and women and children, irrespective of our positions or status, were faced with the threat posed by the Nigerian deadline to crush Biafra by March 31 of that year. That threat was successfully countered by our gallant people, and all enemy plans were frustrated. Since that time the enemy has set many more deadlines for destroying us but has failed. I consider it my duty to alert you of the enemy's present and last desperate effort to carry through its threat of exterminating our people.

You have all heard what Enahoro said in England, namely, "that the war will end only when one side decides to give up." The enemy has long been preparing for its final assault. It launched this final offensive before the start of the Commonwealth Conference in the hope of gaining a dramatic victory to mark the occasion. The enemy failed. It has made further elaborate plans for the future, and those plans are now fully in our hands. It is quite clear that it was in anticipation of the plans that Harold Wilson adopted the indifferent attitude which he did at the last Commonwealth Conference.

We have come a long way. We never wanted, let alone started, this war. We have held back an inveterate enemy virtually with bare hands. We have gained signal successes. We have maintained our faith in God and have not faltered in our cause. As a peace-loving people, we have made many offers for peace. We have made many concessions. In search of peace we traveled to London, Kampala, Niamey, and to Addis Ababa. We approached and pleaded with international organizations, governments, and individuals to tell the Nigerians to leave us alone. Where else can we go? Is there no place on earth where an oppressed people can seek and obtain protection and justice?

Enahoro said that the war will end only when one side decides to give up. Since for us to give up is a fate worse than death, there remain only two alternatives. Either Nigeria and her collaborators call off their mad ambition to deny 14,000,000 people their rights and their lives or we both prepare for a war of attrition.

We cannot give up. We will fight. We will fight Nigeria and all her imperialist collaborators with a ferocity that will shock and frustrate them until they leave us alone. We will fight Gowon and his fellow travelers until they recognize the fact that Biafra is a people, and the land our own. The old will fight, the young will fight, children yet unborn will fight, and their children will fight until they leave us alone. O Gowon! Listen to the voice of reason. Our entire population—chiefs, elders, and people—will fight until you leave us alone. Respected chiefs and elders, this calls for greater sacrifice, greater toil, greater labor. This calls for the noblest form of patriotism. This calls for faith in God and assurance of His divine support.

As for Mr. Harold Wilson, when all his antics failed to impress his inquiring people and an intelligent world, at the end of the last meeting of the Commonwealth Conference he announced that his government has always wanted a cease-fire to be followed by a massive relief but that we the Biafrans have been resisting it. This, of course, is a lie. In my last Christmas message I made proposals for truce, cease-fire, massive relief for the suffering, and accommodation with Nigeria through negotiations. Unbiased and humanitarian people the world over have acclaimed the proposals as realistic and reasonable. How then can Harold Wilson say that we Biafrans have resisted efforts for a cease-fire to be followed by massive relief? It is a fact that the British government has tried to stop relief supplies to Biafra on the grounds that starvation is a legitimate instrument of war; that relief increases the will of the people to resist; that food sustains strength and is therefore ammunition for resistance; that they regard the activity of relief agencies in bringing relief supplies to Biafra as an act of war, and that the aim is to reduce the defenders of Biafra to physical conditions which they can no longer endure.

It is against that background that Nigeria has recently poured abuses and insults on the United States of America for offering planes to relief organizations for relief supplies into Biafra. It is in pursuance of the policy of using starvation as an additional means of genocide against Biafra that Nigeria has bribed the government of Equatorial Guinea to stop the International Red Cross from flying relief into Biafra from Fernando Po. We have received information that all is not well with our nationals now resident in Equatorial Guinea. Nigeria appears to be using the new government of that territory to achieve its political aims through the persecution of Biafran nationals there. I want to assure our brothers and sisters in that territory that we are not insensitive to their plight. Nigeria is trying to do to them even in a foreign country what they have been doing to all of us here at home. I appeal to them to remain calm and to do nothing which can put them in any way to blame. They must do this without compromising their position as true Biafrans.

We must not allow ourselves to be deceived that the British government or Nigeria can be genuinely interested in peace. All their diplomatic actions and talk about peace are designed as a camouflage and for delay to enable them, after each failure to meet their deadline, to retrain and regroup their troops, enlarge their arsenal, before setting their military machinery rolling once again. Their aim is to try like a gambler this final throw of the dice, and having done this, and even if they fail, as they must, to overrun Biafra, they will have gone quite far in destructions; they will have carried out their genocide to the ultimate within their capability.

The British government bears full responsibility for the consequences of the present Nigeria-Biafra conflict; it has obstructed negotiations; it has frustrated moves for peace. It is they who have vitiated all efforts for cessation of bloodshed, suffering, and death in this part of Africa. It is their efforts which have undermined well-meaning peace initiatives by leading world personalities. It was the British government's diplomatic activities which aborted negotiations at Kampala and Addis Ababa; it was the British government's influence which prevented the OAU Summit at Algiers from acting objectively; it is, of course, Harold Wilson who frustrated the known intentions of the Commonwealth leaders, during their recent conference, to try to find a means of ending the current tragic war of genocide against our people.

We have since the start of the current conflict tried to be reasonable and civilized toward the British government and her people. We have, even during the highest moments of provocation, protected their interests in Biafra. We have often appeared quite naïve in respecting their historical claims to justice and fair play. In so doing, we have been influenced by the knowledge that the larger sections of the British public do not support the actions of their government and by our belief that its vaunted claims to democracy would force that government to bow to public opinion. We are now totally convinced that nothing can turn Harold Wilson and his clique from the path of genocide against our peace-loving and progressive people. I therefore make this point crystal clear. As soon as it becomes evident that the latest British-sponsored final offensive against our people is on the move, at that point in time all British interests in Biafra both now and in the future automatically become forfeit.

We are now on the threshold of great events. We are going through the last stages of this bloody war with our heads still high. The end is near—the goal is in sight. We have all denied ourselves everything on our steadfast march toward that goal.

On the battlefields, without pay or reward, our young men and women—the vanguard of the Biafran revolution—are defending with an iron resolve and the highest form of valor our rights to freedom. I salute them.

In the farmlands, our proud farmers, exposed to the bombardment of the Nigeria hordes, are defiant and determined, scorning the enemy to cultivate the land to feed the hungry. I salute them.

In our laboratories, workshops, and factories, our brilliant young men and women are toiling daily, at times without food or money, in order to make available the products of modern technology for our survival. I salute them.

In our offices, directorates, ministries, refugee camps, and win-the-war organizations, thousands of our public servants who are turning the wheels of our civil administration and the administrative machinery of the revolution have demonstrated to the world that no sacrifice is too great for the survival and safety of their fatherland. I salute them.

In our hospitals and sick bays, our dedicated doctors and nurses are working around the clock to bring to

bear the full weight of their medical skill with little or
no drugs to save precious lives. Their only care is the
lives of their fellow men. I salute them.

Our brave and gallant pilots, both Biafrans and foreigners, have defied the elements, conquered the skies,
and flown through fire to bring us relief and comfort.
I salute them.

Foreign missionaries, relief organizations, and our
friends and supporters abroad have faith in our survival
and destiny and remain unshaken even in our darkest
hour. I salute them.

Finally, I urge you all to remain undaunted in your
vigilance and resolution. The survival of Biafra is assured and indestructible. As we prepare for this final
onslaught we pray God to be our shield and pray forgiveness for our enemies. Our reliance is in God. We
shall vanquish!

Diary of Events:
February 4–May 30, 1969

February 4: Biafrans repulse offensive in Ikot Ekpene sector and prevent river-borne invasion of Ndoni.

February 7: Nigerian planes kill more than 300
people, mostly women and children in raid on Afor
Umohiagu village near Owerri.

February 10: Biafran troops regain 60 square miles
in Ahoada sector. . . . Our forces blast enemy strong-
hold in Owerri, capturing 500 Russian-made automatic
rifles and 100 boxes of ammunition.

February 11: I meet New York Senator Charles
Goodell, accompanied by Democratic Congressman,
Allard Lowenstein. In my statement to them I observe
that the Johnson administration had considered the
Biafran situation a nuisance partly because of the Viet-
nam war and partly because of the difficulty of oppos-

ing British policy. . . . I address troops in the Okigwi war sector.

February 13: United States Congressional fact-finding team arrives in Biafra.

February 16: Mr. Winston Churchill (grandson of of the wartime British Prime Minister) makes stirring reports in the *Times* of London on the constant raids by Nigeria air force planes on civilian targets in Biafra.

February 17: I visit hospitals in Orlu Province and distribute cigarettes to patients. . . . Biafran forces gain 10 miles in Ahoada sector.

February 20: Sixty Biafrans killed in air raid in Umuahia.

February 21: Five pregnant women killed in Nigerian air raid on a clinic at Amokwe Item.

February 27: I send a message of condolence to Israel on the death of Prime Minister Levi Eshkol. . . . I join a village Land Army in a neighboring Umuahia village to clear farm land. Correspondents (Lloyd Garrison of the New York *Times,* Winston Churchill of the London *Times,* Dr. Ruth Bowert of West Germany, etc.) who later track me down in the village appear startled to see me without a shirt. . . . I visit refugee camp near Umuahia and distribute vegetables grown by State House Land Army.

February 28: Mass demonstrations in Umuahia and Orlu, calling on the new American President, Mr. Richard Nixon, to reverse the former administration's policy of rubber-stamping British policy on the Nigeria-Biafra conflict.

March 5: Soviet warships arrive in Lagos. Convoy comprises two guided missile destroyers, a submarine and a supply ship.

March 6: Mass demonstrations throughout Biafra against Soviet Union military opportunistic adventurism in Africa.

March 7: Biafra forces encircle Nigerian brigade in Owerri township. I discuss with Biafran field commanders in Owerri war sector on how to deal the final blow on the enemy. . . . I tell a British Labor member of Parliament, Mr. Frank Allen, that we are prepared to accept a cease-fire without preconditions and that the war can end only by negotiation.

March 10:   I address a People's Seminar on the ills of Biafran society at Umudike. . . . Russian jet fighters kill 98 people in air raid on villages in Annang Province.

March 11:   I visit victims of Nigerian air raids in Umuahia hospitals.

March 12:   In a letter to the six European Common Market members, I propose a month's truce in the Nigeria-Biafra war to allow both sides to meet and negotiate a cease-fire.

March 14:   I lead another village in Udo-Mbaise in communal farming, in an attempt to popularize the Biafra Land Army. . . . I address the inaugural meeting of the Biafra Economic Planning Commission and charge it with the task of coordinating Biafra's human and economic resources for effective use.

March 13–19:   Visit to Biafra of a six-man Zambian goodwill mission led by Ambassador H. Simbule, Zambian Ambassador to Ivory Coast.

March 19:   A pro-Biafra sit-down demonstration in the English city of Bristol. Twenty-two people arrested, including a university lecturer.

March 21:   I receive a member of the Dutch Parliament and comment on Mr. Harold Wilson's proposed visit to Nigeria which I said was not to bring peace but to reestablish British influence and to dispel American concern about Russian intervention in Nigeria.

March 22:   The Republic of Haiti becomes the fifth country in the world, and the first outside Africa, to accord diplomatic recognition to Biafra.

March 23:   I visit Onitsha war front to talk to Biafran troops due to cross the River Niger to the Republic of Benin.

March 24:   I send messages of good will to Senators Edward Kennedy and Charles Goodell and two American Congressmen, Lukens and Lowenstein, saying that ocean-going vessels could come as far as the River Niger estuary from where smaller boats would transport supplies up the River to Oguta, in Biafra.

March 25: Biafran troops in Republic of Benin capture three oil fields in two days. . . . Dr. Clyde Ferguson, American Relief Coordinator for Biafra and Nigeria, says in Lagos that the determination of Biafrans was attributable to the indiscriminate bombing of civilian targets by the Nigerian Air Force.

March 27: The Biafra Action Committee in the Federal Republic of Germany initiates an emergency program designed to aid agricultural production in Biafra.

March 30: A white woman in Paris burns herself to death near the Nigerian Embassy in protest against the Nigerian genocidal war against Biafra. . . . Biafran forces capture three British armored vehicles, two Ferrets, one Saracen and a Panhard in Azumini sector, near Aba.

March 31: Night in Owerri war front with the Infantry. Forces of Biafra's crack 14th Division and the Thunder Division smash Nigerian forces and occupy 70 percent of Owerri town.

April 3: I meet delegates of the United States National Students Association.

April 4: I visit the Uzuakoli war front and spend whole day with fighting forces. I attend midnight mass.

April 5: Grueling battle for the strategic town of Uzuakoli, twelve miles from Umuahia. Recapture of the town by Biafran forces.

April 7: In Afikpo sector Biafran anti-tank guns knock out one Saladin and one Ferret armored car, destroy heavy Nigerian artillery gun (number NA.103) and capture 18,000 rounds of 7.92mm and 7.62 NATO ammunition.

April 10: I visit refugee camps around Umuahia to distribute food and toys to the children.

April 14: Enemy thrust to Umuahia led by British tanks intensified.

April 20:   Enemy radio message reveals Brigade Major trapped in Owerri is killed.

April 22:   Nigerian troops enter Umuahia and fighting begins in the town. I spend the morning with the troops in Umuahia war front and later visit nearby military hospital to talk to the wounded.

April 23:   Biafran forces sweep into Owerri and recapture the strategic town from Nigeria's 3d Commando Division. They capture several hundred cases of British- and Russian-made ammunition buried by Nigerians in the town. . . . The French government reaffirms her support for Biafra's right to self-determination.

April 26:   A Ministry of Defense statement announces our capture of Aboh town on the west bank of River Niger in the Republic of Benin.

April 30:   I send a message to General Charles de Gaulle on relinquishing his post as French President. I say: "My people and I will never forget that in our hour of distress we could count on the understanding and support of the great people of France under your leadership. . . ." I send a message to President Nyerere of Tanzania on the fifth anniversary of the United Republic of Tanzania, saying that Biafrans are proud that the noble principles which motivated the creation of the United Republic were reflected in the attitude of the President and his government to the Biafran struggle for self-determination.

May 2:   A Swedish Red Cross international quarterly, *Vart Rodakors,* calls on all lovers of freedom throughout the world to spare no effort in coming to the aid of suffering humanity in Biafra.

May 3:   Biafran women launch the Women's Front. They call on Biafran government to allow Biafran women to enlist in the infantry.

May 4:   Biafran forces capture Okpuala junction, 15 miles from Aba.

May 8:   I send a message of gratitude to President Bongo of Gabon on the first anniversary of the diplomatic recognition of Biafra by Gabon.

May 9: Eighteen oilmen are captured in Kwale town of the Republic of Benin by Biafran infantrymen.

May 17: Senator Eugene McCarthy in a speech made in the Senate calls on the United States government to recognize Biafra.

May 22: Biafra Air Force planes raid Port Harcourt airport and destroy two Soviet-built MIG fighters and one Ilyushin bomber. The Port Harcourt Oil Refinery and airport control tower set ablaze.

May 24: Biafra Air Force planes raid Benin Airport and destroy the notorious Nigerian night bomber— the "Intruder"—loaded with bombs, two MIG fighters, and the airport control tower.

May 27: Biafra Air Force planes rocket Enugu Airport, detroying five Federal Nigerian planes—two bombers, two MIG fighters, and one civilian aircraft. . . . I address Armed Forces Seminar on the Biafran Revolution.

May 29: A requiem mass is held in Freetown, capital of Sierra Leone, in memory of the 50,000 Biafrans killed in various parts of Nigeria during the 1966 pogroms. . . . Dr. Auguste Lindt, the International Red Cross representative for Nigerian-Biafran Refugee Aid, is arrested and detained at Lagos airport, Nigeria. . . . Biafra Air Force raids Ughelli power station, setting it ablaze.

May 30: In New York, an American boy, David Mayrock, burns himself to death carrying a placard on which is written: "Stop Genocide, Save Nine Million Biafrans." May his soul rest in peace. May his death not be in vain. . . . Second Independence Anniversary.

2
Random Thoughts

Contents

RANDOM THOUGHTS

I

On Nigeria

THE FLAG OF SHAME

Nigeria was the creation of British imperialists out of the many and diverse national units which they grouped together in what were called Northern Nigeria and Southern Nigeria and which, until 1914, were administered as separate territories. All through the period 1914–1966, Nigeria was plagued by the unfortunate consequences of the amalgamation which the former Premier of Northern Nigeria, Sir Ahmadu Bello, called "the mistake of 1914." While speaking of the political and social unrest of the early 1950's, he declared: "The mistake of 1914 has come to light and I should like to go no further." From this period, the Northern Nigerians began to think of repudiating the unfortunate merging of their region with the South. As Sir Ahmadu Bello put it: *"We should set up on our own; we should cease to have anything more to do with the Southern people; we should take our own way."*

This line of thought was encouraged by the imperial and religious ambitions of the Northern Nigerian rulers, including Sir Abubakar Tafawa Balewa, the former Prime Minister of Nigeria.

The constitutional and social development of Nigeria was held up for many years by this arrogant attitude of the Northerners and their refusal to be involved in the search for stronger ties within the country. Their desire, moreover, to dominate the country continued to frustrate all efforts at constitutional advance.

1

The people of the then Eastern Nigeria were held responsible for the failure of the North to dominate the country. In 1945 and in 1953, organized riots in Northern Nigeria led to the massacre of hundreds of "unwanted" people of Eastern Nigeria origin. Even as late as December 1964, the manifesto of the government party in Northern Nigeria read, in part: "The time has come. We are going to show these intellectual fools that we are only in the morning of our leadership of this country. . . . Our only obstacles are the Ibos. They have overplayed their card. They will sink."

Nigeria in the end came to be run by compromises made and broken between the Northerners and consenting Southern politicians. This led to interminable violent crises, to corruption and nepotism, and to the arbitrary use of power. The coup of January 15, 1966, was hailed as the God-sent salvation for a dying Federation.

International press conference, Umuahia,
January 28, 1968

I think a most important point of our struggle which a number of people tend to miss is the fact that what was known to the world as Nigeria originally was not one country. It never became one country—our colonial experience was different. The North was governed by indirect rule; the South by direct colonial administration. The people of the South could never mix with the people of the North. If a Southerner went to the North, he lived in a reservation, and his children could not go to the same school as the children of the Northerners. He had freedom of movement but only a limited freedom of association. The Southerner in the North was made to feel a stranger to the North. The system of law in the North was completely different from the system of law in the South. In the South it was the British type: Western European law with magistrates and judges; in the North, it was the Muslim system of law known as the Sharia Court system, where one was dealt with according to Muslim tradition.

> Interview with Cliff Robertson, United States
> actor, Umuahia, December 9, 1968

This war is a war imposed on us by the feudal slave-masters. In the old Federation some of you here will remember quite vividly what the contribution of the people from this area, now known as Biafra, was to the betterment of the areas in which we chose to reside and believed was our country. Socially we gave our best in Nigeria. Politically, we led the struggle for independence and sustained it. Economically, the hope of Nigeria was embedded deeply in this area and we contributed everything for the common good of Nigeria.

Our people moved from this area to all parts of the old Federation, and particularly to Northern Nigeria. Where there was darkness we gave them light! In Northern Nigeria, where they had no shelter we gave them houses. Where they were sick, as indeed most Northerners are, we brought them health. Where there was backwardness we brought progress. And where there was ignorance we brought them education. As a result of all this, we became people marked out in the various communities in which we lived.

Initially we were marked out as people who were progressive. Next, as people who were successful. Finally, as people who should be the object of jealousy— people who were to be hated, and this hatred arose as a result of our success. Nobody who hates the Biafran has been able to say that a Biafran committed an act of injustice against him. Nigerians hate us simply because where they failed, the Biafran succeeded. Our crime in the old Nigeria was that we succeeded. We were relegated to the position of second-class citizens and later to slavery—yes, slavery—because as we worked our masters enjoyed the fruits of our labor.

We reached a stage where the people from this part were fast losing their identity. They hid away the fact that they came from this area. If you had a job to give, so as to show your master that you were really a good servant, you made sure that his brother got the opportunity first before any other, irrespective of experience and qualifications. This process gathered speed, and soon we began to obliterate any outward sign indicating that we were not Northern Nigerians. We hid our own identities.

How many of you looked in dismay at our own sons slowly shaving off their hair and putting on Northern Nigerian robes and passing as Northerners? Some of our senior men in public office considered very seriously whether to go to Mecca or not even though they were not Muslims. It became shameful to be an Eastern Nigerian! Those of you who lived in Lagos would probably remember that if you wanted to be able to ride over the law with impunity, all you had to do was to put on the Northern Nigerian gown and pretend to be a Northerner. How many of you watched with dismay the fact that cars did not normally park in front of Kingsway Stores, Lagos, but as soon as an Alhaji came up with his regalia and discolored teeth, he would be allowed parking space? You all remember that if a Northern Nigerian ran into your car and damaged it, the police would release the Northerner who was at fault and arrest you whose car was damaged by the careless Northerner. This was the state of affairs in the old Nigeria.

The Northern attitude is the attitude of horse and rider. If you look at the map, this becomes very clear. We were carrying the North physically, economically, and in every other way. For all that we received no thanks. They only got furious if we did not travel fast enough. Then they would kick. But, for every mule, there comes a time when it bucks and says, "No, I will

carry no more." We have bucked. We will carry Northern Nigeria no more! They must leave us alone and find another beast of burden. They must let us live our quiet lives alone. Typical of the horse and the rider, the North gave us three lashes [three pogroms], but we refused to budge. They kicked us in the rump—economic blockade —but we still refused. In frustration they now want to destroy us. They are trying to destroy us right now. They will not be satisfied until every one of us is dead.
Address to Port Harcourt Leaders of Thought,
Port Harcourt, October 17, 1967

The fight for independence in this country was fought by men and women who showed great devotion to the cause of freedom. Their activities, at the time of the country's assumption of independence, demonstrated great promise and hope, but, unfortunately, that promise was never fulfilled. Our first essay in democracy was brought to a grinding halt by petty jealousies.

Our leaders in the fight for freedom very soon realized the corrupt possibilities of power, the temptation of which proved too strong for their weak frames. The country was thus thrown into a power conflict—region versus region, ethnic group versus ethnic group, clan versus clan—until finally the country began to disintegrate.

In the disintegration, individuals began to maneuver for positions, throwing overboard all consideration for the progress of the nation and doing only those things which would bring personal aggrandizement to themselves. The masses of this country were exploited for the benefit of the few, and a personality cult became the sole object of government.

In this state of affairs, it was inevitable that our leaders should become alienated from the people they were supposed to serve. They built for themselves palaces of marble, and made grandiose plans directed purely at the glory of individuals. They became indifferent to public opinion. They believed that the only way to silence opposition was a slight increase in the membership of this club that perpetrated the exploitation.

Those who were supposed to be our servants became our masters, then our owners. This was not enough. They even strove to become our gods. In this attempt, they mobilized and geared all efforts toward the acquisition of power—the acquisition of wealth and influence. In search of wealth, they became even more corrupt and bribery became rampant. In search of influence, they indulged in nepotism and tribalism, fanning all sectional antagonisms until the conflagration threatened to devour the whole country.

They practiced deceit and abuse of office and kept bad faith with the people. Their individual greed and avarice threatened the destruction of the fatherland. They raped the Constitution, practiced thuggery at elections, and finally robbed the people at the polls. In all this, they were heedless of the people's cry. They were shameless before the world and reduced Nigeria to a state of being the laughing-stock of the entire world.

When the people revolted, they paid no heed. Murder and arson became the order of the day and they abandoned their responsibilities.

> Address to the students and staff of the
> University of Nigeria (now Biafra),
> Nsukka, February 25, 1966

POGROM

The people of the former Eastern Region of Nigeria had believed, as if it were an article of faith, in the concept of a united Nigeria. No section of the then Federation of Nigeria worked as assiduously for the attainment of this ideal as did Eastern Nigeria and her people. No section made as many and varied positive contributions toward the realization of true unity.

Having, over the years, spearheaded the movement

for closer union, having demonstrated our faith in Nigeria in concrete terms by allowing our sons and daughters to sojourn in other parts of the country, thereby contributing tremendously to the development of such areas to the neglect of our own, it was a hard decision for us to opt out of a Federation in which we had invested so much. But we had no other choice.

Over the years, our erstwhile compatriots made it clear in unmistakable terms that they did not want us in the Federation. Since the 1950's our people were expropriated and discriminated against in parts of Nigeria other than their own. Furthermore, the experience of three harrowing waves of remorseless genocide in 1945, 1953, and especially in 1966, involving a total of nearly 50,000 dead and countless others maimed or destitute, provided an object lesson which could not but be taken seriously.

Self-preservation is probably the strongest human instinct, and it is this that has compelled the harassed and persecuted people of Eastern Nigeria to seek refuge in their own home and among their kindred. As a proverb of one of our Biafran languages has it, "A man who is rejected by others cannot reject himself."

Message to Biafran students in the United States
of America, November 24, 1967

CONTROL OF THE CENTER

A sort of apartheid policy was in vogue in Northern Nigeria against the people of Southern origin, who were kept in "sabon-garis." The children of the two sections were kept in separate schools and not allowed to mix, a situation which, if it had been otherwise, would have led to better understanding.

Recent history has shown that most of the troubles and conflicts among the regions have arisen from a struggle to control the center, and this has in turn been the direct offshoot of suspicion and fear, buttressed by

ambitions for power. Our delegation to the Ad Hoc
Constitutional Conference in Lagos has been given the
mandate to work on the following broad principles:

   (a) The fact of very deep-rooted differences in religion,
       cultured attitude, outlook, and rate of development
       existing in the country should be recognized and
       accepted.
   (b) The necessity of allowing each region to develop in
       its own way and at its own pace should also be rec-
       ognized and accepted.
   (c) Since the control of the center has ever been the
       main cause of friction and tension between the dif-
       ferent regions, thereby threatening national soli-
       darity and integrity, the distribution of functions
       between the regions and the center should be re-
       viewed and so arranged that only such subjects and
       functions as will engender the minimum of suspi-
       cion and friction among different groups are allowed
       in the hands of the federal government.
   (d) The composition of the organs of the federal gov-
       ernment should be so arranged as to give no one
       region an advantage over the other.
   (e) The subject of representation and the method of
       selecting such representatives should be carefully
       gone into. We would like to see the practice of the
       federal general election abandoned.

The acceptance and application of the above principles will inevitably, if regretably, lead to a looser form
of association than anything we have known before.
We believe that there is no other course to adopt, but
we hope that with time Nigerians managing their affairs
separately will come to learn how profitable it is to live
together in peace, oneness, and brotherliness. That is
why our delegation will also insist that whatever constitution ensues from the present discussions should
have a clause for its automatic review after a stipulated
period. I wish to assure you that the East [now Biafra]
believes in self-determination for all groups, and cannot
therefore be opposed to the creation of more states, pro-

vided the basis for such is mutually agreed upon. We do not here in the East wish for, neither have we worked for, secession. If, however, circumstances place us outside what is now known as Nigeria, you may be certain then that we should have been forced out.

Address to diplomatic representatives of the
United States and the United Kingdom,
Enugu, September 22, 1966

JOURNEY TO THE SLAUGHTERHOUSE

The coup of January 15, 1966, caught me by surprise. The first thing that hit me was—here I am in the northernmost part of Nigeria surrounded completely by troops and I have not even tried to find out their allegiance. The telegram that informed me about the coup came to me at the parade ground. The first thing was to try to get some sense from Lagos. For about fourteen hours I called numbers, but people were telling me nothing. I did not realize the suspicion everybody had in everybody. I suppose it was my persistence that got Ironsi [the late Supreme Commander of former Nigeria] to speak to me. He told me what actually happened. He said that the Cabinet [the disturbed civilian federal government] was meeting. The federal government later handed over power to the army to stabilize the situation. I found this extremely confusing. Nobody knew where any other person in the army was.

After Ironsi's first broadcast, I immediately spoke, as the most senior officer in Northern Nigeria, to the North. Somebody else spoke to the West. Ejoor spoke to the East. The announcements had a snowball effect. They helped in restoring confidence and a sense of direction in the army. The country also became clear about the change.

After that announcement I got on to Nzeogwu [one of the leaders of the coup], then in Kaduna, and said, *"You are now famous. You should now demonstrate to the world that you have no personal motive in the*

*coup. Now that the G.O.C. has called, all you have to
do is to get back into line."* Before then there had
been friction between Nzeogwu and myself because I
maintained my independence. . . . The announcement
affected him [Nzeogwu]. This is how I got involved in
government. Nzeogwu found it difficult to accept my
advice, though he realized it was already a *fait accompli*.
I continued to talk. . . . I wanted him to fall in line,
and quite suddenly he said to me, "If you say so, I
agree." I told Ironsi that Nzeogwu had agreed. Later, I
was ordered to Lagos and appointed [military gover-
nor] for the East, Fajuyi for the West, Ejoor for the
Midwest, and Hasan Katsina for the North.

Ironsi tried very hard to unify the country. Personally, I think he went too fast. Or rather, he delayed too
long, and when he started he went too fast without
explaining. If the unification of the country had been
done within the first week of the coup, perhaps the
popular impact and the enthusiasm [generated by the
January 15 coup] would have carried it through. Subsequent events, however, clearly indicated that the
violent reaction of Northern Nigeria could have been
only a delayed action and that the North could never
have allowed any form of unity which sought to broad-
en the Northerners' national outlook and turn them
into Nigerians. When Ironsi moved, he was quite
willing to give a blank decree unifying everything. I
resisted that quite a bit. Assets of the then Eastern
Region were seized. I maintained that we should get
the constitutional proposals first agreed before the
assets were put into the common pool. The North did
not agree with me.

I got myself more and more involved in the politics
of the change—more involved because I think really I
was perhaps better equipped than most of the military
leaders to handle political issues owing to my background, education, and training in administration before
joining the army. So I really got quite involved. The
Supreme Military Council tried a number of things to

inspire confidence and strengthen the unity of the country, but actually there was much to do, and before the whole place could be stabilized the North struck on May 29, 1966.

I still harbored hopes for unity, but I told Ironsi then that this was the last sacrifice the people of former Eastern Nigeria could be expected to make.

In spite of this pogrom, I still thought that the army had a chance to keep Nigeria together, and that chance was to try to get everybody looking upon the government as the government. All I asked of the Supreme Military Council was a Commission of Inquiry on the May massacre. I did not quite realize how far Northern Nigeria was prepared to go. If I knew, perhaps my suggestion would have been different. The council decided on the method of inquiry. But as soon as it was announced, the Northern emirs met and told us that the instructions from Lagos would only be carried out over their dead bodies.

My whole attitude then was to establish once and for all that there was a government. For this reason, we insisted and set August 2, 1966, for the beginning of the inquiry. In doing this, the council [the Supreme Military Council] wanted also to demonstrate that it was going to be fair—a British judge would be the chairman and there would be commissioners from Northern Nigeria. On July 29, 1966, they [the Northerners] struck again. This time they killed Ironsi.

After that, I knew that the end had come. The murder of 3,000 people, by any stretch of imagination, was terrible. 30,000 was the third massacre [September 29, 1966, pogrom], but there was nothing in the past to match the cruelty and sadism of the last massacre.

After the July 29, 1966, mutiny, I tried to get Lagos on the phone. All efforts failed. When eventually I got Lagos, nobody was willing to tell me what was happening. At last I got and spoke to the next most senior officer in Lagos [Brigadier Ogundipe]. I said to Brigadier Ogundipe: "What are you doing? Get the army

together; don't let it disintegrate." He said it was very
difficult because he could not get the soldiers to obey
him. But I told him to take a risk and shout at them;
to get on the air and say something to the country.
"Tell them that you are next most senior officer, you
do not know where the Supreme Commander is, but
you are trying to control the situation." After a long
time, he said: "OK, I will do it." When the statement
was made over the air, *it was a most supine statement.*
He said something like this: "Perhaps you do not
know me, my name is Femi Ogundipe. I am trying to
do my best," and that was the end! This only added
to the confusion. Again, I got on the phone to Brigadier Ogundipe, who said, "These people [Northern Nigerian soldiers] want to go [secede]; they say they cannot
stop killing people unless we allow them to separate." I
advised that if that would stop the bloodshed, he should
let them go. On another occasion after this I tried once
again to contact him on the telephone—I waited for
nearly half an hour without success—the man had fled.

   Now, what could I do? Luckily, both coups had not
affected the then East. I thought of it, talked to Ejoor
and even Katsina, but could not get any sense out of
them. So I decided to phone Gowon. I rang him, but
Mohammed [Colonel Mohammed] answered. He fetched
Gowon, and as we were talking, it was quite clear a
number of people [Northern Nigerian officers] were
standing with them. Gowon could not answer any point
unless he discussed it with the people standing around.
I got this conversation taped. He insisted that he was
going to announce that his boys would only be satisfied
if he took over, and I told him that he could do so,
but not the East. "If you want, as Chief of Staff, and
only as Chief of Staff in Lagos, I will cooperate with
you to enable you to stabilize the situation so that
Ogundipe or whoever is next in seniority to him can
assume power." He replied that the other governors
had agreed with him to take over. He told me that he
was going to make a statement at 7 o'clock. I phoned

Ejoor; he was not very coherent, and he said that all this slaughter must stop and that he left me to do what I could to help the situation.

Gowon announced himself the Supreme Commander, and immediately I decided with the few people available that if we once got under him we would not be able to get anything and all our people would be massacred under the legal cover of the assumed legitimacy of his rebellion. But if we stayed out and negotiated we could save our people. So I spoke out immediately that I did not recognize him as the head of the government. Later, I sent a team to Lagos to the Ad Hoc Constitutional Conference. While the team was discussing our Constitution, we endured another massacre on September 29, 1966.

Ever since, I have made many suggestions to bring about a solution. But each time a suggestion was made it was rejected and more bitterness was generated.

When we found ourselves at Aburi, Ghana, it was our last chance. Those decisions at Aburi could have saved the situation, but again Gowon was very badly advised. He was very badly advised, though he was carried along by the way we all talked. My last statement to the group was: "I know what is worrying you. We cannot solve this problem by hitting each other across the face. If we keep the agreements made here, Jack, I would probably ask this body to appoint you the Supreme Commander." This you can ask General Ankrah. Gowon left his seat, came over to me, and embraced me. It was then that Ankrah said: "All right, let us shake hands." When we ended the meeting, and came out of the hall, Gowon and Ankrah and I sat in Ankrah's car and there he took my hand and placed it on Gowon's hand and said, "Both of you have got fifty-six million people to look after. If you keep to these agreements you will achieve peace; if you don't, then whatever comes is your fault. You have seen the way, it is up to you."

As a gesture of peace, I made a short visit to the

Midwest before coming back to the East. I must say this for Gowon: The first three days after our return to Nigeria he did all right. But on the fourth day, he mentioned that there was one publication he wanted to publish: *Crisis '66.* I said, "Why publish it now? If you do so, my people would now want me to answer and the whole problem would begin all over again." I suggested, "collect them, keep them, if I misbehave publish it." He agreed. The next day the publication was announced all over the world. I rang him and he explained it as a leak. I spent the whole day discussing with him how to punish the director of the Ministry of Information. That night, tuning the various radio stations, I discovered that the book was formally launched by ambassadors in London, Washington, and Ghana; it was not a leak!

Then the various attempts to implement Aburi failed, the refusal to pay our money came, the economic blockade followed, and finally came the fragmentation of the country.

It was under these circumstances that Biafra was born. When it was born I made a statement and said it was going to be a hard time. I thought possibly that Gowon would try after that to bring us together very quickly. Intelligence reports spoke about the massing of troops by Gowon on Biafra's borders. He declared war. There had been an opportunity to strike first, but I knew that no matter what our temporary advantage, eventually with the Nigerian resources they would be able to push us back. So it became very important to me that the world should know that I was not the aggressor. We fought well for six weeks; then we were at par. British help came to Nigeria, and then Russian. Attempts at subversion, and then the journey to the slaughterhouse resumed. This was a journey that started from the Northernmost part of the country and then slowly came to this place.

It is not power I wanted. I initially came to this post as a routine military duty. Looking back at it, I do not

think I had a choice. Each time I felt perhaps that I
had a choice. Could I, after the July 29 massacre, say
to the people of the East, "I resign, I am going"?

Interview with Jim Wilde of *Time* magazine,
Umuahia, August 16, 1968

When I addressed you at the last convocation none
of us foresaw the subsequent course of events. We
were then installing Alhaji Ado Bayero, the Emir of
Kano, as your new chancellor. The appointment of a
Northern Nigerian to that high office was one of our
many manifestations of good will, and of our faith in
and drive toward the goal of unity in Nigeria. Indeed,
that installation took place a few weeks after the organized massacre of May 29, 1966, of our kith and
kin in Northern Nigeria, an event tragic and dam-
nable enough to make us abhor Northern Nigerians.
But at the state banquet I gave in honor of the Emir,
I expressed our readiness to forgive and to forget.

I was concerned that the task of reconstruction which
we had begun should proceed, unhampered by bitterness and recrimination. The military, as the last hope
of every nation, had assumed political power five
months earlier, in order to rescue the former federation of Nigeria from falling into utter chaos and
anarchy.

As you will recall, the Federation had floundered
from one crisis to another as a result of the inordinate
ambition of a reactionary and feudal section of the
country to dominate the rest. The faulty constitution
which had been drawn up under colonial tutelage
enabled this reactionary and feudal section to attempt
to perpetuate their hold on the political strings of the
country. Nigerian politics left much to be desired in
other ways. Politicians abused their offices, enriched
themselves at the expense of the common people, and
imprisoned or massacred their political opponents.
Corruption and nepotism were rife, and so was the
molestation of innocent citizens by the hired thugs of

politicians. Census figures were flagrantly falsified and general elections impudently rigged. In short, those in power flouted all norms of decency and democracy.

And so in spite of the May, 1966, massacre, I considered it better to hold out to the masses the fulfillment of their hope for a more stable future in which peace, justice, and honor would prevail.

Before these massacres, the military regime had taken bold and decisive steps to eradicate the evil practices of the past and to consolidate the various units of the country into a strong, virile, and united nation. The disorders in the Tiv Division of Northern Nigeria had been brought to an end. Peace had been restored to Western Nigeria, which had for long been torn by bloody internal strife. Judicial commissions of inquiry were set up to uncover the malpractices of former politicians with a view to recovering their ill-gotten gains. The military regime sought to provide a lasting solution to the perennial crises which had bedeviled the health of the Nigerian body politic. The regime believed that true unity could only be achieved when, among other things, the even development of the country was guaranteed and its resources, human and material, pooled for the benefit of all sections. In conformity with the unified administration of the armed forces of the country, the Supreme Military Council unanimously promulgated the unification decree [No. 34] of May, 1966.

The reaction of Northern Nigeria is now history: a cold-blooded and systematic genocide calculated to exterminate the progressive people of Biafra everywhere in the now-dismembered Federation of Nigeria. On Sunday, May 29, 1966, Northern Nigerians surprised and butchered to death innocent Biafrans resident in their midst—men, women, and children praying in churches or relaxing in the privacy of their homes. On July 29, 1966, after expressing the hope that there would be no recurrence of the May massacres, Northern Nigerian soldiers murdered Major General Aguiyi-Ironsi, the Supreme Commander of the Nigerian armed forces, and attempted to annihilate all military officers and men of Biafran origin. The atrocities were continued and intensified in the following weeks, reaching a climax on September 29, 1966, when combined teams of Northern Nigerian civilians, soldiers, and native police extended the massacre to Biafran civilians—men, women, and children throughout the Federation. More than 50,000 Biafrans lost their lives and nearly 2,000,000 became refugees.

The pretext for the pogrom was Decree No. 34, the unification decree, which Northern Nigerians feared was introducing a strong, effective central government based in Lagos. Since this decree was the unanimous decision of the Supreme Military Council on which all the regions of the former Nigerian Federation were represented, why, it might be asked, did unholy wrath descend solely on Biafrans?

In any case, following the recent proclamation of himself as the dictator of Nigeria, Lieutenant Colonel Gowon has gone far beyond anything that was ever contemplated in Decree No. 34. He has placed what remained of Nigeria under a unitary and totalitarian regime and deprived the citizens of their basic human rights to liberty and freedom. The treacherous murder of Major General Aguiyi-Ironsi on July 29, 1966, demanded that the next senior military officer should temporarily assume command of the army and headship of the Federal Military Government until the Supreme Military Council should determine the headship of the army and the country. But on August 1, 1966, Lieutenant Colonel Gowon, the leader of the Northern army rebels, announced that he had assumed the offices of the Supreme Commander and Head of the Federal Military Government, although there were at least half a dozen military officers senior to him. This abandonment by the Northern Nigeria army rebels of the principle of succession by seniority strongly underlines the determination of the North to take control of the federal government.

Indeed, since the nineteenth century, the Fulani-Hausa ruling clique in Northern Nigeria entertained the hope of conquering Southern Nigeria but made little headway until the advent of British colonial rule. Subsequently, by emphasizing the differences in their customs, traditions, and religion from the rest of Nigeria, they secured a separate identity for themselves within the country. When the time came for the British to surrender power to Nigerians, the Northern Nigerian leaders, by using the threat of secession, succeeded in obtaining concessions which tended to ensure their permanent domination of the government of the now defunct Federation. It was when they felt that their dominating influence was threatened that they resorted to the pogrom against the traditionally democratic people of Biafra. The Northern Nigeria aim was to destroy us or to reduce us to a state of backwardness worse than their own. Once this was achieved, the way would be clear for them to lord it over the whole country, making use of our resources to better their lot exclusively.

In the face of the unprovoked Northern onslaught, Biafrans remained calm and restrained. They stoically shouldered the burden of rehabilitating their refugees while seeking a peaceful solution to the constitutional problem which the recent and earlier events had posed. That solution, it was hoped, would finally put a stop to the massacres which were the latest repetitions of the earlier ones of 1945 and 1953. The innocent blood of thousands of Biafrans was the supreme sacrifice for the cause of Nigerian unity. Biafrans were determined that never again would they be hounded, humiliated, and butchered. They wished to keep the Nigerian Federation together but on terms which would guarantee their safety and protect their legitimate interests.

But the military leaders of Northern Nigeria, having usurped power in Lagos, and with their troops in occupation of Western Nigeria and menacing Midwestern Nigeria, were unwilling to yield any ground or implement any agreement mutually agreed. Northern Nigerians consistently pursued the path of dishonor and perfidy. They remained contemptuously indifferent to the sufferings of Biafrans and ignored our pleading for realistic settlement. When we took measures to ensure our survival, they attempted to strangle us economically, politically, and diplomatically.

It then became evident that the former Nigerian Federation could not offer Biafrans safety and protection or guarantee them the atmosphere essential for the development of their innate capabilities. Biafrans perceived that their continued association in so-called Nigeria meant acquiescence to intimidation by Northern feudalists. On May 30, 1967, consequent upon spontaneous and widespread demands and demonstrations, the Biafrans therefore resolved to assert their inalienable right to self-determination, and upon the solemn and unequivocal resolution of the accredited representatives and traditional rulers of the people, the sovereign and independent Republic of Biafra was proclaimed.

Address to convocation of University of Biafra,
Nsukka, July 1, 1967

II
On Genocide

"THEY WILL SINK. . . ."

In 1945 and 1953 organized riots in Northern Nigeria led to the massacre of hundreds of "unwanted" people of former Eastern Nigeria origin. Even as late as December, 1964, the manifesto to the government party in Northern Nigeria read, in part:

> The time has come. We are going to show these intellectual fools that we are only in the morning of our leadership of this country. . . . Our only obstacles are the Ibos. They have overplayed their card. They will sink.
>
> International Press Conference,
> ABA, January 1, 1968

From police reports, I know that the May, 1966, riots claimed more than 3,000 lives. Indeed, the police reports say 3,300. I know also that on the first night in Zaria, Northern Nigeria, 670 people were killed. I know also that in Kano, also in the North, on the same first day of the riot, we lost over a thousand people, including women and children.

> International Press Conference, Enugu,
> October 11, 1966

It was as a result of this massacre [May 29 pogrom] that I went to Lagos to try to get justice for our people. A fact I have not made public very often is that at that meeting there was quite a lot of argument as to what we should do and I said to General Ironsi that I would

20

not go back to Enugu without concrete assurances from the Supreme Military Council. After a lot of discussion, the assurance came only in the form that we were going to hold a Commission of Inquiry into the disturbances and that those who were to blame would receive punishment. If you remember, the meeting of the Supreme Military Council was held throughout the night. We received from the Northern emirs two sentences and they read something like: "We have received with dismay your intention to hold a Commission of Inquiry. We wish to inform you that this would be held over our dead bodies."

> Address to Port Harcourt Leaders of Thought,
> Port Harcourt, October 17, 1967

JULY 29

On July 29, 1966, Northern Nigerian soldiers lined up our men in the armed forces and shot them. Riots do occur in any society, but this one within the army was perhaps deeper than the one of May, 1966.

I do not know whether you understand really how we live in the army. An officer is a brother to the next officer. When you are moving around, as soon as you arrive in a garrison, you automatically go to the officers' mess and there you eat and drink with everybody. If you spend the night there, you have to share bed with any officer, but if the officer is married he will leave the bed for his wife and you two will sleep on the mat. This is how close we were, and this is how the army functions. You eat together, live together, and act together. One man's friend is the other officer's friend. We were almost the same, and this system went on and on until the darkness of July 29, 1966.

That evening people ate together and went out together, and then suddenly, at the appointed time, the same people with whom you ate and drank invited you outside and there machine-gun fire was opened up. In fact, all the officers who are here (now in Biafra) came back, not because nobody fired at them but because they were fired at and missed. Some of them escaped. Some still had hopes of one Nigerian army after the first strike of the enemy and after Gowon's assurances. But when they returned to the barracks, they were again shot at by the rebel soldiers. The blood-bath started and our people were killed like rats by a group of Northern soldiers and thugs whose only contribution to Nigeria is savagery.

> Address to Port Harcourt Leaders of Thought,
> Port Harcourt, October 17, 1967

On July 29, they murdered Ironsi. They were not satisfied. Indeed, any senior men you find in the armed forces now were those who escaped, running between bullets, to get back home. I got a phone call from Abeokuta warning me of the situation, and by the time I got to the barracks [at Enugu] the Hausa soldiers were already in battle dress, going to pick their weapons. It was through our defiance of the primitive and cowardly Northern hordes that we escaped.

> International Press Conference,
> Umuahia, November 18, 1967

SEPTEMBER 29 AND AFTER

Eastern Nigerians returning to their homes from other parts of the Federation in eighteen coaches were stopped at Oturkpo near Makurdi in Northern Nigeria. A telegram sent to Enugu, purporting to come from "the O/C Troops Makurdi," demanded a ransom of eleven railway tankers (about 100,000 gallons) of petrol or else they would kill thousands of our people in the eighteen coaches. I later learned that the failure to send the petrol led to our people in the coaches being attacked. A great number of them were injured. There was the ghastly sight of a head severed from the body and the blood-crazed rioters dancing around the train with the head on a spike. There were expatriates there. If you find them, they will tell you the disgraceful story.

The cause of the massacre, I learned, was a broadcast made by Radio Cotonou. The broadcast said that there was some disturbance in Eastern Nigeria and that Northerners had been killed. I have lived in the North for many years, and it is rather gratifying to know that they are now so sophisticated that they listen to Radio Cotonou. Further on, I understand that this report was rebroadcast by Radio-Television Kaduna. Why that was necessary I do not know. But perhaps the most significant thing about this is that according to the Northern story, as soon as they heard this, they found their bows and arrows at their hands and moved out immediately to look for Easterners. What I am saying is that it was a planned operation. The reason for it I do not know. This was what I have been weighing in my mind —how this utter waste could be explained. We were holding a conference which most people thought we had reason not to attend, and yet because we felt it was necessary to resolve our differences by dialogue, we went. The meeting had ended three days previously, and the delegates were just preparing their communiqué when this massacre happened.

International Press Conference,
Enugu, October 11, 1966

EXODUS

They came back. They returned from Northern Nigeria—after the May, 1966, massacre. In quest of Nigerian unity, I sent them back again to the North to continue their work. I sent them back because I sincerely believed the North would change. I was wrong. Indeed, in September, 1966, they were again massacred.

Those in the West and in Lagos, because of the presence of Northern troops and indeed the savage activities of Northern troops, in a number of cases resulting in the killing of civilians of Eastern origin, they too had to come back.

They came back to the East because they had discovered at very great cost that the government of the

Federation was unable to give them protection outside
their ethnic group of origin. My job here is to give
them that protection.

International Press Conference,
Enugu, December 9, 1966

All families in Eastern Nigeria have experienced
some bereavement. Tragic, also, was the sad return of
some of their kinsmen and women who had given many
years of useful service in other parts of Nigeria, and
who are now coming home without clothing, property,
sometimes without their husbands and parents. In order
to minimize this suffering, I have established a high-
powered commission—the Rehabilitation Commission
—for the resettlement of these people. The sum of
£1,000,000 is being made immediately available for
this task, and this sum will be augmented from time to
time, as and when it becomes necessary.

The Commission will consider, among other things,
the establishment of a Land Bank with credit facilities
for refugees, the expansion of the cooperative movement, and the allocation of plots and market stalls in
our urban areas. The Committee will consider also
the establishment of new towns and the extension of
existing urban communities. All government and non-
government organizations, voluntary agencies, and commercial enterprises are requested to cooperate with the
government of Eastern Nigeria in order to minimize the
hardship for these people and accelerate their absorption into suitable appointments and their eventual rehabilitation.

I have already issued directives to the Ministry of
Education to expand enrollment in all our educational
institutions to ensure that all students returning to Eastern Nigeria are found places. All our other refugees
have been requested to report to their district officers,
who are maintaining a register for this purpose.

Finally, I know that I speak for all of you when I
call for mourning and dedication for all our sons and

daughters who lost their lives as a result of the tragic events of May 29 and July 29. In view of the significance of the events of the last few months, I hereby declare Monday, August 29, 1966, a day of mourning for all our dead. All flags will fly at half-mast, one minute's silence will be observed at 12 noon, and religious services will be held in their memory at 6 o'clock in the evening of the same day.

Address to Rehabilitation Commission,
Enugu, August 28, 1966

The people of Biafra feel very strongly that they were rejected from the erstwhile Federation of Nigeria. In that rejection they were brutalized. Those of us who were left in the area which is now Biafra only did what was natural in the circumstances—that was to create a home for our fleeing people to come back to. Biafra came into being for this reason, to put an end to the flight of our people. They came back from all sides. They concentrated here, not seeking for revenge. They came back here to forget the past, to roll up their sleeves and bend down to work and to build a new life for themselves. But our aggressors pursued us to our doorsteps and to the privacy of our homes and sought to slaughter us before our very houses. There is a saying here in this part of the world that goes: "It is only a tree that stands still when it knows that it is to be cut." We are not trees. The people of Biafra are very human.

Interview with Canadian and Dutch
Parliamentarians, Umuahia, November 13, 1968

When it became clear by March 31, 1967, that Lagos was not willing to abide by the Aburi Agreement, thus depriving the people of Eastern Nigeria of the protection afforded them under the accord, the joint meeting of the Consultative Assembly and the Council of Chiefs and Elders mandated the government of Eastern Nigeria to take steps to protect the legitimate personal, political, and economic interests of the region. In furtherance

of his wicked plans to eliminate the people of Eastern
Nigeria, impose a blackout on our activities, and destroy
the foundations of our economy, Gowon imposed a
blockade on Eastern Nigeria, confiscated revenues due
to Eastern Nigeria, refused to pay the salaries of federal
government officials and the staff of statutory corporations in Eastern Nigeria, and embarked on a campaign
of denigration of the leaders of Eastern Nigeria. Finally,
without consultation or mandate, he announced the
division of Nigeria into twelve states including three in
Eastern Nigeria.

International Press Conference,
Umuahia, January 28, 1968

When our own people were being killed, three prominent men from Biafra were sent to Lagos to seek ways
and means of putting a halt to the bloodshed. At that
early stage I said to Gowon: "I will find it extremely
difficult, indeed impossible, to join you in your Government, but I will cooperate with you if that will stop
bloodshed." At that time our people started coming
back.

The Ad Hoc Constitutional Conference, after a lot
of fencing and parrying, got down to the core of the
matter, and it was quite clear what the entirety of
Nigeria wanted. They wanted a looser form of association. *They wanted cooperation, not unity.* Indeed, it was
because of unity that our people were killed in May.
It was again because of this unity that they were killed
in July, and when we met in conference, it was decided
that the various regions were to move slightly apart.
But the Northerners could not accept that. After all,
this was their father's vineyard; it was from here that
they would take, gather where they did not sow, and
then squander it in their annual pilgrimage to Mecca.
Between one of these discussions, they unleashed what
has now come to be known as the great pogrom of
September 29. Indeed, the men we sent to Lagos as
delegates were detained in Lagos during this pogrom,
and they had to escape. Thank God, some Biafrans

escaped and came back, but during that escape, too, we lost more than 30,000 men, women, and children. Is this not enough to show any sane being that these people do not want to be together with us? What other proof do we want? What other proof does the world want?

> Address to Aba Leaders of Thought,
> Aba, November 18, 1967

GENOCIDE THROUGH WAR

If Gowon's military campaign has achieved anything, it is only a confirmation of the fact that Biafrans have nothing to expect but destruction from the hands of their erstwhile Nigerian compatriots. In the border towns which fell into the hands of the Nigerian forces, Biafrans were pillaged and what could not be stolen was destroyed. Then men were shot and tortured, and the women defiled.

> Message to Biafran Students in the United States
> of America, November 24, 1967

In desperation and sheer manifestation of inherent wickedness, Gowon has resorted to an indiscriminate bombing of our civilian population in order to destroy what he cannot hold. Gowon's Soviet planes, piloted by British and Egyptian adventurers, have chosen as their targets our villages, hospitals, marketplaces, homes for disabled children, Red Cross centers, schools and residential areas, and even refugee camps for their bombing raids.

True to this Hausa-Fulani tradition of hate for all Biafrans, irrespective of linguistic grouping, Gowon has only discriminated in his bombing spree to the extent that he has made the so-called minority people of Biafra, whom he professes to love, his special target. It is these people who have suffered most from Gowon's current massive destruction of life and property.

> Message to Biafran Union in the United Kingdom
> and Ireland, March 19, 1968

This is a war of survival. It is so, because every day it has become plainer to us that the enemy we have to fight is an enemy intent on destroying every one of us and everything we have and everything we hold dear. They have demonstrated it often enough. They demonstrated it in May, 1966, and in July, 1966; they demonstrated it on arrival in Nsukka in early July, 1967; they demonstrated it in their entry into the Republic of Benin; they have continually demonstrated it in all the areas in which they have landed or got a foothold in our Republic. Just before coming up to see you, I had been going through the recent intercepts. You might perhaps have heard that our operations are now going on in the Republic of Benin, and the orders that came through from Lagos are: "If you find it difficult, destroy everything in sight." This is typical.

Our people are fighting with vigor, because we have our backs to the wall and death stares us in the face.

Interview with Britain/Biafra Association,
Umuahia, April 18, 1968

Northern Nigerian leaders decided in 1966 that if they had to complete this conquest or domination, they probably would have to apply a final solution to the problem, which was genocide. They decided to destroy completely every living Biafran. Now you wonder why they chose Biafrans? Because it was clear that Biafrans were the only people who really stood up against them.

We made compromises. We continued to make them in the hope that these people would learn and later treat us as human beings, but we discovered to our cost that they considered our compromises evidence of weakness. It reached a point where every single Biafran had agreed in his own mind that it was enough. As far as our people were concerned there was nothing to try to recover, it was just enough, leave us alone!

So came 1966. The first lot of our people were killed in May, the second in July, and while we were discussing the future they killed more in September and throughout October. Throughout you will see the pattern. It was never their intention to destroy houses as normal rioting does; they were after killing the individual Biafrans. They hunted them out of their churches and killed them. Their intention was that no Biafran would remain alive so that they could have an easy run of what was then Nigeria.

This destruction of property came only at the later stages. Indeed, during this war any Hausa soldier you question will tell you that they were promised that when they came to Enugu, capital of Biafra, they would have any two houses they chose. This is what this people are out for. The arrival of the Nigerian vandals in Bonny, our oil terminal, is a story of horror, plunder, and rampage which the people of that area will never forgive or forget. The traditional ruler of this island was lucky to escape with his life. He is still in Biafra.

Response to Address of Welcome by Okigwe
Province, Okigwe, December 27, 1967

Genocide, though it means the wiping out of a people individually, does not restrict itself to that meaning. To destroy a people—if you remove that which makes them a people—is to commit genocide. The Nigerian attitude to us has been one certainly which aims directly at removing, destroying, those things that make us a people—our institutions, our leadership, our organization, and our capacity to resuscitate those institutions. In the course of it, one way is to kill as many as possible.

Nigeria has certainly some three times our population, and in the real sense of it, their economic potential would probably total three times our own potential. Their problem, however, is how to apply their manpower to their resources. They have always been incapable of this and they have been intensely jealous of anybody who can apply himself to industry. I think perhaps this war has taught them a lesson. If it has, the only worthwhile lesson they should have learned is that it is up to them to make for themselves what they want. If they have not learned it, after this war, then, of course, there is danger. There is danger of continued friction, casting one's eyes over another's vineyard and feeling that what is over there belongs to both of them.

What should happen if the Nigerians succeed [in overrunning Biafra]? They would, with their present attitude, have to hold down physically everybody here. Biafrans are very versatile, very hard-working, and I think are adept at finding opportunities. I think that any time, if the heart of the nation was not destroyed, the Biafrans can build up. It will take a long time, and it would be for Africa a major disaster. I think it would be a major catastrophe.

> Interview with Mr. M. Kupfer of *Newsweek*
> magazine, and David Robison, United States
> free-lance journalist, Umuahia, February 13, 1969

WHEN GENOCIDE IS GENOCIDE

In 1945 a group of eminent world statesmen, appalled by the wanton destruction of human life which the world had just witnessed, sat together and solemnly bound themselves to intervene and stop acts of genocide wherever they might occur in the world.

It is pertinent at this period of time in the history of Biafra that one should be permitted to ask what stage must be reached in the systematic massacre of a people before it can be adjudged as amounting to genocide? Has the massacre of 3,000 Biafran men, women, and children in May, 1966, satisfied the criteria? Could the slaughter of 50,000 Biafrans from May, 1966, to October, 1966, and the flight of 2,000,000 maimed and destitute others be accepted as the necessary criteria? What about the fate of 100,000 Biafran civilians who have lost their lives through aerial bombing, strafing, and shelling as well as 4,500,000 refugees who are fast starving to death? In short, when will world statesmen awaken to the fact that the Biafran race is being systematically wiped out? Can they, being responsible and honorable men, sit back and wait until genocide is completed before they realize that it is actually being committed with impunity?

International press conference,
Owerri, July 18, 1968

Genocide is a hard word, very difficult to prove unless of course the act is complete. To prove genocide fully the people must all be dead, and since nobody wants that sort of proof, naturally the intent, the desire, to commit genocide is the crime of genocide. It is left to us as human beings to look at the whole evidence and see whether the whole series of actions are indicative of a state of mind that can commit genocide. Take, for instance, the indiscriminate murder of our people without any recourse to law, the continued massacre of our people, the statements of the officials of the Nigerian government, their radio broadcasts—all these show a clear state of mind, a desire to wipe out the people of Biafra. That is genocide.

When in the actual killing would there be genocide? A hundred people? 3,000? 50,000 or 100,000? When that is put side by side with our history of periodic pogroms, massacres, and subsequent history of threats and actions that are so indiscriminate, one is left with nothing else but the conclusion that, given enough opportunity, the Nigerians would complete the crime because of their state of mind. In this case, the crime has been committed. This question of starvation can be considered the same way. Again, the totality of our people are forced into starvation.

Another aspect of genocide is the complete dispossession of our people of their life savings. This, according to the United Nations conventions, is genocide. We go further on this question of killing 14,000,000 people:

once that which makes them a people is killed, the crime of genocide is committed and that is in fact the situation we are in today.

Interview with Canadian television group,
Umuahia, September 16, 1968

What are the International Observer Team observing? Is war a good thing? Have we reached such a level in our civilization that we really have to go and watch whether killing is properly done? I suppose there are prescribed ways of killing human beings. One must tie the hands behind their backs and administer one cut of the knife! You must make sure that he is properly dressed before you put the bullet through his head. Is that what world civilization has come to?

Another point about the observer team is this: I think one of the observers really put his finger on it when he said that, having visited Colonel Adekunle of the Nigerian Third Commando Division, he reported to the press that Adekunle did not show him any evidence of genocide. One would not expect Adekunle to show it!

If you really want to find out whether genocide is being committed against the people of Biafra, you then have to come across to Biafra to see this problem from the receiving end. I am sure really that during the last war if one talked exclusively to Hitler's cabinet there would be no evidence of genocide, but those who saw it looked at the problem from the Jewish point of view, at least from the Jewish standpoint. It was then, taking the Jewish massacre side by side with the German protestations, that they came to a rough assessment of the situation and made their verdict.

If it is really necessary to prove genocide, a prerequisite is, of course, to view from both sides without which there is no possibility of finding any objective answer or verdict, and this has been so clearly shown in this struggle. Name the country, name the party, whoever goes to one side alone comes out saying one thing only. Send the same party from the same country over to this side, and they come back saying a diametrically opposite thing. It is human. We have been rather lucky, and it has in fact enhanced our confidence that when somebody had been to the other side and has been here, generally they report their views favorably to Biafra.

How can anybody who for sixteen months has faced the entire fury of Nigeria, Russia, Britain, and to a large extent the United States in the way the people of Biafra have, not really understand the word *genocide?* To us, genocide is an everyday affair. Look everywhere, there is evidence.

But the world seeks for proof of genocide. Whenever somebody seeks for this proof, it is a death wish for our people. If you want to prove genocide the only proof is death of the group; that is the only true proof. If you accept that it is a crime, and something has to be done to stop it, then your demands must be somewhat less than absolute proof; otherwise there would be nothing to rectify—the people would be dead already. We are left with circumstantial evidence. We are left with proof of intention. We are left with a number of acts which when put together are indicative of a frame of mind.

Genocide is the killing of a people. What constitutes for the world that killing of a people? Is it the destruction of the leadership of that group? That indeed is genocide. Is it killing of a hundred or a hundred thousand or one million? Once you have seen and you are satisfied that the number is large it becomes genocide. Is it the destruction of their institutions? That which makes the people a people? If you are satisfied that there is an effort to destroy that, it is genocide. If you see a pattern of behavior, like Nigerians getting to a Biafran village and slaughtering all males, getting to a place and lining them up and shooting them, when you

see such constant evidence you have got no other alternative but to accept genocide.

One final point on this. When you listen to the other
side and everything they say—all the education, the
propaganda they give to their people—when it shows
you quite clearly that they are getting their people in
a frame of mind to commit genocide, then it is genocide.
Or is it the splitting of a people, dispossession of their
wealth, an overnight changeover of currency, making
the total savings of a people cease to be legal tender?
In fact, in the United Nations convention these things
are listed. Take any of them and you will find at least
five or six direct pieces of evidence that there has been
an intention, and if so genocide has been committed. If
still one is not satisfied, then perhaps the answer is to
really get the experts to look at it in a formal way in
which both sides can really state their cases. If that is
possible, I am absolutely certain that again the answer
will be that genocide has been committed against the
people of this area.

From the first day of the war, the conduct of Gowon's
soldiers and his officers was marked by the same genocidal instincts. When the Nigerians entered Ogoja on
July 14, 1967, they proceeded to murder all captured
males and to assault or abduct their wives and children. In the Nsukka sector, it was the same story.
Catholic priests who fled the area with their parishioners
told ghastly tales of mass shooting and indiscriminate
bloodletting. Whole families were bundled into their
thatch-roof houses; the houses were then set ablaze.
Those who struggled to escape were shot or else captured and forced to undergo the ordeal in another
thatch-roof hut.

In Bonny, our oil terminal, the atrocities were even
worse. Owing to difficulties of transport in the creeks,
thousands of Biafran civilians were trapped in the island
when the Nigerians entered. They were subjected to
unbelievable tortures—including branding with hot
coals—before being shot. Our experience of this war has

confirmed our previous fears that the Nigerians are not fighting to capture territory or to defeat an army but to find their opportunity to complete the pogroms of earlier years.

In Calabar, in October, 1967, the Nigerian army shot more than 2,000 civilians caught in the town. According to an eye witness, the Reverend David T. Craig (see *Presbyterian Record*, December, 1967), a further 150 prisoners of war were shot on orders from the Nigerian commander. "I referred them to the Geneva Convention," Reverend Craig observed, "and one laughed and said: 'They gave us a copy before we left but I ripped up mine—never read it.'" Reports from correspondents in Nigeria confirm that several hundred children were carried away from Calabar to camps in Lagos. There are no lists of these children or of their parents. Nobody knows how many of these children will survive.

At first, our protests against this genocidal trend were dismissed as exaggerations. Fortunately, independent observers are now confirming our earlier charge. In the *New York Review,* the *New York Times,* and elsewhere, reports and articles are now appearing expressing concern over the pace of mass massacre in those areas occupied by the Nigerian army. "A question which must be posed," Dr. Shepherd of the Presbyterian Church (in the *British Weekly,* November 16, 1967) has remarked, "is whether there is an uncontrollable genocidal movement in the Nigeria Army. Evidence of indiscriminate killing of non-combatant Biafrans is now incontrovertible."

You can then understand why Biafrans feel so terribly abandoned when the reaction of the world to such obvious genocide is indifference and apathy. Genocide is, after all, a crime against all mankind. The Nuremberg Trials after World War II, held even before there was a Genocide Convention (1948), were conducted on the assumption that the deliberate extermination of a marked group of people by whatever power and on whatever pretext was a crime against mankind as a whole. The United Nations Convention on Genocide is specific on what Genocide is:

Any of the following acts committed with intent to destroy, in whole or in part, a national, ethnical, racial, or religious group, as such:
  a. Killing members of the group;
  b. Causing serious bodily or mental harm to members of the group;
  c. Deliberately inflicting on the group conditions of life calculated to bring about its physical destruction in whole or in part;
  d. Imposing measures intended to prevent births within the group;
  e. Forcibly transferring children of the group to another group.

Nigeria has been guilty of genocide in all five ways listed above. It might interest you to know that the Hausa chant which follows the "One Nigeria" slogan on Radio Nigeria is an exhortation to the Northerners to "go and kill them [the Biafrans], loot their property, and leave those left crying helplessly." The tragedy of our situation in Biafra is that the world literally only listens to the abstract slogan "One Nigeria" but has no way of also understanding the language of mass murder involved in the indigenous Hausa war chant.

As you are all aware, the recent trial of four Soviet writers received the attention of the world press and the condemnation of the International Council of Jurists. Is it not remarkable that this simple event involving four people evoked such widespread condemnation compared with the world reaction to the genocidal activities of Gowon and his collaborators involving thousands of lives and the fate of millions?

International Press Conference,
Umuahia, January 28, 1968

III
On the War

We are fighting a war which for us is one of survival. We have used this term now and again, but what actually does it mean? It means that we are fighting for everything that makes our life worthwhile, so that we may breathe God's air. It is my pride and honor that I happen to be on the scene at this time, but I believe that whether I was here or not this war would have come sometime and Biafra would still have survived.

This war began as a result of a futile attempt by the British imperialists to amalgamate the people of the North with those of the South in 1914 into an entity they called Nigeria. From the start, it was quite clear that the amalgamation could only exist on paper. Northern Nigeria had a different idea about fellowship; theirs, according to their religion, was that of slave and master —no more. Before the advent of the British, they had tried to invade the South, and on the Western side had made some success which was only halted by the advent of the British. But a thing which they have always forgotten is that every effort they had made to penetrate into what became Eastern Nigeria had met with failure and disaster. From time immemorial, our people have always stood against slavery. It is an abomination for a full-blooded Biafran to accept, while there is still breath in him, to live as a slave. This is one reason why we are fighting.

We are fighting that we shall not be slaves, so that our children will not be slaves.

Despite this paper amalgamation, our people left

37

their own hometown for what was then Nigeria, in an
attempt, again traditional to our society, to bring people together to live in harmony. As I look in front of
me, I can see the original founders of those developed
areas of Northern Nigeria. They arrived in Northern
Nigeria and gave light to the people there. Our people
lent their full weight in so many other ways in developing a healthy society in the ill-fated Nigeria. To all our
contributions, the Northern Nigerians showed apathy
that later grew into hate. In their mad hate, they turned
on our innocent people and massacred them. Biafra is
the end result of the fruitlessness of the Nigerian experiment which sought to turn our people into vegetables,
into slaves that could be disposed of at will.

Address to the people of Orlu Province,
Orlu, December 30, 1967

Through various crises, slowly it became evident to
us that we were speaking different languages, that our
erstwhile brothers were actually our enemies. Systematically, like clockwork, they massacred our kith and kin
and demonstrated to the world that their association
with us was based on hate.

They wanted, without any equivocation, to destroy
us, and in destroying, they wanted to destroy every
living Biafran. The proofs are quite clear.

They said that their anger arose from the January
15, 1966, revolution. We have ample evidence and
well documented records that the events of January 15,
1966, were applauded not only by Biafrans but by all
organizations in the erstwhile Nigeria. The Northern
People's Congress, the Action Group, the Northern
Elements Progressive Union—all the political parties
that were in existence—applauded them.

The various organizations, the student bodies, the
trade unions, all applauded. The newspapers—it didn't
matter what shade of opinion they represented—applauded it. Outside Nigeria, the world applauded.

British newspapers applauded and gave out a message of hope to the world and to our people and, in

fact, said again without equivocation that this was the beginning of true progress for Africa. That in itself is quite clear. The documents are there.

The subsequent action of the first military government under Major General J. T. U. Aguiyi-Ironsi was blatantly Nigerian; every stage of it was applauded until Britain started surreptitiously to sow seeds of distrust and suspicion.

They were not satisfied with this. They went on and began later by using their personnel and agents, mainly based in the Ahmadu Bello University at Zaria, to tutor our erstwhile brothers into action based on hate.

May 29 came, and they rose, massacred our people. We sought for justice in the law courts. They refused. We insisted on a commission of inquiry. They struck again, this time killing Ironsi and the cream of our youth.

Even at that time we had hopes, and we continued to hope that we could heal the fissure and at least start again, based on a different understanding.

But, of course, the Northern oligarchy, which has controlled the government of the Federation, wanted to seize power again—either they dominate or they move away—and as if to punish us for daring to challenge their authority, on September 29, they unleashed a pogrom in which we lost 30,000.

It was the breakdown of the Aburi Agreements that finally brought about this war. Even though we could not be together again, it was that final breach that caused the present situation.

From then until July 6, 1967, it was purely a question of deciding how much we could postpone what was obvious—the Northern attack—since negotiations had failed. It was in our interest to postpone it because we were not ready. . . . We had nothing to fight with. This war, I have said often enough, was forced upon us. We did everything to avoid it because we are a very peace-loving people.

Address to Delegates of the Biafra Union in
Britain, Umuahia, March 2, 1968

When in July, 1966, the Northern Nigerians decided
first to separate from the then Nigeria, the way and
manner they approached it made it clear to me that
the best thing would be to let them go. It is true we
had sacrificed everything to keep the country together,
yet seeing the ruthless way in which they conducted
their supposed coup, it became obvious that if one did
not let the Northern Nigerians go, Nigeria would be
plunged into utter destruction. They nearly succeeded
in breaking away at that time and, in fact, were on
their way out. They had set up their flag, commandeered airplanes, and started shipping their people up
to the North until the representatives of the British
government in Lagos interfered and halted them and
told them that they had got everything they wanted
and more: they were now in control again of the then
Nigeria; there was only one faint voice in the East which
could easily be silenced. In this they were mistaken. . . .
That voice was not prepared to be silenced. The confusion in Nigeria ensued from that moment.

By the time the war started we had about 150 rifles,
but then, when you consider it all, what alternative had
we? Every effort we made was frustrated because nothing less than absolute domination of the entire country
was acceptable to the Northern Nigerians. It was clear
to us too that each crisis was caused because Northern
Nigeria had never learned from the mistakes of past
crises. Since bloodshed had come into it, it became
obvious that if we did not stand firm the next round
would be either the complete destruction of our people
or servitude for us forever. Whichever one, it was not
acceptable to us.

Meeting with Biafra Nurses Association,
Umuahia, March 21, 1968

Let us not forget, nor allow the world to forget, the
real causes of this war. We never started this war. We
were attacked by Nigeria. Indeed, we are fighting purely
in self-defense and for our security and survival. Despite all our efforts and contributions right through our

unfortunate association with the peoples of Nigeria, we had been suspected, provoked, persecuted, and oftentimes killed.

The climax came in 1966 when, with clocklike regularity in May, July, August, September, and October, our people, in a manner most brutal, were massacred in different parts of Nigeria. In search of safety and security, we returned home and abandoned every material thing we had earned and possessed in every part of that ill-conceived federation. We made strenuous efforts for peace but were ridiculed and subjected to perfidy, ill faith, and physical hazards.

Our people who had been in salaried employment in Nigeria were denied their salaries. Our share of public funds in Nigeria, running into several million pounds, was denied us. We were blockaded. We were threatened. And we were insulted. At our own initiative, we sought respite around the Aburi conference table. At our own insistence, top government officials of the erstwhile Federation had met to discuss mutual accommodation. At our further initiative, the advisers to the military governors held a meeting in Lagos to search for peace. The Aburi Agreements were torn asunder by Yakubu Gowon. All subsequent agreements—indeed the very constitution, were trampled under foot with impunity by Yakubu Gowon. One Hitlerite act followed another. Our people, in the face of mounting sufferings and under threat of death, with no hope of justice, met and decided to assert our right to self-determination.

On May 30, 1967, we proclaimed the Republic of Biafra. That proclamation, taking full cognizance of our geographical proximity, extended a hand of fellowship and cooperation to our former colleagues of the Nigerian Federation. Gowon's response was to march across our boundaries on July 6, 1967, in armed aggression against our injured and defenseless people. Today, after eighteen months of heroic resistance, with victory clearly eluding the aggressor, we have justified our claims and our right to survival as a nation.

End of Year Message, 1968

This invasion of Biafra by the Nigerians was mounted because the people of the former Eastern Region of Nigeria were forced on May 30, 1967, to declare themselves the Independent State of Biafra in order to ensure the security of their lives and property.

The inordinate ambition of the Hausa-Fulani oligarchy to continue to dominate the whole of what was formerly the Federation of Nigeria, the unrealistic desire to acquire the wealth and resources of Biafra while rejecting her people, the mad and homicidal desire to exterminate from the face of the earth 14,000,000 Biafrans, drove Gowon and his clique toward unleashing a costly war to attain the unattainable—the subjugation of this young and promising Republic.

Even with the vast resources of the former Federation of Nigeria with which to prosecute the war, with the active collaboration of those international opportunists—Britain and the Soviet Union—an unholy alliance of vested interests, with the attempt to subvert our government by suborning some of our highly placed military and civilian personnel, an attempt which was foiled at the nick of time, Gowon has failed to make good his boast "to crush" Biafra. A campaign which Gowon bragged would take only 48 hours to accomplish has now dragged on for almost five months and will drag on for as long as it takes Gowon and his clique, both Nigerian and others, to realize that nothing can shake the will, or crush the spirit, of a determined people.

Message to Biafra students in the United States
of America, November 24, 1967

WAR AIMS AND TACTICS

Right from the start, my orders to the Biafran army commanders were quite simple. First, we were not going to be the aggressors. All we have asked of humanity is to be left alone. If the Nigerians just left us alone, there would be no fight. But if they came again (having thrown us out of Nigeria) to throw us out of, or kill us in, our homes, then we would have to resist. I said, too, that ours would have to be a policy of reaction. We would react to enemy aggression, and in reacting to enemy aggression, we would first contain the enemy, and when we were sure we had contained the enemy, then we would strike hard, and this has been happening.

For two solid months, we contained the enemy. *When the army commanders reported back to me that they had contained the enemy, I said, "Wait, let us see what they can throw in more." The enemy continued throwing in what they had and, suddenly, we started seeing Northern policemen at the battlefront; next, we saw their court messengers—Dandokas—at the battlefront. And finally, we were only convinced when they started throwing in Yoruba soldiers to the battlefront.* It was then quite clear to me that they had nothing else to throw in.

It was then that we struck, and by doing so, as I said before, made history a second time. Our first historic achievement was creating an army in such a short time, out of nothing. Our second was the lightning operation in which our gallant forces completely overran the Midwest Region of Nigeria. Just imagine it: Nigeria, an entire nation, sleeping while a whole region was completely taken from it. When Lieutenant Colonel David Ejoor, the then military governor of Midwestern Nigeria, woke up and found Biafran troops in front of his own palace, what was he in? He was in his pajamas. That was the speed.

By this single operation it was then clear that we had beaten Nigeria. Yes, after two months, we had beaten Nigeria completely. They know it. Then they tried getting outside help. They got the British, the unscrupulous Wilson administration, and the Russians, always ready to fish in troubled waters, to assist them.

Address at a mass rally,
Aba, November 18, 1967

Since we are not the aggressors, our war aims are quite limited. All we seek is to maintain the territorial integrity of Biafra. Ours is not to conquer Lagos or to take Kaduna or Zaria: that is not our aim. We are a peace-loving people. It is because of this that we have been surviving; it is because of this that God loves us. As far as I am, and indeed every Biafran is, concerned, this war will be won the day these vandals are pushed out of our territory. We are not seeking anything else. After that, we can talk of what we lost. But right now what we are seeking is the territorial integrity of Biafra and our freedom as a people. If you consider the war in this fashion then you will understand that victory is very much in sight.

After a month of the war, it became quite clear to everybody that Nigeria would not win. Indeed, after eight weeks I was very confident and I would have even announced to everybody that we had won the war. We did win the war. Lagos knows it. But then, of course, Lagos went around seeking help, and the prolongation of this war is only due to British and Russian aid.

Address to the people of Okigwe Province,
Okigwe, December 27, 1967

We are holding the line. Winning or losing depends on the military aims of the parties. Considered from the military aims of Biafra, we are winning. Our military aims are to hold the enemy, to delay him for as long as possible until we can generate outside opinion in solving this problem of ours. In that context you can see what I mean by winning. If one looks at the movement of troops one might be inclined to say that Nigeria is winning, and indeed they have made some significant advances into our territory. The territory has somewhat shrunk from what it was originally, but this is only one facet of the war. Our people, our troops, and our guerrilla fighters are still in the northernmost, westernmost, and easternmost parts of Biafra, still operating with great, but perhaps not dramatic, effect. When all these

are considered and then one looks at the innate potentials of the two fighting groups, for us certainly we have
no cause for dismay. Our people are still fighting very
well indeed. They are fighting better now than ever.

I said that as far as we were concerned we would
maintain formal operations but employ guerrilla tactics
more extensively behind the enemy line. It is necessary
that we maintain a voice internationally, since one of
our major aims is to get people to understand the truth
of our case. We have not been able to match the enemy
man for man or weapon for weapon, and that means
the extensive employment of rather unconventional
means of fighting.

I think actually that the Nigerians have overreached
themselves. The Divisions and the formations are over-
stretched. I also think they have got us truly with our
backs to the wall and that the resistance from now on
will be much grimmer than anything they have ever seen
or contemplated. In fact, this has had the effect of
making Gowon postpone the victory of his final offensive about three times now. We will resist the threats,
and I am sure that very, very soon we will in fact start
rolling the enemy back.

Interview with Canadian television,
Umuahia, September 16, 1968

As I have said before, the war aims of Biafra are
very simple: to delay the enemy for as long as possible
until world conscience is aroused and then to seek
world support in what is essentially a human problem.
I think that as far as world sympathy and conscience
is concerned, one of our major objectives has been won.

We are trying very hard to turn that sympathy and
understanding into practical terms, to direct their efforts
to bringing pressure to bear on Gowon and to make
him sit down at a conference table. . . . Everybody
must agree that no matter the bitterness and what happens in this war, it will end around the mahogany table.
This is the position we have always maintained, and I

feel that as more and more countries understand the problem the pressures on Gowon will grow. . . .

. . . The few arms we have today are purely propaganda, yet even that frightens the enemy. We get some arms but not sufficient for the noise that is made about them. The great thing is the way this is affecting the enemy. You notice that for the past six weeks there has been nowhere we got together and pushed the enemy that he did not scuttle back. Reason: he has by his own propaganda destroyed himself. He has told his own troops about the "massive military supply" that comes into Biafra. Both the people in Biafra and the enemy troops in their trenches listen at night and count the relief planes that come in and calculate that each one carries eleven tons of arms and ammunition! This— together with the ignorant Nigeria propaganda that Tanzania is helping us, that there are 800 French men in the Biafra army, and so on—completely frightens the enemy.

International press conference,
Umuahia, October 28, 1968

Today, everybody talks about increased firepower, therefore all commanders on the Nigerian side that get pushed back immediately have a ready excuse—it is the increased Biafran firepower! It has reached a stage now that, in any encounter, if you can maintain a volume of fire for five minutes the enemy abandons his position and runs. This is precisely what is happening, and, of course, our boys are beginning to exploit it. Yes, Nigeria has destroyed itself with its own propaganda.

Our tactic should now be the straightforward one of using the divisions for holding the ground so that we can continue to maintain a government that the world can see, negotiate and discuss with. This is being done . . . We know that the whole of Biafra belongs to us, therefore the holding of ground by the enemy within Biafra means nothing. The problem in this war is the presence of the enemy in our territory. Therefore, our aim should not be to recapture all these lands but to destroy the enemy, that is, remove him in the absolute sense from wherever he is.

That leads me on to finding the ways and means of ensuring the destruction of the enemy. If the enemy comes to you in Brigade strength, then let whatever force is on the ground play that game with the enemy. Instead of looking for a battalion or a brigade to go and fight with an enemy of equivalent strength, and take the chance of pushing them back with the capture of a few weapons, we must take a force which is many times bigger than that to destroy the enemy completely. A Division to destroy a Battalion—a Brigade for a Company. That is the only way we can fight this war. If you take them on with equal force, you might push them back, but they will regroup and come at you again. But, if you go at them with a large force, strike, and destroy them, you will find a large gap behind them unguarded. You can always push the enemy once you use maximum force on them. At Oguta, near the Uli Airport, we did not have the men but we had the equipment, and we let them have it. It did not take long and they were cleared. At Adazi, near Nnewi, it had the same effect.

Address to Provincial Police Officers' Conference,
Umuahia, December 6, 1968

THE PEOPLE'S WAR

This has been the people's war. Our people know that their struggle is a race for life. In such a race, nobody ever tires. We have a united people. We have a clear goal. We have a just cause.

International press conference,
Umuahia, January 28, 1968

Our struggle is a people's fight for survival. It is the people's assertion of their rights to self-determination. It is an African struggle against neocolonialism, against oppression, against exploitation, against the comfortable myth of racial superiority practiced and sustained by our one-time colonial masters.

Our people have demonstrated completely their own involvement in this struggle. There is nothing they have not done. It is normally in the fight for freedom that people build the background which sustains the life of their nation. It is during a period like this that nations set their own patterns for the future.

When you consider our own struggle you will find that we have, as a nation, demonstrated our determination to survive. It is for us a matter of great pride that the Biafra army is completely supported by volunteers.

Meeting with Health Visitors Association
of Biafra, Umuahia, January 18, 1968

Our people have sacrificed a great deal. Indeed, this is the first time in history that an army has been put to war and yet the government spends nothing in feeding that army. It reflects the feeling of our people in this war. This is the first time a government has not spent money in clothing its armed forces. This is the first time in history that a government has not made special budget for warfare and has been fighting a war through voluntary contributions of the common men and women of the state. . . . What you have demonstrated to the world is that to the people of Biafra this war is just.

Address to the people of Okigwe Province,
Okigwe, December 27, 1967

We have shown that when a people are so oppressed that they unanimously decide to fight for their freedom, they will always win, no matter the odds. This war has taught us a great lesson, and after the war we

as a people will be completely different. Our sense of values will change, so also our sense of public morality.
Address to people of Orlu Province,
Orlu, December 30, 1967

At the time the war broke out, the total armament in the area now called Biafra was about 150 rifles, and yet we have survived until today. I am really proud of our people. Our resistance has been classic—with bare hands. Our people have given massive support and sacrificed everything, knowing that life without freedom is not life at all. The degree of solidarity in Biafra throughout this crisis has been an eye-opener to the world, and people who have come here have been amazed at our indigenous African organization.

The Nigerians thought that they would destroy us in 48 hours. Eight months have elapsed and they are still fighting and will never get near their objective, not even with their collaborators—Britain and Russia.

We will suffer as we are doing now, but the spirit of the Biafran is such that with each action of the enemy he gets stronger and stronger. That is why every day we grow from strength to strength.

I know our students abroad have been wondering about our progress, and from the BBC propaganda you sometimes feel that things are very bad. But think of it this way: Biafra is our own. The only part of Biafra that the enemy controls is that part on which his troops stand; no more. The enemy says he controls Nsukka, but he controls only the house in which he lives. And right now the enemy goes into the main road and lures the men. We cut their communication line into bits. It is obvious that they cannot defeat us unless they bring in 20,000,000 soldiers.

Some people thought it was a boast when I said that when they come into Biafra they would see 14,000,000 soldiers. Today it is not just a mere boast. I have not paid the army yet from government funds. We have

clothed our army by voluntary contributions. Our entire
armed forces are not being fed by the government.
They are being fed by our women. At every stage of
this war at least 16,000 people are waiting ready to go
and fight. This excludes the entirety of our boys abroad
who are also waiting to return home and fight.

Even while they are abroad our brothers are playing
an invaluable role in our struggle for survival. While
most of our equipment is made locally, some students
sit in their digs abroad and work out some formulae
and send them home for our use too. With that sort
of attitude at home and abroad, I have every confidence
we will come out successful.

Message to Biafra Union in Britain,
March 2, 1968

We have fought, as it were, with our bare hands.
We have continued for ten months to fight against overwhelming odds. Most countries in the world have, at
one time or the other, written us off completely. Why?
Because they have done the normal arithmetic; they
have added up the weapons, they have added up support, and decided that we could not survive. One little
thing they have forgotten and they always seem to forget—and this has been the reason for their various
miscalculations—is the spirit of the people of Biafra,
their unconquerable will to live.

Personally, I consider the slaughter too bad. I think
the magnitude of it is really too great, and this is why
I have throughout been calling very fervently for peace.
But this war is a war in which all the people of Biafra
are involved. No matter the amount of carnage, I have
each time, in fact stage by stage, always gone back to
the people to seek their mandate. And each time for
the past four Consultative Assemblies I have put the
same question: "Whenever you are tired let me know."
And our people still remain very solidly behind a
continuation.

The danger of mass destruction is so very real. We feel that even if one says "stop," the outcome will be death for all of us. There will be nothing to shake us from that belief. All evidence points to the same fate, and as human beings, we prefer to take a chance right up to the last with our rifles in our hands. But knowing my people and their ability, I do not think we will ever reach the point of the last man.

Meeting with a delegation of Britain/Biafra
Association, Umuahia, April 18, 1968

The biggest change in the past few months in Biafra has been the absolute conviction of our people that we are going the right way and are going to survive. That reflects itself in everything, even in the economic field. Our people are coming out in the thousands, almost treating this war as incidental. People are seeking licenses for importation. "How do you do it?" Never mind, we will find a way, they reply. Our people are becoming used to the stresses of the war. This, to me, has been the most important change that one has seen.

The bomb raids no longer affect trade. Our general attitude to death here now is a bit different. A trader goes to market today; there is a bomb raid, 30 people are killed, he goes home. It is bad luck. Tomorrow he goes back to market! You have your clerk in the office; in the course of putting a file before you he says, "The air raid yesterday killed my mother"—that is, it is one of the vicissitudes of war. He expects it! All these little things add to our general potential for survival.

I do not expect that in a short time we will suddenly start rolling the enemy back. Rather this is a war of attrition in which we expect that our resistance will wear down the enemy so much that he will give up the struggle. We are not going to give up. Our people have manifested in such a remarkable way their strength of will. Another significant change has been what is happening on the other side. Now, we are beginning to see a crack in their internal alliance. This is becoming each day increasingly manifest. With this, the determination of our people, of course, gets stronger.

Meeting with delegation of the American Committee
to Keep Biafra Alive, Umuahia, January 21, 1969

I think the confidence of the people is very apparent. The way they have withstood everything up till now is truly magnificent. The biggest test, I think, was the sudden switch of currency when we had few days to collect back all the old currency. Our people came forward to anybody who would collect the money and gave everything they had. Their names were written in a ledger—no receipts. In this act the people immortalized their confidence in the government. We are fighting a war, and our people, knowing the difficulties, the odds against us, do show a certain element of fatalism—the people feel: Well, if the world chooses to abandon us, then perhaps it is better we all perish. They do not ever consider a Biafra not free. They believe in either Biafra free or no Biafra at all—that means none of us living to see it.

Interview with British ITV,
Umuahia, January 28, 1968

Somewhere outside Biafra, people who feel sympathetic toward us have been taking children from this area. A certain ambassador representing his country had a Biafran girl of about three years staying with his family. He had a series of visitors and the wife of the ambassador chose this little girl to present the bouquets to the visitors. The various visitors came and the child presented a bouquet to each, until one came and she was told the gentleman came from Niger. The sound of Niger sounded so very much like Nigeria—the little girl threw the flowers down, burst into tears, and refused completely to present the bouquet despite all attempts to convince her that Niger was different from Nigeria.

Can you see that? The other story is about an old woman in the village who lost her husband in an air raid, two children—boys—in the Army. When I visited the village, the woman came down, pressed her rosary beads into my hands, and asked me to take her only remaining son of fifteen. It gives you the two ends of our society.

> Interview with M. Kupfer of *Newsweek* and
> David Robison, United States free-lance
> journalist, Umuahia, February 13, 1969

The events of the passing year leave me with a deep feeling of pride and sorrow.

As I speak, my mind turns with joyous pride to all those who have through their blood and toil saved our dear fatherland from total destruction.

I think with pride of the members of our fighting forces, in the different sectors of the war, who are laying down their lives and all that they hold dear in defense of our freedom.

I think of our scientists, engineers, doctors, and nurses employing with a determined patriotic zeal all the skills of modern science and technology to ensure that both our human and natural resources are fully geared toward the struggle for the preservation of our sovereignty.

I think of the farmers who labor around the seasons, day and night, making available products of their labor to ensure we do not all perish through hunger and starvation.

I think of the volunteer workers, the foreign missionaries in our midst, the public servants, trade unions, our supply directorates, the various international relief bodies and their indomitable pilots, and engineers.

I think of our local leaders and many more who have dedicated their time and lives to either helping victims of Nigerian atrocities or in sustaining the Biafran revolution.

I also remember with deep sorrow all the victims of

this cruel and unjust war—the bereaved, our refugees, thousands of our own kith and kin behind the enemy lines, our brave and gallant men and women who are daily being tortured in Nigerian prisons because they are determined to die as proud Biafrans and not as slaves. I salute them all. I salute them again in the firm conviction that their sacrifices will not be in vain, as the goal—Biafra, the land of the rising sun—holds the promise of all that we price so dear and cherish.

End of Year Message, 1968

No war is ever won by arms alone; though, of course, arms help. Whenever I am in doubt about Biafra's ultimate victory all I do is get into a car and drive through the streets of Biafra. I look at the people's faces. From their reaction I come back absolutely convinced. As long as our people persist in their determination to carry this struggle to a victorious end, then victory must be theirs. We've got many historical examples to prove this point.

Talking in real terms about this war, we have already gone over the hump. Right now the imperialist conspiracy has put in everything it can. It has failed. Anything else it can put in will be a mere combination —different combinations of what it has already put in. And I have absolute confidence that the Biafran will always find antidotes to whatever poison they bring. We have done so for the past two years. Indications even up until today are that we will continue to do so.

Biafra has already succeeded. No question of it. In fact, the little thing that bothers me and should bother some people is how many of us here will be alive to celebrate the formal establishment of Biafra. The whole concept of Biafra is firmly established in the minds of the world. Some of you who have been abroad can testify to this. Even our enemies realize that Biafra now is a living fact. All they are trying to do right now is to inhibit the progress of Biafra. It is not to destroy Biafra any more, because they cannot destroy Biafra.

I have a friend who spends all his time making fore-casts. That friend of mine almost sets daily deadlines. The more he finds his deadlines false the more his determinaton to set a true one. I do not wish to and cannot compete with him in this futile exercise.

But, generally, looking at the future, the immediate future, the next twelve months, I think the area firmly under the control of the Biafran government will be much larger than today. Secondly, I think that the enemy will find it increasingly difficult to administer the towns under his control. I think also that in the course of the next twelve months, world opinion will have so much crystallized in favor of Biafra that more governments will come out openly in support of the struggle of the people of Biafra for self-determination. I believe also that in the next twelve months we will have learned to live better with our various shortages and our various sufferings. I think that in the next twelve months our society will have been a little bit better sifted; already chaff is beginning to blow away in the wind. I think that in the next twelve months we will begin to see the luster of the true, the real Biafran glistering in the basket as we sift. I am sure of this. I cannot say that at the end of the next twelve months we will have peace. I do hope that we will. But I can-not say so. What I can promise is that from now on things will be better. Definitely better.

Interview with national press and information
media, Umuahia, November 4, 1968

THE COST

War generally is a wasteful occupation. This one between Nigeria and Biafra is perhaps more wasteful than most.

With regard to human resources, so many people have died—civilians and military personnel—on both sides. A lot that we could use to develop our country is being diverted to prosecuting a senseless war. Our technicians, our scientists, our teachers who should be teaching children, are all fighting this war. It is a complete waste. And I call it a waste because this war can achieve nothing.

War cannot force Biafra back into Nigeria. I don't think Biafra, on the other hand, can conquer Nigeria. This is not our aim. Our aim is to be left alone to look after our own business.

In financial resources, its cost is also quite clear; somebody once in Nigeria talked in terms of £160,-000,000 as what the war has so far cost them. More recently they talked in terms of £250,000,000. The way they have been pursuing this war (which one has to realize is perhaps the biggest war that could be fought in Africa) has been total, and they have committed everything they have to it.

Here, we have committed everything but the amount is less. The amount is less because we have contracted our economy and we have depended entirely on what we ourselves can produce.

It is difficult to assess figures, very difficult. I always avoid mentioning figures unless I can authenticate them. The war has cost us a lot in actual spending on foreign exchange. I would say probably, everything put into consideration, around £10,000,000—no more. Everything else has been internal—what our own scientists can produce and whatever was here prior to the start of the war.

Since the war started, I think there must have been 100,000, both military and civilians, killed. Of the 100,000 the situation would be—give or take 10 percent —around 60 percent Nigerian, 40 percent Biafran.

Whatever one says of the figure, it is heavy, and secondly, it is unnecessary.

Interview with Dr. B. da Silva of *Diario Popular* of
Lisbon, Umuahia, March 14, 1968

So far the independence of Biafra has cost a great deal, but when one considers the problem one then finds that it is not really the independence that has cost these lives but genocide perpetrated by Lagos, the attempt to destroy our people.

What does one do if one finds one's arm locked in the jaws of the lion? The arm is there, and pulling it out is painful, but you still have to find a way of getting it out. Our struggle for freedom has cost us hundreds and thousands of lives. If we do not struggle for our independence we will all die; that is the problem. We have to balance slow death and the possibility of life. That is why we are fighting.

Interview with Jean Martel of the Swiss TV,
Owerri, August 21, 1968

FOREIGN INVOLVEMENT

Britain

Peace, indeed everything pertaining to this war, depends on one man and one man only, and that person is Harold Wilson. It is he who decided for Nigeria whether to continue the war or to seek peace. No matter how reasonable the others are eventually, Harold Wilson will have to decide and Nigeria will accept. Only recently he got up in the House of Commons and pontificated that his government would wish to found a federal system for Nigeria.

Wilson's attitude continues to consider Nigeria as private property, and this is the crux of the matter. If the British government had kept neutral in this war, granted that Biafra has never had material support, this war would certainly have ended within four weeks of its start. But Britain, under Harold Wilson, has continued to support and arm Nigeria with weapons more sophisticated than the Nigerians themselves. The sum total of it is the continued killing and massacre.

I accuse Harold Wilson of being a direct accomplice in the crime of genocide. Nigerians could never have done one-hundredth of what they are doing today but for Harold Wilson. It is unfortunate that in this matter he has chosen to flout all British opinion and the

House of Commons. The British representatives and
their people have made quite clear their feelings about
this, but Mr. Harold Wilson has refused. He is at the
bottom of this war.

International press interview,
Umuahia, October 28, 1968

There is no aspect of this war in which Britain is not
involved. I do not even know where to start. The problems that bedeviled the old Nigerian Federation were
implanted in that society by Britain.

It was Britain, first, that amalgamated the country
in 1914, unwilling as the people of the North were. It
was Britain that forced a federation of Nigeria, even
when the people of the North objected to it very
strongly. It was Britain, while keeping Nigeria together,
that made it impossible for the people to know themselves and get close to each other, by maintaining an
apartheid policy in Northern Nigeria which herded all
Southerners into little reserves called *Sabon-garis,* bar-
ring them from Northern Nigerian schools, and maintaining different systems of justice in a country they
claimed to be one.

It was Britain, for her economic interest, that put
the various nations in Nigeria side by side and called
it a federation, so as to have a large market.

It was Britain, in the year 1966, when Northern
Nigeria finally made an attempt to separate itself from
Nigeria, that forced her into holding to the federation.

It was Britain, having thus forced Northern Nigeria
into staying in the federation, that promised help to
the North (the military rulers of Nigeria) the sort of
help that enabled them to unleash this war of genocide.
British diplomats have boasted, and have continued to
boast, of their involvement in this war. Sir David Hunt,
and, only yesterday, his deputy high commissioner in
Benin, boast of British involvement.

It is British arms, British bombs, British technical
assistance, British mercenaries, that have been sustain-

ing Nigeria in the battlefront. A British officer boasted of having led the capture of Calabar. The same British officer boasted of having led the invasion of Bonny.

It was Britain that did, and has continued to do, Nigeria's overseas publicity, through the BBC.

I said sometime ago that it might have been more realistic at the Kampala peace talks for Biafra to sit across a table, with Britain on the other side, to negotiate terms for peace.

This war will not end until Britain wants the war to end. The day Britain feels that enough is enough, Gowon cannot continue for six hours.

International press conference,
Owerri, June 5, 1968

It was at this point in the war, four weeks after Nigeria declared it, that our forces crossed the river Niger at Onitsha and took over Midwestern Nigeria on August 9, 1967. The operation took our soldiers to the capital, Benin City, to Warri and Sapele in the South, to Auchi and Agenebode in the Northwest, and to several towns beyond the boundary of the Midwest and Western Nigeria in the direction of Ijebu-Ode, Ondo and Owo and Oshogbo.

At this point, Britain became heavily involved in the war. Heavy equipment and large quantities of ammunition were delivered to the Nigerian army. At about the same time Russia began to supply planes and other military equipment to the army of aggression. Biafrans, for their part, continued to struggle on their own resources. Our scientists began to design and produce our weapons of war, including grenades, rockets, armored cars, and several categories of ammunition. With these resources we were able to face the enemy.

International press conference,
Umuahia, January 26, 1968

Britain does not want anything honorable to come out of this, and that is why they sent Ferrets, Saladins,

mortar and artillery bombs to Nigeria and called them
"defensive weapons."

Audience with Papal Delegates,
Umuahia, February 12, 1968

How do you assess the Anglo-Soviet military support
for Nigeria? Which of the two has helped Nigeria more?
The most significant is probably the moral support of
Britain because, when all is said and done, this area
is considered a British sphere of influence, and the
attitude of Britain does, in a large measure, set the
attitudes of other countries.

Interview with West German journalist,
Dr. Ruth Bowert, Umuahia, March 25, 1968

It is a fact that Lagos is heavily planning for a final
onslaught on our people. Last week a shipload of
British armored cars and ammunition left a Dutch port
bound for Lagos—a further evidence in support of our
assertion that the British government's insistence on the
so-called land and sea corridors is to create routes for
the movement of the armored cars supplied by them to
Nigeria. Only a few days ago a Boeing 707 carrying a
full load of ammunition crashed near Lagos.

International press conference,
Umuahia, January 18, 1968

The only reason that Gowon is fighting is because
he not only has the wherewithal to fight but he feels
that the magnitude of what he gets is enough to overrun
this place and achieve military victory. Even if he overran Biafra, the problem would not end there. The day
Britain exerts the little influence it has on Gowon to stop
the war or Britain refuses to give arms to Nigeria, from
that day we start approaching peace and the solution
to the humanitarian problem. I have said it often
enough that I would accept a total arms embargo.
(That would mean possibly that Nigeria still has more

than we have, but I am forward-looking. Our resistance
will continue and eventually we shall cut down what
Nigeria has and then go to the mahogany table.)

Meeting with Dr. John Dunwoody, British
(Labour) M.P., Umuahia, December 4, 1968

. . . Today, you are living witnesses to the vandalism
implicit in the Lagos junta's concept of the term "liberation." Today you realize the wickedness implicit in
Harold Wilson's advice to accept Gowon's guarantees
and to lay down our arms. Only yesterday, Lagos
finally accepted that this town of Owerri was no longer
in their hands, giving as a reason a withdrawal by them
necessitated for tactical reasons. Already within twenty-
four hours after the enemy had been driven out of this
town, the work of reconstruction and rehabilitation
began. The civilian population have been streaming
back, and it is significant and typical of Biafran enterprise that the first civilian set up shop here barely
twelve hours after the expulsion of the vandals.

The last two weeks have been a most trying period in
our current struggle. Perhaps the most serious event of
that period was the enemy's preparation. This assault
on Umuahia was planned for January this year, but
was postponed after a review by certain British hire-
lings operating as technical advisers for the vandal
army. The British government had advised Gowon that
the capture of Umuahia would have such a psychological, propaganda, and political effect on our people
that it would bring the war to a grinding halt, and for
this reason they spared neither effort nor material
toward the achievement of that goal.

The campaign for Umuahia started immediately
after Harold Wilson's announcement in the British
House of Commons that he intended to visit Nigeria.
Two clear weeks' notice were given with the aim apparently of enabling Harold Wilson to arrive in Nigeria
after the capture of Umuahia, so that he could fly in
triumph into the city. For this reason, he came and

took with him a number of helicopters and small aircraft to carry his aides and members of the international
press who had come to record and give credence to his
latest political gimmick, designed to appease the growing disaffection of his Cabinet, his Parliament and his
people. . . .

. . . The British government, with its accustomed
vicious propaganda, had always been accusing France
of supplying us with arms. In the recent past, they have
said that France has stopped the supply of arms. The
aim of the propaganda is clearly to embarrass France,
which has repeatedly denied supplying us with arms,
and to demoralize our people and fighting troops. Be
that as it may, since Britain now feels that France no
longer supplies us with arms, she should take the
honorable step of following the French example by
stopping the supply of arms to Nigeria. . . .

. . . Mr. Wilson tried to mislead the world about his
intention to visit Biafra or to meet me at some accepted venue. For our part, we promptly expressed our
willingness to meet Mr. Wilson. He must have been
quite embarrassed by our reaction. He had thought
that, influenced by our knowledge and experience of
his insincerity and duplicity, we would refuse to meet
him, let alone receive him in Biafra. *I emphasize here
that Mr. Wilson never intended to meet me except as
a Nigerian prisoner of war.* His visit to Nigeria was
principally to reduce Russian influence in Lagos and
to re-establish British influence, to soothe United States
worry over the marriage of Russia in this part of Africa,
to enable him to have a personal appraisal of the military situation on the spot, and to discuss with the
Nigerian junta what further support they needed in
order to effect their policy of "quick kill."

Immediately after his departure from Lagos, Harold
Wilson proceeded to Addis Ababa to prepare the mind
of the Emperor for the OAU meeting in Monrovia.
Besides this, the British government sent out emissaries to many African countries, including those who

have shown sympathy for Biafra, in order to subvert their interest and sympathy toward us. This was exactly what it did on the two previous occasions when the OAU committee tried to look for a settlement of the current conflict.

This vain little man Wilson does not want Nigeria to lose the war the British government has been servicing, and at the same time he would like the world to believe that it is he who will ultimately find a way of settling the matter. . . .

Address to joint meeting of Elders and
Chiefs and Consultative Assembly at
Owerri, Umuahia, May 1, 1969

Russia

I spent, as a Nigerian, two of my most important years trying to track down Russian involvement in Nigeria. When I was the commander of the battalion in Kano I was the number two man there in the security committee, and our major task was to track down Russian influence. From then on, I warned about the real danger point in Northern Nigeria.

Most schoolteachers in Northern Nigeria are in correspondence with Moscow. All the communist literature that came into the then Nigeria came through Kano. I have watched this and the abortive attempt through Dr. Otegbeye, a leading Nigerian communist, to infiltrate the Western Region and Lagos. I do not know if you realized it, but when the Russians wanted to come to Nigeria they attempted to do so through the then Eastern Region.

There is no day for the past three months, except one day—that was in fact Christmas day—that there was no raid at our airfield. This is the number one target in their strategy. They have in recent weeks concentrated their air strike power in Port Harcourt. As I speak to you they have at the moment fourteen planes in Port Harcourt. They have more, but it has become

necessary to keep certain craft at alert in Lagos. It
seems that Russia is quite prepared to send into Nigeria any amount of their obsolete aircraft, knowing
full well that we have not got antiair capability.

We have lived under this threat for a long time, and
we feel somehow that they will not succeed. From time
to time they make some holes in the runway. Once they
go at low level, which is the only effective way of
putting the airfield out of action, then they come under
a barrage of machine-gun fire, and luckily for us, every
time they have attempted it, they have lost at least
one craft.

The Russians have supplied a great deal more—in
fact almost the entire Nigeria air force is Russian; and
Russian personnel. Oh, yes. They have supplied some
500 technicians—so-called—who have been around
training the Nigerians, helping them, and in fact sometimes fighting for them. The Second Division of the
Nigerian army, which is just on the point of complete
destruction in front of Onitsha right now, has, as a
hard core, 1,000 men trained in Russia.

But politically—and this is essentially a political
problem—the British support turns the scale more than
the Russian.

Interview with West German journalist,
Dr. Ruth Bowert, Umuahia, March 25, 1968

Revisionist Russia, in an unholy collaboration with
the imperialists, has been supplying Nigeria with jet
bombers and fighters. They have continued to arm the
Nigerians since then, and our people have been massacred by British mortars and shells, armored cars and
ammunitions, and bombed and strafed by Russian jets.
Undaunted, our people have continued to resist, relying
on our resources and in our sincere belief that eventually the progressive socialist ideals which inspired the
birth of our Republic will prevail.

Message to Mao Tse-tung,
September 27, 1968

Egypt

In the last week of June, 1968, three Egyptian ships unloaded their cargo, which included 300 tons of half-ton bombs. Three more Ilyushin jet bombers have been delivered to Nigeria, and 48 Egyptian technicians and pilots have arrived there to relieve those who have been manning the Nigerian jet war planes. This is only part of the massive arsenal being assembled by a country [Nigeria] which is playing politics with the transportation of relief supplies to Biafran refugees.

International Press Conference,
Umuahia, October 28, 1968

IV

On Relief
and Starvation

LAND ARMY

A major aspect of this war, which everybody has talked about, is the question of starvation. There have been arguments for and against, whether or not it is a legitimate weapon of war.

The fact is that with the contraction of the areas under our firm control, with the other difficulties of currency and movement, we have reached a stage where one does get apprehensive about the food supply problem in the Republic. In fact, the danger is greater along this line than along the line of enemy weapons.

Food shortage is a problem we have had to face all these months. It is another challenge to us as a people. It is a challenge to our friends. It is a challenge to our own physical prowess. It is a challenge to our own initiative. And I think it is a challenge which we can overcome quite easily by applying ourselves to the problem—food. There are three basic ingredients needed to solve this problem. First, you need the land, then you need the people to do the cultivation, and finally you need the seeds to plant. As I look at Biafra (and I have been doing quite a lot of traveling recently), I do see a lot of land not cultivated, I see a lot of waste all over the place, I see a lot of people around not fully employed. The purpose of this meeting is to put the three elements together and overcome the challenge of the present moment.

It has been said that seed yams have been eaten. It has been said that from now on, the next four months, will be the most critical period. We cannot sit back and expect the relief organizations to feed us. What can they bring in? A plane brings in ten tons, and at the most you get twenty planes a night—that is, two hundred tons. This is like a drop in the ocean. We cannot rely on this supply alone. Our survival cannot depend on it. The best way to look at relief is purely as a bonus. The day we took the decision to move out and establish our own separate existence we knew from then that we had to do everything on our own. Whatever problems we have should be faced by putting our heads together and finding ways and means of solving them. If we had waited for somebody in the world to start arming us when the Nigerians attacked us, where would we be now? In a national mass grave! But we did not wait for anybody. We donated money. Volunteered ourselves and fought back. Every success in Biafra has been a result of our putting our heads together. The major problem today is how to get more food for Biafra. We must again put our heads together.

Whatever I say here today is intended to stimulate discussion and suggestions, and at the end you will have to work out a program, suited to your own needs and situation, for emergency food production for Biafra. What we are trying to do now is to work out and co-ordinate all these and see the most efficient way to get more food in Biafra. There is nothing on earth that is beyond the Biafran.

First of all, what are the key needs? To me it seems, because of kwashiorkor, everybody's mind would go immediately to protein, meat or beans. Chicken would probably be the easiest way of getting meat, but that has been made rather difficult by the shortage of chicken feed. I am told that we can in fact produce our own chicken feed—you will be told how it is done later. And if you take care of the protein needs then what about the carbohydrates? Corn, yams, I think, are the key answers, and then also cassava and perhaps vegetables.

Conscious of the fact that our people have a rather peculiar land tenure, I think that you should, also in your deliberation, explore ways and means of getting over the problems of our system of land ownership, to enable us to cultivate as much as we need to get us over this food problem. I think that if we made a start on the individual level—with every householder planting his own vegetables around his house—we would go a long way to solving the vegetable problem. We should not just leave it to people to think or decide for themselves. We should mount a crusade to make our people interested. We have to mount a crusade to get our people doing what is right for our national existence. I think you will agree with me that the question of cultivation of vegetables is not a difficult one if everybody does his own bit. I think too that one should probably allow everybody who is a farmer to farm what normally he would want to farm. If this is done, a great deal of our land would have been cultivated; but a lot still would lie waste—waste, perhaps, because the farmer, for needs of crop rotation, has allowed the land to lie fallow for some time. Well, in normal times that would be all right, but right now I consider it a luxury. I feel, therefore, that communities should get together and organize the use of this unused area for an emergency period of, say, one year. In this emergency, it should be recognized that the land belongs completely to the owner who, in turn, will lend it to the community for the one year only in order to get us through this period of danger. If that is done, you will find that a large land area will be under cultivation.

There is a third point, and this relates to areas—and I take Onitsha Province, places like Atani and Aguleri—not very thickly populated but with vast farmlands which have all along been merely supplementing what other areas produce. I feel there should be a national move for the complete cultivation of these areas, again, as an emergency measure. We will not acquire the land, but it should be made available either to the local community or to the nation as a whole for this farming season.

We have talked about land and about the possibilities of using areas, but the problem really is: Who does the cultivation? I think there are very many people available for this. About your own vegetable garden there is no problem. You and your wife and sons and daughters will look after this. Luckily, too, the areas still remaining with us have got a lot of water.

I am told by the experts that this question of protein can be solved very easily. I am told that a family with six chickens could get three eggs a day, and it is very simple to run a small poultry farm. I am told also that with the manpower available it is possible to keep in every local community a central poultry house for broilers, holding at a time some five or ten thousand chickens. I am told also that the question of day-old chicks is not beyond us, and to maintain poultry it is now a question of how much corn we have or cassava. This opens quite a wide vista for us. For the central poultry farms you can get young girls to run them. For the family poultry, with good feed we might get four or five eggs a day for each family and with that be able to keep kwashiorkor away for some time, if not indefinitely.

One should also recognize that there are areas that no matter what you do, no matter the consultation, the owners of the land would not allow the actual use of their land by nonmembers of the community. This, in a way, is not too bad. One regrets it, but we have got to take it into consideration. I feel that provided our aim is to make sure that every available bit of land is cultivated, it should not matter too much who does the cultivation. Within this seminar you can find the ways

and means to encourage such communities, make people available to them to cultivate the land, and then
perhaps devise different systems of sharing the harvest.
My point being that it is not impossible for us to work
out a system of soil cultivation which would enable us
to get more food on an emergency basis.

I know what happens when things are centralized,
when the government puts its heavy hand on national
activity. I know that generally it takes no less than six
months to get moving, and I would suggest for this
problem of food that the widest scope be given the local
communities. I think the government should only feature in an advisory capacity. I suggest that you should
all go home and talk to your people, telling them what
the possibilities are, decide to do something, and then
you can call on the government for advice. I think the
government should not step in to run it centrally. If it
does, it would succeed, but by then probably half our
population would have died. What I am saying to you
then is that it is up to you.

For example, before I came here I held a meeting
with the leaders of Olokoro (near Umuahia) and I find
that they have gone quite far with their own project.
They are doing all this at least to prevent their local
community from starving. Look at it that way. Your
own community, does it deserve to starve? Are you
going to watch your own children perish? It is a personal decision.

You are the leaders. You are the ones that the
local community brings presents to from time to time;
they expect something from you in return. The day they
see you with your hoe in your hands, that day they will
know that Biafra means business. So I tell you, ladies
and gentlemen, the question you must continue asking
yourself is this: Do our children deserve to die? If the
answer is no, then you must do something about it. I
have told you it can be done. The rest is left to you.

To assist in getting the young people mobilized, it

is my intention to set up an organization to be known as the Biafra Land Army, which our young ones will join and know that they belong to a national organization. They will be trained, regimented sufficiently for them to be called out for work and to go back to their homes at night. The contingents of the land army will depend on you. You go to your community, mobilize them, and when they are ready, they will register with the government. We will assist you to organize it, but they will belong to you in your various communities. If you can get 2,000 volunteers, all well and good. If you can get 10,000, better still. I am not going to limit any community on what they could do about tilling the land. The volunteers will be recognized by the government as contributing to the war effort.

Now let us talk about other important issues that could arise. Our people love profit. So, let us start on that basis. If you have farmed all the area you can, that is yours, nobody should interfere; I think nobody should interfere with the little bit around your house. But going beyond that, I think, once you have taken land from a group, you should work out among yourselves in your local communities what amount of the harvest goes to the owner of the land. I personally feel that as an incentive, 50 percent should be left to the community, and the rest for purchase by the government. In this way you make profit for other needs. In this way you feed your own people freely. In this way you also make a national contribution. These are symbolic of our revolution; from the individual to the group to the nation.

One problem that keeps cropping up all the time is the question of seed yams. It is true that seed yams are vital for cultivation on a large scale, but the head of every yam is really a seed, and there are thousands of yams being eaten in Biafra today. Where are their heads? The answer is to collect these heads. To begin with, you should ask the children to go and collect all

the yam heads. Every cook must produce the head of
the yam he cooks. It is now five weeks since in my own
household heads of yams have been collected, and we
have been using these and other bits and pieces to cultivate the little patch of land behind the State House. It
is really amazing what people waste by casting away
yam heads in refuse dumps. If we collect all that we
can, I am sure the Ministry will be able to supplement.
The Food Production Directorate and Ministry of
Agriculture will provide technical aid and advice.

I have not talked about the specialized type of cultivation. I have not talked about rice that can only be
produced in special areas. All you do is to use your
land force to do the cultivation, but instead of yams
perhaps you produce rice, or instead of that you produce groundnuts.

It is now time for the experts to put things in their
proper place. We have done very well so far. We have
met all challenges. If I have not given you expert advice,
I think I have generated enough enthusiasm. I am sure
you will do the rest with your people. If you talk to
them, appeal to their patriotic sense. If you link up this
movement with the general war effort, you will get the
type of reaction that we need. A lot depends on you.
Today, in launching this scheme, the government really
is playing its traditional role, and I think by the end
you will find that the government has done its bit as
teacher and guide. We cannot force you. We don't intend to force you. The Biafran revolution has never
depended on coercion. If you recall the way you faced
the attempt of the enemy to overrun us, I am sure you
will all rise up, in the same spirit, now that the enemy
wants to starve us to death.

I think also there should be a slogan for this emergency food production program. I do not know what
the experts have thought of it, but it appears to me that
the slogan should be: *Turn the earth and bury Gowon.*
By growing more food for this Republic you are bury-
ing Gowon. Gowon has tried to kill us with bullets. He

has tried to starve us. He has tried everything and this is his last. I am absolutely confident that as a people we will survive.

Address at the Biafran Agricultural Seminar,
Afor-Ugiri, January 17, 1969

I have not left the protein issue entirely to the relief agencies. In the same way we have gone about cultivation, we have insisted on families maintaining poultry. We have arranged with organizations that will bring the day-old chicks and the initial feed, so that each family can maintain six birds in a little chicken pen that will be made locally and mass produced. From that, we expect that one can get three to four eggs a day for each family. Besides, each population center, each village, will have its own central poultry farm. We feel that with rice, cassava, yams, and garri, together with vegetables in each person's garden, and poultry, we should be able to make it.

Interview with Marvin Kupfer of *Newsweek*
magazine, and David Robison, United States
free-lance journalist, Umuahia, February 13, 1969

FOREIGN RELIEF

Food, medicine, personnel, clothing—all the necessities of life. Even to teach us to build shelters, temporary shelters for my people. In the rainy season, if we do not die of starvation, we will probably catch pneumonia. All these have to be considered, and we need any help we can get.

International press conference,
Owerri, June 5, 1968

In its efforts to confuse and mislead the world, the British government has tried to misrepresent and distort our position with regard to: (a) our refusal to accept its hypocritical and propaganda-motivated offer of re-

lief; and (b) our refusal to accept relief through the
enemy by means of the so-called land corridor.

Our position on the question of relief remains unmis-
takably clear. We welcome and appreciate offers of relief from all genuine sources including the British public and the British humanitarian organizations not associated with the British government. But we shall never
accept such relief and assistance, either directly or
indirectly, from the British government so long as that
government continues to supply to Nigeria arms with
which to increase the very conditions the British government professes or desires to relieve. By ignoring the
logic of our stand, the British government has betrayed
its utter contempt for African intelligence and sense of
honor. What is the sense in the attempt of the Harold
Wilson government to relieve the sufferings of 4,500,000
people today while at the same time ensuring that by
tomorrow the number will swell to 6,000,000 or more?
With the British government as a faithful ally of Nigeria, how does the British government expect us, as
reasonable beings, to treat it as a friend by accepting
its relief supplies?

Here I must say something about the British government's proposal that Lord Hunt and his team should
visit Biafra. We have nothing but respect for those who
constitute this delegation. Our refusal to welcome a
visit by the team stems directly from our well-known
stand about British government mercy supplies while
that government is still supplying Nigeria with arms.
We rightly felt that the visit, the sole purpose of which
was to discuss relief from the Wilson government, could
not produce any useful result since the relief would not
be accepted by us.

But even after we had made our position known, and
having regard to our desire to let the world see the
effects of British government policy on our people, we
were reconsidering our stand when Mr. George Thompson, the British Commonwealth Secretary, came out

with a statement openly endorsing the Lagos insistence that supplies for Biafra must come through Lagos. It became clear that the British government had already taken a firm decision, leaving Lord Hunt with no discretion. At that point we were left with no alternative but to drop the whole question. Thus, it is evident that Mr. Thompson was responsible for the failure of Lord Hunt to visit Biafra.

The strategy of the British government in insisting on supplies coming to us through Lagos and the so-called land and sea corridors is intended to achieve both political and military objectives. The aim is to establish that Lagos alone can control and influence the welfare of our people. Furthermore, the British government knows that bridges have been destroyed and channels blocked along wherever the so-called land and sea corridors ways may be established. Besides, in none of any such routes within the Biafran territory, including those areas where the enemy has established its presence, has the enemy been in full control. All these have combined to retard and frustrate enemy progress into the Biafran heartland. The establishment of the so-called land and sea corridors would remove those obstacles and create routes through which Gowon's war machine could roll easily into our homeland.

All sincere and disinterested visitors, even from Britain, who have examined the situation in its stark reality have been unanimous in stressing the urgent need for quickly sending relief supplies to Biafra. They have emphasized that the best way of doing this is by air. They realize that even if the idea of land and sea corridors were acceptable it would take at least four or five weeks of the hardest industry to restore normal communications before supplies could get through. By this time at least a million people would have perished. Is that not what the British government wants? Are the British government's aims not further revealed by its efforts to stop British humanitarian and private organizations, who have been sending relief to us by air, from doing so, and its attempt to induce them to send such reliefs through Lagos, Nigeria?

Apart from political and military reasons, there is also the question of the need to safeguard the people of Biafra from mass extermination through the poisoning of food reaching them from areas occupied by the Nigerians. As disinterested observers who have visited this Republic have noted, items of food like salt, milk, and sugar which have found their way to us from Nigeria have been proved to contain arsenic. In the circumstances, it would be the height of folly for the government of Biafra to throw its borders open to relief supplies that have passed through Nigerian hands.

No, we cannot be deceived. Anyone genuinely interested in sending relief to us should do so direct to Biafra by air. To this end, we have set aside an airport for that purpose. Our airports can carry any aircraft capable of landing at the Lagos airport and are, in certain respects, better than the Enugu and Port Harcourt airports. The truth is that Lagos, backed by the British government, does not want relief to come to Biafra since they are pursuing a policy of genocide. Hence they are threatening to shoot down any planes carrying mercy supplies direct to Biafra. Hence also the British government, of all the governments of the world, was swift to explain and rationalize that revolting and wicked threat by Gowon's government.

We maintain that the quickest and most realistic means of sending relief to us is by air. We agree, however, that in order to ensure sufficient supplies, airlifts should be supplemented with those by sea and land. In order to facilitate the latter, we are suggesting two routes for the use of our benefactors. First, supplies could be sent through the River Niger up to Oguta where they can be discharged direct into Biafra. Ocean-going vessels could carry their cargoes to the estuary of the River Niger, from where the cargoes would be transferred into smaller craft through the River Nun and up to the Niger to Oguta. Alternatively, Port Harcourt and the road to Igrita, as well as the channels leading to Port Harcourt, should be demilitarized up to ten miles on both flanks (i.e., outside shelling range) and should remain so for the duration of the war, to enable supplies to be delivered through Port Harcourt. Either of these alternatives would be quicker, cheaper, and more realistic than landing the supplies first in Lagos and then operating a shuttle air service to Enugu before carrying the supplies by road to other parts of Biafra. The attitude of Lagos and London to these proposals will prove their good faith.

It is to be hoped that the International Red Cross will not lend itself to the Anglo-Nigerian political maneuvers. Up until now, and before the British government's intervention, the Red Cross has been dealing direct with us without having to seek approval of Lagos. In this way, they have brought us a lot of relief supplies. They have a representative here in Biafra who is in a position to advise them best. We sincerely believe that that universally respected and trusted international humanitarian organization will live up to its tradition in spite of the pressures of international politics.

But what kind of respect has Gowon for the International Red Cross? It is now a well-known fact that his planes have bombed and strafed Red Cross hospitals and destroyed its other establishments in Biafra. The latest example is that of Awgu. That area had been declared a Red Cross zone and consequently we had virtually demilitarized it. Gowon knows this. But he had no scruples in ordering his troops to launch a massive attack and occupy the area.

There were also attempts by Nigeria on more than one occasion to destroy Red Cross planes bringing supplies to Port Harcourt. Nigeria knew that those planes normally landed at 1 A.M. and so they sent their jet aircraft to menace the airport with a view to destroying Red Cross planes landing there.

It is fair that the world should know what we ourselves are doing to help save our starving refugees. The impression which the British government and its agencies, particularly the British Broadcasting Corporation, have tried to make on the British public and the world is that Biafra is finished and all that is now necessary is to send relief and medicines to its war victims.

Biafra is not finished either militarily or otherwise. It is true that our people, particularly children, are dying in scores and hundreds, daily, from exposure, hunger, disease. But we are not sitting back helplessly waiting for a fairy god-mother to help us. True to our character and tradition, we are doing our best to relieve the situation as far as lies in our power. Those of you who have been here for some days have seen with your eyes what is happening. You must have seen even the refugees themselves doing something to help themselves by planting crops and engaging in other occupations.

In our country this is normally the farming season of the year, but even so, villagers are helping to alleviate the sufferings of the refugees by sharing with them whatever food they have. Those in salaried employments have, for months now, voluntarily given up half, and in some cases two-thirds, of their salaries as their contributions toward the needs of war and of the refugees. This week a "Save the Children" program has been launched in the Republic through which individual Biafrans are going to adopt children from refugee camps for personal care.

It is because these efforts cannot possibly cope with the mounting problem of refugees that we have appealed to the world for help. For example, our people have been denied their accustomed protein from fish and meat following the abandonment of their livestock as a result of their flight from the enemy, and the sixteen-month blockade imposed by Nigeria.

But no amount of efforts or assistance can meet the tragic needs of the refugees until our people are able to return to their homes and live normal lives. And that will be possible only with a cease-fire and the removal of enemy troops from our territory.

International press conference,
Aba, July 18, 1968

For weeks now the Nigerian junta and Mr. Harold Weaseling have been conducting vile propaganda against us on the subject of daylight flights of relief into Biafra. Their aim is, of course, to assuage mounting world opinion against their practice of genocidal aggression. Fortunately, they have not been able to deceive the world, which cannot forget their persistent claims that starvation is a legitimate instrument of warfare. The truth is that Mr. Harold Wilson and Nigeria want to use daylight flights of relief as a cover for fulfilling their cherished and passionate ambition of destroying our main airfield.

Under the present circumstances it would be, to say the least, irresponsible for this government to trifle with the security of its people.

Having said this, I want to make it quite clear that we have no objection in principle to daylight flights of relief into Biafra. To this end, we are prepared to make available to any relief organization, which does not find the existing night facilities adequate, any areas in Biafra where they can build an airport for daylight flights. With the blockade we have neither sufficient money nor materials to do this. But we have the skilled manpower and expertise—engineers and other technicians—which we are prepared to place at the disposal of any organization wishing to take up this offer. Besides this, we shall make available any other facilities within our competence. With money and materials available, the construction of the airfield for daylight flights can be completed within a very short time—and I speak from proven experience.

Broadcast, December 22, 1968

On relief, let me repeat that we welcome relief from any well-meaning quarters so long as its receipt does not place the recipients in jeopardy. Biafra will, however, never accept relief through Nigeria or from the British and Russian governments, which are supporting Nigeria in this war. We have never objected to air, sea, and land routes for relief. But it must be emphasized that relief, no matter how massive, can only serve as a palliative. Only the end of the conflict can bring real relief.

On the question of day flights, I repeat the offer which I made a week ago in my Christmas message, to make land available to any relief organization which finds the present night facilities inadequate, to build an airport or airstrip for daylight flights. The government of Biafra has never been opposed to daylight flights. It was in order to facilitate daylight flights into Biafra that we built and equipped an airstrip in Uturu and handed it over completely to the International Red Cross. This airport was subsequently assaulted and seized by the criminal junta in Lagos.

On the question of land and sea corridors, our government has never opposed in principle any such corridors provided the security of our people is not placed in jeopardy. For this reason we continue to propose a corridor by sea using the River Niger to Oguta. It has to be remembered that the only reason Gowon's boasts have come to naught has been the effectiveness of our land route obstacles. Nobody in his right mind would therefore expect, under an atmosphere fraught with bad faith and complete insensitivity to world opinion, that the leadership of this country would hand over this key to our survival to a faithless enemy.

On the vital question of cease-fire and negotiations, we submit that a cease-fire more than any other plan or proposal is the surest and most effective means of bringing relief to the people. Hitherto, we have insisted that there must be a cease-fire before any negotiations; but considering the difficulties and delays associated with a cease-fire before it can be made effective, we propose a truce for a limited and specified period during which arrangements for a cease-fire can be made. During that period too, the much-needed relief supplies for the suffering on both sides of the conflict can be brought in without impediments.

End of Year Message, 1968

OBSTACLES TO RELIEF

Our struggle is a struggle to establish our existence. The International Red Cross does not believe in our existence, it is as simple as that. All their actions toward Biafra show that basic difference in our ideas and opinions. The International Red Cross has not been able to get itself clearly cut off from the diplomatic technicalities imposed by our diplomatic position. We look forward, very much of course, to greater understanding, and I am confident that as time goes on and indeed as the fact of our existence gets more formalized the International Red Cross will find no points of friction.

Meeting with parliamentary delegates from
Canada, Holland, and Denmark,
Umuahia, November 13, 1968

First of all, you have to understand the Lagos attitude to relief. The war was started off by an attempt to starve us Biafrans into submission, hence the economic blockade. They did not want to appear wicked to the outside world, and for a long time they tried very hard to gloss over the real issues and to pretend that they were "anxious" for the welfare of the civilians. You have to understand the question of relief in the context of our charge of genocide against Lagos in this conflict.

Nigerians have throughout this war shown complete lack of discrimination in the large-scale slaughter and indeed, massacre of civilians they have perpetrated. Whenever they are able to raid our area by air, they concentrate on civilians, as has been witnessed by international correspondents who have been here. Whenever their "peace" propaganda has had some effect and lured the people out, instead of dealing with the people as friends they have in fact chosen to massacre them; hence the biggest slaughter in the Midwest area and the Ibibio areas.

A big example, a very clear example, of their attitude to hunger and the suffering of civilians can be seen in the Ikot Ekpene sector, where in the course of some twelve weeks' occupation they reduced every single living human being that remained behind into a mere skeleton through ruthless starvation.

The problem really arises from the fact that Nigeria believes that hunger is a legitimate weapon of warfare. They believe that if they can make the Biafran civilian masses suffer this hunger extremely and long enough, it is possible to bring our people to their knees. In the United States of America, Chief Enahoro, the Nigerian Information Commissioner, said that starvation was a legitimate weapon of warfare. In Niamey, Mr. Ayida, the Permanent Secretary in the Nigerian Ministry of Economic Planning, said that it was a legitimate weapon of warfare and that it was used effectively against Germany in the last world war and they would use it against us.

We have made every effort to accommodate even the Nigerian wishes on this question of relief, but at each stage they move away from the real point. The pile of relief materials rotting away in Lagos while people are dying in both areas—Lagos-occupied and our areas —symbolizes Nigeria's politics with relief and her hypocrisy.

When the ordinary humanitarian organizations saw the problem here they were quite happy to give us direct help—including, in fact, the International Red Cross at the beginning. There was then no politics. This system worked for months until the British government decided to interfere with the grant of £250,000. At this stage the British immediately trumped up this red herring that all aid must go through the International

Red Cross and that the International Red Cross flights must receive Lagos approval. And then, of course, politics came into it completely.

I will give you an instance of politics in the question of International Red Cross relief. We said we wanted direct airlifts as a minimum measure; to be followed up by a land-sea corridor. Immediately Lagos insisted on only a land corridor, at the same time agreeing that it would take a long time to get the corridor established. The International Red Cross, without further consideration or negotiation, immediately started dumping relief in Lagos and Fernando Po. When these were dumped in those places, Lagos switched from the discussion on the land corridor to one on the air corridor. We accepted, "Well, fly in direct," and, of course, Lagos said, "We will shoot down any plane that tries to fly in direct."

The British Broadcasting Corporation and the British government, rather than being shocked at a country shooting down relief planes, immediately warned off all organizations that were willing to bring in relief. I have offered a separate airfield. I have offered inspection at source by both Lagos and Biafrans if necessary. The whole problem, Lagos said, was the possibility of the International Red Cross carrying arms to Biafra— a thing that has never been heard of. Nonetheless, I said, since the distance from Fernando Po to our airfield is shorter than to Lagos and then Enugu and to us, let the Nigerians put somebody on the plane until it lands in Biafra. Lagos said no, the plane must first land in their airfield. Now the only reason for saying all this is to exercise some form of air rights, and this is politics. This has always been the pattern: whenever it appeared as if we could work out something, Lagos broke off the discussions.

Finally, as far as we are concerned and in view of what I have told you very sketchily, it does appear that, in view of the way the International Red Cross has found itself hamstrung by diplomatic considerations,

those insisting on relief seem to be only paying conscience money and not yet helping Biafra. There is no
point in collecting money if, when it has been collected,
and given to the International Red Cross, the relief will
only stop in Lagos and the materials rot.

Indeed, the International Committee of the Red
Cross is organized and run by individuals who do this
through the goodness of their hearts. They have been
sucked into a political-diplomatic maneuver by Lagos
and the British government. The International Red
Cross is being used. In fairness, it is because they have
not been completely sucked in that relief has come in
at all. This is also evidence of their attempt to resist
this Anglo-Nigerian conspiracy.

Interview with Girardet publishing group,
Düsseldorf, Western Germany,
Owerri, August 18, 1968

The International Red Cross, an organization of great
international repute, has, as it were, reluctantly been
bringing relief items into Biafra. It has found itself
greatly hamstrung by political and diplomatic technicalities. Plain logic tells one that if you want to give
something to somebody, the most efficient way of doing
it is to hand it direct to that person and not to give it
to a middleman to deliver. If you then go further and
hand it to his enemy to give to him, the likelihood is
that he will not get enough or even any at all. From
their operations, therefore, the International Red Cross
is not as efficient as it could be in the present circumstances.

Caritas International, the World Council of Churches,
and other various humanitarian organizations who have
tried against very difficult odds to bring relief in here
are indeed bringing in items efficiently. When I say efficiently, I mean within the scope allowed them by this
situation. There is another point and that is that these
charitable organizations deal directly with their Biafran
counterparts. I believe that the International Red Cross

could be more efficient if it dealt directly with the Biafra National Red Cross. Incidentally, there are other national Red Cross bodies that have been dealing direct with the Biafra Red Cross, and their operations have been very efficient and their relief items reach the poor people for whom they are intended.

International press conference,
Umuahia, October 28, 1968

There have been various efforts to alleviate the suffering in Biafra. Regarding the relief organizations, particularly the private ones, I have complete admiration for their courage, their tenacity of purpose, their humanitarian ideals of the highest caliber. Sometime ago, I said that they were the true heroes of this struggle— the pilots that fly the relief materials in. I still maintain it.

The International Red Cross, unfortunately, is perhaps so large and tyrannized by diplomatic clichés and the complications of a large cumbersome organization that they have not been able to do as much as they could, or even thought. I think that, based on their contribution, one would say that the efficiency of the International Red Cross here is down to around 10 percent. They have not been able to get themselves away from red tape and political controversy.

Our feeling about relief is that it is not an alternative to the solution of the problem. You give food to 14,000,-000 people under the threat of starvation and imminent death, but having given them food, what else? What Biafra needs is an understanding of the true cause of this war, an understanding of a simple cause and the justness of our cause, and help to keep away the enemy that threatens to swallow us up. The day the war ends, you will immediately see the end of starvation and the end of misery. What brings about the starvation? Biafra used to be the granary of not only Nigeria but indeed other parts of West Africa. Once you can bring the farmer back to his farm again, the trouble ends. You might say that this is an oversimplification; but it is a fact that the problem today is war, not really starvation, and people who are anxious to put an end to this face the problem of war. One way I think to neutralize the effectiveness of the enemy is by either stopping them or by giving us the wherewithal to protect ourselves. Because for us this war is basically protective. Relief is all right, we welcome it and will always be grateful, but relief cannot solve the problem.

Interview with Cliff Robertson, United States
actor, Umuahia, December 9, 1968

RELIEF AND WAR

You ask me: Are the Biafrans fighting for milk and butter? No. We are fighting for higher ideals.

We are fighting because of a total rejection of Nigeria and all she stands for.

We are fighting because, as men, we feel that we have the right to map out our course in life, to control our own destiny.

We are fighting because we were rejected by Nigeria.

We are fighting to protect our own lives and property.

We are fighting to enable our children to live free, to develop at our own pace, to contribute to the world the best of their abilities.

This war came suddenly on us. In fact we went into the war most reluctantly. We hoped and continued to hope that Nigeria would not be so mad as to launch the war. It is true that on this matter of relief our objection has been partly one of lack of trust of the Nigerians. We have got sufficient evidence to prove their interference with relief materials. There is enough evidence also to show that the Nigerians are no believers in international convention when it comes to matters affecting the International Red Cross. But this is not the main reason for this war. . . .

Interview with Marvin Kupfer of *Newsweek*
magazine, Umuahia, February 13, 1969

Suppose the British government sent us milk. Should we accept it? Not while she is fighting us. Right now, the British government of Harold Wilson is the enemy. There is nothing that Nigeria does today that it could have done without the Wilson administration. We would not accept milk from Wilson. It would probably be poisoned, since he is a direct accomplice in genocide. It would not be beyond him to find a more subtle way to kill us.

Meeting with a parliamentary delegation from
Canada, Holland, and Denmark,
Umuahia, November 13, 1968

One comes in and sees a very cruel picture and feels immediately that something ought to be done very urgently. We have lived with misery for virtually two years now; and each day it increases in intensity.

You cannot solve the humanitarian problem without its political and the military concomitant. In fact, the Nigerian is operating a policy of siege warfare; it is this that has prolonged this war. Without solving the question of the war you cannot succeed in solving the humanitarian problem. Various people all over the world sit back and say that there is shortage of carbohydrates here, so give Biafra a thousand tons of the stuff. When this is done, have you solved the problem? You give the carbohydrates and the fight continues. What happens next? How long will you continue giving the carbohydrates? It is grossly unfair when people say that Biafra is playing politics with starvation. We have looked at the problem, and we know that it is political and military and if we do not solve these the conditions will continue.

Every day the situation deteriorates. The answer to this is a meeting around a polished mahogany table. We know also that the cause of this starvation is the presence of the enemy in our territory. If these people were not in our territory, our people would go back, and within a very short time the need for massive relief

would recede to a point where it would be no longer
a problem.

Nigeria does not want cease-fire: Nigeria wants to
overrun Biafra. We know they can't. And regarding
this question of relief supplies, Nigeria has said often
enough that starvation is a legitimate weapon of war—
a view which, to my surprise, the British Parliament
has tended to endorse. Nigeria and Britain believe that
starvation will bring the people of Biafra to their knees.
On our own side, we do not of course, for one minute,
believe that the situation will come to that [surrender],
the reason being that our own effectiveness in the battlefield has more than shown that before such a state of
affairs will be reached, our own military situation will
be far better improved. The enemy right now has lost
a great number of their soldiers. What they have now
is just massive ammunition and weapons and a few
mercenaries from other countries. I think they have
done their worst.

> Meeting with Dr. John Dunwoody,
> British (Labour) M.P.,
> Umuahia, December 4, 1968

The question of famine is a result of this war. There
is no logic that can turn it the other way. War
brought blockade. War made for the vast population
movement, and it is this that has created the disruption of the economy—that brings about famine. This
area used to feed not only Nigeria but quite a lot of
West Africa. On this question of relief, what really can
the world bring in and for how long would the world
feed 14,000,000 people? Forgive me for saying this
again, but to me relief is like paying conscience money.
One likes to say: I have done this and therefore, like
Pontius Pilate, I wash my hands of it. I do not believe
that any relief organization can afford to feed the
people of Biafra indefinitely.

So why don't we really face the problem? The problem is war. Although it is the gory consequence cf the

conflict that has drawn people to this place, it is most unfortunate that world conscience can be roused only by such gory details. Let us get at the problem—war. The answer is: Stop the war. If our people get peace today, after one month we would cease to starve. The true problem is war, not relief.

Meeting with parliamentary delegates from
Canada, Holland, and Denmark,
Umuahia, November 13, 1968

It would not be right to say that the United States [Johnson administration] has not taken a position in this conflict. I specifically directed that American equipment should be shown to you yesterday—items captured from the enemy. What else do you expect to find to prove partisanship? The 116-mm. gun and ammunition is produced by only the U.S. and it is being used extensively against us by the enemy.

I think too that you will agree with me that the United States has brought diplomatic pressure to bear in favor of Nigeria. This has been a great asset to the Nigerians. Earlier in the conflict, the U.S. ambassador [Mr. E. Mathews] in the then Nigeria indicated quite clearly where he stood. I got letters [from him] telling me what the U.S. government felt I should do and what I should not do.

The U.S. statement on relief, I consider something like paying conscience money. The only way to solve this problem is to stop the war, and forgive me saying this, it would appear that the U.S. present administration is abdicating its position as one of the custodians of world peace, and the leader of our civilization. To see such barbarity and do nothing effective to stop it is complicity.

The U.S. gives me milk and butter so that when I am a corpse, as needs I must be, my skin will still be smooth? No. Let us not deceive ourselves about this humanitarian aid. There is a problem, a problem that affects the world, a problem to be solved, and all lead-

ers of this world should face that problem. Thousands
of people are being killed by the people who, but for
the support of those relief-offering leaders, would not
be in a position to do the killing.

The U.S. has a great responsibility to put a halt to
this carnage. The U.S. is a leading member of the
United Nations and has the moral obligation to see
that the conventions of the United Nations are not
being trampled upon.

> Interview with Canadian, Dutch, and Danish
> parliamentarians and accompanying journalists,
> Umuahia, November 13, 1968

V
On Peace

We have made all attempts at a democratic solution of this crisis. I have offered open elections, plebiscite and referendum. I have offered a prize to anybody who can find another democratic way of finding the wishes of the people, and given assurance that we would go for it.

Interview with Cliff Robertson, United States actor, Umuahia, December 9, 1968

When this crisis began and as I saw it developing, I believed we could get around a table and negotiate a way of living together in a form of association. By September 29, 1966, it had become quite clear to me that we had reached the end of the road, and only then did I change our policy and sought cooperation.

No matter what happens in the future, geography has placed us side by side with the Nigerians, and we either cooperate or both of us perish. The longer this war lasts the more difficult it is to cooperate. I believe that there are avenues—economic avenues—where we can cooperate with mutual advantage. I believe that even in a new set of circumstances, more acceptable circumstances, we can accommodate a free passage of trade. I think there are certain services that we can coordinate. Biafra has always been willing to negotiate on these bases.

International press conference, Aba, November 18, 1967

I have always believed that the crisis between Nigeria and Biafra could be settled by peaceful negotiation around a conference table. Lieutenant Colonel Gowon thought otherwise and declared war. Even after seven months of war, I still believe that the present conflict can be resolved by peaceful negotiations, provided agreement can be reached on the venue and the agenda. Such negotiations can be fruitful if they begin with a proper recognition of the basis of our struggle. In this connection, I can do no better than refer you to the preamble to our Proclamation of Independence:

Conscious of the supreme authority of Almighty God over all mankind, of our duty to (ourselves) and posterity;

Aware that (we) can no longer be protected in (our lives) and in (our property) by any Government based outside Eastern Nigeria;

Believing that (we) are born free and have certain inalienable rights which can best be preserved by ourselves;

Unwilling to be unfree partners in any association of a political or economic nature.

We need peace to enable us to reconstruct the ravaged areas of our land and to resettle the millions who have been displaced and dispossessed of all their properties in Nigeria. We need peace to revive our economy and build a human community where every citizen will make his contribution to the development of a strong, prosperous, and happy nation.

Some foreign pressmen have asked me, *"What will Biafra do with her sovereignty?"* My answer has always been, "A great deal." With it we could restore dignity to our harassed millions who are the citizens of this new Republic. Our sovereignty will secure for them the freedoms of political, economic, and spiritual life which the victimization and the uncertainty of their recent history has denied them.

As a member of the family of nations, Biafra can hope to make worthwhile contribution to the material and the spiritual well-being of mankind. The spiritual characteristics which made us champions of a truly united Nigeria in former years will then have their chance to be made available to Africa and the rest of the free world.

We in Biafra have been fighting to protect ourselves and our institutions against a plunder that is most brutal, a tyranny that is monstrous, and a genocide that is total. The survival of this young Republic as a nation will be a permanent testimony to the supremacy and dignity of human life. It will be a guarantee against genocide and related crimes in Africa and elsewhere. All we ask of the world is to bear witness to the justice of our cause and to grant us the opportunity— surely due to men everywhere—for dignity, security, peace, and happiness.

We, as a people, suffered constant persecution and victimization throughout the period of our association with Nigeria. The climax of this persecution came with genocide of 1966 and 1967. In the eight months of our separate existence as a nation, we have, as it were, acquired the experience of many centuries. It has been most instructive. From our trials, we founded a nation-state composed of people who have a common background, who have undergone a common experience, and who share a common desire to live together. That achievement, surely, has significance for world peace and international understanding.

International press conference,
Umuahia, January 28, 1968

As a world power, the United States has a great potential for peace in this struggle. She can certainly, if she decides to do so, bring about peace in record time. I am sure of this.

Left to Nigeria alone, there would be no negotiated settlement, Yet, if Britain or, as we have always indicated, America, supported a peace move, it would have a very strong chance of success. Reluctantly we are

fighting a war, and as soon as it becomes clear to us
that the whole crisis can be discussed around a table,
we will go to it.

Interview with United Press International
of Bonn, Umuahia, January 28, 1968

We have no territorial ambitions. We don't want to
capture anybody or to punish anybody. We just want
to be left alone. If you leave us alone, then there is no
need to fight. If you continue fighting, we will strike
back anywhere we can.

I cannot say: Because you are not fighting me here
but fighting me over there, therefore I must only take
advantage in the very front you are fighting at. No.
This probably will explain to you the reason why at a
certain stage it became necessary for the Biafran troops
to move across into Nigeria and to take over the Midwest.

Interview with D. B. da Silva of *Diario Popular*
of Lisbon, Umuahia, March 14, 1968

Our detractors and enemies have tried to deceive the
world by paying lip service to the need for peace, and
of relieving the sufferings of our people. We cannot be
deceived by their hypocrisy and dishonesty. Nor can
they claim to be more concerned about the peace and
happiness of our people than we ourselves. It is therefore my earnest hope that all those who have lately
talked too much about peace, particularly the British
government, will find this Christmas an opportunity to
demonstrate and convince the world about their sincerity by ending actions which nourish war rather than
peace.

Our position and conviction remain that war and
bloodshed can achieve nothing except the deepening
and perpetuation of hate and ill will, and the frustration of peace and progress. As a people, we Biafrans
hate conflict and war, and cherish harmony and peace.

Appropriately, all men of goodwill and lovers of

peace and concord have cried out for a cease-fire or, failing that, a truce in the current Biafra-Nigeria conflict during this Christmas season. His Holiness the Pope and the world Catholic leadership have made the appeal. The leaders of Protestant churches the world over have done the same. His Imperial Majesty, Haile Selassie of Ethiopia, supported by President Johnson of the United States, has proposed a truce of at least one week, and so have two well-known humanitarians, Lord Fenner Brockway and Mr. James Griffiths of the United Kingdom—to mention just a few.

In response to these world appeals, and as an earnest of Biafra's dedication to peace, I have today issued an order to the Biafran armed forces to observe as of midnight of December 23/24, 1968, an eight-day truce lasting to midnight of January 1, 1969. During this period, the Biafra armed forces will remain in their positions, make no attack on the enemy, and fire only in self-defense. I have further invited members of international humanitarian organizations resident in Biafra to come forward and observe independently the conduct of both forces during this period of truce.

One would wish that this could be the beginning of a permanent cease-fire, leading to peaceful negotiations. Unfortunately and regrettably, past and current experiences do nothing but show that this might be too much to expect of Nigeria, whose sole interest is that of a military solution.

In this connection, it is worth recalling that, four and a half months ago, on Saturday, August 3, 1968, I unilaterally ordered a truce for the duration of the abortive Addis Ababa talks. Nigeria's response to that well-meaning gesture was to intensify their aggressive activities by land, air, and sea. Nigeria has, of course, consistently spurned every idea and suggestion about a truce or cease-fire. It is to be hoped that Nigeria and the *Weaseling* government of Britain will on this occasion prove their sincerity toward peace by reciprocating.

Yesterday, I received a message from Lord Brock-

way that the Lagos government had agreed to a truce
over Christmas and the end of the Ramadam fast. I am
informed that yesterday, December 21, was the end of
the Ramadam fast and so the day on which Nigeria
promised to observe a truce. But it was, in fact, the day
which witnessed the most intensified enemy activities on
every front. What is more, it was the day which witnessed the longest and heaviest air raids of the war.

Our position and conviction have remained that this
is a futile war which can settle nothing except to widen
the gulf between the people of Biafra and those of Nigeria, as well as deepen hatred and increase suffering.
It is for this reason that we have spared no pains in
working toward the end of the present conflict and the
beginning of peaceful negotiations. I have made two
journeys in search of peace. I have twice offered truce.
I have made countless proposals for peace which have
all been brushed aside by the Lagos junta now crazed
by bloodlust. The Lagos junta is not interested in peace
other than the peace of death. Their attitude to negotiation is only to exact surrender.

Since we ask nothing other than to be left alone,
since we are no trees that remain fixed in face of the
woodman's ax, ours must be to fight and continue
fighting until the threat to our very existence is removed. For us, it is a people's war. It is a war being
fought with the totality of our people behind their
government, and a government demonstrating at every
turn its true position as the servant of the people. Our
struggle is nothing new in history. It is the traditional
struggle of men in society to which everybody is dedicated. If anybody is in doubt, we say again, as we have
always said, that we accept a plebiscite or referendum
conducted or observed by an impartial agent.

This war is a futile one. It can achieve nothing except
misery and waste on both sides of the conflict. It is
nothing but a disgrace to Africa and can delight no
one but the neocolonialists. Already, in addition to this
war against Biafra, Nigeria is now facing upheavals

which are bound to cause additional misery and suffering to the people of that unfortunate country. The people of Western Nigeria, fed up with the war, have come to realize, though a little too late, its futility. They now live under curfews and martial law, and their attempts to express their views or demonstrate their feelings have met with military repression. Armies have been let loose in their midst. War planes have practiced their murderous skills on their unsuspecting civilians.

In Biafra our people continue to suffer. Our institutions continue to stagnate. Our progress has remained at a standstill. Our hoes are rusting. The wheels of our industry have since stopped with lack of use. Our men and women, for long separated, begin to forget the joys of family life with its beautiful laughter.

I think of mothers bereaved of their children, children deprived of their parents, the maimed, the sick and the dying. I think of husbands, I think of wives— all these are my concern. It is for this reason that I sincerely pray that the beginning of the new year may be a time for every one of us, not only on both sides of the conflict but also in the world at large, to take stock. It is incumbent upon all to dedicate themselves anew to the efforts of peace, to the alleviation of human sufferings, and to the creation of an atmosphere of peace, progress and happiness. We must not forget that history will be the final judge.

No matter what people may say or do, future progress and permanent peace lie only through three things —cease-fire, relief of suffering, and negotiations for a peaceful settlement.

The current war of genocide, I repeat, will continue to deepen bitterness and frustrate aspects of harmony unless immediately brought to an end. Every day of delay hardens attitudes, deepens bitterness, and creates obstacles to peace. We must all seize the opportunity of the New Year and this season of good will and peace to cut our losses while sanity still remains.

As for us Biafrans, we stand, in spite of all provocations, all deprivations, all misrepresentations, slanders, and libels, for peace. We do this not because we are in doubt of ultimate victory and survival, but because of our genuine consideration for humanity.

End of Year Message, 1968

THE COURSE FOR PEACE

For us, a just solution would be a solution based on a recognition of our right to self-determination. As a prerequisite to this, we think a cease-fire is necessary. No matter what we do, no matter how long this war rages, eventually its settlement must be around a mahogany table. We have always believed in this. Even if the Nigerians took over every town and village of Biafra, sooner or later a group of people from this side and a group from the other would have to get around a mahogany table and hammer out a settlement.

The vandals would like very much to force Biafra into a surrender. We are fighting a war, and I suppose that is a way of looking at it. But that cannot solve this particular question, which is one of rejection, as I said before. If they take the towns and the villages, we will take to the bushes. And if they come after us into the bushes, they will need a huge army to garrison the whole area—about one soldier per man in Biafra—to ensure that we behave the way the Nigerians would want us! The whole purpose of the war is, of course, to maintain the economic integrity of the old Nigerian unit. Even this cannot be forced on an unwilling people.

What sort of life, what sort of commerce, can go on in Biafra with 14,000,000 people rejecting the Nigerians? What sort of safety can anybody who comes here to work enjoy? Inevitably, this problem will have to be negotiated. Only on this basis, provided the other is willing, can we have a solution.

Interview with Dutch, Canadian, and Danish
parliamentarians and accompanying journalists,
Umuahia, November 13, 1968

If we agree in principle that a cease-fire is necessary, then it is a conference talking point. I personally have not held a meeting with my advisers to work out our own details. Therefore, what I say are my own individual feelings. As an individual, I believe there is no question of a cease-fire on the present lines unless the enemy pulls back to the boundaries proclaimed Biafra. Perhaps in conversation and discussion while you are here you may find other views. But I think a worthwhile conference can be held very quickly.

> Meeting with Lord Brockway and
> Mr. James Griffiths, British (Labour) M.P.,
> Umuahia, December 10, 1968

I believe the Nigerians are tired. Their continuing to fight right now is by reflex: having got into the war, they continue fighting. I believe also that because they continue to get the flow of arms they feel they have not much to lose by continuing. The arms are coming in. If they throw the arms in and they do not win, they will cause more destruction at least. They will continue, therefore, to try whatever they have. Until the arms supply stops, I do not think the Nigerians will stop. The Nigerians would like, if possible, to find a way out of this. This is why I insist very much on this question of cease-fire. I believe that once there is a cease-fire, it will be very difficult, in fact impossible, to restart hostilities again.

I believe that the points of negotiation would range around economic matters. Nigeria has her fears, and in a way they are genuine fears. They are probably worried about their national debt. They are probably worried about their contractual obligations for certain economic projects entered into even prior to the dissolution of the Federation. They are possibly worried about the vacuum created by the exodus of the highest quality manpower in the former Federation. These are points that I am sure, in reverse, as it were, they would want to discuss.

I think also, because of our colonial experience and

the fact that we jointly built our vehicles of commerce, the roads, the ports and so on, they would probably like a discussion on these points in order to be more definitive about their use. Territorially, we would like to establish exactly what is in fact Biafra. This would obviate the continued necessity, we hope, of border skirmishes. I think there will be discussion about Biafra west of the Niger. I think, too, because of the great deal of confusion emanating from the way this war began, there would be a necessity of definition of citizenship. Who is a Nigerian? Who is a Biafran? These are important matters. But you will notice that most of these matters are matters with deep-rooted emotional attachment. It is for this reason that I prefer a cooling-off period to enable us to look at the matters objectively.

Interview with a delegation sponsored by the
American Committee to Keep Biafra Alive,
Umuahia, January 21, 1969

Peace-Keeping Force

The composition of a peace-keeping force must be mutually agreed. Their control must be mutually agreed. Deployment must be mutually agreed, and finally the only organization that I see in the present circumstance that can look after all the forces, and that will be acceptable to us, is probably that of the United Nations. Unless, of course, both sides can agree on just one force. We would, of course, like to see that in the peace-keeping force no contingent comes from countries that have openly shown themselves to be against Biafra. We would like to be involved in the control of the peace-keeping force. We would like, before the arrival of the peace-keeping force, to have agreed on a prescribed method of getting that peace-keeping force to withdraw. These are essentials for any discussion on a peace-keeping force.

The United Nations is the only organization with a large enough peace-keeping force. I wonder if after two years of fighting we can get agreement on any one country. Local control would involve the warring parties. If the force comes from one country, a committee of three would be necessary, and will sit permanently during the period that force is in position.

Meeting with Lord Brockway and
Mr. James Griffiths, British (Labour) M.P.,
Umuahia, December 4, 1968

Plebiscite or Referendum

I am willing to accept the fact that the peoples on both sides have not formally been asked to say whether they like to stay in Biafra or to go with Nigeria. I am aware of this, and I have suggested often enough that perhaps the answer would be to get an international organization which would devise the fairest means of ascertaining the people's wishes and then for the people to be left to decide.

I am also willing to accept that I came here, as it were, by accident, and that perhaps the mandate given to me by the Consultative Assembly should be retested. I am willing, therefore, once there is a cessation of hostilities, that there should be a time lag to enable both sides to go to the people, for the people to vote and get their true representatives out to decide their future. Whatever it is that is suggested, I am willing to accept. Let the other side do the same.

But if you examine both sides you will find that it is easier to believe that the minorities support this government than it is to believe that they don't. I say this because on our side there is constant consultation with the entirety of the people. *Today, for example, there will be a Consultative Assembly meeting. Nigerians have never had one since January 15, 1966, and there does not appear to be any intention of their ever holding one.*

Meeting with Stephen Lewis, Canadian M.P.,
Umuahia, February 10, 1969

The government and people of Biafra believe that the only acceptable form of rule is that deriving from the will of the people. The principle of self-determination for all peoples is the foundation of a stable government, be it democratic or totalitarian.

Biafra has proposed that where there is any genuine doubt as to the wishes of any people to remain in Biafra or Nigeria, a plebiscite should be held.

Claims have been made from Lagos that it is their moral responsibility to look after the interests of the so-called minorities in Biafra. But it is those very people who cannot stand the sight of their troops and have had to run into refugee camps in areas not within reach of Nigerian troops. Even the British Broadcasting Corporation's Nigerian correspondent, Mr. Peter Stewart, was recently forced to admit this fact when he described his experience around Uyo where natives were seen to come in to harvest their crops and then run back into Biafran-held areas.

International press conference,
Umuahia, January 18, 1968

We know who the Biafrans are. Unfortunately, during the period of a military regime, all these areas cannot be accepted as truly represented in our consultations. We have therefore suggested a plebiscite. I say there is no established policy because nobody has since really made the suggestion, really taken it up, and so we have never considered it in detail. But we are quite certain [of the result of such a plebiscite] and will continue to offer a plebiscite. Let the people somehow indicate their wishes; get outside organizations to supervise or to conduct it. We know the Biafrans, and certainly they will vote to remain together.

Nigeria, on the other hand, has consistently said there would be no plebiscite, there was no need for it, and so we have this impasse. I am sure there can be other ways. In fact, some months ago I proposed elections. First, civilianize the governments. Let the representatives of the people come in on both sides and then decide on what the people want. This, again, the Nigerians refused. Any impartial means of determining the wishes of the people, we will accept.

Interview with the American Committee to Keep
Biafra Alive, Umuahia, January 21, 1969

Commonwealth of Biafra and Nigeria

What I mean is a commonwealth that specifies the two countries, with the nature of their relationship to be negotiated and defined at the conference table. What makes this commonwealth? It is the commonwealth as we know it, the British Commonwealth, or some other form of commonwealth. All these are negotiable at the conference table. It is really the degree of cooperation between the two peoples that matters.

There are certain things that experience has taught us not to risk. If I may, I will talk about those things a little bit. We have seen what an armed force jointly owned but not controlled by us can do to our people. We cannot want to put ourselves in a position where there is argument on a matter such as this. We have seen how useless it is to call for independent international organizations to come to our assistance in the time of trouble [waves of pogroms in former Nigeria]. We would never again want to place ourselves in a position where we cannot, as soon as there is a sign of danger, call on these organizations to take note and to assist if need be.

Meeting with British Members of Parliament,
Michael Barnes and Alexander Lyon,
Umuahia, February 12, 1969

Any political arrangement must be such as to assure Biafrans absolute control of their internal and external security, including an independent international identity to prevent a repetition of the gruesome events of the recent past and to ensure that any such acts are brought to the attention of the international community without delay. Nigeria, under the plea of domestic jurisdiction, has successfully prevented the world community from taking any effective action for peace and security.

Message to the American Committee to Keep
Biafra Alive, New York, December 7, 1968

Economic Cooperation

We have always said that the end of the struggle would come with economic cooperation between the two countries. It sounds odd in view of the bitterness and emotional upheaval engendered by this war. People who have come here have been startled by the lack of bitterness that one finds in Biafra. We faced the struggle and have not dissipated our energies in bitterness. You will find among our people a high degree of charity toward even individuals known to be actively against us.

My attitude has always been that whether we like it or not, Nature has put us geographically side by side with Nigeria. The only way for the two countries to remain side by side is to remain good neighbors. We cannot opt out of this area; neither can they. If we continue fighting we can only destroy whatever little we have. I believe that soon after the war and once we have turned our minds to reconstruction, we will seek mutual accommodation in economic fields. As an individual, it is quite clear to me that if the emotions of this war are carried beyond the war, the actions will be tantamount to cutting off one's nose to spite one's face.

We are dealing with human beings, and it is possible that economic association cannot be entered into within one month of the end of the war or three months. In fact, I have suggested that in order to have meaningful talks that would bring us a lasting solution, the answer would be to halt the exchange of bullets in the battlefield, to have a cooling-off period before meeting face to face to discuss.

Meeting with delegation sponsored by the
American Committee to Keep Biafra Alive,
Umuahia, January 21, 1969

Nigeria has not solved the internal ills which brought about the birth of Biafra. Northern Nigeria has not really changed. It would only wish to separate if it cannot dominate the rest of Nigeria. Though restive, the Yorubas are not likely to disintegrate. There will be a lot of in-fighting among them.

As to the future of Nigeria, I believe it can become a stable federation if the leaders have learned the lesson of the last two years, but that is not yet evident. Economically, Nigeria can do without Biafra and must learn to do so. In the past, Nigeria was considered well off because she had cocoa, groundnuts, and other things; now, she has in addition a good source of electric power and oil. The problem with Nigeria has always been that her people were unwilling to work due to the ever-availability of Biafrans. They have the resources to be a great country if they now begin to work.

Meeting with delegates of Friends of
Biafra Association, Umuahia, March 18, 1968

Through its worldwide diplomatic machinery, originally established with our joint resources, Nigeria has succeeded in deceiving and blackmailing the world. The deceit and blackmail, rather surprisingly, seem to have gripped world conscience. While one can readily understand and appreciate the antics of ideological and economic imperialism, it is difficult to understand the attitude and antics of some of our sister African states. . . .

For our part, our stand is that our sovereignty is not negotiable. What we have done today by inaugurating this Court of Appeal should be further evidence to the world of our determination in this regard. . . . We shall regard no sacrifice, no price, too high to pay for our freedom. We shall continue the fight until our enemy—Nigeria—is vanquished and our sovereignty acknowledged and assured.

Inauguration of Biafra Court of Appeal,
December 8, 1967

THE INTERNATIONAL CONSPIRACY

Harold Wilson

Harold Wilson is the real obstacle to peace. His attitude and conduct throughout this war have shown that he regards Nigeria and Biafra as markets rather than countries, their peoples as chattel rather than human beings, inanimate, with no aspirations and pride. Harold Wilson's attitude in supporting the Nigerian war of genocide against our people has been as contemptuous and mean as it has been subjective and denigrating.

While arrangements for the abortive Addis Ababa peace negotiations were going on, Harold Wilson was busy with the Lagos junta, finalizing plans for a "quick kill" of the people of Biafra. He shipped to Nigeria by air and sea, and on an unprecedented scale, tons of the most sophisticated weapons for use against our people. The agreement by Nigeria to attend the Addis Ababa talks was nothing but a hoax. Harold Wilson's support for this conference was a mere alibi for a crime of murder.

Against mounting British disgust, Harold Wilson, as a diversion, proposed an international observer team, appointed its leader Major General Alexander, and announced it even before Lagos made public her decision to invite such a team. Alexander went to Lagos with clear orders—to whitewash the crime and to manipulate and obtain a report favorable to Mr. Harold Wilson.

Harold Wilson's latest trick has again been exposed by no other person than Major General Alexander himself. While addressing a meeting in London recently, he spoke of Wilson's plans for total victory for Nigeria by January, 1969. He spoke of Harold Wilson's plan for a massive "quick kill" which would necessitate, first, the complete destruction of our airports, the strengthening of the Nigerian air force with better pilots to facilitate this, and a further supply of armored vehicles from Britain and personnel to man them. He spoke of plans to mount more intensified propaganda, accusing me of being responsible for the starvation of our people. He spoke of advice to Gowon to abandon what is left of his Sandhurst days and to conduct the war with appropriate brutality and ruthlessness.

On the question of relief, Major General Alexander said it was the position of the British government and Nigeria to insist on a land corridor, which they knew might not be acceptable to us, in order to ensure further starvation which would then be blamed on me personally, at the same time ensuring the success of their military operations. He spoke of the quick end to the conflict, after which all relief would be handed over to the Nigerian government for distribution by the Nigerian Red Cross. As a necessary preparation for this, Major General Alexander flew to Geneva on Friday, December 20, 1968, in a bid to get the World Council of Churches to hand over their relief program to the International Committee of the Red Cross. Finally, he indicated that he would soon be going back to Nigeria to supervise the final operations. As I speak to you now, this plan is gathering momentum.

I have throughout this statement referred to Harold Wilson as an indication of our conviction that he is the real enemy of the defenseless Biafran people. I say this with full knowledge that the public in Britain do not support him.

The Labour Party and its executives do not support Harold Wilson.

The Labour Parliamentary group does not support Harold Wilson.

His Cabinet, judging from private utterances of its members, does not support Harold Wilson.

The Church in England does not support Harold Wilson. Russia cannot support Harold Wilson.

The United States in reviewing its policy is not convinced of Harold Wilson.

Europe does not support Harold Wilson.

Nigeria does not support Harold Wilson.

Men, women, and children, the maimed and the un-
maimed, the sick and the dying, the fit and the fighting
in Biafra, do not, and cannot, support Harold Wilson.

Humanity does not support Harold Wilson.

The Almighty God, surely, must have to abandon
Harold Wilson.

End of Year Message, 1968

Nigeria

It is quite clear Nigeria does not want to negotiate.
Gowon says tie your hands, truss yourself up, roast
yourself, garnish yourself, serve yourself up to me, and
I will talk peace. I will not be hungry. . . .

International press conference, Aba,
April 22, 1968

I was never convinced that Nigeria was prepared for
peace. Nigeria is only a pawn. Nigeria is a puppet.
Whitehall holds the strings. You pull one string, the
arm jerks up. You pull another, the leg goes up, and
so on. Nigeria has no initiative of its own.

As your illustrious administrator [Professor Eyo Bas-
sey Ndem] has said, this war will end and peace will
come only when Harold Wilson's administration decides that there should be peace or that the war should
end.

Response to an address by Efik community,
Umuahia, June 11, 1968

The main obstacles to a peaceful settlement have
come from the Nigerian attitude of belligerence, lack
of faith in agreements mutually reached, and the backing of the British government, which has claimed to
be committed to the principle of "founding a federal
Nigeria." Wrong premises have been adduced to support the argument that the territorial integrity of Nigeria must be maintained, no matter the cost in human
lives. The recent utterances by British government

spokesmen, notably Lord Shepherd and Mr. Thompson, clearly indicate that the British government has still not altered its colonialist attitude, which places no premium on African lives if it means compromising its own selfish economic interests. They have stated that they will continue to support Nigeria so long as there is no "unnecessary" destruction of lives, and that they will stop supplying arms to Lagos only when there is a "catastrophe."

Nigeria sees the pogrom, the expulsion of Biafrans from Nigeria, the economic blockade, sanctions and other hostile acts against Biafrans, as steps in the final military solution of the "Ibo" problem, that is, the extermination of 14,000,000 Biafrans. Thus the obstacles in the way of peace may be summarized as follows:

1. The British government's desire to maintain her economic dominance over the single Nigeria she had created and her open support and encouragement of Gowon by:
   (a) continued supply of arms to Nigeria;
   (b) economic, diplomatic, and propaganda offensives on behalf of Nigeria;
   (c) dishonest representation of the facts to the British Parliament and public.
2. Nigeria's intransigence, which has resulted in:
   (a) her refusal to agree to a cease-fire;
   (b) her insistence that Biafra must renounce her sovereignty and accept a twelve-state structure created without consultation of the people or their representatives;
   (c) her provocative request in the twelve-point proposal at Kampala for virtual surrender;
   (d) her continued rejection of all appeals and blackmailing of reasonable African heads of state and international organizations.
3. Russia's ambition to establish a communist sphere of influence in West Africa. Consequently, Russia, Britain, and the United States of America—countries with diametrically opposed ideologies—are competing to maintain an influence in Nigeria by supplying arms for the genocide of Biafrans.
4. The unrealistic attitude of the Organization of African

Unity. The OAU had the unique opportunity of proving to the world and to the member states that African independent countries were capable not only of ruling themselves but also of solving African problems. The OAU Mediation Committee failed because of its unrealistic approach of attempting to solve an African problem in an un-African manner. Until a couple of days ago they had not indicated their willingness to to listen to both sides in the dispute.

5. The United Nations, which has turned a blind eye to evident genocide. The United Nations Organization, whose charter on human rights empowers it to intercede in cases of genocide, refused to accept Biafra's application for intercession to halt Nigeria's genocidal war against Biafra.

In spite of all these obstacles to peace, Biafra has offered peace terms which, if accepted, would achieve a lasting peace in this part of Africa. These proposals are:

(i) immediate cessation of fighting on land, sea, and air. We are prepared to discuss with Nigeria the terms rather than the conditions for a cease-fire;

(ii) immediate removal of the economic blockade mounted by Nigeria against Biafra;

(iii) the withdrawal of troops to behind the prewar boundaries to enable refugees to return to their homes.

With regard to (i), cessation of fighting, Biafra will agree to:

(a) the policing of the cease-fire line by an international force, the composition of which must be agreed to by both sides;

(b) a supervisory body, the composition and power of which are to be agreed, which will be stationed in the areas from which troops are withdrawn to ensure that the local population are not in any way victimized.

With regard to (ii), the removal of the blockade, we shall be ready, if it is agreed, to accept the supervision at points of entry into Nigeria and Biafra to ensure that there is no arms buildup by either side while talks on arrangements for a permanent settlement continue. The aim should be to restore civilian life and administration back to normal in the war-ravaged areas as soon as possible. Biafra is still willing to discuss:

(i) maximum economic cooperation and common services with Nigeria;

(ii) problems relating to the sharing of assets and liabilities (including the external public debt) of the former Federation of Nigeria;

(iii) problems relating to the payment of compensation for the lives and property of Biafrans which were lost during the pogrom and as a result of the war;

(iv) the holding of a plebiscite in the disputed areas inside and outside Biafra to determine the true wishes of the people.

Address to international press,
February 18, 1968

The position of the United States in this struggle until now has been, to say the least, quite puzzling. I think that it would not be fair to talk about government policy, for the U.S. has not considered the problem as such: that is the puzzling aspect of it. Whatever the position of the U.S. government, it is a position merely by default.

I think also that the U.S. has, and that is not the first time, let herself into a wrong policy as a result of a peculiar "most favored friend" relationship between herself and Britain. I do not think the Johnson administration actually studied this problem, and therefore the first thing I think the new American administration should do is to study the problem objectively.

I think the next contribution, which would have a startling effect in this struggle, is for the U.S. government, without even going into the merits and demerits of the struggle, to call for peace. For the U.S. to say that this is an internal matter or an African matter is a dereliction of duty.

What else can the American government do? The American government has tremendous influence in the world, particularly in Africa, where governments look up to her for leadership. I think that, should the United States government find that as a people we have a right to exist on God's earth and should they have the courage to say so, the whole of Africa would probably come to reason. If having studied the case, the Americans really feel that the long-term interest of America lies with our survival and the American government recognizes that fact, the war would come to an end.

Talking to a friend last night, I said that perhaps the most dramatic way of halting this fight would be a statement, on the lines of the famous De Gaulle declaration, from the American administration without blame but recognizing all basic principles, such as that of a people to self-determination. A statement of that nature would probably bring this war to a grinding halt.

Interview with the American Committee to Keep
Biafra Alive, Umuahia, January 21, 1969

VI

On the Nation and the State

LEADERSHIP

A number of people have said that Ojukwu is the leader of the secessionists. I am no leader in the right sense of it. Indeed, what I have become, in this struggle, is the mouthpiece of my people. I go where they push and no more. The day I think otherwise, the day I act otherwise, that day my people, without compromising the struggle, will find another person to express their aspirations.

Interview with Canadian and Dutch
parliamentarians and accompanying journalists,
November 13, 1968

. . . To be a good leader, you must serve the people. The day a leader becomes a slave to the people (God bless him!) he is not worthy of the leadership. He must stand uncompromisingly for right and justice at the expense of losing his leadership. This is what I call true greatness. If you compromise justice, then justice becomes politics, and for a society this would be catastrophic. This is what people mean by the loneliness of a leader, because at that point of time the leader stands alone to decide. At every stage you will be pitching your leadership against the challenge of injustice, and each time you break through you succeed.

If what you are doing is right, it should bear complete light of day. Your actions and motives should be searched by anybody who wants to. If you are not found wanting, you will emerge more confident. I really do have that confidence. Call it naïve. I like it that way. Some do talk about martyrdom for everybody. Martyrdom for everybody? No. A leader should have a pronounced streak of martyrdom.

If a leader accepts himself as already dead to society, there will be no reason for cowardice in his leadership. One thing that frightens leaders and leads them to a number of excesses is usually fear of death. No leader should fear death. In fact, you should accept the fact that from the moment of leadership you are sacrificed to death. Each subsequent day becomes a bonus for the preparation of one's memorial. This is my own idea of leadership.

Discussion at the Biafra People's Seminar,
Umuahia, February 16, 1969

How does one respond personally to the sight of victims of air raids, starving kids, and elders? I suppose an answer to this will give psychiatrists plenty to analyze. But, generally, what does one feel? What does a human being feel when you see misery? What do you feel when you see a baby six months old with a limb cut off? A market woman with her legs shattered? I went to Aba Government Hospital to see the effect of that massive bombing in Aba township. I think "shock" is the word to describe my feeling. Yes, one feels numb. There is nothing you can do. It is so final. For a time you move from body to body; this is what happens to me. You really don't know what you are thinking of— the pictures are just registering in your mind. This is unfortunate because later it all comes back in such rapid succession all too soon—the look on the faces.

I remember one very clearly—a head separated from the body. The head looked restless. In my position, I wonder: Am I really responsible? What could I have done? Could I have stopped it? I come to the inescapable answer that I really could not, and then anger starts. That means, you first find peace for yourself and then you look forward. You get very angry. You wish that you could do something. Then you think of your limited resources. You go out, you put on a bright face and try to make people forget their miseries. You get them again to think about the real reasons for this war. Generally, our people, and I suppose they are not different from any other, pick up from where they left off. At the end of it all, when I have gone through all these mental processes, I come out with a stronger determination—a determination that this will never again occur to our people with impunity. That is how I feel. I know the process—the numbness, the thought wondering whether or not it is my fault, coming out, putting on a bright face, and then the determination. It seems to be the process . . . every time.

International press conference,
Umuahia, February 13, 1969

Right now, I think, what I would most like of the Biafrans is a stronger determination in their minds to wage this war, to conduct this struggle and as true Biafrans. I have found that in the past we have done very well, but I feel we could have done much better. I would like the Biafran to look again at himself and perhaps to recognize the fact that he has been fighting this war against Nigeria as a Nigerian. His attitude of mind, his approach to problems, has been completely Nigerian, and that has tended to inhibit the pace of his success. If the Biafran would as a result of this become more progressive, more critical of certain things that happened within our society, then I think I should have had the best gift of all for this time. I don't think you want me to go into details.

I have been talking quite a bit about this for the past, say, three weeks. I feel that there is a lot of room for improvement. I feel that our attitude to the Biafran revolution is very much wanting generally. I feel that the Biafran is still very much attracted by money. I feel that his sense of values is not yet fully in tune with the revolution. I feel also that his sense of priorities is not yet in tune with the new age—the new Biafra. If the Biafran wants to give me a gift it is to give me a change of heart, a heart more critical of himself.

As a people, the Biafrans have shown themselves to be very courageous. Their solidarity has been stupendous. They have shown basically that they do understand what it means to be men. They have shown loyalty to themselves and to outsiders. The only fault is that our people have not really educated themselves sufficiently for the new age. Now as an individual I feel very proud and honored. My job has been very simple. I don't even have to initiate any new policies. I get, as it were, pushed ahead by the voice of our people, and I have found that this voice has always been the right course. It has not led us to any mistakes.

The youth normally are great pioneers. The youth of this country feel a sense of identity with me; personally, I think not just because of my age—thirty-five —but arising from our identity of attitudes to problems. The youths want a change. They have wanted this change for some time, and it appears to them that here is an opportunity to have the change. They have usually been very critical and I want to think that I haven't let them down. For me I feel the youth have been perhaps the biggest support this government has had. And so it should be, because when all is said and done, this struggle is their struggle. The future one talks about is the future of the young.

What worries me is what the future holds for our future generation. I think that the youths recognize this and they want to be completely involved in mapping out their future. They support this government because the government does give them the opportunity to do just that.

I have refused to be promoted to ranks higher than lieutenant colonel* when I promoted others to ranks of colonels, brigadiers, and major generals, because I don't really think I deserve the promotion. I don't know what you think. But everybody that has been promoted so far merits it. I have seen these officers conduct campaigns. I have seen them resist the enemy with nothing. I have admired their courage. I have admired their ability to organize men, and I think in every way they merit their promotions. For myself, I have continued to look to see whether I do merit it. In this matter, I am afraid I have to be the sole judge and up until now, I don't think I do. I might merit promotion in the field of politics. I have done certain things militarily, but I don't think that those are enough for military promotion.

Gowon and his collaborators have consistently accused me of being ambitious and wanting to have an empire of my own. It is through sheer providence that I find myself head of state of the Republic of Biafra. I had planned out my life hoping that after a few more years in the army I would then retire. In fact, I had hoped to retire at the age of thirty-five to join my father in business.

I came to the then Eastern Region by way of duty. As an army officer I was posted to assume special duties in the Eastern Region. I accepted and went. Ever since, I have tried to do my duty to the best of my ability.

As to ambition, certainly I am ambitious. Every living man ought to be ambitious. Any man without ambitions can only end up being like Gowon. A medi-

---

* *Text of Resolution No. 13 passed at the Joint Meeting of Elders and Chiefs and Consultative Assembly in the recaptured City of Owerri on 1st May, 1969:* Since out of modesty and personal consideration our respected and gallant Head of State Lt. Colonel C. Odumegwu Ojukwu, has not seen to the implementation of our previous resolution in these terms, we hereby unanimously confer on him on behalf of this Republic, the rank and title of General of the Biafran Army.

ocrity at best, a nonentity, as has been so plainly obvious to us in the past two years. No, I am ambitious. I am ambitious for the freedom of our people. I am ambitious to see our people out of bondage. I am ambitious to protect the lives of our people—the men, women and children that make up the 14,000,000 people of Biafra. I am ambitious to indicate the way to progress for the 14,000,000 people. I am ambitious to establish that the African can do what his white counterpart can do. I am certainly ambitious as a black man, to arrive at the stage where I would be considered by every living human being as a man. I don't think there is anything wrong with ambition. One thing I am not ambitious for is blood. I am not ambitious for destruction. I don't want to make a name by the enormity of my crime and by committing genocide. In one sentence, I am ambitious for good.

I think my good health is certainly 70 percent attributable to God and His protection. The other 30 percent comes from my own inner satisfaction that what I am doing is something that has to be done, comes from my own conviction of ultimate victory, comes from my intimate and detailed knowledge of the true state of affairs which at least enables me to avoid being harassed as many people are by unfounded rumors, and finally, from the solicitude of my wife and family.

Interview with national press and information
media, Umuahia, November 4, 1968

THE GOVERNMENT

The military regime has been in power for eighteen months. It is not normally the function of the armed forces to govern but to defend their country. We must therefore begin to think of putting into motion the machinery which will restore civilian rule so that the armed forces can revert to their role in the life of the nation. The military government of Biafra has already taken the first steps in this direction by appointing civilians to the Executive Council, to the Provincial Executive Committee, and as provincial administrators. The process of injection into the government of civilians of proven ability and integrity will continue.

A Constitutional Drafting Committee will soon be appointed to work on the recommendations of the Consultative Assembly and to produce a draft constitution for the approval of the Assembly. Thereafter, a Constituent Assembly will be elected to approve the draft constitution and work out the procedure for the handover of power to civilians. An electoral roll will then be prepared which will form the basis for the election of the Chief Executive of the Republic and members of the national and provincial legislative bodies.

At every stage the army will ensure that the elections are free and fair. It is envisaged that all the processes for the return to civilian rule will be completed within eighteen months from the commencement of the program.

Address to the convocation of the University
of Biafra, Nsukka, July 1, 1967

How does your government function during this war? How does Biafra live and breathe during this whole experience? How do you run the everyday job of government in this war? How do you preserve government in some of the villages? Is there a representation of all the people in your government during this war?

In replying to these questions, one has to trace the evolution of our present government to understand what is happening and why it has been possible. This area was a self-governing region in the old Nigeria. On January 15, 1966, there was an attempted coup in Lagos. This coup affected the senior of the five governments of the federation. Personnel-wise, it affected also members of government in Lagos, in the West and in the North. The remnants of that senior government took a quick decision and handed over government to the army in order to bring about stability. The army then invited the armed forces. The change was an orderly transition, it was not a coup, because if you remember, those who conducted that coup were rounded up and imprisoned. There was then no necessity for a formal recognition of the post-January 15 government. International verdict accepted that it was an orderly transition.

Another coup came in July, 1966, and with it a government which had tried not to unite the country but only to centralize its administration. To achieve complete success, the coup should have overthrown the five governments of the Federation: it took over the government of the West and garrisoned the West, but it did not take over the Midwest; it did not even affect the East (now Biafra). This coup was inspired from the North. The North was in control of the mutineers. So you had Northern Nigeria, Lagos (the capital city), and Western Nigeria effectively controlled by the rebels. The time between that and Aburi was utilized by the head of the rebels, that is Gowon, in trying to complete his unfinished coup. Antagonistic world opinion made it really impracticable for him to continue the bloody orgy. Gowon, after the sudden action of the coup, set about trying to cajole the rest of the Federation into submission. He got to a position where Midwestern Nigeria was not quite sure of itself. Quite early I made it clear that I would not accept the legality of the coup in the region under my control. I made that very clear to him. I was not prepared to be cajoled, and when it appeared as though this would cause greater bloodshed we tried to get some negotiation. This I know is a different story, but what I am driving at is the evolution of the government here.

I was left with the Eastern Region still intact, that is, the self-governing Eastern Nigeria still intact. We now had to negotiate a *modus vivendi* with the Nigerian central government. We had to because we had certain reservations and would no longer accept everything that went on before. We had suffered a great deal, but our administration was intact, our leadership remained intact, in fact the only new element was myself. At a certain stage when Lagos proved quite impossible to deal with and when the junta would not be reasonable, I summoned the Consultative Assembly. I'll have to explain.

Because of the fact that no coup ever succeeded in overrunning the former Eastern Nigeria, I did not at any stage really impose a military government on this area. It was not necessary. While believing that we could form a central administration and forge unity, I felt that unity must be based on willingness and therefore it had to be fully discussed and agreed. It was while arguing on this that the July, 1966, coup occurred. After that coup and my rejection of Gowon, I had to seek a basis for the administration in the Eastern Region.

The Parliament had been disbanded. A number of the leaders were discredited. I had to find new leadership here, and the first thing I did therefore was to set up the Consultative Assembly, which has in fact wider representation than in the political days. This then became, as it were, our legislative body, though it was advisory, for all our own legislation.

We continued with this until after Aburi and it became clear that we were sliding down into war. Then I began to give thoughts to an Executive for Biafra. I did not relinquish the powers I held as military governor, but I set up a council which was advisory, and this was a civilian council. This became significant later as a result of the transition from a military to civilian rule. Many people did not realize this. When our problem with Gowon got to crisis point, the accredited representatives of our people met in joint session with the Council of Chiefs and Elders and there mandated me to do a series of things if Lagos did not do certain things. This is my mandate. From then the choice was open—to derive power from Lagos or to derive power from my people. My first action was an acceptance of the people's sovereignty. This I accepted and carried out their wishes. From then the government in Biafra technically became fully a civilian government.

By evolution it turned out to be a form which is nearer the American pattern than the Westminster pattern. I did not choose new people, but I widened the Executive Council and appointed more civilians. In the Executive Council there are 28 people—24 appointees from the various provinces and my 3 advisers and the Chief of General Staff. What emerges is an executive on top and the legislature. Our administration continued completely undisrupted, and the judiciary was, of course, intact. From this it was easy to continue as near normal as possible.

Before the split from Nigeria it became clear to me that perhaps the most important question was the question of the various minorities. I set up a committee entirely composed of the minorities, headed by Okoi Arikpo (now Nigerian Commissioner for External Affairs), to let me know what they would wish for themselves, what type of association they would wish with the center in the regional context. They produced a paper which, I am glad, needed no amendment. The original is still there, signed by Arikpo. I can now remember the ovation in the house when I reported that I accepted Arikpo's report without modification. From that point onward we got real cohesion.

Another asset has been Gowon himself. His attitude to the minorities in this war has been such that it has really made the minorities, rather than look the other way, look more to this side. At the beginning of the war I would have said that probably I had around 70 percent of the minorities; right now, without fear of contradiction, I can say that I have 90 percent support. Out of the 10 percent left I would say 8 percent are on the other side.

If you ask me what gives me the feeling that such a high percentage support me, considering that before the war the minorities were considered anti-Ibo, I hope that it will be enough to say that I get reports weekly from Calabar, or that I get reports from Ogoja once a week, and that right through, our people are meeting and sending reports about the imposed vandal administration. That people from the so-called minority areas are still sending money here to be exchanged for them. That people are running away from the Nigerian-held areas and coming to this side.

I can go on, but I am always so aware of my position in this struggle and realize that the more cynical will say: "What do you expect him to say?" I have looked at the minority problem and have noted the high passions it generates. So I am prepared to throw it back again to the people and let them decide. I suggested a referendum. I am not just saying a referendum that I will organize. I accept a third party that will set up the rules and present them to both of us to amend and accept. I accept that a third party should supervise the exercise and present results to both of us. Naïve? No, confidence.

I am even willing to concede that a man with a rifle in his hands is a very persuasive man. I am willing to throw away the rifle and say to the people, all the people—including the minority people—"Choose for yourselves your representatives provided Gowon will do so on the other side." I agree that those representatives should negotiate and decide their own future. I am also prepared to listen to any other formula for ascertaining the people's true wishes, and, if eminently fair, I will accept. This I believe is the real way to find out, instead of arguments that will never resolve anything except to create delay while more and more people are being killed.

Interview with Marvin Kupfer, of *Newsweek* magazine, and David Robison, a United States free-lance journalist, Umuaha, February 13, 1969

Our sovereignty is complete in every sense of the word. In fact, from August 1, 1966, when Gowon usurped power in Lagos, to our Declaration of Sovereignty on May 30, 1967, the government of then Eastern Nigeria consistently refused to recognize the illegal regime in Lagos. And no law enforcement agencies within our territory took cognizance of any Decree promulgated by the Lagos junta. The latest Decree of Gowon and his Lagos military junta creating states in the Republic of Biafra is not only a futile gesture but also has been ignored by the people with feelings of insult from, and contempt for, Lieutenant Colonel Gowon.

Since our proclamation of sovereignty the 14,000,000 people who inhabit the 29,400 square miles of our territory have not only expressed but demonstrated their unswerving allegiance to the government of the Republic. Our civil service, the armed forces, the police, and the judiciary have all taken their oath of allegiance to our government and obey only its laws and decrees. All sections of the people, including the traditional chiefs, elders, the working class, farmers and traders, have not only openly and willingly pledged their allegiance to the government of the Republic but have also made voluntary and substantial contribution and sacrifices toward the defense of the Republic and the maintenance of our sovereignty. Within our territory our sovereignty is unhindered and unfettered by any external forces. No foreign jurisdiction is exercised in the Republic of Biafra, and no appeals from our courts lie anywhere outside our well-defined territorial boundaries.

The peace which reigns within our borders can only surprise and baffle our detractors, who have spared no pains to undermine our solidarity. As is demonstrated in a recent publication of my government entitled *Introducing the Republic of Biafra*, we, the people of this nation, have lived peacefully side by side for more than 2,000 years. During this period we have traded together, intermarried, and acquired the cultural traits of one another. We recognize the fact of our interdependence and common destiny. We would no doubt have emerged, in due course, as a nation-state but for the advent of colonial rule which retarded this logical and natural development. As was the case elsewhere, the partition of Africa around the conference tables of Europe had lumped our emerging nation with others of different religion and culture generally in order to satisfy the interests of the powers concerned. The willingness of the peoples involved to coexist was not sought; indeed, that consideration was ignored. Nor did the colonial policies adopted in many cases encourage the emergence of a common national outlook within the artificially created countries. The period of colonial rule, in any event, was too short to break age-long loyalties, traditions, and affiliations.

With the removal of the imperial mold, cracks naturally appeared in the structures. In some cases, where a measure of willingness to live together had been achieved and a national outlook had developed, the cracks were minimal and the structure held together. But in others, notably in the former Federation of Nigeria, which has one of the biggest and certainly the most populous and complex of the political agglomerations in Africa, the colonial boundaries have had to be readjusted in the light of historical experience, so as to avoid perpetual strife and bloodshed.

Our strength, therefore, lies in the indisputable fact that upholding our unique oneness we had the courage to take the irrevocable step out of the British creation called Nigeria. By taking this bold, resolute, and irrevocable step Biafrans have called into being the first nation-state in Africa carved out by the indigenous people themselves from the political dispensations handed over by European powers.

> Address to the convocation of the University
> of Biafra, Nsukka, July 1, 1967

The Government is the servant of the people, not their master. I maintain that the people, being masters, delegate or give over some part of their authority to the government as one would give a certain part of one's property to one's servant to look after. This relationship between master and servant I consider very essential. Remember I said "servant" and not "slave." The servant has rights; so the people in leadership of government do have rights. Remember in this question of servant-master relationship that the servant is not a good servant unless he does certain things. Implicit in the term "servant" is the idea of preservation in good repair. This is very important to the idea of government, as I see it.

My view is that those entrusted with powers by the people must at all times strive to embellish that power. If you don't do so, then you are failing somewhere. And particularly in the Biafran society, I think that it is very important that we always realize that those placed in positions of leadership derive that leadership from the people, and their guiding light is always the consensus. I have said these things primarily to give you an idea of my attitude of mind.

From this, we have gone on to discuss Biafran people, the individual, the community. And I find that people so very easily do two things: (a) They point out the ills of society. Everyone would be quite willing to indicate the ills of our society. (b) Everyone would appear to be prepared to push everything onto the government.

I think this is a wrong attitude. Although the government is not saturated with hearing what it should do, I think, to maintain a balance, it is necessary for us to think really of our own individual contribution— what we should do as individuals for this new society. I know that you all like to see a new society. I presume that the type of society you want is something different from the one you knew in the old Federation of Nigeria. I should think that most of you would want to avoid things like corruption, bribery, nepotism, all the various things we have all talked about. We wouldn't like to see hoarding in our society. We wouldn't like to see indolence and inefficiency in our offices. To achieve this, we have to work very hard, and I am sure you

would like to see many changes made. But as soon as
I say to you, "How do we get over this?" immediately
you start telling me the government has to reform the
police; the government has to pass this law; the government has to punish such and such people. Is that really
the answer? How does the government deal with
14,000,000 people? If 14,000,000 people want to be corrupt, how does the government really stop them? Perhaps you may say it isn't logical. Right. If about 13,-
900,000 people want to be dishonest, how do the few
good ones in government set about correcting the re-
mainder? Near impossible. This in a way is what, in
fact, we have been saying to Gowon. This is the basis of
our fight. Gowon cannot make 14,000,000 people do
what they don't want to do. Now, having accepted this
guiding principle in our struggle, let us turn it to the
good of our own society. What do we find? We are told
so many things that government should do. How the
government should do this and that, and so I have
decided today to put this question around this way:
What does the individual do? I believe this is the more
important consideration. In any case, society is made
up of individuals. I believe that if every individual does
what he ought to do, the job of the government will be
a lot easier. . . .

Address at Biafra People's Seminar,
Umuahia, February 12, 1969

The Dictator

The Nigerian government is a classic example of a
complete military dictatorship. If Yakubu Gowon, whom
I know from the days when he was a junior officer
under my command, had been elected to his position
of power, one could rightly say that his determination
to beat Biafra represented the will of the people of
Nigeria. If he stood for all those things that Britain
holds dear—peace, justice, liberty, and democracy—
one could say that his course of action was for the best.

Gowon came to power following one of the bloodiest coups Africa has ever seen. With his full knowledge and approval, 380 officers and men of the federal army, whose opposition to him had been presumed before the act, were marched out of their barracks by their colleagues, put up against walls, and machine-gunned. Nor have twenty months in power moderated his way of dealing with opposition.

Democracy in Nigeria is out—once and for all. No meetings are allowed. No expression of opinion may be made that does not reflect his government's opinion. Justice is dead. The courts are suspended. Arrest is automatic for the slightest misdemeanor. Detention is frequent, without trial and often accompanied by savage beatings. When Nigeria's foremost playwright, Wole Soyinka, suggested in a letter to a newspaper that a solution to this war might be negotiated, he was picked up by the army, taken to a Lagos jail, and nearly beaten to death. When Peter Elstos of Hampstead, Secretary General of PEN, flew to Lagos to try and see Soyinka, he too came within an inch of a beating for not disclosing to the army the details of his talks with Cabinet ministers. Such is Nigeria today.

Gowon's regime is reminiscent of Vietnamese dictator Ngo Dinh Diem's regime in the early days. Like Ngo, he came to power with a gun in his hand and remains there by the same means. Like Ngo, he has railroaded his people into a war he claims they want, but for which they have no stomach. Like Ngo, he will not consider a negotiated peace because he thinks he can win in a short, sharp campaign. Like Ngo, he is heavily backed by Western big business because he claims he can extend the monopolistic mineral and produce concessions which enable the controlling strings of the Vietnamese economy to be pulled in Wall Street and the strings of the Nigerian economy to be pulled in Lombard and Cornhill. Like Ngo, he has put his economy in hock to buy arms for a war that could, and eventually must, be settled around a piece of polished mahogany. The only difference is that we are not Vietcong, we are not Communists, we do not want to take over one inch of another man's land or endanger another man's life. We just want to be left alone to live our lives in peace.

Letter to a British Member of Parliament,
March 12, 1968

PROVINCIAL SYSTEM AND MINORITIES

I have spoken earlier of the need to reorientate our attitudes and establish a new social and political order which will ensure an even development of the Republic. To this end the machinery of government has to be galvanized and streamlined to provide the conditions for the revolutionary change we envisage. I have already taken steps to implement the Provincial Administration Decree, which marks a new departure in the evolution of our political institutions. The objectives of the Decree, as stated in the government White Paper on the subject, are:

a. To eliminate the fear of domination;
b. To promote national unity by providing a halfway house between the provincial autonomy and complete unity;
c. To enable contiguous units to develop in their own environment while at the same time keeping pace with others under the umbrella of the national government; and
d. To provide an opportunity for even development throughout the Republic.

To attain these objectives the Decree devolves on the provinces' legislative and executive powers over the following subjects: local government and chieftaincy affairs; town and country planning; health and sanitation; education at primary and secondary levels (excluding the maintenance of standards); customary marriages and succession; markets; roads; water supply; agricul-

ture and fisheries; cooperatives; and local devclopment
gencrally. The national government will make available
the necessary funds to ensure that these functions are
successfully performed. Special subventions for the
rapid development of the less developed provinces will
be provided.

In the past there have been complaints in some sections of the Republic of neglect in the distribution of
amenities. The new system will remove the basis of
such complaints by enabling people to use their local
knowledge to tackle effectively the economic and social
problems posed by their environment. I am gratified
that the spirit of the new provincial administration system has been acclaimed everywhere in the Republic.

Address to the convocation of the University
of Biafra, Nsukka, July 1, 1967

The provincial system is perhaps the real savior of
Biafra in this crisis. Very earlier on, when it became
quite clear that our ideas were moving away from those
of Lagos, we had to look inward and try to cure our
own society.

The manner in which the provincial setup was introduced was quite simple. I threw it open to every community in the land and I asked them what they wanted.
And as it happened, my own original suggestion was
that we should have eight provinces. In the course of
the consultation, the number rose to thirteen. After further consultation and debates, the people and the Consultative Assembly finished up with twenty.

The great thing is that it does satisfy the people.
Here they have a government of their own, with their
own sons heading their local administration. We did not
call them states purely out of pride because Lagos has
done so much and talked so much about states. We
called them provinces. Having solved our minority
problem, we did not want to confuse issues by using
the same term as Lagos. That is the only reason why
they are not called states.

Their powers are wide—legislative and executive on matters that affect them in their own areas, matters of welfare. These are the points that used to cause friction.

How about scholarships? What is your education policy? What happens to money that is derived from the area? That sort of thing we have left to a large measure to the provinces.

By internationally accepted standards, one could really say that there are twenty states in Biafra. Even in the last Consultative Assembly before the proclamation of the sovereignty of Biafra, one of the resolutions was that I should proclaim the Republic and take steps to ensure that we have a federation of Biafra. I think when this occurs, it will be a tight federation, a true federation, one part never being able to dictate to the others. The provinces will be more or less the same size. They will have more or less the same potentials provided they work as hard as one other.

It will make for healthy competition, without those destructive tendencies of hoarding everything for oneself and without any turning its back on the others, because none is really big enough to stand on its own.

I look forward to the end of the war, when we can implement it fully.

Right now we have only got, as it were, the super-structure, just nucleus organizations. We have not really got down to the detailed implementation yet.

Interview with West German journalist,
Dr. Ruth Bowert, March 25, 1968

I am deeply touched by your expressions of loyalty, support, and solidarity. I am quite amazed by your generosity, particularly knowing, as I do, that as refugees things are not easy to come by. To be able, in the midst of all this, to raise this generous sum of £200 in itself is very symbolic of the support which the Efik community has throughout this struggle given to this government.

Some time ago when it was possible for me to visit

Calabar, I did say that perhaps the most loyal of the areas in Biafra was the Efik area. I have not changed from that. It is most unfortunate that the first action of the enemy in the early days before we were able to contain him was to strike at Calabar. Nevertheless, they are there, and I am glad that they are not having any joy. Every intelligence report points to the fact that the enemy is not having any joy in Calabar. They have committed a great number of atrocities. They have tried to force the locals into following them. Apart from a few Judases, the feeling of the Efik people has remained, even behind the enemy line and under enemy control, solidly loyal to Biafra.

If this were not so, there would be no need for the massive shipment of Efik people to Lagos. This is clearly as a result of the vandals' inability to control the area or to have support of the people.

Lagos talks about a twelve-state structure based on no known established wish of any people. We had the Calabar-Ogoja-Rivers state movement a long time ago. It later broke up into the Calabar state movement, Rivers and Ogoja movements, and so on. What the people want is quite clear. We had a minorities commission which investigated this problem and which established the various ethnic areas and their compatibility or otherwise. The Efiks never even said they wanted to remain with the Ibibios. And with all this, Gowon stays in Lagos and pontificates.

The problem, the real tragedy of the whole war, is that the Nigerian government has been so remote from the people they claim to rule that they just wallow in the sentiments of the past, and the ignorance of the leadership is such too that they can only pick on odd names they remembered from their childhood.

There is no such thing as a Calabar-Ogoja state. It means absolutely nothing. If Gowon were open to advice, the only advice I would give him is to try to just ask the people what they want. And it is for this reason, and with the confidence I have, that I said that as far as I am concerned, in any disputed area I am willing to accept an impartial plebiscite. Let the people decide. There is no attempt here in Biafra to impose. We did, with the best of our own knowledge, what the people wanted. We found out the wishes of the people. But if anybody feels that this is not complete, we are still willing to have a plebiscite. And I would like Gowon to try a plebiscite on his own side to find out the true wishes of the people. After all, that is the only basis of sovereignty.

Response to address by the Efik community,
Umuahia, June 11, 1968

There are no problems now between the minorities and the major tribes, or ethnic groups, in Biafra. Yet I am not so naïve as to believe that safeguards are not necessary, because ours is a new experiment. Today, without boasting, I suppose one thing is absolutely certain: As long as I am on the scene (and this is a personal attachment which the minorities have) there will be no problem. Their confidence, their faith, is personalized. I know this, but I think it is a necessary stage in the evolution of a type of cohesion which one needs for nation-building. It will be one of my prime duties to ensure that this becomes a permanent feature in our society, with or without me. When I have done that I have succeeded.

Interview with John Horgan of the Irish *Times*,
Umuahia, February 20, 1968

Having failed all around, the Nigerians have raised the bogey of a minority in Biafra being forced into independence against their wish. This again is far from the truth. Our people, irrespective of their ethnic grouping, have shown conclusively their commitment to, and support of, the territorial integrity and sovereignty of Biafra by their sacrifice in blood and contribution to the war effort.

The decision to declare the sovereign and independ-

ent state of Biafra was a unanimous one made by the
chiefs, leaders, and representatives of all communities
in Biafra at the Consultative Assembly and Council of
Chiefs and Elders. The so-called representatives of the
minorities in Lagos have never had any popular backing. They were defeated in elections in their own homes
during the civilian era and have since been denounced
by their own people. Some of them, like the Nigerian
Commissioner for External Affairs, Okoi Arikpo, are
themselves guilty of intellectual dishonesty, since they
were party to or sponsors of the constitutional proposals
creating the present provinces of the Republic of Biafra
in order to allay minority fears.

Our people know enough of Lagos and can testify
that the massacre of thousands of then Eastern Nigerians was irrespective of tribal affiliation. The bombing
and other military brutalities since Biafran independence have followed the same pattern. Having suffered
together, they are now united together in a solidarity
to fight on to victory to ensure a place of honor and
respect for themselves and their children.

Message to Biafran students in the United States
of America, November 24, 1967

I would like to touch on one other point which appears to have worried a great number of people, and
that is the question of minorities in our midst. There
are minority problems everywhere. I can see an example in Britain. In Britain, even with so many years of
togetherness, you still have the Welsh nationals. You
still have the Scottish nationals. The demand for home
rule for Scotland has always been one of those cries
that cause a ripple in British society. How to deal with
minorities is the point, not whether minorities exist. In
a federation where we were a minority we were not
dealt with fairly.

In Biafra today there are people who could be called
minorities, but I am glad to say that they are happy
in Biafra. They are happy because they, more than anybody else, fashioned what constitution Biafra has today.

The constitutional committee that suggested the establishment of the state of Biafra was in fact headed by none other than Okoi Arikpo. The first document of separation was signed by him as the chairman of the committee. While I do not want to be presumptuous to think that I have got all the minorities behind me, I think when one looks around generally one would tend to believe that they are happier here than on the Nigerian side.

How does one find out if one does not give them a chance to declare their wishes? One has to look at the way the war is raging. Here, in spite of all the hardships of the war and Gowon's blockade, there has been no breakdown of law and order in Biafra. It is significant that the so-called minorities, to whom the strains and stresses of the war have offered every opportunity to desert Biafra if they are so inclined, choose to remain and suffer and fight with Biafrans.

Interview with U.S. Senator Charles Goodell,
Umuahia, February 11, 1969

It is worth drawing attention here to the fact that all the refugees now starving and dying have come from areas occupied by Nigerians. These include the non-Ibo areas which Gowon's forces claim to have "liberated." Indeed, Colonel Adekunle, the commander of the Nigerian forces in that sector, recently admitted that the people there normally run into Biafran-held territories even after obtaining food from Nigerian forces. In contrast, we are proud to say that, right through the period of our stay in the Republic of Benin (Midwest) in 1967, there was no refugee problem in any part of the whole territory.

International press conference,
Aba, July 18, 1967

THE ECONOMY

What has been the effect of the blockade and the war itself on Biafra's economy? In modern terms, one says that since the blockade there has been no economy. That is in modern terms. But when you assess in basic terms, you will find that the blockade has not really had much effect. This is theoretically so because Biafra's economic potential is essentially what is innate in Biafra, and this is still there, still to be exploited. It only needs a period of peace and again we shall leap forward.

If you consider it in social terms, you will find in fact that the war has had again very little effect. But this is not a result of the emotion attached to this war. Many things we do not have any more. For instance, instead of feeding our babies on tinned baby food, we now use local foodstuffs. We have not had imports, and therefore we do not really worry over any balance of payments problem. Our people are quite content.

No, I do not think the blockade, though disruptive in its effect, has completely destroyed our economy. It has only put it in a state of suspended animation.

Interview with Britain-Biafran Association
delegates, April 18, 1968

It is very difficult to assess in international terms the shape of the Biafran economy. Remember we have been blockaded for more than two years. We have been fighting the war with Nigerian foreign exchange, plus, of course, what we converted or what we acquired earlier on. We have no international trade to talk about. But the potential for a buoyant economy is innate in our country. Our own resources are still there and make a very good backing for a strong economy. We have the confidence that once we start international trade we can rebuild our economy very fast.

Interview with Marvin Kupfer of *Newsweek*
magazine and Mr. David Robison, United States
free-lance journalist, Umuahia, February 13, 1969

Foreign oil companies have not made financial contributions to our cause. It was the question of royalties and rents that sparked off the hostilities, and so far, with

Gowon's propaganda and war, we have not really had
contact with the various concerns that operated here.
Actually, when you talk about oil companies, I imagine
you mean the two controversial oil companies. These
are the two oil companies in a position to pay something—Shell BP, which not only has refused categorically to pay but has indeed paid Lagos. Then there is
SAFRAP, the French enterprise. Only a week ago, I
sent somebody abroad to try to make contact and see
whether they would pay. The amount is very little, but
at this time it would be welcome.

There are many other commercial concessions: produce concessions, shipping concessions, and so on.
There are so many. We are a new country just starting
off. The opportunities are limitless. The concessions of
Shell are still valid. What will come out at the end of
this war I do not know, but at the moment as I sit here
their concessions are still valid.

The economic aspect of the effects of the blockade
is heavy. There is no trade going back and forth—
certainly not the way we knew it before. Ships do not
come in. We depend on our local ingenuity. We depend
on a tenuous line of supplies which I must say has held
out magnificently throughout the course of this war. I
have every confidence, of course, that it will continue.
The great thing about this struggle is that here, spiritually, our people understand the war; they believe in
the war and therefore ask for nothing much. On the
other side, the Nigerians are feeling the pinch because
their mental approach to the war is entirely different.
In Nigeria, this is a war being fought by soldiers, and
her civilians feel the loss of certain luxury items.

I will now talk about our currency. The new Biafran
currency is backed up by the entire resources of Biafra.
This is nothing new. Potentially in resources, mineral
resources, any forms of resources, Biafra can be considered in wealth terms a rich country. The new currency in Lagos is supposedly backed by an ever diminishing foreign exchange reserve to the tune of, I think,

25 percent. Taking our resources in monetary terms, the Biafran currency would probably be backed 100 percent by available Biafran resources.

International press conference,
Umuahia, January 28, 1968

In order to achieve these objectives [welfare state] we must generate a more rapid rate of growth in our agricultural and industrial output so as to be able to pay for these amenities. We cannot increase our pace of development unless we possess the necessary skills and techniques. This is where the University of Biafra and its sister institution, the University of Science and Technology, Port Harcourt, have a vital role to play. Our institutions of higher learning must endeavor to provide the highest and best education and training necessary for the achievement of our technological revolution.

We must at the same time facilitate the accumulation of capital for the implementation of our development projects. Biafrans will, therefore, be encouraged to improve their savings habit in order to participate more effectively in the economic activities of the nation. Biafrans should endeavor to form more cooperative societies and thus be better able to pool their financial resources and compete on a more favorable footing with foreign firms. Those engaged in various aspects of trade and industry will benefit from the new measures which the government hopes to initiate in the near future. These measures will facilitate increased participation of Biafrans in the retail trade as well as in the industrial development of the Republic.

It is recognized that agriculture is the most important single sector of our economy. We must aim at increasing our agricultural output by continuing to encourage our people to adopt modern methods of farming. We must press on with the expansion and diversification of our cash crops production while at the same time ensuring an adequate production of food crops both for local needs and for export. In this connection, the government will intensify agricultural research and extension services and encourage the development of cooperative farming.

The government fully recognizes the important role which foreign technical aid and capital investment can play in improving our economic and social life. We shall therefore continue to welcome assistance and investment from all friendly countries throughout the world so long as these accord with the interest and aspirations of Biafra. We will ensure that our independence and sovereignty are meaningful and will therefore strive to remove in the shortest possible time all vestiges of exploitation reminiscent of the colonial era.

During the difficult period we have been passing through, a number of foreign aid establishments, conscious of the justice of our cause, have been cooperating fully with us in our struggle. We appreciate their assistance. My government has recently issued the Revenue Collection Decree No. 2 of 1967, providing that all revenue derived from company profits, petroleum profits, oil pipelines, mineral oil, and gas be paid to the government of Biafra. This will ensure that the people enjoy to the fullest the wealth of the land which God has given them. On the provisions of this decree there can be no compromise.

> Address to convocation of the University of
> Biafra, Nsukka, July 1, 1967

It is hoped that a number of our old partners will come back at the end of the war to negotiate with us. In this way we can hurry our task of reconstruction. But then you understand that the war is still on—we don't know what their attitudes in the future will be. The problem is not one-sided. I think the future will be vastly dictated by the foreign companies themselves by their attitudes to our survival.

We have not made a firm policy except in general terms. We hope that they do not get themselves involved in the conflict and so make it impossible for us to work together.

As for Shell BP, the position is quite straightforward. Shell BP owes Biafra some money. Indeed, very shortly I hope to demand again payment of that amount. I hope that this time they will see what they claim not to have seen before, that the government of Biafra is in control. I think after nine months they would have seen that. It is my sincere hope that they will pay up. If they do, it makes things easier for both ourselves and for Shell BP.

As of now, Shell property is being given maximum protection by the government of Biafra. The future will depend on them, how they react to the fact of our existence as a nation.

> Interview with Dr. B. da Silva of *Diario Popular*
> of Lisbon, Umuahia, March 14, 1968

There will be a free enterprise society in Biafra. The only limitations to the freedom of the enterprise will be cash, as in all underdeveloped countries—the question of availability of capital. It is this lack of capital that in fact induces government involvement in industrial enterprise. If, on the other hand, we find other means of generating and building up capital for the enterprises, the tendency here will be to leave it free to the individual. Direction from the government will be a diminishing factor.

> Interview with West German journalist,
> Dr. Ruth Bowert, Umuahia, March 25, 1968

THE ARMY

There is a terrible fallacy abroad in the world today that the strength of an army lies in the equipment, the weapons, and the ammunition available to the force. The true strength of an army lies in the caliber of its men, in their hearts. It is the heart that decides, not the rifle. You can carry five rifles to the field, but if you don't shoot any of them, the enemy with his bow and arrows will put you to flight. You can, and this has been demonstrated in this war, give any amount of MIG fighters to an army without heart, or to a force without a soul; if you do that, the resulting success will still be nil. Our people have succeeded mainly because they have confidence in themselves. They knew, right from the start, the difficulties that would face them, and they have a strong belief in the justice of their cause.

Our people have succeeded in the war because they have relied entirely on themselves. Whatever comes to them from outside they have considered truly a bonus. They are, therefore, not surprised by anything that the enemy throws at them. The Biafran army has expected the worst possible from the enemy, which is the right military approach. The army today believes that what the enemy does not throw against them the enemy has not got.

Our army, therefore, fights with the desperation of a people who are threatened with extermination. The secret of success of the Biafra army is the soul of Biafra. When I talk about the soul of the army and the spirit of the army, these can in no way exist in a vacuum. The spirit of the Biafra army arises from the spirit of the Biafran people.

Our army has been popularized and has become a people's army. Who are the people in the army today? They are the clerks, the stewards, the farmers, the petty traders, the teachers, the lecturers and professionals. These normally are considered the masses of the population. They have not been changd. Two weeks from putting away their hoes, putting aside their old dresses, and putting on khaki uniforms, still keeps them, in essence, part of the people. Their soul is the soul of our people. In Nigeria it is not quite the same. The Nigerian people might feel one way, and that feeling of the people might not be completely in consonance with their army, because they have not popularized their army. They, for example, run a class-structured army that conscripts the common people to make up the numbers, whereas we in Biafra have a volunteer army in the widest possible sense. Even our salaries are donated by our people. This is the essential difference. The Biafra army is the citizenry of Biafra.

Meeting with Youth and Labor leaders,
Umuahia, April 4, 1968

A foreign correspondent once told me that if Nigeria wanted they could wipe out Biafra, but they had to wait to see if starvation could change Biafrans. I made it clear that I considered his statement an arrant nonsense, the illogicality of cheap, sensational, ignorant journalism, Nigeria's apologia for incompetence. I have never heard of an army not wanting victory. Sometimes when whites talk of soldiers, you immediately think of the Western officers, and all the various attributes of a European army come to mind. When you, a foreign correspondent, report about the Nigerian division, as far as he is concerned it is the modern division. There may be some differences, but by and large, it is a division. Herein lies the mistake.

Nigeria set out on this war from the beginning totally to overrun Biafra, to find a military solution to their problem. That they have not done it so far is only because they are incapable of doing so. There can be no other rationalization of their policy. It is so easy to assess our shortage of arms—you see Nigerians with all the preponderance of arms; on top of it, you see them with MIGS, Ilyushins in the air, therefore with European logic, so used to seeing efficient armies, you decide that the reason for their failure is compassion for Biafra. If it is, why do they keep collecting arms?

Even those who give them arms are making terrible miscalculations. Those of them who have had experience in Africa tend to equate Nigeria with Biafra, forgetting that both are quite different. Biafrans are basically of superior intelligence to the Nigerians. What I am driving at is that no matter what you give to the

Nigerians, unless you do the fighting yourself they will not succeed. Nigerians are not capable of victory. They are wasteful, they are lazy. They are just populous. A Nigerian division, seeing a platoon of our own infantry, rather than move would for the next three days shell and bombard every inch of the area before daring to sally forth.

> Interview with Marvin Kupfer of *Newsweek*
> magazine and David Robison, United States
> free-lance journalist, Umuahia, February 13, 1969

As a Christian and Godly people, we do not accept the British theory that God is always on the side of big battalions. We believe in the crushing power of truth and justice. The very Nigeria that Britain professes to preserve can be saved only with an immediate end to the war and not by a military defeat of Biafra.

> Address to the Armed Forces,
> Onitsha Warfront, November 4, 1968

The Biafran army and our guerrilla forces are the same thing.

The guerrilla is another specialized arm in the army. You notice I use the term "specialized." The basic soldier is an infantryman. The guerrilla, being a specialist, is therefore an infantryman who has the added ability to operate behind enemy lines, an ability to operate deep into the enemy rear. Normally, you find that in a war such as we are involved in, where we find ourselves with so much less than the enemy, the classical strategy for conducting warfare is to employ fully guerrilla tactics.

In the Biafran struggle I have considered the advantages and the disadvantages of turning over completely to guerrilla warfare as opposed to what I am doing today, which is to use the traditional army side by side with the guerrilla, each complementing the other's efforts. I have come to the conclusion that my method is the answer, particularly in a situation in which a war of aggression was suddenly thrust on an unprepared people.

The reason why Biafra today stands a chance of fighting a war of self-determination and emerging from it in record time is because you have available for the world to see a state to negotiate with, to discuss with, with all the accoutrements of statehood. The only thing that we have not got in our march to fully accepted statehood is a firm immovable frontier. I feel that if we lose this definition, the war will then become a protracted war that will go on for many many years to come. Our ultimate victory, of course, is never in question. The problem is the suffering, its duration. By maintaining a state and therefore a regular army, the regular army maintains for us a territorial definition, no matter how small, of a state, while the guerrilla forces operate behind the enemy lines, making it impossible for the enemy to enjoy his aggression and wreaking havoc at his bases in the rear and making him very uncomfortable.

Ours is the classical story of the elephant and the ant. The elephant is driven frantic with ants all over its enormous bulk. The elephant has its powerful tusk but can find no respite. The elephant is so harassed that in an attempt to dislodge all the ants, he dashes himself, crashing headlong against a tree trunk, and possibly commits suicide. By employing the guerrilla in harassing the enemy at every point where he has set his venomous foot, I expect the enemy sooner or later to commit suicide. Already, indications are that the enemy is going that way. I believe that at the end of this war we will come out having won a war of self-determination in record time, and our contribution to revolutionary theory will be, in the fact of this phenomenon, our ability to fight an orthodox war while at the same time using extensively unorthodox methods in an imperialist, not civil, war.

Interview with Biafra national press,
February 27, 1969

The strongest point in the Biafra army is the belief in our cause. Another strong point is fighting in our own land. A third point is our marked ability to improvise. A fourth arises from the second; because we are fighting in our own land we can walk around the enemy. Another point is that we are fighting among a population that is dedicated to our success. Sixth, our morale rises with the increased tide of favorable public opinion in the outside world. The troops are very much aware of whatever is said about Biafra abroad, and we have, as I said at the Consultative Assembly, been able to improve our weapons position. . . .

The Biafran army, by Western standards, is weak, but they make up for their weakness by their determination. Judging the Biafran army by European standards, you immediately see the disparity in training and armament. Hence the inevitable verdict that our people cannot last. When Europeans in our forces see acts of courage, they term them suicidal. Our troops go to war with five bullets in their rifles. I suppose in Western Germany or anywhere else in Europe, if one went to a battle with five rounds, it would be suicide. In this case, we go to battle because we have to. The history of Europe is replete with instances of such heroism bordering on martyrdom. Our troops go to the battle hoping to delay the enemy. Remember, the war aims of the warring parties are basically different. Nigeria's is to conquer and overrun; ours is to delay. With long delay, we hope that we will have sufficiently established not only our rights to self-determination but our ability to remain as a nation. We think that the world will have had sufficient opportunity to understand the reasons, the causes of this struggle, and to appreciate not only the justness of our cause but that their interest, world interest, lies in the survival of Biafra. That is, world interest for peace can be best served in the acceptance of the right of all peoples to self-determination.

The potential for a "quick kill" is greater on this

side than on the other side because here you have a
force that knows the reason they are fighting, and
therefore a dramatic push, a quick dash, can put the
other side more easily into disarray than a like move
directed at this side, as has been witnessed when the
enemy took Aba, Owerri, and Okigwi. If anything like
that happened to the other side they would collapse.
Not here.

Interview with Marvin Kupfer of *Newsweek*
magazine and David Robison, United States
free-lance journalist, Umuahia, February 13, 1969

The Biafran army, like the Biafran people, has
emerged out of a series of factors that built them up.
The Biafran army is the product of a long period of
colonialism and a period of neocolonialism. They find
themselves, like the Biafran people, in the midst of an
upheaval, an upheaval which we Biafran people have
now called the Biafran revolution. Since this is the
people's war, and since it is on the people that we
depend for victory, I think the revolution, which we
are trying to guide, should also sweep through the
army. You will find that our officers have been trained
in a particular way and are tied to stereotyped military
maneuvers. They have a rather pronounced class consciousness, and a feeling of superiority to other human
beings. This must be discouraged, particularly in our
situation, where the only thing that matters is how
well you serve the people and the state.

The army would appear not to have yet adapted
themselves. They tend to believe that by mere wearing
of uniform and putting ranks on their shoulders, they
have an automatic right to leadership. We are in a
revolution! Everybody, including the soldiers, must be
tested. They have not got any rights other than as a
result of how well they serve the people in our revolution.

There is a lot to be done about the army. We have
to popularize the army. The army has to recognize the

fact that it is one of the leadership groups in the revolution. The army has to demonstrate its love for the people by virtue of its leadership, to show that truly the army is the servant of the people.

There are instances of indiscipline and intimidation of our people by our own forces. The sum total effect of this could be alienation, and alienation in a state of war reduces our chances of victory. We curb excesses in our political life by education, so I find that with the army we have to educate the leaders and the rank and file to understand the precepts of our revolution, and hope through this education to change their attitude, to make new men of the individuals and a new army for the Republic.

Address to officers and troops,
Ikot-Ekpene war front, August 2, 1968

What the army should not do is very obvious. Anything that makes the army an enemy of the people is wrong. How do you correct it? There are two ways. There is the hard way, which is purely a demonstration of government antipathy toward certain actions. If a soldier does something inappropriate for a revolutionary Biafran, and you punish him harshly and publicly, that acts as a deterrent sometimes, but at other times it brings about resentment and disaffection unless one really understands the danger inherent in these acts. To cure this, we have to find the causes. I believe the cause is ignorance of the revolution, and therefore the real solution must come from educating the army. This is why every single army officer that passed out for the past six months in Biafra is subjected to a long course of education on the state of the nation, physically and spiritually—the war and the revolution. That is why you find that for the past three months I have brought the leadership of the army closer to the people.

Every time we have seminars I draw the available leadership of the army into these seminars, to listen and to feel with the people. You find also that in the

past month I have given an order that the leadership
of the army must get involved in the mass activity of
our people so that when there is a public demonstration
I encourage the army to take part in public demonstration, to get this experience of the masses. I do not want
the army to be shy of the masses. I want them to feel
part of the masses. I am actively pushing the army
that way, and it is a difficult thing because there are
so many old prejudices that one has to break, such as
the idea of class, the feeling of being an elite group. I
am encouraged, however, because I now discover that
wherever an army leader is put into a position where
he has to justify his leadership in the society, he usually
finds a solution in identifying himself with the masses.
This is a very healthy sign. I have not come across one
that goes before the masses and puts himself against
them—that, to say the least, would be imprudent.

> Address to volunteers, Enugu war sector,
> August 7, 1967

The idea that the army should be a classless army
does in no way imply that the army should not have a
rank structure. No army can function without definite
responsibilities which, of course, really are according
to ranks.

But this class system of thinking that you are born
to the officer class, thinking that once you are an officer
you are automatically a gentleman, whatever a gentleman means in our context, these are the things that
must stop. Anybody, by virtue of being a citizen of
Biafra, has a right to the officer corps of the Biafra
armed forces, has a right to a position of leadership
within the Biafran society. The demands on leadership
by virtue of the fact of the dangers attendant upon
holding a rifle have to be very, very strictly adhered
to; the various criteria have to be very strictly adhered
to when considering the army. Whereas you can be
forgiven for laxity in the selection of leaders, say, in
the civil service, in the army the dangers are too great.

I expect, therefore, that the army should be an army of revolutionaries. The leadership of the army, of course, has to be almost the same as the political and economic leadership of the revolution, all working in their various fields.

Within the leadership group there are many functions —there is a political leadership, there is military leadership—but all of them are leading the masses in our revolution. When I say that the army is a leader group, one has to know first the people's attitude to the army, what they expect of the army leadership particularly in a state of war. If the army cannot give the leadership, then it is inadequate. Armies can, but armies of the old type, the British-type army, cannot give progressive leadership. The British army was specifically designed to be a buffer between a people's desire for progress and their own establishment. The army in Britain was created as a lower adjunct of the establishment. The old Nigerian army was modeled on this for other reasons.

Because of certain privileges in the Nigerian army, the British found it easy to create a reactionary group within the army that would stultify any innate desire of the people to change the various myths on which neocolonialism thrives. The British colonialists have therefore created in the army an elite corps—elite by name, but without any contributive power in socio-economic terms, nor in progress. It is a maxim of our present-day circumstance that the more incompetent one is, the greater his adherence to position. This appears to be the rule in Africa today.

The army, particularly the British-trained army, has had young people transplanted very quickly from obscurity into positions of pre-eminence; they find themselves automatically in the so-called senior cadre of society, with more money than is good for them, less responsibility than is good for them. These men develop in time only a marked ability to hang on to their seats. Wherever you find people like that, people who can do so much, tied down or hampered by this form of training and experience—men so aware of their own inadequacy and so afraid of social displacement—you find the most fertile ground for neocolonialist puppetry. If a group like the army, they remain ever grateful to their neocolonialist patrons.

The patronage affords them ample opportunity for exploiting their own people without any form of challenge. This is what has happened. The army can, if properly reorganized, if properly educated, give leadership; after all, if it is a people's army, the mere fact of wearing a uniform does not reduce the capacity of the people to evolve leadership; they can evolve leadership in any sphere of life.

Address at Biafra People's Seminar,
Umuahia, November 1, 1967

You owe it to your people to lead the Biafran revolution. More than anybody else, you have a stake, you are sacrificing your entire being—your life—for something that will be good in the future. Therefore, you cannot take this revolution for granted. You must strive to educate yourself and improve your education with all the principles of the Biafran revolution. You must get yourselves involved in all the activities directed toward the efficiency of this revolution. You must undertake an individual crusade for a cleaner Biafra. The government can do a lot, the leaders can do a lot, but by far the greatest responsibility lies on the shoulders of the individual. Remember that our position is that the Biafran revolution is based on love, on trust —one Biafran for the other.

Address to under-officers, Afor-Ugiri,
January 5, 1969

I see the army in a postwar situation assisting the people in their return to normalcy. I say this in the widest possible sense. Everything that is necessary to bring normalcy to the people can be assisted by the armed forces. For instance, the armed forces will be involved in every aspect of reconstruction.

I see the army physically clearing our roads, building our new towns.

I see the army setting up and operating the postwar emergency medical service.

I see the army already evacuating our produce, starting off our economy again.

I see the army constructing schools, maternity homes, orphanages.

I see the army providing emergency transport services for our society. There are really limitless avenues through which the army could get involved in national projects.

Politically, I see the army, too, exemplifying to our people the ideal of service to the community. It is necessary because here you have a force available, a force which does not work for pay other than just enough to keep body and soul together, a force of dedicated men. They do work, and do it fast. They achieve results. I think by this method the productivity of the army will act as a constant challenge to the other organizations in the state. I said that the new Biafran, the revolutionary Biafran, has his own place in a peace situation, and when there is an emergency, automatically he fits into the national contingency plan. This implies that every man and woman in Biafra will have a dual role—peace role, emergency role—and each must be trained for these two roles. In whichever role the Biafran is performing, he must have the opportunity to refresh himself on the other. Only in this way can we maintain the type of force that is necessary to protect the revolution, and at the same time do the necessaries such as reconstruction and general economic progress. An army that is cut off from the general economic progress of its nation becomes really a parasite of that society. It becomes a parasite army, a waste-pipe—everything that goes into it is lost to the nation. But an army that does things other than fighting, a very rare necessity in a peaceful country, is worth its weight in gold.

One other point about the army. I don't envisage a situation where it would be necessary ever to turn the national army against its own people. Armies are for combating external aggression. Police forces are for maintenance of law and order. I would like to see this clear demarcation of functions. If you agree with me that there is a need for this demarcation, then, of course, it underlines the necessity of making the army productive in a peace situation; otherwise, if there is no war, what do you find? A large army taking a large percentage of the national budget and producing nothing. People will go there, have their careers, die, and all the money spent and the efforts made will have been wasted. You get no production.

A country like ours, and indeed any country in Africa, cannot afford the luxury of an unproductive army.

Address at Biafra People's Seminar,
Umudike, December 4, 1968

THE JUDICIARY

Today is ushering in yet another important and significant landmark in our history as a sovereign and independent nation. For we meet today to inaugurate the Court of Appeal for this Republic as well as swear in the president and members of that court. It gives me great pleasure to see all of you who have come to witness this ceremony, as a concrete evidence to the world of our determination to keep our sovereignty.

The Edict establishing the Court of Appeal for what was then Eastern Nigeria was published in April this year. Even at that time, when we were still part of the defunct Federation of Nigeria, the need had become clear and pressing for establishing our own Court of Appeal, under the constitution of the defunct Federation of Nigeria. That previous governments had not taken steps to establish a regional Court of Appeal for the then Eastern Nigeria before that time sprang from our misguided belief in a united country.

Since February, 1965, the Supreme Court of the former Federation of Nigeria had held no sitting in our territory, even though it had done so in other parts of the former federation. The events of 1966 had made it impossible for our lawyers and their clients to go to Lagos to prosecute cases pending in the Nigerian Supreme Court. The insecurity of life, persons, and property which faced our people made it necessary even for our representative in the Supreme Court to leave Lagos and return home. The tragic circumstances of that fateful and fatal year, 1966, also made it necessary for us to establish a School of Legal Education for our young men and women whose studies could not be continued in Lagos.

These were the reasons behind the passing of the edict in April. But since the passing of that edict we have since May 30 severed all political and administrative connections with the defunct Federation of Nigeria. This factor alone, overriding even the reasons which prompted the passing of the edict in April, has further justified the existence of the court. I have made these preliminary remarks as a matter of historical interest, not as an apology for our action. We owe nobody any apology and have none whatsoever to give. We take full pride in what we have done and shall ever continue to do so.

Recent years have been marked by the expansion of our judiciary in this Republic. The aim is, as far as possible, to bring justice to the doorstep of every citizen. It is my desire that the independence of the judiciary should not be compromised. That is the surest guarantee of individual freedom, and I am happy to say that we in Biafra are determined to uphold this principle fully at all times.

I have received a number of petitions from people in custody about delays in the disposal of their cases. This has been brought about by the present war situation, which has meant movement of people and law enforcement agencies from one place to the other. In such a situation in any country, there is bound to be some delay in the disposal of cases. Their complaints have been brought to the notice of the Chief Justice, who has assured me that everything possible is being done to deal with them.

The interest of Biafrans in the due administration of justice is reflected in the number of barristers of Biafran origin now enrolled and practicing in Biafra. Only a fortnight ago, 52 more members of the bar who passed through our law school were enrolled to practice in our courts. This brings the number of Biafran lawyers practicing in our courts to well over 600. This is a measure of the interest which the citizens of Biafra take in the application of the rule of law and in the preservation of individual rights and liberty. I wish to remind the members of the bar of their responsibility in this respect.

We look upon this new court as a citadel of justice, freedom, and protection for the rights of our people.

We look upon it as the very symbol and custodian of our liberties and all that goes with a free society. Indeed, a society of equality between its different peoples and individuals. A society guaranteeing the safety and sanctity of life and property, freedom of movement and association, fairness and equity for all.

We look upon this as an institution which will be free from all the ills which shook confidence in its counterpart in Nigeria and contributed to the disintegration of that ill-fated country. It must be a court bold and courageous to defend its rights and powers and ensure that it is not converted into an instrument of oppression and political vandalism.

Inauguration of the Biafran Court of
Appeal, December 8, 1967

THE REVOLUTION

I wish to restate that the military came to power as a corrective regime dedicated to the elimination from our national life of all forms of injustice, corruption, nepotism, and abuse of office. The military was resolved to create a society in which every individual would be free to develop to the fullest his or her natural talents and enjoy the fruits of honest labor. The military envisaged a nation so reconstructed as to win respect and admiration for the black race. It has been one of my deepest regrets that the attention of the military regime was diverted from these objectives through the evil machinations of the enemies of progress.

I wish to affirm that the military government intends to pursue vigorously the task of purging the nation of the ills of the last civilian regime. It is my determination that the Republic of Biafra shall thrive and prosper on grounds cleared of the malpractices and malversations which plagued the defunct Federation of Nigeria. Though tainted by our previous associations, we, as a progressive and revolutionary people, must now create and sustain a new national image in a society shorn of the pernicious accretions of the colonial and postcolonial era. We must fashion new codes of moral behavior in public and private life, eliminate pockets of privilege, and secure for all, as far as our means allow, the enjoyment of the amenities of modern civilization, of which we are a part.

This task calls for a reorientation of outlook. Ours is a society in which by tradition everyone is his brother's keeper. This spirit of selflessness was put to the test last year with the return of 2,000,000 refugees who today have shelter and sustenance in Biafra. We must foster this spirit by establishing the machinery necessary to ensure that prosperity diffuses to everyone and that social and economic development is evenly spread throughout the Republic. Our main objective in this direction is to transform our nation, within the minimum

time possible, into a modern welfare state, and thus
guarantee for the people some of the basic necessities
of life. Within the resources available to us we shall
introduce measures to ensure that medical treatment is
within the reach of the common people, that employment opportunities are provided for every able-bodied
Biafran, and that the right to education is extended to
every citizen. This government is determined to introduce measures for social security and, as soon as our
economic circumstances can, sustain them.

Address to convocation of the University
of Biafra, Nsukka, July 1, 1967

One other issue which demands an early attention is
the organization and place of the working class in our
national life. The working class is the backbone of any
progressive state. The moribund Federation of Nigeria
inherited and encouraged friction and antagonism between labor on the one hand and management and government on the other.

We had begun to witness the growing gap between
the rich and the poor as well as the evils attendant upon
mounting unemployment. We began to witness poor
and inefficient output, wages and salaries unrelated to
production, introduction and promotion of privilege
unrelated to merit, and increasing disparity between
town and countryside.

Under the civilian regime our labor movement had
fallen into disarray, since some of its leaders had betrayed the cause of the workers to the corrupt politicians
or allowed themselves to be seduced by local or foreign
vested interests. These leaders became as corrupt as the
regime they pretended to attack. The result was that the
role of the labor organizations in the defunct Federation
of Nigeria constituted a direct negation of the real interests of the workers.

It will be the duty of this government, by eliminating
all forms of oppression, exploitation, and injustice, to
offer the workers their rightful place in society. The

workers of this Republic will come to occupy an important position and play a healthy role in the mechanics of nation-building. We envisage that the position of our trade union movement will be one of complete cooperation with, and full participation in, government economic policies.

We consider as obsolete the separation of labor from management in industrial and, indeed, all economic activity. Such separation often creates two warring camps engaged in a power tussle which leads to strikes, retrenchments, and the frustration of economic targets. We hope to strive to achieve harmony between the two, so that the working class can itself become the driving force of our economic resurgence. To this end, the government intends to take steps to set up the necessary machinery for the effective participation of Biafran workers, through their accredited bodies, in the planning and execution of our economic policy. Such machinery, by constantly watching production, output, and national viability, will be in a position to advise on related problems of wage structure and conditions of work.

In order to play the leading role which the new society demands of the workers, it is necessary that they rid themselves of bribery and corruption, clannishness, recklessness, and indolence. They must realize the absolute necessity for the solidarity of the working class in a framework that cuts across ethnic groupings and religious affiliations. Equally important is the need for the workers to form a stable, well-organized, and well-oriented central labor organization under able, honest, and informed leadership. It is only under the aegis of such a body that the workers can effectively tackle the responsibilities which will be theirs under the new dispensation. The arrangement will also give the trade unions financial stability which will insulate them from the tempting bait of foreign money and enable them to develop their own image within the context of Africa's struggle for freedom and equality.

Like the trade unions, the youth movements have a
significant contribution to make toward the attainment
of our national goals. Previously, the youth have been
neglected and their energies frittered away in pastimes
which are not relevant to our national aims and objectives. It is necessary to reeducate and organize them so
that they, too, will be able to channel their energies toward our national ideals and efforts. This, in fact, is
the principal work of the Biafra Youth Committee,
which the government recently established.

The government of Biafra is taking steps to involve
every Biafran directly in the task of national reconstruction. Every individual Biafran must adopt a genial mental approach to his fellow Biafran in the interest of
peace, harmony, and orderly development. The ideal
Biafran must be a disciplined citizen who is ready to
render selfless service at all times. He must be civil
and courteous in his dealings with his neighbors and
perform his job honestly, efficiently, cheerfully, and
with pride.

> Address to convocation of the University
> of Biafra, Nsukka, July 1, 1967

What is a revolution? Simply, it is quick change—a
quick change that has implicit in itself a change for the
better—that is what I understand by revolution. I find,
too, that things do not just change for the better, that
people usually try to make things better. I find that the
government has to help to make things better. I analyzed all our problems and could very easily lay them
on the doorstep of what I call Nigerianism. That is all
those ills that plagued the old Federation—bribery, corruption, nepotism, indolence, blind adherence to the
naked pursuit of money, money-grabbing, irresponsibility, inability to keep official secrets, a marked pro-
pensity for exploiting the female sex in our public life.
All these things were present in Nigeria. Biafra rejects
and must reject them. The need for a change in Nigeria
is not as urgent because they have many friends that

are supporting them, so they can afford the inefficiencies. For us, it is vital.

The only way to make sure of this change is by education—a national education—an understanding of the true meaning of the struggle. I say that if we finish this fight still the same as we are, without a change for the better, then we have lost 50 percent, if not more, of the reasons for this fight. If we arrive at the end not changed, there is no worse disaster for this nation, because I can promise you that the same problems that brought about the breakup of our old society in Federal Nigeria, now confined in a smaller space, will still set up the same chain reaction and destroy our new society.

Have we yet accepted ourselves as brothers? Does the Nnewi man accept fully the man from Ikot Ekpene? Does he think that fighting in Uyo is equally important as fighting in Nnobi? Think on these things. There are others. Do we, having fought for this Republic, now accept that everybody has an equal stake in the society of Biafra? Do we give employment on merit? Are we honest in our dealings with our fellow Biafran? These are the beginnings of our change.

Gradually, I came to accept the fact that we have a revolutionary situation and that the society demands of me a leadership of that revolution. I say "society" because I am well aware of the fact that our people have not had the opportunity really to select or mandate somebody to lead them. I happened to be on the scene, they were threatened, and they said: "Go on, having everything you need to carry on." I don't forget this fact. I don't have a peculiar right to the position that I hold other than that society demands of me to do certain things.

To be able to prosecute the Biafran revolution there are various prerequisites. First of all, to prosecute the Biafran revolution, you must believe in Biafra. What do you mean by Biafra? What is it to you? Do you believe in the Biafran? You have to, because revolution is something from within. You believe in yourself, you believe in your environment, your people. You love your people. The Biafran revolution, therefore, is based on love, not on hate. A number of revolutions in history have been based on hate—a clique hating certain groups or seeking to wipe them out. Ours is a revolution that came about in our attempt to prevent the tragedies of the past ever repeating themselves.

The starting point of our revolution is a recognition of our oneness as a nation. The Biafran revolution starts off by accepting everybody born within the territorial confines of the proclaimed Biafra, or whose parents were born or come from that area, as Biafrans. While this is all right for the purpose of this struggle, it appears to me that the true Biafran will be not just somebody who happens to be a Biafran by accident but the Biafran who has struggled in the Biafran revolution. He is the type of Biafran we really want, and he is the man we are after.

To be a true Biafran, you must know your rights; not only know your rights, you must have the confidence of the Biafran to assert your rights; not only the confidence to assert your rights, you must demand of every Biafran the right and assistance to obtain your rights.

When you see in the new Biafran society that somebody's right has been trampled upon, it is not enough to just shake your head in sympathy. The Biafran revolution demands of you to stake your life and see to it that that right is not trampled upon because of our fundamental belief that every Biafran is personally responsible for the society in which he finds himself. It is only in this way—our being our brother's keeper—that we can really purge ourselves of the ills that threaten to engulf our society.

If you are a true Biafran, when you go to the bank and you see somebody jump the queue and go straight to the front, and you see him obtain service, your duty is clear—you should push that person out and make sure that he does not trample on other people's rights. But that is not enough; the others in the queue should assist you. To be a revolutionary in our society, you must have the confidence to carry through your conviction. How many times have you helped to solve other people's problems? How many times have you stopped, instead of driving through, to give your fellow Biafran a lift? You have seen others starving—what have you done about it? These are some of my basic beliefs about the Biafran revolution.

The most important thing really in an organized society is the position of power and the exercise of that power. The Biafran revolutionary believes that power is rightly the power of the people. The revolutionary believes that all power derives from the people. Who are the people? All of us. We believe that people in positions of authority are merely acting as agents of the people. When you appoint somebody to an office, he is your agent. You have given him an assignment to exercise certain of your powers for you.

The leadership group in the Biafran revolutionary society, therefore, comes to be the servant group. I believe I am the biggest servant in Biafra, and all the people that assist me are, in that degree, servants to the community. At no stage must the leadership ever forget the fact that the people are masters and they servants. In the Biafran society of the future, that society created by the Biafran revolution, the people retain the right at all times to demand of their leaders an account of their stewardship. We do not believe that this stewardship is an assignment you give to somebody and then resign your authority until the end of the stewardship. No. At every stage the people reserve the right to question the leadership.

The Biafran revolutionary believes that the more your responsibility in leadership the less your freedom.

Not the other way around, as we found in the old society that the people in authority could do anything and
the followership virtually nothing. No! *Power belongs
to the people*. The man who is in a position of leadership is limited. He is less free because of the dangers
inherent in what has been entrusted to him; he therefore
has limitations. Your steward cannot do anything he
likes in your house; so also the leaders of the revolution
cannot do what they like in our state. The more the
power the people give to you as an individual, the less
room you have to maneuver.

One more point on the question of power. Every
leader in the Biafran revolution accepts as a basic principle that he holds power only just as long as the people find satisfaction in his exercise of the power, not
one minute longer. So you will find that the government
that will emerge after the revolutionary struggle will not
be a government that is self-perpetuating like what we
have had before. Indeed, it is a principle of this revolution that anybody in power should not seek to perpetuate his control of that power, but to hold power just
as long as the people find him exercising the power well
on their behalf.

Followership in the revolutionary Biafra must comprise people who know their rights and have confidence
in those rights. But there is more than that to it. The Biafran followership, because the power is theirs, have to
be trained to understand the essence of power. We cannot accept the situation where a large proportion of our
society do not exercise their democratic right. It is in-
tolerable in a revolutionary society. Indeed, it is the
duty of the leadership to educate the masses. For this
reason, I have insisted on seminars and discussions as
a means of educating our masses. This is how some of
those problems are being solved.

The Biafran is equal to any other Biafran in our society. Let us not just pay lip service to this tenet of our

belief. Equality means equality in all respects, equality before the law, and so on. Once we accept this, then we have a basic platform from which we can set about correcting a number of ills.

Considering the ills of our society, it occurred to me some time ago that our biggest ills arose from politics. Think back. Those avaricious individuals with long robes, very long cars—they were in essence parasites in our society, sucking our blood, sucking the people dry, living in affluence while the people were suffering and not having even the slightest thought for the good of the people.

You remember the old-type politician with a very sweet tongue who came at election time and promised you heaven, even insisting that he could put God in your lap, and then, having got your vote, turned out to be your oppressor? The Biafran revolution is out to ensure that this type of being never again smells the seat of power in our society. How do we achieve that? It has been possible for opportunists to get themselves into various positions because of the structure of our politics. We found that people who were voted into power, who were voted in to represent the people, used that as a stepping-stone to other things. In the Biafran society of the future, one is selected for a specific job and that job only. When we send a man to Parliament in the future, I hope to see that that man, by virtue of that selection, aspires to nothing else beyond representing the people. That means he cannot use this as a lever to climb into a ministerial post.

If he is going to represent the people, he stands election to represent the people. What I envisage, therefore, is a split of the executive from the legislative. The two should be completely separated so that our people will have the opportunity to vote for the leader *per se* and then give him scope to choose the people who will assist him. The reason why you choose him is that basically you accept his program. A thing that has bedeviled politics for a long time is that we find this preoccupation with program without its being tied to any time span for completion.

I think that politics in the future should be dependent on a program which has a timetable which the people consider in its entirety. For instance, at the end of this war we should have a reconstruction program. Whoever gets to head this state, I would like to see him work out a program of reconstruction with a time span of, say, five or ten years, then present that to the people and say: "This is my program for ten years."

The leader, being chosen, should select those he needs to do the job with him. He has no limitation. He will not have to look up to his own party or any organization to choose his men. He will not be tied to the legislature or the judiciary but will be completely free to choose from the entire society.

Having been selected, these men resign their various appointments or whatever jobs they already have in the society. So that, if you are a professional representative of the people or a politician, once you are chosen to a ministerial appointment, you resign your membership of Parliament and immediately a by-election is held and somebody gets in and takes over that seat. If you are a judge and you are selected, you resign from the judiciary and become a commissioner or a minister. Those in the legislature would be able to act independently and also as safeguards for the excesses of the executive. Every program of the executive will be debated in the legislature and a majority decision taken. It would of course be in the interests of the executive to work for a legislature that would at least allow it to carry out its program. I think, in this way, you would reduce the incidence of political jobbery in our society.

Nepotism and tribalism are twin evils. I believe that these can be avoided if we set about making sure that every appointment in our society is based on one and only one criterion—merit. We should ensure that this term "merit" is no mumbo-jumbo. It should be something that is obvious for everyone to see: that is, when you have given somebody a job, the reason for giving that job to that person in preference to others must be generally clear. There must be an avenue for our people to find out, if they want, the reason why this man got the job as opposed to that other man. If they do not have that avenue, we go back to the same problem.

All posts should be advertised. If experience is needed, you list the type of experience that is required. That is what I envisage in the future. If you go to an interview and it is decided that you will not get the post because you look scruffy, let the interviewers write it down and let people have the opportunity to know that you did not get that job because you looked scruffy. It is in this way that enlightened opinion can be brought to bear on our corrupt situation.

I believe that there must be some form of commission in our society to which the common man can go for redress without going through administrative red tape, which in fact only ensures one thing—that he does not get redress. Various systems have tried this—some people call it the *ombudsman*. There must be something out of the legislative which will be a power on its own, having the right to look at any problem posed by the individual, particularly when he feels that his rights are being trampled upon.

This will go a long way to cut down nepotism.

Tribalism is, perhaps, more deeply rooted. This idea of considering some of our people foreigners in some parts of our own country, this question of ethnic territorial boundaries, all these things have to be looked into very carefully to see whether they enhance the concept of the Biafran nation. When I first came to this area as the military governor, one of the first things I did was to erase tribe from all public documents. We are all Bi-

afrans. "Where do you come from?" you are asked, and
the answer is simple: "I come from Biafra." The government must not emphasize tribal origin if it is trying
to stamp out tribalism. If you ever find tribe on a document, take no note of it. One legitimately may want to
know where you were born. Write that. A man whose
parents come from Calabar could quite easily be born
in Aba, but since he has equal rights in Biafra, he is an
Aba person and he should be able to exercise his political rights in Aba. I believe that you have rights only
where you live and work, where you were born, not
where you have been extracted from. Every effort
should be made by future governments to educate our
people away from tribalism. I would like to see movement of people across tribal frontiers. The government
should encourage people to move from their own areas
to be educated elsewhere. Yes, I would even go further
to support government measures to encourage intertribal marriages. It is one way. One cannot force it on
people. Today, I find that where a woman has triplets,
the government pays bounty to her. I think that a lot
can be done this way to encourage intertribal marriages.
It is only a gesture, but if the government really believes
that tribalism could be wiped out, something like a
bounty should be given to that young man who marries
across tribe, to show that the government appreciates
what he has done. Incidentally, it will not be done in
retrospect!—the bounty, I mean.

Absentee politicians would, of course, be rejected
now by the people. The only time you see such men in
the villages is at election time. They all lived in Lagos,
Kano, all over the place, and never came home; but as
soon as there was an election, they rushed home. All
they knew of was their own streets and houses in Kano
and in Lagos. If by legislation we make sure that the
people who will represent Aba are only people who live
in Aba, things will be better. We would stipulate a min-

imum residential period of, say, three to five years, as
the case may be, for qualification to vote anywhere.

I also believe that this question of land has to be
looked at very carefully. Who really owns land?

A lot has been said about this problem without getting truly into it. Most of our problems in society come
from land ownership or the desire to own land. I believe that land properly belongs to the community. Nobody, no single individual, has absolute right over land.
You will notice that I did not say "belongs to the government," because the government could be a bad
government. I say "to the community." If this is so,
how does it solve our problem later on? A number of
people here now say: "I come from Onitsha, people
must not take my land." I remember that the two greatest soldiers that fought for Onitsha came from Annang
and Eket provinces: these were Archibong and Nsudo.
There were others also. Some of them lost their limbs
fighting for Onitsha. Many died, from Awka, from
Orlu, all over the place, to save Onitsha. Now, if at the
end of the war they have saved Onitsha, do you really
believe that the people of Onitsha have exclusive right
to the land, more than those who have sacrificed their
limbs and lives?

We are now trying to move into Ikot Ekpene. We are
trying to move back into Enugu. Nobody in his right
mind will say to the owners of the land: "Go and bring
back your land, then join us." If we did that, we would
lose very fast the whole of Biafra.

I do not conceive of a situation where people will be
ejected from their sources of revenue and income or
homes. No. But the community has a right to see
that the use of land by those who have proprietary
rights over the land is done properly to the benefit of
the entire public. This is the point. It does not mean
that you will not own your house, that you will not cultivate your farm. It does not mean that on your death

your son cannot move into your farm. I am not advocating confiscation of land and cutting it all into pieces, or all this irresponsible talk about one man one acre, and one man half an acre. No! The government must have full right to say that this land here will be used for industrial development, this land here is good for farming. If you cannot farm it, then people can lease it under prescribed terms and farm it. You cannot say because his mother comes from somewhere else you will not lease the land to him. This is the way I see it. If we accept that land belongs to the community, then, of course, the most important thing becomes the community. You have to be at peace with the community to get the best out of the community. That means you have to be a good citizen.

People have talked about language, suggesting that everybody should learn two or three languages. I say that the new Biafran has quite a lot to learn. I would not like to see it mandatory for everybody to learn two or three Biafran languages. Rather than that, I would prefer to make facilities available for any Biafran to learn any Biafran language he wants to.

I had my incentive as a Nigerian this way. As a young officer, I found it extremely difficult to live within my means—it is true. My father did not give me any extra pocket money. Suddenly I discovered something in the general orders which said that if you could speak a language not your own, you got something at each level—for the lower level you got £40, for the intermediate level you got another £40, and for the professional level, £80. I thanked God. I found that this was really God-sent. Every six months, I took one stage of a Nigerian language. Take Yoruba—I took the lower level and got my £40. It covered my debts for some time! Next three months, the intermediate level, another £40; later, the professional level, I then got my £80. I then pushed Yoruba aside. I started on

Hausa, passed the lower level, and collected my £40, but I did not get around to the intermediate level.

I spent a long time arguing that since I went to school in England, perhaps Ibo would be considered a language not my own to enable me to do the three!

Now, I say that rather than force anybody to learn these languages, if this form of incentive continued for people essentially in administrative jobs, people in the armed forces, people in all the public services where they are dealing with the public, that those people, because of their economic needs, would find it necessary to learn the language and therefore be able to deal with the people better. I find that an easier way. In this way we break down the barrier, but the biggest barrier still is inside. You have truly to believe that the man who speaks a different language is in all respects equal with you in Biafra. Don't wait for the government to do it all. If you believe in it, then go out and practice it.

There are also dangers of tribalism in reverse. There is an oppression in tribalism in reverse. When you see somebody from your own group who is lazy and gets sacked, or who steals and gets sacked, when he comes to complain to you, you should tell him off. If you think that because you come from an area you can exploit that accident to the immediate disadvantage of somebody else, if you proceed to do it, you are a saboteur. If you ask someone, "Why have you been sacked?" and he replies, "They said that I stole, but it is not true, it is because they don't like Orlu people," you have a clear duty to find out what he really did to earn the sack. Don't rush off immediately to call your tribal meeting.

That takes me to another point: tribal meetings. I envisage the new Biafra where there will be none of these tribal meetings. There will be cultural meetings of people from the same ethnic groups, but only to deal with cultural matters, and improvement unions which will be in accordance with locality, not from areas of extraction. Develop Aba, where you live. If you are from Oguta, by all means Oguta women should meet together and produce an Oguta dance. If you are from Awka, see how the designs of your woodcarving would be better. Yes, cultural heritage, but do not use it as a protection group for people from your area. It is in fact subversion of the worst type. In this connection, I plan setting up a commission to handle our cultural exercises, as a means of doing away with many of our mushroom organizations which breed and sustain clannishness and tribalism.

This revolution is a continuing process. It is a revolution that is inevitable for our society—inevitable because of our unique position today. We are a people who find ourselves in a unique position to save the African from neocolonialism. We are a people who by succeeding would ensure for the black man everywhere a place—his right place—under the sun. A place of equality. To be able to do this we have to canalize all our energies and we must be able to root out all those things that distract and dissipate.

Look at yourselves. You are, each and every one of you, a very important individual in Africa. All Africa is watching us. This is the first time in history that a black people are forging ahead together, taking their own destiny in their own hands and making something out of it.

Look at the nations of the world. What is it that makes them big and important? There is nothing that they do that we have not done, under worse circumstances. We are fighting against oppression as men. We are not waiting for somebody to hand victory and freedom to us on a platter of gold. That in itself is a new dimension to African emergence. We are fighting a war—the biggest test of nationhood. We are the only people in Africa, black Africa, the only black people, that have truly fought a war of liberation. We are fighting the stooges of neocolonialism. We are fighting the imperialist powers, Britain and Russia and, in a way, America.

Has it ever occurred to you that the reason why the Eastern and Western bloc countries can get together on our problems is the racial line that has been drawn, across which they are looking at our problems? Everything we have done in this war, indeed from the beginning of the crisis until today, if only our skins had been white, would have earned for us a place of unique honor in the world. We have done it. We have done it everywhere down the line. We have shown that everything the white man can do we can do also, even in the fields of modern science and technology.

We have a historical role to play. Take Britain: What makes Britain? It is the fact that Britain has the ability to exploit us; it is the fact that Britain has the cunning to take from us our raw materials at a price dictated by her and manufacture these raw materials and then sell back to us at a price dictated by her. In order to be able to continue exploiting us, they have created a lot of myths about the black man.

Talking to somebody last week, I described the black man as an unfortunate being. Born a giant, he finds himself in chains. He finds himself in iron chains fastened around his ankles, left to toil in the garden of the white man. From time to time from the garden, through the doors of the mansion, he would see the white man, his master, who was free, enjoying the fruits of his labor. He cursed the God that made him a slave. He saw the white man and his ladies at cocktail parties. He saw them at their dinner parties. He saw them in their finery. And he began to think that cocktails, dinners, and finery were, in fact, the essence of freedom. He looked at them more closely and found them bedecked with glittering gold. The shining metal became to him the symbol of freedom.

He paused. He looked again and again at himself,
his nakedness, his chains—iron around his ankles. He
swore. He cursed. He wept. He prayed for that day
when he would be free. He prayed for that day when
he would have his own gold ornaments. He prayed for
that day when he too would move into the mansion
and sleep, and wake up late in the morning and enter-
tain beautiful ladies.

He then began to think seriously and plan about his
freedom. One day the white man—his master—was
passing through to the plantation and he called on him
and asked, "Master, why am I like this? I want to be
free." The white man looked at him and smiled. "Yes,
Simba, you will be free," he said. "I want to be free.
I want to have gold like you." "Yes, Simba, you will
have some gold." The white man went back and got a
chain of gold. Looking at Simba, he said, "This is your
gold." When he saw the gold, Simba jumped up in
excitement. He put the gold chain on his head. He put
it around his neck. He put it all over his body. He was
delirious. The white man stood near him and watched.
The white man called Simba, worn out with joy, "Come
and let me remove your iron chains of slavery." Simba
moved closer to his white master. The white man bent
down and removed the iron chains around Simba's
ankles. "Please, give me the gold chain," the white man
said. He took the gold chain and tied it around Simba's
ankles. The black man jumped up with joy, shouting,
"I am free. I am free. I am free." He then attempted to
go into the sitting room and stumbled. He fell. He fell
on his face. He found he was still chained: a glorified
slave.

The story illustrates the African dilemma of today.
It dramatizes the farce of the independence of African
states. It paints the picture of a black agony—what I
advocate is breaking of the chains and not changing
of the chains. I call for an African revolution which
would ensure that the chains are broken asunder and
not replaced by a gold chain. I say to the black man,

"Stand up. You have to break your chains, and these chains are in the form of the various myths which have been created to keep us in a position of perpetual servility."

We are the nearest blacks to breaking our chains. We have ourselves fashioned the tools with which to break those chains. We are building. We are fighting with equipment fashioned by ourselves. We are doing everything. We are building a society which will destroy the myth that the black man cannot organize his own society.

We are involved in an indigenous revolution, not borrowed from Mao Tse-tung, or from Whitehall or the White House. We are taking our rightful place in the world as human beings. The white world is watching us with trepidation. They are afraid of the unknown. They do not know what will happen. You see, for a long time there have been so many inhibitions. The black man cannot progress until he can point at a progressive black society. Until a society, a virile society entirely black, is established, the black man, whether he is in America, whether he is in Africa, will never be able to take his place side by side with the white man. We have the unique opportunity today of breaking our chains.

If we fail, the white man, who has been so surprised by our movement, the white man, who has entirely miscalculated every facet of this struggle, will have garnered a new range of knowledge about the potential of the black man and prepared himself to combat us should we ever again rear our ugly head. We owe it, therefore, to Africa not to fail. Africa needs a Biafra. Biafra is the breaking of the chains.

It is not enough just to fight the Nigerians or their friends. We have to fight as a starting point of the African revolution. We are very well equipped for this role. Here in Africa we have the greatest concentration of manpower of the requisite caliber. We are endowed in Biafra with many resources, so that if the size and quality of the manpower available to us is applied to the quality and size of the resources available, the outcome can only be one thing—greatness. Other countries in Africa have not got that combination.

If the revolution fails, we do a disservice to our race. *But, perhaps, more important, and what really frightens the white man, is this whole challenge to the direction of international economy.* The whites have created a system which is a one-way traffic—raw materials to Europe. If that is so, logic tells me that sooner or later, Africa will be sucked dry. The flow of manufactured goods is also a one-way traffic: Europe, America, to Africa. But Biafra, born in blood and revolution, is determined and poised to reverse the trend and challenge this economic imperialism. We are the one black country that today has the capability and capacity to buy raw materials from Europe to manufacture in Africa for selling back to Europeans. I do not say this because I believe the black man is greater. No. I believe that this is the way things should go. They should buy from us. We should buy from them. They should buy our raw materials and we should also buy their own. We should cooperate not as slaves of the European economic oligarchy but as equal partners in a world of progress and not of piracy.

> Address at the passing-out parade of officer
> cadets, Afor-Ugiri, March 2, 1969

A NEW NATION

The flag of Biafra proudly flies high in all corners of the Republic and shall never be hurled down. The flag, depicting our people oppressed by the forces of darkness and redeemed by the blood of our compatriots, bears the sun of a new nation rising from the greens of our fertile lands to herald the birth of the Republic of Biafra. Nor shall we ever cease to play and sing our national anthem, which bears the spirit of a revolutionary people who have freed themselves from the

shackles of feudalism and oppression. We are determined to defend our sovereignty with every ounce of
our strength and with all the resources at our disposal.
Address to convocation of the University of
Biafra, Nsukka, July 1, 1967

From the Northern part of Nigeria our people were
slaughtered. We began running. From the West of
Nigeria and from other parts of the defunct federation
we ran. Many returned by road, dispossessed, brutalized
and helpless. Some returned by rail, harassed, hacked,
and humiliated. The lucky few, women and children,
were squeezed into foreign commercial planes and returned to their fatherland as ghosts of their former
selves: broken, penniless, and bitter.

All I did was to set up an organization, a place, and
to inspire a hopeful vision which would sustain them in
their flight. Having crossed the line, they settled in a
place they could call home. *This is what Biafra is—an
end to a journey, an end to a flight.*
Interview with Marvin Kupfer of *Newsweek*
magazine and David Robison, United States
free-lance journalist, Umuahia, February 13, 1969

Out of the carnage and wrecks of the past will emerge
a new breed of men and women: resolute, powerful
and prosperous.
Foreword: *Pogrom—Crisis '66*

You are in Biafra, you have talked to people and
widely enough, but you ask me what is Biafra? Biafra
was created out of difficulties, but it has a beginning
which is far deeper than the difficulties of 1966. Biafra
came at a time in our history when our people, scat-
tered all over the old Nigerian Federation, were being
hounded everywhere. Very quickly we got together,
those of us who were here, and tried to give direction
to the flight of our people. We got together and decided
that a people in flight must have a goal and a home;

they must have somewhere demarcated where once they have crossed, they can heave a sigh of relief and then face any difficulty with some satisfaction that this is the last area to which they can flee. So, Biafra came as an end to a journey for our people.

One does not talk so much about the material losses —they mean very little to us; what now means something to us is to be left alone to start again to build up. Our attempt at building a large unit has been met with such high cost that our people have gradually realized that the answer perhaps is for us to get together here, roll up our sleeves, find a way of life which will enable us to have the various basic freedoms, enable us to map our own course, to follow it, to make our own mistakes and successes, and, above all, to develop at our own pace and to be in a position to contribute something to the development of the world.

. . . Right now what we are trying to do is to establish in Africa a state that exercises all the attributes of statehood, decides for herself her destiny, stands by that decision, and resolves any difficulties that may arise. If we don't it will take a long time for another Biafra to arise.

What we have demonstrated, especially to those people nervous about their independence, what we have demonstrated very clearly to Africa, is how not to treat their minorities. I think even now every leader in Africa is very much aware of how far and no further he can go in dealing with the minorities. I think Africa has therefore gained a certain wisdom arising from this conflict. I do not think anybody would want to face this problem again.

Meeting with American Congressmen,
Umuahia, February 15, 1969

Our achievements and resolve are something which will go down in world history to the credit of all Biafrans. This will be true whether we think in terms of our young men actually engaged in the battlefronts, our scientists producing weapons and other needs for our existence (incidentally, we have started to produce our own Biafran-made quality salt which is in every way as good as any produced elsewhere in the world), women cooking for the fighting forces, farmers producing food, the police and the civil authorities conducting normal administration, the peasants helping in various ways, indeed everybody without exception. We have every reason to feel proud. God is on our side. Our cause is just.

Inauguration of the Biafran Court of Appeal,
December 8, 1967

There have been a lot of comparisons between us and the Jews. There are, of course, the obvious points—a people persecuted; a people misunderstood grossly; a people haunted by the specter of diaspora; a people upon whom genocide has been visited. There are other points, quite apparent too but not often mentioned—very hard-working people and a people deeply religious.

I do not know which comes first, whether it is religion itself or the persecution that brings about the religion, but there are these similarities.

We travel a lot; so do the Jews; the Jews move around to places and assimilate quite a lot without themselves being assimilated. I think we are the same. And the final point is that the Jews crown all their efforts with success. Now, this applies equally to the Biafran. The Jews get persecuted as a result, basically out of jealousy. That again is true in Biafra.

Interview with John Horgan of the Irish *Times*,
Umuahia, February 20, 1968

What proof does anybody want of solidarity in Biafra? The decision to form the state of Biafra was taken at a meeting of representatives of both sides—that is, the majority and the so-called minorities. In fact, the committee that drafted our pro tem constitution was headed by a "minority" man, Mr. Okoi Arikpo, Nigerian Commissioner for External Affairs.

The war brought with it complex problems and hardships, and people have suffered many deprivations that normally would bring unrest, but there has been no unrest, no breakdown of law and order. That, in itself, is indicative of the people's feelings. The war is a perfect time for those who do not really believe in Biafra to pull out. But there has been no such thing.

Biafra is not a tribal state. It is a group of people who have willingly come together to work out their own destiny. To find out the feelings of these people, the answer obviously is to talk to them. But in case there is any doubt, we have said here that a referendum should be held for them to decide for themselves whether or not to stay as part of Biafra.

Interview with Canadian, Dutch, and Danish
parliamentarians and accompanying journalists,
Umuahia, November 13, 1968

Gowon has tried everything. He has fought us by land and found it more difficult than he expected. He has tried by sea and found it quite disastrous. He has tried to intimidate us from the air and failed. He has tried subversion, but each time our people have shown that nothing will daunt them in their determination to survive. I think perhaps the most diabolic thing Gowon and his clique have done is this question of withdrawal of the Nigerian currency, by which he hoped, just by a stroke of the pen, to complete the dispossession of all 14,000,000 people of Biafra. I am glad of the way our people have remained solid in their determination.

After the announcement of the currency switch, the whole world expected Biafra to go up in flames, in riots, in demonstrations, to frustrate the action of the government to such an extent that we would lay down our arms and surrender to Nigerian domination. As it has happened, the only place there has been a riot about money is in Kaduna. It has not affected us. Our people have remained solidly behind the government. Biafra has shown that this is a war of the people. This is the greatest test of nationhood, and our people have come out of it with their heads held up high in the air. I understand that some women in the villages said that if this money [during the recall of Nigerian currency for Biafran currency] was wanted for the war they did not mind; the government should take all. It shows the degree of our total involvement in this war.

> Response to Health Visitors of Biafra,
> Umuahia, January 18, 1968

The Nigerians appear not to know that by unleashing a war of aggression in addition to several past injuries, they have aroused a whole people against them. This is a people's war for freedom. Biafra has come to stay, and the fact of our independence is irreversible.

Ours is a nation of 14,000,000 people, with various ethnic groupings, united together by past suffering and present freedom, and nothing can shake our determination. Conscious of the justness of our cause, and with God on our side, our people are determined to fight to the last man, confident of eventual success.

> Message to Biafran students in the United States
> of America, November 24, 1967

The Biafran society is such that you cannot stay in office probably longer than six months without having to consult the people. There are many checks and balances here.

And all the attributes of Nigeria which fired the imagination of the world prior to the revolution of January, 1966, are in fact, as it were, exclusive to the people of this area.

The people who make up Biafra were the ones who won freedom for Nigeria and preached the concept of equality and all the various ideals. With the people now concentrated here, I think we could build, quite easily, a state which would be a model in Africa.

> Interview with West German journalist
> Dr. Ruth Bowert, Umuahia, March 25, 1968

VII

On Africa

African Initiative

Africa belongs to Africans. The world belongs to humanity. Africans own Africa, and to improve Africa in a world context they need the world to help them. I believe Africa is large enough to accommodate a number of people, provided the spirit is right, provided they come in as partners in progress, provided one knows here that the African is the host and the visitor is the guest.

Interview with Dr. B. da Silva of *Diario Popular*
of Lisbon, Umuahia, March 14, 1968

When Biafra is fully recognized there will be opportunity to share the benefits of our vast mineral and manpower resources with other African countries. Before this war, when Zambia asked for locomotive drivers, we were ready to send them 100. This is an indication of our African attitude. Our sovereignty will give us protection within and outside Biafra, but the benefit will be extended to others. Even with our enemy, Nigeria, there is also a vast area of possible accommodation.

Meeting with delegates and of Friends of Biafra
Association (Britain), Umuahia, March 18, 1968

I understand that to get diplomatic recognition for Biafra, African countries will have to take the lead. I understand also that very few African countries have sufficient independence for an initiative of this nature.

So it works in a vicious circle: the African countries should do it; they cannot because the greater powers (that is, the patron states) have not given the approval. Now, the patron states themselves say they are inhibited because the client states have not taken an initiative they know they cannot take.

Countries in Africa that have shown a more independent line in their policies are the more progressive states. They are likely to recognize Biafra first.

States like Senegal and the Ivory Coast, states like some of the East African countries, have shown a marked understanding of our problems. This sort of understanding should be a prelude to a definite action by the states, and certainly one would expect that sort of action [recognition] from those who have indicated an understanding of our problem.

Interview with John Horgan of the Irish *Times*,
Umuahia, February 20, 1968

The diplomatic recognition of Biafra by Tanzania is having a great effect, even now. It is the first time an African country has demonstrated its independence. Indeed, President Julius Nyerere has shown tremendous courage. I think the effect of this will grow with time. A number of countries are now considering: (1) why Tanzania took this action, (2) what action they themselves should take.

I think that the position that Tanzania has taken certainly will affect the Organization of African Unity itself. Of course, anything that affects OAU as a body does affect a large portion of the world. I think the major powers, the European powers, if not alive to the problem here, are now actively studying it, because for the first time they see the possibility of a new member of the comity of nations.

I think that Tanzania having, as it were, broken the ice, the true feeling of Africa will now be demonstrated. I think those who now feel that we are right will come forward and speak. I feel, too, that this obvious split in African opinion will make Lagos think more realistically on the issues involved in this war, and possibly enhance the possibility of getting around to the conference table.

I think that the stand taken by Tanzania will definitely excite a lot of interest in the Commonwealth too, and that the question of Biafra, by this bold stroke, has ceased to be an internal problem of Nigeria. This is a great thing that President Nyerere has done.

> Meeting with delegates of Britain-Biafra
> Association, Umuahia, April 18, 1968

Recognition by four friendly African states (Tanzania, Gabon, Ivory Coast, and Zambia) has helped, because it opened the lid of this struggle to the world. It has brought the problem to an international audience. But more important, it has quite clearly forced Gowon to a conference table. Though the conference did not achieve much result, it is a step in the right direction. But for the recognition, we would not have had the opportunity of getting around the table to discuss the problem.

The recognition, too, has clearly shown to the world that there is not just one African opinion, which is anti-Biafran. It has clearly shown to the world that there is a conflict and this has made people consider the merits and demerits of the two sides. For us this is encouraging! It has made us at least feel that we are not entirely alone. In practical ways, it has made it possible for more relief to come here.

> Interview with Cliff Robertson, United States
> actor, Umuahia, December 9, 1968

The Organization of African Unity we recognize as an essential instrument for the achievement of meaningful African unity. Unlike the defunct Nigerian Federation, the Republic of Biafra must work more positively for the realization of the objectives of the organization which have thus far eluded it.

We believe that true unity will eventually emerge from the association if African states, while maintaining their popular character and institutions, enter into free association with one another to serve their common economic interests. In due course, this form of association will help to build up an African political union.

Biafrans must play a dynamic role by their readiness to share their human and material resources with other African peoples even if it means some sacrifice on our part. We shall adopt an open-door policy toward all Africans who may wish to sojourn here and benefit from any facilities we may possess. It is through such free association and exchange of ideas among African peoples that the unity we all desire can materialize.

Broadcast, August 10, 1967

THE ORGANIZATION OF AFRICAN UNITY

The Organization of African Unity is merely a title—a marionette show—plenty of pomp but no circumstance. It has many slogans but no sense of purpose and makes no pretense of satisfying African needs. Indeed, it might be an Organization of African Eunuchs.

Interview with Biafra Information Complex,
December 31, 1968

The Organization of African Unity, by its inability to find a solution to the Biafran problem, has demonstrated its impotence as an organization, its impotence in resolving African conflicts. The reasons for this failure arise from the type of independence the countries that compose this organization have.

The OAU was expected to give an African solution, yet, in a sense, the OAU is not African. The OAU has African skin, but this is only a mask for neocolonialism. It is a mask for established imperialism—Arab—British—Russian.

Interview with Biafra Information Complex,
Umuahia, December 31, 1968

What can Africa do? African leaders have made attempts to find a solution but throughout they have been
handicapped by a knowledge of their own inadequacy.
A knowledge of their own shortcoming. They have not
been able to do anything because they have had to
await their patrons' pleasure.

They have in a number of cases had to toe the line
of their patrons—the major powers. The Organization
of African Unity has tried for over a year and has
failed. I do not think the OAU can now do much about
this struggle. The Western powers which are more independent can individually have a critical appraisal of
the situation and act as individual countries, either to
bring pressure to bear on Lagos to seek a peaceful
solution or to neutralize aggression by stopping the
supply of arms to Nigeria.

> Interview with Cliff Robertson, United States
> actor, Umuahia, December 9, 1968

I do not believe that the impotence of the Organization of African Unity is due to lack of initiative by
African states or the OAU Secretariat. It is not the
structure. The present structure is not relevant to the
point because African states are not independent. Only
truly independent African states can develop, each in
its way, to enable the OAU to have the type of machinery necessary for maintaining African peace. If peace in
Africa depends on borrowed might, is it not then clear
that peace in Africa would depend on the interests of
the outside world which gives the wherewithal to maintain that peace?

> Interview with Biafra Information Complex,
> Umuahia, December 31, 1968

As long as you find in Africa an Organization of
African Unity that has a preponderance of non-Africans, you cannot get anything out of it.

African unity should, at least at the beginning, be
African unity of purpose. I do not see in the immediate
future a surrendering of the various sovereign rights

completely into a fusion of one large African sovereignty. I can see cultural exchanges. I can see uniform systems and patterns evolving in Africa for progressive activity. I can see economic cooperation, a common market. I can see free interchange and outlets of commerce. I can see customs unions. I can see eventually a parliament for Africa, in which sovereign states would be represented, which would not have rights over sovereignties but enable African states to thrash out their differences so as to achieve a unity of purpose.

Unfortunately, a lot of confusing definitions have been made about this question of unity. Everybody has talked about African unity without clearly showing what it means. It was, in fact, in avoiding this definition that the OAU was created from the Monrovia and Casablanca groups of states.

At every turn, Africa has suffered from the inability to differentiate adornment from substance. You will always find the same thing in meetings of the OAU. As soon as there is a problem, either the OAU does not meet or the OAU meets and discusses technicalities. It is more important to appear united without actually tackling any problem. These meetings normally end with the issue of a high-sounding communiqué which, if examined in detail, is meaningless or a mass of contradictions. The member states go back to their patrons to report on the meeting. It is only then that various interpretations are given to the slogan which was indeed their communiqué. The only thing that comes out from the meeting, in real substance, is what the patron states want to emerge. This is the problem of Africa today.

The colonial divisions or boundaries in Africa are wrong. They bear no relationship to our national needs or interests. They only tend to make it impossible for our societies to stay together in unity. The Biafran experience has dramatized this fact—the fact that certain prescribed factors make for disunity and any attempt to bring about unity by force would only lead to conflicts.

Biafra is a warning to all Africans on how not to

treat small groups within large groups. If Africans learn as a result of our struggle to tolerate, then wider unity becomes easier; such unity would be realistic. But if Africa persists in treating minorities as though they had no rights at all, despite the Biafran example, then there will be greater friction and inevitable breakdown of larger entities. For example, the conflict in Sudan is one where it has become very clear that there must be a separation. The Northern Sudanese have not recognized the fact that the blacks in the South have any rights, let alone equal rights.

Interview with Biafra Information Complex,
Umuahia, December 31, 1968

The real obstacle to a realistic approach to the problem has remained Mr. Diallo Telli, the Secretary General of the OAU. His destructive and unhelpful influence has been evident on all occasions where the OAU has tried to tackle the problem of the current war. So absolutely and prejudicially committed to the Nigerian cause is Diallo Telli that he, sometimes, seems more pro-Nigeria than the Nigerians themselves. In order not to leave any room for flexibility in the minds of the members of the OAU Committee, Mr. Diallo Telli, consistently and almost in a way bordering on blackmail, pinned them down to the letter of OAU resolutions in Kinshasa and Algiers, resolutions accepted in unprejudiced circles the world over as one-sided and unrealistic.

. . . As might be expected, the British government, its agents and allies, have embarked on their vicious propaganda to show the world that Biafra was responsible for the failure of the OAU Committee in Monrovia to find a solution to the conflict, or at least bring about a cease-fire. The head of the Biafran delegation to the meeting did immediately issue a statement in Monrovia which accurately and faithfully represented our position.

In his letter of invitation to us, President Tubman of Liberia wrote that the purpose of the meeting was, and I quote, "to explore the possibility of further talks between both parties in the Nigeria-Biafra conflict without preconditions or agenda." In briefing our delegates for the meeting we had nothing else in mind but what President Tubman clearly stated to be the purpose of the meeting. Our delegation therefore went to Monrovia to *explore* the possibility of further talks with Nigeria without preconditions. The government statement issued just before the departure of our delegation made the point clear. I have no reason to doubt that the contents of President Tubman's letter represented the minds and intentions of all the members of the committee.

To the surprise of our delegation, the final proposal of the OAU went quite contrary to what had been given out as the purpose of the meeting. It imposed the condition that our people must accept the Nigerian position by renouncing our sovereignty, or what they call secession, before there could be a cease-fire and talks. The terms "United Nigeria" and "citizens" contained in the OAU Committee proposals mean nothing else but that. It is significant that the OAU proposals spoke of guarantees for all citizens. This is clearly an acceptance of the point we have always stressed, namely, that we are a wronged people to whom guarantees hold out no prospects of security.

To accept the OAU Committee proposals as offered would mean our acceptance of Nigeria's and the British government's position that the present conflict is an internal problem. It would mean a surrender to Nigeria when we know that unity with Nigeria cannot: (a) bring back the lives of millions who were murdered in 1966 or perished as a result of this war, (b) compensate us for all the property destroyed, (c) rebuild Owerri and other cities equally devastated, (d) compensate us for the hundreds and millions of pounds which our people lost as a result of the Nigerian wicked currency switch last year.

I personally see no advantage in such a situation. The fact is that Nigeria is not interested in a peaceful settlement. It is still poised for a military solution, and that is why they put in everything in order to capture

Umuahia in the belief that such a capture would mean the capitulation of Biafra. Having claimed to have captured Umuahia, what they now expect is nothing but the surrender of Biafra.

I have repeatedly made it clear that Biafra is willing to enter into meaningful talks with Nigeria without preconditions. A talk without preconditions offers the best possibility of resolving the conflict. What do we mean by talk without preconditions? Gowon says Biafra is part of Nigeria and must be integrated into Nigeria. Let him keep to that position and we shall not expect him to accept the fact of our sovereignty before proceeding to the conference table. We say that Biafra is sovereign and no longer part of Nigeria. Let Gowon and the world allow us the right to say so, and not expect us to recant our position, before proceeding to the conference table. At the conference, we shall put forward and discuss our positions, and whatever comes out of such discussions will be the factual position. Why is Nigeria afraid of arguments and discussions? Could it be that Nigeria is conscious that her case could not bear the light and test of reason?

In order to create the right atmosphere for discussions there must be a cease-fire, or failing that, a truce for a limited period. Our delegation suggested two weeks for such a truce, thereby trying to meet Nigeria's fears that we might use the period of truce to accumulate arms or reorganize our troops. One, however, wonders, in the light of current events, whether such fear would not be more justified for us than for Nigeria. In his opening speech, President Tubman accepted the need for a cease-fire to enable negotiations to proceed. Why did he and other members of the committee eventually act differently?

It is now absolutely clear from this last performance of the OAU Committee that that Organization has failed. It has neither the will nor the ability to bring about peace. If, therefore, the present conflict is to be brought to an end by Africa, then, perhaps, the best approach would be to adopt true African methods, shorn of extraneous trappings, toward a settlement. One such method might be to ask the two parties to nominate two or three friends each to go into the matter on their behalf. Such friends could meet, possibly under the chairmanship of the Emperor, to find an acceptable solution on behalf of the two parties.

I wish once again to emphasize that the present conflict between Nigeria and Biafra has ceased to be a regional or African problem, just as Vietnam is not an Asian problem or the Middle East an Arab problem. It is nonsense to talk of the problem being African in the face of the barefaced and direct involvement of Britain and Russia, and the less obvious involvement of Algeria and Egypt and Sudan.

Now that events have shown that Nigeria can never win this war and its policy of quick kill also is a farce, it is left to the world to step in and stop the current bloodshed. America should cease to look at the problem merely in terms of relief, which, as I have often repeated, can be no more than a palliative.

Our policy remains unchanged. We remain prepared to reach an accommodation with Nigeria, provided our internal and external security are guaranteed, along with an international presence. We cannot ever again entrust our security into the hands of other people, and cannot accept a situation where, should events similar to those of the recent past repeat themselves, we shall not be able to reach direct to the world for a hearing.

Since the OAU has failed and the UNO has decided to bury its head in the sand, and since the grumblings of the nations have not crystallized into action to end a crime against humanity, we have no alternative but to continue the struggle, until Nigeria is finally compelled to abandon her militarism and maniacal ambition.

In search of peace, in search of honor, we have already tramped the capitals of the world. In search of peace we have approached public men of proclaimed good will. Individuals have called for peace. Groups have called for peace. Governments have called for peace. International organizations have called for peace. Only the Organization of African Unity has stood out for and distinguished itself in pursuance of policies which can only promote war. The OAU as an organization has shown itself not capable of and to a certain degree not interested in solving problems of any magnitude.

Address to joint meeting of Elders and Chiefs
and Consultative Assembly, Owerri, May 1, 1969

BALKANIZATION

A country never disintegrates because another one did; otherwise there would be only fragments of countries left in the world today—after all there have been many precedents for disintegration. The world by now would have been reduced to a conglomeration of family sovereignties. I think the disintegration of Nigeria will serve as a warning, a very necessary warning, to African states on how not to treat their citizens, no matter whether or not they are ethnic minorities or other forms of minorities. I believe this to be the true lesson of the Biafran independence.

There is no state that has no minority. Even in the State of Biafra, there are minorities. But as you have seen here, if anything, separation from Nigeria has welded us far closer together than before the separation of Biafra from the larger entity.

Meeting with delegates of Britain-Biafra
Association, Umuahia, April 18, 1968

Our detractors have also confused African, and indeed world, opinion by propagandizing the despicable falsehood that our independence will be a precedent for separatist movement in other African states. They have not bothered to ask themselves, for instance, what was the precedent for the alleged Biafran "secession." The truth is that one so-called secession does not necessarily lead to another.

Throughout history, there has been a long list of empires that broke up into nations, and federations which split into sovereign states. The union of Great Britain and (Northern) Ireland, the federations of Mali, Malaysia, West Indies, and Central Africa, are recent examples of this: the disintegration occurred on account of unique local factors or grave linguistic and religious differences. Biafra, however, remains a lesson to all countries of what could happen if they were to unleash a pogrom against a section of their own community.

Among other spurious arguments trumped up by the Lagos clique is that Nigeria is a single interdependent economic unit and that its disintegration would disrupt established market trends and leave the separate economies so much poorer. It is true that between the regions of the former Nigerian Federation the economic pattern was one of interdependence, but this is equally true of all world economies which are complementary. But this should not make us try to force unworkable political units on an unwilling people merely to create a large market.

It is enough for both states to enter into trade and technical agreements. With more efficient planning, these separate units could even be made economically more prosperous. This also disproves the argument that Nigeria would not be viable without Biafra. Perhaps, Nigeria may be poorer for it, and it should have occurred to its leaders to be more tolerant of people who they now admit constituted their wealth. But the rest of Nigeria has enough potentiality to remain a great and united African state, if only its leaders will show realism and imagination in harnessing their vast potential resources.

Message to Biafran students in the United States of America, November 24, 1967

On the question of nationalism, it would be a pity if Africa considers as final present political subdivisions of Africa without ascertaining the wishes of Africans. Present boundaries were imposed by imperialists—every member of the club receiving his share of the loot. Size, shape, and quality of the loot reflected the relative importance of the imperial state, not the needs of the African who, incidentally, owns the place. Peace was maintained with the finger on the trigger. With the departure of the colonial master, without his pistol, readjustments became inevitable—readjustments of either boundaries or the basis of association within the political entity. Or else a dominant group has to acquire a pistol to maintain some cohesion. The easiest and most ready-to-hand form of acquisition is by borrowing from the ex-colonial masters . . . at a price. I call that price neocolonialism. To strive to maintain these artificial boundaries is to set the stage for neocolonialist exploitation. This explains in a way the reason for the Nigerian aggression.

In Biafra we have been bold. In Biafra you find a people, not just a drawing on a map, a people willingly bound together to seek their own salvation. Biafra is a nation-state and it will survive. Its emergence will act as a warning to Africa. It will warn African states not to treat their minorities the way Nigeria treated Biafra. In any country anywhere in the world, given the same set of circumstances, the reaction will be exactly the same. Readjustment of nationalities within state boundaries is inevitable—it is a prerequisite of modernization and progress; it is a necessary stage of development. The period of this adjustment in European history is indeed what is commonly known as "modern history." We have in Biafra shown the world this fact about ourselves that we are tolerant. No country in the world could have suffered what we have and bear it for so long.

International press conference,
Umuahia, November 18, 1967

Larger unities? It is very difficult in a short space of time to explain away the complexities of neocolonialism.

Our attitude of mind is so much dictated by the prescribed notions imposed upon us by our erstwhile colonial masters. One such idea is the emphasis on the quantitative as opposed to the qualitative. This is what gives rise to this romantic idea of larger unities. I normally call this the elephantine theory of politics—the larger the state the better. If you want a large state, then create the state of Sahara! It extends from the east coast to the west coast of Africa. If nothing else, it would be large. The white man implanted this notion, half-baked as it is, in order to keep us for a long period under his tutelage. He, in his own society, has not founded larger unities—his prescribed answer to this problem of self-fulfillment. If the emphasis should be on larger unities, I would have thought the white man had a beautiful starting point: the Holy Roman Empire. The white man should perhaps in Europe be forced back into the Empire; he should learn that in such large unity he would find fulfillment. Today, why not blindly unite the whole of Europe? This would then be a larger unity.

No, what I am trying to break away from is the blind acceptance of half-digested thoughts handed out from outside. The white man says large unities are a good thing. The African, the black man, should ask himself, "Good for what?" Are large unities merely good just for the sake of largeness? Or, in the case of Nigeria, good for genocide and neocolonialist exploitation? A large unity, whether it has the essentials of freedom and true independence or not? The size of a nation is not the important thing but the quality of the nation. In any case, Nigeria was large, but what benefit did the black man derive from that size? Ghana is small, and at a time the black man got certainly far more from the existence of Ghana than the black man ever got from the existence of Nigeria. Quality is what matters, not quantity.

National seminar, Umuahia,
December 9, 1968

How much do larger unities enhance the African revolution? This is what one has to find out. I do not think that the black man has yet examined the various state organizations to find out whether the states are democratic or not, to find out whether basic human dignities are respected or not, to find out whether the ultimate goal of the state—the security and welfare of its citizens—is attained. The Biafran revolution serves as a warning that answers to these questions should not be taken lightly.

What I really support would be closer associations of progressive forces in Africa. I would like to see a situation where truly independent African states unite culturally, associate socially, cooperate economically, and coordinate in political and diplomatic matters: It would be dangerous at this stage, since many African countries are tied to the apron strings of some major power, to join an association other than in the loosest form. It must be borne in mind that a headlong dive into such associations, such unities, will inevitably invite the imperial powers back to Africa. At the moment, the Organization of African Unity is a lower platform for the ex-colonial powers to meet and also a place where the ex-colonies can let off steam. Most meetings in Africa are really oversimplified versions of meetings in European capitals, and this is what Africa should avoid. Decisions in the OAU still continue to be taken in Europe. We Africans should be able to get together, to plan independently, take only our own African interests into consideration, and face the European, the American, the Chinese, the Russian, the Asian, and the Arab with our own body of interests and mutually find a formula for mutual progress. I do not support blind unity, unity without substance, unity without the essentials of African independence.

National seminar, Umuahia, December 9, 1968

When will Americans get off their neocolonialism hobbyhorse? What rights have the Americans to dictate to us what is right for our people here? Somebody sits in Washington and pontificates about what will be good for Africa! The same voice we hear from Whitehall telling us: *"We intend to found a stable federation."*

Do countries act just because another country has acted this or that way? I do not think so. There is always the question of cause and effect. When a series of tragic events have taken place, then there is a reaction. If you want to stop the reaction then stop the series of tragic events.

I think that rather than being a cause for fragmentation of Africa, Biafra will be a warning to Africa against ill treatment of a minority. The world has been terrorized by clichés and words that have very little bearing on some of its problems. So many words have got so many connotations now that objective analyses give way to sloganization. Nobody ever finds solutions in slogans. You don't know a product ever by merely reading the advertisement or commercial.

Now, let us get back to the question of Balkanization. What we have in Biafra is not a weak, unstable entity. If you take the manpower quality, I believe we are around number one in Africa. And when I talk of Africa I mean real Africa. When you talk about population, you will probably find us within the first five in all of Africa. By size, I do not think we are the smallest. By resources, I think we would probably be within the first five also. Therefore, the question of weakness and instability does not affect us.

Balkanization implies weakness, but I have tried to show that this is not true. But if by Balkanization you mean division, secession inclusive, then I say to you: "Look at Europe." For a time there were endless wars in Europe, incessant conflicts until the old European empires were dismantled, until the Balkans were Balkanized—then came peace. Why would one think that Balkanization for Europe and Biafranization for Africa would produce different results? I do not think it would. While not advocating that every country be split into bits, I think we should look at Biafra objectively. Biafra has a message for Africa.

Interview with Marvin Kupfer of *Newsweek*
magazine and David Robison, United States
free-lance journalist, Umuahia, February 13, 1969

IMPERIALISM

Imperialism means the silencing of the moral voice of a people by force of arms from outside and the continued exploitation arising from it.

> Interview with Biafra Information Complex,
> Umuahia, December 31, 1968

The war has continued to this day because of the determination of Harold Wilson to crush a people of progress, of talent and initiative, in an area of Africa which his government would like forever to keep under its direct economic control and indirect political subservience.

> End of Year Message, December 31, 1968

The Russians want a foothold in Africa. Their plan now seems to be to link up this foothold in Nigeria with their communist militant Arab satellites in North Africa. This is an extension—a logical extension—of the Middle East conflict.

> Meeting with Dr. J. Dunwoody, British
> (Labour) M.P., December 4, 1968

Our true enemy is imperialism and its insatiable greed to plunder, to loot, to rampage Africa and the African people, and, if possible, to use African puppets to achieve their selfish ends.

As I have said before, and I repeat, the war we are fighting is an imperialist war, waged by Britain and Russia in an unholy alliance and with the tacit acquiescence of the United States of America and fought by proxy. The Nigerians are merely tools deserving not of hatred but pity.

Born into a world dominated by narrow and selfish national interests, into a world where fair humanity has been ravished of any conscience, in a world where megalomaniac materialism has usurped the position of all spiritually ennobling virtues, we have emerged with our heads bloody but unbowed. The success of this day has come as a result of our togetherness in this struggle. No more should we fear the bullets in the borrowed arsenal of our enemies.

Address to a joint meeting of Elders and Chiefs and Consultative Assembly, Owerri, May 1, 1969

VIII
On the Black Man

"The sky above belongs to God, and down below gathering strength from the earth is the black man and, between him and God stands the white man." That is our predicament. We reach out to go beyond the white man to get to God himself. To get the white man to one side and go straight to God is our problem. In this African [Sengalese] proverb you see everything of the African predicament and his aspirations.

Interview with Alan Grossman of *Time* magazine, Umuahia, April 25, 1968

To be an African means to be handicapped. The old African was considered something at par with the animal. The present African is considered somewhat subhuman. We are hoping (and every African has this struggle to face) and trying very hard to prove to the world that the African is a man. That he and his ancestors have made important contributions to human progress and civilization. I do not think the African asks for more.

To be truly African in the present-day context is, at all times, to be proving to the world that you are a man, a human being; no more, no less. In Biafra, we are trying to establish the fact that, despite the color of our skin, we are men, human beings, to be accepted as such.

Interview with John Horgan of the Irish *Times,* Umuahia, February 20, 1968

The origin of conflict is rooted in the desire to dominate. This desire for dominance is the fundamental cause of all conflicts between states, the cause of all wars.

The acceptance of equality is conducive to peace— it is a recognition of this very fact that evolved the international concept of sovereignty, allowing a group, no matter how small, to be equal with another group, no matter how big. This assertion by the black man of his equality certainly will bring about a clash if the white man continues to maintain that the black man is not equal to him. It is the resistance to this basic fact of equality that will bring about the clash, not just the fact of the assertion. I am hopeful, I am convinced, that once the Biafran experiment is fully established, once its acceptance is established, once Biafra takes her place and the black man can point to it, then the lie will have been given to the white myth of black inferiority.

Address to National Seminar, Umuahia,
December 6, 1968

. . . It worries me, it worries me very much, that our black brothers and sisters in America do not in fact see this struggle for what it really is. What we are trying to do here is for this small area called Biafra to stay on its own; and the whole concept has significance for Africa and the black race. Black men have always struggled to establish themselves as men, to be accepted as equal to all men.

We have a unique opportunity here. Our history is such that it has been possible for us to develop in a unique way.

Biafra is a viable organization that is truly black. We derive great pride from this fact. We feel very sure that, had the things we have done here been done by people whose skins were white, our heroism would be universally heralded. An unflinching commitment to the noble concept of self-determination, to a people's right to independence, the setting up by a people of a nation and the institutional structures that will enable them to work out their own destiny—these are what we have done.

We have fought this battle without funds. Despite the international conspiracy against our people, we have shown that what has been done by the whites can be done by our people. It is for this reason that I feel sad that our struggle is not fully understood by those for whom it is essential.

The reason for the lack of understanding is quite simple. It is an imperialist conspiracy, that is, the attempt by neocolonialists to bamboozle African governments, frighten them, particularly when a number of these governments choose not to use their own judgment. What has happened is that the bogey of Balkanization has been evoked on these governments; and since the governments are not truly representative and very afraid of their own shadows, they have succumbed.

I believe that with real understanding—and the only way to do it is for people to come and see for themselves—the black man would derive an inspiration from the Biafran struggle.

I repeat that this is the first time that the Biafran humanity is being put to trial and we are not doing badly. Sooner or later this revolution will be recognized. I am well aware too that the imperialist interests are all wondering what will come out of all this. They fear that the whole basis of their economic grip is being threatened. The imperialists do not know how this will affect their various vested interests. They suffer from a terrible fear of the unknown. We are faced with problems basically arising from their fright against what they sometimes see as a new threat to their continued domination of the black man.

Meeting with Charles Kenyatta, American leader,
Umuahia, November 11, 1968

THE SIGNIFICANCE OF BIAFRA

I see Biafra as the crystallization of the black man's search for identity and recognition.

I see Biafra as the starting point of the black man's march to his rightful place under the sun—his march to his destiny. His march to a tomorrow of promise, progress, and equal opportunity.

I see Biafra as a symbol of black resistance in a world dominated by narrow national selfish interest and inhumanity.

I see Biafra as a bastion of the free in an age in which freedom and self-determination are conditioned by the color of the skin.

I see Biafra as a challenge to the color myths of the centuries which relegate the black man to the role of a serf without brains, without pride, without dignity.

I would even go further to say that for the acceptance of the black race, there must be a Biafra. Without Biafra the black man cannot establish as fully equal with other men. The black man must be able to point to a social organization which stands equally as erect as others. Possibly, it might not be this Biafra. If this Biafra is stifled, then perhaps in twenty years another will emerge.

Interview with Charles Kenyatta, American leader,
Umuahia, November 11, 1968

What we are trying to do here is to establish the fact that despite this black color of our skin, we are human beings. Had the color of our skin been white, everything we have done in Biafra from the beginning to the end would have meant the complete rewrite of all schoolbooks for children to emulate and study. Our struggle would have been a classic in literature, an epic in our civilization. But, unfortunately, all these seem misplaced; they fall on the wrong side of the color bar. What is more, it has tended to create certain fears. Fear in the realization that this is indeed a revolution. The fear that when the revolution does succeed a whole world of clichés will be cast asunder, a whole list of myths will be debunked. More important, the entire direction of economic transaction would change, or rather the indication of the change would be manifest.

Our eventual success shows that for once in Africa you will find a country that will go out seeking raw materials with which to manufacture. That change in economic direction is an important one. It is something that has to come.

Interview with Cliff Robertson, United States
actor, Umuahia, December 9, 1968

What is the significance of Biafra? Biafra is the first true attempt of the black man to set up his own society, to set it up by himself, to rely on himself for protecting that society, to develop that society, and to nurture that society. This is what Biafra is. Without this, whatever Negroes do elsewhere will just be beating about the bush. To destroy a myth, one has to expose the abject fallacy of that myth.

It is not enough to preach to the world that the African or the black man is equal to his white counterpart. No. The African must be able to point at a success which is truly his own. He must be able to say: "This is our own African society. This is our own progressive society, this is our own fast-developing society. This is our own society that can take its place with other societies on earth, this is our society that can contribute equally with the other societies to the store of civilized knowledge." There is need for this success in Africa.

I see Biafra as the beginning of an African revolution. I say this because, somehow, nature has conspired to put Biafra in a unique position to carry through this revolution, to carry through this change.

Here, circumstances have forced us into a position of self-reliance. We have achieved a measure of success in establishing our own society. We have here adequate manpower of the right quality, the requisite quality. We have here sufficient endowment. We have sufficient innate capacity for applying ourselves to our resources. We have been tested in war, the sort of war no other black society has been tested in. The chances are that we are nearer success than any other black society has been. Once we succeed, then our continued existence gives a lie to all the myths which enable the whites to continue to dominate. The myths that enable the whites to rule us, as it were, by remote control. The fact of Biafra already indicates that one of the basic myths— that of direction of economy which for all time must always be from Africa to Europe—will have been changed.

Address at Biafra People's Seminar,
Umuahia, January 22, 1969

This is the one black society that on its own can go out and seek raw material, process the raw materials, manufacture finished products, and sell them with absolute equality in the open world market. Once this has been demonstrated, you will find that the basis of neo-colonialism has been removed; which is, continued economic dominance. Biafra is a starting point in that the black man must be able to point at the Biafra success as a precedent before he can obtain total acceptance in a world that considers him inferior.

The concept of Biafra, to me, is one that transcends our own territorial confines. It goes beyond Africa. It goes on and finds its roots in the aspiration of the black man to find a place for himself on this God-given earth. I feel that the black man has suffered for a long time. He has been a victim of political domination, exploitation, and social indignities.

The whites have been able to keep the blacks back because of the series of myths they have created about the black race. The whites, for example, believe that the term "Negro" is the same as servility; to them the term "Negro" immediately spells permanent dependence and a lesser being than the white.

Throughout history, the black man has been in chains. The indications are there that the black man has never liked the chains he finds himself in. One has only to go back into history to see valiant attempts by black men to assert themselves, to find acceptance in the world, to find a place of equality in the world. In doing this, the black man has tried, by tackling various facets of his disability, to demonstrate that the myths are truly myths, not facts. In the field of culture he has tried by developing his own. Some have tried to do this by an almost blind effort at discovering their roots in Africa. He has tried in the field of economics to build up certain economic entities. There had been, as well, a political attempt at coming back to Africa. *With the passage of time, it became clearer that to obtain this acceptance the black man needs freedom—absolute freedom, black freedom.* The various political attempts are in fact a recognition of this need.

A man can progress only if he is truly free. A man is himself only in a free atmosphere, in a free environment. A man can develop fully when he is free. Any restriction on his freedom inhibits his development. So it is with the African. A search for his own identity became for him a search for freedom, or rather an attempt to place himself in a position which is truly his on earth; to be accepted, not just as a black man, but to be accepted as *man* with no other adjective describing him.

We have got to shed all those things that make us, the Africans, a lesser breed. We must shed the slave complex.

. . . The whites feel very strongly about the emergence of an independent state in Africa or an independent black state. They see such a state as the biggest threat to their position in the world establishment. Like all establishments, they are very nervous of anything that might tend to shake or to ruffle the status quo. Most of them are not really sure of what they are afraid of. Right now, they feel that this black state, this unknown quantity, somehow must affect them. If you think of our problems in this way, there is then a clear logic running through the activities of our white brothers all over the world. The racial unity of interest among the whites is more important to them than humanity. It is more important to them than their liberalism or even their ideologies.

Address at Biafra People's Seminar,
Umuahia, March 5, 1969

IX
On the World

INDIFFERENCE

Blockaded, besieged, we had no alternative but to cry out as loud as we could so that, should we perish, somewhere, some people in the world, men of good will, will at least record the fact that at one time we did exist.

Interview with Lloyd Garrison, *New York Times,*
Umuahia, February 27, 1969

A people have been killed so systematically and no question has been raised anywhere in the world. In Biafra we find genocide staring us in the face, and the world has no conscience and people merely sit back and rationalize [the final push-out, May, 1967]. What was there to rationalize? The world would continue rationalizing until we were all dead. But our people said no, we have had enough: and from then we made arrangements to face the inevitable. Right from then I told the people of Biafra that we would probably have to fight to save ourselves from genocide. Then I assured them, too, that as long as their hearts were strong, no matter the difficulties, we would carry this fight to a successful conclusion.

Address to Aba Leaders of Thought, Aba,
November 18, 1967

The Biafran problem, to most major powers, is a nuisance. They would rather not have to deal with it in a world already gripped with the Vietnam war, economic crises, monetary crises, election fever here and there. There is an initial resentment against Biafra for

205

leading them into another problem when they have got so much to deal with.

Secondly, the Biafran problem was not regarded a major problem in the world, and it is only recently that people began to understand the fullness of the problem. Originally people regarded the problem as that small Biafra—so tiny Biafra—fighting for oil. That impression is, of course, ridiculous.

We are sure that this fight is a fight for Africa and, in a way, a fight for the black man. What we are trying to do here is to establish the fact that despite this black color of our skin, we are men, human beings, to be accepted as such.

It has always seemed somewhat strange to us here in Biafra that the tragic events which occurred in what was the former Federation of Nigeria and which are being reenacted during the current Nigeria-Biafra conflict, have hardly raised a murmur in the civilized world. This apparent indifference or apathy seems even more strange when we recall, or are witness to, the feverish concern often shown over similar situations in other parts of the world which—though reprehensible enough and deserving of condemnation—pale into insignificance in comparison to the tragic experiences of the people of Biafra in the last few years.

No people within recent history, with the possible exception of Jews during the Second World War, have suffered so much injury or faced such a grim possibility of certain death and extermination in their God-given land. The silence of the world was therefore a matter for great disappointment and sorrow for us.

I have noted the joint appeal by your organization—the World Council of Churches and the Roman Catholic Church—to us and Nigeria, urging an end to the present armed conflict. This humanitarian appeal is indeed welcome, the more so since the past nine months have clearly shown that the war is a futile attempt to resolve in the battlefield what, in the first place, is a human problem that should be resolved around the conference table.

History abounds with instances where the world rallied to uphold the sanctity of human lives. This was the case in the creation of the state of Israel, after the Jews had been subjected to atrocious massacres like ours. The only difference here is that the world statesmen have only acted where the lives of non-Africans are involved. It is against this background of world apathy that we must view this urgent appeal of the world's largest Christian bodies.

> Address to delegation of World Council of
> Churches, Umuahia, March 28, 1968

If you walked into my place here and perhaps you stopped at the gate and you saw a pile of rubbish, what would you do? You would step aside and go on. The world, faced with the present disaster, would prefer to sidetrack it. This is why it has taken fourteen months for the world to become alive to our problem.

I believe that the reasons why the world has not looked at this problem objectively is racial. The white man picks up his newspaper and exclaims, "Oh, another problem in Africa." In the clubroom someone drinking will say, "Oh, it is a pity these Biafrans are dying in thousands." Someone else will answer, "Never mind, if the bastards did not die as a result of war they would die of malaria anyway!" Nobody bothered about our problem until we yelled blue murder.

As a university student I thought that the world was a fair place with people of various standards in economic growth and various patterns of behavior. But now I find that in politics there are no moral issues. What you have is a constant conflict of interests, self-interest. Let us not be naïve about this. It is this sort of naïveté that makes people bitter. If you understand that (a) the problem is your own problem, (b) you have to rouse the interest of the world in your problem in order to obtain help, and (c) the world has nothing to do with you and that they can continue living without you—if you understand these three points—you cannot be betrayed. We are not bitter. In short, by the time you have spent forty-eight hours [in Biafra] you will be amazed at the openhanded way the people have received visitors, black or white.

Interview with Jim Wilde of *Time* magazine,

Umuahia, August 16, 1968

The world should know our case. Biafra is a people, not a tribe.

The church must speak out and not just deplore the enormity of the crime. The World Council of Churches has sent a mission; let the world hear the church condemn genocide.

It is paradoxical that a war of genocide was going on here but no voice was heard condemning it, but when four writers got prison sentences in Russia, the whole world was nearly in flames with pious indignation.

Informal meeting with the Papal delegates,

Umuahia, February 2, 1968

FOREIGN COUNTRIES

We have fought an enemy determined to exterminate us. We have fought this war with nothing in our hands, only our stout hearts. And in this fight we have drawn a great deal of inspiration from the fact of French sympathy and understanding of our cause.

I know that a great number of people have tried to make of this struggle a complex issue, but in actual fact it is very straightforward. Ours is a problem that the world has faced a number of times over and over again, a problem of what happens to a people when they have been rejected by a society they were part of. The problem facing a people in their decision on how they should be governed.

Our problem today is a problem arising from the assumption of our sovereignty, our assertion of our right to self-determination. For certain reasons, these rights have not been recognized. For reasons which are basically economic and short-termed, a number of countries are lending their support to what is tantamount to a crime against humanity.

We are proud that the French people, the French government, despite a blockade which shut us off from the normal channels of information, have been able to penetrate and understand the real issues. We are proud of the fact and very grateful that your moral support has brought much relief to our people who are suffering and dying.

Our people are grateful for all this help, but, of course, we have always said, and we still maintain, that relief is a short-term solution, indeed not a solution but merely a palliative. It does not solve the problem though it alleviates the problem for a short time. Our problem here is war, war that is most vicious, and the solution to war is peace, nothing else. We would be grateful therefore for any help that would bring about peace.

I welcome you here particularly, since your visit in a way represents the increased attention which the Parliament of France is paying to the struggle in this part of the world. We have our hopes that through such visits as yours it will be possible for a greater understanding to be generated, a greater understanding which will bring about peace, but more important perhaps, a greater understanding which will bring about greater cooperation toward the more important task of reconstruction after the war.

One more point: we have been fighting a conspiracy, a conspiracy which the circumstances of our growth have forced us to take note of. I would like to take this opportunity to appeal to French men and women to help us on a problem which does not attract diplomatic complexities. As this war goes on, it becomes increasingly clear to us that we must find an alternative door to Western civilization. To enable us to gain from the experience of Europe, to gain from your experience, I feel it is vital for us to open up cooperation in the cultural fields with France—particularly in the field of language. If nothing else, I would very much appeal to those Frenchmen who understand and speak English to come forward to teach our people to communicate with your great and sympathetic people.

Meeting with French Deputies, Mr. Offroy
and Mr. Marette, Umuahia, March 7, 1969

We as a people, and I want you to know this, are very proud that so faraway a people [the French] are so confident of our survival that without actually being here they declared support for our aspirations. Our case is quite simple. We have experienced everything: suffered massacre, suffered genocide, suffered wicked war in its most vicious form. The threat is ever before us, right at our doorsteps, and therefore our reactions are by reflex. But for a people so faraway and so different to find sympathy for us at a time like this really gives us very strong inspiration and reassures us of the equality of man. Like the great philosophers of France, we believe here that all men are equal. It is to assert this that you find us involved in this war. I personally believe that the biggest problem in the world is how to curb man's desire to dominate his fellow man. An acceptance of equality brings peace, but a desire for domination always brings war.

I like to thank you [visiting French deputies, Mr. Offroy and Mr. Marette] for demonstrating your solidarity with us by coming here. I personally admire your courage to come to an unknown country such as this, to run the gauntlet of antiaircraft fire, to run beneath the ever menacing enemy jet arsenal, and to come because you believe in man. This fills me with admiration. I feel most honored this evening to have the opportunity of conveying to you the entire gratitude of my people.

While you are here, I want to say just one word about relief. Our feelings about relief, of course, are well known. Our people are dying, they are suffering.

We need relief. We are very grateful to the French people for the way they have risen to this occasion and the way the French Red Cross, particularly, and the ancillary French organizations have been struggling to bring relief to us and in fact risking their lives too. Please convey to your people that here at least, if nowhere else on earth, you find a grateful people.

Our fight is a fight against enslavement. We have had to fight with all the means at our disposal, which is very little. We have not got much. Our desires are not much either. All we want is to prevent ourselves from being killed. We ask nothing. We do know that we cannot ask, as of right, for people to help us, yet the fact that you have helped us morally is something that fills us with gratitude.

If I continue in this vein I will just be cataloging the points of gratitude to you. This is as it should be. At a time when we were written off as a people dead, a forgotten past, the French people rose and said: No, these are human beings, they therefore have human rights. This is the way I understand your great leader's statement. He has told the world that we too are human beings, that these are men who have their own rights as men. We are grateful. You have, of course, seen the effect that declaration [President Charles de Gaulle's statement] had on the whole situation.

People marvel from time to time about how we survive. I do not think they should. We draw inspiration from your great tradition—your tradition of humanism and, indeed, your tradition of resistance. We draw inspiration from your great leader—a man who, when the whole world seemed to have written off your great Republic of France as dead, had his vision, stood up with his head high, and defended France and brought her to the position of tremendous power and undisputed leadership.

You have seen us here. It is true we are fighting this war, but we are not so materialistic as one might expect. Oh, yes! when you look at the enemy with his arsenal,

when you see him menacing the skies, bullying a defenseless people, perpetrating huge atrocities, you would
expect to find us a people devoting every ounce of their
energy just to one thing—to save their necks. I hope
that in the course of your visit you will see that it is not
so. We have time. We find time to study the deeper
meaning of this struggle, because life after all is tran-
sient. One is alive today; tomorrow one might be dead.
But the only thing that matters is what one leaves for
future generations. What is that? For Biafra it is that
black or white, yellow or pink, men are men everywhere.

Finally, forgive me for what I want to do now. I
must apologize that my education is lacking in this aspect, my knowledge of the French language is poor, and
I cannot speak to you in your own tongue. But in offering my apologies, I shall still try to make some points
in your own language [English translation follows].

I hope that you have had an opportunity to see us as
we truly are, a people alive and struggling against tremendous odds. We have no apologies to make for this
war, only to restate that we are fighting for our rights
as human beings. We are fighting for our rights to self-
determination; we are fighting for our rights to chart
our course and pursue our chosen paths; we are fighting
for our rights to make our own mistakes and to correct
them ourselves.

We did not start this war. When we were slaughtered
we did not seek revenge; all we asked and are still asking is to be left alone. In a world so lost to human passion, a world which has sacrificed humanity on the
altar of interest, we are proud that civilization still has
a chance. We are proud that France has remained
proudly true to her noble traditions. We are proud of
the sympathy of that colossus of a man, your proud
leader, that great institution, General Charles de Gaulle.

> After-dinner speech in honor of French
> Deputies, Mr. Offroy and Mr. Marette,
> Umuahia, March 6, 1969

The allegation about French aid to Biafra is the usual unimaginative propaganda of Nigeria following the well-known Russian pattern: they say America is financing us and blame everything on America—"It is all American big business interest that is keeping Biafra on."

We have been fighting this war, using a very marginal budget. For every pound sterling we spend in this war I am absolutely certain that Nigeria spends twenty, and this has its effect. Also, we had and we still have a certain amount of money. Remember that Biafrans are the travelers of West Africa, and foreign exchange is not so foreign to us. There is no Biafran, except in Nigeria, who does not contribute to this war. This always happens in a war like this. We have received odd amounts from certain individuals. There have been financial discussions, sometimes for a debt, sometimes for a credit.

If France were really helping, I think by now the war situation would have been very different. France, right now, is giving only moral support. As soon as General de Gaulle makes a statement, the world jerks to a halt. When that statement affects small powers or small countries, then it is not just a pause, it has significant effect. The specter of French help is one factor that frightens Nigeria. Nigeria fears what could happen should this moral support be translated to physical support. When it does it will be to our own advantage and we are doing everything to induce the change.

Interview with Philip de Craene of *Le Monde,*
Umuahia, April 13, 1969

The story of British hypocrisy and duplicity is as old as the rocks. The British government will lie, cheat, kill, defraud without any shame, when its economic interests are involved. For instance, it is clear that Britain produced the most active and notorious slave traders, and today all men and women of color are made to believe that the British government stopped the slave trade for humanitarian reasons when in fact it was for purely selfish economic reasons. The truth is that Britain wanted a market for its manufactured goods and also a source for raw materials. The only way to foster and sustain such an economic imperialism was to stop the selling of Africans to the Americas. The Africans remained in Africa virtually as slaves producing raw materials for British industries and becoming consumers of British goods. The educational system was also tailored to serve British economic interests. For exactly the same reasons and motive, the Wilson administration is doing everything possible to destroy Biafra and frustrate our national aspirations so as to protect British economic interests in Biafra. Britain needs the oil from Biafra to bolster its bankrupt economy.

What is left of British influence, prestige, and honor has been completely wrecked by Harold Wilson. No British administration or government has ever brought the British people so close to chaos or to its lowest ebb as that of Harold Wilson. No British administration has ever made the Britons the subject of contempt, distrust, and hatred around the world as that of the present Labor government led by Wilson. No other past government in Britain has the record of disastrous foreign and national policies or of economic chaos and bankruptcy of the present Wilson administration. Overnight Britain, once a respected world power, has suddenly become the subject of weekly attacks in the past three years in every corner of the globe as a sly and double-faced nation. The British Lion and Britannia which once ruled the waves have become a sick beast, and a third-rate debtor nation under Harold Wilson.

British hypocrisy, deceit, and duplicity are not only confined to matters involving its national interests, but also on moral issues. Take a look at the legislations and statements of the British establishments. They condemn miniskirts, perversion, and prostitution, and yet members of the same establishments are the most notorious perverts and patronize private sex clubs of naked girls and notorious call girls. Only recently an important member of the British establishment shared a common prostitute with a Russian diplomat and spy. In Nigeria there is the same unholy marriage between the British and the Russians, even though communism is denounced from British pulpits!

This brings me to the subject of the Nigeria-Biafra war. After the first two months of the war, we beat Nigeria completely. The Nigerians know it. Gowon was ready to escape to Northern Nigeria in his jet plane. Then shameless Britain came to their rescue. The British government hotly denied supplying arms and ammunition to Nigeria until the *Financial Times* exposed the British government's falsehood and duplicity.

With a finger in every pie in the world, even in the desolate regions of the North Pole, the Antarctic, and the Sahara Desert, so it is being burned at every turn and in every country.

I will give you another example of British bad faith and double-dealing. You all remember that Britain created Nigeria and brought Christianity to the country. We were taught the tenets of Western democracy, British justice, and fair play. We were taught to be gentlemen, to play cricket and polo. Britain also introduced in Nigeria its parliamentary system and helped fashion a number of constitutions designed, according to the British government, to foster Nigerian unity and progress. But the disunity in Nigeria was implanted by the British. Our fate today is a logical consequence of British perfidy. And yet, with no conscience, they turn around to give arms to Nigerians to enslave, oppress, and murder us in our home.

As far as I am concerned, the British are worse than the Northern Nigerians because the British government should know better than that you do not foster unity and progress with armored cars and bullets. There is no question of the British government coming to say: We are impartial, we are your friends. How can you be my friend when you have given weapons of war to somebody to kill me? This point we have always made and will continue to make. As far as Biafra is concerned the British government is our enemy in this war.

Address to the Aba Leaders of Thought,
Aba, November 18, 1967

In all honesty, I was very much gratified by the statement made by President Nixon in which, during his election campaign, he used the word "genocide" to describe the carnage of the present conflict. I am optimistic in that I see in him a man with sympathy. That optimism is a bit inhibited by my own knowledge that changes in policy are perhaps the most difficult thing in politics for a great power. I also know that the bigger a country the more difficult the change. I say I am optimistic, but I do not think there will be a dramatic change. As a people, we are hopeful.

There is one aspect of the struggle to which there are certainly positive indications. This concerns Russian involvement. Once the Soviet involvement launches the struggle along the cold war line, I believe from past records that it is likely that President Nixon would look more intimately into the problem. We have always maintained that a dispassionate study of the problem results always in our favor, and we therefore anticipate this hopefully. I do not want to say more now.

Interview with the American Committee to Keep
Biafra Alive, Umuahia, January 21, 1969

Canada is one country that has had past association with us and still has remained completely neutral. I know that Biafra listens respectfully to what Canada says, and I feel that Nigeria also listens to Canada. There would appear to be a great deal that Canada can do to help resolve this conflict. I would like to see Canada take an initiative in bringing about a cease-fire in order to stop the wanton massacre of so many human beings. But I think the war involves human problems that Canada can very easily raise before the United Nations.

I do not think Canada could have recognized Biafra by now because originally everybody thought it would be best to leave this problem to Africa to solve. It is only recently, after the failure of the Africans to solve the matter, that it became properly international.

I think too that Canada has not had an intimate knowledge, a sufficient knowledge, of the problems to enable her to come to an individual decision. I think that if Canada, having now got an intimate knowledge of the problem, should recognize Biafra, the effect would be to deter the bloodlust of Nigeria. I believe that recognition by Canada would crystallize world opinion. I think it would also stimulate other countries to look more critically at the problem instead of getting completely terrorized by such clichés as "internal affairs," "Balkanization," domestic jurisdiction, territorial integrity, and One Nigeria. I believe that because of her position, and particularly her internal problem, Canada's recognition would destroy one myth—the myth that countries react to problems purely because other countries do so; the fact that Canada, with her own Quebec problem, has looked at this problem and seen that it is not the same and has recognized Biafra would stimulate others to action and stop the present sloganizing of the whole conflict.

Interview with Canadian TV,
September 16, 1968

The Israeli nation has spent its entire life fighting the Arabs. The problem stems from fanatic Arab nationalism buttressed by communism. This is what you have been fighting. If the Arabs succeed in this part of the world, then you have the same problem in front of you and behind you. Countries that oppose you will get

progressively wider. It is to Israel's permanent interest
that this Arab-Russian collusion should not spread in
Africa.

Interview with Abe Nathan, director of
Fund for Children of Biafra in Israel,
Umuahia, July 29, 1968

The question of recognition has worried many during
this crisis. I think we have demonstrated in our charac-
teristic manner our ability to maintain our independence. I think too that the world generally is waiting
for who will bell the cat.

The Western powers think that this is an African
problem. The African says, "We are not really truly independent; we are not strong enough; let's go back to
our patron states and find out what they feel." So this
table tennis game goes on. In the meantime people are
suffering.

You had just said to me: France, Tanzania, Zambia,
Ivory Coast, and I say to you why not Germany? Why
not? Germany has not got any reason for not recognizing Biafra. Germany is independent and sovereign,
and sufficiently so to maintain whatever she decides is
right. Germany should now ask herself why she has not
recognized Biafra. It isn't a question of if we can only
get country A, B, or C to do it, then we'll come in. Why
cannot Western Germany do it, knowing now what she
knows about the problem in Biafra?

There is a danger in the attitude of many so-called
small countries because really what this leads to is
leaving all initiatives in world affairs to two countries
[U.S.A. and U.S.S.R.]. Eventually this can only lead
to all decisions affecting the world being made by either
America or Russia. The danger of such a state of affairs
is quite obvious. It only needs a madman to make a
wrong decision and we all sink with him.

I think the future, if it is going to be peaceful, will be
a future in which sovereignty really means sovereignty

and is exercisable by those nations that are sovereign. I believe that if there is going to be peace in the world, it will come through the action of the small countries, not the big ones.

Interview with West German journalist,
Dr. Ruth Bowert, Umuahia, March 25, 1968

I think, like most countries, there is a lot that the Irish can do. Perhaps it is too much to expect Ireland to step out immediately and recognize Biafra. I think, first, she has to understand our problem, show understanding and sympathy, and then bring pressure to bear on Nigeria directly, since she is diplomatically represented there, and in other countries, to effect a cessation of hostilities and a committal to negotiation as the only way of solving our problem. I think too that when there is very little a country can do, she can probably get a hearing in the world on a moral basis. I think she could cry out against the crime being committed against humanity in this area. I do not think any country should sit by and watch this act of genocide.

Interview with John Horgan of Irish *Times*
and David Robison, United States free-lance
journalist, Umuahia, February 20, 1968

We would not want to interfere in Nigeria's internal affairs. We are not in control of the destiny of Nigerians. We would find it extremely difficult to do much about it, if the Nigerians should accept the Russians. I know that right now the Russians are very keen on getting certain facilities in Nigeria, such as strategic bases, in pursuance of their policy of trying to dot the Atlantic with bases and staging posts.

I know that right now they have fully under their control the Kano airport. I know right now they are negotiating the movement of commerce and traffic in the Lagos harbor to a place toward Badagry and to use Lagos as a base for their Atlantic fleet. I know also that

there have been attempts to tie the future economy of
Nigeria to Russia. I know that eventually what Russia
wants is to get at the strategic resources of the country.
I think eventually they will want to have a strong lien
on the oil. This would be an easy matter for them because of the lack of cohesion in Nigeria. I do not think
they have sufficient time to consolidate their hold, but
if this war lasts much longer they would have the opportunity.

Before I came to this part [Biafra], I was working in
Northern Nigeria. I was commanding the battalion in
Kano and at the time the major security problem was
the influence of communism in the North. Kano then
was the Russian bridgehead into Nigeria. Drawing on
their experience, on their ability to find some platform
of collusion between a type of Arabism as it is in
North Africa, and Russian communism. For the Russians this was a long-term program. But with the disruption caused by this war, they found an opportunity
to get a foothold in the South.

I do not think they will willingly relinquish that hold.
Indeed, from the way the Russian hold is growing in
Nigeria, it appears that the Russians will fight if there
is an attempt to dislodge them. I believe they can be
halted if this war stops before they consolidate. I am
quite alarmed at the prospect for the future. If nothing
else, I can see already for Biafra a waste of resources
in holding back Russian-oriented Nigerians.

The problem that we are dealing with basically is the
problem that is visible in almost all the countries of
West Africa and in places where you have a predominantly Arab-oriented people as against the purely black
Southern peoples. A lot will depend on the outcome of
this struggle. If the Arab-oriented Lagos regime, in collusion with the Russians, succeeds [in crushing Biafra],
I believe it will give some form of impetus to a Russian
attempt to push through from North to South in the
other countries of West Africa. I can see this problem

already in Senegal, Sierra Leone, and, of course, in Sudan.

Interview with Marvin Kupfer of *Newsweek*
magazine and David Robison, United States
free-lance journalist, Umuahia,
February 13, 1969

The recognition of Biafra by the Haitian government brings out a new dimension—the black dimension of our struggle. It shows an understanding by our race. It focuses the attention of the other side to the black problem on this side of the world. It is the first non-African state to recognize Biafra.

Interview with Philip de Craene of *Le Monde,*
Umuahia, April 13, 1969

A DIVIDED WORLD

The world community is today beset by many complex and intractable problems. It is deeply divided by rival political ideologies, differing racial backgrounds, apparently irreconcilable religious dogmas, and divergent rates of economic growth.

In the resulting clash of interests two powerful blocs have emerged, each led by a superpower and possessing enough deadly weapons to destroy the entire human race. It must be our determination as a progressive people to pursue a dynamic foreign policy which avoids interference in the internal affairs of other states and ensures the peaceful coexistence of all. We will not be drawn into the ideological conflict between the East and the West, but we will actively cooperate with all progressive nations to ensure world peace.

Our idea of nonalignment will not at any time mean neutrality or indifference. We shall always feel free to act in accordance with our own interest and that of humanity, supporting whatever cause is just and taking sides with those who pursue that cause. Ours will be a policy of friendship and respect for all nations who are willing to reciprocate such feelings and gestures.

We recognize that the cause of world peace can never be successful unless every nation and every people are accorded the right to self-determination. Experience has shown that it is only through free and voluntary associations of races and peoples that strife and bloodshed can be avoided.

We are therefore strongly opposed to all forms of discrimination and all ideologies or practices which detract from the fundamental principle that all men are equal and that all peoples should enjoy the free and unfettered right to develop their potentialities, human and material. We shall therefore join all forces of progress and justice to oppose discrimination on any ground whatsoever. We shall not hesitate to point out and condemn acts of oppression and inhumanity, appealing at all times to the conscience of the world. Biafra must identify herself with the cause of the national liberation movements in Africa. We intend to join hands with other progressive African countries in ensuring that the nationalists are victorious and that the African is master in his continent.

We believe that the United Nations Organization and its agencies constitute man's best hope for peace and progress. We shall uphold the principles embodied in the charter of that world body. We shall also retain our membership of the British Commonwealth of Nations as an independent and sovereign country because it is consonant with our interests and promotes peace and racial understanding.

One great barrier which hinders progress toward interstate understanding and cooperation in Africa is language; that is, the inability of French- and English-speaking Africans to freely communicate their thoughts to each other. We in this Republic must take positive steps to break down this barrier by ensuring that the present generation of Biafrans have a working knowledge of the French language. This will further enable

Biafrans to benefit from the rich culture of the French-speaking world which otherwise would be lost to them. Consequently, it will be our policy to make the study of French compulsory in our secondary, technical, and teacher-training institutions, and actively encourage those who have the aptitude to pursue the study at university level.

We are fortunate in Biafra to have sizable natural resources, some of which are being developed. We also have an appreciable reservoir of manpower trained in many skills. We seem to be poised for an economic takeoff which will ensure prosperity for our Republic. We must not, however, think of ourselves alone but must contribute toward the upliftment and betterment of all Africa. Previously our role in this direction had been largely confined to the borders of the former Federation of Nigeria. We ought not to be daunted by our past experience and so become entirely introspective. Now that we have freed ourselves from the shackles of reactionaries, we must be prepared to extend our horizon to embrace the entire African continent. Biafrans must play a dynamic role by their readiness to share their human and material resources with other African peoples, even if it means some sacrifice on our part. Our young men and women must be ready to offer their services whenever and wherever they are wanted, and we must be willing to provide material assistance to our African brothers in distress. We must also adopt an open door policy toward all Africans who may wish to sojourn here and benefit from any facilities we may possess.

Broadcast, August 10, 1967

About the Author

The General of the People's Army, Chukwuemeka Odumegwu Ojukwu, was born in November, 1933. Son of a business millionaire, he had his early education in Roman Catholic School, Anglican Grammar School and Kings College in Lagos, Nigeria, and in 1947 gained admission into Epsom College, a reputable British Public School, where apart from his academic attainments he won colors in Rugby and athletics. From Epsom he went to Lincoln College, Oxford, in 1952 where he graduated in 1955. He holds the M.A. degree in Modern History.

He served as a Government Administrative Officer in the then Eastern Nigeria. He joined the Nigerian Army in 1957 as the first indigenous University graduate and in the same year he entered Eaton Hall Officer Cadet School in Chester, England, where he was commissioned with the rank of Second Lieutenant. He later attended officers courses at Hythe and Warminster and returned to Nigeria in December, 1958 and was instantly appointed Company Commander of Fifth Battalion of the Nigeria Army.

For the next six years, he crowded into his military career an impressive variety of activities and responsibilities, such as the Cameroun Campaign (1959) against armed uprisings in the Bamaliki area of the French Cameroun, his task being to guard that sector of the Nigerian border; Lecturer (then as a full Lieutenant) in tactics and military law at the Officers Training School of the Royal West African Frontier Force in Teshie, Ghana (1959); Deputy Assistant Adjutant and Quartermaster (with the rank of Major) to the First Nigerian Brigade (1961); Congo (Kinshasa) U.N. Operations in Luluabourg (1962).

In May, 1962, he attended the Joint Services Staff College in Latimer, England. In December, 1962, he was promoted to Lieutenant-Colonel and was appointed Quartermaster-General of the Nigerian Army, the first Nigerian to hold the post. By the end of the second year at the post, he was transferred to Kano to assume the command of the Fifth Battalion. His first difference with the Army authorities occurred in March, 1965 while commanding a composite Battalion to quell a communal uprising in the Tiv Division of Northern Nigeria. Appalled by the brutality ordered against the local population, he sought and was granted permission to return to his Battalion headquarters after only two weeks in this special command. While still in Kano, he was on January 19, 1966, appointed Military Governor of Eastern Nigeria following the January 15, 1966, military coup, and later Head of State, Republic of Biafra and Commander-in-Chief of its Armed Forces. He was promoted General in May, 1969 by a unanimous resolution of the Biafra Consultative Assembly.

Though born wealthy, he is an advocate of the Welfare State, a confirmed anti-imperialist and firm believer in the destiny of the black man. His philosophical concept finds manifestation in his personal standard which reads: "To Thy Own Self Be True." He enjoys lawn and table tennis. He is an avid reader of historical and philosophical books, plays and poetry, Milton being his favorite poet. He has maintained his interest in art. The General is married and has three children—a son, a daughter and a step-daughter.

69 70 71 72 73 10 9 8 7 6 5 4 3 2 1